D 307 - BUILDING

Designing High-Density Cities

Designing High-Density Cities
for Social and Environmental Sustainability

Edited by Edward Ng

publishing for a sustainable future
London • Sterling, VA

First published by Earthscan in the UK and USA in 2010

Copyright © Edward Ng, 2010

ISBN: 978-1-84407-460-0

Typeset by Domex e-Data, India
Cover design by Rob Watts

For a full list of publications please contact:

Earthscan
Dunstan House
14a St Cross St
London, EC1N 8XA, UK
Tel: +44 (0)20 7841 1930
Fax: +44 (0)20 7242 1474
Email: earthinfo@earthscan.co.uk
Web: **www.earthscan.co.uk**

22883 Quicksilver Drive, Sterling, VA 20166-2012, USA

Earthscan publishes in association with the International Institute for Environment and Development

A catalogue record for this book is available from the British Library

Library of Congress Cataloging-in-Publication Data

Designing high-density cities for social and environmental sustainability / edited by Edward Ng.
  p. cm.
 Includes bibliographical references and index.
 ISBN 978-1-84407-460-0 (hardback)
 1. City planning--Environmental aspects. 2. Sustainable urban development. 3. Urban ecology (Sociology) I.
Ng, Edward.
 HT166.D3869 2009
 307.1'216--dc22
        2009012710

At Earthscan we strive to minimize our environmental impacts and carbon footprint through reducing waste, recycling and offsetting our CO_2 emissions, including those created through publication of this book. For more details of our environmental policy, see www.earthscan.co.uk.

This book was printed in the UK by
The Cromwell Press Group. The paper
used is FSC certified.

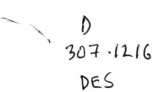

Contents

List of Figures and Tables   *xi*
List of Contributors   *xxi*
Foreword by Sir David Akers Jones   *xxix*
Preface   *xxxi*
Acknowledgements   *xxxvii*
List of Acronyms and Abbreviations   *xxxix*

PART I: AN UNDERSTANDING OF HIGH DENSITY

1   Understanding Density and High Density   3
Vicky Cheng
Physical density   3
Building density and urban morphology   9
Perceived density   12
High density   13
Conclusions   16

2   Is the High-Density City the Only Option?   19
Brenda Vale and Robert Vale
The post-oil scenario   19
The food equation   20
Wastes and fertility   23
Low density or high density?   24
Conclusions   24

3   The Sustainability of High Density   27
Susan Roaf
Population and the people problem   27
Resource depletion   33
Pollution   36
Conclusions: Avoid the Ozymandias syndrome   37

4   Density and Urban Sustainability: An Exploration of Critical Issues   41
Chye Kiang Heng and Lai Choo Malone-Lee
Sustainability and planning   41
Historical review   42
Density and sustainability   43
Conclusions   50

PART II: CLIMATE AND HIGH-DENSITY DESIGN

5   **Climate Changes Brought About by Urban Living**   55
    Chiu-Ying Lam
    Temperature   55
    On climate changes brought about by urban living   55
    Wind   57
    State of the sky   57
    Evaporation   59
    Thinking about people   60

6   **Urbanization and City Climate: A Diurnal and Seasonal Perspective**   63
    Wing-Mo Leung and Tsz-Cheung Lee
    Urban heat island (UHI) intensity   63
    Diurnal variation of UHI intensity   64
    Seasonal variation of UHI intensity   66
    Favourable conditions for high UHI intensity   67
    Conclusions   67

7   **Urban Climate in Dense Cities**   71
    Lutz Katzschner
    Introduction   71
    Problems   72
    Urban climatic maps   74
    Urban climate and planning   78

PART III: ENVIRONMENTAL ASPECTS OF HIGH-DENSITY DESIGN

8   **Thermal Comfort Issues and Implications in High-Density Cities**   87
    Baruch Givoni
    Thermal comfort   87
    Recent research on comfort   90
    Conclusions: Implications for building design and urban planning   104

9   **Urban Environment Diversity and Human Comfort**   107
    Koen Steemers and Marylis Ramos
    Introduction   107
    Background   108
    Monitoring outdoor comfort   108
    Conclusions   116

10 **Designing for Urban Ventilation** 119
Edward Ng
Introduction 119
Urban ventilation in high-density cities 119
Wind velocity ratio for urban ventilation 120
Building and city morphology for urban ventilation 121
Case study: Hong Kong 124
Design guidelines 130
Conclusions 135

11 **Natural Ventilation in High-Density Cities** 137
Francis Allard, Christian Ghiaus and Agota Szucs
Introduction 137
Role of ventilation 138
Cooling potential by ventilation in a dense urban environment 141
Natural ventilation strategies in a dense urban environment 156

12 **Sound Environment: High- versus Low-Density Cities** 163
Jian Kang
Sound distribution 163
Sound perception 168
Noise reduction 177

13 **Designing for Daylighting** 181
Edward Ng
Introduction 181
Context 181
Graphical tools for design 182
The need for daylight 184
Towards high density 186
A tool for high density 188
The way forward 190
Conclusions 193

14 **Designing for Waste Minimization in High-Density Cities** 195
Chi-Sun Poon and Lara Jaillon
Introduction: Waste management and waste minimization 195
Designing for waste minimization 200
Conclusions 206

15 **Fire Engineering for High-Density Cities** 209
Wan-Ki Chow
Introduction 209
Possible fire hazards 210
Fire safety provisions 211

Performance-based design   213
Atrium sprinkler   214
Structural members under substantial fires   214
Super-tall buildings   217
Glass façade   219
Application of performance-based design in Hong Kong   219
Necessity of full-scale burning tests   220
Fire engineering as a new profession   221
Conclusions   222

16 The Role of Urban Greenery in High-Density Cities   227
    Nyuk-Hien Wong and Yu Chen
Introduction   227
Reducing ambient air temperature with plants   229
Reducing surface temperature with plants   243
Challenges in incorporating urban greenery in high-density cities   257

17 Energy in High-Density Cities   263
    Adrian Pitts
Introduction   263
Energy demand   263
Energy supply   266

18 Environmental Assessment: Shifting Scales   273
    Raymond J. Cole
Introduction   273
Building environmental assessment methods   274
Shifting scales   277
Blurring boundaries   279
High-density urban contexts   280
Conclusions   281

PART IV: HIGH-DENSITY SPACES AND LIVING

19 The Social and Psychological Issues of High-Density City Space   285
    Bryan Lawson
Introduction   285
Privacy   287
Public policy   288
The city territory   289
Evidence-based design   290
Perception of density and satisfaction   291
What have we learned?   291

20 Sustainable Compact Cities and High-Rise Buildings   293
    Sung Woo Shin
    History and background   293
    Current status, direction and effect of high-rise buildings   294
    High-rise buildings – their trend and efficiency in terms of the sustainable compact city   298
    Conclusions   307

21 Microclimate in Public Housing: An Environmental Approach to
        Community Development   309
    John C. Y. Ng
    Introduction   309
    Sustainable community: A holistic approach   310
    Community development: In pursuit of economic sustainability   310
    Community development: In pursuit of social sustainability   311
    Community development: In pursuit of environmental sustainability   311
    Conclusions   319

22 Designing for High-Density Living: High Rise, High Amenity and High Design   321
    Kam-Sing Wong
    High-density living: Best or worst?   321
    1993 – Hong Kong architecture: The aesthetics of density   322
    2003 – Hong Kong's dark age: The outbreak of severe acute respiratory syndrome (SARS)   323
    2004 – Hong Kong's turning point: The rise of 'green sense'   324
    2008 and beyond – Hong Kong's sustainable future: High rise, high amenity and high design   327
    High-density living: Our dream city?   327

List of Figures and Tables

Figures

P.1	Cities with more than 1 million inhabitants	xxxi
P.2	Reasons for high-density living	xxxiii
1.1	People density	3
1.2	Building density	4
1.3	Net residential area	4
1.4	Gross residential area	4
1.5	Plot ratio = 1	5
1.6	Plot ratio = 1.5	5
1.7	Plot ratio = 2	6
1.8	Site coverage = 25 per cent	6
1.9	Site coverage = 50 per cent	6
1.10	Hong Kong population density map	7
1.11	Population density gradient from the town centre towards rural outskirts	7
1.12	Density gradients over time	8
1.13	Density profile calculated over concentric circles of radii of 200m, 400m, 800m and 1600m	8
1.14	Two built forms with the same plot ratio but different proportions of site coverage	9
1.15	Same density in different layouts: (a) multi-storey towers; (b) medium-rise buildings in central courtyard form; (c) parallel rows of single-storey houses	10
1.16	Three different urban forms: (a) courtyard; (b) parallel block; (c) tower	10
1.17	Relationships between building height, plot ratio, site coverage and solar obstruction	11
1.18	Residential densities of four different urban forms	11
1.19	Perceived density is about the interaction between the individual and the space, and between individuals in the space	12
1.20	Architectural features that influence the perception of density	13
1.21	High density in Hong Kong	14
1.22	High density helps to protect the countryside	15
2.1	Areas of land required to support Hong Kong with local food production	23
3.1	Height in metres of the world's tallest buildings	37
4.1	Same density in different forms	44
4.2	The hierarchy of streets, from the Buchanan Report	45
4.3	Contrast between high-rise residential blocks and low-rise houses in Hanoi's Dinh Cong area	47
4.4	Kim Lien Area, Hanoi: (a) 1985; (b) present	48
4.5	Street scenes in Kim Lien	48
4.6	Seoul, Korea	49
5.1	Annual mean temperature recorded at the Hong Kong Observatory headquarters (1947–2005)	56
5.2	Annual mean temperature recorded at (a) Ta Kwu Ling (1989–2005); (b) Lau Fau Shan (1989–2005)	56
5.3	Mean daily maximum and mean daily minimum temperature of Hong Kong Observatory headquarters (1947–2005)	57

5.4   Annual average of 12-hourly 10-minute mean wind speed of King's Park and
        Waglan Island (1968–2005)   58
5.5   Annual total number of hours with visibility at the Hong Kong Observatory
        headquarters below 8km from 1968 to 2005 (not counting rain, mist or fog)   58
5.6   Long-term trend in annual mean of the daily global solar radiation, 1961–2005   59
5.7   Long-term trend in annual total evaporation, 1961–2005   60
5.8   Annual number of hot nights, 1961–2005   61
6.1   Map showing the locations of the Hong Kong Observatory headquarters and Ta Kwu Ling   64
6.2   Diurnal variations of the average (a) T_{HKO} and T_{TKL}; (b) T_{u-r}; and (c) rate of change of
        T_{HKO} and T_{TKL}, 1989–2007   65
6.3   Diurnal variations of average T_{u-r} of Hong Kong in different months of the year (1989–2007)   66
7.1   Sketch of an urban heat island profile   72
7.2   Heat islands in London and Tokyo   73
7.3   Isolines of air temperatures in the city of Karlsruhe, Germany   73
7.4   Correlation between physiological equivalent temperature (PET) >35°C and Tamin >18°C and
        mortality in Vienna (1996–2005)   74
7.5   Hong Kong skyline   74
7.6   Global climate change and air temperature trend for Hong Kong   75
7.7   Variation of air temperature with global warming   75
7.8   Distribution of calculated PET in Hong Kong in January and July   76
7.9   PET values of a street canyon without trees and with trees in Gardaiha   76
7.10   Urban Climatic Analysis Map (UC-AnMap) and Urban Climate Recommendation
        Map (UC-ReMap) from Kassel, Germany, with heat island, ventilation and planning
        classifications   77
7.11   Principal methodology for deriving urban climate maps and the use of GIS layers for
        detailed classification information   79
7.12   An illustration of work flow for creating an urban climatic map   80
7.13   The result of the urban climatic map of Hong Kong   81
7.14   Some examples of buildings adopting green roofs and walls   81
7.15   Urban climate map and planning recommendations   82
7.16   Urban climate map of Kassel with explanations   82
8.1   The four experimental settings   91
8.2   Percentage of thermal responses of subjects at different climatic settings   92
8.3   Effect of changing wind conditions on thermal responses   93
8.4   Effect of changing sun-shading conditions on thermal responses   94
8.5   Relationship between thermal sensation and overall comfort   95
8.6   Comparison of the measured and predicted thermal sensation   95
8.7   Layout of environmental chamber for thermal comfort survey   96
8.8   Observed and computed thermal sensations in the comfort study at the City
        University of Hong Kong   97
8.9   Average effect of air temperature on thermal sensation   98
8.10   Average effect of air speed on thermal sensation   98
8.11   Measured and computed thermal sensations in the chamber study in Singapore   100

8.12	Thermal sensation as a function of temperature, with different symbols for the different air speeds	100
8.13	Thermal sensations as a function of the humidity ratio	101
8.14	Observed and computed thermal sensations (FEEL) in the Singapore survey	101
8.15	Comfort responses (FEEL) as a function of temperature	102
8.16	Comfort responses (FEEL) as a function of air speed	102
8.17	Thermal sensations expressed as a function of temperature, with different symbols for the different wind speeds	103
8.18	Measured and computed thermal sensation in the Thailand study	104
8.19	Temperatures in areas with different plants in a small park in Tel Aviv	105
9.1	Portable field monitoring kit	109
9.2	An example of the analysis of one of the urban case study areas, 200m × 200m (Cambridge), showing (a) sky view factors (SVFs); (b) solar shading; and (c) wind shadows	113
9.3	Simplified threshold images of the data in Figure 9.2	113
9.4	Environmental diversity map, which overlaps the maps in Figure 9.3	114
9.5	Diversity profile and weighting factors for the Cambridge site	115
9.6	Diversity versus desirability for each period of the day, for each season and for the year overall, related to the Cambridge site	115
9.7	Annual diversity of each of the 14 European sites against average ASV	116
10.1	Wind velocity ratio is a relationship between Vp and V∞	121
10.2	Two urban layouts with different wind velocity ratios: lower velocity ratios due to higher building blockage; higher velocity ratios due to more ground level permeability	121
10.3	A geometrical relationship of buildings and air paths	122
10.4	Various street canyons and air circulation vortexes	123
10.5	A city with various building heights is preferable	124
10.6	A comfort outdoor temperature chart based on survey data in tropical cities	126
10.7	An understanding of wind velocity ratio based on 16 directions	127
10.8	An example of an air ventilation assessment (AVA) study showing the boundary of the assessment area, the boundary of the model, and positions of the test points	128
10.9	A flow chart showing the procedures of AVA methodology	129
10.10	Breezeways and air paths when planning a city are better for city air ventilation	131
10.11	Aligning street orientations properly is better for city air ventilation	132
10.12	Linking open spaces with breezeways, low-rise buildings and linear parks is better for city air ventilation	133
10.13	Reducing ground cover and breaking up building podia is better for city air ventilation	134
10.14	Buildings with gaps along the waterfront are better for city air ventilation	134
10.15	Improving air volume near the ground with stepping podia is better for city air ventilation	134
10.16	Varying building heights is better for city air ventilation	134
10.17	Gaps between buildings are better for city air ventilation	135
10.18	Vertical signage is better for city air ventilation	135
11.1	Minimum ventilation rates in the US	138
11.2	ASHRAE ranges of operative temperature and humidity in summer and winter clothing	140
11.3	Comparison of comfort zones for air-conditioned and naturally ventilated buildings	140

11.4   Heating, ventilating and air-conditioning (HVAC) operating zones: (1) heating; (2) ventilation; (3) free cooling; (4) mechanical cooling   142

11.5   Principle of estimating frequency distribution of degree hours for heating, ventilating and cooling   143

11.6   Representation of a building as the difference between indoor and equivalent (sol-air) temperature   144

11.7   Percentage of energy savings when cooling by ventilation is used instead of air conditioning   144

11.8   Wind velocity and wind-induced pressure are reduced in the urban environment   145

11.9   Maximum differences in urban and rural temperature for US and European cities   148

11.10   Contours of noise level at different heights above the street and street widths   152

11.11   Relationship between pollution and development: (a) particles and SO_2 pollution in relation to income; (b) estimated global annual deaths from indoor and outdoor pollution   153

11.12   The variation of indoor–outdoor ozone ratio as a function of (a) air changes per hour; (b) outdoor concentration   154

11.13   Building classification according to permeability   154

11.14   Ozone outdoor–indoor transfer: (a) I/O ratio; (b) precision; (c) degree of confidence   155

11.15 NO_2 outdoor–indoor transfer: (a) I/O ratio; (b) precision; (c) degree of confidence   156

11.16   Particulate matter outdoor–indoor transfer   157

11.17   Top-down or balanced stack natural ventilation systems use high-level supply inlets to access less contaminated air and to place both inlet and outlets in higher wind velocity exposures   158

11.18   Windcatcher for natural ventilation systems   159

11.19   Passive downdraught evaporative cooling stack ventilation   160

12.1   Typical street canyon configurations used in the simulation   164

12.2   Comparison of the sound pressure levels (SPLs) between UK and Hong Kong streets with geometrically reflecting boundaries   165

12.3   Comparison of the SPLs between UK and Hong Kong streets with diffusely reflecting boundaries   166

12.4   Comparison of the RT30 between UK and Hong Kong streets with diffusely reflecting boundaries   167

12.5   Comparison of the SPLs between the UK and Hong Kong streets with mixed boundaries   168

12.6   Comparison of the SPLs in front of a façade between the UK and Hong Kong streets with mixed boundaries, in the case of a line source   169

12.7   Noise maps of the sampled areas in Sheffield and Wuhan   170

12.8   Comparison of the SPLs between Sheffield and Wuhan in the sampled urban areas: (a) L_{avg} and L_{50}; (b) L_{min} and L_{90}; (c) L_{max} and L_{10} 171

12.9   Importance of various factors in choosing a living environment   172

12.10   Noticeability of typical sound sources in residential areas; the standard deviations are also shown   174

12.11   Comparison between the evaluation of sound level and acoustic comfort in Sheffield and Beijing   176

12.12   Comparison of the scatter plot with factor 1 and 2 between Sheffield and Beijing   177

12.13   Examples of self-protection buildings: (a) podium as a noise barrier; (b) using balconies to stop direct sound   178

13.1   Waldram diagram for estimating daylight factor   183

13.2   Lynes' pepper-pot diagram for estimating daylight factor   184

13.3	Hopkinson projectors for understanding building obstructions with tall buildings	184
13.4	Solar envelopes during different times of the year	185
13.5	Vertical obstruction angle restrictions in different cities	187
13.6	A sky component table in 5° intervals based on CIE overcast sky	188
13.7	A study of daylight factor based on Tregenza's dot method	189
13.8	A graph showing the relationship between unobstructed vision area (UVA) and façade heights with various achievable vertical daylight factors	190
13.9	A diagram showing the concept of UVA	191
13.10	A real-life application of UVA in a housing estate design with 15 per cent glazing area	191
13.11	A real-life application of UVA in a housing estate design with 10 per cent glazing area	192
13.12	A design hypothesis based on maximizing UVA	192
14.1	OECD working definition on waste minimization	196
14.2	Waste minimization hierarchy	196
14.3	Construction waste disposed at landfills and public filling areas since 1993	198
14.4	Existing facilities for construction waste management and disposal	200
14.5	Construction waste disposed at the three strategic landfills since 1997, in tonnes per day (tpd)	201
14.6	Electrical and Mechanical Services Department headquarters in Kowloon; adaptive reuse of the former air cargo terminal of Kai Tak Airport	202
14.7	Redevelopment of Upper Ngau Tau Kok completed in 2008, using a site-specific design approach and standard building components and unit configurations	203
14.8	Factors affecting building technology selection	205
14.9	Prefabrication construction adopted at The Orchards in 2003	205
15.1	Crowd movement in a railway station, Shinjuku, Tokyo, Japan	210
15.2	Active fire protection systems: (a) alarm system; (b) selected sprinkler heads; (c) exit signs	212
15.3	Testing smoke management system	212
15.4	Atrium sprinkler: (a) the sprinkler; (b) the atrium	215
15.5	Adverse effects of an atrium sprinkler	215
15.6	Combustibles in an atrium	216
15.7	Long-throw sprinkler: (a) water pattern; (b) installation; (c) testing	216
15.8	Substantial fire test: (a) the substantial fire; (b) positions of thermocouples; (c) temperature–time curve	217
15.9	Evacuation to refuge floor: (a) refuge floors; (b) other examples in Hong Kong; (c) reduction in evacuation time	218
15.10	Fire in a glass building in Dalian, Liaoning, China, 18 September 2005	219
15.11	Airport fire, 1998: (a) full of smoke; (b) not allowed to enter	221
16.1	Model of environment (plants are considered to be the major component of environmental control)	228
16.2	Graphical interpretation of hypothesis 1 and hypothesis 2	228
16.3	The comparison of average air temperatures measured at different locations in Bukit Batok Natural Park (BBNP) (11 January–5 February 2003)	229
16.4	Correlation analysis of locations 6 and 3, as well as locations 9 and 3	230
16.5	Comparison of cooling loads for different locations	231
16.6	The correlation analysis between solar radiation and air temperatures at all locations	231
16.7	The comparison of section views at 12.00 am of scenarios: (a) with woods; (b) without woods; and (c) with buildings replacing woods	232

16.8   Three streets selected in Tuas area: Tuas Avenue 2; Tuas Avenue 8;
         Tuas South Street 3   233
16.9   Box plot of average temperatures (°C) obtained from different locations in the
         Tuas area over a period from 21 March to 14 April 2005   234
16.10   The comparison of average temperatures measured in the Tuas area on 10 April 2005 235
16.11   The comparison of cooling energy consumptions to balance the heat gain from outside
         and potential energy saving caused by road trees   236
16.12   The measurement points in Changi Business Park (CBP) and International Business Park (IBP)   237
16.13   Comparison of average air temperatures obtained at different locations over a
         period of 20 days   237
16.14   Simulation results at midnight: concentrated landscape; scattered landscape   238
16.15   Punggol site and Seng Kang site   238
16.16   The comparison of temperatures between two sites: (site 1) Punggol site; (site 2) Seng Kang site   239
16.17   Rooftop garden C2 with vegetation   239
16.18   Rooftop garden C16 without vegetation   239
16.19   Air ambient temperature and relative humidity plotted over three days   240
16.20   Rooftop garden of the low-rise building   241
16.21   Positions of the field measurements   241
16.22   Comparison of ambient air temperatures measured with and without plants at a height of
         300mm on 3 and 4 November   242
16.23   Comparison of mean radiation temperatures (MRTs) calculated with and without plants at
         a height of 1m on 3 and 4 November   243
16.24   Comparison of surface temperatures measured with different kinds of plants, only soil,
         and without plants on 3 and 4 November   244
16.25   Comparison of heat flux transferred through different roof surfaces on 4 November 245
16.26   Comparison of annual energy consumption, space cooling load component and peak space
         cooling load component for different types of roofs for a five-storey commercial building   246
16.27   The multi-storey car park without and with an extensive rooftop system   247
16.28   Comparison of surface temperatures measured on G4 during the rainy period   247
16.29   Comparison of substrate surface temperatures with exposed surface temperatures   248
16.30   Comparison of G1 and G3 (1 April 2004)   249
16.31   Comparison of G2 and G4 (1 April 2004)   249
16.32   Exposed metal surface and three types of plants measured on the metal roof   250
16.33   Long-term analysis of the surface temperatures measured above the green metal roof 251
16.34   Long-term analysis of the surface temperatures measured above the green metal roof
         (excluding night-time) from 7.00 am to 7.00 pm   251
16.35   Comparison of surface temperatures measured on the green metal roof on a clear day
         (16 September 2005)   252
16.36   Comparison of surface temperatures measured on the green metal roof on a cloudy day
         (3 October 2005)   252
16.37   The two factories involved in the measurements in Changi South Street 1   253
16.38   Comparison of surface temperatures measured on the external walls of F1 and F2 on a clear
         day (20 July 2005)   253

16.39	Comparison of surface temperatures measured on the internal walls of F1 and F2 on a clear day (20 July 2005)	254
16.40	The two factories involved in the measurements in Woodlands Link	254
16.41	A long-term comparison of the surface temperature variations with and without trees from 21 September to 7 December	255
16.42	Comparison of solar radiation and surface temperatures measured with and without shading from trees on 1 November 2005	256
16.43	Comparison of solar radiation and surface temperatures measured with and without shading from trees on 15 November 2005	257
16.44	Comparison of cooling energy consumption to balance the heat gain from outside for a factory	258
16.45	Wall-climbing type on a hotel (natural style) and on an office building (artificial style), Singapore	259
16.46	Hanging-down type on a car park and on a university building, Singapore	260
16.47	Module-type outside hoarding and on a university building, Singapore	260
16.48	The terrace occupied by vertical landscape	261
20.1	City development process: (a) city function expansion; (b) sustainable compact city	294
20.2	Global trend and plans of high-rise buildings	295
20.3	Roppongi Hills model, Tokyo	297
20.4	Canary Wharf and London metropolitan skyline, London	298
20.5	La Défense, Paris	298
20.6	Freedom Tower, New York	299
20.7	Shanghai Pudong skyline	299
20.8	Singapore city high-rise building for vertical public space	301
20.9	Energy costs of 92 office buildings	302
20.10	Consumption pattern based on the nature of construction	302
20.11	Energy consumption ratios within large buildings	303
20.12	Building integrated photovoltaic system with design variation on a high-rise building	304
20.13	Double-skin system design concept and cases	305
20.14	Wind turbine system cases	305
20.15	Phare Tower	306
20.16	Bishopsgate Tower	306
20.17	Bahrain World Trade Centre	306
20.18	Guanzhou Pearl River Tower	306
20.19	Seoul LITE building	307
20.20	Sustainable compact city concept utilizing high-rise buildings	307
21.1	The three dimensions of sustainability	310
21.2	Simulation tools: (a) wind rose; (b) computational fluid dynamics; (c) wind tunnel	312
21.3	Air ventilation assessment to ensure ventilation performance at the pedestrian level	313
21.4	Wind corridor to enhance the wind environment of the plaza	313
21.5	Wind corridor to enhance the wind environment of the housing development and nearby neighbourhoods	314
21.6	Enhancement of wind environment at a pedestrian promenade through built form refinement and disposition of domestic blocks	314

21.7	Podium option discarded for better wind environment at the pedestrian level	315
21.8	The deck garden enhances the microclimate of the domestic tower and integrates the social activities at the ground level	315
21.9	Cross-ventilated re-entrants improve building permeability and facilitate social interaction among tenants at common areas within the domestic blocks	316
21.10	Wing wall enhances natural ventilation in common corridors, improves comfort level and facilitates social interaction among tenants in common areas	316
21.11	Modular design of domestic flats	317
21.12	Daylight simulation for modular flats	317
21.13	Cross-ventilated window openings improve daylight penetration	318
21.14	Sun-shading simulation results for external open space	318
21.15	Environmental façade with design approach to reduce energy consumption	319
22.1	Kowloon Station Development	322
22.2	Verbena Heights public housing estate	323
22.3	Amoy Gardens	324
22.4	Wall effect developments along the waterfront of Tseung Kwan O New Town	325
22.5	Districts in Kowloon	326
22.6	'Lohas Park'	328

Tables

P.1	Urban density	xxxii
P.2	Urban density – new development	xxxii
2.1	Land area required to feed cities of various sizes	21
3.1	Fire safety requirements in Hong Kong	32
3.2	Case study buildings' embodied energy results (GJ/m^2 gross floor area) by element group	34
3.3	Energy consumption of typical traction lifts	35
4.1	Density and distance travelled per person per week by mode	43
4.2	Ratio of employees and self-employed	50
6.1	Statistics of the seasonal variations of T_{u-r} in Hong Kong (1989–2007)	67
6.2	The meteorological observations for the 11 cases with the top ten maximum values of T_{u-r} in Hong Kong (1989–2007)	68
7.1	Urban climate and planning scales	78
7.2	Positive and negative effects on urban climate	79
7.3	Open space planning possibilities with their thermal effects	80
8.1	Subjective scales used in the questionnaires	91
9.1	Summary of correlation indicators for all actual sensation vote (ASV) equations	111
9.2	Summary of t-values for all ASV equations	111
10.1	Height of gradient wind versus wind speed based on the power law with various coefficients	120
10.2	Relationship between height contrast and air change per hour performances	124
11.1	Values for air speed inside the canyon when wind blows along the canyon	147
11.2	Values for air speed inside the canyon when wind blows perpendicular or obliquely to the canyon	147
12.1	Mean ranking orders of various environmental pollutants, with the standard deviations shown in brackets	173

12.2	Mean evaluation of the general living environment, sound quality and health status, with the standard deviations shown in brackets	173
12.3	Main activities at home (percentage), where multiple choices were allowed	173
12.4	Mean preference of various potential positive sounds, with 1 as yes (selected) and 2 as no; standard deviations are shown in brackets	174
12.5	Factor analysis of the soundscape evaluation in Sheffield (Kaiser-Meyar-Olkin (KMO) measure of sampling adequacy: 0.798)	175
12.6	Factor analysis of the soundscape evaluation in Beijing (KMO measure of sampling adequacy: 0.860)	177
14.1	Wastage percentage of various trades for public housing projects and private residential developments	197
14.2	Drivers towards waste minimization in the Hong Kong construction industry	199
14.3	Government waste disposal facilities and disposal charge	199
16.1	Comparison of total heat gain/loss over a clear day (22 February 2004) on the rooftop, before and after	248
16.2	Comparison of four types of vertical landscaping methods	259
20.1	World high-rise buildings – status and plan	296
20.2	Ripple effect of high-rise buildings	297

List of Contributors

Editor

Edward Ng is an architect and a professor at the Chinese University of Hong Kong (CUHK). He has practised as an architect, as well as lectured in various universities around the world. Professor Ng's specialty is in environmental and sustainable design. He is director of the MSc Sustainable and Environmental Design Programme at CUHK. As an environmental consultant to the Hong Kong government, he developed the performance-based daylight design building regulations and the *Air Ventilation Assessment (AVA) Guidelines*. He is currently drafting the Urban Climatic Map for Planning in Hong Kong. Edward is a daylight and solar energy expert adviser to the Chinese government. As a visiting professor of Xian Jiaotong University, China, he currently designs ecological schools and is involved in building sustainable projects in China.

School of Architecture, Chinese University of Hong Kong, Shatin, NT, Hong Kong
Email: edwardng@cuhk.edu.hk
Web: www.edwardng.com

Contributors

Francis Allard, president of REHVA (Federation of European Heating, Ventilating and Air-conditioning Associations), is professor at the University of La Rochelle, France. He is director of LEPTIAB laboratory, one of the most specialized laboratories in France in the area of building physics, transport phenomena in buildings and the energy efficiency of buildings. He serves on numerous national and European scientific and technical committees, and is a frequent lecturer at many international conferences.

LEPTIAB, Pôle Sciences et Technologie, Bâtiment Fourier, Université de La Rochelle, Avenue Michel Crépeau, F-17042 La Rochelle Cedex 1, France
Email: francis.allard@univ-lr.fr

Yu Chen was a research fellow in the Department of Building at the National University of Singapore. His main areas of interest and research include the thermal effects of vegetation placed around buildings and in a built environment. He is currently working at Cobalt Engineering in Canada, conducting building energy simulation and building science-related analysis.

Cobalt Engineering, Suite 305 – 625, Howe Street, Vancouver, BC, V6C 2T6, Canada
Email: ychen@cobaltengineering.com

Vicky Cheng has been a researcher in the field of environmental architecture and urban design for the last six years, having obtained a degree in building services engineering. Dr Cheng has conducted research relating to urban ventilation and outdoor thermal comfort at the Chinese University of Hong Kong before moving to the Department of Architecture at the University of Cambridge, UK, for her doctorate study. She currently works at the University of Cambridge and Cambridge Architectural Research Limited on a range of research and consultancy projects.

Department of Architecture, University of Cambridge, 1–5 Scroope Terrace, Cambridge CB2 1PX, UK
Email: bkc25@cam.ac.uk

Lai Choo Malone-Lee teaches urban planning and environmental planning at the Department of Real Estate, School of Design and Environment, National University of Singapore, Singapore. Ms Malone-Lee is currently director of the Environmental Management Programme. She has published on land-use and urban planning subjects in international refereed journals such as *Land Use Policy, Habitat International, Town Planning Review* and *Cities*. She has extensive public-sector experience prior to joining academia and currently sits on various Singapore government committees and regularly consults for private-sector firms.

Department of Real Estate, School of Design and Environment, National University of Singapore, 4 Architecture Drive, Singapore 117566
Email: rstmalon@nus.edu.sg

Wan-Ki Chow is the chair professor of architectural science and fire engineering (leader of the area of strength: fire safety engineering) and director of the Research Centre for Fire Engineering of Hong Kong Polytechnic University. Professor Chow's main research interests are in architectural science, fire and safety engineering. He has had over 600 papers published in journals and conference proceedings. He has been the founding president of the Hong Kong Chapter, Society of Fire Protection Engineers, since 2002, and was elected president of the Asia-Oceania Association for Fire Science and Technology in 2007. He is active in dealing with performance-based design in the Far East and serves on government committees in Hong Kong and China on fire safety, ventilation and lighting, as well as professional bodies.

Hong Kong Polytechnic University, Hung Hom, Kowloon, Hong Kong
E-mail: bewkchow@polyu.edu.hk

Raymond J. Cole is a professor and director of the School of Architecture and Landscape Architecture at the University of British Columbia, Canada. He has been teaching environmental issues in building design in the architecture programme for the past 30 years. Dr Cole is the academic director of the Design Centre for Sustainability – the focus of sustainability-related research within the school. He was co-founder of the Green Building Challenge – an international collaborative effort to benchmark progress in green building performance and environmental assessment – and has served on numerous national and international committees related to buildings and the environment. Dr Cole was selected as a North American Association of Collegiate Schools of Architecture Distinguished Professor for 'sustained commitment to building environmental research and teaching' in 2001. In 2003 he received the Architectural Institute of British Columbia Barbara Dalrymple Memorial Award for Community Service and the US Green Building Council's Green Public Service Leadership Award. He is currently a director member of the Canadian Green Building Council, a director member of the Canada Solar Buildings Research Network, and holds the University of British Columbia designation of Distinguished University Scholar.

School of Architecture and Landscape Architecture, University of British Columbia,
402-6333 Memorial Road, Vancouver, BC V6T 1Z2, Canada
Email: raycole@arch.ubc.ca

Christian Ghiaus is a professor of building physics at the National Institute of Applied Sciences (INSA) of Lyon, France, involved in research on the control of energy and mass transfer in buildings. His main contributions are on estimating building energy performance, fault detection and diagnosis, and fuzzy and internal model control of airflow in heating, ventilating and air-conditioning (HVAC) systems and buildings.

INSA, Lyon, 9, Rue de la Physique, 69621 Villeurbanne, France
Email: christian.ghiaus@insa-lyon.fr

Baruch Givoni is professor emeritus of architecture in the Graduate School of Architecture and Urban Planning at the University of California, Los Angeles (UCLA), US, and was associated for many years with the Technion in Haifa, and with Ben Gurion University of the Negev in Beer Sheba, both in Israel. Mr Givoni's classic text *Man, Climate and Architecture* (Applied Science Publishers, Ltd, 1969) is considered the most authoritative volume in the field of building climatology. His career also includes teaching assignments at nearly a dozen universities, as well as hundreds of papers and contributions to scholarly works, lectures and symposia. He has assisted the World Health Organization, the World Meteorological Organization, the Israel Ministry of Housing and numerous governments around the world on passive and solar energy design of structures in hot climates.

Department of Architecture, School of Arts and Architecture, UCLA, Los Angeles, CA, US
Email: bgivoni@bezeqint.net

Chye Kiang Heng teaches architecture and urban design at the Department of Architecture, National University of Singapore. Professor Heng is currently dean of the School of Design and Environment; co-leader of Asia Research Institute's Sustainable Cities Cluster; and board member of the Singapore Urban Redevelopment Authority and Centre for Liveable Cities. He publishes widely on urban history, urban design and heritage. His publications include *Cities of Aristocrats and Bureaucrats* (Singapore University Press/University of Hawaii Press, 1999), *The House of Tan Yeok Nee: The Conservation of a National Monument* (Singapore: Winpeak Investment Private Ltd, 2003) and *A Digital Reconstruction of Tang Chang'an* (Beijing: China Architecture and Building Press, 2006). He also consults on urban design and planning and is the conceptual designer of several international urban design/planning competition winning entries in China.

Department of Architecture, School of Design and Environment, National University of Singapore, 4 Architecture Drive, Singapore 117566
Email: akihck@nus.edu; hengck@yahoo.com

Lara Jaillon has completed her studies in architecture in France (University of Paris) and Canada (McGill University) and completed her MSc in Hong Kong. As an architect, she has previously conducted research on construction waste reduction at the design stage, co-writing a guidebook, helping designers to reduce waste by design concepts, material selection and construction methods *A Guide for Minimizing Construction and Demolition Waste at the Design Stage*, (Poon, C. S. and Jaillon, L., The Hong Kong Polytechnic University, Hong Kong. 2002). She is now carrying out her PhD in the Department of Civil and Structural Engineering at the Hong Kong Polytechnic University on the evolution of the use of prefabrication in high-rise buildings in Hong Kong, considering aspects such as construction techniques, materials, design concepts and building performance. She has written articles published in local and international journals and conferences.

Department of Civil and Structural Engineering, Hong Kong Polytechnic University, Hung Hom, Kowloon, Hong Kong
Email: lara.jaillon@polyu.edu.hk

Jian Kang is professor of acoustics at the School of Architecture, University of Sheffield, UK. He obtained his first degree and MSc from Tsinghua University in Beijing, his PhD from the University of Cambridge, UK, and also worked as a Humboldt Postdoctoral Fellow at the Fraunhofer Institute of Building Physics in Germany. His main research fields include environmental acoustics, architectural acoustics, building acoustics and acoustic materials. With over 300 publications, he is a fellow of the UK Institute of Acoustics (IOA), a fellow of the Acoustical Society of America (ASA), and the editor in environmental noise for *Acta Acustica* united with *Acustica – European Journal of Acoustics*. Dr Kang has acted as the principal investigator for over 40 funded research projects, and a consultant for over 40 acoustics and noise-control projects worldwide. He was awarded the 2008 Tyndall Medal by the UK Institute of Acoustics.

School of Architecture, University of Sheffield, Western Bank, Sheffield, S10 2TN, UK
Tel: +44 114 2220325
Fax: +44 114 2220315
Email: j.kang@sheffield.ac.uk

Lutz Katzschner is a meteorologist and professor of environmental meteorology at the University Kassel, Germany, in the Faculty of Architecture and Urban Planning. His main science interest is urban climatic mapping from meso- to micro-scales and their implementation in an urban planning perspective. In this field he is chairman of the Guideline Committee on Climate and Planning in Germany. He is currently carrying out projects on global warming aspects and their effect on urban climatology in different countries.

University Kassel, Faculty of Architecture and Urban Planning, Department of Environmental Meteorology, Henschelstr. 2, 34127 Kassel, Germany
Email: katzschn@uni-kassel.de

Chiu-Ying Lam is ex-director of the Hong Kong Observatory. He is a meteorologist with extensive experience in weather operations and meteorology applications in various sectors. He studied meteorology at Imperial College, London, and has worked at the Hong Kong Observatory since 1974. Mr Lam served as the vice president of Regional Association II (Asia) of the World Meteorological Organization between 2003 and 2008. His interests in recent years include the elucidation of climate trends in Hong Kong and their projection into the future. He was a contributing author of *Climate Change 2007: Fourth Assessment Report* of the United Nations Intergovernmental Panel on Climate Change (Cambridge University Press, 2007).

Hong Kong Observatory, 134A Nathan Road, Tsim Sha Tsui, Kowloon, Hong Kong
Email: lamchiuying@gmail.com

Bryan Lawson is both an architect and a psychologist. His research focuses on the nature of design processes and on the impact of the built environment upon our quality of life. He has been head of department and dean of the Faculty of Architectural Studies at the University of Sheffield, UK, distinguished visiting professor at the National University of Singapore and Universiti Teknologi Malaysia, and visiting professor at the University of Sydney, Australia. He has practised as an architect in both the private and public sectors, and now advises government bodies, architects and developers mainly in the UK, Ireland, Australia and the US.

The Arts Tower, Western Bank, University of Sheffield, Sheffield, S10 2TN, UK
Email: b.lawson@sheffield.ac.uk

Tsz-Cheung Lee is a scientific officer with the Hong Kong Observatory and has been working with the Hong Kong Observatory since 1993. Mr Lee has been variously involved in weather forecasting, tropical cyclone research, climatological information services and climate studies. Present responsibilities include climate change monitoring and research, urban climate studies, and outreach activities on climate change.

Hong Kong Observatory, 134A Nathan Road, Tsim Sha Tsui, Kowloon, Hong Kong
Email: tclee@hko.gov.hk

Wing-Mo Leung is senior scientific officer at Corporation Communication and Tropical Cyclone Studies and has worked in many different areas over the past two decades, including weather forecasting, environmental radiation monitoring and emergency preparedness, implementation of a meteorological observational network, as well as training in meteorology. In recent years, Mr Leung's main areas of interest have been related to corporate communication and tropical cyclone research, as well as climatological studies, particularly on climate change and public education on the issue. He is currently a member of the Commission for Climatology of the World Meteorological Organization (WMO) and a member of the WMO Expert Group on Climate and Health.

Hong Kong Observatory, 134A Nathan Road, Tsim Sha Tsui, Kowloon, Hong Kong
Email: wmleung@hko.gov.hk

John C. Y. Ng is an architect and town planner. He was chief architect with the Hong Kong Housing Authority; has served many years as divisional advisory committee member, Division of Building Science and Technology, City University of Hong Kong; and is currently honorary associate professor in the Department of Architecture, University of Hong Kong. He has more than 30 years of experience in the planning, design, construction and project management of high-density housing and related facilities. A number of awards were won by these projects in architecture, planning, urban design, green building and research. John has been dedicated in the pursuit of innovative design and sustainable development, and believes that planning and architecture must serve the community and enhance the built environment.

Housing Department, Hong Kong Housing Authority Headquarters, 33 Fat Kwong Street, Kowloon, Hong Kong
Email: johnng@me.com

Adrian Pitts is professor of sustainable architecture at Sheffield Hallam University in the UK. He has been teaching and researching in areas of environmentally sensitive design and energy efficiency in relation to the built environment for over 20 years. He has published over 80 refereed articles in journals and conference proceedings and is the author of three books. His activities have received public funding from such sources as research councils in the UK, European Union programmes, commercial organizations and government departments.

Architecture Group, Sheffield Hallam University, City Campus, Howard Street, Sheffield, S1 1WB, UK
Tel: +44 114 225 3608
Email: a.pitts@shu.ac.uk

Chi-Sun Poon obtained his PhD in Environmental Engineering from Imperial College, London University, UK. He is currently professor and director of the Research Centre for Environmental Technology and Management at the Civil and Structural Engineering Department of the Hong Kong Polytechnic University. Professor Poon specializes in the research and development of environmentally friendly construction materials, waste management and recycling technologies, and sustainable construction. He has published over 220 papers in international journals and conferences. He is a Fellow of the Hong Kong Institution of Engineers (HKIE) and is a past chairman of the HKIE Environmental Division. He has also served as chairman of the Hong Kong Waste Management Association.

Department of Civil and Structural Engineering, Hong Kong Polytechnic University, Hung Hom, Hong Kong
Email: cecspoon@polyu.edu.hk

Marylis Ramos has been researching in the field of environmental sustainability over the past five years. She currently works as a senior sustainability consultant at PRP Architects, UK.

PRP Architects Ltd, 10 Lindsey Street, Smithfield, London, EC1A 9HP, UK
Email: mcr29@cam.ac.uk

Susan Roaf is professor of architectural engineering at Heriot Watt University, Edinburgh, Scotland, and visiting professor at the Open University. She spent ten years in the Middle East, and her doctorate was on the wind catchers of Yazd. She has published on Iranian nomadic architecture, excavated for seven years in Iraq and was a landscape consultant in Iraq and the Gulf. Her research interests over the last two decades have centred on thermal comfort, ecological building design, building integrated renewable energy systems, adaptation of the built environment for climate change, carbon accounting and the traditional technologies of the Middle East. She has recently chaired international conferences on solar cities, carbon counting, architectural education, thermal comfort and post-occupancy evaluation. She have written and edited numerous publications, including ten books.

Heriot Watt University, Edinburgh, Scotland, EH14 4AS
Email: s.roaf@sbe.hw.ac.uk

Koen Steemers is the head of the Department of Architecture and professor of sustainable design at the University of Cambridge, UK, carrying out research on the environmental performance of buildings and cities with a particular focus on the role of human agency. As director of the Martin Centre for Architectural and Urban Studies, he coordinated the department's research that resulted in it being ranked top in its field in the UK in 2008. He has published over 120 books and articles, including *Energy and Environment in Architecture* (Taylor & Francis, 2000), *Daylight Design for Buildings* (Earthscan, 2002), *The Selective Environment* (Taylor & Francis, 2002) and *Environmental Diversity in Architecture* (Routledge, 2004).

Department of Architecture, University of Cambridge, 1 Scroope Terrace, Cambridge, CB2 1PX, UK
Tel: +44 1223 332950
Email: kas11@cam.ac.uk

Sung Woo Shin is professor and dean of Hanyang University, Korea, and has been chairman of the Korea Super Tall Building Forum since 2001, as well as the director of Sustainable Building Research Centre (ERC)-funded MEST/KOSEF since 2005. He is a co-organizer SB07 Seoul, a board member of iiSBE and was vice president of the Architecture Institute of Korea. He is a member of the National Academy of Engineering of Korea. Dr Shin is interested in sustainable tall building research, practice and education. He is the chief editor of *Super Tall Building Design and Technology* (kimoondang, 2007) and *Sustainable Building Technology* (kimoondang, 2007), and is the author of over 20 professional books. He is the recipient of research awards from both American and Korean concrete institutes. He won the National Best Scientist and Engineer Award from the National Assembly of the Republic of Korea.

Sustainable Building Research Centre, School of Architecture and Architectural Engineering, Hanyang University, 1271 Sa 1-dong, Sangnok-gu, Ansan-si, Gyeonggi-do, 426-791, Korea
Email: swshin@hanyang.ac.kr

Agota Szucs is an architect and building engineer graduated from the University of Technology and Economics of Budapest, Hungary. She investigated the relation between spectators' comfort in open sports stadia, the climatic parameters and the stadium architecture during her PhD, obtained from La Rochelle University, France. She is now a post-doctoral researcher in LEPTIAB, at La Rochelle University, and works on indoor air quality and ventilation in French educational buildings.

LEPTIAB, Pôle Sciences et Technologie, Bâtiment Fourier, Université de la Rochelle, Avenue Michel Crépeau, F-17042 La Rochelle Cedex 1, France
Email: agota.szucs@univ-lr.fr

Brenda Vale and **Robert Vale** are professorial research fellows at the School of Architecture, Victoria University of Wellington, New Zealand. Their 1975 book *The Autonomous House* (Thames & Hudson) is widely recognized as a basic text in the field of green building. Throughout the 1980s the Vales designed a number of very low-energy commercial buildings in England. During the 1990s the Vales wrote *Green Architecture* (Thames & Hudson, 1991) completed the first autonomous house in the UK and received the UN Global 500 award. They also designed the award-winning zero-emission Hockerton Housing Project. They later developed the National Australian Built Environment Rating System (NABERS). The latest book by the Vales, which deals with the realities of sustainable living, is *Time to Eat the Dog? The Real Guide to Sustainable Living* (Thames & Hudson, 2009).

School of Architecture, Victoria University, Wellington, 139 Vivian Street, PO Box 600, Wellington, New Zealand
Email: brenda.vale@vuw.ac.nz; robert.vale@vuw.ac.nz

Kam-Sing Wong is an architect who integrates research and sustainable design principles in practice, particularly with reference to high-density urban contexts and humid subtropical climates. He teaches part time in various local schools of architecture and participates in joint research, including air ventilation assessment and the urban climate map. He studied architecture at the University of Hong Kong and furthered his research study at the University of British Columbia, Canada. Previous projects include Verbena Heights, an award-winning high-rise public housing estate in Hong Kong. With 20 years of experience in the architectural practice, he is currently director of Sustainable Design in Ronald Lu & Partners, leading architectural and urban design projects at various scales – from designing a centre for healthy life on top of a hospital block, to master planning for urban regeneration in various old and dense districts. A recent consultancy commission by the government was to study building design that supports sustainable urban living space in the dense context of Hong Kong, with recommendations in the form of design guidelines for voluntary or mandatory application. He is currently serving as the chairman of the Professional Green Building Council and vice president of the Hong Kong Institute of Architects.

Ronald Lu & Partners (Hong Kong) Ltd, 33/F Wu Chung House, Wanchai, Hong Kong
Email: kswong@rlphk.com

Nyuk-Hien Wong is an associate professor and deputy head (research) in the Department of Building at the National University of Singapore. He has been the principal investigator for a number of research projects funded by the various Singapore government agencies to study the urban heat island effect in Singapore and to explore the various mitigation measures, such as the effective utilization of urban greenery and cool roof materials. Dr Wong has also been engaged as a member of advisory boards to the various government agencies in Singapore. He has written four books and published more than 150 international refereed journal and conference papers in these related fields.

National University of Singapore, School of Design and Environment, Department of Building, 4 Architecture Drive, Singapore 117566
Email: bdgwnh@nus.edu.sg

Foreword

This book is timely; but I can't help wishing we had had it when Hong Kong was recovering from the Pacific war and post-war reconstruction was about to begin.

Before the war much of the built-up area of the city was guided by the straight length of a China fir pole, which served as a roof beam for the many shop houses that lined our narrow streets and, most importantly, to which their owners had title. Indeed, you can still see some of these strange pencil buildings, which this gave rise to, wedged in between high rises in parts of the city. In the decades after the war it was the lack of familiarity and expense of elevators that limited our buildings to what would be the tolerable height to climb a staircase – nine storeys was about the limit.

At the time, the new runway at Kai Tak Airport in the city centre set a height limit at 60m above principal datum for any future building in Kowloon. This gave rise to a not unpleasing flat-roofed city without ugly competition in height or sight. The closing of the city airport in 1997 and the consequent removal of the height limit without restriction, except that of plot ratio, and without a great deal of thought as to what real estate developers would make of this literally golden opportunity, resulted in environmental destruction on a grand scale. It permitted monster buildings to be built, almost hiding the lovely mountains that encircle our city and are such a scenic feature of Hong Kong, further shutting out views of the harbour.

In addition to these depredations, no one thought about the effect that the growth of traffic or the helter-skelter industrialization of the Pearl River Delta would have on the air we breathe. Pragmatism and profit have influenced policies and good planning. Given that land is in short supply, we could really have done better. Surely we have some fine high-rise buildings; but we have lost so much. Now we have buildings that are packed close together in a wall, flats which never have a ray of sunshine to enjoy, and streets described as 'airless canyons'.

This book brings together expert opinions from many disciplines and many nations to give their experience and advice on these matters together under one cover; it will be a valuable guide, a *vade-mecum* to all of those involved and employed in the work of building our towns and cities not just here, but anywhere in the world. I should like to express my most sincere thanks to them.

A last word: we have not finished building Hong Kong. I pray we make some changes from now on.

Sir David Akers-Jones
Former Chief Secretary (1985–1987) and Acting Governor (1986–1987) of Hong Kong

Preface

● City with at least 1,000,000 inhabitants in 2006

Source: Data from Thomas Brinkhoff – The Principal Agglomerations of the World, www.citypopulation.de

Figure P.1 *Cities with more than 1 million inhabitants*

The year 2006 was a memorable year. From then on, more than 50 per cent of the world's population would live in cities (see Figure P.1). The number of cities and megacities has continued to be on the rise. There are now more than 20 so-called megacities (cities with a population of more than 10 million), and more are being added to the list every day. More than 400 cities worldwide now have populations in excess of 1 million. Urbanization and higher-density living is an irreversible path of human development.

The world's population is not spread evenly across the Earth's land mass. On a per country land area basis, Europe, China and the Asian subcontinent have the higher population density, in the order of 300 to more than 1000 people per square kilometre. However, a low number like this may be misleading. A more telling picture is density in urban areas, sometimes known as urban population density (see Table P.1). New York, for example, has an urban population density of only 1750 individuals per square kilometre; London has 5100; whereas Asian cities such as Delhi and Tehran have higher densities of 10,700 and 12,300 individuals per spare kilometre, respectively. Some cities such as Hong Kong and Mumbai have very high urban densities in excess of 20,000 people per square kilometre.

More affluent Asian cities in Japan and cities in Europe have urban densities in the order of 2000 to 5000 people per square kilometre. City sprawl in the US means that urban densities are low, at around 1000 per square kilometre or less. Except Hong Kong, generally speaking, high-density cities mean poor cities. Of the 20 highest-density urban cities in the world, 16 are in India, with the rest in China, Bangladesh and North Korea. Finding ways of designing high-density cities must therefore be one of our humanitarian goals (Jenson, 1966).

There is another way of looking at urban density, and that is to note the density of urban development (see Tables P.1 and P.2). The most interesting observation is that most cities are now moving towards high-density development. In Canada, for example, newer developments house around 5000 to 7000 people per square kilometre. Higher-density living will continue to be developed and will soon be the norm.

There are commercial and sometimes even political reasons for high-density living (Walker, 2003). Higher and more compact city design conserves valuable land resources, reduces transport distance and, thus, the energy

Table P.1 *Urban density*

City	Urban area (km²)	Urban density (person per km²)
Hong Kong, China	220	29,400
Macau, China	23	23,350
Beijing, China	4300	4300
Shanghai, China	2396	5700
Singapore	479	8350
Manila, Philippines	1425	13,450
Mumbai, India	777	21,900
Delhi, India	1425	10,700
Tokyo-Yokohama	7835	4350
Sydney, Australia	1788	2050
Tehran, Iran	635	12,300
Cairo, Egypt	1269	12,800
São Paulo, Brazil	2590	7200
Paris	3043	3400
London	1623	5100
Berlin	984	3750
New York	11,264	1750
San Francisco–San Jose	2497	2150
Toronto, Canada	2500	2500
Mombasa, Kenya	57	14,050

Source: www.demographia.com

Table P.2 *Urban density – new development*

City	Urban density (person per km²)
Hong Kong, China	54,305
Los Angeles, USA	7744
Singapore	18,622
Manila, Philippines	55,686
Tokyo-Yokohama	16,640
Sydney, Australia	2960
Sacramento, USA	5700
San Francisco–San Jose	6721
Vancouver, Canada	5054
Paris	4516

Source: www.demographia.com

needed, and the density makes public transport more viable (Smith, 1984; Betanzo, 2007). Advocates argue that high-density cities are more efficient economically (see Figure P.2). There are, of course, downsides. 'Experts warn against high-density housing' was a headline of the *Guardian* newspaper on 18 November 2003; it named noise and privacy two of the main drawbacks. There are other concerns (Phoon, 1975). The stress of crowded living is one of them (Freedman, 1975; Travers, 1977); 'high density and low diversity' is another. Doubtless, concerns are mostly based on the past and unhappy episodes of squatters, high-rise council flats and slums. Nonetheless, the message is clear. Can we continue using our traditional wisdom in designing high-density cities and homes? The answer is obviously no.

This book focuses on the socio-environmental dimension of the subject. It attempts to bring together scholars, experts and practitioners of high-density city design to share current experience and knowledge on the subject. One must, however, see this offering as only representing a start. One is only getting there, and there is a long way to go.

It can be difficult to define exactly what high-density living is. In the UK, it probably means a rise from 10 homes to 20 homes per acre. In Australia, it probably means an increase from 1000 to 3000 people per square kilometre. In Hong Kong, it may mean an increase from 40-storey to 60-storey high-rise residential buildings. As such, when we talk about high-density living, there is a good possibility that we are talking about different things. Hence, it is very important to bear this diversity in mind. There is a need to expand understanding of the term 'high density'. In Part I, Vicky Cheng delineates various ways of looking at density in Chapter 1. She argues for a diverse way of looking at perceived density. After all, density is not noticeable unless it is seen. In Chapter 2, Brenda and Robert Vale cast the discourse on high-density living on a wider and perhaps more holistic basis. A high-density city still need its hinterland to supply it with the required resources. As a result, the equation for efficiency may not be as straightforward as at first perceived. High density may not be the only option. Susan Roaf believes that high density (not high rise) is the inevitable future (see Chapter 3). One only needs to find ways to cope with it. Roaf looked at high-density living from health, vulnerability, security and equality points of view. She reckons that there is a limit to high density, and one must be prudent in trying to assess the limit contextually and appropriately. Heng and

- **living closer together encourages more community interaction, and reduces isolation for vulnerable social groups, such as young families;**

- **compact settlements require less transport and reduce car use, with health and environmental benefits;**

- **higher-density development is environmentally beneficial, resulting in lower carbon emissions;**

- **in rural areas, more compact villages could help to stem the decline in rural services, such as shops, post offices and bus services.**

Source: Willis (2008)

Figure P.2 *Reasons for high-density living*

Malone-Lee also caution how the notion of density should be debated and understood. They reckon it is related to building and urban form, and how uses are mixed. The authors discuss diversity and flexibility, complexity and size, and problems with over-determination as ways to dissect the discourse. Roaf, Heng and Malone-Lee highlight the challenges of the quest towards high density. One must not be too simplistic about the potential complexity and unknowns facing researchers, designers and planners. Together, they have set the scene for authors of Part II.

In Part II, the climatic considerations of high-density living are the main thesis of Chiu-Ying Lam's and Wing-Mo Leung and Tsz-Cheung Lee's chapters (Chapters 5 and 6). Urban climate and liveability can be important factors in designing high-density cities. After all, it is people for whom we build our cities, and when failing to provide for inhabitants climatically, high-density cities have no value and little meaning. High-density living, furthermore, has its environmental problems. Heat islands and hot nights are problematic issues. Lam, in particular, vividly argues that the poor and the weak are most in need of our attention when designing high-density cities. The environmental dimensions of high-density cities, especially in tropical and subtropical climatic zones, are important to get right. In Chapter 7, Lutz Katzschner reckons that urban climate is an important consideration. The use of urban climate maps may allow planners and policy-makers a better and strategic view of urban design.

Part III of this book is about various environmental considerations of high-density design. Cities are designed for people. In Chapter 8, Baruch Givoni argues that, environmentally, the thermal comfort of inhabitants should be a key focus. Givoni stresses the importance of research leading to a better understanding of thermal comfort in high-density cites. It is only with better information about what is needed that designers can design appropriately. Koen Steemers and Marylis Ramos further the thesis in Chapter 9, but stress the need to ensure diversity in city design. We are all different. Cities with many people need to provide various kinds of space to address this need for difference. The concept of 'choice' is useful.

Edward Ng's chapters on ventilation and daylight (Chapters 10 and 13) highlight important aspects of high-density designs. Light and air are basic human needs. In high-density cities, the provision of light and air can be difficult. Ng argues that there is a need for a complete rethink when designing high-density cities. A paradigm shift of methodology is required. The topic of environmental degradation is echoed by Francis Allard, Christian Ghiaus and Agota Szucs in Chapter 11. Ventilation for comfort and the cooling potential of ventilation, both indoor and outdoor, in high-density cities are explained.

Apart from air and light, opponents to high-density living have raised the issue of noise. Close proximity of apartment units exaggerates the problem. In Chapter 12, Jian Kang explains a method of looking at noise based on urban morphology. The concept of 'soundscape' may help us to see problems as opportunities. Another environmental issue of high-density living is waste. In Chapter 14, Chi-Sun Poon and Lara Jaillon suggest a few ways of minimizing waste production due to development. Low-waste building technology may be a way out. There is also a need for corresponding policy by the government. The risk of fire that comes from living too close together is the focus of Wan-Ki Chow's chapter (Chapter 15). Performance-based fire engineering is preferable, and Chow elaborates upon the concept of total fire safety.

Urban greenery to alleviate the adverse effects of high-density cities and urban heat islands is discussed in Chapter 16 by Nyuk-Hien Wong and Yu Chen. Greenery and green open spaces not only address the thermal comfort problem; they also offer an alternative to city dwellers seeking an outside oasis.

The energy issue of high-density living is addressed by Adrian Pitts in Chapter 17, such as how renewable energy can be of meaning in high-density city design. A holistic view based on environmental assessment is further offered by Raymond J. Cole in Chapter 18. The need to look beyond a simple building is very important when we are dealing with high-density living. Perhaps it is not the space within building envelopes that matters. It is the spaces in between buildings that test the design of high-density cities.

Apart from environmental considerations, the social aspects of high-density living are dealt with in Part IV by Bryan Lawson (Chapter 19), Sung Woo Shin (Chapter 20), John C. Y. Ng (Chapter 21) and Kam-Sing Wong (Chapter 22). Lawson theorizes that the perception and identity of open spaces in high-density cities are particularly important in providing inhabitants with a sense of belonging.

Can high-density cities also be eco-cities? Shin reckons that much further research is needed. Is sustainable high rise a solution? Shin has raised more questions than one can easily find answers to. Ng, on the other hand, is much more optimistic. He can afford to be so as he has demonstrated with his high-rise high-density residential housing in Hong Kong that the holy grail of high-density living is a definite possibility. It should, however, be noted that this is not an easy path. Ng argues that social acceptability through participation may offer a way out. Lawson has suggested an evidence-based approach with creativity. Last, but not least, Wong's chapter recaps some of the key views expressed. Quality city living in a high-density context means that there is a need for balance. High density is not a one-way path, and there is definitely a limit to it. Using the example of wall buildings in Hong Kong, Wong speculates on the idea of eco-density. There is a need for innovation.

There are many more socio-economic issues regarding high-density cities and high-density living than a single volume can hope to embrace. Nonetheless, the 22 chapters have painted a diverse and yet cohesive picture. The fact is that designing for high-density living is not a straightforward extrapolation of our known wisdom and knowledge base. The adventure needs care and sometimes a paradigm shift of thoughts and operations. As such, this book on high-density living and city density only opens a can of worms that requires further efforts to put it back into order. One thing is sure: the subject will continue to haunt us. There's no easy way out and the discourse has just started.

Edward Ng, November 2009

References

Betanzo, M. (2007) 'Pros and cons of high density urban environments', *Build*, April/May, pp39–40

Freedman, J. L. (1975) 'Crowding and behaviour', *The Psychology of High-Density Living*, Viking Press, New York City

Jenson, R. (1966) *High Density Living*, TBS, The Book Service Ltd, Praeger, Leonard Hill, London

Phoon, W. O. (1975) 'The medical aspect of high-rise and high-density living', *The Nursing Journal of Singapore*, November, vol 15, no 2, pp69–75

Smith, W. S. (1984) 'Mass transport for high-rise high-density living', *Journal of Transportation Engineering*, vol 110, no 6, pp521–535

Travers, L. H. (1977) 'Perception of high density living in Hong Kong', in Heisler, G. M. and Herrington, L. P. (eds) *Proceedings of the Conference on Metropolitan Physical Environment, General Technical Report*, NE-25, US Department of Agriculture, Forest Service, Northeastern Forest Experiment Station, Upper Darby, PA, pp408–414

Walker, B. (2003) *Making Density Desirable*, www.forumforthefuture.org/greenfutures/articles/601476, accessed January 2009

Willis, R. (2008) *The Proximity Principle*, Campaign to Protect Rural England, Green Building Press, www.cpre.org.uk/library/3524

Acknowledgements

I met Guy Robinson of Earthscan at the PALENC05 conference in Greece. After my presentation on designing for better urban ventilation for Hong Kong, the idea of producing a volume that gathers expertise and views on high-density city design came about right away. Amidst all of the chores of living, working and assisting the Hong Kong government in designing one of the world's highest-density cities, weekends and holidays were spent on the book, and it would not have been an easy few years without the help of colleagues, friends and family.

I have to thank all of the contributors. Without your support, effort and scholarship, I am sure this book would still be in cyberspace. I apologize that I have had to send friendly reminders from time to time.

Thanks are due to Polly Tsang, Max Lee, Justin He, Iris Tsang and Chao Yuan, my assistants, who did most of the administrative chores, and who have helped to put the manuscript together for me.

I would like to mention two of my most important mentors. Both now retired, they have, more than anybody else, helped me on my scholarly paths. Professor Peter Tregenza taught me when I was a fresh first-year student at Nottingham University, UK. I owe him everything I know about daylighting design and, more importantly, almost everything I know about scholarship and how to become a scholar. Professor Dean Hawkes was my PhD supervisor. He taught me how to look beyond equations and numbers. There is poetry and beauty to be found if we look and work vigorously – including living in a high-density city. His book *Environmental Imagination* (Taylor and Francis, 2007) has been my source of reference when I am lost.

Last, but not least, my two sons, Michael and Simon, have always been a reminder to me that we need a better Earth upon which to live. Sustainability is not for oneself. My wife Yiwen has tolerated me all of these years, not that I have always been late for dinner; but I have worked too much and neglected her from time to time. I dedicate this book to her, my beloved.

List of Acronyms and Abbreviations

ach	air changes per hour
ANOVA	analysis of variance
ASA	Acoustical Society of America
ASHRAE	American Society of Heating, Refrigerating and Air-Conditioning Engineers
ASV	actual sensation vote
AVA	air ventilation assessment
BBNP	Bukit Batok Natural Park (Singapore)
BEE_{UD}	building environmental efficiency in urban development
BIPV	building integrated photovoltaic
BIPVS	building integrated photovoltaic system
BRE	Building Research Establishment
BREEAM	Building Research Establishment Environmental Assessment Method
C&D	construction and demolition
CAD	computer-aided design
CASBEE	Comprehensive Assessment System for Building Environmental Efficiency
CASBEE-UD	CASBEE for Urban Development
CBP	Changi Business Park (Singapore)
CC	correlation coefficient
CEPAS	Comprehensive Environmental Performance Assessment Scheme (Hong Kong)
CFA	construction floor area
CFD	computational fluid dynamics
CHP	combined heat and power
CIE	Commission Internationale de l'Eclairage
CIRC	Construction Industry Review Committee
CIRIA	Construction Industry Research and Information Association
CityU	City University of Hong Kong
CIWMB	California Integrated Waste Management Board
CNU	Congress for the New Urbanism
CO	carbon monoxide
CO_2	carbon dioxide
CSIR	Council for Scientific and Industrial Research
CUHK	Chinese University of Hong Kong
CWP	Celmenti Woods Park (Singapore)
dB	decibel
DEM	digital elevation model
DF	daylight factor
EDSL TAS	Environmental Design Solutions Limited (EDSL) Thermal Analysis Simulation software
EMSD	Electrical and Mechanical Services Department (Hong Kong)
ERC	external reflected component
ESCo	energy service company
ESSD	environmentally sound and sustainable development
ET	effective temperature
EU	European Union
FEA	fire engineering approach

FRP	fire resistance period
FSE	fire safety engineering
g/h	grams per hour
GFA	gross floor area
GFA	ground floor area
GIS	geographical information system
GWh	gigawatt hour
ha	hectare
HDB	Housing Development Board
HK-BEAM	Hong Kong Building Environmental Assessment Method
HKHA	Hong Kong Housing Authority
HKIE	Hong Kong Institution of Engineers
HKO	Hong Kong Observatory headquarters
HKPSG	Hong Kong Planning Standards and Guidelines
HKSAR	Hong Kong Special Administrative Region
HMSO	Her Majesty's Stationery Office
HR	humidity ratio
HVAC	heating, ventilating and air conditioning
H/W	height-to-width ratio
INSA	National Institute of Applied Sciences (France)
IBP	International Business Park (Singapore)
I/O	indoor–outdoor ratio/input–output ratio
IOA	Institute of Acoustics (UK)
IPCC	Intergovernmental Panel on Climate Change
IUCN	World Conservation Union (*formerly* International Union for Conservation of Nature)
K	Kelvin
K	potassium
KMO	Kaiser-Meyer-Olkin
kHz	kilohertz
kJ	kilojoule
km	kilometres
KPF	Kohn Pederson Fox
kWh	kilowatt hour
LAI	leaf area index
LCA	life-cycle assessment
LCC	life-cycle costing/cost
LEED®	Leadership in Energy & Environmental Design
LEED-ND®	LEED for Neighbourhood Development
L_{UD}	environmental load in urban development
LVRw	local spatial average wind velocity ratio
MIT	Massachusetts Institute of Technology
MJ	megajoule
MRT	mean radiant/radiation temperature (°C)
MW	megawatt
MWh	megawatt hour
MXD	mixed-use development
NASA	US National Aeronautics and Space Administration

NGO	non-governmental organization
NHT	numerical heat transfer
NIST	US National Institute of Standards and Technology
NO_2	nitrogen dioxide
NRDC	Natural Resources Defense Council
NUS	National University of Singapore
O_3	ozone
OECD	Organisation for Economic Co-operation and Development
OTTV	overall thermal transfer value
P	phosphorus
Pa	pascal
Pb	lead
PBD	performance-based design
PCA	principal components analysis
PET	physiological equivalent temperature
PJ	petajoule
PMV	predicted mean vote
ppb	parts per billion
ppm	parts per million
PV	photovoltaic
Q_{UD}	environmental quality and performance in urban development
R	correlation coefficient
R^2	coefficient of determination
REHVA	Federation of European Heating, Ventilating and Air-Conditioning Associations
RH	relative humidity (%)
RHP	rectangular horizontal plane
RT	reverberation time
RUROS	Rediscovering the Urban Realm and Open Spaces project
SARS	severe acute respiratory syndrome
SBAT	Sustainable Building Assessment Tool
SC	sky component
SO_2	sulphur dioxide
SPeAR®	Sustainable Project Assessment Routine
SPL	sound pressure level
SR	solar radiation intensity
SVF	sky view factor
SVRw	average wind velocity ratio
Temp	air temperature
Tglobe	globe temperature (°C)
TKL	Ta Kwu Ling
TS	thermal sensation
TSV	thermal sensation vote
UC-AnMap	Urban Climatic Analysis Map
UCI	cool island effect
UCL	urban canopy layer
UCLA	University of California, Los Angeles
UC-ReMap	Urban Climatic Recommendation Map
UHI	urban heat island

UN	United Nations
UNESCO	United Nations Educational, Scientific and Cultural Organization
UNFPA	United Nations Population Fund
USGBC	The US Green Building Council
UVA	unobstructed vision area
VDF	vertical daylight factor
vel	wind speed (m/s)
VOC	volatile organic compound
VRw	wind velocity ratio
W/h	watt per hour
WHO	World Health Organization
WMO	World Meteorological Organization
WS	wind speed

Part I

An Understanding of High Density

1

Understanding Density and High Density

Vicky Cheng

The word 'density', although familiar at first glance, is a complex concept upon closer examination. The complexity mainly stems from the multitude of definitions of the term in different disciplines and under different contexts. This chapter attempts to untangle the intricate concepts of density according to two perspectives – namely, physical density and perceived density. A thorough comprehension of these two distinct concepts of density will serve as a basis for understanding the meaning of high density. Hopefully, this chapter will establish the ground for the discussions in later chapters on the design of high-density cities with respect to the timeliest social and environmental issues.

Physical density

Physical density is a numerical measure of the concentration of individuals or physical structures within a given geographical unit. It is an objective, quantitative and neutral spatial indicator. However, in practice, physical density takes on a real meaning only if it is related to a specified scale of reference.

For instance, density expressed as ratio of population to land area can vary significantly with reference to different scales of geographical unit. Take Hong Kong as an example: if the land area of the whole territory is taken into account, the overall population density in Hong Kong is about 6300 persons per square kilometre. However, only about 24 per cent of the total area in Hong Kong is built up. Therefore, if the geographical reference is confined to built-up land, then the population density will be about 25,900 individuals per square kilometre, which is four times the overall density of the territory. Hence, it is important that the scales of geographical references be explicitly defined in density calculation, otherwise comparison of density measures will be difficult.

Nevertheless, there is no standard measure of density; there are only measures that are more widely used than

Source: Vicky Cheng

Figure 1.1 *People density*

others. In town planning, measurement of physical density can be broadly divided into two categories: people density and building density. People density is expressed

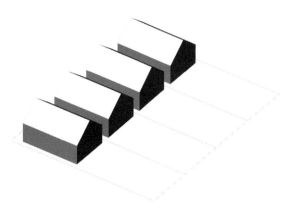

Source: Vicky Cheng

Figure 1.2 *Building density*

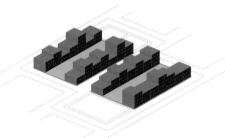

Source: Illustration redrawn by Vicky Cheng, adapted from Greater London Authority (2003, p11)

Figure 1.3 *Net residential area*

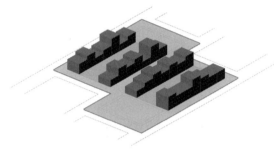

Source: Illustration redrawn by Vicky Cheng, adapted from Greater London Authority (2003, p11)

Figure 1.4 *Gross residential area*

as the number of people or household per given area, while building density is defined as the ratio of building structures to an area unit. Common measures of people and building densities are outlined as follows.

Measures of people density

Regional density

Regional density is the ratio of a population to the land area of a region. The reference area is usually defined by a municipal boundary and includes both developed and undeveloped land. Regional density is often used as an indicator of population distribution in national planning policy.

Residential density

Residential density is the ratio of a population to residential land area. This measure can be further classified in terms of net and gross residential densities based on the definition of the reference area. However, there is no consensus on the definition of net and gross areas; it varies across cities and countries. In the UK, net residential area refers only to land covered by residential development, along with gardens and other spaces that are physically included in it; this usually also takes into account half the width of adjacent roads (TCPA, 2003). In Hong Kong and some states in the US, net residential area only consists of the parcels allocated for residence where internal road, parks and other public lands are excluded (Churchman, 1999; Hong Kong Planning Department, 2003).

The measure of gross residential density considers the residential area in its integrity. In addition to the area allocated for residence, it also takes into account non-residential spaces such as internal roads, parks, schools, community centres and so on which are meant to serve the local community. Nevertheless, in practice, it is difficult to clearly define the extent of these residentially related areas. Some developments may take into account lands for purposes of serving a wider neighbourhood and others may include non-developable land such as steep slopes. This inconsistency of inclusion leads to great ambiguity in gross density measurement and, in turn, makes comparison difficult.

Occupancy density

Occupancy density refers to the ratio of the number of occupants to the floor area of an individual habitable unit. The reference habitable unit can be any kind of private or public space, such as a dwelling, office, theatre and so on. However, the reference area usually refers only to an enclosed area. Occupancy density is an important measure in building services design as it provides an indicator for estimating the services required. For instance, the electricity demand, space cooling and heating load, provision of fire safety facilities, and so forth are estimated based on the occupancy density.

Occupancy rate, which is the inverse measure of occupancy density (i.e. ratio of floor area of individual unit to number of occupants), is commonly used as an indicator of space available for individual occupants. Higher occupancy rate means larger habitable area for individual occupants. Regulation of minimum occupancy rate is often used in building design to safeguard the health and sanitary condition of habitable spaces.

Measures of building density

Plot ratio (floor area ratio)

Plot ratio is the ratio of total gross floor area of a development to its site area. The gross floor area usually takes into account the entire area within the perimeter of the exterior walls of the building, which includes the thickness of internal and external walls, stairs, service ducts, lift shafts, all circulation spaces, and so on.

Site area refers to the total lot area of the development, which, in most cases, is precisely defined in the planning document. Since the definitions of both floor and site areas are relatively clear in the measurement, plot ratio is considered as one of the most unambiguous density measures.

In planning practice, plot ratio is extensively adopted as a standard indicator for the regulation of land-use zoning and development control. Different plot ratios for different types of land uses are often specified in urban master plans as a provision of mixed land use. Furthermore, maximum plot ratio is often controlled in the master plan in order to govern the extent of build-up and to prevent over-development.

In building design, plot ratio is widely used in design briefing and development budgeting as it reflects the amount of floor area to be built and, hence, can be used to estimate the quantity of resources required for construction; consequently, it can forecast the financial balance of investment and returns.

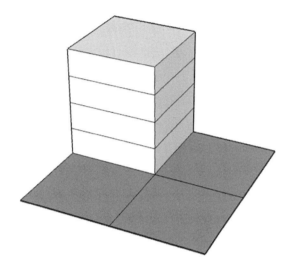

Source: Vicky Cheng

Figure 1.5 *Plot ratio = 1*

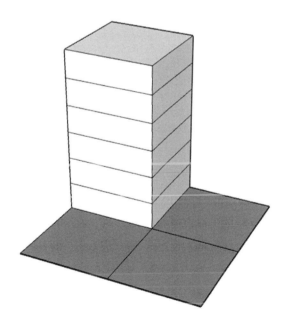

Source: Vicky Cheng

Figure 1.6 *Plot ratio = 1.5*

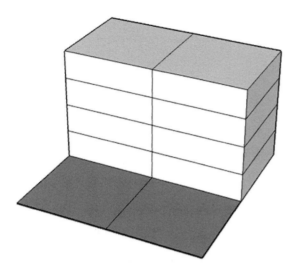

Figure 1.7 *Plot ratio = 2*

Site coverage

Site coverage represents the ratio of the building footprint area to its site area. Therefore, site coverage is a measure of the proportion of the site area covered by the building. Similar to plot ratio, site coverage of individual developments is often controlled in urban master planning in order to prevent over-build and to preserve areas for greenery and landscaping.

The open space ratio, which is the inverse measure of site coverage, indicates the amount of open space available on the development site. However, the term is

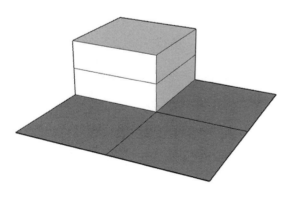

Figure 1.8 *Site coverage = 25 per cent*

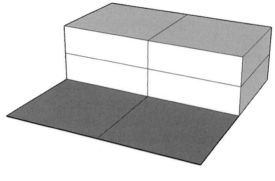

Figure 1.9 *Site coverage = 50 per cent*

sometimes also expressed as area of open space per person and this measure is used by the planning authority to safeguard a reasonable provision of outdoor space for the population.

Apart from plot ratio and site coverage, other density measures, such as regional and residential densities, can also be expressed in terms of building density. Measurement of residential density with respect to number of dwellings per land area is an important indicator in the making of planning policy. In the UK, for instance, the government has set a residential density of 30 dwellings per hectare as the national indicative minimum for new housing development (UK Office of the Deputy Prime Minister, 2006).

Density gradient and density profile

The density measures discussed so far are based on averages over a land area. These measures can properly reflect reality if people or buildings are fairly evenly distributed over the entire area. However, in many cases, especially when the reference geographical unit is large in scale, the distribution pattern of people or buildings can vary significantly.

Take Hong Kong as an example: the average population density over the entire territory is about 6300 persons per square kilometre. Nevertheless, the distribution of the population is very uneven across districts, ranging from 780 people per square kilometre in the outlying islands to 52,000 people per square kilometre in the urban area (Hong Kong Census and Statistics Department, 2006).

Figure 1.10 *Hong Kong population density map (magnitude represented in height): high density in the central urban area and low density in outlying islands*

In order to address the spatial variation of density, other means of density measurements, such as density gradient and density profiles, have been introduced.

Density gradient

Density gradient is defined as the rate at which density falls (according to distance) from the location of reference; therefore, a positive density gradient denotes a decline of density away from the reference location. The density gradient is usually derived from densities measured in a series of concentric rings at a 10m or 20m width, radiating out from the location of the reference (Longley and Mesev, 2002).

Density gradient is a composite measure of density. Comparing the changing pattern of density gradients over time can review the process of spatial evolution. Figure 1.12 shows two changing patterns of density gradient. Figure 1.12 (a) represents a process of progressive decentralization with decreasing population density in the urban centre and increasing density and boarders towards the outskirts. In contrast, Figure 1.12 (b) depicts a process of centralization with growing population density in both the urban centre and outskirts and, at the same time, enlarging borders towards the periphery. Between 1800 and 1945, the North American metropolis exhibited the former process of decentralization, while European counterparts resembled the latter process of centralization (Muller, 2004).

Density profile

Density profile refers to a series of density measurements based on a reference location but calculated in different spatial scales. Similar to density gradient, it is a measure of the rate at which density

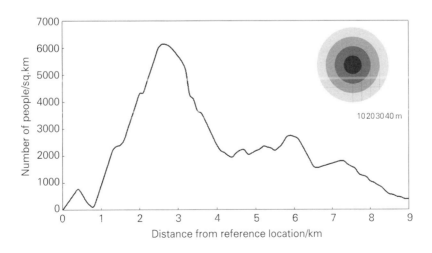

Figure 1.11 *Population density gradient from the town centre towards rural outskirts*

(a)

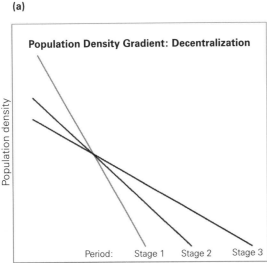

(b)

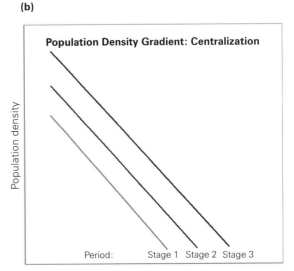

Source: Illustration redrawn by Vicky Cheng and adapted from Muller (2004, p62)

Figure 1.12 *Density gradients over time: progress from stage 1 to stage 3 – (a) progressive decentralization with decreasing population density in the urban centre and increasing density towards the outskirts; (b) centralization with growing population density in the urban centre and outskirts, as well as enlarging borders towards the periphery*

changes away from the reference location and is used as an indicator of settlement structure.

Density profile has been adopted in the UK as the basis for rural definition. In the UK rural classification system, density profile is calculated based on land area enclosed by a series of concentric circles of 200m, 400m, 800m and 1600m radii. The variation of density at these successive scales is then used to characterize the spatial structure of different settlements. For example, a village as defined in the classification system has the following properties:

- a density of greater than 0.18 residences per hectare at the 800m scale;
- a density at least double of that at the 400m scale; and
- a density at the 200m scale at least 1.5 times the density at the 400m scale (Bibby and Shepherd, 2004).

Through comparing the measured density profile with the predefined profiles, settlements of different spatial structures can be classified.

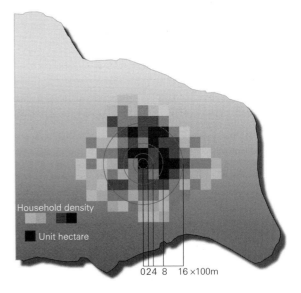

Source: Vicky Cheng

Figure 1.13 *Density profile calculated over concentric circles of radii of 200m, 400m, 800m and 1600m*

Building density and urban morphology

Building density has an intricate relationship with urban morphology; it plays an important role in the shaping of urban form. For instance, different combinations of plot ratio and site coverage will manifest into a variety of different built forms. As illustrated in Figure 1.14, the building transforms from a single-storey building to a multi-storey tower as the proportion of site coverage decreases.

In a similar vein, urban developments of the same density can exhibit very different urban forms. Figure 1.15 shows three settlements with the same residential density of 76 dwellings per hectare, but in different urban forms: multi-storey towers, medium-rise buildings in central courtyard form, and parallel rows of single-storey houses. Intrinsically, the three layouts are different in many aspects; nevertheless, in terms of urban land use, the proportion and organization of ground open space is of particular interest.

The high-rise layout creates large areas of open land that are suitable for expansive communal facilities, such as libraries, sports grounds and community centres. Nevertheless, without efficient land-use planning, these spaces can run the risk of being left over, not properly managed and end up producing problems.

The proportion of open area resulted in the medium-rise courtyard form, although it is less than that of the high-rise layout. However, unlike the former, the courtyard space is enclosed and clearly defined. It can be shaped as the central stage of the community and, thus, encourages full use of space.

The single-storey houses layout, on the other hand, divides open space into tiny parcels for individual uses. In this arrangement, the area for communal facilities is limited; nevertheless, residents can enjoy their own private open space.

In the face of rapid urbanization, the relationship between building density and urban form has attracted wide interest. Growing pressure of land scarcity as a consequence of increasing urban population has initiated extensive investigation on the spatial benefit of multi-storey buildings. Mathematical and geometrical analyses have been conducted to address the issue, particularly concerning the relationships between building height, plot ratio, site coverage and solar obstruction (Gropius, 1935; Beckett, 1942; Segal, 1964; Martin and March, 1972; Evans, 1973; Davidovich, 1968).

For an array of continuous courtyard form at a given plot ratio, increased building height will always lead to reduced solar obstruction, as shown in Figure 1.17. Or, to put it another way, provided that the solar obstruction angle is kept unchanged, increased building height will heighten the plot ratio. Moreover, the site coverage will decrease concurrently, which will lead to more ground open space.

For urban form with an infinite array of parallel tenement blocks, although geometrically different from the courtyard form, the mathematical relationships between building height, plot ratio, site coverage and solar obstruction remain the same. Therefore, the observations obtained from the courtyard form apply to the parallel block form as well.

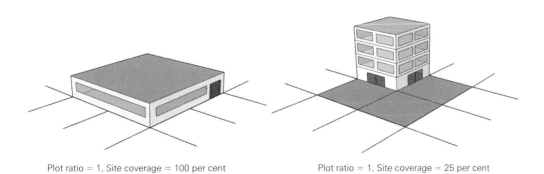

Plot ratio = 1, Site coverage = 100 per cent   Plot ratio = 1, Site coverage = 25 per cent

Source: Vicky Cheng

Figure 1.14 *Two built forms with the same plot ratio but different proportions of site coverage*

(a) High-rise

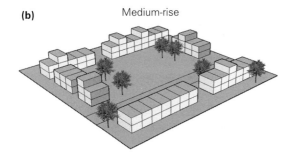

(b) Medium-rise

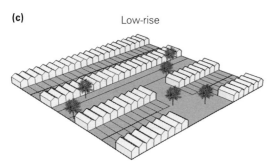

(c) Low-rise

(a)

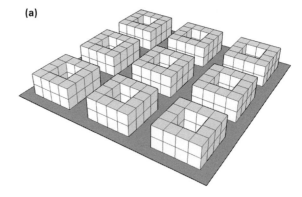

(b)

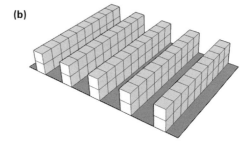

(c)

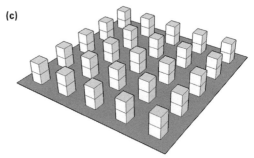

Source: Illustration redrawn by Vicky Cheng and adapted from Rogers (1999, p62)

Figure 1.15 *Same density in different layouts: (a) multi-storey towers; (b) medium-rise buildings in central courtyard form; (c) parallel rows of single-storey houses*

Source: Illustration redrawn by Vicky Cheng and adapted from Martin and March (1972, p36)

Figure 1.16 *Three different urban forms: (a) courtyard; (b) parallel block; (c) tower*

For urban form with an infinite array of towers at a low solar obstruction angle (below approximately 45°), increased building height will always lead to a reduced plot ratio. At high solar obstruction angles (above approximately 55°), increased building height may increase the plot ratio initially, but further increment will result in a reduced plot ratio.

Nevertheless, increased building height will decrease the site coverage in both cases. Finally, compared to the courtyard and the parallel block forms, at a given solar obstruction angle and building height, the tower form will always lead to a lower plot ratio and lower site coverage.

In reality, site area is usually limited and urban form is very often determined by the predefined development density. Figure 1.18 shows the residential densities of

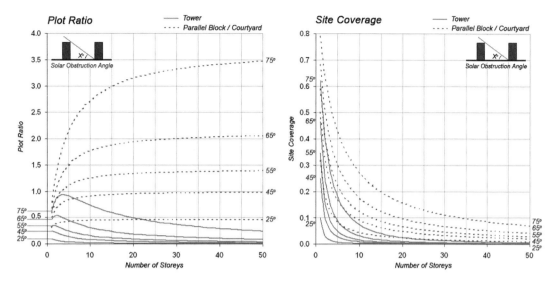

Source: Vicky Cheng

Figure 1.17 *Relationships between building height, plot ratio, site coverage and solar obstruction*

Single family houses
25–40 units/net hectare

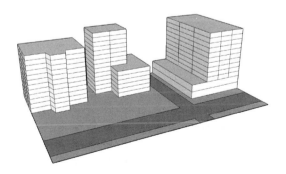

Multi-storey townhouses
50–100 units/net hectare

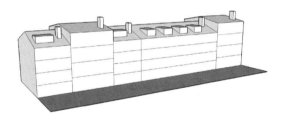

Multi-storey apartment blocks
120–250 units/net hectare

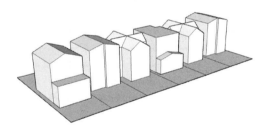

High-rise apartment blocks
1000 units/net hectare

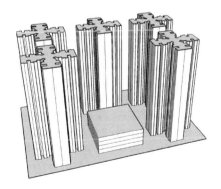

Source: Vicky Cheng

Figure 1.18 *Residential densities of four different urban forms*

several existing urban forms (Alexander, 1993; Ellis, 2004; Campoli and MacLean, 2007).

Perceived density

Perceived density is defined as an individual's perception and estimate of the number of people present in a given area, the space available and its organization (Rapoport, 1975). Spatial characteristic *per se* is important in the perception of density; but in addition, the interaction between the individual and the environment as a whole counts even more. Individual cognitive attributes and socio-cultural norms are also factors that contribute to this interaction (Alexander, 1993).

Furthermore, perceived density not only addresses the relative relationships between individual and space, but also between individuals in the space. For example, suppose there are two spaces with the same occupancy rate of 3 square metres per person; in one case, there is a group of friends in a clubroom, while in another there are several unacquainted people in a small lobby. Clearly, these two situations are very different in social and perceptual terms, even though they show the same physical density (Chan, 1999). In order to distinguish between these two different aspects of perceived density, the concept of spatial density and social density were introduced.

Spatial density refers to the perception of density with respect to the relationship among spatial elements such as height, spacing and juxtaposition. High spatial density is related to environmental qualities, such as

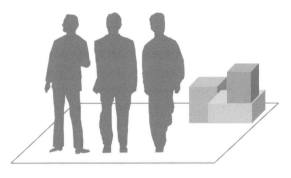

Source: Vicky Cheng

Figure 1.19 *Perceived density is about the interaction between the individual and the space, and between individuals in the space*

high degree of enclosure, intricacy of spaces and high activity levels, in which all of these qualities tend to result in higher rates of information from the environment itself.

Social density describes the interaction between people. It involves the various sensory modalities, the mechanisms for controlling interaction levels such as spacing, physical elements, territorial boundaries, hierarchy, the size and nature of the group involved, its homogeneity and rules for behaviour, in which all of these qualities affect the rates of social interaction (Chan, 1999). In general, for high spatial density, the primary problem is too little space, while for high social density the primary problem is too many people with whom one must interact.

Perceived density, therefore, is subjective as it relies on individual apprehension; nevertheless, it is also neutral as it does not involve any personal evaluation or judgement. Crowding, on the other hand, refers to the state of psychological stress that is associated with a negative appraisal of density (Churchman, 1999). Density, although a necessary antecedent of crowding, is not a sufficient condition for causing the experience of crowding (Stokols, 1972). Apart from physical conditions, crowding also involves the evaluation of situational variables, personal characteristics and coping assets (Baum and Paulus, 1987). Research suggests that as far as crowding is concerned, the influence of social density is more significant than spatial density (McClelland and Auslander, 1978). However, the experience of crowding would be intensified as a consequence of limited space since the freedom of adjusting one's physical proximity to others is reduced (Mackintosh et al, 1975; Saegert, 1979).

Perceived density and architectural features

Perceived density emphasizes the interaction between the individual and the environment; therefore, it is not the actual physical density, but the perception of density through this man–environment interaction that matters. Prior studies concerning the indoor environment have shown that alteration of density and crowding perception is feasible through architectural features such as colour, brightness, room shape, window size, ceiling height, amount of daylight, use of screen and partition, and arrangement of furniture (Desor,

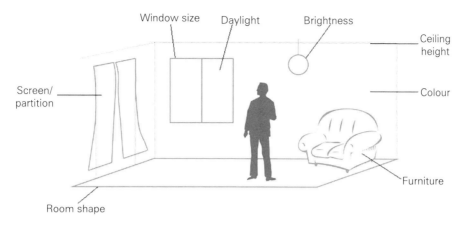

Window size   Daylight   Brightness

Ceiling height

Screen/ partition

Colour

Furniture

Room shape

Source: Vicky Cheng

Figure 1.20 *Architectural features that influence the perception of density*

1972; Baum and Davis, 1976; Schiffenbauer et al, 1977; Bell et al, 2001).

In the urban environment, the perception of density has been found to be associated with the built form and certain urban features. Rapoport (1975) outlined the importance of a list of environmental cues, which are thought to have effects on perceived density; these hypothesized factors include building height-to-space ratio, building height, space openness, space complexity, the number of people, the number of street signs, traffic, light level, naturalness of the environment, and the rhythm of activity.

In a guidebook for housing development authored by Cooper-Marcus and Sarkissian (1988), design attributes such as the overall size of buildings, space between buildings, variety in building façade, and visual access to open and green space are acknowledged as contributing factors to the perception of density. On the other hand, Bonnes et al (1991) pointed out that spatial features such as street width, building height, building size, and balance between built-up and vacant spaces can affect people's perception of density.

Flachsbart (1979) conducted an empirical study to examine the effects of several built-form features upon perceived density. According to his findings, shorter building block lengths and more street intersections could lower perceived density. However, surprisingly, the influence of street width was found insignificant; and other features such as street shape, slope and building block diversity did not show noticeable effects.

Zacharias and Stamps (2004) proposed that perceived density is a function of building layout. Based on the findings of their simulation experiments, building height, number of buildings, spacing and the extent of building coverage have significant effects upon perceived density. Nevertheless, architectural details and landscaping did not show significant influences.

By and large, research to date indicates that the perception of density is related to certain environmental cues; however, it is important to keep in mind that besides physical characteristics, individual-cognitive and socio-cultural factors are also prominent, especially with respect to the notion of high density. There is not an explicit definition of high density; it varies from culture to culture and from person to person. The next section furthers the discussion of density with regard to the phenomenon of high density.

High density

Rapid urbanization since 1950 has exerted tremendous pressure on urban development in many cities and has been confronted with the scarce supply of land in urban areas; densification has also become an important agenda in planning policies around the world. High-density development has consequently been a topic of increasing interest worldwide; it represents different notions in different countries, across different cultures and to different people.

Source: Vicky Cheng

Figure 1.21 *High density in Hong Kong*

The meaning of high density is a matter of perception; it is subjective and depends upon the society or individual's judgement against specific norms. Hence, societies or individuals of different backgrounds and under different contexts come up with different definitions of high density. For example, in the UK, residential development with less than 20 dwellings per net hectare is considered low density; between 30 to 40 dwellings per net hectare is considered medium density; and higher than 60 dwellings per net hectare is considered high density (TCPA, 2003). In the US, low density refers to 25 to 40 dwellings per net hectare; medium density refers to 40 to 60 dwellings per net hectare; and high density refers to development with higher than approximately 110 dwellings per net hectare (Ellis, 2004). In Israel, on the other hand, 20 to 40 dwellings per net hectare is considered low density, and 290 dwellings per net hectare is considered high density (Churchman, 1999).

The term 'high density' is always associated with overcrowding; however, the notion of high density expressed in terms of building density has little to do with overcrowding. High building density measured in terms of plot ratio, for instance, refers to a high proportion of built-up floor area. In the case of larger dwelling size and smaller household size, higher plot ratio may lead to lower occupancy density and, therefore, more habitable area for individuals, in turn mitigating the crowding condition. For instance, the plot ratio of government housing development in Hong Kong rose from about 3 during the 1970s to about 5 in the 1980s; accompanied with this growth in building density, the living space for occupants increased from about 3.2 to 5 square metres per person (Sullivan and Chen, 1997; Ng and Wong, 2004). Thus, higher building density, in this case, actually helped to ease the problem of overcrowding in dwellings.

The phenomenon of overcrowding has resulted from the lack of space for individuals; thus, it is more about high people density. However, as illustrated in the example above, the relationship between building density and people density is not straightforward and depends to a great extent upon how people density is measured. Again, Hong Kong may be taken as an example. The average residential density of government housing projects completed during the 1970s was approximately 2300 individuals per hectare; during the 1980s, it was 2500 persons per hectare (Lai, 1993). Hence, although higher building density reduced occupancy density within the dwelling, it also increased the overall people density on the site.

All in all, the phenomena of high building density and high people density represent very different issues; complicating the matter even further, an increase in building density can have opposite effects on people density depending upon how the latter is measured. Nevertheless, this vital concept is vaguely addressed in the debate concerning high-density development.

Debate on high density

Attitudes towards high-density development are diverse. Some people acknowledge the merits of high density and advocate urban compaction, whereas others criticize the drawbacks and argue strongly against it. The following sections outline the major debate regarding the pros and cons of high-density urban development (Pun, 1994, 1996; Churchman, 1999; Breheny, 2001) and attempts to review them based on the understanding established in the foregoing discussion, particularly on the distinction between building and people densities.

Urban land use and infrastructure

Land is always a scarce resource in urban development; high building density, by providing more built-up space on individual sites, can maximize the utilization of the scarce urban land. High building density, therefore, helps to reduce the pressure to develop open spaces and releases more land for communal facilities and services to improve the quality of urban living. However, some people argue that the opposite is also true. In order to achieve high building density, massive high-rise buildings are inevitable, and these massive structures, crammed into small sites, can conversely result in very little open space and a congested cityscape. This may happen when high-density development is carried out without planning. Therefore, in order to avoid the negative impacts of high density, thorough planning and appropriate density control are essential.

Infrastructure such as roads, drainage and sewerage, electricity, telecommunication networks and so on are substantial in supporting urban development. These infrastructural services, however, are very costly to provide and maintain; and in many cases, a minimum utilization threshold is required in order to operate these systems cost effectively. High people density, by concentrating a population in a smaller area, can make greater use of these infrastructural services and help the systems to run more economically. However, if the population exceeds the system capacity, high people density can contrarily lead to overload of the systems and deteriorate services. Again, in order to achieve the former outcome, it is important that the planning of high density and the provision of infrastructure go hand in hand.

Transportation system

The public transport system is very costly to build and operate; like most infrastructural services, public transport needs a minimum utilization rate in order to be profitable and efficient. High people density, by providing a greater number of users, would sustain the use of the mass transit system and thus improve its efficiency and viability. Furthermore, high building and people density means that both places and people are concentrated and close to each other. This offers more opportunities for walking and cycling, and therefore would reduce the number of car trips, as well as the travel distance per trip. The increase in proximity together with the increased use of public transit would help to reduce traffic congestion in urban centres. However, these benefits will only be realized if transportation systems are well planned. Otherwise, high density can lead to traffic congestion and overcrowding in mass transit facilities if the provision of public transport is deficient.

Environment and preservation

Source: Vicky Cheng

Figure 1.22 *High density helps to protect the countryside*

High building density can help to protect the countryside and agricultural land from urbanization. For instance, as mentioned earlier, only 24 per cent of the land area in Hong Kong is built up; the rest of the land area remains largely rural in character and provides a pleasant recreational outlet for urban dwellers.

High people density can enhance the opportunity for using public transit and thus help to reduce the use of private cars. The reduction of private vehicles can lead to lower gasoline consumption and decreased pollution from traffic. High people density can also facilitate the use of centralized energy systems, such as the combined heat and power plant, which would result in more efficient energy use and decreased emission of pollutants from power generation.

On the other hand, high building density, which is usually in the form of high-rise clusters, may impede the potential of building integrated renewable energy systems. Furthermore, high building density may reduce space for trees and shrubs that purify the air and cool inner urban areas. The high proportion of built-up mass and the loss of greenery are causes of the urban heat island effect.

Personal and social elements

The proximity of people and places brought about by both high building and people density offers a high degree of convenience for work, service and entertainment. However, this proximity, especially between people, may force individuals to undergo some unwanted social contact and cause psychological stress. High people density may also lead to competition for the use of facilities and space and, in turn, create social conflicts. Moreover, high people density may result in reduced privacy and invoke the feeling of loss of control and anxiety. Nevertheless, with proper organization and management, the proximity that arises from high people density can conversely facilitate social interaction and promote good neighbourhood relations.

The unpleasant experience as a result of overcrowding is more related to high people density and not necessarily associated with high building density. As previously illustrated, increased building density as a means of lowering occupancy rate can, in fact, help to mitigate the problem of overcrowding. Furthermore, high building density, which can allow more open space for recreation and communal uses, may also help to establish social interaction and consolidate the sense of community.

Conclusions

This chapter has sought to explain the diverse dimensions of 'density', from the elemental numerical measures to the complex notion of human perception. In terms of physical measurement, density embraces a broad range of definitions; therefore, whenever the term is to be used, an explicit definition of the measure has to be clearly specified in order to avoid unnecessary confusion. In terms of human perception, it is not the physical density *per se* but the interaction between individuals and the physical environment that is important. Nevertheless, individual cognitive attributes and socio-cultural factors are also contributing to the notion of perceived density.

Concerning high density, this concept is a matter of perception, is very subjective and represents different notions in different countries, across different cultures and to different people. It is, therefore, essential to understand the context before the potential of high-density development can be evaluated. In considering the advantages and disadvantages of high density, the distinction between building and people density has to be observed. For the arguments reviewed, not all but most of the propositions are matters of planning. In

order to maximize the benefits of high density, thorough and comprehensive planning strategy is essential; otherwise, high-density development can lead to severe social and environmental problems.

Good planning is important; but as to what makes good planning of high-density cities is another question. The rest of this book will address various social and environmental issues concerning high-density development, accompanied by design strategies corresponding to these issues. Hopefully this chapter has set out the ground for further discussion of high-density issues in later chapters and, altogether, this book can provoke deeper reflection upon the potential of high-density development.

References

Alexander, E. R. (1993) 'Density measures: A review and analysis', *Journal of Architectural and Planning Research*, vol 10, no 3, pp181–202

Baum, A. and Davis, G. E. (1976) 'Spatial and social aspects of crowding perception', *Environment and Behavior*, vol 8, no 4, pp527–544

Baum, A. and Paulus, P. B. (1987) 'Crowding', in D. Stokols and I. Altman (eds) *Handbook of Environmental Psychology, vol I*, John Wiley, New York, NY

Beckett, H. E. (1942) 'Population densities and the heights of buildings', *Illuminating Engineering Society Transactions*, vol 7, no 7, pp75–80

Bell, P. A., Greene, T. C., Fisher, J. D. and Baum, A. (2001) 'High density and crowding', in *Environmental Psychology*, Wadsworth, Thomson Learning, Belmont, CA

Bibby, R. and Shepherd, J. (2004) *Rural Urban Methodology Report*, Department for Environment Food and Rural Affairs, London

Bonnes, M., Bonaiuto, M. and Ercolani, A. P. (1991) 'Crowding and residential satisfaction in the urban environment: A contextual approach', *Environment and Behavior*, vol 23, no 5, pp531–552

Breheny, M. (2001) 'Densities and sustainable cities: The UK experience', in M. Echenique and A. Saint (eds) *Cities for the New Millennium*, Spon Press, London, New York

Campoli, J. and MacLean, A. S. (2007) *Visualizing Density*, Lincoln Institute of Land Policy, Cambridge, MA

Chan, Y. K. (1999) 'Density, crowding and factors intervening in their relationship: Evidence from a hyper-dense metropolis', *Social Indicators Research*, vol 48, pp103–124

Churchman, A. (1999) 'Disentangling the concept of density', *Journal of Planning Literature*, vol 13, no 4, pp389–411

Cooper-Marcus, C. and Sarkissian, W. (1988) *Housing as if People Mattered: Site Design Guidelines for Medium-Density Family Housing*, University of California Press, Berkeley, CA

Davidovich, V. G. (1968) 'Interdependence between height of buildings, density of population and size of towns and settlements', in *Town Planning in Industrial Districts: Engineering and Economics*, Israel Programme for Scientific Translations, Jerusalem

Desor, J. A. (1972) 'Toward a psychological theory of crowding', *Journal of Personality and Social Psychology*, vol 21, pp79–83

Ellis, J. G. (2004) 'Explaining residential density', *Places*, vol 16, no 2, pp34–43

Evans, P. (1973) *Housing Layout and Density*, Land Use and Built Form Studies, Working Paper 75, University of Cambridge, Department of Architecture, Cambridge, UK

Flachsbart, P. G. (1979) 'Residential site planning and perceived densities', *Journal of the Urban Planning and Development Division*, vol 105, no 2, pp103–117

Greater London Authority (2003) Housing for a Compact City, GLA, London

Gropius, W. (1935) *The New Architecture and The Bauhaus*, Faber and Faber Limited, London

Hong Kong Census and Statistics Department (2006) *Population By-Census: Main Report*, vol 1, Hong Kong, Census and Statistics Department, Hong Kong

Hong Kong Planning Department (2003) *Hong Kong Planning Standards and Guidelines*, Planning Department, Hong Kong

Lai, L. W. C. (1993) 'Density policy towards public housing: A Hong Kong theoretical and empirical review', *Habitat International*, vol 17, no 1, pp45–67

Longley, P. A. and Mesev, C. (2002) 'Measurement of density gradients and space-filling in urban systems', *Regional Science*, vol 81, pp1–28

Mackintosh, E., West, S. and Saegert, S. (1975) 'Two studies of crowding in urban public spaces', *Environment and Behavior*, vol 7, no 2, pp159–184

Martin, L. and March, L. (1972) (eds) *Urban Space and Structures*, Cambridge University Press, Cambridge, UK

McClelland, L. and Auslander, N. (1978) 'Perceptions of crowding and pleasantness in public settings', *Environment and Behavior*, vol 10, no 4, pp535–552

Muller, P. O. (2004) 'Transportation and urban form: Stages in the spatial evolution of the American metropolis', in S. Hanson and G. Giuliano (eds) *The Geography of Urban Transportation*, 3rd ed. Guilford Press, New York, NY

Ng, E. and Wong, K. S. (2004) 'Efficiency and livability: Towards sustainable habitation in Hong Kong', in *International Housing Conference Hong Kong*, Hong Kong

Pun, P. K. S. (1994) 'Advantages and disadvantages of high-density urban development', in V. Fouchier and P. Merlin (eds) *High Urban Densities: A Solution for Our Cities?*, Consulate General of France in Hong Kong, Hong Kong

Pun, P. K. S. (1996) 'High density development: The Hong Kong experience', in *Hong Kong: City of Tomorrow – An Exhibition about the Challenge of High Density Living*, Hong Kong Government, City of Edinburgh Museums and Art Galleries

Rapoport, A. (1975) 'Toward a redefinition of density', *Environment and Behavior*, vol 7, no 2, pp133–158

Rogers, R. G. (1999) *Towards an Urban Renaissance: Final Report of the Urban Task Force*, Department of the Environment, Transport and the Regions, London

Saegert, S. (1979) 'A systematic approach to high density settings: Psychological, social, and physical environmental factors', in M. R. Gurkaynak and W. A. LeCompte (eds) *Human Consequences of Crowding*, Plenum Press, New York, NY

Schiffenbauer, A. I., Brown, J. E., Perry, P. L., Shulack, L. K. and Zanzola, A. M. (1977) 'The relationship between density and crowding: Some architectural modifiers', *Environment and Behavior*, vol 9, no 1, pp3–14

Segal, W. (1964) 'The use of land: In relation to building height, coverage and housing density', *Journal of the Architectural Association*, March, pp253–258

Stokols, D. (1972) 'On the distinction between density and crowding: Some implications for future research', *Psychological Review*, vol 79, no 3, pp275–277

Sullivan, B. and Chen, K. (1997) 'Design for tenant fitout: A critical review of public housing flat design in Hong Kong', *Habitat International*, vol 21, no 3, pp291–303

TCPA (Town and Country Planning Association) (2003) *TCPA Policy Statement: Residential Densities*, TCPA, London

UK Office of the Deputy Prime Minister (2006) *Planning Policy Statement 3: Housing*, Department for Communities and Local Government, London

Zacharias, J. and Stamps, A. (2004) 'Perceived building density as a function of layout', *Perceptual and Motor Skills*, vol 98, pp777–784

2

Is the High-Density City the Only Option?

Brenda Vale and Robert Vale

Commoner's fourth law of ecology (Commoner, 1971) should be uppermost in the minds of those trying to decide whether high density, defined as a large number of people living on a small area of land, is a good and potentially sustainable thing. The idea 'there is no such thing as a free lunch' suggests that there are ecological consequences to all human decisions regarding the built environment. This chapter will begin an examination of what these are for both high-density and low-density urban development in an attempt to see whether one has a significant environmental benefit over the other.

The post-oil scenario

Many sources suggest that peak oil is happening (Association for the study of Peak Oil and Gas, undated), and in the future development reliant on fossil fuels will cause increasing competition for these increasingly scarce resources. Expansion of human numbers on Earth also means that more people are in competition for a fixed quantity of land, while development generally signifies that people expect to occupy more land, not just for larger apartments or houses, but for the entire infrastructure that comes with development, such as access to transportation, health facilities, education, leisure activities, etc. Bringing together these two ideas of increased demand for conventional fuels and increased demand for land reveals a very serious problem that is often neglected in debates about density and the compact city. Land is a key resource available to support human development. Land can be used for growing food, for growing fuels, and for conversion to built settlements and infrastructure. In the past, all human settlements that were sustained over a long period of time kept these three aspects of land use in some type of balance. Access to a suitable water supply is also essential for sustained

settlement, and this can be thought of as another land use, especially when land has to be given up to storage of water in purpose-built reservoirs for dry seasons. Most recent planning theory has ignored the vital relationships between food, energy, water and land because of access to cheap and plentiful fossil fuels. This has meant that food can be grown at a long distance from settlements and transported to them and that wastes generated by urban dwellers can also be shipped long distances for disposal. This is all possible because consideration of the ecological consequences of all this movement, now at last being recognized as measurable through measuring carbon dioxide emissions, has never formed part of any economic calculation of whether this is a sensible thing to do.

One way of looking at these ecological consequences is to turn the problem on its head and ask what sort of settlements will be able to be sustained in a post-oil society. Sustainability means nothing but the ability of something to adapt to inevitable changing circumstances over time. The European city could be seen as a good example of this. Medieval cities and towns were based on pedestrian movement and the need for defensive capability, such as when withstanding a siege. This meant having water and food supplies nearby; it meant having the ability to store food in appropriate buildings against siege; it meant having places to grow food within the city. The city was low rise but its use was intensive. Thus, the streets were places for trade, places for movement, places for recreation and celebration. The home place was a workshop as well as a place for family life. The gardens behind the houses were for growing food and for recreation through the presence of greenery within the urban fabric. They were also places for absorbing organic waste and wastewater through composting and growing. The form of the terraced buildings onto the street meant that the home could also become part of a defensive wall in times of war, and the gardens behind formed a movement path for troops defending the city, tactics that were still being promoted during World War II (Levy, 1941). Multiple use of the built form for different purposes meant maximizing the use of the physical resources. This is a very long way from the simplistic separation of functions as found in the modernist cities of Garnier (Wiebenson, no date, Figures 2–3) and Le Corbusier (1929, p179). In a world where resources are in short supply, it will not be the efficient use of resources – the modernist approach – that will be sustainable, but rather one resource supporting many functions, as in the vernacular settlement. This is more to do with intensity of activities within the same place in the city, not just density of people on the ground, and the medieval city is a good illustration of this.

The low-rise pedestrian-focused European city may have had medieval origins, but it has also absorbed industrialized society. The streets have accommodated motorized transport, although often public transport has had to be used for inner-city locations, as the very narrowness of the streets works against the idea of everyone driving about in their own cars. The simple form of terraced buildings, normally of load-bearing masonry, onto the street is also flexible, its required cellular form being put to many uses for dwellings, offices, school, storage, etc. This means the resources that go into the dwellings are useable over centuries, not just decades, making the issue of the energy embodied in them much less significant. For European cities Banham (1969, p22) suggests that they would not have been tenable without the masonry construction as this mass was a climate moderator. Sufficient mass, like the caves that human ancestors

used as dwellings, will stabilize the internal temperature at either the yearly average, or – with less mass – the monthly average temperature. At the same time, massive buildings offered stable shelter against natural disasters such as storm and flood. They also had acoustic properties that meant they could contain numerous people doing different things while ensuring some acoustic privacy. Again, the same piece of built environment has multiple functions, which can be seen as adding to its sustainability. Resource use is intense although density is relatively low.

Just as the European city adapted to change in the past, so it could be changed in a post-oil future. More food could be grown within the city and walking and cycling would be the chief means of getting around. Two other urban forms are also worth considering in a post-oil future: the suburban sprawl that characterizes many North American settlements and the very high-density city that is the subject of this book. The first has available land that could be used for food growing. The roads could be used to support solar collectors or could be dug up to support the growing of trees for fuel, much as the Street Farmers group in London envisaged during the 1970s (Boyle and Harper, 1976). Water could be collected from the roofs of houses and some form of community ethos would be created because people would not be commuting but staying at home, trying to extract the basis of an existence from their surroundings. If there is catastrophic collapse, the high-density city is not going to be as tenable, certainly in the short term, and the most likely scenario is that many people will leave for the surrounding areas in an effort to supply themselves with the basics of life. Any so-called 'sprawl' surrounding the city centre will mean that some land is available to support these urban refugees. In a post-oil world, everything still needs to be brought in and out of the high-density city and the energy to do this may not be there and will definitely be more expensive.

The food equation

Many people would argue that there will not be catastrophic collapse and humanity will find a way of coping with future oil shortages and increases in prices, as well as global warming and other environmental issues. However, since buildings last a long time, what is built now will have to work for changed circumstances in any future time of resource shortages. This raises the question of whether very high-density cities can be made to work. To explore this, one of the essentials of supply for any settlement – food – will be examined in more detail.

Feeding Hong Kong

In 1998, less than 3 per cent of the land in Hong Kong was used for agricultural production (Environmental Protection Department, 2006). The same source also stated that 13.9 per cent of fresh vegetables, the easiest produce to grow locally at a small scale, were produced in Hong Kong. Given the age of this data and the pace of development, the amount of locally grown food has probably decreased. In order to work out the approximate area of land needed to feed a high-density city such as Hong Kong, a more general approach has therefore been taken.

The area of land needed to provide the food for a city's population can be estimated by using ecological footprint data. The ecological footprint figure for food production allows for the growing of the food on a sustainable basis, and is therefore the most appropriate figure to use for 'post-oil' calculations. Estimates of the ecological footprint of a typical Western diet vary from 1.3ha per person according to the Task Force on Planning Healthy and Sustainable Communities at the University of British Columbia in Canada (Wackernagel, 1997) to a more detailed calculation of 1.63ha for a resident of south-west England (SWEET, 2005). This is very close to the often quoted 'fair Earth share' of 1.8ha per person (Wackernagel and Rees, 1996), leaving almost nothing over for shelter, transportation, clothing or items such as leisure activities. In 1997, Friends of the Earth calculated the food footprint of Hong Kong to be 1.6 hectares per person, although the footprint was unusual in having a lower land use per person than the

fair Earth share value, but a much higher sea food footprint exceeding a fair share by nearly 200 per cent (Friends of the Earth, undated). Although the diets may be different, the footprints are similar. Based on these values, and taking an average food footprint of 1.5ha per person, it is possible to calculate the approximate area of land needed to support cities. The results are shown in Table 2.1.

This means that a city of 10 million needs to be at the centre of a circle of productive land 440km in diameter. The city of 1 million needs an area of land with a diameter of 140km, and even the city of only 100,000 people has to be at the centre of a 44km diameter circle.

Hong Kong, with a population of 7 million, currently occupies an area of 1076 square kilometres, of which 75 per cent is open space, so the built area of the city is about 270 square kilometres (Wikipedia, 2007). The area needed for providing the city's food is 105,000 square kilometres, nearly 400 times the built area of the city or 100 times its total area. This would be a circle with a diameter of roughly 360km.

A sustainable city also needs a sustainable source of energy. Hong Kong's energy consumption in 1999 was 17,866 thousand tonnes of oil equivalent, which is around 750 petajoules (PJ) (WRI, 2007). A 1 megawatt (MW) wind turbine will produce 3.9 gigawatt hours (GWh) per year, which is 0.014PJ (New Zealand Wind Energy Association, 2005, p3), so powering Hong Kong from renewable energy will require 54,000 wind turbines, each of 1MW (or 18,000 3MW turbines), assuming the wind regime is suitable. It may not be possible to power a city or country completely by wind power because there are times when there is too little wind and machines must also be turned off when winds are too high. This means that wind is best used with a supply system such as hydropower, which has built-in energy storage. However, for this simple exercise it is assumed that all energy comes from the wind. The

Table 2.1 *Land area required to feed cities of various sizes*

City population	Hectares occupied at density of 300 persons/ha	Hectares of land required to supply food	Square kilometres of land for growing food
100,000	333	150,000	1500
1,000,000	3333	1,500,000	15,000
10,000,000	33,333	15,000,000	150,000

Source: Authors

New York State Energy Research and Development Authority estimates that the total land use for a wind farm is from 17.8 acres to 39 acres (7.2ha to 15.8ha) per megawatt (Wind Power Project Site Identification and Land Requirements, 2005, pp5–6). At 15ha per megawatt, the turbines to power Hong Kong will occupy only 810,000ha (8100 square kilometres).

This energy calculation, based on electricity, also ignores the fact that most of the transport energy currently used in cities comes from oil. In Hong Kong, with its small land area and dense population, electrically powered transport already provides much of the personal transport through trains and trams, and in the future buses and even cars could also be electric. However, if the land surrounding the city is to be used to grow its food, there is the need to transport the food from where it is grown to where it is consumed. This is likely to require a fuel that can act as a substitute for oil.

The two probable alternative fuels at present are ethanol, to replace petrol, and vegetable oil, to replace diesel. Both these fuels can be used in an ordinary engine, but the engine needs to be converted. For example, to burn ethanol instead of petrol means, among other things, changing the size of the carburettor jets, and using vegetable oil means fitting a means of warming it because it is thicker than oil-based diesel. However, assuming that the engine can be converted, what are the implications of these fuels and what land area would be needed to grow enough fuel to transport food to the city?

According to Journey to Forever, an organization promoting sustainability, there is a very wide range of possible plant crops that yield oils, so that oil-bearing plants could be grown in many different climates. Yields range widely; nuts can supply 176 litres oil per hectare from cashews up to Brazil nuts at 2392 litres oil per hectare, while seeds range from cotton at 325 litres oil per hectare to rapeseed at 1190 litres oil per hectare (Journey to Forever, undated). Fruits also yield oils – for example, avocados give 2638 litres oil per hectare. The highest yielding plant is the oil palm, at 5950 litres oil per hectare.

Assuming an average oil yield of 1000 litres per hectare to allow for different climates, it is possible to calculate the land area needed to get the food to the city. Hong Kong (or any city of 7 million) needs an area of 105,000 square kilometres to provide its food.

Assuming that the average travel distance is that over which half the total of all food must be moved, the radius of the hypothetical circle that provides half the food can be calculated and used as the average travel distance. The area of half the total circle is 52,500 square kilometres, so the radius of this half area is 129km. According to the south-west UK study cited above, the average weight of food eaten by one person in a year is 700kg, so the 7 million people in Hong Kong will eat 4.9 million tonnes of food a year. Road freight in 1999 in Europe used 0.067kg oil equivalent per tonne kilometre (EEA, 2002). 1kg oil equivalent is 41.868 megajoules (MJ),[1] so road freight uses 2.8MJ per tonne kilometre. This means that transporting Hong Kong's food from the surrounding food-producing area would use 1.77PJ per year. This figure needs to be doubled to allow for the return trip empty, making 3.5PJ per year.

The energy content of 1 litre of diesel fuel is approximately 30MJ (Clean Energy Educational Trust) and if, for the sake of the calculation, the same value is assumed for vegetable oils, the oil yield will be 30,000MJ per hectare. To grow the fuel to transport the food will need 117,000ha (1170 square kilometres) of land in addition to the land needed for food growing. This area is small in comparison to 105,000 square kilometres for growing the food.

Given that most high-density cities such as Hong Kong do not come with large areas of unused hinterland where food could be grown, it would be useful to look at the situation where all food is imported to the high-density city. New Zealand is a country of few people and a good climate for agriculture so could be used for supplying food to cities which cannot feed themselves. The World's Ports Distances website shows that it is 5053 nautical miles (9357km) from Auckland to Hong Kong.[2] Sea freight is far more efficient than shipping by road, and a container ship uses 0.12MJ per tonne kilometre (IMO, 2005); so if all Hong Kong's food were to be imported from New Zealand by sea, the total energy consumption would be only 5.6PJ.

From all of this it appears that the big issue is the land, or the sea equivalent, to grow the food for those living in cities who cannot feed themselves, rather than the energy needed to bring the food to the city, or the land required for renewable energy supply. These values are summarized in Figure 2.1. However, what these

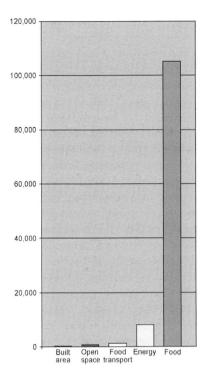

Source: Authors

Figure 2.1 *Areas of land required to support Hong Kong with local food production*

rough calculations do illustrate is the need to consider what will happen to cities that rely on foreign imports in a post-oil world, or a world where access to cheap oil is no longer possible.

Wastes and fertility

It seems clear that the energy needed to transport food to consumers might not be a problem for the high-density city. A greater problem, however, in the post-oil world may be obtaining fertility for growing the food. Nitrogen fertilizer is generally now made from the hydrogen in natural gas, although initially it was fixed from the air by electric arc, using hydroelectric power.[3] It would be possible to move towards making nitrogen fertilizer from renewable energy; but the other two key components of all fertilizers, phosphorus (P) and potassium (K), are derived from naturally occurring minerals, and supplies of these will become depleted. The Fertilizer Institute, an industry group based in Washington, DC, states the following:

The source of phosphorus in fertilizer is fossilized remains of ancient marine life found in rock deposits in North America and North Africa, and volcanic activity in China… Fertilizer producers mine potassium, or potash, from naturally occurring ore deposits that were formed when seas and oceans evaporated, many of which are covered with several thousands of feet of earth. (Fertilizer Institute, undated)

Roberts and Stewart (2002) suggest that phosphorus ores in North America will last 25 years, or 100 years if higher cost ores are used, meaning that phosphorus will also become more expensive in the future, increasing the costs of fertilizer and, hence, food. In contrast, they state that there is sufficient potassium for centuries. These assumptions are based on current rates of consumption, which are likely to rise as population and living standards increase. What this means it that current agriculture based on artificial fertilizers cannot be considered sustainable.

Cities in the past used the sewage of their citizens as the source of fertilizer to grow the food to feed the city. However, a point was reached when the physical size of the city precluded the movement of sewage out to the fields. This happened in London during the first half of the 19th century when the population grew from 1 million to 2.5 million (Cadbury, 2004). Mayhew in *London Labour and the London Poor* (1851) states that before the city outgrew night soil collection from the cesspits when the distance to be travelled made such collection too expensive, the collected waste was mixed in yards with other organic waste, such as hops from brewing, to make a more balanced manure, 75 per cent of which was shipped in barges down the Thames to more distant farms, while some was even shipped overseas in barrels to fertilize sugar growing in distant plantations. The remaining 25 per cent was taken some 5 or 6 miles by cart to fertilize local food production. Although by no means a pleasant practice, it was an attempt to make sure that natural cycles were closed rather than open ended so that essential nutrients were not lost.

The industrialized cities of the past that grew beyond this simple balance, based on the renewable transport of the sailing ship and horse and cart, and the modern high-density city have thrown this fertility away and instead have relied on modern agricultural systems with their artificial fertilizers. In fact, this throwing away of fertility has resulted in the problems and costs associated with sewage disposal. It may be difficult to use the sewage from a modern high-density city as fertilizer for its food production, even if the food were to be grown in an area of land immediately adjacent. However, in a smaller high-density settlement or a decentralized low-density city this practice would be relatively easy. This echoes the argument by Yong Xue (2005) who, in his examination of late imperial Jiangnan, sees the richer urban population increasing the wealth of the surrounding rural population through their night soil and the nutrients contained in it because of their better diet. At the same time, the health of those in the cities was guaranteed because the sewage disposal problem was solved. This could only happen because of the relatively small scale of the dense city settlement.

Low density or high density?

When Howard proposed the garden city as a place that could provide an adequate standard of living, his approach to planning included the land to grow the food for the people living at higher density in the central part of the garden city. He also acknowledged the need for some people to live in agricultural areas at much lower density in order to grow food. In this way he arrived at the ideal figure of 32,000 people: 30,000 in the garden city at a density of 30 persons per acre and 2000 in the agricultural hinterland at a density of 2 persons per 5 acres (Osborn, 1946, p28). This was robust planning as the basic resources of food, as well as water supply, were considered; but it was also looking at the world in a non-capitalist way. Making money was not Howard's objective, even though he did discuss how development and increasing the price of land through development could finance the building of garden cities. His view was to see this money put back into the local communities, who would thus be in charge of their own affairs (Howard, 1965, p127). In a capitalist world, however, it is the price of everything that matters, not the robustness of the system. A capitalist society would operate best with everyone living at high densities so that the maximum number of people would need to buy everything they required, having little opportunity to provide basic services, such as growing food, themselves. A high-density city is necessarily a consumer city; but, as Commoner said, there is no such thing as a free lunch,

and all these goods will be taking up land somewhere and also using labour somewhere. Unlike the garden city model, this supply is not necessarily under the control of those living in the city.

The garden city model would work well in a post-oil society. The garden areas next to the houses could be used for growing food very close to home, as happened in World War II in the UK when Britain grew 10 per cent of its food in private gardens and allotment gardens (London Borough of Sutton, 2006). In addition, the distances into the agricultural hinterland could be walked, so a complete food supply could be maintained. There would also be sufficient land to grow crops for fuel and lower densities such as the 12 houses to the acre of the garden city, making it easy for each individual house to collect solar energy, whether as hot water or as electricity through the use of photovoltaics for direct home consumption. Very high densities mean that most energy supply will have to be centralized even if generated from renewable sources. Low densities also give the chance for sewage to be collected and returned to the soil to support organic agricultural production; ultimately, only organic production is sustainable.

The current rush towards densification in countries with suburban sprawl, such as the US and Australia, seems to be linked primarily to more efficient use of public transport in an effort to reduce the use of the private car. However, this is still based on the use of the capitalist city model and the idea that people will buy all they need, with limited production of goods and food at home. No densification scheme seems to consider food supply and where the land to grow the food is to be located, or the problem of organic food production and the need to return sewage nutrients to the soil. In a post-oil world it may well be the lower-density suburban sprawl developments that can more easily adjust to life either without energy or with expensive energy because they have the land at hand to use. Walking and bicycling are good transport options at low density once the private car that makes them unsafe is priced out of existence.

Conclusions

There is no magic answer to city design. There is, however, a real need for regional planning for a future when cheap oil is no longer available. The worry at present is that high density is perceived as good without ever seeing how it fits into a pattern of resource flows so that the people living in these settlements have secure access to the basic necessities of life, including food. The very high-density city appears to be very efficient in land use and in the use of some resources, such as transport; but the low-density city also has advantages, these being the ability to collect enough energy for home use and to grow food. Historical patterns show that planning for a stable supply of basic resources was always considered, something that seems to have been forgotten in a capitalist globalized society. Who owns resources is already beginning to be a difficult political problem, as the world is seeing with oil. Rather than rushing to ever higher densities, perhaps those who govern cities should consider how such cities can be future-proofed in terms of guaranteeing a secure supply of resources. If Edward I could do this during the 13th century when he was establishing the planned settlements of the bastides in France and towns such as Berwick-on-Tweed in the north of England (Osborn, 1946, p70), maybe 20th-century city councillors and planners could be equally resourceful.

Notes

1   Calculated from data of 1 million tonnes oil equivalent = 41.868PJ given in http://astro.berkeley.edu/~wright/fuel_energy.html, accessed 2 January 2008.
2   World Ports Distances Calculator, www.distances.com/, accessed 3 January 2008.
3   Leigh, G. H. (2004) *The World's Greatest Fix: a history of nitrogen and agriculture*, Oxford University Press, New York, p136.

References

Association for the Study of Peak Oil and Gas (undated) www.peakoil.net/, accessed 10 December 2007

Banham, R. (1969) *The Architecture of the Well-Tempered Environment*, Architectural Press, London

Boyle, G. and Harper, P. (eds) (1976) *Radical Technology*, Wildwood House, London, pp170–171

Cadbury, D. (2004) *Seven Wonders of the Industrial World*, Harper Perennial, New York, NY

Clean Energy Educational Trust (undated) 'Hydrogen produced using UK offshore wind-generated electricity and development of hydrogen-fuelled buses and cars in the UK', www.hydrogen.co.uk/h2/offshore_windpower.htm, accessed 3 January 2008

Commoner, B. (1971) *The Closing Circle*, Knopf, New York, NY

Le Corbusier (1929) *The City of Tomorrow*, John Rodker, London

EEA (European Environment Agency) (2002) *Indicator Fact Sheet TERM 2002 27 EU – Overall Energy Efficiency and Specific CO_2 Emissions for Passenger and Freight Transport (per passenger-km and per tonne-km and by mode)*, EEA, Brussels, Figure 2, p1

Environmental Protection Department (2006) *EA and Planning Strategic Environmental Assessment*, www.epd.gov.hk/epd/english/environmentinhk/, accessed 9 January 2008

Fertilizer Institute (undated) www.tfi.org/factsandstats/fertilizer.cfm, accessed 6 January 2007

Friends of the Earth (undated) 'EcoCity Hong Kong', www.foe.org.hk/welcome/eco_1997ef.asp, accessed 9 January 2008

Howard, E. (1965) (ed) *Garden Cities of Tomorrow*, Faber and Faber, London

IMO (International Maritime Organization) (2005) *International Shipping: Carrier of World Trade*, IMO, London, p3

Journey to Forever (undated) 'Vegetable oil yields', http://journeytoforever.org/biodiesel_yield.html, accessed 3 January 2008

Levy, Y. (1941) *Guerrilla Warfare*, Penguin Books, Middlesex, UK, p86–88

London Borough of Sutton (2006) 'What is an allotment?', www.sutton.gov.uk/leisure/allotments/whatallotments.htm, accessed 6 January 2008

Mayhew, H. (1851) *London Labour and the London Poor*, http://old.perseus.tufts.edu/cgi-bin/ptext?doc=Perseus%3Atext%3A2000.01.0027%3Aid%3Dc.9.179, accessed 9 January 2008

New Zealand Wind Energy Association (2005) *Wind Farm Basics Fact Sheet 1*, August, NZWEA, Wellington, New Zealand

Osborn, F. J. (1946) *Green-Belt Cities*, Faber and Faber, London

Roberts, T. L. and Stewart, W. M. (2002) 'Inorganic phosphorus and potassium production and reserves', *Better Crops*, vol 86, no 2, p6

SWEET (South West England Environment Trust) (2005) 'Food footprint', Table 7, www.steppingforward.org.uk/ef/food.htm, accessed 17 December 2007

Wackernagel, M. (1997) 'How big is our ecological footprint?', Table 1, www.iisd.ca/consume/mwfoot.html, accessed December 2007

Wackernagel, M. and Rees, W. (1996) *Our Ecological Footprint*, New Society Publishers, British Columbia, Canada

Wiebenson, D. (no date) *Tony Garnier: The Cite Industrielle*, Studio Vista, London

Wikipedia (2007) http://en.wikipedia.org/wiki/Ecology_of_Hong_Kong, accessed 10 December 2007

Wind Power Project Site Identification and Land Requirements (2005) NYSERDA Wind Power Toolkit June 2005, Prepared for New York State Energy Research and Development Authority, 17 Columbia Circle, Albany, NY

WRI (World Resources Institute) (2007) *Earth Trends: Environmental Information*, WRI, Washington, DC, http://earthtrends.wri.org/pdf_library/country_profiles/ene_cou_344.pdf, accessed 17 December 2007

Yong Xue (2005) 'Treasure night soil as if it were gold: Economic and ecological links between urban and rural areas in late imperial Jiangnan', *Late Imperial China*, vol 26, no 1, p63

3

The Sustainability of High Density

Susan Roaf

Cities have come and gone across the world for nearly 10,000 years since people first began to live in villages. The first known settlement of actual buildings was at Gange Dareh (Roaf et al, 2009), dating to around 7000BC, high in the Zagros Mountains looking across the plains of Mesopotamia (Iraq) to where Ur, Babylon and Nineveh grew in the Cradle of Civilization – huge dense cities, of which 'Nothing beside remains' (Shelley, 'Ozymandeus') and all had disappeared by the time that Mohammad, Buddha or Christ were born. If you have ever explored the Kasbah of Algiers, the twisting wynds of 18th-century Edinburgh, the alleys of Jerusalem or any other of the great medieval cities, you will know that density in cities is sustainable until, of course, that city falls.

But we live in a high-risk age in which cities face three gargantuan challenges:

1 population and the people problem;
2 resource depletion;
3 pollution and its environmental impacts, including climate change.

Population and the people problem

Urbanization

Two strong forces are shaping our cities today: population growth and escalating rates of urbanization. Over 56 per cent of people in developing countries will live in cities by 2030, whereas in developed countries it may well exceed 84 per cent by then; this process is occurring at a time when vast numbers of city dwellers are already living in substandard conditions. A United Nations Educational, Scientific and Cultural Organization (UNESCO) report on access to water and sanitation based on a sample of 116 cities shows that for Africa, Asia, Latin America and Oceania, a house or yard water connection exists in only 40 to

80 per cent of households, whereas levels of access to a sanitation infrastructure is far worse, at only 18 to 41 per cent (UNDESA, 2004). These numbers imply that the simple vernacular approaches to development may not be capable of achieving the required densification of dwellings, services and infrastructure to house populations in workable, rapidly growing cities (Meir and Roaf, 2005).

Building durability

Conversely, in Europe and North America, with far lower birth rates, the bulk of the increasing population can typically be accommodated by new housing built at significantly lower densities. However, in many of these countries most of the existing housing stock is what will eventually be expected to cover the bulk of housing needs for the next half century or so. A recent report to the Scottish government on housing demonstrated the need to often spend very large sums on the external cladding and other refurbishment measures for the refurbishment of Scottish homes to stop the current level of 20 per cent of the population in fuel poverty (households spending more than 10 per cent of their income on fuel bills) from rising steeply towards the 50 per cent mark. Tower blocks, in particular, are the most expensive to refurbish. In Scotland, these were traditionally social housing blocks (where costs had to be met by local councils and, in turn, the tax payer), usually 10 to 18 storeys in height, costing around UK£2 to £2.5 million each to over-clad and provide efficient heating. These blocks were typically less than 40 years' old and many were already in very poor condition (Roaf and Baker, 2008). In order to create cities that are socially and physically sustainable, city authorities must ensure that the buildings in their cities can be repaired, refurbished and replaced at an affordable price. The only way to do this is via a firm regulation system, an essential ingredient of the sustainable city.

People, en masse, are coming off the land where they grow their own food and can build their own homes into cities where they cannot. Nowhere is this trend clearer than in the emerging mega-economies of China, Latin America and India; but the contrast between how each of these cultures deals with urban migration is very telling and will, in the long term, dictate the long-term health of the culture. India has the disadvantage of never having successfully controlled its exponential population growth rate, while China has put successful controls in place and is committed to providing housing, food and transport for the many in a far more egalitarian, though ostensibly less democratic, society.

Density and health

The need for high-density living in the 21st century is inevitable and has many consequences. The first is that simply putting so many people together increases health risks, just as it does in fish or poultry farms where disease spreads rapidly through densely packed populations. The severe acute respiratory syndrome (SARS) outbreaks of 2003 showed that the infection was rapidly spread between people via the building infrastructure, including lift buttons, but also between buildings in the Amoy complex in Hong Kong in the air (Li et al, 2007).

In a 2007 review paper by Li et al looking at related published evidence of disease spread in the built environment, 15 international authors concluded that there is strong and sufficient evidence to demonstrate the association between ventilation and the control of airflow directions in buildings, and the transmission and spread of infectious diseases such as measles, tuberculosis, chickenpox, anthrax, influenza, smallpox and SARS.

The infection intensity and rates of spread of disease are predicted to significantly increase as climate change affects the habitats of birds, animals, insects, fish, pathogens and plants, exacerbated by terrestrial and atmospheric pollution and extreme weather events such as floods and storms that provide enhanced potentials for the transmission of air- and water-borne diseases (Kovats, 2008, p124). The more people there are in the places where such diseases are brewing, the more individuals will get sick and die; so from this point of view, higher-density cities present a higher risk for the spread of anything from infection. This was always a strong factor in the move of the rich to the suburbs of large cities from the time of the great plagues onwards.

Size and vulnerability

The larger a building and the more centralized its services, the more vulnerable it is to large-scale failure – for instance, to terrorism. We all understand the implications of the attacks on the twin towers on 11 September 2001; but the failures can be much more subtle than that. In buildings with fixed windows and extensive air circulation systems there is an increased hazard from biological agents. Ventilation ducts have proved to be a route of infection; at the US Pentagon, 31 anthrax spores were found in the air-conditioning ducts of the building (Staff and Agencies, 2001). The problem here is that the bigger the building, the bigger the risk. Many tall buildings have centralized circulation, servicing and air-handling units that make them very vulnerable to attack from many different sources.

In many regions of the world, the preference for room-level air-conditioning units will reduce the risk of systemic infection of buildings that is the risk in buildings with centralized air-handling plants. It is not only the density but the resilience of the building form, design and servicing that will drive rates of infection.

The Hilton Hawaiian Village in Honolulu reopened in September 2003, 14 months after it closed, at a cost of US$55 million dollars in repairs because a single tower block became infected with mould. The mould *Eurotium aspergillus* in the centralized air-conditioning system, the same kind of mould seen on bread or cheese, was the cause. It has no effect on most people; some people experience a minor irritation of the nose, while a very few people have severe symptoms that in rare cases can be life threatening. The problem is not confined to the tropics, and, indeed, a problem similar to what Hilton experienced was found in hospitals across Canada in recent years.

Hilton has sued virtually every contractor who had anything to do with the construction of the Kalia Tower, including the architect, all the consulting engineers and other specialists on the project, and even the company that provided the lanai glass doors. It has argued that both the design and the construction of the building made it a 'greenhouse' for growing mould. The entire heating, ventilating and air-conditioning (HVAC) system was rebuilt, mostly to ensure a more frequent turnover of drier air. The insurance industry has subsequently withdrawn 'mould coverage' from many policies and it is claimed that mould will be the 'new asbestos' in terms of payouts. The severity of the problem is reflected in the size of the payout to one family in a mould case, when a Texas jury awarded a family US$4 million in a single toxic mould lawsuit against Farmers Insurance Group in June 2001 (Scott, 2003; Cooper, 2004). Such outbreaks may become more prevalent with climate change and warming, wetter climates, which will make buildings more susceptible to systemic infestations of naturally occurring toxins within large-scale air-handling systems. The need for building resilience is obvious. In Hawaii, with the perfect climate, they could, for instance, just have opened the windows for adequate and often delightful ventilation. The benefits of reducing use of or eliminating air conditioning here are obvious, a lesson that should be widely learned.

Density and security

High-density cities can exacerbate security risks. During the 19th century, town planning became fashionable as people cut wider streets though the dense, crowded and filthy alleyways of the European industrial cities. Not only did the boulevards bring fresh air into the heart of the town, but they also made it more secure. During 1809 to 1891, Georges-Eugene

Haussmann, under the patronage of Napoleon, destroyed the heart of the old city of Paris and rebuilt it with broad roads and parks. He designed the streets 'to ensure the public peace by the creation of large boulevards which will permit the circulation not only of air and light but also of troops'. As more people crowd into cities, they also raise issues of security (Gideon, 1976, p746).

Just as in the Bon Lieu of Paris, with their tower block estates, where in 2003 and 2004 extensive rioting took place, so too is Latin America's densest city well known for its high levels of crime. A recent study by Clark and McGrath (2007) using spatial-temporal analyses of data showed that the structural determinants of violent crime in the São Paulo Metropolitan Area during the last two decades of the 20th century were uncorrelated to structural explanations of crime, such as social disorganization, deprivation and threat models. Rates of violent crime were also uncorrelated with economic levels and conditions or to property crime rates. Instead, they found that rates of violence were concentrated to the urban peripheral areas where policing appears to be overwhelmed.

Conditions in the city are extremely difficult to police, not least because many parts of the city are impassable at various times of day. In response to this problem, and to avoid crime, pollution and delay, many of the rich have developed a new highway and have taken to the skies for their daily commute. The numbers of helicopters rose from 374 to 469 between 1999 and 2008, making São Paulo the helicopter capital of the world ahead of New York or Hong Kong (Gideon, 1976, p746). The city has around 6 million cars, 820 helicopter pilots earning up to US$100,000 a year each and 420 helipads, 75 per cent of all Brazil and 50 per cent more than in the whole of the UK. Below in the streets it is often gridlocked, creating two worlds of the rich and the poor.

Inequality

The last couple of decades have seen the gap between the rich and poor grow in many parts of the world, from India to China, and Europe to the US, and herein lies a problem that relates to density in cities at a time of rapid change.

Richard G. Wilkinson (2005) in his excellent book on *The Impact of Inequality* points out that however rich a country is, it will still be more dysfunctional, violent, sick and sad if the gap between social classes grows too wide. Poorer countries with fairer wealth distribution are healthier and happier than richer, more unequal nations. Homicide rates, and other crimes, including terrorism, track a country's level of inequality, not its overall wealth. The fairest countries have the highest levels of trust and social capital.

Wilkinson's message is that the social environment can be more toxic than any pollutant. Low status and lack of control over one's life is a destroyer of human health and happiness. The wealth gap causes few to vote or participate in anything in a world of fear, conflict and hostility. Poverty in rich nations is not a number or the absence of a particular necessity. A poor man may bring up children well on lentils and respect. But for most people respect is measured in money.

He also argues that one way to cope with a challenge to society is to explicitly reduce the level of social inequality. Therefore, during the war years, in the UK the government explicitly created and imposed a greater degree of social equality, which made society better able and more willing to cope with the challenges that they were faced with.

Similar examples can be found in Europe. During World War II, income differences narrowed dramatically in Britain. This was, of course, partly due to the effect of war on the economy, which led to a decline in unemployment and a diminution of earning differentials among employed people, but also as a result of a deliberate policy pursued by the government to gain the 'cooperation of the masses' in the war effort. Richard Titmuss, in his 1955 essay on war and social policy, points out that 'inequalities had to be reduced and the pyramid of social stratification had to be flattened' (Titmuss, 1976, p86). In order to ensure that the burden of war was seen as fairly shared, taxes on the rich were sharply increased and necessities were subsidized. Luxuries were also taxed, and a wide range of food and other goods was rationed to ensure a fair distribution.

The 1941 Beveridge Report in Britain, which set out plans for the post-war development of the welfare state, including the establishment of the National Health Service, had the same purpose: 'to present a picture of a fairer future and so gain people's support for the war effort'. If people felt the burden of war had fallen disproportionately on the mass of the working population, leaving the rich unaffected, the sense of camaraderie and cooperation would surely turn to resentment and, in turn, civil unrest.

Density: What will people pay for?

By early 2008 property market conditions had become very difficult in the US and Europe, not least in offices, as anticipated in a UK Gensler Report on the very vulnerable property markets of 2005/2006. *Faulty Towers* was published in July 2006 (Johnson et al, 2006) and its authors issued a stark warning to commercial property investors that 75 per cent of property developers believe that impending legislation to grade the energy efficiency of buildings will have a negative impact upon the value and transferability of inefficient buildings when certification under the European Buildings Directive (European Commission, 2008) was imposed from 2007. They claimed that:

> Property fund managers are effectively sitting on an investment time bomb. The introduction of energy performance certificates will shorten the lifespan of commercial buildings constructed before the new regulations, and we expect the capital value of inefficient buildings to fall as a result. We expect to see a shakeup in the market, with investors disposing of inefficient stock, upgrading those buildings which can be adapted and demanding much higher energy efficiency from new buildings.

The report also reveals that 72 per cent of company property directors believe that business is picking up the bill for badly designed inefficient buildings and 26 per cent state that bad office stock is actually damaging UK productivity. However, there is a perception amongst developers that there is no demand for sustainable buildings.

It might be argued that short-sighted and greedy developers have written their own obituary in not understanding the drivers for higher performance in buildings and putting short-term profit before the long-term sustainability of businesses. The value of property portfolios in the UK has fallen by over 50 per cent almost across the board since the publication of *Faulty Towers*; but is the reasoning in it actually explaining the whole picture?

Since around 2000 I have been noticing the growing phenomenon of 'dead building syndrome'. As you pass by the railway stations in cities around the world, you will see from the carriage windows the growing numbers of 'dead buildings'. They are usually a minimum of ten floors and were typically built in the UK during the 1960s and 1970s when the hub of commercial life still revolved around the old centres in towns and cities everywhere. They are empty and often in poor condition. Another type of dead building syndrome has sprouted in the UK over the last year or two, and these are the empty tower blocks of urban flats, usually cheaply built with steel frames and fairly low-cost cladding systems, often with high levels of glazing in the external envelope. You can see them in Manchester, Leeds and a number of other cities. Many are lying empty due to a glut in the market during 2006 to 2007, and the fact that the people for whom the flats were designed cannot get a mortgage any more. They often could not afford them before, but could get easy credit to buy them with cheap mortgages.

The developers' bonanza is magnified where whole new cities of such buildings are being built in the fossil-fuel economies of the world. Astana is the new capital of the oil-rich country of Kazakhstan. Its old Soviet-era city blocks are in poor condition, with four- to six-storey buildings of shops, offices and apartments lining the grid pattern of streets and backing onto the local neighbourhood squares with their children's playground and small parks. Here people meet to enjoy the fresh air and sunshine in these sheltered, communally owned spaces protected from the cruel Siberian winds. An apartment here may commonly cost between US$45,000 and $150,000.

Beyond the old town is the new Astana, dream child of the current president. Huge tracts of the flat Siberian steppes have been criss-crossed by well-laid roads and building plots into the centre of which have been built stand-alone sculptural towers, the land around them blasted by the relentless winter gales and littered by kilometres of car parks. An apartment in these new fancy tower blocks starts at around US$250,000 to $1 million. The average Kazakh family may bring home US$15,000 to $30,000 a year. Thousands of these apartments have been built and many of them sold to investors in the Gulf. But who will live here? 98 per cent of Kazakhs cannot afford to live in them. This is a society breeding inequality.

How much more so in Dubai, where the sea of glass towers rise over the limitless arid desert in some fantasy of a super-rich international community jetting in and out to spend time in their US$250,000 apartments. Will people buy them? Who will service them? Where will the poor live and in what conditions? Is this the greatest level of inequality of any city in the world?

People and businesses alike in the 'worst recession since the Depression' at the end of the 'nice decade' in so many countries today can no longer afford the 'prestige' rents and the very high running costs of keeping commercial or residential premises warm or cool over the year. 20 per cent of the Scottish population is in fuel poverty (spending over 10 per cent of their income on heating or cooling). Many glass box offices lie empty in business parks on the outskirts of towns, while people are moving back into more modest offices in the town centres where public transport is readily available and cheaper than commuting out of town.

You can see the impact of decades of economic recession in the Rust Belt of North America, where the industries that spawned prosperity such as iron and steel, cars, railways, canal-building, typewriters, washing machines and agricultural machinery have died themselves or moved to Taiwan or China. Here, even beautiful, fine tall buildings of stone and brick lie empty in the lifeless hearts of once great cities. Of the 18 towers in Cleveland, Ohio, 8 are completely empty and others only partially occupied; some of these could be counted amongst the world's great buildings built by Rockefeller and Kodak. They have simply lost their economic *raison d'être*.

But in other modern, vibrant, high-density, high-rise cities, what makes one flat or building more viable than another? A recent study of the Hong Kong property market by Kwok and Tse (2006) looked at the Hong Kong market during a seven-month period in 2005 to 2006, during which time the mean monthly growth rate of the economy was 1.5 per cent. The authors looked at the impacts of trading volume upon the price of flats and their turnover rates and found that people are influenced in their purchases by the size of the flats (the bigger the better for the price), their newness, and also quite strongly by how much open space they are associated with. Purchasers also liked the fact that a block had more amenities, like a club house. The study found that contrary to conventional wisdom, people were less attracted by big developments, preferring smaller ones which characteristically had more liquidity (sold faster and better). A mix of buildings and less monolithic developments appeared to be preferred. What the data did suggest is that the market was determined by the quality of the housing units, and it was the quality that drove price premiums. As one would expect, the age of the block was important, with older blocks being more difficult to sell, although the quality factor obviously counts in spite of this.

The higher up a building a flat is, the higher the premium that can be charged. Kwok and Tse (2006) showed that *price* and *floor* are positively correlated and that there is around a 6 per cent premium on floor height over 30 floors in Hong Kong.

Of course, there are a number of factors that will add value to blocks, including location, history and, of course, view. A study by Yu et al (2007) showed that in Singapore, along the east coast area of the island, buyers would pay an average selling price premium of around 15 per cent. The study raised another issue, which is that in the event of new developments being built that could obstruct existing views, buyers need to ensure that they will not end up losing the premium that they paid for (Yu et al, 2007).

However, William C. Wharton, professor at the Massachusetts Institute of Technology (MIT) Department of Economics, US, and one of the world experts on property valuation, warned in 2002 that a view does not necessarily command an attractive premium. Even before 11 September 2001, rents in Lower Manhattan were only 60 per cent of those commanded by comparable midtown properties. Wharton estimated that much of this lost rent is due to the poorer transportation access of Lower Manhattan versus midtown. Rents in Manhattan decline by 30 per cent for each mile to the nearest subway stop, and by an additional 9 per cent for each mile from Grand Central Station. Finally, rents downtown increase only 30 per cent between comparable buildings of 60 storeys in height versus those only 10 storeys tall. This 'view premium' probably, in his words, does not match the required additional construction costs – casting doubt on the economic wisdom of building ever higher (Wharton, 2002).

Who decides how high a building will be?

In governing the height of buildings, the most powerful regulations, apart from specific planning directives, are fire regulations. In the UK, a generally low-rise country, there are strong drivers that keep buildings moderately low. Above six storeys, significant extra costs are incurred in sprinkler systems, and after ten storeys, the need for enhanced fire escape provision means that the extra costs can only be recouped if storey heights push up above 15 storeys. At around 18 storeys the need for upgrading passenger lift systems in the building makes higher buildings (even in expensive areas of London) less than fully economically viable. In London, former Mayor Ken Livingston actually forced developers to push up their planned buildings above this level because he wanted to promote London as a tall city, despite the fact that this seriously reduced their profit levels from the build. The cost efficiency of a high building will vary according to the cost and quality of the build; so, of course, developers will make more profit the higher they go if they build to lower standards.

In Hong Kong, where space is at a premium, building codes for thermal performance are less stringent, resulting in more fire-proof buildings. In the UK, thermal regulations require that cold bridging of the external structure is eliminated by floating the external envelope of the building outside the structure thereby destroying the fire compartmentalization that prevents rapid fire spreading up the outside of towers. In Hong Kong, this is not required, lowering the thermal performance of structures by allowing floor-to-floor construction, but eliminating the potential for fire spread along the inside of the building skin. In Hong Kong, where fatal residential fires do occur, there is a fairly onerous requirement for fire-fighting equipment to be stored at the top of the building (Cheung, 1992, pp47–60) (see Table 3.1).

Again, the high cost implications of upgrading water storage capacity will mean that developers will tend to go up to the maximum floor height achievable for the minimum water storage capacity.

In a developer-driven city, it is interesting that a main fire-fighting regulation relates to the provision, size and location of fire hydrants. If fighting a fire from

Table 3.1 *Fire safety requirements in Hong Kong*

Gross floor area	Required water storage
Not exceeding 230m²	9000 litres
Over 230m² and below 460m²	18,000 litres
Over 460m² and below 920m²	27,000 litres
Over 920m²	36,000 litres

Source: Cheung (1992)

the street, the maximum height of a tall fire ladder is around 30m, or around ten floors. A fully kitted out fire-fighter can climb to a maximum of around ten floors and remain operational, but not above this level. In Hong Kong, the main way to fight fires in towers is either through internal sprinkler systems (ideally at least one per flat) or for firemen to climb with extendable hydrant-fixed fire hoses and portable fire pumps to pump the water to the level of the fire from the street.

In America, where the height of buildings is related to the perceived success of cities and/or organizations and limitations on personal freedoms are not encouraged, fire regulations have evolved with developers' interests at heart. Before 11 September 2001, fire regulations in tall buildings were predicated on the idea that buildings would be evacuated in an orderly phased fashion floor by floor. After 9/11, this was understood not to be the case as it was realized that people would potentially not survive above a catastrophic fire. After a three-year review by the US National Institute of Standards and Technology (NIST), it was recommended, very much against developers' wishes, that an additional stairway exit for buildings over 140m (420feet, or circa 40 floors) and a minimum of one fire service access elevator be required in all new buildings over 40m high (120 feet, or 12 floors), as well as luminous markings to show the exit path in buildings more than 25m high (75 feet, or circa six to eight floors) (NIST, 2007). Developers did not object to the luminous markings. These regulations will result in lower towers in the US.

Costs associated with fire-fighting, lifts provision, crane heights during construction, water-pumping regulations and the cost and quality of construction, etc. influence the economics of building height and, thus, the height to which buildings are built. These limits are a reflection on the culture of the local society. Hubris drives individuals and cash-rich corporations and states to go above these sensible heights.

Resource depletion

Issues around resources depletion are increasingly posing enormous limits on the way in which we design, build and live today and in the future. There are three immediate imperatives on buildings resulting from the growing demand for, scarcity and cost of the Earth's resources:

1   Lower the build cost per square metre of a building.
2   Lower the cost per square metre of running a building.
3   Change lifestyle patterns to lower costs while maintaining quality of life.

The following sections deal with the basic resources of building materials, water and fossil fuels.

Building materials

In 2001, Treloar and colleagues published a classic study of the energy embodied in substructure, superstructure and finish elements for five Melbourne office buildings of the following heights: 3, 7, 15, 42 and 52 storeys. The two high-rise buildings were found to have approximately 60 per cent more energy embodied per unit gross floor area (GFA) in their materials than the low-rise buildings. Increases were evident in building elements such as upper floors, columns, internal walls, external walls and staircases, as well as the direct energy of the construction process and other items not included in the bill of quantities, such as ancillary items, consultants' activities and financial and government services.

Variations in other elements, such as substructure, roof, windows and finishes, did not appear to be influenced by building height. The case study analysis suggested that high-rise buildings require more energy-intensive materials to meet structural requirements and wind load compared to 212 low-rise office buildings also recorded. A combination of two effects occurs:

1   The materials are more energy intensive.
2   More materials are required for high-rise buildings.

The findings of Treloar et al (2001) are reproduced in Table 3.2, and the disparity in the results is striking. The additional 60 per cent costs of the materials and energy embodied energy in them in relation to the potential to charge a 30 per cent view premium backs up Professor Wharton's assumption that the cost of the view does not cover its building costs.

The importance of the embodied energy costs of buildings is more significant in today's markets, where the cost of building materials such as steel and concrete is soaring, bolstered by market shortages driven by the boom economies of China and India and the rising price of oil. Material costs are beginning to reduce the

Table 3.2 *Case study buildings' embodied energy results (GJ/m² gross floor area) by element group*

Height in storeys	3	7	15	42	52
Structure group	5	7	9.9	11.7	11.6
Finishes group	0.6	0.4	0.5	0.4	0.7
Substructure	0.9	0.4	1.2	0.5	0.7
Roof	1	0.8	0.1	0.2	0.4
windows	0.3	0.2	0	0.2	0.1
Non-material group	2.9	3.2	4.4	4.9	5
TOTAL	10.7	11.9	16.1	18	18.4

Source: adapted from Treloar et al (2001)

viability of many building projects, and the 12-month rise in steel costs in the US to August 2008 of 60 to 70 per cent (Scott, 2008) has meant that many projects have been value engineered out of existence. In Las Vegas alone, since 2005, 30 major tower building developments, already given planning permission, were cancelled because they simply would never make a return on investment.[1]

Perhaps the highest profile of these, in all ways, was the super-tall Crown Las Vegas, with a height of 1888 (575m) feet, given planning permission in June 2007 and cancelled in July 2008; it would have been the tallest building in the Western Hemisphere and a solid focal point for the north strip of this entertainment city. Austin-based developer Christopher Milam proposed the US$4.8 billion, 5000 unit, 450,000 gross square metre, 142-storey condo-hotel resort and casino for the land south of the Sahara resort, in a project that was conceived of by Skidmore, Owings and Merrill, and Steelman Design Group. It is a tripod, which is the most efficient structural shape for a super-tall building, and this allows for the maximization of height with minimum penalty for structural weight. It was designed to be of composite steel and concrete for reasons of both speed and cost, whereas the Burj Dubai is all concrete. The apparently cost-efficient design contrasted with Burj Dubai that is very inefficient in its top 80 floors and was never considered commercial as a stand-alone project; but the owners have the financial resources and the 'greater regional objective' to have the tallest building in the world (Milham, 2006). None of the super-tall towers are commercially viable, and developers in the UK typically will not look at a structure over 18 floors if they want to make money.

Water

Las Vegas is a city in trouble because, despite the fact that many of its planned towers have been cancelled, some ten new towers will be completed by 2013 with potentially catastrophic consequences for the viability of the city itself. It is one of those 'cities on the edge of cliffs' that because the settlement has grown in such a way as to exceed the capacity of its hinterland to support it, may simply die itself.

Las Vegas is one of the most energy-hungry cities in the world and nearly all of its electricity is generated by hydropower. Not only is it located in a dry desert which is too hot and dry to support non-acclimatized Western populations without air conditioning, but the types of buildings on 'The Strip' are some of the most energy profligate in the world, with their 'full-view' windows. At a time of growing energy and water shortages in the drought-ridden south-west of America, the city now has over US$30 billion of new developments on its books to be completed, with the first one being the new city centre development, to be completed in late 2010. It is located on the imploded site of the old MGM lot, and the new seven-tower block development will cost approximately US$8 billion, cover 1.8 million square metres and include hotels, casinos and residences. It will eventually house 8000 new visitors and need an additional 12,000 staff to service it. This was planned in a city with high levels of employment, soaring house prices, no free school places, and an electricity and water supply system in crisis.

Each new resident will need around 20,000 kilowatt hours (kWh) of electricity a year. So this single development may need an extra 400,000 megawatts hours (MWh) per annum generation capacity at a cost of US$1 million a year producing 160 million tonnes of carbon dioxide (CO_2) per annum, all generated by turbines at the Hoover, Parker and David dams that serve Nevada, and have a maximum generation capacity of only 200,000MW. The state utilities are building two more coal-powered stations and have commissioned the Solar One plant, a 64MW solar generator in the Nevada Desert. But even this does not cover the energy requirements from the new developments on The Strip.

The real problem is water. Not only is the electricity generated by the water turbines at the dam, but the new demand may create an additional demand for over 1 billion gallons of water per year. This is taking a very conservative assumption of 10,000 people in the development multiplied by the average Las Vegas per capita consumption of around 115,000 gallons of water per year. The warming climate has caused a rapid decrease in the snow pack on the Rockies that feeds the Colorado rivers and its dams. Researchers Barnett and Pierce at Scripps Institution of Oceanography at the University of California, San Diego, calculate that there is a 10 per cent chance that Lake Mead (Hoover Dam) will dry up in six years and a 50 per cent chance that it will be gone by 2021 (Barnett and Pierce, 2008). Professor Hal Rothman of the University of Nevada, Las Vegas, probably spoke for many Americans who find it difficult to deal with issues of climate change when he said: 'Water is unlikely to ever be a major problem for Las Vegas as long as the city's success continues. Water flows uphill to money in the American West' (Krieger, 2006).

Nevada, Las Vegas's home state, is already triggering a water war with neighbouring Utah as it tries to purloin its underground water reserves by drilling in areas in the north of the state, such as Snake Valley. Despite the lack of resolution on future water resources, Las Vegas just gets more and more water- and energy-greedy as it begins to plunder the adjacent landscapes to feed its ever-rising needs (DJ, 2008).

Oil

The cost of energy changes everything. In April 2005 there was a global price spike for oil that went through the US$60 a barrel level; in April 2006 the price spike hit US$80 dollars a barrel in the wake of the devastation wrought by Hurricane Katrina in the Gulf of Mexico, and in July 2008 its price spiked to US$147 a barrel. No one actually knows where this price is heading and how fast, but it changes the way in which we build and live in our cities.

Middle-class people in warm countries around the world are beginning not to be able to afford to run their cooling systems as much as they would like, because they can no longer afford the steeply rising electricity prices for them. In higher buildings in many cities, including Hong Kong or São Paulo, not only are the prices rising for basic food commodities, petrol and services, but there is the additional energy burden of paying for lifts. Lifts also use a large amount of energy to run. For buildings that are largely served by lifts, you can add a rough figure of 5 to 15 per cent onto building energy running costs. Nipkow and Schalcher (2006) showed that lifts can account for a significant proportion of energy consumption in buildings with surprisingly high standby consumption, accounting for between 25 and 83 per cent of total consumption (see Table 3.3).

So, a twelve-storey residential block with two lifts might use up to 40,000kWh just to get to the flats. In addition, there are higher operation and maintenance costs in taller buildings and, as has been found in Scottish social housing blocks, a significant 'concierge cost' to

Table 3.3 *Energy consumption of typical traction lifts*

Type of Building/ Purpose	Capacity kg	Speed m/s	Wh per cycle	No. of stops	No. of Travel p.a.	kWh pa. including standby	% in mode standby
Small apartment building	630kg	1 m/s	6	4	40,000	950	83%
Office block/med sized apart. block	1000kg	1.5 m/s	8	13	200,000	4350	40%
Hospital, large office block	2000kg	2 m/s	12	19	700,000	17,700	25%

Source: Nipkow and Schalcher (2006)

provide security to the higher, more densely populated blocks (Meir and Roaf, 2005).

There are also significant costs in raising water in a block where water is used for fire sprinkler systems, for hot and cold water supplies and for cooling systems. Perhaps this is best illustrated with figures for the highest building in the world, the Burj Dubai Tower. The 160-storey tower of 344,000 square metres will include 45.7MW of cooling alone with a chilled water system and a subsidiary ice storage system to reduce installed chiller capacity to lower the capital costs (Twickline, 2008). This tower uses the outputs of two major power stations just to keep the lights on.

The energy subsidy problem

Kuwait, has only been a state since 1913 and is now one of the richest countries per capita in the world. It is also one of the most vulnerable for the very reason of the inequality between the rich and the poor, or, in this case, the very very rich and the rich. Kuwait has for decades subsidized the price of electricity, which is sold now for the unbelievably low price of around US$0.06 a unit (kWh) to the citizens of Kuwait. This may have been an affordable gesture as little as ten years ago when oil was around US$10 dollars a barrel; but in 2008 with oil at US$147 a barrel it was beginning to look seriously untenable. In 1995 the population of Kuwait was 1.8 million; in 2005 had it reached 2.4 million; and it is predicted by the Kuwaiti government to rise to 4.2 million by 2025 and to 6.4 million by 2050.

The Kuwaiti nationals, encouraged by cheap energy, typically live in large air-conditioned houses. If they paid the UK going rate for energy, it would now cost them approximately UK£15,000 to run a medium-sized house a year just to pay the electricity bills at 2005 prices. The average income for a teacher there is around UK£40,000 to £50,000 a year, and house costs are high. One consequence of subsidies is the lack of investment in generation capacity. Today, the largest per capita power users are increasingly found in the Middle East where there are subsidies. Per capita power use in Kuwait now surpasses the US, while in Dubai, one of the region's key economic engines, the level is now nearly twice what it is in the US. Even in countries which still lag behind the US, demand is fast catching up. Saudi power consumption, for example, has grown at an average 7 per cent annual rate during

the last half decade, four times as fast as in the US, and its huge expansion plans for water desalination plants are about to raise power consumption and costs (Reddy and Ghaffour, 2007). The energy needed to desalinate 1000 cubic metres of sea water varies with the system: for the multi-stage flash systems it is 3MWh to 6MWh; by vapour compression, around 8MWh to 12MWh; and by reverse osmosis, 5MWh to 10MWh.

The Kuwaitis who look so secure in their oil wealth are perhaps some of the most vulnerable people in the world to the impact of the peak oil problem and soaring energy prices; but the possibility of removing the subsidies for electricity is not discussed because of fears that it may lead to a revolution. In the summer, every year now blackouts are experienced in cities along the Gulf because electricity generation capacity is exceeded by demand as summer temperatures rise to over 54°C. Yet, despite this, they are building more glass towers, announcing in April 2008 that in Subiya, in Madinat al-Hareer in Kuwait, they are planning to erect the world's tallest tower, stealing the crown from Dubai, in addition to planning on creating a hugely ambitious rail network that would link the Middle East with China.

But there is a considerable reality gap in the Gulf, where power consumption is expected to rise 50 per cent over the next five years in the region, while power generation will only increase by 30 per cent over the same period. Already industrial projects are being scrapped, hospital wards are blacking out, and otherwise completed residential units are lying empty without the means to power lifts or even light bulbs.

Pollution

Against this backdrop we hear the words of dedicated scientists such as James Hansen of the US National Aeronautics and Space Administration (NASA)/ Goddard Institute of Space Studies in New York who tell us that if humanity wishes to preserve a planet similar to that on which civilization developed and to which life on Earth is adapted, palaeoclimatic evidence and ongoing climate change suggest that CO_2 will need to be reduced from its current 385 parts per million (ppm) to at most 350ppm. The largest uncertainty in the target arises from possible changes of non-CO_2 forcings. An initial 350ppm CO_2 target may be achievable by phasing out coal use except where CO_2 is

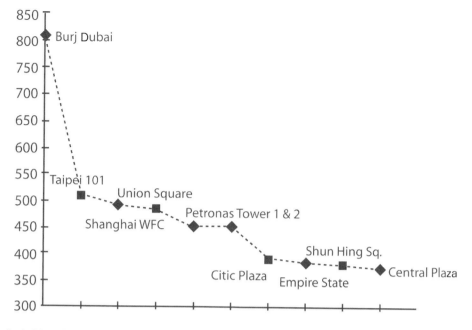

Source: www.tallestbuildingintheworld.com/

Figure 3.1 *Height in metres of the world's tallest buildings*

captured and by adopting agricultural and forestry practices that sequester carbon. If the present overshoot of this target CO_2 is not brief, there is a possibility of seeding irreversible catastrophic effects (Hansen et al, 2007; Hansen et al, 2008). High-density living need not be high-energy living, as the dense cities of the past demonstrate; but in today's machine age they inevitably are. We are currently on track to reach over 700ppm by 2100.

To prevent the planet from passing catastrophic trigger points that will accelerate climate change, and if we are to avoid the untenable increases in global temperatures outlined in the Fourth Report of the Intergovernmental Panel on Climate Change (IPCC, 2007), then we are going to have to reduce our carbon emissions by over 90 per cent of today's emissions levels. Climate change will exacerbate many of the factors outlined above (Oil Depletion Analysis and the Post Carbon Institute, 2008), and the severity of their impacts will become insurmountable for many, not least those in dense and (particularly) high-rise cities, as we can no longer buy our way out of problems with cheap oil (IPCC, 2007).

Conclusions: Avoid the Ozymandias syndrome

With global populations exponentially increasing and urbanizing, we can see that traditional vernacular solutions for building and city form are not capable of achieving the required densification of dwellings, services and infrastructure needed to support workable and rapidly growing cities.

Quite simply put, if we are to survive with a decent standard of living, we will all have to get an effective plan for the density at which we build our emerging cities. The question is not 'are high-density settlements sustainable'; rather, for any place and people on this Earth, 'what is the optimal density for this city'. The answer depends upon the capacity of, and the constraints in, the supporting social, economic and ecosystems of that city. Welcome to the new age of the capacity calculators.

For each city we need careful calculations of the population level that it is capable of supporting in relation to available water, energy and food; sewage and waste disposal systems; transport and social infrastructure; and work opportunities for current and future conditions.

Underlying every calculation must be an assumption of what constitutes either a minimum for, or adequate supply of, a necessary resource or service. This assumption will vary for each location and culture; in addition, the rate of change for rapidly changing global drivers, such as politics and the need to produce shareholder profit, climate change and fossil-fuel depletion, must also be taken into account. The prime imperative of the 21st century is the need to reduce energy use for reasons of its associated costs and emissions impacts.

This imperative favours both walkable cities and walkable buildings. It favours energy efficiency and renewable energy. It makes energy profligate buildings into 'time bomb' investments, waiting to go off. Cities and regions with effective public transport and service infrastructures and amenities will find it easier to maintain secure, healthy and civilized operational conditions within their boundaries. The quality of the environment we can provide today will be reflected in its social, economic and environmental durability in the future.

The most important questions of all are: can you build a sustainable society here? And how do you make that society happen? Perhaps in the quest for a sustainable city we should put social equality at the top of our design brief. The sustainable city is the equitable city and the quality city, not a city full of vainglorious kings such as Shelley's Ozymandias. Invest in the future and in the quality of life of the people on the street. The optimal densities will follow.

Note

1   For the 30 tall buildings projects cancelled since 2005 in Las Vegas, see www.vegastodayandtomorrow.com/dreams3.htm; see also Never Built Visionary Projects, http://forum.skyscraperpage.com/forumdisplay.php?f=342, accessed July 2008.

References

Barnett, T. P. and Pierce, D. W. (2008) 'When will Lake Mead run dry?', *Journal of Water Resources Research*, vol 44, American Geophysical Union, Washington DC

Cheung, K. P. (1992) *Fire Safety in Tall Buildings*, Council on Tall Buildings, McGraw Hill, New York

Clark, T. W. and McGrath, S. (2007) 'Spatial temporal dimensions of violent crime in São Paulo, Brazil, Paper presented at the annual meeting of the American Society of Criminology, Atlanta Marriott Marquis, Atlanta, Georgia, www.allacademic.com/meta/p196287_index.html, accessed August 2008

Cooper, S. and Buettner, M. (2004) *The Truth about Mold*, Dearborn Real Estate Education, published by EPA, Washington State Department of Health, Washington DC

DJ (2008) 'Another battle in the NV–UT water war', blog posted August 2008, http://asymptoticlife.com/2008/08/08/another-battle-in-the-nvut-water-war.aspx, accessed September 2008

European Commission (2008) *EPBD Buildings Platform: Your Information Resource on the Energy Performance of Buildings Directive*, www.buildingsplatform.org/ cms/, accessed August 2008

Gensler (2006) Faulty towers: Is the British office Sustainable?, Gensler, London, www.gensler.com/uploads/documents/FaultyTowers_07_17_2008.pdf

Gideon, S. (1976) *Space, Time and Architecture*, 5th edition (1st edition published in 1941), Harvard University Press, Cambridge, US

Hansen, J., Sato, M. Ruedy, R., Kharecha, P., Lacis, A., Miller, R. L., Nazarenko, L., Lo, K., Schmidt, G. A., Russell, G., Aleinov, I., Bauer, S., Baum, E., Cairns, B., Canuto, V., Chandler, M., Cheng, Y., Cohen, A., Del Genio, A., Faluvegi, G., Fleming, E., Friend, A., Hall, T., Jackman, C., Jonas, J., Kelley, M., Kiang, N. Y., Koch, D., Labow, G., Lerner, J., Menon, S., Novakov, T., Oinas, V., Perlwitz, Ja., Perlwitz, Ju., Rind, D., Romanou, A., Schmunk, R., Shindell, D., Stone, P., Sun, S., Streets, D., Tausnev, N., Thresher, D., Unger, N., Yao, M., and Zhang, S. (2007) 'Dangerous human-made interference with climate: A GISS model E study', *Atmospheric Chemistry and Physics*, vol 7, pp2287–2312

Hansen, J., Sato, M., Kharecha, P., Beerling, D., Berner, R., Masson-Delmotte, V., Pagani, M., Raymo, M., Royer, D. L., and Zachos, J. C. (2008) 'Target atmospheric CO_2: Where should humanity aim?', *Science*, vol 310, pp1029–1031

IPCC (Intergovernmental Panel on Climate Change) (2007) *Fourth Report on Climate Change*, www.ipcc.ch/ipccreports/ar4-syr.htm, accessed September 2008

Johnson, C. et al (2006) 'Faulty towers: Is the British office sustainable?', Gensler, London, www.gensler.com/uploads/documents/FaultyTowers_07_17_2008.pdf

Kovats, S. (2008) *The Health Effects of Climate Change 2008*, UK Department of Health Protection Agency, UK

Krieger, S. (2006) 'Water shortage looms for Vegas', www.allbusiness.com/transportation-communications-electric-gas/4239405-1.html, assessed May 2006

Kwok, H. and Tse, C.-Y. (2006) *Estimating Liquidity Effects in the Housing Market*, University of Hong Kong, www.econ.hku.hk/~tsechung/Estimating%20Liquidity%20Premium%20in%20the%20Housing%20Market.pdf

Li, Y., Leung, G., Tang, J., Yang, X., Chao, C., Lin, J., Lu, J., Nielsen, P., Niu, J., Qian, H., Sleigh, A., Su, H-J., Sundell, J., Wong, T., and Yuen, P. (2007) 'Role of ventilation in airborne transmission of infectious agents in the built environment – a multidisciplinary systematic review', *Indoor Air*, vol 2007, no 17, pp2–18

Meir, S. and Roaf, S. (2005) 'The future of the vernacular: Towards new methodologies for the understanding and optimisation of the performance of vernacular buildings', in L. Asquith and M. Vellinga (eds) *Vernacular Architecture in the Twenty-First Century: Theory, Education and Practice*, Spon, London

Milham, C. (2006) 'Las Vegas Tower – 1888' tall', blog posted December 2006, http://forum.skyscraperpage.com/archive/index.php/t-121563.html, accessed September 2008

Nipkow, J. and Schalcher, M. (2006) *Energy Consumption and Efficiency Potentials of Lifts*, Report to the Swiss Agency for Efficient Energy Use (SAFE), http://mail.mtprog.com/CD_Layout/Poster_Session/ID131_Nipkow_Lifts_final.pdf , accessed September 2008

NIST (National Institute of Standard and Technology and the International) (2007) *High-Rise Safety, International Codes and all Buildings: Rising to Meet the Challenge*, www.buildings.com/articles/detail.aspx?contentID= 4931, accessed July 2007

Oil Depletion Analysis and the Post Carbon Institute (2008) *Preparing for Peak Oil: Local Authorities and the Energy Crisis*, www.odac-info.org/sites/odac.postcarbon.org/files/Preparing_for_Peak_Oil.pdf, accessed September 2008

Reddy, K. and Ghaffour, N. (2007) Overview of the Cost of Desalinated Water and Costing Methodologies, *Desalination*, vol 205, pp340–353

Roaf, S., Baker, K. and Peacock, A. (2008) *Experience of Refurbishment of Hard to Treat Housing in Scotland*, Report to the Scottish Government, July, Scotland

Roaf, S., Crichton, D. and Nicol, F. (2009) *Adapting Buildings and Cities for Climate Change*, 2nd edition, Architectural Press, Oxford

Scott, B. (2003) '$32 million award in toxic mold suit slashed', www.mold-help.org/content/view/294/, accessed September 2008

Scott, M. (2008) 'Rising cost of steel stresses building projects', www.mlive.com/businessreview/tricities/index.ssf/2008/08/rising_cost_of_steel_stresses.html, accessed in August 2008

Shelley, P. B. (1818) 'Ozymandias', sonnet, widely reprinted and anthologized, e.g. http://en.wikipedia.org/wiki/Ozymandias

Staff and Agencies (2001) 'Anthrax found in Pentagon Complex', *The Guardian*, 5 November, www.guardian.co.uk/world/ 2001/nov/05/anthrax.uk, accessed September 2008

Titmuss, R. M. (1976) *Essays on the Welfare State*, George Allen & Unwin Ltd, Museum Street, London, Chapter 4

Treloar, G. J., Fay, R., Ilozor, B. and Love, P. E. D. (2001) 'An analysis of the embodied energy of office buildings by height', *Facilities*, vol 19, nos 5–6, pp204–214

Twickline (2008) 'Keeping Burj Dubai cool', http://dubai-tower.blogspot.com/2008/04/keeping-burj-dubai-cool.html, accessed September 2008

UNDESA (United Nations Department of Economic and Social Affairs) (2004) *World Urbanization Prospects: 2003 Revision*, www.un.org/esa/population/publications/wup2003/2003wup.htm/, accessed September 2008

Wharton, W. C. (2002) The Future of Manhattan: Signals from the marketplace, Conference on the Future of Lower Manhattan, Institute for Urban Design, New York City, 10 January 2002; data and analysis are courtesy of Torto-Wheaton Research, http://web.mit.edu/cre/news-archive/ncnyc.html, accessed 2002

Wilkinson, R. (2005) *The Impact of Inequality: How to Make Sick Societies Healthier*, Routledge, London

Yu, S.-M., Han, S.-S. and Chai, C.-H. (2007) 'Modeling the value of view in high-rise apartments: A 3D GIS approach', *Environment and Planning B: Planning and Design*, vol 34, pp139–153

4

Density and Urban Sustainability: An Exploration of Critical Issues

Chye Kiang Heng and Lai Choo Malone-Lee

Sustainability and planning

The issue of sustainability has made a profound impact upon every aspect of life in society. The notion, first popularized in the *World Conservation Strategy* (IUCN, 1980), embodies the idea that conserving the Earth's resources is integral to future human well-being. Its subsequent form in the Brundtland Commission, expressed as the pursuit of 'development which meets the needs of the present without compromising the ability of future generations to meet their own needs' (WCED, 1987, p43), has become widely accepted as an overarching principle that will guide the actions of governments, corporations and individuals in all aspects of social, economic and political life. The urban environment, in particular, has become the focus of discussion and exploration, and planners have long begun to apply varying notions of 'sustainability' to the contemporary debate on how cities and regions should be revitalized, redeveloped and reformed. From the 1980s, few planning and urban policy documents would omit reference to this concept (Briassoulis, 1999), and 'sustainability' was variously upheld as either the proper means to, or the proper end of, urban development (Basiago, 1999).

However, 'sustainable development' remains a concept that is intuitively understood by all, but still very difficult to express in concrete and operational terms (Briassoulis, 1999). The general consensus is that it is all encompassing and has to include the three aspects of economic, social and environmental sustainability. In more specific expositions from both the academic and practical perspectives, economic sustainability has referred to the potential of a city 'to reach qualitatively a new level of socio-economic, demographic and technological output which in the long run reinforces the foundations of the urban system'; social sustainability was generally acknowledged to embody the principles of futurity, equity, participation empowerment, accessibility, cultural identity and institutional stability; while environmental sustainability embraces the notion of the sensitive pursuit of urban development that synthesizes land and resources use with nature conservation (Basiago, 1999).

Fundamentally, planning and sustainability are complementary, given that they share two quintessential perspectives of cities and societies: the temporal and the spatial (Owens, 1994). In the context of this relationship, sustainability can hardly be divorced from mainstream planning programmes and activities (see Healey and Shaw, 1994), although it is still acknowledged that the tasks required to fulfil the high aspirations embodied in this supra-concept would be enormous. From a pragmatic viewpoint, planners have generally sought to transcend the esoteric arguments in favour of more practical means to 'cross the sustainability transition' (Selman, 2000), rather than be mired in the unending debates on achieving the lofty ideals that are inherent in the concept.

At the level of cities, the area of debate has often distilled down to the relationship between urban density, form and sustainability, and how their multifarious interlinkages can be explored to achieve better utilization of the Earth's resources and quality of human life. In particular, urban density, which denotes the level of concentration of population and activity in an urban area as measured by floor area ratio, population density or residential density, is a subject that has been widely deliberated in research and practice. This chapter is a further attempt to elucidate the relevance of density to the sustainability discourse and to explore the qualitative aspects of higher-density development that may not have been adequately addressed in current urban research and planning practice.

Historical review

The history of 20th-century planning 'represents a reaction to the evils of the 19th-century city' (Hall, 1988, p7). Many pioneering modernist urban proposals were positive and earnest responses to the overcrowded and uninhabitable urban environments of the early industrial cities. The utopian concept of the garden city, for example, was a classic response in the form of a highly organized construct of a human settlement, a highly determined form and expression that embraces the ideals of harmonious man–environment relationship while upholding the notions of self-governance and personal fulfilment. It is an un-sung hero of the earliest and perhaps most thoughtful attempt to plan and build 'sustainable' communities.

However, such zealous attempts to create 'more liveable' environments, particularly in 'new towns' away from the city, have tended to overemphasize the evils of the city, and in rejecting the degradation of inner city live–work environments, planners run the risk of 'throwing the baby out with the bathwater'. In the name of urban renewal and introducing healthier urban living environments, planners have inadvertently neglected and even destroyed the social elements of the vibrant urban life of the traditional city. In parallel, post-war urban sprawl and the resultant monotonous environment of dispersion as epitomized by the homogeneous low-density residential suburbs in many developed countries have now raised further concern of their negative impacts upon the urban environment and its social life.

The problems of urban sprawl are well documented. The more insidious and persistent ones relating to urban sustainability are high car dependency, expensive infrastructure costs and inefficient city structures. Even in less developed countries, planners have become enamoured by the more visual and functional attractiveness of 'new towns', and have tended to continue building them on greenfield sites, leading to loss of good agriculture land and incurring higher transport costs for residents.

Critiques of modernist planning have also focused on land-use zoning, which divides the city arbitrarily into separate functional districts, causing waste of land resources, inefficient material and energy use, and excessive travel time. Many now see the pre-industrial traditional cities as offering viable models of urban development, whose size was decided by comfortable walking distance, urban forms organized in fine grain networks composed of narrower streets and public spaces, and urban life richly intertwined in an organic way across a relatively dense and compact urban fabric.

This compelling image has led to a retrospection and introspection on high-density living as more people begin to regain an appreciation of the liveliness of cities with compact and dense urban form. Close observation of cities such as Paris reveals that it is the densest parts of the city that have the greatest vitality.

Following the United Nation's Agenda 21, the 1990 Green Paper on Urban Environment adopted by the European Commission in Brussels advocated a 'return' to the compact city. The debate was in favour of a development model with relatively high densities around public transportation nodes, and clearly delineated to establish a defined urban boundary to contain sprawl and car use. Urban planners and designers are actively exploring how spatial strategies should be reconstructed to achieve more dense urban environments and how design can be better programmed to cope with the ever-increasing complexity of the activities in such cities (see Frey, 1999). The dominant thinking as embodied in the compact city model is to promote urban regeneration, revitalization of town centres, restraint on development in rural areas, higher densities, mixed-use development, public transport, and the concentration of urban development at public transport nodes (Breheny, 1997; McLaren, 2000; Newman, 2000). Even in already dense environments, arguments have been advanced in favour of the concept by way of dispersal strategies involving networks of dense compact settlements away from core areas, linked by public transport systems (see Frey, 1999).

Density and sustainability

Opinions regarding the definition of an ideal level of density and the detailed strategies to achieve such density vary and there are still concerns about the negative aspects of high-density living, such as congestion, noise, localized pollution, negative human perception caused by urban cramming, and social withdrawal for privacy. However, there seems to be a general consensus regarding the benefits associated with higher density and its potential contribution to urban sustainability. Basiago (1999), for example, analysed three of the most densely populated urban centres in developing countries – namely, Curitiba in Brazil, Kerala in India, and Nayarit in Mexico – and used a range of qualitative sustainability assessments, highlighting their outstanding performance in achieving various aspects of economic, social and environmental sustainability.

In developed countries, evidence from the UK has suggested that higher densities seem to be strongly associated with lower levels of total travel and with increased use of transport modes other than the motor car (see Table 4.1).

Other benefits achievable from promoting a higher density of buildings and public spaces in urban design have been well documented. They include cost savings in land, infrastructure and energy; reduced economic costs of travel time; concentration of knowledge and innovative activity in the core of the city; lower crime and greater safety; the preservation of green spaces in conjunction with certain kinds of urban development; reduced runoff from vehicles to water courses, and emissions to the air and atmosphere; greater physical activity, with consequent health benefits; and social connectedness and vitality (Ministry for the Environment of New Zealand, 2005).

However, it is also obvious that density as a sole criterion for urban quality has its limitations. As illustrated by Figure 4.1, the same density can be obtained via a variety of urban forms whose social implications and impacts upon the quality of urban life may vary substantially. Density alone cannot deliver environmental benefits unless other important design issues are also addressed – for example, mixed land and building uses. Mixed-use areas are places where different activities take place in the same building, street or neighbourhood. Urban design that supports mixed-use areas is expected to be able to allow parking and transport infrastructure to be used more efficiently; lower household expenditure on transport; increase the viability of local shops and facilities; encourage walking and cycling, bringing health benefits; reduce the need to own a car, thus reducing emissions; enhance social equity; increase personal safety; and offer people convenience, choices and opportunity that lead to a sense of personal well-being (Ministry for the Environment of New Zealand, 2005).

The critical questions

We may be able to achieve a higher level of density and mixed use; but have we ignored something that this higher density is expected to bring? Are we running the risk of simplifying a complex and continually unfolding phenomenon in the process of searching for an 'ideal' land-use planning pattern or an optimal density for the city? (Thomas and Cousins, 1996) The nature of contemporary urban life is very different from that of

Table 4.1 *Density and distance travelled per person per week by mode (km): UK 1985/1986*

Density (persons/ha)	All Modes	Car	Local Bus	Rail	Walk	Other
Under 1	206.3	159.3	5.2	8.9	4.0	28.8
1 – 4.99	190.5	146.7	7.7	9.1	4.9	21.9
5 – 14.99	176.2	131.7	8.6	12.3	4.3	18.2
15 – 29.99	152.6	105.4	9.6	10.2	6.6	20.6
30 – 49.99	143.2	100.4	9.9	10.8	6.4	15.5
50 and +	129.2	79.9	11.9	15.2	6.7	15.4
All Areas	159.6	113.8	9.3	11.3	5.9	19.1

Source: ECOTEC (1993, Table 6)

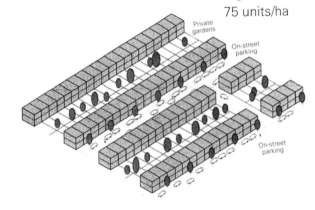

**High rise –
low coverage**
75 units/ha

Surface parking

Landscaped gardens

NOISE

Children's play area

NOISE

**Low rise –
high coverage**
75 units/ha

Private gardens

On-street parking

On-street parking

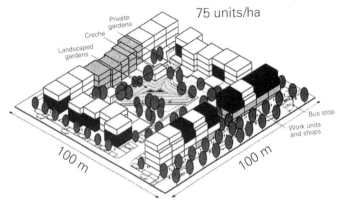

**Medium rise –
medium coverage**
75 units/ha

Private gardens

Creche

Landscaped gardens

Bus stop

Work units and shops

100 m

100 m

Key

*Target a mix of activities
include a variety of house types*

○ Community facilities
◉ Shops and workspaces
● Maisoneties
◐ Houses
○ Apartments

Source: Andrew Wright Associates, cited in Rogers and Urban Task Force (1999, p62)

Figure 4.1 *Same density in different forms*

the traditional city. It is far more complex, heterogeneous, interrelated and dynamic. Therefore, it is necessary to consider whether we have overemphasized the quantitative measures of density, used in an overly simplistic way to dictate design, and overlooked the qualitative aspects of density, which may have equivalent, and maybe even greater, pertinence to the issue of sustainability in the context of urban design.

Diversity and flexibility

Many researchers and practitioners have delved into the issue of density and diversity. In her seminal work *The Death and Life of Great American Cities* (1961), Jane Jacobs identified four conditions that foster a vital city:

1   the need for districts to serve more than one primary function and preferably more than two to encourage different users to use common facilities on different schedules;
2   smaller urban building blocks for ease of access and movement;
3   a mixture of buildings of varying ages and conditions to encourage a variety of enterprises; and
4   a dense concentration of population to support diverse activities.

What Jacobs envisaged is a vibrant urban community as perhaps best represented by the dense mixed-used Greenwich Village in New York City. Sennett (2006) believed that Jacobs's encouragement of quirky jerry-built adaptations or additions to existing building or uses of public spaces that do not fit neatly together represents an appreciation of dissonance or, as Jacobs put it, a sense of unevenness, as opposed to the determinate, predictable and balanced form generally favoured by mass capitalism.

Hall (2004) wrote that 'the short blocks on through-trafficked streets [are] ... the ideal for encouraging the quintessentially urban qualities of sociability and spontaneity'. This design approach as also advocated by Jacobs represents an urban model that is in sharp contradiction to that proposed by Buchanan (Minister of Transport, and Steering Group and Working Group, 1963), in which a highly hierarchical traffic system composed of primary access, district connectors and local roads was superimposed upon an area, dividing it into several environmental zones of approximately similar size (see Figure 4.2). This has been criticized for not taking into account the urban

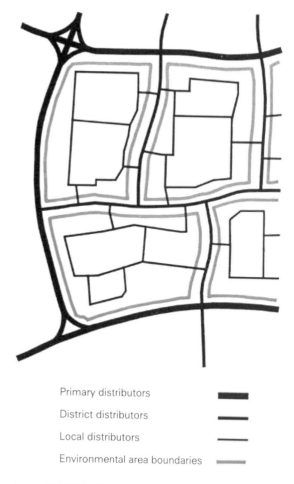

Primary distributors

District distributors

Local distributors

Environmental area boundaries

Source: Hall (2004, p9)

Figure 4.2 *The hierarchy of streets, from the Buchanan Report*

dynamics represented by the continual diffusion of people and employment in cities. Such rigid hierarchical structure, which emphasized functionality based on traffic movement, has resulted in many cities having segregated districts of homogeneous uses within which spontaneous communication and interaction of people and services are difficult to be realized. Such patterns, which are replicated extensively during the suburban explosion in the US, are in sharp contrast to the less hierarchical street structure of many traditional European cities such as Paris and Barcelona, which seem to have coped with the issue of density and diversity in a better way. Their less structured street networks offer equal opportunities of access and communication, in both physical and social terms, to both sides of the road, thus creating a better seedbed for the proliferation of mixed use in a relatively dense urban setting. These examples suggest that higher-density development must imply a certain kind of urban form and transportation relationship of a non-hierarchical nature if it is meant to serve mixed use better and foster diversity.

Complexity and size

The issue of complexity and diversity in urban design was also addressed by other scholars, who observed a disturbing phenomenon in many contemporary urban projects whose increasingly large and monolithic scale is accompanied by a decrease of richness of the mix of activities and uses. Bender (1993) described such projects as 'elephants turned loose in the city'. He argued that an urban strategy analogous to an Inuit dog-sledge is needed to cope with the complexity of dealing with a variety of overlapping and conflicting relationships involving people, institutions and uses in urban development. As he illustrated, the strength of dog-sledge strategy lies in the distributed motive power among the team of dogs that can easily adjust to the uneven surface of the ice flow, the ease of self-adjustment of each dog when there is casual collision with others, the minor influence of the absence of an individual dog to the whole journey, the ease of renewing the energy of the team, and the potential of expansion of the dog family through reproduction. In the worst case, an individual dog can even be sacrificed to keep the whole team moving on. On the other hand, a lot of disadvantages will emerge if the sledge is driven by an elephant. The bulky animal will stumble its way across the uneven terrain and run the risk of breaking the ice at any moment. The injury or illness of the elephant will cause a halt and even termination of the whole journey, not to mention the load of food that the sledge has to carry in order to feed the carrier itself. Bender highlighted the problems presented by the large footprint of many current urban mega-projects, which include their inflexibility for change, the huge amount of resources needed to sustain their performance, and the tremendous impacts upon the surrounding micro-climate. The 'dog-sledge' approach could better serve many of our waterfronts and city centres if they can thus be designed as a complex agglomeration of organisms whose many parts interact in rich and complex ways to synergistically meet urban functions.

Built, managed and adapted incrementally, these projects can accommodate a wide range of uses and users, adapt their form to the context, and thus distinguish themselves from the gigantic and clumsy 'elephants' that can only stress the existing urban fabric.

Similar concern about the increasing scale of the urban projects and the accompanying decrease of their social complexity was also expressed by other urban scholars. Sennett (2007) advocated taking the Hippocratic Oath of 'Do no harm' and proposed three ideas to face the challenges to recover the art of urban design. First, citing the impact inflicted by large urban projects in Shanghai, he argued that we should use complexity as a measure of quality and, in particular, we should use street grain as the first point of reference when we build in cities. Second, he criticized the intention to create a perfect fit between form and function in current urban development that produces very rigid, inflexible built objects that are resistant to adaptation and growth. Accordingly, he suggested that we should, instead, 'seek for forms which are ambiguous, whose ambiguities mean that change can occur in the physical fabric'. Third, in addressing social segregation in many cities, he suggested that we may need to shift our focus from the centre of the community to the edges of public space where different identities confront each other. Urban development and resources deployed along the edges can thus help to facilitate recognition and interaction that can be derived from this kind of propinquity. In such a situation, contact perhaps matters more than identity in fostering a more socially cohesive city.

Problems with over-determination

What the above scholars' arguments have in common are their rejection of over-determination, both of the contemporary cities' visual forms and their social functions (Sennett, 2006), and an appreciation of the diversity derived from relatively dense urban development with certain flexibility. Over-determination will result in a 'brittle city', a term used by Sennett (2006) to denote a city that is fragile in face of the dynamism of urban life. On the other hand, places which can allow for a variety of functions and which are often undesigned and unregulated are 'loose-fit' environments (Dovey and Fitzgerald, 2000; Franck, 2000; Rivlin, 2000), as opposed to precisely planned places based on order and control, and these are the places that could be more sustainable physically and socially in the long term. They are spaces of 'becoming' and 'found' spaces, which are not necessarily places with no rules, but places where new rules can be continually invented, places that allow for unexpected uses, and places whose purposes are intentionally left ambiguous. Researchers (e.g. Thompson, 2002) who discussed the value of such indeterminate areas in the context of urban open space have argued that although these informal spaces may seem to be unmanaged and derelict, they can accommodate a variety of adventurous activities that usually are not well served by formal spaces. Their multiple uses enable them to be resilient and enduring spaces that give cities the quality of familiarity in the face of rapid social and technological change. Moreover, pioneering and opportunistic vegetation often found exuberantly in these places may better serve the urban ecology of cities than formal parks and playgrounds, thus rendering to them the distinctive character that can only come from allowing nature to take its course.

Learning from the ordinary

The vibrant urban character that can be derived from a flexible framework of urban development, as advocated by the aforementioned scholars, can be seen in many cities in Asia. Two such examples are presented here from the city of Hanoi. In the first example from the Dinh Cong area, the sharp contrast between two adjacent residential developments is clearly illustrated (see Figure 4.3). In this case, on one side of the road are typical slabs and towers of 'high-density' residential blocks with the same unified façade design and layout plan repeated floor after floor. On the other side of the road are urban blocks of low-rise 'medium-density' residential houses, each taking up a slice of about a 6m wide façade and sharing the side walls with its neighbours. The variety of the styles in the elevations of these four-storey houses, which are designed in either historical or traditional architectural idioms, presents a striking contrast to its monolithic and monotonous neighbours across the street. Over time, some of these houses adapted their ground level to various new functions, such as restaurants and shops, thus opening the access to the street and enriching the street life with a variety of activities. This also presented a sharp contrast to the pedestrian-unfriendly, fortress-like ground-level environment of the adjoining high-rise

Source: Author

Figure 4.3 *Contrast between high-rise residential blocks and low-rise houses in Hanoi's Dinh Cong area*

blocks. What is demonstrated in this case is the different choice of building typology corresponding to similar densities but yielding vastly different streetscape and fabric. It is a value-laden dichotomy – with sterile monotony on the one hand and a rich diversity fostered by a flexible urban housing typology on the other. The latter is a choice that allowed for the coexistence of heterogeneous expressions, ease of adaptation and change of use.

The second example is the Kim Lien area in Hanoi, which was originally composed of a series of parallel north–south-facing low-rise linear blocks arranged in an army-camp fashion with large distances set between them (see Figure 4.4a). Since its completion in 1985, many individual and spontaneous constructions were carried out by local residents, who gradually filled the empty spaces between this orderly array of blocks with small-scale expansions, resulting in a far denser and livelier urban district than it used to be (see Figure 4.4b). Shops and new rooms were added on the ground floor in close proximity to each other along the streets. Front yards with storage room were created by enclosing the ground area in front of each unit. In some cases, even new balconies were attached to the upper floor rooms, and roof areas were reclaimed as covered roof decks, forming new platforms for living above ground (see Figure 4.5). Compared with the clustered low-rise houses in the previous case, which is still developed in a controlled way, development in the Kim Lien area is

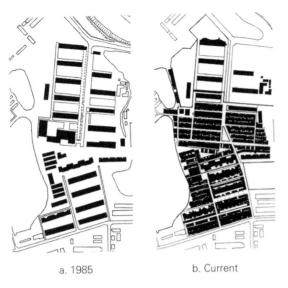

a. 1985   b. Current

Source: François Decoster

Figure 4.4 *Kim Lien Area, Hanoi:*
(a) 1985; (b) present

informal and autonomous. The new expansions offer residents a variety of opportunities of customization and individualization according to their own needs. The shops developed along the streets not only cater to local residents' diverse routine needs in a more convenient way, but also provide various job opportunities for local people. The small-scale additions help to reorganize the public space and

reformat it into a more fine-grained hierarchy suggesting clearer gradation from public, semi-public and semi-private, to private space. In doing so, these additions transform the scale of the dispersed modernist residential blocks to an intimate and pleasant level and reweave them back into an urban fabric of finer texture. Being an incremental process, these spontaneous developments constantly adjust themselves to the situation of the immediate physical and social context, thus making them more adaptable to changes and, therefore, more resilient.

These simple examples illustrate high-density urban districts in which diversity is a salient characteristic. While seemingly disorganized from the outside, they demonstrate the qualities of flexibility and resilience that are essential to sustain a city socially and economically. While planners must be cautious of the biases derived from romanticizing the negative aspects of this phenomenon of autonomous development, they should not ignore the important principles that can be drawn from these everyday living environments, which are beacons of sustainability in their own right.

Inward versus outward densification

The two examples above illustrate a kind of inward densification process, as described by Rodrigo Pérez de Arce (1978) and epitomized as growth by additive transformation as opposed to urban growth by extension in the form of outward expansion. The latter

Source: Author's photographs

Figure 4.5 *Street scenes in Kim Lien*

involves claiming new lands for urban use, and growth by substitution as characterized by replacement of pre-existing urban elements through complete demolition. What is important in understanding the difference in the two approaches is the planner's sensitivity to the scale of substitution. In many instances, especially in rapidly developing cities, the scale of substitution effectively means the eradication or complete demolition of entire stretches of the city. In the name of urban renewal, it is not uncommon to find entire stretches of a city being wiped out to be replaced by denser and, presumably, more economic land uses.

We can draw many lessons from the transformation processes of urban buildings in historic European cities, in which ruins of ancient temples, triumphal arches, amphitheatres, palaces and public spaces were reused in construction or reinhabited by civilian functions. Pérez de Arce (1978) pointed out that this is a common mechanism by which many traditional towns evolved in history and one that is often ignored in contemporary urban development practice. He argued that this kind of transformation process presents many important lessons in our understanding of urban quality: first, incremental incorporation of parts into an existing core extends the likelihood of continued use of pre-existing structure for a prolonged period; second, being based on the retention

of what already exists, additive transformation is a low-cost development option in both social and material terms, and by doing so it maintains the continuity of the normal rhythm of life in the affected area; third, by being a sedimentary process, it ensures a sense of continuity in the construction of the town, thus contributing to the formation of a sense of 'place' in both historical and spatial terms. In this manner of 'inward densification', buildings and places become repositories of successive interventions. In this incremental process, a true complexity and a meaningful variety may arise from the gradual accumulation of elements that confirm and reinforce the space over a period of time. This is the sense of continuity in time and space that is so critical to the paradigm of sustainability, but is an aspect that has all too often eluded the attention of planners and urban designers in their quest for new developments to support contemporary urban life.

Density, form and urban employment

Similar high-density development with great diversity can also be found in other compact Asian cities such as Seoul, where monumental skyscrapers exist amidst a mosaic landscape of low-rise, small-scale buildings (see Figure 4.6). Seen from above, the undulating roofs of

Source: Author's photograph

Figure 4.6 *Seoul, Korea*

Table 4.2 *Ratio of employees and self-employed*

	Employees	Self-Employed	Self-Employed (Wholesale, retail, hotel, restaurant, etc.)
US	93.2	6.8	1.3
Japan	85.4	14.6	2.4
Germany	88.8	11.2	3.2
UK	87.4	12.6	3.8
Italy	75.5	24.5	9.1
Mexico	70.9	29.1	12.6
Korea	66.4	33.6	14.6

Source: OECD (2005), provided by KIM Sung Hong, University of Seoul

these buildings seem to suggest a rather chaotic live–work environment. In effect, they accommodate a diverse variety of businesses and activities in a very dense environment that has its internal order and rhythm. More importantly, the urban form is congruent with the economic structure of the city in which self-employment takes up a relatively large proportion of the total employed compared with other cities (see Table 4.2). The dense and fine-grained urban fabric provides an easily adaptable physical environment for the small- and medium-scale self-employed businesses, which, due to their nature, require a flexible and low-cost platform for their ever-changing activities that cannot be provided by the expensive skyscrapers in the city. Thus, in this case there is a symbiotic relationship that interlocks the adaptability offered by the urban form and the flexibility and cost efficiency required by the local economic activities.

In urban planning, it is often thought that meticulous layout and design is necessary to achieve order, which in turn supports economic functions and efficiency. Underlying this assumption is that economic activities generally follow the Fordist regime of mass production and mechanized output systems that can be accommodated in highly structured built forms. Greater sensitivity to local production processes, trading systems, service functions and employment structures is necessary to create work–live environments that are responsive to local culture and the informal sectors. More importantly, it must be recognized that across cities and within cities, economic transition continues to take place, and urban sustainability in such a context must be interpreted with reference to the evolving economic and social landscape. In the final analysis, densification must be a process that creates opportunities for local employment, harnesses the more sustainable use of local resources and provides the context for social exchange and support.

Conclusions

It is clear that increasing density is not a panacea and urban developments that overemphasize high density in a simple quantitative way could give rise to serious environmental and social ramifications. Density needs to work in conjunction with other conditions and approaches such as mixed use, building form and design, and public space layouts. What is more important in higher-density development is a flexible framework in which self-adjustment, though sensitively regulated, is allowed. The group of distinct but related concepts such as adaptability, robustness, resilience and choice all suggest a kind of quality of being responsive to changes over time, a quality of embracing choices and nurturing opportunities, a quality of being inclusive rather than exclusive, and a quality that helps to avert, avoid or delay the loss of vitality and functionality. It is by acquiring this characteristic of flexibility that higher-density development can be said to have been brought closer towards the objective of sustainability.

The challenge facing planners, designers and decision-makers is the profound mind shift that is necessary to enable them to treat complexity in dense environments as an indicator of quality rather than a negative aspect to be avoided. Too often, planners take the less demanding route to achieve efficiency by simplification, segregation and compartmentalization. The examples point to the need to pay more attention to the informal and the unregulated, and to learn to appreciate the diversity as exhibited in those less orderly environments. The transition to sustainability (Selman, 2000) involves reforming current urban planning processes at the practice, policy and even legislation levels so that the city, while being planned, can also accommodate and facilitate the flexibility needed to achieve a rich and diverse environment. For this, more empirical research needs to be conducted to investigate the mechanisms that underlie and determine the dynamism inherent in existing high-density urban areas. This will enable multi-prong strategies to be drawn up in order to attain not just higher densities, but optimal density ranges for different urban forms and characteristics, and to attain urban sustainability in its most holistic form. Planners have a major role to play to promulgate solutions that are within a community's means and that are relevant to the local context in order to facilitate the transition to sustainability.

Acknowledgement

This article was written with the research assistance of Dr Zhang Ji.

References

Basiago, A. D. (1999) 'Economic, social, and environmental sustainability in development theory and urban planning practice', *The Environmentalist*, vol 19, pp145–161

Bender, R. (1993) 'Where the city meets the shore', in R. Bruttomesso (ed) *Waterfronts: A New Frontier for Cities on Water*, International Centre Cities on Water, Venice, pp32–35

Breheny, M. (1997) 'Urban compaction: Feasible and acceptable?' *Cities*, vol 14, no 4, pp209–217

Briassoulis, H. (1999) 'Who plans whose sustainability? Alternative roles for planners', *Journal of Environmental Planning and Management*, vol 42, no 6, pp889–902

Dovey, K. and Fitzgerald, J. (2000) 'Spaces of "becoming"', in G. Moser, E. Pol, Y. Bernard, M. Bonnes, J. Corraliza and M. V. Giuliani (eds) *IAPS 16 Conference Proceedings: Metropolis 2000 – Which Perspectives? Cities, Social Life and Sustainable Development*, 4–7 July 2000, Paris

ECOTEC (1993) *Reducing Transport Emissions Through Planning*, HMSO, London

Franck, K. A. (2000) 'When are spaces loose?', in G. Moser, E. Pol, Y. Bernard, M. Bonnes, J. Corraliza and M. V. Giuliani (eds) *IAPS 16 Conference Proceedings: Metropolis 2000 – Which Perspectives? Cities, Social Life and Sustainable Development*, 4–7 July, Paris

Frey, H. (1999) *Designing the City: Towards a More Sustainable Urban Form*, Routledge, New York, NY

Hall, P. (1988) *Cities of Tomorrow: An Intellectual History of Urban Planning and Design in the Twentieth Century*, Blackwell, Oxford, UK and New York, NY

Hall, P. (2004) 'The Buchanan Report: 40 years on', *Transport*, vol 157, no 1, pp7–14

Healey, P. and Shaw, T. (1994) 'Changing meanings of "environment" in the British planning system', *Transactions of the Institute of British Geographers*, vol 19, no 4, pp425–438

IUCN (World Conservation Union) (1980) *World Conservation Strategy*, IUCN, Gland, Switzerland

Jacobs, J. (1961) *The Death and Life of Great American Cities*, Random House, New York, NY

McLaren, D. (2000) 'Compact or dispersed? Dilution is no solution', *Built Environment*, vol 18, no 4, pp268–284

Minister of Transport, and Steering Group and Working Group (1963) *Traffic in Towns: A Study of the Long Term Problems of Traffic in Urban Areas*, HMSO, London

Ministry for the Environment of New Zealand (2005) *Summary of the Value of Urban Design: The Economic, Environmental and Social Benefits of Urban Design*, www.mfe.govt.nz/publications/urban/value-urban-design-summary-jun05/value-of-urban-design-summary-jun05.pdf, accessed December 2008

Newman, P. (2000) 'The compact city: An Australian perspective', *Built Environment*, vol 18, no 4, pp285–300

Owens, S. (1994) 'Land limits and sustainability: A conceptual framework and some dilemmas for the planning system', *Transactions of the Institute of British Geographers*, Royal Geographical Society, vol 19, pp439–456

Pérez de Arce, R. (1978) 'Urban transformations and architecture of additions', *AD Profiles 12: Urban Transformations*, vol 49, no 4, pp237–266

Rivlin, L. G. (2000) 'The nature of found spaces', in G. Moser, E. Pol, Y. Bernard, M. Bonnes, J. Corraliza and M. V. Giuliani (eds) *IAPS 16 Conference Proceedings: Metropolis 2000 – Which Perspectives? Cities, Social Life and Sustainable Development*, 4–7 July, Paris

Rogers, R. G. and Urban Task Force (1999) 'Towards an Urban Renaissance' Final report of the Urban Task Force, Department for the Environment, Transport and the Regions, London

Selman, P. (2000) *Environmental Planning*, Sage, London

Sennett, R. (2006) 'The open city', Paper presented at the Urban Age: A Worldwide Series of Conferences Investigating the Future of Cities (Berlin), www.urban-age.net/0_downloads/archive/Berlin_Richard_Sennett_2006-The_Open_City.pdf, accessed December 2008

Sennett, R. (2007) 'Urban inequality', Lecture given at the Urban Age: A Worldwide Series of Conferences Investigating the Future of Cities (Mumbai), www.urbanage.net/10_cities/07_mumbai/_videos/UI/RS_video1.html accessed December 2008

Thomas, L. and Cousins, W. (1996) 'The compact city: A successful, desirable and achievable urban form? ', in M. Jenks, E. Burton and K. Williams (eds) *The Compact City: A Sustainable Urban Form?* E. & F. N. Spon, London, New York, pp53–65

Thompson, C. W. (2002) 'Urban open space in the 21st century', *Landscape and Urban Planning*, vol 60, no 2, pp59–72

WCED (World Commission on Environment and Development) (1987) *Our Common Future*, Oxford University Press, Oxford, New York

Part II

Climate and High-Density Design

5

Climate Changes Brought About by Urban Living

Chiu-Ying Lam

Hong Kong went through a period of major urbanization during the past half century. Much more land than before is now under concrete. Clusters of tall buildings have invaded into previously open country. At the same time, the increase in population as well as per capita energy consumption in this affluent society has meant the burning of much more coal and petrol than before, with the attendant emissions of gases and particulates. The atmosphere overlying Hong Kong cannot escape interacting with these changes. In the process of doing so, the climate in Hong Kong has changed. Leung et al (2004a) have documented the long-term changes in various observed parameters up to 2002. This chapter extends the data series to 2005 and also looks at a couple of aspects not covered before.

Temperature

The aspect of change in Hong Kong which is most obvious to all is the generally warmer climate in urban areas. Figure 5.1 shows the time series of the annual mean temperature recorded at the headquarters of the Hong Kong Observatory between 1947 and 2005. The observatory is situated at the heart of Tsimshatsui and is characteristic of a location where urbanization has been at its most active in Hong Kong over the past half century. Over the entire period, the temperature rose at 0.17°C per decade. However, towards the end of the period, between 1989 and 2005, the rate increased sharply to 0.37°C per decade. In order to contrast with stations in locations less affected by urbanization, the temperature series at Ta Kwu Ling and Lau Fau Shan, which are situated in the north-eastern and north-western New Territories, respectively, are shown in Figure 5.2. The rates of temperature rise at these two stations over the same period of 1989 to 2005 were 0.08°C and 0.25°C per decade, respectively. The fact

that the urban area has been warming up much more rapidly than the 'countryside' is thus evident.

On climate changes brought about by urban living

It is well established that where urbanization bears on the long-term temperature trend, the effect is more on the daily minimum temperature than on the daily maximum temperature (Karl et al, 1993). This is related to the increase in the thermal capacity of the urban area where concrete stores the heat absorbed during the day and releases it during the night, thus holding the temperature at a level higher than it would be in the absence of so much concrete. Figure 5.3 portrays the trends in mean daily maximum and minimum temperature at the headquarters of the Hong Kong Observatory over the period of 1947 to 2005 – that is, the post-war development years. The trend in daily maximum temperature was nearly flat, the

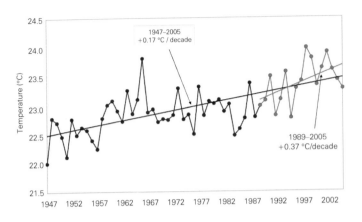

Source: Hong Kong Observatory

Figure 5.1 *Annual mean temperature recorded at the Hong Kong Observatory headquarters (1947–2005)*

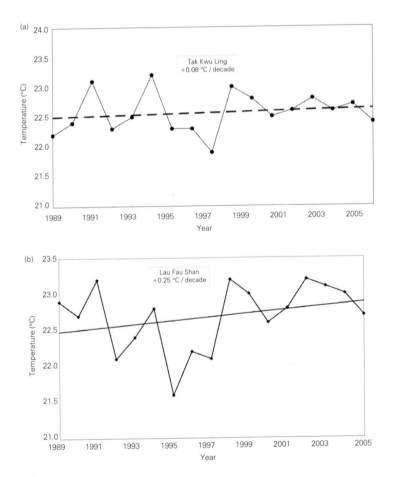

Source: Hong Kong Observatory

Figure 5.2 *Annual mean temperature recorded at (a) Ta Kwu Ling (1989–2005); (b) Lau Fau Shan (1989–2005)*

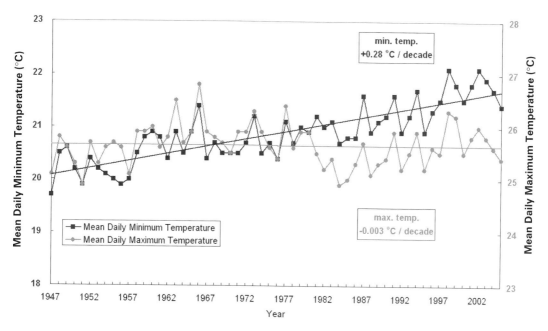

Source: Hong Kong Observatory

Figure 5.3 *Mean daily maximum (black) and mean daily minimum (grey) temperature of Hong Kong Observatory headquarters (1947–2005)*

influence of general global warming having been overshadowed by the increasingly turbid sky (a point which we will return to later). In contrast, the mean daily minimum temperature has been rising steadily throughout the period, at a rate of 0.28°C per decade. The signature of urbanization in the temperature trend is thus abundantly clear.

Wind

Another hallmark of urbanization is the growing number of buildings. It increases the roughness of the surface underlying the atmosphere and exerts a drag on the low-level winds. The tendency, therefore, is to see wind speed near the ground decreasing in the long run. Figure 5.4 shows the time series of wind speed measured at King's Park and Waglan Island in 1968 to 2005. For technical reasons and in order to compare like with like, the data points represent the annual average of 10-minute wind speed readings taken twice daily, at 8.00 am and 8.00 pm. Waglan Island is an offshore location and so the observations there reflect purely the background climate without the impact of

urbanization. There was no significant long-term trend in the wind speed there. However, at King's Park, which is situated on a knoll surrounded by Yaumatei, Mongkok, Homantin and, slightly further afield, Hunghom, there has been a steady decrease in the wind speed. Because the anemometer at King's Park meteorological station was relocated (within the station) in 1996, two segments of the time series are shown in the figure. But the sustained decrease in wind speed remains evident. By contrasting the two time series, it is clear that urbanization in the broad vicinity of King's Park has brought down the wind speed in the boundary layer of the atmosphere around the station. The urban area is therefore generally less well ventilated than before.

State of the sky

One visible aspect of climate change is the turbidity in the sky, which more and more local people are concerned about. It is caused by suspended particulates of one kind or another thrown up by human activities in the city. It may be purely dust and natural

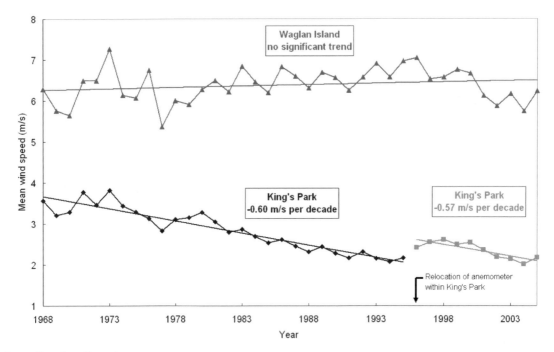

Source: Hong Kong Observatory

Figure 5.4 *Annual average of 12-hourly 10-minute mean wind speed of King's Park and Waglan Island (1968–2005)*

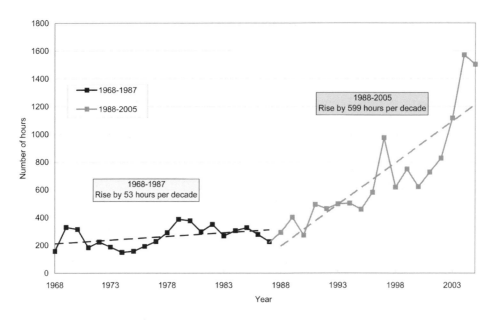

Source: Hong Kong Observatory

Figure 5.5 *Annual total number of hours with visibility at the Hong Kong Observatory headquarters below 8km from 1968 to 2005 (not counting rain, mist or fog)*

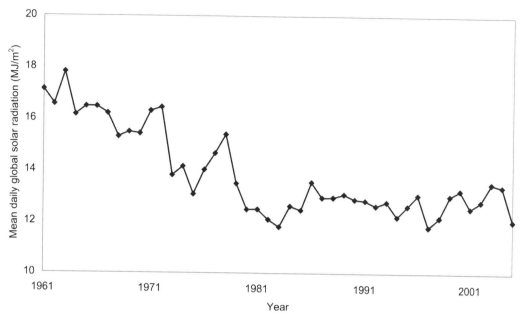

Source: Hong Kong Observatory

Figure 5.6 *Long-term trend in annual mean of the daily global solar radiation, 1961–2005*

(e.g. loess from northern China). It could also be particulates formed from combustion products (e.g. vehicle exhaust, kitchens and power generation) through photochemical processes. Figure 5.5 shows the time series of the annual total number of hours with visibility at the Hong Kong Observatory headquarters below 8km from 1968 to 2005. Cases of reduced visibility due to rain or mist or associated with high relative humidity are excluded because those would be more like 'natural' weather. Until the late 1980s, there was no significant trend. But from then onwards, there has been a dramatic rise in the frequency of reduced visibility. By 2005, the frequency was five times that in the 1970s and 1980s. It could be argued that some of this increased turbidity of the atmosphere is transported to Hong Kong from outside. But considering the large consumption of energy within Hong Kong itself, which invariably involves combustion of one form or another with its attendant emissions, there is no question that some of this turbidity is locally generated by the urban form of living practised here. Leung et al (2004a) also reported that the annual mean cloud amount observed at the Hong Kong Observatory headquarters has been increasing at a rate

of 1.8 per cent per decade during the period 1961 to 2002. One potential cause could be the increase in the concentration of condensation nuclei in the air (a factor favourable to the formation of cloud), which is known to be associated with urbanization. Increased turbidity and increased cloud amount reduce the amount of solar radiation reaching the ground. Figure 5.6 shows the time series of the annual mean of the daily amount of solar radiation measured at King's Park between 1961 and 2005. There has been a clear, broad falling trend. With the lesser amount of solar energy reaching the ground, the urban heat island effect during the day has therefore been suppressed. This provides the context for us to view the nearly flat trend in the daily maximum temperature in Figure 5.3. It also prompts us to think what the consequences might be in terms of reduced illumination in buildings and reduced ability to kill germs potentially harmful to human beings.

Evaporation

One aspect of climate change in cities less noticed by people is the decreasing trend in evaporation. Meteorologists measure evaporation by placing a pan of

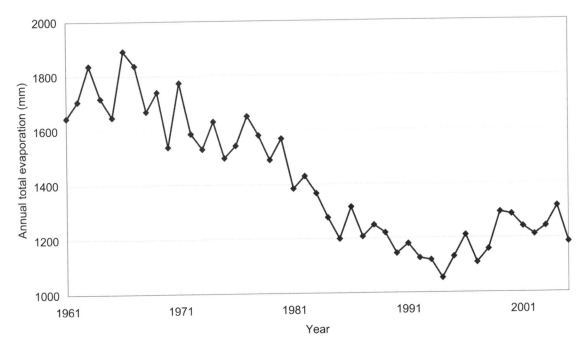

Source: Hong Kong Observatory

Figure 5.7 *Long-term trend in annual total evaporation, 1961–2005*

water lying low on the ground and exposing it to the winds and to the sunshine. The time series of annual total evaporation measured at King's Park between 1961 and 2005 is shown in Figure 5.7. The broad decreasing trend is evident. It could be attributed to the greatly decreased prevailing wind speed and the reduced amount of solar radiation reaching the ground during the day. Thus, it is another signature of urbanization. Again, one wonders whether it could mean damp corners remaining damp more than before, providing a favourable environment for germs.

Thinking about people

In tandem with urbanization in Hong Kong, urban temperature has risen faster than in the countryside, winds have slowed, visibility has deteriorated, less solar radiation is reaching the ground, evaporation rates have gone down, and so on. But does it matter? For the rich and the elite, it probably does not. They could switch on air conditioning throughout the year, watch high-definition TV instead of looking at the sky, employ artificial sunlight to get a tan, dry their clothes with electrical devices, etc. Unfortunately, this would raise urban living to an even higher level in terms of high energy consumption, which would, in turn, cause even greater climate change. For people with lesser means, especially the old and the weak, it could, however, become a life-threatening issue. One aspect of climate change that could 'kill' people with chronic diseases and old people living alone is the increasing number of hot nights. Figure 5.8 shows the rise in the number of hot nights – that is, nights with a minimum temperature above 28°C, based on Hong Kong Observatory headquarters data from 1961 to 2005. During the 1960s, it was just a few days a year. Now it is roughly 20 days a year.

According to the projection of Leung et al (2004b), the figure would rise to 30 by the end of the century. This city is heading towards a hot, stuffy state of atmosphere. In future summers, the old and the weak living in their tiny rooms in urban areas will have to face an increasing number of hot nights with no air conditioning, little wind and the dampness arising

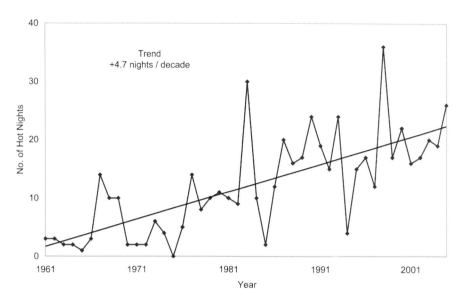

Source: Hong Kong Observatory

Figure 5.8 *Annual number of hot nights, 1961–2005*

from little sun and little evaporation. They also have to fear the attack of more germs than there used to be since their natural enemies – namely, fresh air and sunshine – have been reduced in strength. Unfortunately, the underprivileged have to look forward to even more tall buildings along the shore or even right at the heart of the urban areas to block the little wind and sunshine left. Buildings are meant to benefit people. But we have seen in the meteorological records presented above that buildings have collectively modified the urban climate in a way unfavourable to healthy living. It is high time for us to rethink the fundamentals of what urban living should look like. Much is in the hands of architects and engineers.

References

Karl, T. R., Jones, P. D., Knight, R. W., Kukla, G., Plummer, N., Razuvayev, V., Gallo, K. P., Lindseay, J., Charlson, R. J., and Peterson, T. C. (1993) 'A new perspective on recent global warming: Asymmetric trends of daily maximum and minimum temperature', *Bulletin of the American Meteorological Society*, vol 74, pp1007–1023

Leung, Y. K., Yeung, K. H., Ginn, E. W. L. and Leung, W. M. (2004) *Climate Change in Hong Kong, Technical Note,* no 107, Hong Kong Observatory, Hong Kong, p41

PGBC (2006) *PGBC Symposium 2006 on Urban Climate and Urban Greenery*, 2 December 2006

6

Urbanization and City Climate: A Diurnal and Seasonal Perspective

Wing-Mo Leung and Tsz-Cheung Lee

Over the years, a number of researchers have reported that urban development, as the major land-use change in human history, has a great impact upon the local climate of a city (Landsberg, 1981; Arnfield, 2003). One of the best-known effects of urbanization is the urban heat island (UHI) effect, which develops when rural cooling rates are greater than urban ones (Oke and Maxwell, 1975). Factors that may bring about the difference in temperatures between urban and rural areas include (Kalande and Oke, 1980; Oke, 1982; Grimmond, 2007):

- *the different thermal (heat capacity and thermal conductivity) and radiative (reflectivity and emissivity) properties of construction materials used in urban development compared to surrounding rural areas, resulting in more of the sun's energy being absorbed and stored in urban compared to rural surfaces;*
- *in urban areas, anthropogenic heat emissions by buildings, air conditioning, transportation and industries, contributing to the development of UHI;*
- *the increase of impermeable surfaces in urban areas, which results in a decrease in evapotranspiration and loss of latent heat from the ground, causing warming there;*
- *the tendency of high-density buildings in urban areas to block the view of the sky and to affect the release of heat as long-wave radiation at night; and*
- *dense development in urban areas, which reduces wind speeds and inhibits cooling by convection.*

Urban heat island (UHI) intensity

The strength of the UHI effect is commonly measured by the 'urban heat island intensity', which describes the urban-to-rural temperature difference at a given time period (Karl et al, 1988; Arnfield, 2003). Here, the urban-to-rural temperature difference (T_{u-r}) is defined as:

$$T_{u-r} = T_u - T_r \qquad [6.1]$$

where T_u and T_r are, respectively, the air temperature of the urban and rural sites. As such, a positive (negative) T_{u-r} represents a higher (lower) temperature at the urban station than that of the rural station.

Studies have also suggested that the UHI intensity of a city could exhibit seasonal and diurnal variations (Haeger-Eugensson and Holmer, 1999; Wilby 2003; Weng and Yang, 2004; Sakakibara and Owa, 2005; Chow and Roth, 2006). In general, the urban-to-rural temperature difference is larger at night than during the day, larger in winter than in summer, and is most apparent when winds are weak and under a clear sky. However, each city has its own unique UHI characteristics, depending upon its land use, building density, population size, landscape, ambient climate, etc.

Like many other metropolises, Hong Kong is densely developed with many skyscrapers in the urban area. Hong Kong also has a large population, with an average density of some 6000 people per square kilometre (HKSARG, 2007), and the corresponding figure in the centre of the urban area is significantly higher. Urban climate studies in Hong Kong have shown that the rapid urban development in the last few decades has had significant effects on the temperature and other meteorological elements in Hong Kong (Leung et al, 2004; Lam, 2006).

In Hong Kong, the Hong Kong Observatory headquarters (HKO) in the centre of the urban area of the Kowloon Peninsula is a representative urban station. For the rural station, the meteorological station in Ta Kwu Ling (TKL) in the northern New Territories could be taken as a typical rural station (Leung et al, 2007). This is because there has been no significant change in the immediate environment for TKL since observations commenced in 1989. As HKO is only 17m higher than TKL, no temperature adjustment is required for this difference in elevation. The relative locations of HKO and TKL in Hong Kong are shown in Figure 6.1. For

Hong Kong, the UHI intensity can thus be estimated by $T_{u\text{-}r} = T_{HKO} - T_{TKL}$, where T_{HKO} and T_{TKL} are the temperature of HKO and TKL, respectively.

The data used to study the UHI intensity are the hourly temperatures recorded at HKO and TKL from 1989 to 2007. The time coordinate used in the following discussion refers to Hong Kong local time (h).

Diurnal variation of UHI intensity

Figure 6.2a shows the diurnal variations of the average T_{HKO} and T_{TKL} from 1989 to 2007. The corresponding diurnal variation of the average UHI intensity (i.e. $T_{u\text{-}r}$) is shown in Figure 6.2b. The UHI intensity has a large diurnal variation with positive values during night-time and negative values during the day. The positive values of $T_{u\text{-}r}$ represent a higher temperature in the urban area than that of the rural area at night, and vice versa for the negative values observed during the day. As there are over 16 hours in a day with $T_{u\text{-}r} > 0$, the daily average $T_{u\text{-}r}$ is positive (i.e. the urban area is warmer than the rural on average).

The average UHI reaches a maximum at around 6.00 am (around dawn) with $T_{u\text{-}r}$ of about 2°C. In Hong Kong, this nocturnal UHI effect is mainly due to the high heat capacity of the buildings, the anthropogenic heat emission in the urban area and the small sky view factor resulting from the dense and tall urban development. However, after 7.00 am, the positive UHI dissipates gradually and becomes a negative value in the afternoon, resulting in a 'cool island effect' (UCI), which peaks at around 2.00 pm (or 1400 h). This daytime 'negative UHI' or UCI effect was also observed in UHI studies of other cities, such as Salamanca in Spain, London, Singapore, etc. (Alonso et al, 2003; Mayor of London, 2006; Chow and Roth, 2006). It is probably caused by the daytime shading effects that block part of the sunshine from reaching the ground in the urban area. The higher heat capacity and conductivity in the urban area may also be another cause of the UCI effect (Bornstein, 1968; Oke, 1982).

The rates of change of T_{HKO} and T_{TKL} were also calculated to analyse the temporal development of the UHI. As shown in Figure 6.2c, cooling of both the urban and rural areas starts at around 3.00 pm (or 1500 h). The cooling rate of the rural area (line with triangular points) is significantly faster than that of the urban area

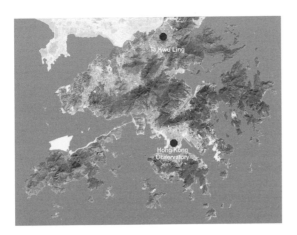

Source: Hong Kong Observatory

Figure 6.1 *Map showing the locations of the Hong Kong Observatory headquarters and Ta Kwu Ling*

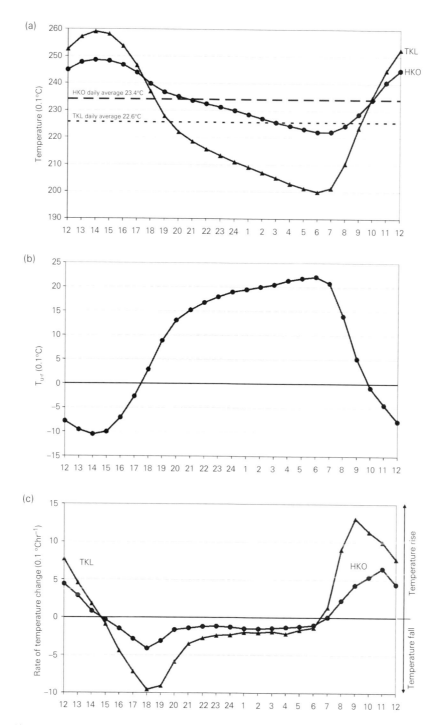

Source: Hong Kong Observatory

Figure 6.2 *Diurnal variations of the average (a) T_{HKO} and T_{TKL}; (b) T_{u-r}; and (c) rate of change of T_{HKO} and T_{TKL} (i.e. $\dfrac{\partial}{\partial t}T_{HKO}$ and $\dfrac{\partial}{\partial t}T_{TKL}$), 1989–2007* (line with circular points) between 4.00 pm (1600 h) and 12.00 am (2400 h), with the largest difference occurring at around 6.00 pm (1800 h) (around sunset) at over 0.5°C per hour. Moreover, it can be seen in Figure 6.2b and Figure 6.2c that the maximum T_{u-r} occurs when the rates of cooling at the urban area and rural area are equal. This is explained mathematically as follows. Since $T_{u-r} = T_{HKO} - T_{TKL}$, the rate of change of T_{u-r} equals:

$$\frac{\partial}{\partial t}T_{u-r} \equiv \frac{\partial}{\partial t}T_{HKO} - \frac{\partial}{\partial t}T_{TKL} \qquad [6.2]$$

and T_{u-r} reaches a maximum when:

$$\frac{\partial}{\partial t}T_{u-r} = 0 \text{, or when } \frac{\partial}{\partial t}T_{HKO} = \frac{\partial}{\partial t}T_{TKL} . \qquad [6.3]$$

Overall, in Hong Kong, the urban area is warmer than the rural area during night-time, but the situation reverses during daytime. The UHI intensity is highest around dawn due to the large difference in the cooling rate between the urban and rural area after sunset.

Seasonal variation of UHI intensity

The diurnal variations of the average T_{u-r} of Hong Kong in different months are shown in Figure 6.3. Statistics of the seasonal variations of T_{u-r} are summarized in Table 6.1.

As shown in Figure 6.3, although the diurnal variation of average T_{u-r} in different months/seasons generally follows a similar pattern (i.e. positive at night and negative during the day), the duration with positive (negative) T_{u-r} in winter is longer (shorter) than in summer. Furthermore, there is a marked seasonal variation in the UHI intensity with a maximum in winter (December) and a minimum in spring (April). The annual average daily maximum T_{u-r} of 2.9°C is nearly three times the annual average of 0.8°C. The absolute maximum T_{u-r} in winter months could reach 10°C or above (see Table 6.1). Similar features were also reported in the UHI studies for major cities in China Mainland and Seoul (Kim and Baik, 2002; Weng and Yang, 2004; Hua et al, 2007; Liu et al, 2007). Roth (2007) also indicated that the seasonal

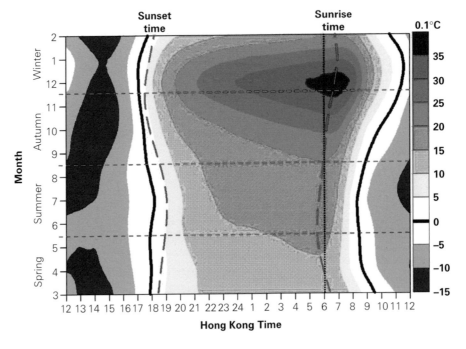

Source: Hong Kong Observatory

Figure 6.3 *Diurnal variations of average T_{u-r} (in units of 0.1°C: solid shading denotes +ve; dotted shading denotes −ve; the thick black line denotes T_{u-r} = 0) of Hong Kong in different months of the year (1989–2007)*

Table 6.1 *Statistics of the seasonal variations of T_{u-r} in Hong Kong (1989–2007)*

Different T_{u-r} parameters (°c)	Month												Annual
	Spring			Summer			Autumn			Winter			
	3	4	5	6	7	8	9	10	11	12	1	2	
Absolute daily maximum[1]	8.9	6.8	7.2	4.7	4.9	4.7	6.5	7.9	11.0	11.5	11.0	9.1	11.5
Average daily maximum[2]	2.1	1.9	2.1	2.4	2.6	2.6	2.7	3.2	3.9	4.4	3.7	2.7	2.9
(time of most frequent occurrence)[3]	(7)	(6)	(6)	(6)	(6)	(6)	(6)	(6)	(7)	(7)	(7)	(7)	(6)
Average at 6 am	1.3	1.2	1.6	1.8	1.9	1.9	2.1	2.6	3.2	3.7	2.8	1.9	2.2
Daily average	0.4	0.3	0.4	0.6	0.5	0.6	0.7	1.0	1.4	1.8	1.4	0.7	0.8

Note: bracketed figures represent local time in the morning.
Source: Hong Kong Observatory
Remarks:
[1] Only the data between 5 am and 7 am were considered. The dates with rainfall recorded were also excluded.
[2] Negative values were not included in the computation.
[3] The mode value is given.

differences in UHI are likely to be largest in places where the seasonal contrast in rural moisture properties is large (i.e. in climates with a pronounced dry season, such as the winter in Hong Kong).

The UHI intensity also has a noticeable correlation with the sunset/sunrise time in different seasons. Following the change in the sunrise time, (dashed line in Figure 6.3), the time of occurrence of the maximum T_{u-r} in winter shifted from 6.00 am in summer to 7.00 am in winter (see Table 6.1). Similarly, the time when T_{u-r} changes sign (from positive to negative: solid line in Figure 6.3) in the morning is also postponed from 9.00 am in summer to 11.00 am in winter.

Favourable conditions for high UHI intensity

As shown in Table 6.1, the absolute maximum UHI intensity in Hong Kong can reach 10°C or above in autumn and winter. In order to investigate the meteorological conditions favourable for the occurrence of high UHI intensity in Hong Kong, 11 cases with the top ten maximum values of T_{u-r} during the study period from 1989 to 2007 were identified and the corresponding meteorological observations extracted for study (see Table 6.2). It was observed that all the top ten maximum T_{u-r} cases happened between 5.00 am and 8.00 am in December or January. The maximum T_{u-r} from 1989 to 2007 was 11.5°C, which occurred at 6.00 am on 24 December 2001. The temperatures of HKO and TKL at

that time were 12.8°C and 1.3°C, respectively. All of these cases have a $T_{u-r} > 10°C$, and occurred under the following meteorological conditions:

- a moderating north-east monsoon affecting southern China;
- clear sky conditions with cloud amount less than or equal to 2 okta;
- stable atmosphere with K-index below 0 (George, 1960); and
- light north or north-easterly winds with wind speeds of 2.5m/s or below.

The high UHI intensity observed in these cases is mainly due to the large difference in the urban-to-rural cooling rates. Under clear skies, light winds and stable conditions, temperatures at exposed rural areas can drop appreciably overnight because of radiation cooling. On the other hand, in urban areas, the heat generated from human activities and limited sky view from the tall buildings results in a much slower cooling rate when compared with that of the rural area.

Conclusions

From the above analysis using temperature data recorded at HKO and TKL from 1989 to 2007, it can be observed that:

- The UHI effect in Hong Kong is primarily a night-time phenomenon. The maximum UHI intensity

Table 6.2 *The meteorological observations for the 11 cases with the top ten maximum values of* T_{u-r} *in Hong Kong (1989–2007)*

Time	HKO					TKL				King's Park	
	Temperature (°C)	Wind direction (°)	Wind speed (ms⁻¹)	Rainfall (mm)	Cloud Amount (okta)	Temperature (°C)	Wind direction (°)	Wind speed (ms⁻¹)	Rainfall (mm)	K-index at 8 am	T_{u-r}(°C)
2001122406	12.8	70	0.5	0	1	1.3	Variable	0.2	N/A	–43	11.5
1995123107	12.7	60	0.5	0	2	1.4	0	0	0	–21	11.3
1996010108	14.5	30	0.5	0	0	3.2	0	0	0	–38	11.3
1996010307	16	230	0.5	0	0	5	Variable	0.1	0	–4.1	11
2007113007	15.1	80	2.4	0	1	4.1	Variable	0.1	0	–44	11
1993122608	14.2	270	0.5	0	0	3.3	240	0.2	0	–69	10.9
1989120507	16.7	90	0.5	0	0	6.2	310	0.4	0	–30	10.5
2005122305	12.1	360	0.1	0	0	1.6	Variable	0.1	0	–47	10.5
1993013106	12.9	110	2	0	0	2.5	360	0.1	N/A	–64	10.4
1996010207	15	60	0.5	0	1	4.6	0	0	0	–28	10.4
1999122606	12.4	70	2	0	0	2	Variable	0.1	0	–64	10.4

Note: N/A – Data not available

Source: Hong Kong Observatory

usually occurs at approximately 6.00 am (around dawn). There is also a noticeable 'urban cool island' effect during the day, especially around 2.00 pm (1400 h).

- There is a distinct seasonal variation in the UHI intensity in Hong Kong. Higher UHI intensity was observed during winter (the dry season), particularly in December. The time of occurrence of maximum UHI intensity also shifts with the change in the sunrise time in different seasons.
- The absolute maximum UHI intensity can reach 10°C or higher in winter in Hong Kong. Stable atmosphere, light winds and a clear sky are favourable meteorological conditions conducive to high UHI intensity in Hong Kong.

References

Alonso, M. S., Labajo, J. L. and Fidalgo, M. R. (2003) 'Characteristics of the urban heat island in the city of Salamanca, Spain', *Atmosphere*, pp137–148

Arnfield, A. J. (2003) 'Two decades of urban climate research: a review of turbulence, exchanges of energy and water, and the urban heat island', *International Journal of Climatology*, vol 23, pp1–26

Bornstein, R. D. (1968) 'Observations of the urban heat island effect in New York City', *Journal of Applied Meteorology*, vol 7, pp575–582

Chow, W. T. L. and Roth, M. (2006) 'Temporal dynamics of the urban heat island of Singapore', *International Journal of Climatology*, vol 26, pp2243–2260

George, J. J. (1960) *Weather Forecasting for Aeronautics*, Academic Press, New York, p673

Grimmond, S. (2007) 'Urbanization and global environmental change: Local effects of urban warming', *The Geographical Journal*, vol 173, no 1, pp83–88

Haeger-Eugennsson, H. and Holmer, B. (1999) 'Advection caused by the urban heat island circulation as a regulating factor on the nocturnal urban heat island', *International Journal of Climatology*, vol 19, pp975–988

HKSARG (2007) *Hong Kong in Brief 2006*, www.info.gov.hk/info/hkbrief/eng/ahk.htm, accessed November 2008

Hua, L. J., Ma, Z. G. and Guo, W. D. (2007) 'The impact of urbanization on air temperature across China', *Theoretical and Applied Climatology*, vol 93 pp179–197

Kalande, B. D. and Oke, T. R. (1980) 'Suburban energy balance estimates for Vancouver, BC, using the Bowen ratio energy balance approach', *Journal of Applied Meteorology*, vol 19, pp791–802

Karl, T. R., Diaz, H. F. and Kukla, G. (1988) 'Urbanization: Its detection and effect in the United States climate record', *Journal of Climate*, vol 11, pp1099–1123

Kim, Y. H. and Baik, J. J. (2002) 'Maximum urban heat island intensity in Seoul', *Journal of Applied Meteorology*, vol 41, pp651–659

Lam, C. Y. (2006) 'On the climate changes brought about by urban living', *Bulletin of the Hong Kong Meteorology Society*, vol 16, pp15–27

Landsberg, H. E. (1981) *The Urban Climate*, Academic Press, New York, NY

Leung, Y. K., Yeung, K. H., Ginn, E. W. L. and Leung, W. M. (2004) 'Climate change in Hong Kong*', Hong Kong Observatory Technical Note,* vol 107, p41

Leung, Y. K., Wu, M. C., Yeung, K. K. and Leung, W. M. (2007) 'Temperature projections for Hong Kong in the 21st century – based on IPCC 2007 Assessment Report', *Bulletin of the Hong Kong Meteorology Society*, vol 17, pp13–22

Liu, W., Ji, C., Zhong, J., Jiang, X. and Zheng, Z. (2007) 'Temporal characteristics of Beijing urban heat island', *Theoretical and Applied Climatology*, vol 87, pp213–221

Mayor of London (2006) 'London's urban heat island: A summary for decision makers', Greater London Authority,

www.london.gov.uk/mayor/environment/climate_change/, accessed November 2008

Oke, T. R. (1982) 'The energetic basis of the urban heat island', *Quarterly Journal of the Royal Meteorological Society,* vol 108, pp1–24

Oke, T. R. and Maxwell, G. B. (1975) 'Urban heat island dynamics in Montreal and Vancouver', *Atmospheric Environment*, vol 9, pp191–200

Roth, M., (2007) 'Review of urban climate research in (sub)tropical regions', *International Journal of Climatology*, vol 27, 1859–1873

Sakakibara, Y. and Owa, K. (2005) 'Urban–rural temperature differences in coastal cities: Influence of rural sites', *International Journal of Climatology*, vol 25, pp811–820

Weng, Q. and Yang, S. (2004) 'Managing the adverse thermal effects of urban development in a densely populated Chinese city', *Journal of Environmental Management*, vol 70, pp145–156

Wilby, R. (2003) 'Past and projected trends in London's urban heat island', *Weather*, vol 58, pp251–260

7

Urban Climate in Dense Cities

Lutz Katzschner

Introduction

The rapid urbanization and emergence of many megacities triggers a number of environmental issues. The urban climate, and with it the well-known urban heat island phenomenon, has to be seen as a negative factor for thermal comfort and air pollution. The reasons for a special urban climate are heat storage, trapping of radiation, increasing roughness and less evaporation, which are seen in cities worldwide but are most evident in densely built-up megacities. With this the urban heat island is a storage of solar energy in the urban fabric during the day and the release of energy into the atmosphere at night. The process of urbanization and development alters the balance between the energy from the sun used for raising air temperature (heating process) and that used for evaporation (cooling process).

In today's moderate climate, the urban heat island (UHI) is experienced only in summer and air pollution caused by reduced ventilation occurs in winter. The UHI refers to the phenomenon where the temperature in an urban environment is always higher than that in surrounding rural areas, especially on calm and cloudless nights. Figure 7.1 illustrates an idealized heat island profile for a city, showing temperature rising from the rural fringe and peaking in the city centre. The profile also demonstrates how temperature can vary across a city depending upon the nature of the land cover, such that urban parks and lakes are cooler than adjacent areas covered by buildings.

According to Landsberg (1981), the urban heat island, as the most obvious climatic manifestation of urbanization, can be observed in every town and city. In dense cities these factors tend to become extreme; in cities situated in tropical climates, negative urban climate effects become even worse.

The urban heat island can have a positive effect during short winters in cities north or south of the 23rd latitude, producing thermally neutral city temperatures, making citizens comfortable and decreasing energy consumption for heating. Most megacities lie in subtropical regions and experience very long, hot and humid summers, so that in such cases the heat island and air mass exchange effect are negative outcomes. Planners, architects, urban designers and developers should keep in mind that urban heat island intensities should be mitigated, and planning and construction should not worsen the heat condition.

Generally, dense tropical cities cannot compare to European cities in terms of density and height. But European studies have shown that climate change in cities has a certain pattern, which has to be determined. Comparison of the spatial distribution of the urban heat island shows certain similarities in many cities due to the city fabric. Figure 7.2 demonstrates that in London and Tokyo the maximum heat island in these city centres is not always linear to the city centre but has hot spots, where heat storage and low albedo have a major effect and are directly dependent upon the density of buildings in relation to their heights. Therefore, the height–width ratio is widely used to express urban heat storage and urban heat island effects throughout the world (Oke, 1987). Figure 7.3 shows that in European cities heat islands occur. In the example of Karlsruhe, Germany, two separate heat islands can be seen following the densely built-up areas of the city.

Modelling of climate change has already shown the extreme heat load of Asia, Latin America and Africa,

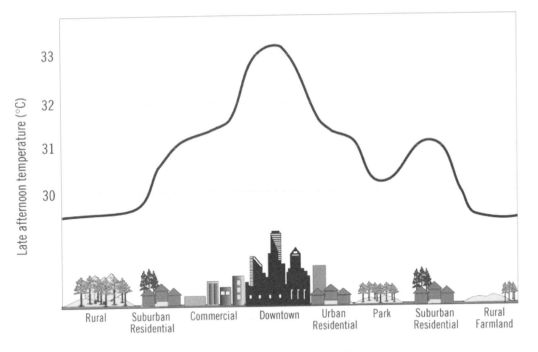

Source: http://eande.lbl.gov/HeatIsland/HighTemps/, assessed 23 July 2008

Figure 7.1 *Sketch of an urban heat island profile*

where nearly all of the world's megacities are located. One can thus see how global climate change and urbanization have synergistic effects and will increase the heat load considerably above the calculated stress factors. The importance and urgency of urban climate studies to reduce the urban heat load, and therefore PET, can be seen from Figure 7.4. There is a clear correlation that exists between increasing thermal load, as expressed through the thermal index PET, and mortality.

Problems

The urban climate, which is influenced by an increasing heat storage (heat balance), on the one hand, and the barrier effect with reduced ventilation, on the other, has to be seen as a problem for health in terms of thermal stress and air pollution. Since there is a direct dependency from heat stress to mortality (see Figure 7.4; Rudel et al, 2007), the urban heat island has to be resolved and mitigated through ventilation or cooling materials, especially in cities such as Hong Kong (see Figure 7.5) or in the big cities of Latin America and others where sea breeze potentials are often blocked and lead to heat stress inside the urban canopy layer. This

effect increases as a result of global warming. For Hong Kong, this is evidenced in a comparison between the long-term surrounding temperature and a station located inside the city (see Figure 7.6). The urban heat island is a permanent factor, but varies, of course, during the season. The situation in London shows how global warming will considerably increase the days of heat stress. An increasing heat island and the incidence of global warming both compound risks to individual health. As a result of the changing meso-climate in urban areas, increases in thermal stress combined with increased air pollution must be considered. Figure 7.7 shows the trend of hot days. This again illustrates the importance and urgency of planning actions in cities. Urban climate-related heat load and global climate change discussion must be coupled.

Thermal component

As mentioned above, the urban heat island (UHI) is not the principal indicator of thermal stress; rather, it is thermal indices. One of these thermal indices is the physiological equivalent temperature (PET), which is used to describe the effective temperature by

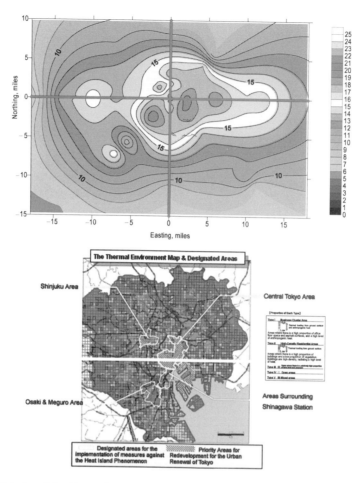

Source: top: Endlicher (2007); bottom: Tokyo Metropolitan Government (2006)

Figure 7.2 *Heat islands in London and Tokyo*

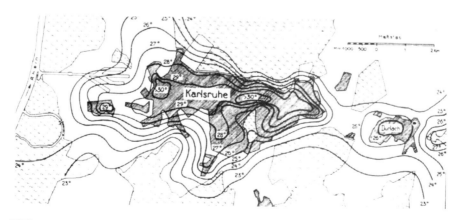

Source: Peppler (1979)

Figure 7.3 *Isolines of air temperatures in the city of Karlsruhe, Germany*

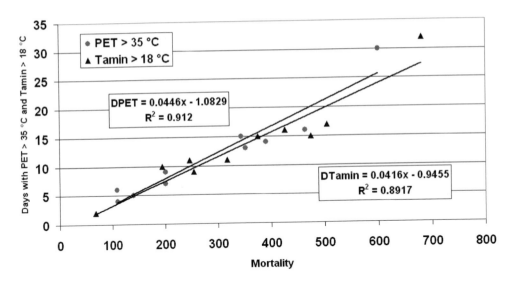

Source: Rudel et al (2007)

Figure 7.4 *Correlation between physiological equivalent temperature (PET) > 35°C and Tamin >18°C and mortality in Vienna (1996–2005)*

Source: Katzschner 2007

Figure 7.5 *Hong Kong skyline*

considering all environmental factors, such as temperature, solar radiation, wind speed, humidity, etc. PET is an effective thermal index for urban planners and architects to evaluate environmental conditions. An example of the PET distribution in Hong Kong with 1km × 1km resolution is shown in Figure 7.8.

For people walking in streets and open spaces, this resolution is not sufficient for mitigation and planning

processes, especially since planning requires detailed spatial results in terms of urban climate investigations. One should first, however, determine the small-scale effects of planning measures on thermal conditions. This is demonstrated, for example, through the ENVI-met calculations for a hot climate in Gardaiha, Algeria, which show the considerable influence of trees in a street canyon causing a decrease in temperature of over 10°C (see Figure 7.9).

Urban climatic maps

The urban climatic map is a scientific tool that helps planners to achieve their aims. There are typically two maps: the Urban Climatic Analysis Map (UC-AnMap) and the Urban Climatic Recommendation Map (UC-ReMap). The UC-AnMap scientifically presents the climate of a city. It synergizes the scientific understanding of urban heat islands, urban ventilation and outdoor human thermal comfort. Based on the UC-AnMap and working with planners, the UC-ReMap could be further developed. The map resolves scientific climatic understandings into guidelines and planning recommendations and could be used to guide planning actions and decision-making.

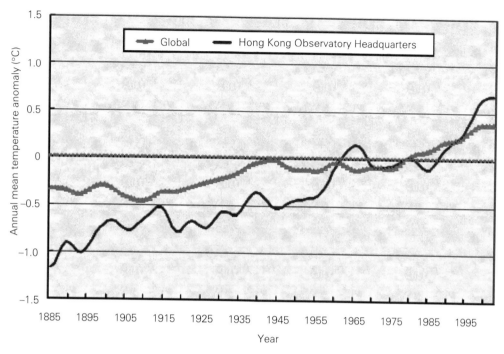

Source: Lam (2006)

Figure 7.6 *Global climate change and air temperature trend for Hong Kong*

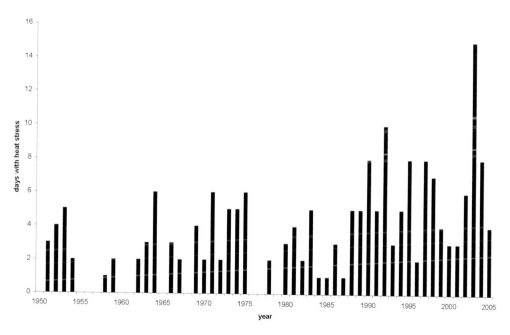

Source: Katzschner et al, 2009

Figure 7.7 *Increase in the number of hot days in Frankfurt, Germany*

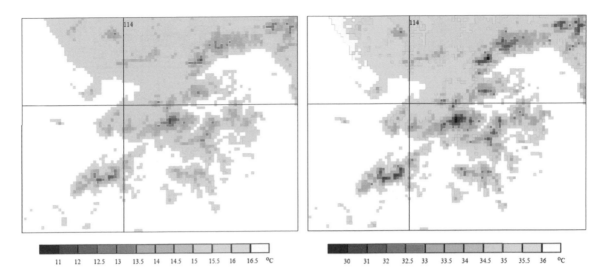

Source: Professor A. Matzarakis

Figure 7.8 *Distribution of calculated PET in Hong Kong in January (left) and July (right)*

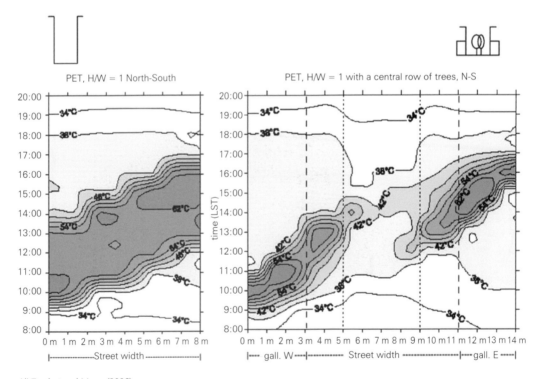

Source: Ali-Toudert and Mayer (2006)

Figure 7.9 *PET values of a street canyon without trees (left) and with trees (right) in Gardaiha*

(a)

(b)

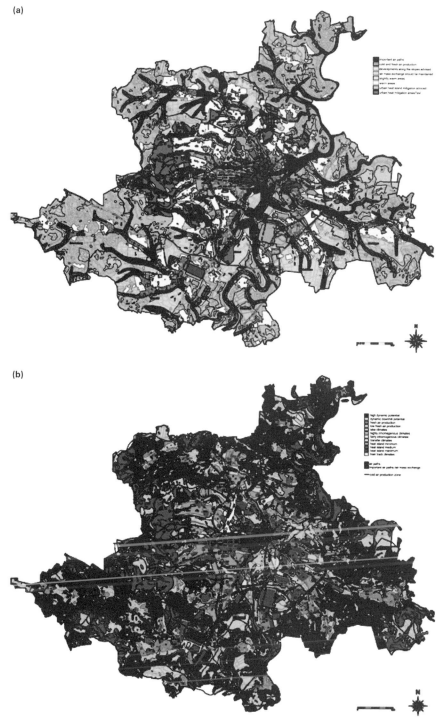

Source: Bosch et al (1999)

Figure 7.10 *(a) Urban Climatic Analysis Map (UC-AnMap) and (b) Urban Climate Recommendation Map (UC-ReMap) from Kassel, Germany, with heat island, ventilation and planning classifications*

The concept of the urban climatic map was developed in Germany during the early 1980s. There was intense public support and political will to plan for the future responsibly and sensitively with respect to the natural environment. In Germany, the law explicitly stated that no new development should negatively affect the natural environment. Within this ambit, planners, meteorologists and scientists began to draft urban climatic maps, and have attempted to synergize climatic, topographical and urban parameters in order to more objectively guide the planning decision process.

The UC-AnMap provides a 'synthetic' as opposed to an 'analytic' understanding of the factors affecting the urban environment. That is to say, it attempts to balance, prioritize and weight the combined effects of the parameters appropriately in view of the outcome of the planning decisions that need to be made. The UC-ReMap is useful in assisting planning decision-making, ranging from the regional scale of 1:100,000 to the urban scale of 1:5000. The UC-ReMap provides a holistic and strategic understanding upon which detailed and further micro-scale studies could be identified and conducted.

For the use of urban climate results, urban climatic maps are an important tool: both the analysis and the recommendations derived from the maps are significant. Planning relies on spatial climatic information of a high resolution in classification systems following thermal and ventilation criteria that aim to find urban climatic characteristics. Two steps can be identified in this process: first, an urban climate analysis and, second, an urban climate evaluation map (see Figure 7.10). Scale is important for any use (see Table 7.1). Here the city planning level for urban development plans (master plans) of 1:25,000 and for zoning plans of 1:5000 can be used.

Geographical information system (GIS) data and land-use data were classified and transformed to meet urban climate functions, such as thermal aspects (i.e. heat and cooling rates), a wind classification with ventilation paths and topographically influenced downhill air movements. The building fabric was classified according to roughness length and thermal radiation processes.

The following factors were used:

- land-use classifications for thermal and radiation data with categories of city structures, industrial areas, gardens and parks, forests, greenland and agricultural areas; lakes were the only water features used, while train tracks received a special classification as they have a large daily variation in surface temperature and, therefore, radiation differences;
- topographical and geographical data that influence the local circulation pattern; and
- ventilation according to an analysis of the roughness length.

The urban climatic map can therefore outline patterns that affect the human urban thermal comfort of a city. The use of a human urban thermal comfort indicator as a synergistic element to collate data from the urban climatic map of the city seems appropriate and indicates the likely elevation of thermal heat stress. Based on a parameter's magnitude of increasing or decreasing PET (whether land use, building volume or urban green space), classification values can be defined.

After the analysis, an evaluation is carried out using GIS and based on a calculation method that calculates weighting factors following the scheme from Figure 7.11; for every grid, a result for thermal and dynamic potentials is mapped. The classification of climatopes is directly derived from PET values (see Figure 7.12).

The study process results in the urban climate map (Figure 7.13). The climate functions are illustrated spatially. This forms the basis of planning recommendation works.

Urban climate and planning

For any planning discussions, urban climate results have to be translated to general planning aims in terms

Table 7.1 *Urban climate and planning scales*

Administration level		Planning level	Urban climate issue	Climatic scale
city	1:25,000	urban development; master plan	heat island effects; ventilation paths	meso scale
neighbourhood	1:5000	urban structures	thermal comfort, air pollution	meso scale
block	1:2000	open space design	thermal comfort	micro scale
single building	1:500	building design	radiation and ventilation effects	micro scale

Source: Author's unpublished work

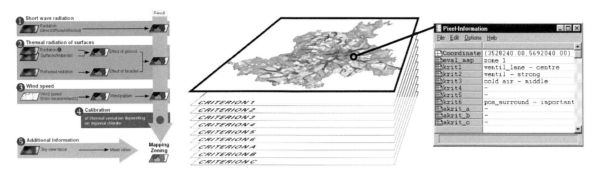

Source: Bosch et al (1999)

Figure 7.11 *Principal methodology for deriving urban climate maps and the use of GIS layers for detailed classification information*

Table 7.2 *Positive and negative effects on urban climate*

Positive climate effects	Negative climate effects
Ventilation paths	Heat island (building bulk)
Downhill air movement	Anthropogenic heat
Air mass exchange	Reduced ventilation
Bioclimatic effects from vegetation	Lack of air path effect
Neighbourhood effects	
Altitude and elevation	

Source: Schiller et al (2001)

of the well-being of people. To what extent do dense building sites affect the heat island and thermal conditions of open spaces, and what potential does the concept have to improve thermal conditions and air mass exchange – for example, along roads and parks?

Before discussing some conflicts between planning and urban climate, it is important to examine the interactions between climate and the use of spaces. Investigations through interviews in previous studies (Katzschner et al, 2002) showed very clearly the existence of microclimates in neighbourhoods. From the example of Kassel, Germany, the ideal thermal conditions could be derived as follows:

- The use of open spaces is more frequent in the centre of the heat island and increases with high values of thermal indices.
- Streets are seen as more comfortable for pedestrians if there is a choice between sun and shadow.

- Ventilation areas have to be evaluated in the context of the whole city in order to have an appropriate influence on planning.

The definition of the ideal urban climate by Mayer (1990) considers the areas and time concept as important evaluation criteria:

The 'ideal urban climate' is an atmospheric situation within the UCL [urban canopy layer] with a high variation in time and space to develop inhomogeneous thermal conditions for man within a distance of 150m. It should be free from air pollution and thermal stress by means of more shadow and ventilation (tropical areas) or wind protection (moderate and cold climates).

Schiller et al (2001) have already developed some proposals for architects and planners on how to achieve this situation on a micro-scale level. These general proposals should be devoted to concrete urban places, as outlined in Table 7.3.

Policies designed to mitigate the most extreme urban climate conditions may need to balance the need to manage heat at building, neighbourhood and city scales, taking into account the nature of development (new versus existing) and what is achievable in reality. Focus should also be placed on ventilation and the albedo of houses in order to reduce the radiation trap. Urban designers and planners need to acknowledge this, and in doing so base design criteria on data that describe the current and projected future climate of any city, being especially aware of the critical importance of minimum temperature for human thermal comfort, health and patterns of energy consumption.

The main problem is to use data from cities such as ventilation paths, sea breeze and mountain wind to mitigate urban heat islands. Therefore, information on aerial distribution is needed. With the example from Hong Kong, one can see how the thermal situation and dynamic potentials were combined into a single map in order to determine planning proposals which use general knowledge, such as green spaces or land sea breezes, but locate this to specific conditions.

From this point on, proposals directed at materials such as cool roofs and walls, cool pavements, or planting trees and vegetation can be carried out. Further on in the recommendation map, the urban geometry, such as the sky view factor (SVF) height–width ratio, and can

Table 7.3 *Open space planning possibilities with their thermal effects*

Planning possibilities	Thermal effect
Width of streets	Using shadow and sun for daily and annual variation
Pergolas and arcades	Sun protection in summer, using winter radiation
Vegetation	Sun and wind protection; long-wave radiation
Colours	Reflection and daylight
Materials	Heat storage; dust

Source: Schiller et al (2001)

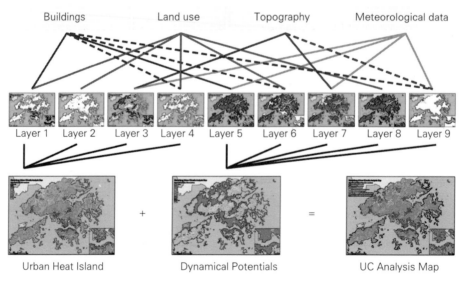

Source: Ng et al (2008)

Figure 7.12 *An illustration of work flow for creating an urban climatic map*

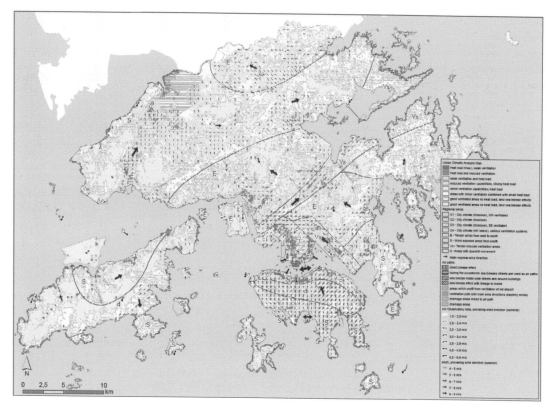

Source: Ng et al (2008)

Figure 7.13 *The result of the urban climatic map of Hong Kong*

Source: www.stadtentwicklung.berlin.de/umwelt/umweltatlas/

Figure 7.14 *Some examples of buildings adopting green roofs and walls*

be used to influence the formation of urban climate conditions. Finally, the reduction of anthropogenic heat release can help to lessen difficulties.

One can see in Figure 7.15 the elements of the urban climatic map characteristics, such as densely built areas with highly developed thermal stresses, as well as areas that profit either from sea breezes in the north or from downhill air movements in the south. Urban planning has to respect these factors and to find a way for city development which has enough gaps for ventilation in certain spots. Some areas now block wind, so that neighbouring sides require a higher permeability.

The example from Kassel in Figure 7.16 shows how one can focus and zoom in on a local spot where reconstruction is planned or where new buildings are to be erected, including the surrounding climatic conditions (such as wind direction and hot environments).

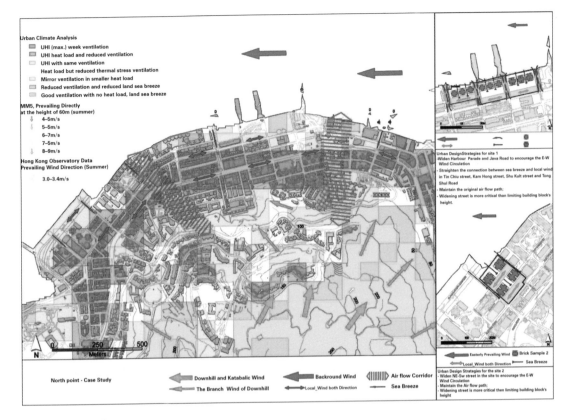

Source: Bosch et al (1999)

Figure 7.15 *Urban climate map and planning recommendations*

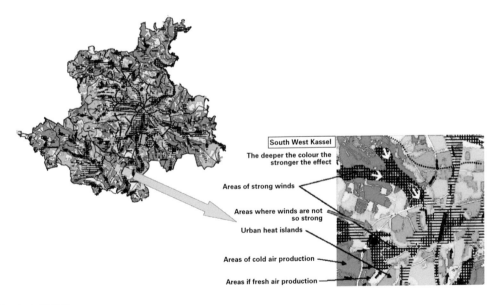

Source: Bosch et al (1999)

Figure 7.16 *Urban climate map of Kassel with explanations*

References

Ali-Toudert, F. and Mayer, H. (2006) 'Numerical study on the effects of aspect ratio and orientation of an urban street canyon on outdoor thermal comfort in hot and dry climate', *Building and Environment*, vol 41, pp94–108

Bosch, U., Katzschner, L., Reinhold, M. and Röttgen, M. (1999) *Urban Climatic Map*, Planning Institute for the Region of Kassel, Kassel, Germany

Bosch, U. Katzschner, L. Reinhold, M. Röttgen, M. (1999) Vertiefende Klimaanalyse und Klimabewertung für den Raum des Zweckverbandes Raum, Kassel, Germany

Endlicher, W. and Nickson, A. (2007) 'Hot places – cool spaces', Paper presented at the Symposium on Klimaatcentrum Vrije Universiteit/Fac. der Aard- en Levenswetenschappen, Amsterdam, 25 October 2007

Katzschner, L., Bosch, U. and Röttgen, M. (2002) *Analyse der thermischen Komponente des Stadtklimas für die Freiraumplanung, UVP Report,* vol 3, Hamm, Germany

Katzschner, L., Maas, T. and Schneider, A. (2009) Das Städtische Mikroklima: Analyse für die Stadt und Gebäudeplanung, *Bauphysik*, vol 31, no 1

Lam, C. Y. (2006) *Proceedings of PGBC Symposium 2006, Urban Climate and Urban Greenery,* 2 December 2006, Hong Kong, Published by the Professional Green Building Council, Hong Kong, pp14–17, www. hkpgbc.org

Landsberg, H. E. (1981) 'The urban climate', *International Geophysics Series*, vol 28, pp84–99

Mayer, H. (1990) *Die humanbiometeorologische Bewertung des Stadtklimas*, VDI-Reihe Umweltmeteorologie Bd, 15 Düsseldorf, Germany

Ng, E., Chao R. and Katzschner, L. (2008) 'Urban climate studies for hot and humid tropical coastal city of Hong Kong', *Berichte des Meteorologischen Instituts der Universität*, Freiburg, no 18, pp265–271

Oke, T. R. (1987) *Boundary Layer Climates*, 2nd edition, Methuen, US

Peppler, A. (1979) 'Modifikation der luftfeuche im Stadtgebiet', *Promet*, vol 9, no 4, pp14–20

Rudel, E., Matzarakis, A. and Koch, E. (2007) 'Bioclimate and mortality in Vienna', *Berichte des Meteorologischen Institutes der Universität Freiburg*, vol 16, Fachtagung Biomet, Freiburg, Germany

Schiller, S., Evans, M. and Katzschner, L. (2001) 'Isla de calor, microclima urbano y variables de diseno estudios en Buenos Aires', *Avances en Engerieas Renovables y Medio Ambiente*, Buenos Aires, vol 5, pp45–50

Tokyo Metropolitan Government (2006) www.metro. tokyo.jp/ENGLISH/TOPICS/2005/ftf56100.htm

Part III

Environmental Aspects of High-Density Design

8

Thermal Comfort Issues and Implications in High-Density Cities

Baruch Givoni

Thermal comfort

Thermal comfort is a subjective sensation, but it is related to the physiological condition of thermal balance between the body and the surrounding environment. A narrow definition may define thermal comfort as the absence of discomfort from heat or from cold. A wider definition also includes some specific factors related to climate that enhance enjoyment from the thermal environment. This chapter will deal not only with the conditions of maintaining comfort, but also with minimizing discomfort when the indoor or outdoor conditions are beyond the comfort zone.

The body produces heat from food ingestion through the process of metabolism. This internal heat production should be balanced by heat loss to the surrounding environment in order to keep the inner body temperature within a very narrow range. The rate of metabolic heat production depends upon the physical activity of the person (Givoni and Goldman, 1971). The heat exchange with the environment, which may include components of heat gain in addition to the essential heat loss, takes place through the physical processes of heat flow and depends upon climatic conditions as well as upon the properties of clothing. However, in variance with inert materials, the human body has several physiological processes that can modify the rate and pattern of various modes of heat flow from and to the body in order to provide better adaptation to different climatic conditions.

Maintaining thermal balance is a pre-required, although not a sufficient, condition for feeling thermal comfort because thermal balance can also be maintained under uncomfortable thermal conditions.

Comfort and heat exchange of the human body

The heat exchange of the human body with the environment is governed by physical processes of heat flow (convection and radiation) and by heat loss through evaporation, and takes place at the skin's surface. Skin temperature over the body is not constant. The differences between the various parts of the body are smallest under hot conditions. Under cold conditions, on the other hand, skin temperature differences are much greater (see below for details). Under cold exposure conditions, the extremities, especially hands and feet, as well as the nose, are the coldest parts and often these body parts are the source of localized cold discomfort.

Convection

Convection is the process of heat exchange between the skin and the surrounding air. It can be either positive (heat gain) or negative (heat loss), depending upon the relationship between the skin and air temperatures. Convection heat flow is proportional to the temperature difference between the skin and the air, and its rate depends upon the speed of the air around the body and upon the thermal resistance of the clothing (their clo value). Under comfortable conditions, skin temperature is about 32°C to 33°C. However, the body has a physiological process for modifying skin temperature under different stressful climatic conditions and thus for modifying physiological heat gain or loss. This is accomplished by changing the blood flow distribution between the inner parts of the body and the skin layer (vasomotor regulation). Under hot conditions, more blood is directed to the skin and less to the inner parts of the body. This brings up the skin temperature and lowers the heat gain by convection (and also by radiation). Under cold conditions, blood flow is directed mainly to the inner parts of the body, which are essential for maintaining life, at the expense of blood flow to the skin and to the extremities (hands and feet). Consequently, the average skin temperature and the temperature of the extremities are lowered and physiological heat loss is reduced; but this process is accompanied by subjective cold discomfort.

The effect of air speed on convective heat exchange, and on comfort, is not linear. The change from still air (speed of about 0.2m/s) to a speed of 1m/s has a much greater effect on convection, as well as directly on comfort, than, for instance, the change from 2m/s to 3m/s. This pattern is of special interest when dealing with comfort in a high-density city, where outdoor wind speed is often very low, resulting in extremely low indoor air speed in outdoor spaces, as well as in ventilated houses.

Air speed and evaporative cooling

The speed of air around the body also affects the rate of sweat evaporation, per unit area, from the skin. However, its effect on the total rate of sweat evaporation from the skin is more complex.

Every gram of water, or sweat, that is evaporated consumes in the process about 0.68Wh. Physiological cooling by evaporation occurs in two ways: first, continuous cooling by water evaporation in the lungs and then cooling of the skin by sweat evaporation. The cooling in the lungs is proportional to the breathing rate providing oxygen to the body, which in turn is proportional to the metabolic rate. The evaporation rate is also proportional to the difference between the vapour pressure in the lungs (about 42mmHg) and the vapour pressure in the air, as we exhale nearly saturated air at 37°C and take in air with the ambient water vapour content. Evaporative cooling in the lungs is not related to the ambient air temperature.

Evaporative cooling of the skin, on the other hand, is closely related to the ambient air temperature. Some minor amounts of water diffuse from the skin even under thermal comfort conditions, when the sweat glands are not activated. Activity of the sweat glands and sweat secretion occurs only at temperatures above the comfort zone.

The rate of sweat secretion is not necessarily related to the subjective feeling of wetness of the skin. Thus, for example, on a hot day in a desert, with air temperature of 37°C, high winds and very low humidity level, the skin of a resting person may feel very dry, but measurements may show a rate of sweat secretion, and evaporation, of about 300 grams per hour. On the other hand, on days of about 27°C, with still air and very high humidity, the skin may feel very moist, even with sweat covering parts of the body, although measured sweat rate and evaporation may only be about 150g/h (Givoni, 1971). When air temperature is above about 30°C, sweat evaporation is the major cooling factor enabling the body to maintain thermal balance.

Radiation

Two types of radiation have to be considered when dealing with comfort in the context of cities: solar radiation when dealing with comfort in outdoor spaces, and infrared (heat) radiation when dealing with comfort inside buildings. Inside buildings the body exchanges heat with the surrounding surfaces by infrared radiation. The temperatures of the various surfaces around a space may be at different temperatures than the indoor air temperature. For example, the ceiling temperature of a room with an uninsulated concrete roof may be much higher in summer than the other surfaces and the indoor air temperature. The surface temperature of a window may be much lower in a cold winter than the indoor air. Thus, when dealing with indoor comfort, the mean radiant temperature (MRT) of a space – namely, the area-weighted mean of all the indoor spaces – is the relevant factor. Often, the temperature of a globe thermometer (a sensor placed inside a black metal globe) is substituted in comfort studies for the calculation of the MRT.

Outdoor surfaces often have temperatures much higher than air temperature at about 1m height – for instance, dark-coloured pavements on a sunny summer day may be 10°C to 20°C above the air temperature. Thus, the MRT may be a factor in outdoor comfort as well.

Comfort issues in high-density cities

The main urban climatic features in high-density cities that affect thermal comfort are lower urban wind speed, higher temperatures (the urban heat island, or UHI) and restricted access to solar energy compared with the climatic conditions in low-density cities placed in a similar natural climate. The actual impact of these features upon thermal comfort may be reversed in summer and winter. Lower wind speeds and higher temperatures tend to increase thermal discomfort in summer, especially of people staying outdoors. Lower outdoor wind speed also reduces ventilation rate and the indoor air speed of naturally ventilated buildings. The higher outdoor temperature elevates the indoor temperatures of buildings, thus increasing the likelihood and severity of indoor thermal discomfort. This worsening of comfort may be encountered mostly in high-density cities located in a hot humid climate.

When dealing with outdoor comfort, exposure to solar radiation is a very important factor. In winter, it usually greatly enhances comfort, while in summer such exposure may be a major source of heat discomfort. From an urban design aspect the problem often is how to provide exposure to the sun in outdoor spaces in winter while providing shading in summer.

The thermal comfort of individuals staying outdoors is one of the factors that may affect the level of outdoor activities in streets, plazas, playgrounds, urban parks, etc. The amount and intensity of such activities are affected by the level of discomfort experienced by inhabitants when they are exposed to climatic conditions in outdoor spaces.

Thus, for example, on a hot summer day the thermal discomfort of people staying outdoors exposed to the sun may discourage them from utilizing available urban parks, depending upon the particular combination of the air temperature, the surface temperature of the surrounding areas, the wind speed and the humidity level. The availability of shaded outdoor areas may result in greater utilization of open space by the public. In a similar way, in a cold region, a high wind speed and obstruction of the sun in shaded areas may discourage people from staying outdoors while the provision of sunny areas protected from the prevailing winds may encourage public activities in that outdoor space (Givoni et al, 2003).

The effect of direct exposure to solar radiation is not limited to thermal sensation. In winter it may produce pleasure; on a hot summer's day it may produce discomfort beyond the heat sensation. In unshaded areas pedestrians may also be exposed to surface temperatures much higher in summer and lower in winter than the ambient air temperature. Outdoors, wind speeds are much higher than the air speeds occurring indoors. Wind in summer, up to a certain speed, may be very pleasant, while in winter it may be very annoying. These factors have to be included in evaluating overall subjective responses to the outdoor environment.

Recent research on thermal comfort was conducted both on outdoor comfort and on indoor comfort in Hong Kong, Singapore, Indonesia and Thailand. These studies are summarized below and the implications of their findings for high-density cities will be discussed. Because of the personal experience of the author, the emphasis in this chapter will be on comfort in high-density cities located in hot climates.

Methodologies of comfort research

There are several different procedures for conducting comfort research, differing in the nature of the information collected, the amount of control and the cost, as well as the human subjects used in the research.

One objective of comfort research might be to find out the 'comfort temperature' of a given population in a given location and season. This means: what is the range of temperatures in which the largest fraction of the population would feel comfortable? A complementary finding of such research is the statistical distribution of thermal sensations at that temperature, from 'cold', through 'neutral' to 'hot'. In order to obtain information representative of the population, the size of the sample should be as large as practical financially, and each person should be interviewed only once ('once through', or transverse, procedure). Typically, several hundred people are interviewed in such studies.

A different objective, calling for a different research procedure, might be to find out directly how people respond to *changes* in climatic conditions: changes in solar radiation, temperature, humidity and wind speed. A complementary objective can be to find out what is the relative effect of changes in one climatic element (e.g. wind speed) relative to changes in another climatic element (such as temperature).

The following is a discussion and comparison of advantages and limitations of different research methodologies on human comfort from the aspect of the information and insight that can be gained from the research work. The evaluations expressed in this discussion are the personal opinions of the author.

Methodologies

The methodologies include the following:

- Controlled extended experiments with a group of the same test subjects, over periods lasting from several days to one week or more. The overall number of subjects is limited, but each subject is tested under different combinations of temperature, humidity and air speed. This methodology is common in environmental physiological research.

  Such research can be conducted only where a climatic chamber is available. With this procedure every test subject experiences directly the effects of climatic changes or other variables such as clothing, metabolic rate, etc. The number of people who can be tested is fewer in comparison with other methodologies. On the other hand, the estimation of the effect of climatic changes and other variables is more accurate.

- Semi-controlled experiments in an unconditioned room, where indoor temperatures and humidity are changing with the outdoor climate. The subjects are tested under naturally changing indoor temperatures during the day. It is possible to change indoor air speed through the use of fans and thus to investigate the effect of air speed under changing indoor temperature and humidity conditions. It is also possible to elevate indoor temperature through a heating device in order to observe responses to various temperatures.

  With this procedure there is no use of a climatic chamber, so it can be conducted with limited financial resources. With respect to the effect of air speed, it is possible to evaluate the effects of temperature and humidity under specific levels of air speed. On the other hand, temperature and humidity conditions are not controlled.

- Comfort surveys of occupants in a given indoor or outdoor location, where occupants stay at the time of the survey. Each person is interviewed only once, under the prevailing climatic conditions at the survey time. With this methodology no person experiences the effect of *changes* in climatic

conditions. The quantitative evaluation of the effect of *changes* in climatic elements by this methodology can be evaluated only by statistical analysis of the distribution of the data because no test subject actually felt the effect of such changes during the survey.

Recent research on comfort

In this section the results of recent studies on comfort, with potential implications for high-density cities, are reviewed. These studies were conducted at the following universities:

- Chinese University of Hong Kong, China;
- City University of Hong Kong, China;
- National University of Singapore;
- King Mongkut University of Technology in Bangkok, Thailand.

Research on outdoor comfort at the Chinese University of Hong Kong

The objective of this project (Cheng et al, 2007) was to evaluate the effects of solar radiation, air temperature and wind speed on the comfort of individuals staying outdoors. Special interest was in the effects of wind speed and solar radiation, factors that can be modified by urban design. It was also of interest to observe any gender and age effect in the comfort responses to the different exposure conditions. This comfort research utilized a 'longitudinal' methodology, where several groups of subjects took part in experiments over an extended time (one or more full day), and experienced and responded to natural or induced changes in some climatic elements, such as air temperature, solar radiation and wind speed. This procedure obtains the thermal comfort responses of the same subjects in changing experimental climatic conditions.

The experimental set-up consisted of four exposure settings, close to each other, located in an open area. In setting 1, the subjects sat under a sun umbrella, exposed to the local wind. In setting 2, subjects sat behind a vertical windbreak made of transparent polyethylene sheets supported by aluminium frames, which greatly reduced the wind speed. In setting 3, subjects sat under a sun umbrella and behind a windbreak. In setting 4, subjects sat under direct sun and exposed to the wind (see Figure 8.1 for all four settings).

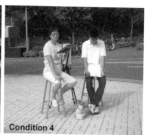

Source: Cheng et al (2007)

Figure 8.1 *The four experimental settings*

The subjects group consisted of eight individuals: four males and four females. For each gender group, half of the subjects were in their 20s and half in their 50s. The eight subjects worked in four pairs in the survey. The common summer outdoor clothing in Hong Kong is short-sleeved T-shirts and shorts or light trousers; the average clothing index measured in this study was 0.35clo. In an experimental session, each pair was instructed to sit in a designated climatic condition for 15 minutes; each subject was then asked to complete a thermal comfort questionnaire before moving to the next setting. With this procedure all the eight subjects experienced within an hour approximately the same exposure conditions, so that the groups' average comfort responses, under the average climatic conditions in each setting during the same hour, could be obtained.

The microclimatic condition in each experimental setting was measured using a mobile meteorological station. The meteorological station included sensors for measuring air temperature, globe temperature, wind

Table 8.1 *Subjective scales used in the questionnaires*

Thermal sensation: How do you feel with respect to heat and cold?

Very hot	Hot	Too warm	Neutral	Too cool	Cold	Very cold
3	2	1	0	−1	−2	−3

Exposure to the sun: How about exposure to the sun?

Sun makes me uncomfortable	Just fine	I'd like to get more sun
1	0	−1

Wind speed: How is the air in terms of wind?

Much too windy	Too windy	Slightly windy	Just OK	Slightly still	Too still	Stagnant
3	2	1	0	−1	−2	−3

Humidity of the air: How does the air feel?

Too humid	Just OK	Too dry
1	0	−1

Skin wetness: How is your skin in terms of wetness?

Drops of sweat	Moist	Normal	Dry	Very dry
2	1	0	−1	−2

Overall comfort

Very uncomfortable	Uncomfortable	Comfortable	Very comfortable
−2	−1	1	2

Source: Cheng (2008)

speed, relative humidity and solar radiation. Wind speed was measured using a hot wire anemometer. The questionnaire dealt with the subjects' sensations of the microclimatic environment and their overall comfort. The votes included subjective sensation or rating the attitude with respect to the thermal environment, solar intensity, wind speed, humidity of air, wetness of skin and overall comfort. A total of 190 questionnaires were included in the final analysis. The subjective scales are shown in Table 8.1.

Main finding of the research (from Cheng, 2008)

Thermal responses of subjects

Figure 8.2 (Cheng et al, 2007) shows the thermal responses of the subjects under the four different experimental conditions. The central category '0' (neutral thermal sensation) is often associated with the feeling of comfort.

As can be seen in Figure 8.2, setting 2 with sun exposure and suppressed wind speed has the lowest

percentage of comfortable votes, and was most frequently voted by the subjects as hot and very hot; on the other hand, the subjects in setting 1, with sun shade and exposure to the wind, had the highest percentage of comfortable votes and was least frequently voted hot.

When the subjects were exposed to direct sun and the wind in setting 4, the rate of neutral sensation vote dropped from 38 to 29 per cent. However, when the sun umbrella was retained but the wind was suppressed in setting 3, the rate of neutral sensation vote reduced remarkably from 38 to 19 per cent. It appears that wind was the most influential environmental factor in relating to the thermal responses of subjects in this research.

The effect of changing wind conditions

Figure 8.3 (Cheng et al, 2007) shows the effect of changing wind conditions on the thermal responses of subjects as a function of air temperature and with corresponding regression lines. The average wind speed in settings with a windbreak was approximately 0.3m/s,

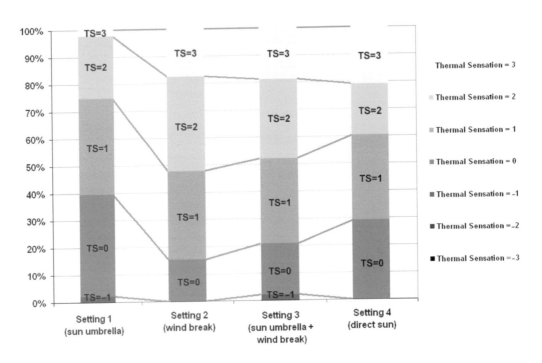

Figure 8.2 *Percentage of thermal responses of subjects at different climatic settings*

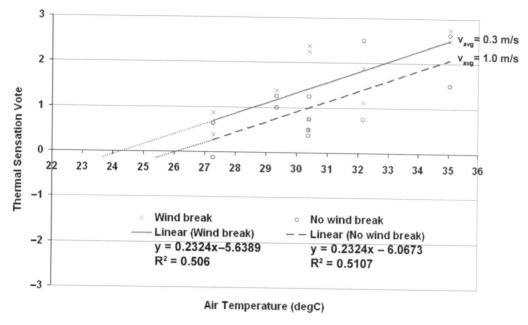

Source: Cheng et al (2007)

Figure 8.3 *Effect of changing wind conditions on thermal responses*

while that without a windbreak was about 1m/s. The average slope of the thermal responses with changes in the air temperature was 0.23 units/°C. The difference between the average thermal responses in the 'windbreak' and 'no windbreak' settings was 0.43 units. Thus, the effect of increasing wind speed from 0.3m/s to 1m/s was equivalent to about a 1.9°C drop in air temperature. This relative effect of wind speed is very close to the relative effects that were found in the indoor comfort studies of the City University of Hong Kong and the National University of Singapore, discussed below. Similar results were also obtained in the research in Thailand.

The highest wind speed measured in the exposed setting in this study was about 1.5m/s, reflecting the suppression of the regional winds by the high urban density of Hong Kong. Based on the data of the wind sensation vote, the subjects generally rated the wind speed, even without the windbreak, as less than appropriate. On average, the wind condition in settings with a windbreak was rated as too still, and that without a windbreak was rated as slightly still. This means that in climatic conditions common in Hong Kong, people

prefer wind speeds higher than 1.5m/s, suggesting that wind speeds of about 2m/s or even higher may be pleasant outdoors in this climate.

The effect of sun shading

Figure 8.4 (Cheng et al, 2007) shows the effect of changing sun-shading conditions on the thermal responses of subjects as a function of air temperature and with corresponding regression lines. The average solar radiation intensity in settings with sun shade was about 136W/m², while that without sun shade was about 300W/m². The average slope of the thermal responses with changes in the air temperature was 0.23 units/°C. The difference between the average thermal responses in the 'sun shade' and 'no sun shade' settings was 0.55 units. Therefore, it can be inferred that the effect of increasing solar radiation exposure from about 130W/m² to 300W/m² was equivalent to an approximately 2.4°C increase in air temperature.

Based on the data of the solar sensation vote, the subjects under shade, on average, rated the solar exposure condition as just fine. On the other hand, the

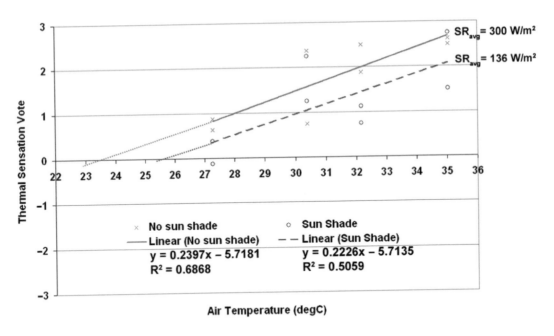

Source: Cheng et al (2007)

Figure 8.4 *Effect of changing sun-shading conditions on thermal responses*

subjects under direct sun exposure generally rated the solar exposure condition as slightly too much.

Thermal sensation and overall comfort

Figure 8.5 (Cheng et al, 2007) shows the relationship between thermal sensation (TS) and overall comfort as observed in this study. The overall comfort was rated on a four-point scale from –2 (very uncomfortable) to +2 (very comfortable). The neutral point zero has been taken out from the scale. Since the study was conducted in summer, the relationship shown in Figure 8.5 only represents the thermally warm scenarios.

Based on the data collected in this study, thermal sensation vote exhibits high correlation with overall comfort (R^2 = 0.82). The feeling of discomfort disappeared when the thermal condition was rated as cooler than slightly warm (TS < 1). Moreover, the comfort level increased as the thermal condition approaching the neutral sensation point (TS = 0). The regression line intercepts the y-axis at comfort rating equal to 1; it means that the subjects felt comfortable in thermally neutral conditions.

Predictive formula for thermal sensation vote

A multifactor regression analysis has been performed on the collected data. Based on the results, a formula for predicting the subjective thermal sensation vote has been developed. The formula is a function of air temperature, wind speed, solar radiation intensity and absolute humidity; the resulting formula is as follows:

$$TS = 0.1895 \times Ta - 0.7754 \times WS + 0.0028 \times SR + 0.1953 \times H - 8.23. \qquad [8.1]$$

TS is the predicted thermal sensation vote on a seven-point scale ranging from –3 (too cold) to +3 (too hot) with the thermally neutral sensation point at 0. Ta is the dry bulb air temperature in degrees Celsius; WS is the wind speed in m/s; SR is the solar radiation intensity in W/m²; and H is the absolute humidity in g/kg air.

Figure 8.6 (Cheng et al, 2007) shows the correlation between the thermal responses given by the subjects and those predicted by the formula. The correlation coefficient between the measured and

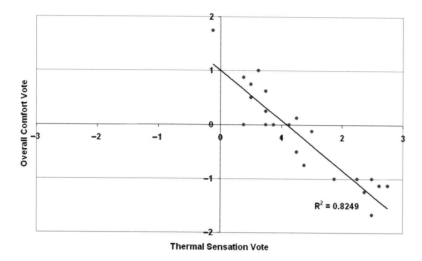

Source: Cheng et al (2007)

Figure 8.5 *Relationship between thermal sensation and overall comfort*

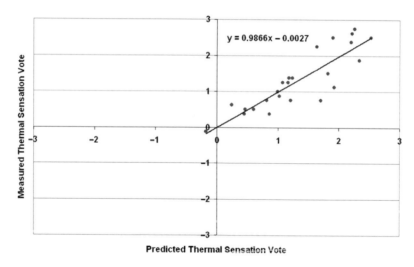

Source: Cheng et al (2007)

Figure 8.6 *Comparison of the measured and predicted thermal sensation*

the predicted data is 0.87. This suggests that the predictive formula performed well in estimating the thermal responses of subjects. However, it should be stressed that the formula was developed based on a very small number of subjects; therefore, it should be considered only as a rough indication of the subjective thermal sensation and may not be generalized to a larger population.

The formula provides a means for estimating the wind speed required to produce neutral thermal sensation in different environmental conditions. As an illustration, on a typical summer day in Hong Kong where air temperature is around 28°C and relative humidity 80 per cent, a person with light summer clothing sitting under shade will require a wind speed of 1.8m/s in order to obtain a neutral thermal sensation.

Indoor comfort research at the City University of Hong Kong

The objective of the research at the City University of Hong Kong (CityU) was to see if it would be possible to maintain indoor comfort, for persons acclimatized in the hot humid climate of Hong Kong, at higher temperatures and humidity levels than those currently practised in air-conditioned buildings in Hong Kong (Fong et al, 2008). The idea was to provide higher air speed, without the occurrence of uncomfortable draught. From both the thermal comfort and energy saving perspectives, it is essential to have an optimal setting of air temperature and air speed to provide comfortable but not overcooled buildings.

The research at the CityU was conducted in the environmental chamber of the university in August 2007. In this survey, 48 human subjects participated (24 males and 24 females) in the age group of 19 to 25. All of the subjects were requested to wear local typical summer clothing, including polo shirts, long trousers, underwear, socks and shoes. This would have an expected clo-value of 0.55. The air temperatures were between 25°C and 30°C, air speeds from 0.5m/s to 3m/s, and relative humidity of 50, 65 and 80 per cent.

Environmental chamber and equipment arrangement

A thermally insulated environmental chamber (7.9m × 5.9m × 2.4m) was used for this thermal comfort survey in the CityU, as shown in Figure 8.7 (Fong et al, 2008). Two existing fan coil units with room thermostats were installed for general air-conditioning purposes. There was a waiting area outside the environmental chamber, where the subjects could settle themselves down before the survey.

In each session, four subjects could be involved at the same time. Each subject had a working desk and sat comfortably to carry out light office work, such as reading and writing, during the survey period. There was a tower fan beside each person and the air speed

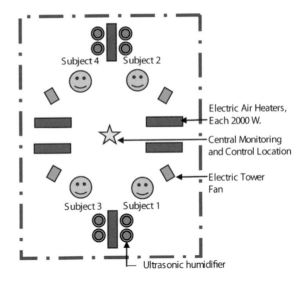

Source: Fong et al (2008)

Figure 8.7 *Layout of environmental chamber for thermal comfort survey*

could be changed according to the setting at 0.5m/s, 1m/s, 1.5m/s, 2m/s, 2.5m/s and 3m/s. The actual location of each fan was commissioned in the preparation stage. Four 2000W air heaters with a thermostat control were installed evenly inside the environmental chamber in order to provide the required temperature setting at 25°C, 26°C, 27°C, 28°C, 29°C and 30°C. Eight ultrasonic humidifiers were also installed and divided into two groups in order to maintain the prescribed humidity at 50, 65 and 80 per cent for different temperature settings without contributing any space-sensible heat gain. In each group of humidifiers, an additional air heater was used to enhance evaporation of the emitted water mist. In all, 108 climatic combinations of air temperature, air speed and relative humidity were tested in this study. In the whole research process, the air temperature, air speed, humidity, operative temperature and radiant temperature asymmetry were logged at the 0.6m level of the representative monitoring location inside the environmental chamber.

Each session of the study involved the six air speed settings at a certain temperature and humidity. The whole survey session lasted for 3.5 hours. Initially, the four human subjects had a rest in the waiting area outside the environmental chamber. Then they were briefed about the objectives and procedures of the thermal comfort survey, and asked to fill in their general information on the questionnaire. They were also asked to declare their health in good condition. Then the subjects were arranged to sit comfortably inside the environmental chamber so that they would perform a sedentary activity naturally.

The session for each air speed setting was conducted for 30 minutes in order to achieve the steadiness of thermal sensation. Throughout this 30-minute period, the subjects were asked to give their thermal sensation based on the American Society of Heating, Refrigerating and Air-Conditioning Engineers (ASHRAE) seven-point scale at five-minute intervals. Therefore, six thermal sensation responses would be collected for each air speed: altogether 36 responses for six air speeds in the entire three-hour survey session. The subjects did provide their responses in each sub-session independently, without the influence of the previous response.

A formula expressing the average thermal sensation of the group of four subjects in a session, as a function of air temperature, air speed and humidity ratio, was generated by multiple regression analysis:

$$TS = -9.3 + 0.3645 \times Ta - 0.6187 \times AS + 2.349 \times HR \quad [8.2]$$

where:

- TS = thermal sensation;
- Ta = air temperature (°C);
- AS = air speed (m/s);
- HR = humidity ratio (g/g).

The correlation coefficient (CC) between the observed and the computed thermal sensations is 0.9018.

Figure 8.8 shows the observed and the computed thermal sensations.

Figure 8.9 shows the average effect of air temperature on thermal sensation. As can be seen in Figure 8.9, the average elevation in the thermal sensation with temperature was 0.2245 units of TS/°C.

Figure 8.10 shows the average effect of air speed on thermal sensation. As can be seen in Figure 8.10, the average drop in thermal sensation with air speed was 0.4653 units of TS per m/s. Thus, the relative effect of air speed on thermal sensation, relative to the effect of temperature, is 0.4653/0.2245 = 2.1. This relative

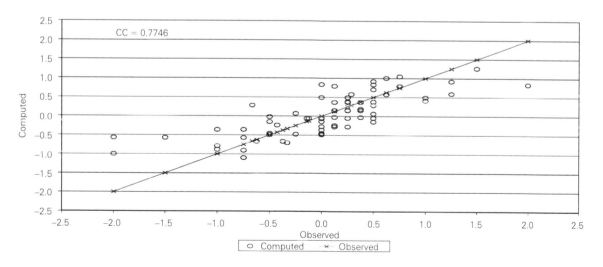

Source: Author, based on the data of Kwong Fai Fong, Tin Tai Chow and B. Givoni

Figure 8.8 *Observed and computed thermal sensations in the comfort study at the City University of Hong Kong*

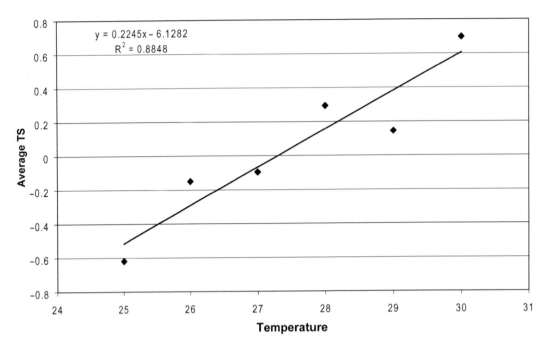

Source: Author, based on the data of Kwong Fai Fong, Tin Tai Chow and B. Givoni

Figure 8.9 *Average effect of air temperature on thermal sensation*

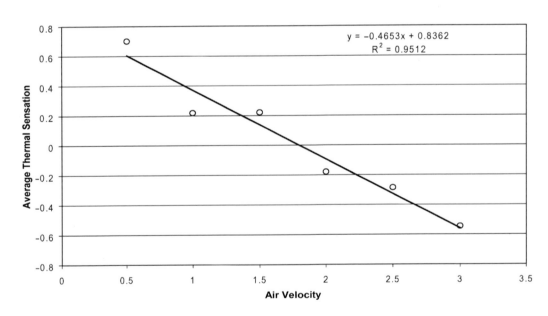

Source: Author, based on the data of Kwong Fai Fong, Tin Tai Chow and B. Givoni

Figure 8.10 *Average effect of air speed on thermal sensation*

effect is very close to the one found in the outdoor comfort studies discussed in this chapter.

Comfort research in Singapore

Two comfort studies were conducted at the National University of Singapore (NUS). The first study was a controlled research experiment in a climatic chamber and the second study was a 'once through' comfort survey of occupants in their residences.

Climatic chamber research in Singapore

A semi-lab comfort research experiment was conducted in the climatic chamber of the National University of Singapore (Wong and Tanamas, 2002). Air conditioning controlled the air temperature and humidity conditions. Wind speeds of 0m/s, 0.2m/s, 0.5m/s, 1.0m/s, 2.0m/s, 3.0m/s and 4.0m/s were generated by the wind-tunnel fans. The globe temperature of the chamber was also measured. The experiment was carried out between 22 August and 1 September 2001. The range of the air temperatures in this study was from about 22°C to 29°C. The range of relative humidity was from 45 to 75 per cent, with a corresponding range of humidity ratio from 7g/kg to 19g/kg.

The experimental subjects were 16 males and 16 females. The subjects were divided into eight groups with each group consisting of two males and two females. Each group was required to attend two sessions in the study. The first session represented the lower range of air temperature, mean radiant temperature and relative humidity conditions while the second session represented the higher range of air temperature, mean radiant temperature and relative humidity conditions. Thus, a total of 28 different experimental conditions, in which they had no control, were experienced by each subject.

The data on the subjective variables experienced by the subjects were collected by means of questionnaire surveys. The votes of thermal sensations of the subjects were according to the following seven-point scale:

- −3 = cold;
- −2 = cool;
- −1 = slightly cool;
- 0 = neutral;
- 1 = slightly warm;
- 2 = warm;
- 3 = hot.

A multiple regression formula was generated from the data of Wong and Tanamas (2002):

$$TS = 0.2358 \times Ta - 0.6707 \times AS + 0.0164 \times HR - 6.33 \qquad [8.3]$$

where:

- TS (scale) = thermal sensation;
- Ta = air temperature;
- °C;
- AS = air speed (m/s); and
- HR = humidity ratio (g/kg).

Figure 8.11 shows the groups' average thermal sensations as a function of the values computed by the formula. The measured sensations are marked differently, according to the air speeds. There is no separation between data with the different air speeds. The correlation coefficient (CC) between the computed and the measured TS is 0.9252.

From Equation 8.3 it is possible to evaluate the cooling effect of air speed relative to the effect of temperature: 0.5707/0.2358 = 2.8. It means that an increase of 1m/s in air speed has a cooling effect similar to that of a drop of 2.8°C in temperature. The very strong effect of air speed can be seen in Figure 8.12, which shows the thermal sensation as a function of temperature, with different symbols for the different air speeds. People exposed to temperatures of 29°C and air speeds of 2m/s to 3m/s had about the same thermal sensation as people at 22°C and with an air speed of 0.2m/s.

It is of interest to see the effect of humidity, relative to the effect of air speed, in the Singapore study. Figure 8.13 shows the thermal sensations as a function of the humidity ratio, with different symbols for the different air speeds. The elevation of humidity ratio from 8g/kg to 19g/kg (a very large range) had a smaller effect than the reduction of 1m/s in the air speed.

Singapore comfort survey in residences

A comfort survey was also conducted in Singapore (Wong et al, 2002). The survey was designed as cross-sectional data collection (once-off sampling of many respondents) and it was conducted in the residences of the subjects. A total of 538 respondents participated in the Singapore survey, wearing the clothing they were used to at home. Physical measurements in each

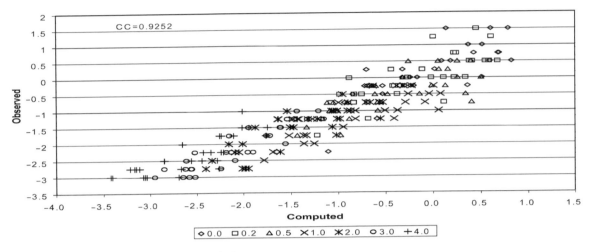

Source: Author, based on the data of N. H. Wong and J. Tanamas

Figure 8.11 *Measured and computed thermal sensations in the chamber study in Singapore*

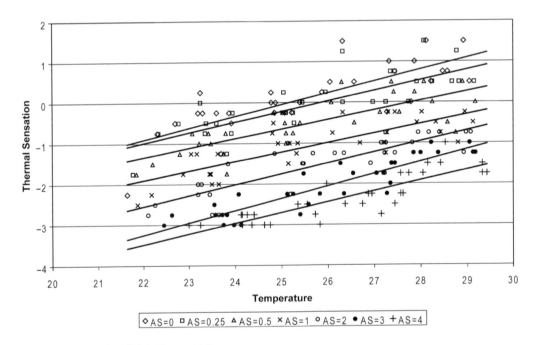

Source: Author, based on the data of N. H. Wong and J. Tanamas

Figure 8.12 *Thermal sensation as a function of temperature, with different symbols for the different air speeds*

dwelling included air temperature, relative humidity, globe temperature and wind speed.

The formula expressing the thermal sensation in the Singapore comfort survey is:

$$TS = 0.3253 \times Ta - 2.1116 \times AS^{0.5} + 0.1495 \times (Tg-Ta) + 0.0432 \times HR - 0.3,$$

with a correlation coefficient (CC) of 0.8360.

[8.4]

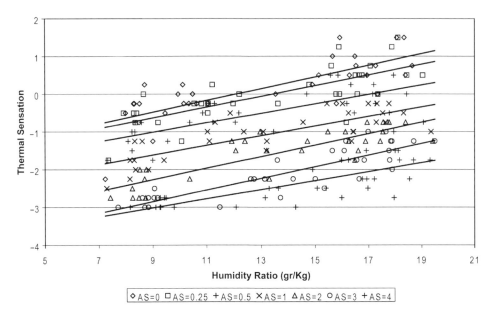

Source: Author, based on the data of N. H. Wong and J. Tanamas

Figure 8.13 *Thermal sensations as a function of the humidity ratio*

In order to see more clearly the relative effects of air speed and temperature on the comfort response (FEEL) of the occupants, the comfort response was expressed first as a function of temperature (see Figure 8.15) and then as a function of air speed (see Figure 8.16), and regression lines were generated in each case.

In the regression in Figure 8.15, the slope of the comfort response with temperature is 0.4561. In the

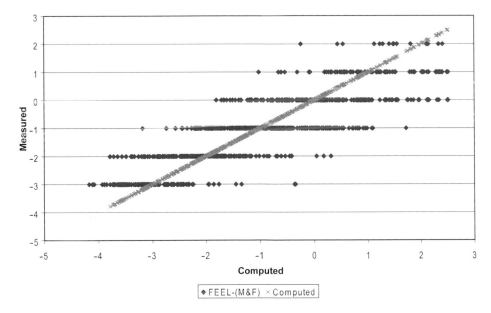

Source: Author, based on the data of N. H. Wong, H. Feriadi, P. Y. Lim, K. W. Tham, C. Sekhar and K. W. Cheong

Figure 8.14 *Observed and computed thermal sensations (FEEL) in the Singapore survey*

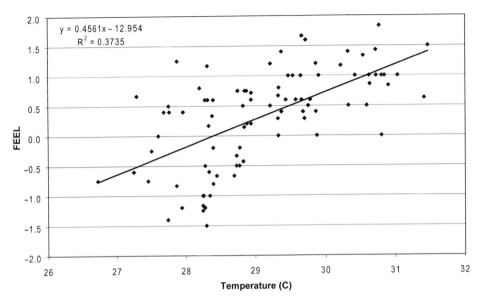

Source: Author, based on the data of N. H. Wong, H. Feriadi, P. Y. Lim, K. W. Tham, C. Sekhar and K. W. Cheong

Figure 8.15 *Comfort responses (FEEL) as a function of temperature*

regression of Figure 8.16, the slope of the comfort response with air speed is −1.28. Thus, the ratio of the cooling effect of the air speed to the heating effect of temperature is 1.28/0.4561 = 2.8.

It is of interest to note that the same values (2.8) of the ratio of air speed cooling effect to the heating effect of temperature rise were obtained in the two different comfort studies conducted by the National

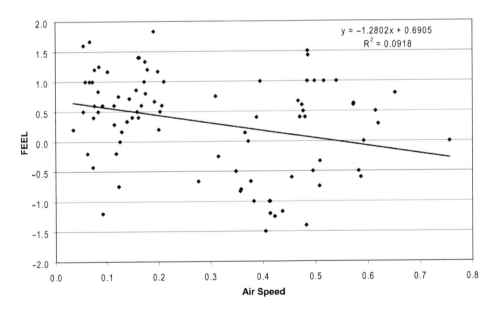

Source: Author, based on the data of N. H. Wong, H. Feriadi, P. Y. Lim, K. W. Tham, C. Sekhar and K. W. Cheong

Figure 8.16 *Comfort responses (FEEL) as a function of air speed*

University of Singapore, using very different research methodologies.

Research at King Mongkut University of Technology in Bangkok, Thailand

The Thailand research (Khedari et al, 2003) was conducted in a classroom. A total of 288 subjects (183 males and 105 females) took part in the study. Six subjects per group were in each experiment. Subjects wore normal clothing (0.54–0.55clo) and were engaged in sedentary activities. Indoor air temperature and humidity were determined by the naturally changing climatic conditions (free running). Variable indoor air speeds have been created by six desk fans. The speed controllers adjusted air speed individually for each subject, at one of six levels: 0.2m/s, 0.5m/s, 1.0m/s, 1.5m/s, 2.0m/s and 3.0m/s. The fans adjusted the air speed so that the speed was the same for all six subjects in each test. The votes of thermal sensations of the subjects were according to the following scale:

- −2 = cool;
- −1 = slightly cool;
-   0 = neutral;

- 1 = slightly warm;
- 2 = warm;
- 3 = hot;
- 4 = very hot.

In the Thailand study every subject had experienced directly the effect of changes in the wind speed under different conditions of temperature and humidity. An interaction was observed between the wind speed and the effect of temperature: as the wind speed increased, the effect of changes in temperature was reduced (smaller slope of regression lines). This interaction could be expressed by the following formula (Givoni et al, 2004):

$$\text{Slope} = 0.4441 - 0.0777 \times \text{WS}^{0.5} \times \quad \text{with } R^2 = 0.9973. \qquad [8.5]$$

The formula expressing the thermal sensation (TS) of the Thailand subjects as a function of the interaction between air temperature (Temp) and wind speed (WS) was:

$$\text{TS} = (0.444 - 0.0777 \times \text{WS}^{0.5}) \times \text{Temp} - 11, \text{ with a correlation coefficient of } 0.9418. \qquad [8.6]$$

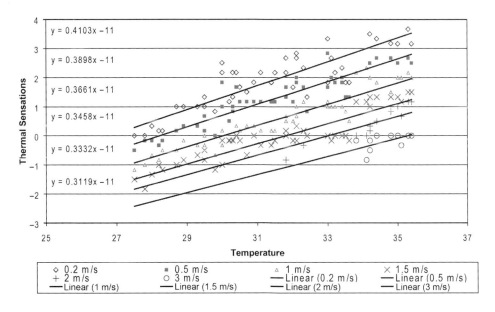

Source: Givoni et al (2004)

Figure 8.17 *Thermal sensations expressed as a function of temperature, with different symbols for the different wind speeds*

Figure 8.17 (Givoni et al, 2004) shows the thermal sensations expressed as a function of temperature, with different symbols for the different wind speeds.

It can be seen in Figure 8.17 that the neutral temperature (TS = 0) with a wind speed of 0.5m/s is about 28°C; with 1m/s it is about 29.5°C; with 1.5m/s it is about 31.5°C; and with a wind speed of 2m/s it is about 32.5°C. Thus, on average, an increase of wind speed of 1m/s has a cooling effect greater than a decrease of 2°C in temperature, similar to the results in the other comfort studies discussed above.

Figure 8.18 (Givoni et al, 2004) shows the measured thermal sensation as a function of the computed values, with the different air speeds marked differently. The correlation coefficient between the measured and the computed values is 0.9418.

Conclusions: Implications for building design and urban planning

As indicated above, in the discussion of comfort issues in high-density cities, the main urban climatic features in such cities that affect thermal comfort are the lower urban wind speed and the higher temperatures – the urban heat island (UHI) – compared with the climatic conditions in low-density cities located in a similar climate. The common finding in all of the comfort studies reviewed in this chapter is the large impact of

air speed upon comfort, both indoors and outdoors. In all of these studies it was found that increasing the air speed by 1m/s had a cooling effect equivalent to lowering the temperature by more than 2°C. This finding has implications for high-density cities, both in terms of urban planning and in terms of building design, in all types of climates. However, the actual implications are different in hot and in cold climates.

Implications in hot climates

Comfort issues are somewhat different in hot dry and in hot humid climates. In hot dry climates the daytime summer temperatures are often around and above 40°C and thus the houses should not be ventilated during the hot hours. In many hot dry regions, dust storms, especially during the afternoon hours, are common, making it necessary to close windows even if the outdoor temperatures are comfortable. Whenever indoor temperatures in the closed buildings are uncomfortable, a higher indoor air speed, produced by ceiling fans or other types of fans, can significantly improve the comfort of inhabitants or reduce the level of their discomfort. In most hot humid regions, on the other hand, summer temperatures are lower and the humidity is higher. Under these conditions natural ventilation is more important for comfort (Givoni, 1991).

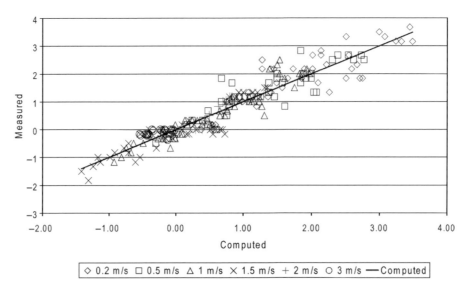

Source: Givoni et al (2004)

Figure 8.18 *Measured and computed thermal sensation in the Thailand study*

From the viewpoint of enhancing comfort in high-density cities located in hot humid climates, the findings of the comfort studies reviewed in this chapter call for ensuring the best urban ventilation conditions possible under regional wind conditions and a high-density situation. Street layout and orientation should enable the penetration of the regional winds into the interior of the built-up area. Open spaces between building blocks should take into account the regional wind directions in order to enable wind flow between and around buildings. This will improve the ventilation potential of the buildings and the comfort of the occupants of the buildings.

Enhancing comfort in private and public parks in hot regions

Comfort objectives of landscaping in hot regions, especially in hot humid climates, should be as follows:

* Minimize the blockage of wind by plants.
* Provide shade for the users of public parks.
* Lower air and ground surface temperatures compared with built-up areas.

In hot dry climates there is another comfort objective in public parks: minimize the dust level.

The impact of green areas on temperatures, within the green areas and around them, is discussed in Chapter 16, where the emphasis is on the impact of plants on wind conditions. The impact of plants on human comfort in hot areas can be a mixed bag. Shading provided by trees is always welcome. However, blockage of wind and the contribution to humidity at ground level by evaporation from the leaves of plants may increase human discomfort, especially during hours with still air and with high humidity.

Trees with a high trunk and a wide canopy are the most effective plants in providing usable shade. If densely placed on the windward side of a house they block the wind. Therefore, the best strategy with such trees is to have them only in spots where their shade will be utilized without blocking the wind, such as near the walls but not in front of windows. Pergolas of vines in front of and above windows can also provide effective shading without blocking the wind. If the trees and the vines are deciduous, they enable daylight and solar gain in winter. However, one should be careful to prevent low-growing trees and high shrubs in front of windows on the windward sides of building. Such plants can, in effect, act as windbreak and greatly reduce the ventilation potential.

High shrubs and trees with low trunks block the wind and 'contribute' to the humidity level without providing useful shade. According to the research of Potchter et al (1999), in a small urban park in Tel Aviv, Israel, it was demonstrated that in an area surrounded by low trees the wind speed was lower and the temperature and humidity were higher than in an area under trees with high trunks ('well trees') or in open grassed area. Figure 8.19 shows the temperature in the areas with different plants in this small park (Potchter et al, 1999). Therefore, the introduction of high shrubs and low trees should be minimal, especially at the windward parts of the site, except when they are placed alongside walls without windows. A combination of grasses, low flower beds and shade trees with high trunks is, thus, the most appropriate plant combination in landscaping in hot humid climates.

Implications for building design in high-density cities in cold climates

Cold cities are defined in this chapter as cities located in regions where the main comfort issues occur during winter. With this definition, cold cities can be divided into two types, according to their summer climate:

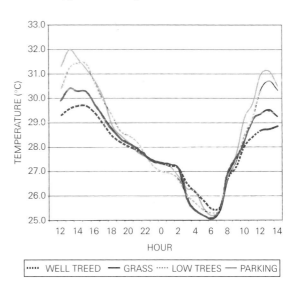

Source: Potchter et al (1999)

Figure 8.19 *Temperatures in areas with different plants in a small park in Tel Aviv*

1   regions where the summers are cool or comfortable;
2   regions with hot summers (often hot humid summers).

During the winter, the main comfort implications for urban and building design, in both types, are protection from wind and access to the sun. In cold cities, buildings are usually well insulated, so that comfort issues are mainly related to the outdoors and concern pedestrians in the street and people using public parks.

Comfort issues during the summer, in cities with the two types of summer climate, may be different. In cities with cool or comfortable summers, the main planning and design considerations are governed by winter comfort needs. On the other hand, in cold cities with hot summers, especially hot humid summers, there seems to be a conflict between the need for wind protection in winter and the comfort need for enhanced urban ventilation in summer. Fortunately, in most regions with cold winters and hot summers there is a clear change in the main wind direction during the two seasons. In the northern hemisphere, the cold winter winds are mainly from the north, while the hot summer winds are mainly from the south. This situation enables urban planners and building designers to have urban schemes protected from the north and open to the south, and thus to meet the comfort needs in both seasons. U-shape configurations open to the south (in the northern hemisphere), both of buildings and of urban blocks, offer a very attractive design solution. They provide protection from the winter winds, are open to the summer winds and provide some exposure to the low winter sun.

A special comfort problem may occur when high buildings are located next to lower buildings. Wind striking the high building, at levels above the height of the lower buildings located upwind, causes a strong wind flowing downward. This air down-flow may cause severe discomfort even in comfortable climates.

Concerning urban parks, although the main season in which parks are used by the public in cold regions is the summer, they may also be used in winter for such outdoor activities as ice skating, etc. The main climatic considerations in the design of public parks are protection from wind and exposure to the sun in winter. U-shaped belts of evergreen high shrubs and low trees open to the south, around rest areas and areas

mostly used by the public, can thus provide optimum comfort both in winter and summer.

References

Cheng, V. (2008) *Urban Climatic Map and Standards for Wind Environment: Feasibility Study*, Technical Input Report No 1: Methodologies and Findings of User's Wind Comfort Level Survey, November, Chinese University, Hong Kong.

Cheng, V., Ng, E. and Givoni, B. (2007) 'Outdoor thermal comfort for Hong Kong people: A longitudinal study', in *Proceedings of the 24th Passive and Low Energy Architecture (PLEA 2007) Conference*, November 2007, Singapore

Fong, K. F., Chow, T. T. and Givoni, B. (2008) *Optimal Air Temperature and Air Speed for Built Environment in Hong Kong from Thermal Comfort and Energy Saving Perspectives*, World Sustainable Building Conference, Australia, September

Givoni, B. (1971) *Man, Climate and Architecture*, Elsevier Publishing Co, London (second enlarged edition) (French translation, 1978; paperback edition, 1981; Chinese translation, 1987)

Givoni, B. (1991) 'Impact of planted areas on urban environment quality: A review', *Atmospheric Environment*, vol 25B, no 3, pp289–299

Givoni, B. and R. F. Goldman. (1971) Predicting metabolic energy cost, *Journal of Applied Physiology*, vol 30, no 3, pp429–433

Givoni, B., Noguchi, M., Saaroni, H., Pochter, O., Yaacov, Y., Feller, N. and Becker, S. (2003) 'Outdoor comfort research issues', *Energy and Buildings*, vol 35, pp77–86

Givoni, B., Khedari, J. and Hirunlabh, J. (2004) *Comfort Formula for Thailand*, Proceedings, ASES 2004 Conference, July, Portland, OR, pp1113–1117

Khedari, J., Yamtraipat, N., Pratintong, N., and Hirunlabh, J. (2003) 'Thailand ventilation comfort chart', *Energy and Buildings*, vol 32, no 3, pp245–250.

Potchter, O., Yaacov Y. and Bitan A. 1999. 'Daily and seasonal climatic behavior of small urban parks in a Mediterranean climate: A case study of Gan-Meir Park, Tel-Aviv, Israel', in *Proceedings of the 15th International Congress of Biometeor and International Conference on Urban Climatology*, Sydney, Australia, 8–12 November; ICUC 6.3

Wong, N. H. and Tanamas, J. (2002) 'The effect of wind on thermal comfort in naturally ventilated environment in the tropics', in T. H. Karyono, F. Nicol and S. Roaf (eds) *Proceedings of the International Symposium on Building Research and the Sustainability of the Built Environment in the Tropics*, Jakarta, Indonesia, 14 October, pp192, 206

Wong, N. H., Feriadi, H., Lim, P. Y., Tham, K. W., Sekhar, C. and Cheong, K. W. (2002) 'Thermal comfort evaluation of naturally ventilated public housing in Singapore', *Building and Environment*, vol 37, pp1267–1277

9

Urban Environment Diversity and Human Comfort

Koen Steemers and Marylis Ramos

Introduction

This chapter explores the relationships between urban form and human comfort. It starts by identifying the ways in which this area of research falls into the gap between theoretical modelling and empirical fieldwork. The argument is that environmental diversity in real urban spaces is the result of a complex urban morphology, and that this diversity correlates with freedom of choice and an overall expression of comfort. Based on the monitoring, surveying and modelling of 14 urban sites in Europe and a database of nearly 10,000 respondents to outdoor comfort surveys, this hypothesis is tested and implications for high-density cities are discussed. Spatial and temporal environmental diversity is defined in simple terms – related to parameters of temperature, sun and wind – using graphic image-processing techniques and computer-aided design (CAD) models by way of demonstration. We aim, thus, to reveal potential relationships between urban climatology, on the one hand, and human comfort in outdoor spaces, on the other. These relationships are mediated by urban built form. Urban forms are described – typically by physical scientists – in various ways, including density (e.g. floor–area ratio); height-to-width ratios; roughness; or as regular arrays of blocks. Alternatively, urban form is represented by case study cities, urban neighbourhoods or public spaces, etc. and thus is also explored in social-scientific terms. Both approaches provide valuable insights: the former offering generic correlations between physical parameters such as height-to-width

ratios of streets and the maximum urban heat island temperature, and the latter giving information related to more complex and real urban microclimates as well as the people within them. Both approaches can be useful with respect to urban planning, although there is a risk that the two sectors remain separate: one addressing physical science aspects and the other focusing on the social and behavioural.

Pearlmutter et al (2006) exemplify the former technical approach, where meticulous analysis of regular urban arrays is used to predict theoretical comfort in the centre of the street as a function of height-to-width ratios and orientation. This is then used to explore the comfort implications of different urban forms. For example, such work for hot arid climates shows that north–south streets are theoretically better than west–east streets.

Nikolopoulou and Lykoudis (2006) represent the other end of the spectrum where the focus is on empirical evidence from surveying human comfort in real urban spaces while monitoring the physical parameters traditionally associated with thermal comfort (air and globe temperature, wind, etc.). However, discussion of urban form in this work is limited. The key finding of such research is that outdoor comfort is determined by a complex combination of physical and psychological conditions presented by the urban environment. The implications are that the urban context is even further removed from comfort-chamber research findings than the interior environment of a building: in other words, the physiology of human comfort can only partially explain comfort perception in the urban environment.

This chapter, then, highlights the links between the physical effects of built form, on the one hand, and the perception of comfort on the other. The correlation between diversity and average comfort votes is shown to be strong by comparison to correlations between singular physical parameters of comfort. It is suggested that this is because environmental diversity in urban settings leads to a greater freedom of choice and, thus, greater comfort.

Background

A key variable that has a significant bearing on comfort is choice, sometimes expressed as 'perceived control' (e.g. Campbell, 1983; Paciuc, 1990; Nikolopoulou and Lykoudis, 2006) or 'adaptive potential' (e.g. Baker and Standeven, 1996; de Dear et al, 1997). Most of the research to date, including almost all of the above references, relate to interior environments and are used to explain differences between physiological models and actual comfort. Typically, 'control' in these cases is related to human interactions with the building (e.g. opening windows and drawing blinds) and its environmental systems (e.g. light switching and thermostat adjustments). An overview of findings from research in this field suggests that the more control the user has, even if this control is perceived and not exercised, the greater the tolerance is to swings away from theoretical comfort, particularly where these swings are supported by expectations (Baker, 2004).

Thus, research in comfort chambers, offering the occupants an artificial environment with extremely constrained (if any) freedom of choice, gives results that are dramatically different from real building environments. One suspects that the difference is even greater with respect to outdoor environments. However, this latter point is not evident: do outdoor conditions present more adaptive opportunities and choice than indoor environments? Nikolopoulou and Lykoudis (2006) suggest that 'actual control over the microclimate is minimal, perceived control having the biggest weighting'. It is true that opportunities for control at a given point in an urban environment (e.g. the deployment of parasols or windbreaks) are less than in adaptive interiors. However, this may be more than compensated for by the fundamental choice to be outside or not, as well as the spatial range of conditions that can be chosen compared to an interior (where

spatial location is fixed in a typical office context). This spatial variability might mean that someone can choose to move into or out of the sun, the breeze, etc. in order to improve their comfort conditions. Furthermore, there is a greater freedom of choice regarding clothing (office culture often dictating dress codes), physical activity (i.e. sitting, walking or exercising all affecting metabolic rate) and food or drink consumption (also affecting metabolic rate). The above physical parameters related to choice can be shown to contribute significantly to physiological comfort. Work by Baker and Standeven (1996) demonstrates that even minor incremental alterations to temperature, wind speed, clothing and metabolic rate have a pronounced effect on comfort.

The notion of spatial choices influencing comfort is further demonstrated by the study of traditional courtyard houses in a hot arid climate. Merghani (2004) shows that the temperatures chosen by the occupants from the range available in courtyard houses clearly tend to be those nearer the comfort zone. Furthermore, he demonstrates that the courtyard is occupied during the season and time of day in a way that corresponds to the most comfortable temperature conditions. Such spatially adaptive inhabitation is particularly noteworthy because it is integrated within a clearly established set of domestic rituals of the region, culture and religion. This is not to say that there is climatic determinism with respect to the design and use of space, but that socio-cultural and environmental behaviour are closely intertwined.

The evidence from the examples discussed above suggests that offering an appropriate range of conditions can improve comfort and that people will tend to exercise their freedom of choice to do so. Does the urban microclimate in real and complex built form, as opposed to simplified arrays, offer this diversity, and can this help to explain why reported comfort is far greater than physiological comfort? This chapter draws on two approaches to explore this question:

1   detailed data from comfort surveys;
2   simplified models of urban climatic conditions.

Monitoring outdoor comfort

The approach adopted for this study is to monitor and survey a large number of people who choose to stay in a wide range of urban spaces. Much of this work stems from the European research project RUROS (Rediscovering the Urban Realm and Open Spaces), which addresses socio-economic and environmental issues with respect to the use of outdoor space. Apart from thermal aspects, the visual and acoustic perspectives were included in the assessment of comfort in sites across Europe. Overall, a total of 14 sites were studied and nearly 10,000 people were surveyed over a period of 15 months. Cities included in the research covered the range of latitudes from 38 to 54 degrees throughout Europe, including: Athens (Greece), Thessaloniki (Greece), Milan (Italy), Fribourg (Switzerland), Kassel (Germany), Cambridge (UK) and Sheffield (UK). The sites represent a range of urban morphologies and conditions, from compact medieval cores to large contemporary open squares.

The microclimate was monitored using portable weather stations, such as the one in Figure 9.1 developed in Cambridge.

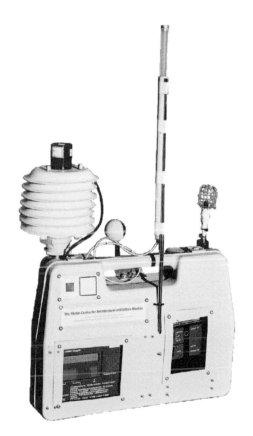

Source: Authors

Figure 9.1 *Portable field monitoring kit*

This portable kit was designed to have a fast response and to be lightweight in order to encourage easy mobility and, thus, proximity to the locations of each interview. As a result the physical measurements were directly related to each individual survey and thus represented conditions in each respondent's spatial location and their available choice (where they had one) of environmental conditions. Pedestrians are not central to this study and present an interesting challenge in terms of monitoring and transient effects of conditions. Readings were recorded at 5-second intervals. It was found that the standard black globe thermometer for indoor use had a response time that was too slow and, thus, the data risked lagging behind the time of the actual interviews, particularly noticeable when moving from sunny to shady conditions and back again. For this study we used a globe thermometer with a shorter response time appropriate for outdoor use, replacing the traditional thicker black plastic globe with a thin ball with a grey coating, representative of average clothing reflectance. This aspect of the research is reported in detail in a paper by Nikolopoulou et al (1999).

The fieldwork covered representative periods for each season for a minimum length of one week and for four two-hour sections of the day (morning, midday, afternoon and evening). This allowed seasonal and diurnal variations to be observed, as well as changes in weekly patterns (e.g. differences between weekdays and weekends).

The fieldwork consisted of both environmental monitoring and surveys of people. The thermal comfort-related parameters that were monitored include air temperature, globe temperature, solar radiation, wind speed and humidity. Additional acoustic and luminous data were also collected, but are not discussed in this chapter.

The surveys consisted of two parts: a questionnaire and an observation sheet. The questionnaire recorded various aspects of people's perception of the environment on a five-point or three-point scale. Thus, the scale for thermal sensation is: very cold; cool; neither cool nor warm; warm; and very hot. Questions related to temperature, sun, wind, humidity and overall thermal comfort. Alongside the structured questions related to thermal, visual and aural comfort, issues of social background and those related to space use (such as reasons for being in the space, how long they had been there, etc.) were also addressed through semi-structured questions. The observation sheet allowed the interviewer to record location, date and time, clothing levels, activity, food or drink consumption, etc.

A point to raise is that the population available for interview is, to an extent, self-selecting. This is particularly noticeable on cold winter days in Northern Europe when the population size is substantially lower than on summer days. For example, average interview numbers in Kassel and Cambridge dropped from 321 in summer to 80 in winter. However, this change was not noticed in Fribourg, where, in fact, the population peaked in the winter, partially due to mild conditions and perhaps because the people are more used to going outdoors during the winter skiing season. Furthermore, the population that was easiest to interview consisted of people who were standing or sitting still in the space, rather than passing through. The results show that a large proportion of those interviewed – 75 per cent, on average, for all cities – reported being comfortable. This figure was lowest (43 per cent) for Kassel in the winter.

Results of surveys

Despite the above limitations, the project represents a wealth of valuable information – probably the largest database of its kind – that is beginning to reveal new insights related to outdoor comfort. An overview of the project has been published (Nikolopoulou, 2004), with visual comfort findings discussed by Compagnon and Goyette (2005) and acoustic conditions detailed in numerous publications (Yang and Kang, 2005a and 2005b; Kang, 2006).

This chapter draws on the responses to the thermal comfort questions and uses these 'actual sensation votes' (ASVs) for the thermal conditions recorded from the interviews. The ASVs, as opposed to the predicted mean vote (a theoretical measure of comfort based on physiological parameters), provides a true measure of comfort in the sites. This database is used to study actual comfort in real urban contexts.

It is noticeable that a significant proportion of the responses lie in the comfort zone between cool and warm, reflecting the fact that 75 per cent of respondents said that they were comfortable. This is particularly interesting to note in the context of the wide variations of microclimatic conditions measured during the interviews. Past work on outdoor comfort has suggested that there is a wide discrepancy between physiological comfort as defined by indoor comfort theory, and actual comfort reported in outdoor spaces (Nikolopoulou and Steemers, 2003). This is confirmed in this study which shows that the correlation between the surveyed ASV (actual sensation vote) and the calculated PMV (predicted mean vote, defined in ISO 7730) or TSV (thermal sensation vote, based on the effective temperature – ET) has a correlation coefficient (R) of only 0.32 and 0.37, respectively.

Backward stepwise regression was used to determine which variables from the data set – including air temperature, globe temperature, wind speed, relative humidity, mean radiant temperature, metabolic rate and clo value – could be used to predict the actual thermal sensation vote, or ASV. Using this method, it was determined that the parameters that had the most influence on the prediction of the ASV were:

- globe temperature;
- wind speed;
- relative humidity;
- mean radiant temperature.

Using multiple linear regression, the following equation was obtained, which shows the relationship of these variables to ASV:

$$ASV = -1.465 + (0.0332 \times tglobe) - (0.0761 \times vel) + (0.00256 \times rh) + (0.0233 \times mrt) \qquad [9.1]$$

where:

- $tglobe$ = globe temperature (°C);
- vel = wind speed (m/s);
- rh = relative humidity (percentage);
- mrt = mean radiant temperature (°C) (calculated using the ASHRAE formula).

This equation has a correlation coefficient (R) of 0.516, and a coefficient of determination (R^2) of 0.266: relatively low, suggesting that the temperate conditions exert only a modest influence on comfort (in more extreme conditions one would expect these coefficients to be higher). R^2_{adj}, which is the R^2 adjusted to take into consideration the number of independent variables, is also 0.266. The standard error is 0.778. All of the variables appear to be positively correlated to ASV with the exception of wind speed, which is inversely correlated in this data set. An analysis of variance (ANOVA) test shows that F = 863.892. The F-test statistic gauges the ability of the regression equation, containing all independent variables, to predict the dependent variable. If F is a large number, as it is here, it may be concluded that the independent variables contribute to the prediction of the dependent variable. An F value of 1.0 means that there is no association between the variables.

In summary, the actual responses for all the sites correlate best with the globe temperature, which is itself a function of the radiant conditions and air temperature. Wind is also perceived as a significant variable. This is confirmed in the statistical analysis of a similar data set carried out by Nikolopoulou and Lykoudis (2006), which shows that ASV correlates better with globe temperature (R = 0.53) than air temperature (R = 0.43), and that solar radiation (R = 0.23) and wind speed (R = 0.26) also play a role.

Overall, the theoretical equation for ASV shown above correlates reasonably well with the actual data, with a correlation of R = 0.51, which is an improvement on R = 0.32 for the PMV calculation based on the same data. For cooler climates (notably Switzerland and the UK) the equation results in better correlation (see Tables 9.1 and 9.2). The ASV correlation is improved to R = 0.61 when using country-specific versions of the equation.

The t-values in Table 9.2 summarize the significant parameters for each of the case study locations. A common trend across all ASV equations is that wind speed is inversely proportional to the thermal sensation vote, which strongly indicates that as wind speeds decrease, the voting approaches 'warm' or 'hot', which makes a lot of sense. Also, at least one thermal variable, whether it be globe temperature, air temperature or mean radiant temperature, is always significant in the ASV equation, as is wind speed.

Mapping urban diversity

The physical parameters outlined above – particularly those to do with radiation, temperature and wind – go some way in explaining reported comfort in outdoor spaces, with the remaining spread of results usually being explained in terms of adaptive processes. One might expect there to be a link between a measure of the diversity of physical parameters and the perceived control in terms of the range of choices that is available, which is what we explore next in this chapter.

What we will aim to achieve in the next part of this chapter is to:

- define urban environmental diversity in terms of temperature, radiation and wind conditions;
- explore the correlation between environmental diversity for the urban spaces and reported comfort in those space.

Table 9.1 *Summary of correlation indicators for all actual sensation vote (ASV) equations*

	Greece	Switzerland	Italy	UK	Germany
R	0.511	0.696	0.568	0.691	0.502
R^2	0.261	0.484	0.322	0.477	0.253
R^2_{adj}	0.260	0.484	0.319	0.476	0.250
Standard Error	0.808	0.607	0.558	0.763	0.544
F	191.877	900.475	110.994	355.957	66.827

Source: Authors

Table 9.2 *Summary of t-values for all ASV equations*

Variable	Greece	Switzerland	Italy	UK	Germany
tair	insignificant	insignificant	10.110	insignificant	insignificant
tglobe	10.398	42.332	insignificant	17.068	3.312
vel	−6.854	−4.747	−8.670	−4.611	−3.318
rh	7.271	insignificant	insignificant	−4.390	insignificant
mrt	8.460	insignificant	7.801	3.168	2.808

Source: Authors

The aim is to see if it is possible to graphically map environmental diversity over space (an urban area) and time (seasonally or annually) initially in simple terms to demonstrate the principles. Given that outdoor thermal comfort has been shown to correlate primarily to globe temperature (incorporating air temperature and radiant energy) and wind, it is not unreasonable to suggest that temperature difference, sunshine hours and wind patterns might be useful simplified indicators. The reason for opting for these indicators is that we are primarily interested in variance over space and time, and not concerned with absolute values at a given moment in time. If the latter issues were of interest then existing models, such as ENVI-met, CTTC, CFD or Radiance, could be appropriate for detailed simulation of urban conditions. The aim here is to demonstrate in principle a simplified method of defining diversity and exploring the implications: a proof of concept rather than a simulation tool.

The advantage of using temperature difference, sunshine availability and wind as variables is that they are all relatively easily defined in relation to urban form. We note that peak temperature difference can be assessed in terms of height-to-width ratios (H/W) or sky view factors (SVFs) (Oke, 1987). It is also clear that sunshine will create areas of shade as a function of urban built form and can be determined using simple solar geometry. Finally, wind in urban environments, though complex, can be based on prevailing wind conditions (which vary seasonally in direction and frequency) and can be modelled using increasingly readily available software. However, combining even these three simplified parameters is rarely carried out at the urban scale.

In the first instance, the approach to modelling a range of urban parameters was to use digital elevation models (DEMs) of urban form and analyse them using image-processing techniques. This method is reported in detail in a series of papers dealing with the theory (Ratti and Richens, 2004), microclimatic parameters (Steemers et al, 1997; Baker and Ratti, 1999), energy (Ratti et al, 2005) and wind (Ratti et al, 2006). The analysis of the DEMs has generally been carried out using Matlab software – in particular, its image-processing toolbox in combination with sophisticated graphics outputs that can then reveal the result on a pixel-by-pixel basis for an urban area. The software allows simple algorithms to be written to determine SVFs and hourly shadows, but it is not appropriate to assess wind patterns within the urban area. As a result, the work has more recently used existing CAD and

image-based software, notably 3D Studio and Maya, which are common tools used in architecture and other design professions. Maya has a simple wind modeller that uses Navier-Stokes equations and is adequate for the purpose of demonstrating the strategic ideas of diversity discussed here, although more sophisticated computational fluid dynamics (CFD) modelling would provide greater accuracy and detail. The input data are based on hourly wind directions and frequency for each location and presented in terms of wind shadows (defined here as those areas where wind is reduced to less than 20 per cent of the synoptic wind speed data).

Each of the 14 sites in Europe has been modelled for days that represent each of the seasons and for the year overall. To reduce the number of figures in this chapter, the method is demonstrated for one site; but the overall results and correlations that are presented include all 14 sites. Using a site in Cambridge as an example, the mapping of SVFs, annual hourly shadows and annual hourly wind shadows is shown below (see Figure 9.2). What becomes evident is that each image shows a complex range of conditions over the period of a year; but this is equally the case when considering individual days. In terms of the SVF, certain outdoor spaces are highly occluded, and thus with reduced temperature fluctuations, whereas other parts are much more open to the sky and thus will follow synoptic temperature swings more closely. Similarly, solar shading is dense over some areas but almost in continual sunlight only a matter of metres away. Wind patterns also reveal areas continually exposed to prevailing wind and other areas that are sheltered.

In order to draw a clear map of discreet combinations of the three parameters, it is useful to create threshold bands of values for each parameter. For the purpose of this exercise we will use binary conditions to demonstrate the concept: open–closed to the sky, sunny–shady and windy–still, as shown in Figure 9.3. The threshold values for this test are set at the mean value of the range for each parameter (e.g. six hours of sunlight). It would be possible to define threshold levels more precisely, ideally related to values of significance to perception (e.g. wind speeds below 0.2m/s are imperceptible), and to weight them separately; but in this chapter the aim is to see if a simplified definition of diversity has potential. The three simplified images in Figure 9.3 are combined to create a composite map of the range of environmental conditions, or the 'environmental diversity map' (see Figure 9.4).

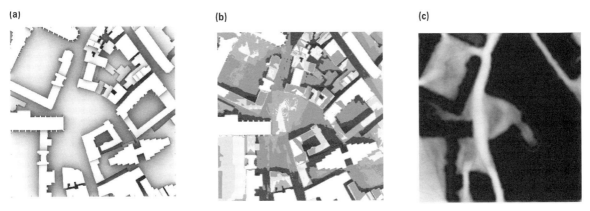

Source: Authors

Figure 9.2 *An example of the analysis of one of the urban case study areas, 200m × 200m (Cambridge), showing (a) sky view factors (SVFs); (b) solar shading; and (c) wind shadows*

Source: Authors

Figure 9.3 *Simplified threshold images of the data in Figure 9.2*

Source: Authors

Figure 9.4 *Environmental diversity map, which overlaps the maps in Figure 9.3*

An environmental diversity map can be created for any timeframe (hour, day, season or year) and for any urban configuration. A limitation is that currently the DEMs do not include colonnades or arcades below buildings, although they have been studied separately (Sinou and Steemers, 2004), nor the effects of trees, which can be used to significantly alter the urban microclimate.

Using image processing it is a simple step to create a graphical representation the diversity, which we refer

to as the 'diversity profile'. Figure 9.5 is an example of such a diversity profile, based on data extracted from Figure 9.4, and reveals the relative proportions of areas with certain environmental characteristics. In this example we can see that the 'closed–shaded–still' combination is largest, typical for dense medieval urban centres. Clearly such conditions may be particularly appropriate for hot arid climates where the 'closed' characteristic is correlated with cool islands, shade is clearly preferred and hot winds are

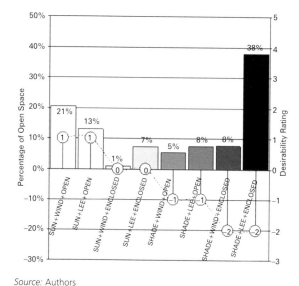

Source: Authors

Figure 9.5 *Diversity profile and weighting factors for the Cambridge site*

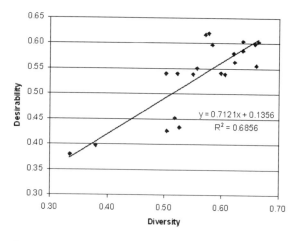

Source: Authors

Figure 9.6 *Diversity versus desirability for each period of the day, for each season and for the year overall, related to the Cambridge site*

ideally excluded. However, in more temperate climates such a condition is not so desirable with respect to outdoor comfort. Each variable, and combination of variables, may thus be desirable or not and is therefore rated according to the prevailing climatic context. Values for such 'desirability factors' have been adapted from Brown and DeKay (2001) – from 0 (undesirable), 1 (moderately undesirable), 2 (moderately desirable) to 3 (desirable) – and used to derive a 'desirability index' (Des) for each urban condition and time period.

The diversity profile can be reduced to a diversity factor, which we define simply as being related to the standard deviation between the columns in the diversity profile. A high diversity factor means that all combinations of environmental parameters are equally represented. Conversely, if the profile is strongly skewed with one combination of conditions being predominant, then the index is low. Figure 9.6 shows an example of the relationship between diversity and desirability for the one site in Cambridge with points representing each of the four periods in the day (morning, midday, afternoon and evening), for each season (summer, autumn, winter and spring), an average day for each season and average for the year. The graph suggests that there is a relationship between diversity (Div) and desirably (Des) with a relatively

strong correlation coefficient (R) of 0.83. Diversity is correlated to desirability, particularly in winter conditions, but less so for spring and autumn conditions. This is, in part, due to the fact that in winter the environmental desirability is suppressed because of low sun angles (with a resulting average Des = 0.48), whereas spring and autumn (with an average Des = 0.70) tend to result in more diversity. There are, however, interesting local effects that are best discussed with reference to the specific example.

Studying the sample data for the temperate climate of Cambridge city centre more closely, by way of an example, reveals that spring and autumn data score high desirability and winter low, the two lowest points being winter morning (Des = 0.40) and evening (Des = 0.38). Furthermore, within the seasons the midday desirability values are generally higher except in the summer where the value is lower than in the morning or afternoon. The highest desirability score is achieved during autumn and spring at midday (0.62), followed by autumn and spring mornings and afternoons (0.60). The overall ranking of seasons from highest to lowest desirability is autumn (0.60), spring (0.58), summer (0.55) and, finally, winter (0.43), with a significantly lower score. The annual overall desirability score is 0.54, which is at the low end of the range of the 14 sites where values range from 0.53 to 0.74. These insights are valuable as they suggest that this piece of urban form responds moderately well under most climatic conditions except winter, and this could have implications for planning strategies. However, further detailed analysis and comparisons of all the sites, urban forms and data are warranted and will be reported in future publications.

The next step in the research is to explore whether what is modelled as diverse actually has some relationship with the reported comfort (ASV) for the sites studied. The initial results show that the annual environmental diversity for each site against the average comfort vote for the year correlates moderately with the absolute value of ASV, as shown in Figure 9.7. Although not strong, there is, nevertheless, a correlation suggesting that increasing diversity improves comfort. The value of the correlation coefficient is comparable to those found for purely physical parameters of temperature and wind. In the light of the simplistic approach taken to derive the diversity index at this point, it gives us some confidence that this work is worth pursuing and refining.

The linear line fits moderately well (R = 0.64), showing that as diversity increases comfort improves (i.e. ASV approaches 0 or 'neither warm nor cold'). It interesting to note that the better fitting polynomial line (R = 0.90) suggests an optimum diversity of approximately 0.6. As diversity continues to increase above 0.6 (i.e. notably for spring and autumn periods), the diversity begins to become too great, resulting in reduced comfort. This might be explained by the fact

that increasing diversity beyond a certain 'optimal' point will mean that the ideal combination of environmental conditions is displaced by more options. As diversity reduces below 0.6 (i.e. typically for winter conditions), a reduced range of appropriate conditions limits freedom of choice. Also noteworthy is that a small increase in diversity from a low base has a significant effect; but as diversity increases, further changes become less significant. This is understandable if one considers, for example, that a small amount of sun in an otherwise overshadowed area is particularly welcome compared to the same amount of sun in an already sunny environment.

As the density of a city increases, typically the opportunities for creating environmental diversity diminish. It becomes more challenging to create a variety of types and dimensions of open spaces within easy reach or view of pedestrians. Buildings are typically tall and even where there is an increase in spatial dimensions on plan, the impact upon the sky view and access to sun or wind remains modest. In other words, the relative horizontal spatial variation is diminished by the vertical dimensions. Where dense urban development meets an edge – for example, at a harbour or riverside, or at a large urban park (such as Central Park in New York) – there is a very clear but abrupt change in environmental condition. However, despite the benefits, such a change is sudden and typically not articulated or varied. Research has shown that strong variation in built form, even in dense urban environments, brings with it significant environmental potential (Cheng et al, 2006). Implementing such diversity in built form through planning control presents challenges, but can deliver significant benefits to the environmental performance – in terms of energy, health and well-being – of our cities.

Conclusions

This chapter started by outlining the research context related to comfort in urban microclimates and noted that activities in this sector tended either to study theoretical built form and comfort simulation, or used empirical research methods to monitor and survey respondents in urban environments. In this work we have highlighted the link between built form and actual comfort using simplified environmental analysis of real urban morphology. In particular, we have demonstrated

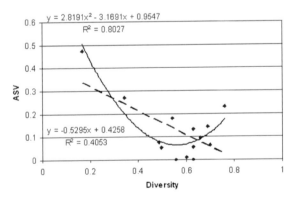

Source: Authors

Figure 9.7 *Annual diversity of each of the 14 European sites against average ASV (which reads as more comfortable as it approaches 0: neither warm nor cold)*

that environmental diversity, even defined in simple terms, correlates well – in some cases, better than singular parameters such as air and globe temperature or wind – with reported comfort data.

Appropriate environmental diversity increases the freedom of choice and results in increased levels of satisfaction. This work is important because it establishes that environmental diversity correlates with comfort. We strongly believe that environmentally diverse urban spaces – spatially and temporally – provide a richer and more enjoyable environment. This is particularly important in high-density cities where a small improvement can deliver great potential. We have begun to use the techniques reported here in a number of master plans for sustainable urban development and have found that the methods offer valuable insights – for example, into the seasonal performance of public squares – and raise general awareness and level of debate of how design projects impact upon the urban microclimate and vice versa.

Acknowledgements

We would like to acknowledge the financial support of the European Union (EU) for funding the research project upon which much of this chapter is based: EU research contract, Fifth Framework Programme, Key Action 4: City of Tomorrow and Cultural Heritage from the programme Energy, Environment and Sustainable Development; Project title: RUROS: Rediscovering the Urban Realm and Open Spaces.

We would also wish to thank all of the teams involved for their role in the project, particularly for the fieldwork. Their team leaders (PIs) are: Marialena Nikolopoulou (CRES, Greece, and now at Bath University, UK) who coordinated the research project; Niobe Chrissomalidou (Aristotle University of Thessaloniki, Greece); Raphael Compagnon (Ecole d'Ingénieurs et d'Architectes de Fribourg, Switzerland); Jian Kang (University of Sheffield, UK); Lutz Katzschner (University of Kassel, Germany); Eleni Kovani (National Centre of Social Research, Athens, Greece); and Giovanni Scudo (Politecnico di Milano, Italy).

References

Baker, N. (2004) 'Human nature', in K. Steemers and M. A. Steane (eds) *Environmental Diversity in Architecture*, Spon, London, pp47–64

Baker, N. and Ratti, C. (1999) 'Simplified urban climate models from medium-scale morphological parameters', in *Proceedings of the International Conference on Urban Climatology, ICUC 1999*, Sydney, Australia

Baker, N. and Standeven, M. (1996) 'Thermal comfort in free-running buildings', *Energy and Buildings*, vol 23, no 3, pp175–182

Brown, G. Z. and DeKay, M. (2001) *Sun, Wind and Light: Architectural Design Strategies,* 2nd edition, John Wiley & Sons, New York, NY

Campbell, J. (1983) 'Ambient stressors', *Environment and Behavior*, vol 15, no 3, pp355–380

Cheng, V., Steemers, K., Montavon, M. and Compagnon, R. (2006) 'Urban form, density and solar potential', in *PLEA 2006: 23rd International Conference on Passive and Low Energy Architecture*, Geneva, Switzerland, 6–8 September, pp701–706

Compagnon, R. and Goyette, J. (2005) 'Il comfort visivo negli spazi urbani', in *Il comfort ambientale negli spazi aperti*, Edicom Edizioni, Monfalcone (Gorizia), pp63–73

de Dear, R., Brager, G. S. and Cooper, D. (1997) 'Developing an adaptive model of thermal comfort and preference', final report ASHRAE RP-884

Kang, J. (2006) *Urban Sound Environment*, Taylor & Francis, London

Merghani, A. (2004) 'Exploring thermal comfort and spatial diversity', in K. Steemers and M. A. Steane (eds) *Environmental Diversity in Architecture*, Spon, London, pp195–213

Nikolopoulou, M. (ed) (2004) *Designing Open Spaces in the Urban Environment: A Bioclimatic Approach*, CRES, Athens

Nikolopoulou, M. and Lykoudis, S. (2006) 'Thermal comfort in outdoor urban spaces: Analysis across different European countries', *Building and Environment*, vol 41, no 11, pp1455–1470

Nikolopoulou, M. and Steemers, K. (2003) 'Thermal comfort and psychological adaptation as a guide for designing urban spaces', *Energy and Building*, vol 35, no 1, pp95–101

Nikolopoulou, M., Baker, N. and Steemers, K. (1999) 'Improvements to the globe thermometer for outdoor use', *Architectural Science Review*, vol 42, no 1, pp27–34

Oke, T. (1987) *Boundary Layer Climates*, Routledge, London

Paciuc, M. (1990) 'The role of personal control of the environment in thermal comfort and satisfaction at the workplace', in R. I. Selby, K. H. Anthony, J. Choi and B. Orland (eds) *Coming of Age*, Environment Design Research Association 21, Oklahoma, USA

Pearlmutter, D., Berliner, P. and Shaviv, E. (2006) 'Physical modeling of pedestrian energy exchange within the urban canopy', *Building and Environment*, vol 41, no 6, pp783–795

Ratti, C. and Richens, P. (2004) 'Raster analysis of urban form', *Environment and Planning B: Planning and Design*, vol 31, no 2, pp297–309

Ratti, C., Baker, N. and Steemers, K. (2005) 'Energy consumption and urban texture', *Energy and Buildings*, vol 37, no 8, pp824–835

Ratti, C., Di Sabatino, R. and Britter, R. (2006) 'Urban texture analysis with image processing techniques: Winds and dispersion', *Theoretical and Applied Climatology*, vol 84, no 1–3, pp77–90

Sinou, M. and Steemers, K. (2004) 'Intermediate space and environmental diversity', *Urban Design International*, vol 9, no 2, pp61–71

Steemers, K., Baker, N., Crowther, D., Dubiel, J., Nikolopoulou, M. and Ratti, C. (1997) 'City texture and microclimate', *Urban Design Studies*, vol 3, pp25–50

Yang, W. and Kang, J. (2005a) 'Soundscape and sound preferences in urban squares', *Journal of Urban Design*, vol 10, no 1, pp61–80

Yang, W. and Kang, J. (2005b) 'Acoustic comfort evaluation in urban open public spaces', *Applied Acoustics*, vol 66, pp211–229

10
Designing for Urban Ventilation

Edward Ng

Introduction

In many high-density cities in subtropical and tropical regions, such as Singapore, Hong Kong, Tokyo and so on, the hot summer can cause thermal stress, which is unhealthy to inhabitants. Buildings add to the problem as they increase the thermal capacity and, thus, add to the urban heat island intensity, reduce trans-evaporation, and increase roughness, slowing down incoming wind. (Avissar, 1996; Golany, 1996; Tso, 1996)

Besides the obvious health hazard, there are two further consequences of the city for not providing thermally comfortable outdoor spaces. First, less people will spend their time outdoors, hence reducing the spatial efficacy of the city. Second, people will try to stay indoors and, due to the not so desirable outdoor environment, will use air conditioning more, greatly increasing energy consumption.

Urban ventilation is important for the following purposes:

- indoor ventilation for free-running buildings;
- pollution dispersion; and
- urban thermal comfort.

For urban planners, while pollution issues can best be tackled at source in order to reduce emissions, urban ventilation needs for thermal comfort during the summer months can only be optimized with appropriate city design and building layouts.

Urban ventilation over human bodies increases heat lost and reduces heat stress in hot and humid urban conditions. For example, during the summer months in cities such as Tokyo, Hong Kong or Singapore, summer mean temperature can average

26°C to 30°C. Givoni has studied with Japanese subjects and proposed the following thermal sensation equation (Givoni and Noguchi, 2004):

$$TS = 1.2 + 0.1115 \times T_a + 0.0019 \times S - 0.3185 \times u \quad [10.1]$$

where:

- TS = thermal sensation scale from 1 (very cold) to 7 (very hot); TS = 4 is neutral;
- T_a = air temperature (°C);
- S = solar radiation (W/m²);
- u = wind speed (m/s).

Based on Equation 10.1, for an average person under the environmental condition of air temperature = 28°C, solar radiation = 150W/m², one would need a wind speed of 1.9m/s over the body to remain in neutral thermal sensation condition (Cheng and Ng, 2006) The example illustrated is not atypical in the summer months of tropical and subtropical cities. Hence, wind is a very important environmental parameter to design for urban thermal comfort.

Urban ventilation in high-density cities

The urban boundary level is typically regarded as the layer of the atmosphere from ground to about 1000m. The energy and mass exchange in this layer determines the climatic conditions of the city (Oke, 1987). The urban atmosphere over the city has an urban boundary layer and underneath it an urban canopy layer (UCL), which is typically regarded as at the mean roof height of the city. Due to the higher volume, and typically taller buildings in the UCL, the urban air temperature is normally higher, and the wind field weaker and more turbulent. For tropically and subtropically located high-density cities, this can mean poor urban thermal comfort for inhabitants. In order to alleviate the negative effects, it is very useful to design the high-density city in such a way that the natural elements (e.g. wind) can penetrate the city. Based on the power law, the percentage of the gradient wind at pedestrian level (2m above ground) given the ground roughness can be summarized as in Table 10.1 (Landsberg, 1981).

Compared to suburban cities and towns, in urban morphological terms, high-density cities enjoy much less of the available wind at ground level. For example, given an incoming wind of 15m/s, not atypical realistically, by the time it comes to the middle of the city over its roughness, it would have already reduced to less than 1m/s. This is already less than the 1.9m/s needed for comfort in the example illustrated above. In reality, the wind speed at pedestrian level can be substantially less due to buildings blocking the winds and creating stagnant zones locally.

The study of the pedestrian wind environment around buildings in urban areas has traditionally focused on the effect of strong winds on comfort (Hunt et al, 1976; Melbourne, 1978; Murakami, 1982; Bloeken and Carmeliet, 2004). The consideration is particularly important for sites in windy conditions with a few tall towers. The buildings in a certain relationship with each others could inadvertently create wind-channelling effects that create amplification conditions that are uncomfortable or even unsafe for pedestrian activities. Wind engineers, when conducting wind environment assessments for a site, mostly concentrate on mitigating wind gust conditions. Hence, it is normal for wind engineers to look for areas

that might have wind gust problems – for instance, at the corners of the windward side of the building, at the bottom of the windward side of the main building façade, and at building gaps and tunnels. Except for pollution dispersion studies, few wind engineers examine the ground-level urban environment for the purpose of weak wind urban thermal comfort. For weak wind studies, it is important to locate study focuses within the urban canyon, in streets and in wake areas, and to position test points appropriately.

Wind velocity ratio for urban ventilation

In order to understand the concept of wind for urban ventilation, the wind velocity ratio (VRw) is a useful and simple model. Figure 10.1 outlines how VRw could be schematically conceptualized.

Consider the wind available to a city coming from the left. The wind profile as illustrated can be devised using the aforementioned power law with the coefficient appropriate for the approaching terrains. At the gradient height of this profile, wind is assumed to be not affected by the friction of the ground. This is commonly known as V∞ or V (infinity). For high-density cities, this can be conveniently assumed to be about 500m above ground – hence, V_{500}. At the pedestrian level inside the city at, say, 2m above ground, city activities commonly take place. Wind at this level is V_p or V_2. The ratio between V_2 and V_{500} is known as the wind velocity ratio (VRw). The ratio indicates how much of the available wind to the city is enjoyed by pedestrians on the ground. It is immediately obvious that the buildings and structures between 2m and 500m dictate the magnitude of this ratio. How well architects and planners design for city

Table 10.1 *Height of gradient wind versus wind speed based on the power law with various coefficients*

α	Description	Height of gradient wind (m)	Wind speed % of gradient wind
0.10	Open sea	200	63
0.15	Open landscape	300	47
0.3	Suburban	400	20
0.4	City with some tall buildings	500	11
0.5	High-density city	500	6

Source: Landsberg (1981)

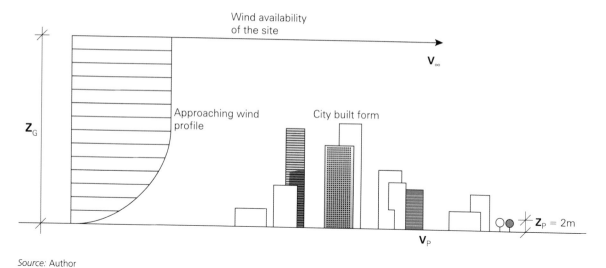

Figure 10.1 *Wind velocity ratio is a relationship between Vp and V∞*

ventilation can be assessed by the magnitude of the VRw; the higher the VRw, the better the available site wind is captured for pedestrians. Consider the simplified urban forms in Figure 10.2. The arrangement on the left has a spatial average VRw of 0.18, whereas the layout on the right has an average VRw of 0.28. In this case, the city layout on the right is better designed for wind.

Building and city morphology for urban ventilation

In high-density cities, especially in hot summers, designing for wind is a city planning and urban design issue. If the city is not designed properly, it is very difficult, if not impossible, for the building designer to 'create' wind in one's own site.

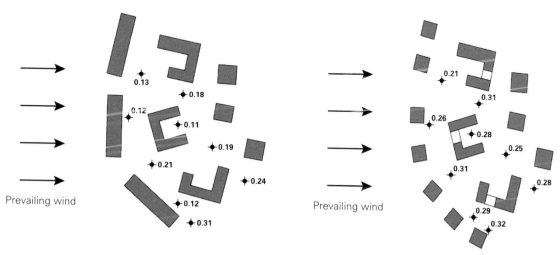

Figure 10.2 *Two urban layouts with different wind velocity ratios: (left) lower velocity ratios due to higher building blockage; (right) higher velocity ratios due to more ground level permeability*

For high-density city design, the following design parameters are worth bearing in mind:

- air paths;
- deep street canyons;
- street orientations;
- ground coverage ratio; and
- building height differentials.

Air paths

Due to the fact that high-density cities typically have tall buildings of approximately 60m to 100m in Singapore, or 100m to 150m in Hong Kong, it can be very difficult for planners to design streets wide enough for wind to flow to the ground from the rooftop. For isolated roughness flow or wake interference flow,

the building height to street width ratios have to be less than 0.7 – that is to say, the width of the street must be wider than the height of the building, otherwise skimming flow will dominate (Oke, 1987). Therefore, when building heights are generally tall in high-density cities, it is far more effective to introduce wind into the city through gaps between buildings in the form of air paths (Givoni, 1998). For the air path to be effective, the width of the air path at the windward side should be at least, and on average, 50 per cent of the total widths of the buildings on both sides. The width needs to be increased when the heights of the buildings increase. In addition, the length of the air path needs to be considered. A preliminary suggestion is that width (W) be increased to around 2W when height (H) > 3W and length (L) > 10W (see Figure 10.3).

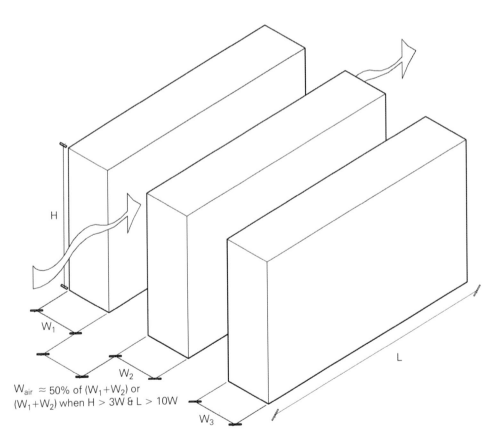

$W_{air} \approx 50\%$ of (W_1+W_2) or (W_1+W_2) when $H > 3W$ & $L > 10W$

Source: Author

Figure 10.3 *A geometrical relationship of buildings and air paths*

Deep street canyons

Parametric studies of wind flow in canyons have been conducted by many researchers (Plate, 1995). However, most studies stopped at canyons with an H/W ratio of 2 or less (Nakamura and Oke, 1989; Santamouris et al, 1999). A few studies go beyond H/W = 2 (Kovar-Panskus et al, 2002), as can be summarized in Figure 10.4, and report the observation of primary and secondary vortexes in the canyon due to the ambient wind blowing perpendicular to the canyon (Kovar-Panskus et al, 2002). Once the secondary vortexes developed, the ground-level wind became weak (DePaul and Sheih, 1986). It is apparent that

with high-density cities of tall buildings, the H/W ratio is likely to have exceeded an H/W of 3. For example, in Hong Kong, an H/W ratio of 5:1 is not uncommon; occasionally, it can go to as much as 10:1.

Street orientations

Based on an understanding of air path and canyon wind flows explained above, it is apparent that streets aligning with the prevailing winds during the critical summer months are extremely important for city ventilation. In a nutshell, the difference in terms of VRw in the streets can be as much as ten times. For streets that cannot be orientated directly towards the

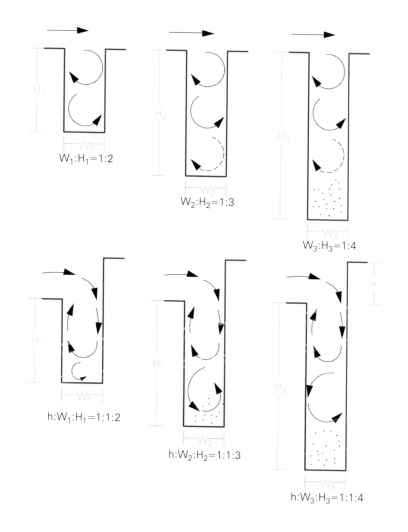

Source: Author

Figure 10.4 *Various street canyons and air circulation vortexes*

prevailing wind, it is useful to limit the deviation to less than 30°. However, in reality, the proper orientation of the street has to take into account many other factors – for example, topography or solar access. In recent research, Mayer et al (2008) demonstrated that north–south-orientated streets have a higher probability of areas that are thermally comfortable than east–west-orientated streets. This has a lot to do with how the sun and its shadow move across the street on a typical summer's day (Mayer et al, 2008).

Ground coverage ratio

For high-density cities, one of the most useful indicators of the city wind environment parametrically is to refer to the ground coverage ratio. The ratio is basically the percentage of the ground area in, for example, 100m × 100m that is occupied by buildings of at least a few storeys tall. Wind tunnel experiments indicate that the VRw of a city, in general, would halve if the ground coverage increased from 10 to 30 per cent. Experimental evidence also suggests that the relationship is linear – that is to say, for a high-density city with a high ground coverage of 60 per cent (which is not uncommon in Hong Kong), then the VRw will be halved again (Kubota, 2008). The concept of ground coverage ratio roughly corresponds with the ideas of air paths. In addition, experimental results also indicate that spatial porosity and permeability at the ground level is very effective in improving city ventilation (Ng and Wong, 2006).

Building height differentials

Another important concept with city ventilation in high-density cities is that given the same building volume, a city with larger differences between the taller and the lower buildings tends to have better city ventilation (see Table 10.2). It appears that the taller buildings catch the wind passing through the city and downwash it down to the city. This downwash effect not only happens on the windward façades of buildings, it also happens at the leeward façades via spiralling vortexes towards the ground. In addition, buildings that are of different heights induce positive and negative pressures on the two sides of a slab-like building (see Figure 10.5). This, in turn, creates air movement parallel to the building façades and improves urban city ventilation (Ng and Wong, 2005).

Table 10.2 *Relationship between height contrast and air change per hour performances*

Height contrast	Height difference Max:Min	Air changes per hour
0	4:4	10.5
3	3:6	10.8
4	3:7	11.9
6	2:8	13.8
7	2:9	11.2
8	1:9	13.3
10	1:11	13.4
10	0:10	17.9
14	0:14	17.0

Source: Data from author's experiment

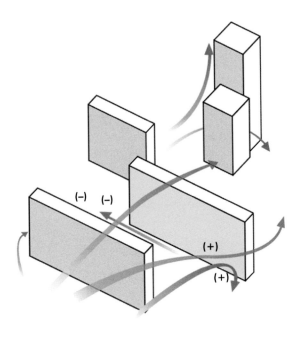

Source: Author

Figure 10.5 *A city with various building heights is preferable*

Case study: Hong Kong

Hong Kong is one of the most densely populated cities in the world. High-density living has the advantages of efficient land use, public transport and infrastructure, as well as the benefits of closer proximity to daily amenities. The 'sunk cost' of high-density living is that it is more difficult to optimize urban design for the benefits of the natural environment – daylight and natural air/wind ventilation. Good planning and building designs are critically important. The unique urban fabric of Hong Kong – its pattern of streets, building heights, open spaces, density, features, landscape and so on – determine the environmental quality both within buildings and outside.

Since the unfortunate event of severe acute respiratory syndrome (SARS) in Hong Kong in 2003, there have been calls from the community for measures to improve the quality of our urban living environment. Among the recommendations in the *Team Clean Final Report* of the Hong Kong government, it has been proposed to examine the practicality of stipulating air ventilation assessment as one of the considerations for all major development or redevelopment proposals and for future planning.

A qualitative review of the existing urban fabric in Hong Kong by a number of experts invited to Hong Kong in 2004 – Professor Baruch Givoni, Professor Shuzo Murakami, Professor Mat Santamouris and Dr N. H. Wong – can be summarized as follows (Ng et al, 2004). There is/there are:

- a lack of well-considered networks of breezeways and air paths towards the prevailing wind;
- tall and bulky buildings closely packed together forming undesirable windbreaks to the urban fabric behind;
- uniform building heights resulting in wind skimming over the top and not being re-routed into the urban fabric;
- tight, narrow streets not aligning with the prevailing wind, and with very tall buildings on both sides, resulting in very deep urban canyons;
- a lack of general urban permeability: few open spaces, no (or minimal) gaps between buildings or within large and continuous buildings, and excessive podium structure reducing the air volume at pedestrian level;
- large building lots with insufficient air spaces, and with buildings on them not generally designed for wind permeability and forming wind barriers;
- projections from buildings and obstruction on narrow streets further intruding into the breezeways and air paths; and
- a general lack of greenery, shading and soft landscape in urban areas.

The expert review resolved that urban ventilation in the city has not been optimized. Stagnant or slow air movements often occur. The study recommended that it is important to initiate steps to improve the situation.

Urban ventilation for thermal comfort

Outdoor thermal comfort could be achieved when the following factors are balanced: air temperature, wind speed, humidity, activity, clothing and solar radiation. For designers, it is possible to design the outdoor environment to maximize wind speed and minimize solar radiation in order to achieve comfort during the hot tropical summer months of Hong Kong. A higher wind speed might be needed if a pedestrian is only partly shaded; likewise, a lower wind speed might be desired if the air temperature is lower. Based on Ng's researches (Cheng and Ng, 2006), Figure 10.6 shows, for example, that when a pedestrian is under shade, a steady mean wind at pedestrian level of around 1.5m/s will be beneficial for providing thermal relief and a comfortable outdoor urban environment during summer in Hong Kong. Factoring in the macro-wind availability of Hong Kong, it might be stated statistically that a good probability (50 per cent median) of achieving this 1.5m/s mean wind speed is desirable.

Referring to Hong Kong's general macro-wind availability data from the Hong Kong Observatory, in order to capture this 'mean 1.5m/s wind over 50 per cent of the time', it is desirable to have a city morphology that is optimized and, as much as possible, designed to capture the incoming wind availability. Properly laid out urban patterns and street widths, careful disposition of building bulks and heights, open spaces and their configurations, breezeways and air paths, and so on are all important design parameters. Achieving a quality outdoor thermal environment for Hong Kong is an important planning consideration. A well-designed urban wind environment will also benefit the individual buildings and their probability of achieving indoor comfort, as well as contribute to other benefits, such as the dispersion of anthropogenic wastes.

Air ventilation assessment system

Air ventilation assessment (AVA) is a design methodology promulgated by the Hong Kong

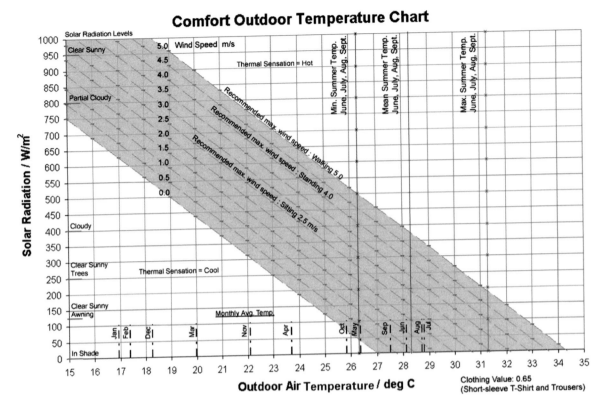

Source: Author

Figure 10.6 *A comfort outdoor temperature chart based on survey data in tropical cities*

government in 2006 to deal with the weak pedestrian conditions of Hong Kong (Ng et al, 2004). It aims to objectively evaluate how a proposed development affects the surrounding wind environment. Taking into account the above 'wind for urban thermal comfort' considerations, as well as various climatic and urban factors, and given Hong Kong's high-density conditions, it is suggested that, for planning considerations, optimizing or maximizing air ventilation through the city fabric should be the focus of AVA. In general, 'the more city ventilation the better' – save some isolated gust problems that, in most cases, could be dealt with locally.

The AVA methodology states that given the natural wind availability of the site, a high probability of a gentle breeze at pedestrian level of some 1.5m/s is a useful 'criterion'. Taking into account the general high-density urban morphology of Hong Kong and the macro-wind availability, the methodology recommends that the city

fabric should, in general, be as permeable and porous as possible. As such, the AVA system has been developed to encourage this permeability to happen.

Wind velocity ratio as an indicator

The key purpose of an indicator is to address what minimum wind environment information, and in what form, is needed to guide design and planning in order to achieve a better wind penetration into (and, hence, air ventilation of) the city, especially at the pedestrian level. The focus of the methodology to be introduced is about providing information based on a simple indicator to permit better layout design of developments and planning of the urban fabric. The wind velocity ratio (VRw) has been used as the indicator.

The basic concept of VRw has to be elaborated upon further since wind comes from all directions (see Equations 10.2 and 10.3) It is a common practice in wind engineering study to account for wind coming from 16 main directions (see Figure 10.7):

$$VRi = \frac{Vpi}{V\infty i} \qquad [10.2]$$

$$VRw = \sum_{i=1}^{16} Fi \times VRi \qquad [10.3]$$

where:

- Vpi is the pedestrian wind velocity of the location when wind comes from direction i;
- V∞i is the available wind velocity of the site when wind comes from direction i;
- VRi is the velocity ratio of the location when wind comes from direction i;
- Fi is the frequency occurrence of wind from direction i (16 directions are considered);
- VRw is the wind velocity ratio.

The wind velocity ratio VRw is the sum of the wind velocity ratio of wind from direction i (VRi) multiplied by the probability (Fi) of wind coming from that direction. For example, if, say, 60 per cent of the wind at the site comes from the south and 40 per cent comes from the east, and the velocity ratio when wind comes from the south is 0.2 and when wind comes from the east is 0.4, then VRw = 0.60×0.2 + 0.40×0.4 = 0.28. VRw is a simple indicator to signify the effects of developments on the wind environment. In general, with reference to 'the more, the better' for Hong Kong, higher VRw is better. Higher VRw means that the buildings design captures better the wind available to the site.

In some circumstances, it may be necessary to mitigate the adverse effect of strong wind gust for the safety of pedestrians. For buildings situated in an exposed location where there is no apparent shielding from the approaching wind, such as those with a frontage of an open fetch of water, parkland or low-rise

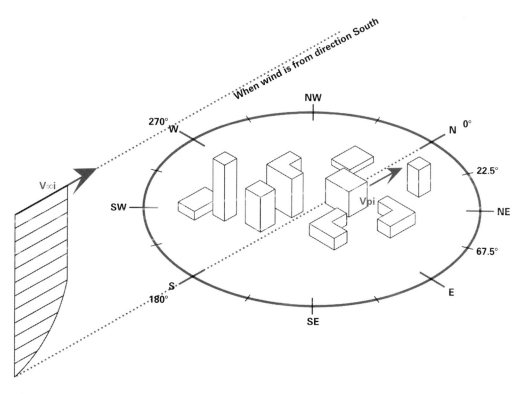

Source: Author

Figure 10.7 *An understanding of wind velocity ratio based on 16 directions*

structures, on hill slope or hill top, an assessment of the potential occurrence of windy conditions that may affect the safety of pedestrians is strongly recommended. Careful examination of the individual test points and their respective VRw has been useful.

AVA study methodology

The AVA utilizes the VRw as an indicator. The methodology allows designs to be systematically evaluated and objectively assessed. A design with a higher resultant VRw is generally a better design as far as the urban wind environment is concerned:

- Take a test site in the city as in Figure 10.8 (within the grey boundary). A number of buildings have been designed and require assessment. The height of the tallest building on site is H (in some cases, it is possible to define H as the average height of the taller buildings of the test site). A model (physical or digital) has to be constructed to truthfully represent the 'surrounding area'. The radius of this model is approximately 2H (from the base of the tallest building or from the test site boundary in cases of many tall buildings on site). All existing buildings within this 2H radius must be faithfully modelled.

- As shown in Figure 10.8, the shaded circle (the 'assessment area') is within a radius of H from the base of the tallest building, or from the test site boundary in cases of many tall buildings on site. Typically, the designed buildings 'significantly' affect the wind environment within this area. A number of test points are planted, and their results give an indication of the impact of the design on the wind environment in this assessment area.

- Test points are positioned where pedestrians are likely to congregate. For a detailed study, the total number of test points is approximately 60–100 for a 2ha site. More test points are needed for bigger sites, except when doing a rough initial study, or when the site condition is simpler. In general, more test points give better detailed results.

Source: Author

Figure 10.8 *An example of an air ventilation assessment (AVA) study showing the boundary of the assessment area, the boundary of the model, and positions of the test points*

- Along the boundary of the site, a number of perimeter test points are planted. They can be about 10m to 50m apart, depending upon the site condition, surrounding the test site and evenly distributed. Test points must be planted at the junctions of all roads leading to the test site, at corners, as well as at the main entrances of the test site. This set of test points will be known as perimeter test points. They will later provide data to calculate the site spatial average wind velocity ratio (SVRw).

- Additional test points are evenly distributed over the assessment area of the model. For a detailed study, one test point per 200 to 300 square metres of the assessment area would typically suffice, except when doing a rough initial study or when the site condition is simpler. Test points are positioned where pedestrians can or will mostly access the area. This may include pavement, open spaces, piazzas, concourses and so on, but will exclude back lanes or minor alleyways. For streets, the tests point should be located on their centrelines. Some of the test points are located at major entrances, as well as identified areas where people are known to congregate. This group of test points will be known as overall test points, together with the perimeter test points, and will provide data to calculate the local spatial average wind velocity ratio (LVRw).

- On a case-by-case basis, wind engineers may advise locating additional special test points to assess the impact of the development upon areas of special concern (e.g. waterfront promenades or exposed areas). These additional special test points are not included in the SVRw or LVRw air ventilation assessment calculation because they might be used to further study the detail and reveal information for a particular concern.

Once the model and the test points are defined, it can be tested in a wind tunnel. The test procedures are well documented (ASCE, 2001; AWES, 2001). Figure 10.9 captures the essential steps of the performance-based air ventilation assessment (AVA) methodology.

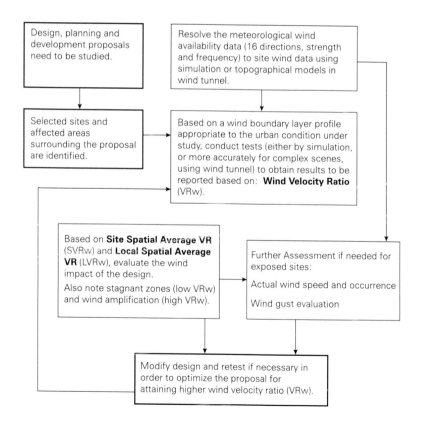

Source: Author

Figure 10.9 *A flow chart showing the procedures of AVA methodology*

AVA implementation

Since December 2006, the government/quasi-governmental organizations in Hong Kong have been required to undertake AVA, where practicable, under any one of the following circumstances:

- preparation of new town plans and major revision of such plans;
- development that deviates from the statutory development restriction(s) other than minor relaxations;
- erection of building structures within a designated breezeway;
- urban renewal development that involves agglomeration of sites together with closure and building over of existing streets;
- development with shielding effect on waterfronts, particularly in confined air sheds;
- large-scale development with a high density (e.g. site area over 2ha and an overall plot ratio of 5 or above; development with a total ground floor area (GFA) of 100,000 square metres or above);
- massive elevated structures over a road in dense urban areas; and
- for developments situated in an exposed location where there is no apparent shielding from the approaching wind, an assessment of the potential occurrence of windy conditions that may affect the safety of pedestrians should be included.

It has been recommended that AVA be carried out for different design options in order to identify better design scenarios and potential problem areas, based on VRw as an indicator. A design having a higher VRw would be considered as a better design than one with a lower VRw. At the stage of implementation in 2006, only the better design option is known; but whether the better design option meets a standard cannot be known due to the lack of benchmarking. The aim of AVA is to move 'towards a better future' rather than for precision.

Design guidelines

For the initial design, some forms of qualitative guidelines are useful for planners and designers. Apart from the AVA methodology, the government of

Hong Kong has also promulgated a number of guidelines in the Hong Kong Planning Standards and Guidelines (HKPSG). It contains, among others, the following.

Breezeway/air path

It is important for better urban air ventilation in a dense, hot humid city to let more wind penetrate through the urban district. Breezeways can occur in the form of roads, open spaces and low-rise building corridors through which air reaches inner parts of urbanized areas largely occupied by high-rise buildings. Projecting obstructions over breezeways/air paths should be avoided to minimize wind blockage.

Orientation of street grids

An array of main streets, wide main avenues and/or breezeways should be aligned in parallel, or up to 30 degrees to the prevailing wind direction, in order to maximize the penetration of prevailing wind through the district.

Linkage of open spaces

Where possible, open spaces may be linked and aligned in such a way as to form breezeways or ventilation corridors. Structures along breezeways/ventilation corridors should be low rise.

Non-building area

The tendency for many developments to maximize views and site development potential often results in congested building masses and minimum space between buildings to meet building (planning) regulations in Hong Kong. Large sites with compact developments particularly impede air movement. Development plots should be laid out and orientated to maximize air penetration by aligning the longer frontage in parallel to the wind direction and by introducing non-building areas and setbacks where appropriate.

Waterfront sites

Waterfront sites are the gateways of sea breezes and land breezes due to sea cooling and sun warming

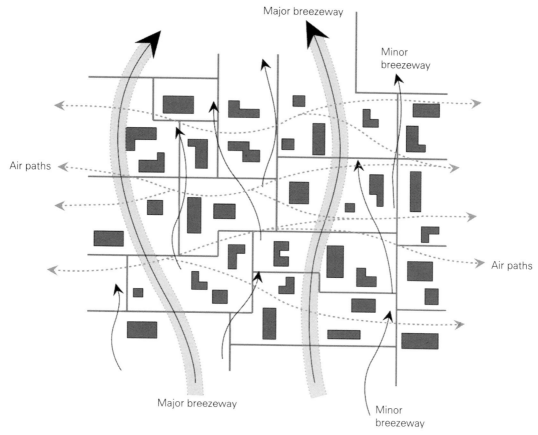

Source: Author

Figure 10.10 *Breezeways and air paths when planning a city are better for city air ventilation*

effects. Buildings along the waterfront should avoid blockage of sea/land breezes and prevailing winds.

Scale of podium

The 100 per cent site coverage for non-domestic developments up to some 15m high as permitted under the building (planning) regulations often results in large podia. For large development/ redevelopment sites, particularly in existing urban areas, it is critical to increase permeability of the podium structure at street levels by providing some ventilation corridors or setback in parallel to the prevailing wind. Where appropriate, a terraced podium design should be adopted to direct downward airflow, which can help to enhance air movement at

the pedestrian level and to disperse the pollutants emitted by vehicles.

Building heights

Height variation should be considered as much as possible with the principle that the height decreases towards the direction where prevailing wind comes from. The stepped height concept can help to optimize the wind-capturing potential of the development itself.

Building disposition

Where practicable, adequately wide gaps should be provided between building blocks to maximize the air permeability of the development and to minimize its

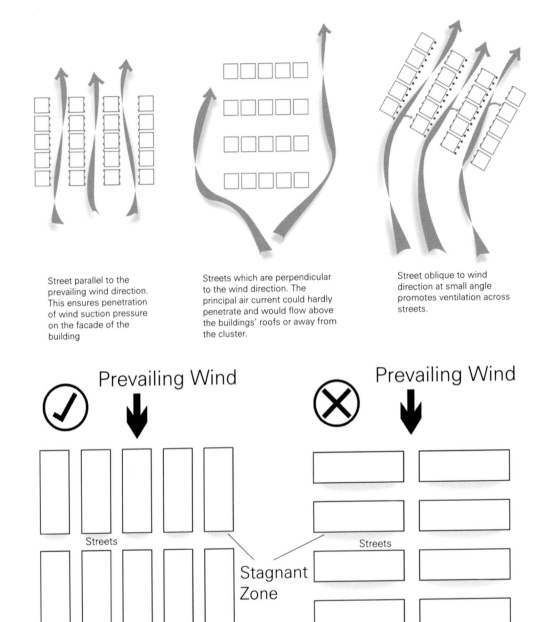

Street parallel to the prevailing wind direction. This ensures penetration of wind suction pressure on the facade of the building

Streets which are perpendicular to the wind direction. The principal air current could hardly penetrate and would flow above the buildings' roofs or away from the cluster.

Street oblique to wind direction at small angle promotes ventilation across streets.

Source: Author

Figure 10.11 *Aligning street orientations properly is better for city air ventilation*

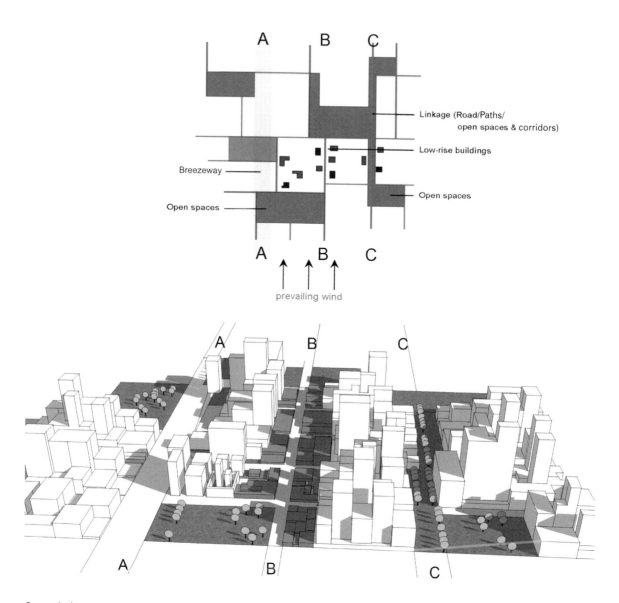

Figure 10.12 *Linking open spaces with breezeways (A-A), low-rise buildings (B-B) and linear parks (C-C) is better for city air ventilation*

impact upon the wind-capturing potential of adjacent developments. The gaps for enhancing air permeability are preferably at a face perpendicular to the prevailing wind. Towers should preferably abut the podium edge that faces the concerned pedestrian area/street in order to enable most of the downwash wind to reach the street level.

Projecting obstructions

Massive projecting obstructions, such as elevated walkways, may adversely affect the wind environment at pedestrian level, as observed in Mongkok. Signage is preferably of the vertical type in order to minimize

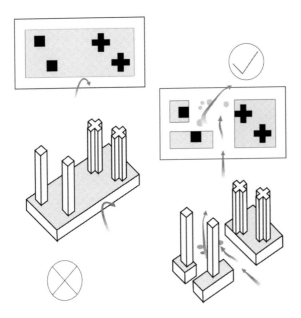

Source: Author

Figure 10.13 *Reducing ground cover and breaking up building podia is better for city air ventilation*

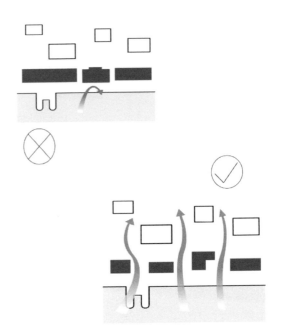

Source: Author

Figure 10.14 *Buildings with gaps along the waterfront are better for city air ventilation*

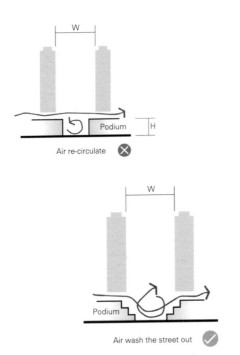

Source: Author

Figure 10.15 *Improving air volume near the ground with stepping podia is better for city air ventilation*

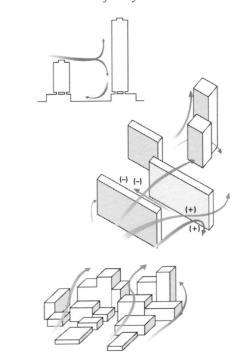

Source: Author

Figure 10.16 *Varying building heights is better for city air ventilation*

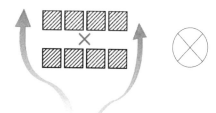

Prevailing Wind

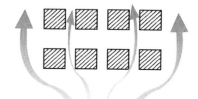

Prevailing Wind

Source: Author

Figure 10.17 *Gaps between buildings are better for city air ventilation*

wind blockage, particularly in those areas with a high density of projecting signs over streets.

Conclusions

The *Technical Guide for Air Ventilation Assessment for Developments in Hong Kong* allows design options to be compared on a scientific and objective basis with respect to the effect on air ventilation. A technical circular, based on the technical guide, setting out guidance for applying air ventilation assessments to major government projects was promulgated by the Hong Kong government in July 2006. In addition, Chapter 11 of HKPSG on urban design guidelines was expanded to incorporate guidelines on air ventilation in August 2006.

Improving air ventilation for a better wind environment is only one of the many considerations towards sustainable development in Hong Kong. In planning, one must, of course, also try to balance other equally if not more important considerations and as far as possible synergize needs to result in an optimized design.

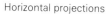

Horizontal projections

Vertical projections

Source: Author

Figure 10.18 *Vertical signage is better for city air ventilation*

Acknowledgements

The air ventilation assessment study reported in this chapter is funded by the Planning Department, HKSAR government. Apart from the researchers at the Chinese University of Hong Kong (CUHK), thanks are due to Professor Baruch Givoni, Professor Lutz Katzschner, Professor Kenny Kwok, Professor Shuzo Murakami, Professor Mat Santamouris, Dr Wong Nyuk Hien and Professor Phil Jones.

References

ASCE (American Society of Civil Engineers) (2001) *Wind Tunnel Studies of Buildings and Structures* and *Australasian Wind Engineering Society*, ASCE, Virginia, USA

Avissar, R. (1996) 'Potential effects of vegetation on the urban thermal environment', *Atmospheric Environment*, vol 30, pp437–448

AWES (2001) *Wind Engineering Studies of Buildings*, AWES-QAM-1-2001, Published by the Australasian Wind Engineering Society, Australia

Bloeken, B. and Carmeliet, J. (2004) 'Pedestrian wind environment around buildings: Literature review and practical examples', *Journal of Thermal Environment and Building Science*, vol 28, no 2, October, pp107–159

Cheng, V. and Ng, E. (2006) 'Thermal comfort in urban open spaces for Hong Kong', *Architectural Science Review*, vol 49, no 3, pp236–242

DePaul, F. T. and Sheih, C. M. (1986) 'Measurements of wind velocities in a street canyon', *Atmospheric Environment*, vol 20, issue 3, pp455–459

Givoni, B. (1998) *Climatic Considerations in Building and Urban Design*, John Wiley & Sons, Inc, New York, NY, p440

Givoni, B. and Noguchi, M. (2004) 'Outdoor comfort responses of Japanese persons', in *Proceedings of the American Solar Energy Society: National Solar Energy Conference 2004*, 9–14 July, Portland, OR

Golany, G. S. (1996) 'Urban design morphology and thermal performance', *Atmospheric Environment*, vol 30, pp455–465

Hunt, J. C. R., Poulton, E. C. and Mumford, J. C. (1976) 'The effects of wind on people: New criteria based upon wind tunnel experiments', *Building and Environment*, vol 11, pp15–28

Kovar-Panskus, A., Louika, P., Sini, J. F., Savory, E., Czech, M., Abdelqari, A., Mestayer, P. G. and Toy, N. (2002) 'Influence of geometry on the mean flow within urban street canyons – a comparison of wind tunnel experiments and numerical simulations', in *Water, Air and Soil Pollution*, Focus 2, Kluwer Academic Publishers, The Netherlands, pp365–380

Kubota, T. (2008) 'Wind tunnel tests on the relationship between building density and pedestrian-level wind velocity: Development of guidelines for realizing acceptable wind environment in residential neighbourhoods', *Building and Environment*, October, pp1699–1708

Landsberg, H. E. (1981) 'The urban climate', *International Geophysics Series*, vol 28, Academic Press, Harcourt Brace Jovanovich Publishers, New York, NY

Mayer, H., Holst, J., Dostal, P., Imbery, F. and Schindler, D. (2008) 'Human thermal comfort in summer within an urban street canyon in Central Europe', *Meteorologische Zeitschrift*, vol 17, no 3, pp241–250

Melbourne, W. H. (1978) 'Criteria for environmental wind conditions', *Journal of Industrial Aerodynamics*, vol 3, pp241–249

Murakami, S. (1982) 'Wind tunnel modelling applied to pedestrian comfort', in Timothy A. Reinhold (ed) *Wind Tunnel Modelling for Civil Engineering Applications*, Cambridge University Press, New York, NY, p688

Nakamura, Y. and Oke, T. R. (1989) 'Wind, temperature and stability conditions in an E–W oriented urban canyon', *Atmospheric Environment*, vol 22, issue 12, pp2691–2700

Ng, E. and Wong, N. H. (2005) 'Building heights and better ventilated design for high density cities', in *Proceedings of PLEA International Conference 2005*, Lebanon, 13–16 November 2005, pp607–612

Ng, E. and Wong, N. H. (2006) 'Permeability, porosity and better ventilated design for high density cities', in *Proceedings of PLEA International Conference 2006*, Geneva, Switzerland, 6–8 September 2006, vol 1, p329

Ng, E., Tam, I., Ng, A., Givoni, B., Katzschner, L., Kwok, K., Murakami, S., Wong, N. H., Wong, K. S., Cheng, V., Davis, A., Tsou, J. Y. and Chow, B. (2004) *Final Report – Feasibility Study for Establishment of Air Ventilation Assessment System*, Technical Report for Planning Department HKSAR, Hong Kong

Oke, T. R. (1987) *Boundary Layer Climates*, 2nd edition, Halsted Press, New York, NY

Plate, E. J. (1995) 'Urban climates and urban climate modelling: An introduction', in J. E. Cermak and A. D. Davenport (eds) *Wind Climate in Cities*, Kluwer Academic Publishers, The Netherlands, pp23–39

Santamouris M., Papanikolaou N., Koronakis I., Livada I. and Asimakopoulos D. (1999) 'Thermal and air flow characteristics in a deep pedestrian canyon under hot weather conditions', *Atmospheric Environment*, vol 33, issue 27, pp4503–4521

Tso, C. P. (1996) 'A survey of urban heat island studies in two tropical cities', *Atmospheric Environment*, vol 30, pp507–519

11

Natural Ventilation in High-Density Cities

Francis Allard, Christian Ghiaus and Agota Szucs

Introduction

During the second half of the last century, urban population increased tremendously. While during the 1950s urban residents did not exceeded 200 million, at the end of the century their total number was close to 3 billion and it is expected to increase to about 9.2 billion by 2050 (UNFPA, 2006). Transfer of people to cities has mainly happened and will continue to happen in the so-called less developed countries as the result of increased economic and social opportunities offered in urban areas and the degradation of rural economies and societies.

The growth rate of urban populations is much faster than rural populations. It has been reported that almost 80 per cent of the world's population growth between 1990 and 2010 will occur in cities and most probably in Africa, Asia and Latin America (UNFPA, 1998). In other words, there is a current addition of 60 million urban citizens a year – the equivalent of adding another Paris, Beijing or Cairo every other month.

This extremely rapid urbanization has resulted in the dramatic increase of the size of the world's urban agglomerations. According to the United Nations (UNFPA, 2001), our planet hosts 19 cities with 10 million or more people, 22 cities with 5 to 10 million people, 370 cities with 1 to 5 million people and 433 cities with 0.5 to 1 million people. This phenomenon has led to the construction of high-density cities.

This very rapid urbanization has also resulted in extremely important environmental, social, political, economic, institutional, demographic and cultural problems. A detailed discussion of these problems is given by Santamouris (2001). In developed countries, overconsumption of resources (mainly of energy); increased air pollution (mainly from motor vehicles); the urban heat island effect and an increase in ambient temperatures due to positive heat balances in cities; noise pollution; and solid waste management seem to be the more important problems. On the contrary, poverty, environmental degradation, lack of sanitary and other urban services, lack of access to land and adequate shelter are among the more serious issues in developing countries. Energy is the most important engine to improve quality of life and fight poverty. Given that by 2020 almost 70 per cent of the world's population will be living in cities, and 60 per cent will be below the poverty line, it is estimated by the World Bank that many of those will be energy poor. Thus, for the next decades, thousands of megawatts of new electrical capacity have to be added. Estimates (Serageldim et al, 1995) show that the cost of the new power generation plants over the next 30 years will amount to over US$2 trillion. However, developing countries already pay too much for energy. Citizens in these countries spend 12 per cent of their income on energy services (i.e. five times more than the average in Organisation for Economic Co-operation and Development (OECD) countries). In parallel, energy imports are one of the major sources of foreign debt. As reported during the Johannesburg summit, 'in over 30 countries, energy imports exceed 10 per cent of the value of all exports', while 'in about 20 countries, payments for oil imports exceed those for debt servicing'.

It is thus evident that alternative energy patterns have to be used. The use of renewable sources in combination with energy-efficient technologies can provide the necessary energy supply to two-thirds of the world's population to improve their quality of life, while contributing substantially to decreasing overconsumption of resources in developed countries. Ventilation and, in particular, natural ventilation are among these technologies.

The main strategies for natural ventilation in high-density urban climates are the same as for open area locations: single-sided, cross-ventilation and stack ventilation (Allard, 1997). Combinations and adaptations of these strategies make them more suitable to the urban climate (Ghiaus and Allard, 2006).

When it is used for free cooling, natural ventilation can replace air-conditioning systems for much of the year. The potential of natural ventilation is related to the energy saved for cooling if natural ventilation is used instead of cooling. But dense urban environments present disadvantages for the application of natural ventilation: lower wind speeds, higher temperatures due to the effect of the urban heat island, noise and pollution.

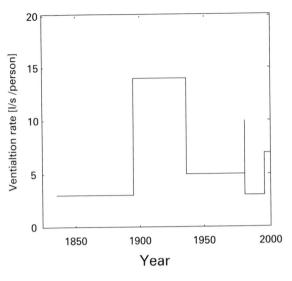

Source: Awbi (1998)

Figure 11.1 *Minimum ventilation rates in the US*

Role of ventilation

The ventilation of buildings is necessary in order to maintain indoor air quality and thermal comfort. These aims are achieved by controlling airflow rate. The airflow rate should be large enough to ensure that the maximal concentration of any pollutant is lower than the maximal limit admitted. Airflow rate also influences thermal comfort. Environmental factors (e.g. air temperature and velocity, and relative humidity) may be controlled by the airflow rate. Thermal comfort is a sensation and recent research studies have demonstrated that either excessive stimuli amplitude or insufficient adaptive opportunities cause dissatisfaction. Since naturally ventilated buildings provide more means for adaptation, people accept wider indoor temperature fluctuations with direct benefits for energy consumption.

Indoor air quality and comfort standards are important in the design phase, when inappropriate criteria may result in adopting high-energy air-conditioning solutions. After the building is built, air quality and comfort are assessed by the occupants and the criteria become less critical (Baker and Standeven, 1996).

Indoor air quality

The first signs of insufficient ventilation are odours (and other contaminants) and heat. Afterwards, indoor air humidity increases, producing condensation

on walls, starting with thermal bridges, which may result in mould growth. Later on, there is insufficient oxygen.

Not enough ventilation causes 'sick building syndrome', which was first identified during the 1970s. During the worldwide oil embargo, high-rise office buildings were designed to be airtight and very little fresh air from outdoors was introduced in buildings for energy saving reasons.

Thermal comfort in naturally ventilated buildings

Thermal comfort is a complex sensation of satisfaction with the environment related to the physiological effort of thermoregulation. In general, comfort is felt when body temperature is held within a narrow range and skin humidity is low.

Body temperature and skin humidity result from energy and mass balance. The metabolic activity of the body produces about 70W to 100W of heat, which must be evacuated through the skin: about 35 per cent by convection, 35 per cent by radiation and 24 per cent by evaporation; conduction heat transfer is negligible (1 per cent) (Liébard and De Herde, 2006). Heat transferred by convection, advection, radiation and conduction due to temperature difference is called sensible heat. Heat transferred due to water evaporation through breathing and sweating is called latent heat. These two forms of heat show the importance of environmental factors of thermal comfort: air and surface temperatures, air humidity and air velocity. Generally, the thermal comfort sensation is unchanged in a temperature range of 3°C, water vapour pressure range of 3kPa and air velocity range of 0.1m/s. Thermal comfort is also influenced by individual factors, such as metabolic rate and clothing. Metabolic rate varies with the type of activity of the person; it is measured in met: 1met = 58.1W/m². Clothing determines the thermal insulation of a person; it is measured in clo: 1clo = 0.155m²K/W.

Comfort indices

Environmental variables are directly or indirectly measurable, while air temperature is easily measurable. Relative humidity and humidity ratios may be obtained by measuring the bulb temperature and the dew point temperature. Air velocity may be measured and estimated by using fluid mechanics theory. However, the estimation of thermal radiation needs the values of surface temperature and view factors. The value used to characterize the thermal radiation is the *mean radiant temperature*, which is defined as the surface temperature of a fictitious enclosure in which the radiant heat transfer of the human body is equal to the radiant heat transfer in the actual enclosure. An acceptable approximation of the mean radiant temperature at a point is the *globe temperature*, which is the temperature of a black sphere of 15cm in diameter (ISO 7243, 1982).

Two or more environmental variables may be combined to obtain *environmental indices*. The dry bulb temperature, T_a[K], the globe temperature, T_g[K], and air velocity, v[m/s], can be combined to estimate the mean radiant temperature:

$$\overline{T}_r^{\,4} = T_g^{\,4} + Cv^{1/2}(T_g - T_a)$$ [11.1]

where C = 0.247.10⁹ s⁰·⁵/m⁰·⁵. The *operative temperature* is the temperature of a homogeneous environment that would produce the same sensible heat exchange as the real environment. It may be estimated as the weighted mean of the mean radiant temperature, $\overline{\theta}_r$, and air temperature, θ_a, (Berglund, 2001):

$$\theta_o = \frac{h_r \overline{\theta}_o + h_c \theta_a}{h_r + h_c}$$ [11.2]

where h_r and h_c are the coefficients for heat transfer by radiation and by convection, respectively. An acceptable approximation of the operative temperature is:

$$\theta_o = \frac{\overline{\theta}_r + \theta_a}{2}$$ [11.3]

where $\overline{\theta}_r$ may be approximated by the mean wall temperatures weighted by their surfaces. The *effective temperature, ET**, is the temperature that at a relative humidity of 50 per cent produces the same thermal sensation as the combination of operative temperature and the relative humidity (RH) of the real environment, provided that the air velocity is the same.

ASHRAE Standard 55 provides acceptable ranges of operative temperature and humidity for people in summer clothing (0.5clo = 0.078m²K/W) and winter clothing (0.9clo = 0.14m²K/W) with a metabolic rate between 1.0 and 1.3met (58.15 to 75.6W/m²) in an environment with air speed less than 0.20m/s (see Figure 11.2). The separate comfort zones are due to the assumption of different clothing in winter and in summer, which might not be the case for spaces in which people dress similarly all year round.

Field research based on measurements in office buildings around the world has shown that in naturally ventilated buildings, people feel comfortable in larger temperature limits (de Dear et al, 1997; de Dear and Brager, 2002). The explanation of this difference seems to be the 'adaptive opportunities' in naturally ventilated buildings where thermal conditions are controlled mainly by the occupants (Baker and Standeven, 1996).

The comfort limits of Figure 11.2 may be changed by modifying the individual: by 0.6K for each 0.1clo and by 1.4K for each 1.2met, and by modifying the environmental factors, especially the mean air velocity (ASHRAE, 2001).

Control of air quality and comfort through ventilation

The airflow rate may be used to control indoor air quality and thermal comfort. The outdoor airflow rate should be enough to dilute the contaminants. In a steady-state condition, the airflow rate, $\dot{V}$, is:

$$\dot{V} = \frac{I}{\rho_o (C_{\text{lim}} - C_o)}$$ [11.4]

where I is the intensity of the contaminant source, C_{lim} and C_o are the limit value and the outdoor value of the

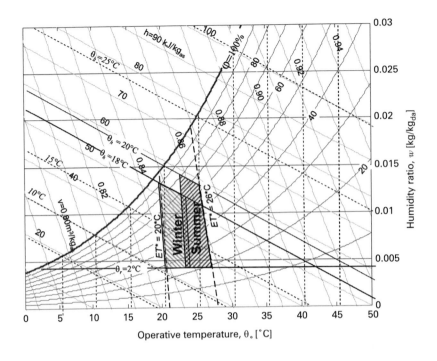

Source: ASHRAE (2001)

Figure 11.2 *ASHRAE ranges of operative temperature and humidity in summer and winter clothing*

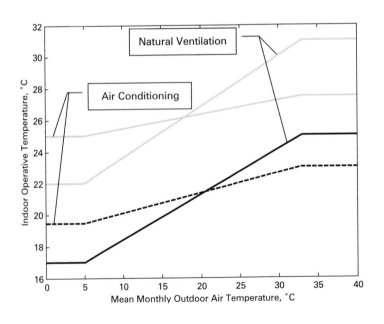

Source: Authors

Figure 11.3 *Comparison of comfort zones for air-conditioned and naturally ventilated buildings*

contaminant concentration, respectively, and ρ_o is the external contaminant density. The contaminant may be water vapour, odours, volatile organic compounds (VOCs), etc. If there are more contaminants, the airflow should dilute all of them.

During the heating season, the occupants are the main source of contaminants (mostly odours and humidity). In this case, the airflow rate should be between 6L/s person and 15L/s person (prEN 13779, 2004).

Outdoor air may be used for thermal control of the building. The outdoor airflow rate needed for cooling is given by an expression similar to Equation 11.4:

$$\dot{V} = \frac{Q}{c_p \rho_o (\theta_{\lim} - \theta_o)} \qquad [11.5]$$

where c_p is the air heat capacity at constant pressure and Q is the sensible cooling load.

Cooling potential by ventilation in a dense urban environment

Improved thermal insulation and the air tightness of buildings have alleviated certain heating problems, but have augmented cooling needs. Therefore, it is of practical interest to assess the potential for cooling by ventilation. Lower wind speed and higher pollution and noise levels of urban environment changes the cooling potential through ventilation.

Cooling potential of natural ventilation

Currently, the energy performance of buildings is assessed by using two types of methods: steady state and dynamic. The steady-state approach is appropriate if the building operation and the efficiency of heating, ventilating and air-conditioning (HVAC) systems are constant, at least for intervals of time and/or outdoor temperature. Dynamic analysis, which uses building thermal simulation, requires exhaustive information about the building construction and operation. The results are usually given in the form of time series. Steady-state methods based on temperatures or on heating/cooling curves can be adapted to characterize the dynamic behaviour by considering their frequency or probability distributions. The heating/cooling curves and temperatures can be used separately in analysing the

building performance. However, the heating/cooling curve and the free-running temperature are equivalent, which enables analysis of the building's heating, ventilation and cooling regimes by using a single concept. The advantage of this method is that the three main factors that influence the energy consumption of the building (the thermal behaviour of the building, the thermal comfort range and climate) are decoupled (Ghiaus, 2006b). Energy consumption for the whole range of variation of the outdoor temperature is:

$$\sum_{T_o} \lfloor q_h \rfloor = \mathbf{F}^T \times \overline{\mathbf{K}} * (\mathbf{T}_o - \overline{T}_b) \qquad [11.6]$$

where $\mathbf{T}_o = [T_{o1} \ T_{o2} \ ... \ T_{ok}]^T$ is the vector which represents the centres of the bins of outdoor temperature, $\mathbf{F} = [F(T_{o1}) \ F(T_{o2}) \ ... \ F(T_{ok})]^T$ is the vector of frequencies of occurrences of outdoor temperature in the bins $\mathbf{T}_o$, and $\overline{\mathbf{K}} = [\overline{K}(T_{o1}) \ \overline{K}(T_{o2}) \ ... \ \overline{K}(T_{ok})]^T$ is the vector of mean global conductance values corresponding to the bins $\mathbf{T}_o$. The operator × represents the matrix multiplication and the operator * represents the array multiplication (i.e. the element-by-element product of arrays):

$$\overline{\mathbf{K}} * \mathbf{T}_o = [\overline{K}(T_{o1}) \cdot T_{o1} \quad \overline{K}(T_{o2}) \cdot T_{o2} \quad ... \quad \overline{K}(T_{ok}) \cdot T_{ok}]^T \qquad [11.7]$$

and the brackets $\lfloor \ \rfloor$ indicate the operation:

$$\lfloor f \rfloor = \begin{cases} f \text{ if } f < 0 \\ 0 \text{ otherwise} \end{cases} \qquad [11.8]$$

If the values of the vector $\overline{\mathbf{K}}$ are constant, then:

$$\overline{\mathbf{K}} * \mathbf{T}_o = \overline{K} \mathbf{T}_o \qquad [11.9]$$

and Equation 11.6 becomes:

$$\sum_{T_o} \lfloor q_h \rfloor = \mathbf{F}^T \times \overline{\mathbf{K}} (\mathbf{T}_o - \overline{T}_b) \qquad [11.10]$$

This expression delivers a condensed representation of the building performance during heating, ventilation and cooling. The conditions for heating, ventilation and cooling can be expressed as:

$$\delta_h = \begin{cases} 1, \text{ if } T_{fr} < T_{cl} \\ 0, \text{ if } T_{fr} \geq T_{cl} \end{cases} \qquad [11.11]$$

$$\delta_v = \begin{cases} 1, \text{ if } T_{fr} > T_{cl} \text{ and } T_o < T_{cu} \\ 0, \text{ if not.} \end{cases} \qquad [11.12]$$

and:

$$\delta_c = \begin{cases} 1, \text{if } T_{fr} > T_{cu} \\ 0, \text{if not.} \end{cases} \quad [11.13]$$

The condition for free cooling (cooling by ventilation) is a sub-domain of ventilation:

$$\delta_{fc} = \begin{cases} 1, \text{if } T_{fr} > T_{cu} \text{ and } T_o < T_{cu} \\ 0, \text{if not.} \end{cases} \quad [11.14]$$

These domains are shown in Figure 11.4. The principle of estimating frequency distribution of degree hours for heating, ventilating and cooling is shown in Figure 11.5. For a given outdoor temperature, the product of the difference between the free-running temperature and the comfort limit (see Figure 11.5 top), and the number of occurrences of the outdoor temperature (which is equal to the product of the probability of occurrences and the number of values – Figure 11.5 middle), gives the frequency distribution for heating and cooling (see Figure 11.5, bottom). If the outdoor

temperature, T_o, is lower than the upper limit of comfort, T_{cu} (Figure 11.5, top), cooling by ventilation is possible (Ghiaus, 2003).

The advantage of representing the data as frequency distributions over a time series is two fold. First, the data has a condensed representation; interpretation of time variation over large intervals such as ten years (which is a lower limit for statistical significance) is very difficult. Second, the adaptive opportunities of the comfort, building and climate are simpler to visualize. The variation of comfort limits with the environmental factors (mean radiant temperature, air velocity and humidity) and personal factors (clothing and metabolism) are easily figured on the top panel of Figure 11.5. Sol-air temperature and its variations due to the urban environment appear on the middle panel of Figure 11.5. The thermal behaviour of the building is described by the difference between the indoor temperature of the building when free running and the outdoor temperature (see Figure 11.6). This difference may be seen as a summation of different effects represented as monthly (Figure 11.6b) and daily variations (Figure 11.6c). These

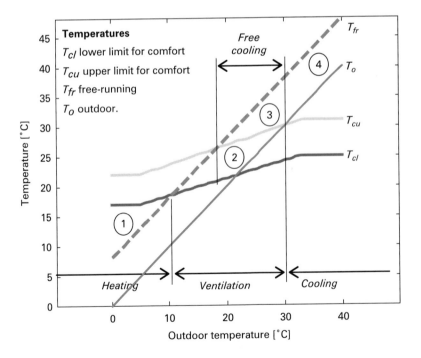

Source: Authors

Figure 11.4 *Heating, ventilating and air-conditioning (HVAC) operating zones: (1) heating; (2) ventilation; (3) free cooling; (4) mechanical cooling*

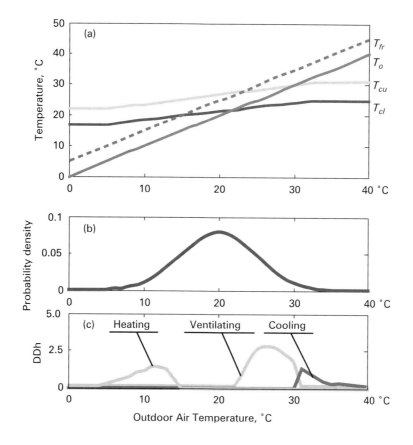

Source: Authors

Figure 11.5 *Principle of estimating frequency distribution of degree hours for heating, ventilating and cooling*

variations may be summed to give the building thermal fingerprint (Figure 11.6a and d). The inertia of the building and the effect of night cooling as expressed in terms of the reduction of the difference between the indoor and the outdoor temperature may be easily integrated in the thermal fingerprint of the building.

Free-running temperatures may be obtained in three ways by:

1 expert estimation;
2 model simulation; and
3 measurements in real buildings (Ghiaus, 2006a).

The example data reveal that the free-cooling potential is not fully used since there are many points plotted for mechanical cooling in the free-cooling domain.

Based on these considerations, the cooling potential of ventilation may be estimated based on statistical weather data (Ghiaus and Allard, 2006). An estimation of the cooling potential of ventilation in Europe and North America is given in Figure 11.7. This potential is modified by the urban environment: wind speed, temperature, noise and pollution.

Airflow and temperatures in street canyons

In urban environments, although eddies and turbulence are important, the mean velocity of wind is often reduced significantly by about an order of magnitude. As a result, wind-induced pressure on building surfaces is also reduced. In order to have an approximate idea of the extent of this reduction, let us consider the case of a building having a height of 20m and a much larger length, exposed to a perpendicular wind, having a reference velocity of 4m/s at 10m over the building. The

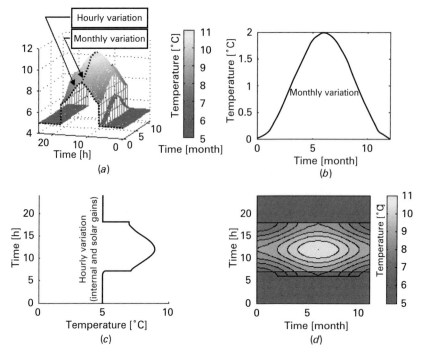

Source: Ghiaus (2003)

Figure 11.6 *Representation of a building as the difference between the indoor and the equivalent (sol-air) temperature: (a) 3D representation; (b) monthly variation; (c) hourly variation; (d) cumulative effects of monthly and hourly variations*

pressure difference between two opposite façades is then about 10Pa to 15Pa in the case of an isolated or exposed building and about zero for a building located in a dense urban environment (see Figure 11.8).

Airflow in street canyons

The wind field in urban environments may be divided into two vertical layers: the urban canopy and the

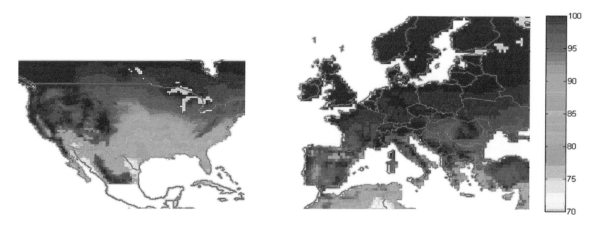

Source: Authors

Figure 11.7 *Percentage of energy savings when cooling by ventilation is used instead of air conditioning*

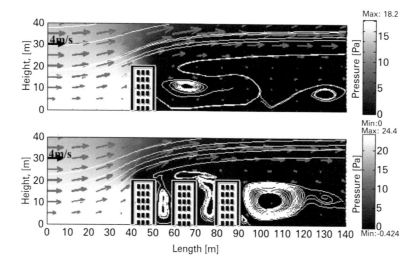

Source: Authors

Figure 11.8 *Wind velocity and wind-induced pressure are reduced in the urban environment*

urban boundary. The first layer extends from the ground surface up to the upper level of the buildings; the second is above the buildings (Oke, 1987). The flow in the canopy layer is influenced by the wind in the urban boundary layer; but it also depends upon the geometry of the buildings and of the streets, upon the presence of other obstacles such as trees, and upon traffic. Generally, the speed in the canopy layer is lower than in the boundary layer. Airflow and temperatures in street canyons were studied by Georgakis and Santamouris (2003) in street canyons in Athens under the framework of the URBVENT project. A synthesis of their findings is given further on in this chapter.

Airflow around isolated buildings is better known. It presents a lee eddy and a wake characterized by lower velocity but higher turbulence compared with the undisturbed wind. The airflow in urban canyons is less known, especially for lower velocities of the undisturbed wind and for oblique directions.

The geometry of street canyons is characterized by H, the mean height of the buildings in the canyon; by W, the canyon width; and by L, the canyon length. Based on these values, the street canyon is characterized by aspect ratio H/W and the building by the aspect ratio L/H.

Wind perpendicular to the canyon axis

When the predominant direction of the airflow is approximately normal (± 15°) to the long axis of the street canyon, three types of airflow regimes are observed as a function of the building (L/H) and canyon (H/W) geometry (Oke, 1987). When the buildings are well apart, (H/W > 0.05), their flow fields do not interact. At closer spacing, the wakes in the canyon are disturbed and the downward flow of the cavity eddy is reinforced. At even greater H/W and density, a stable circulatory vortex is established in the canyon because of the transfer of momentum across a shear layer of roof height. Because high H/W ratios are very common in cities, skimming airflow regime has attracted considerable attention.

The velocity of the vortex depends upon the undisturbed wind speed. If the undisturbed wind has values higher than 1.5m/s to 2m/s and the aspect ratio is H/W = 1...1.5, the speed of the vortex increases with the speed of the wind (DePaul and Sheih, 1986; Yamartino and Wiegand, 1986; Arnfield and Mills, 1994). If the aspect ratio is higher, a secondary vortex was observed for H/W = 2 and even a tertiary for H/W = 3 (Hoydysh and Dabbert, 1988; Nakamura and Oke, 1988). Since the lower vortexes are driven by the upper ones, their velocity is five to ten times lower.

For wind speed larger than 5m/s, the relation between the undisturbed wind, u_{out}, and the air velocity in the street canyon, u_{in}, is almost linear:

$$u_{in} = p \cdot u_{out}$$

[11.15]

For H/W = 1, the coefficient p has values between 0.66 and 0.75, air speed u_{in} being measured at about 0.06H and u_{out} at 1.2H (Nakamura and Oke, 1988).

Wind parallel to the canyon axis

As in the case of perpendicular winds, the airflow in the canyon has to be seen as a secondary circulation feature driven by the flow imposed above the roof (Nakamura and Oke, 1988). If the wind speed outside the canyon is below some threshold values (close to 2m/s), the coupling between the upper and secondary flow is lost and the relation between wind speed above the roof and the air speed inside the canyon is characterized by a considerable scatter (Nakamura and Oke, 1988). For higher wind speeds, the main results and conclusions resulting from the existing studies are that parallel ambient flow generates a mean wind along the canyon axis (Wedding et al, 1977; Nakamura and Oke, 1988), with possible uplift along the canyon walls as airflow is retarded by friction by the building walls and street surface (Nunez and Oke, 1977). This is verified by Arnfield and Mills (1994), who found that for winds that blow along the canyon, the mean vertical canyon velocity is close to zero. Measurements performed in a deep canyon (Santamouris et al, 1999) have also shown an along-canyon flow of the same direction.

Yamartino and Wiegand (1986) reported that the along-canyon wind component, v, in the canyon is directly proportional to the above-roof along-canyon component through the constant of proportionality that is a function of the azimuth of the approaching flow. The same authors found that, at least in a first approximation, $v = U \cdot \cos \theta$, where θ is the incidence angle and U the horizontal wind speed out of the canyon. For wind up to 5m/s, it was reported that the general relation between the two wind speeds appear to be linear: $v = p \cdot U$ (Nakamura and Oke, 1988). For wind parallel to the canyon axis, and for a symmetric canyon with H/W = 1, it was found that p varies between 0.37 and 0.68, air speed being measured at about 0.06H and 1.2H, respectively. Low p values are obtained because of the deflection of the flow by a side canyon. Measurements performed in a deep canyon of H/W = 2.5 (Santamouris et al, 1999) have not shown any clear threshold value where coupling is lost. For wind speed lower than 4m/s, the correlation between

the wind parallel to the canyon and the air velocity along the canyon was not clear. However, statistical analysis has shown that there is a correlation between them.

The mean vertical velocity at the canyon top resulting from mass convergence or divergence in the along-canyon component of flow, w, can be expressed as $w = -H \cdot \partial v / \partial x$, where H is the height of the lower canyon wall, x is the along-canyon coordinate, and v is the x-component of motion within the canyon, averaged over time and the canyon cross-section (Arnfield and Mills, 1994). A linear relationship between the in-canyon wind gradient $\partial v / \partial x$ and the along-canyon wind speed was found. According to Arnfield and Mills (1994), the value of $\partial v / \partial x$ varies between -6.8×10^{-2} and $1.7 \times 10^{-2} s^{-1}$, while according to Nunez and Oke (1977), $\partial v / \partial x$ varies between -7.1×10^{-2} and $0 s^{-1}$.

Wind oblique to the canyon axis

The more common case is when the wind blows at a certain angle relative to the long axis of the canyon. Unfortunately, the existing information on this topic is considerably sparse compared to information on perpendicular and along-canyon flows. Existing results are available through limited field experiments and mainly through wind tunnel and numerical calculations. The main results drawn from the existing research have concluded that when the flow above the roof is at some angle of attack to the canyon axis, a spiral vortex is induced along the length of the canyon – a corkscrew type of action (Nakamura and Oke, 1988; Santamouris et al, 1999).

Wind tunnel research has also shown that a helical flow pattern develops in the canyon (Dabberdt et al, 1973; Wedding et al, 1977). For intermediate angles of incidence to the canyon long axis, the canyon airflow is the product of both the transverse and parallel components of the ambient wind, where the former drives the canyon vortex and the later determines the along-canyon stretching of the vortex (Yamartino and Wiegand, 1986).

Regarding the wind speed inside the canyon, Lee et al (1994) report the results of numerical studies in a canyon with H/W = 1 and a free-stream wind speed equal to 5m/s, flowing at 45° relative to the long axis of the canyon. They report that a vortex is developed inside the canyon whose strength is less than the wind speed above the roof level by about an order of magnitude. Inside the canyon, the maximum across canyon air speed was 0.6m/s, occurring at the highest part of the canyon. The vortex was centred at the upper middle part of the cavity, particularly to about 0.65 of the building height. The maximum wind speeds along canyon were close to 0.8m/s. Much higher along-canyon wind speeds are reported for the downward façade (0.6–0.8m/s) than for the upward façade (0.2m/s). The maximum vertical wind speed inside the canyon was close to 1.0m/s. Much higher vertical velocities are reported for the downward façade (0.8–1.0m/s) than for the upward one (0.6m/s). Studies have shown that an increase of the ambient wind speed corresponds almost always to an increase of the along-canyon wind speed for both the median and the lower and upper quartiles of the speed (Santamouris et al, 1999).

Regarding the distribution of pollutant concentrations in symmetric, even, step-down and step-up canyons, when the wind flows at a certain angle to the canyon axis, Hoydysh and Dabberdt (1988) report results of wind tunnel studies. The authors have calculated the wind angle for which the minimum of the concentration occurs. They report that for the step-down configuration, the minimum concentration occurs for along-canyon winds (incidence angle equal to 90°). For the symmetric configuration, the minimum on the leeward façade occurs for an incidence angle of 30°, while on the windward, the minimum is achieved for angles of between 20° and 70°. Finally, for step-up canyon configurations, the minimum on the leeward façade occurs at incidence angles of between 0° and 40°, while for the windward façade the minimum is found for incidence angles of between 0° and 60°.

Experimental values for low velocities of the undisturbed wind

When wind speed outside the canyon is less than 4m/s but greater than 0.5m/s, although the flow inside the street canyon may appear to have chaotic characteristics, extended analysis of the experimental data resulted in two empirical models (Georgakis and Santamouris, 2003). When the direction of the undisturbed wind is along the main axis of the canyon, the values from Table 11.1 can be used. When the direction of the undisturbed wind is perpendicular or oblique to the canyon, the values from Table 11.2 can be used.

Table 11.1 *Values for air speed inside the canyon when wind blows along the canyon*

Wind speed outside canyon (U)	Wind speed inside canyon	Typical values in the canyon	
		lowest part	highest part
$0 < U < 1$	0.3m/s–0.7 m/s	0.3 m/s	0.7 m/s
$1 < U < 2$	0.4m/s–1.3 m/s	0.4 m/s	1.3 m/s
$2 < U < 3$	0.4m/s–1.5 m/s	0.4 m/s	1.5 m/s
$3 < U < 4$	0.4m/s–2.2 m/s	0.4 m/s	2.2 m/s

Source: Georgakis and Santamouris (2003)

Table 11.2 *Values for air speed inside the canyon when wind blows perpendicular or obliquely to the canyon*

Wind speed outside the canyon (U)	Wind speed inside the canyon		near the upwind façade
	near the windward façade of the canyon		
	at the lowest part	at the highest part	
$0 < U < 1$	0.4 m/s	0.7 m/s	0.4 m/s
$1 < U < 2$	0.4 m/s	1.3 m/s	0.4 m/s
$2 < U < 3$	0.6 m/s	1.5 m/s	0.6 m/s
$3 < U < 4$	0.7 m/s	3 m/s	0.7 m/s

Source: Georgakis and Santamouris (2003)

Airflows in high-density cities

Few studies refer to this important problem of predicting local velocities in high-density cities. Much research has been performed on structural aspects, focusing on high wind velocities. The problem of weak winds, which is the leading problem for ventilation purposes, has not yet been solved.

Ng (2009) studied this question in terms of optimizing the benefits of the natural environment in high-density cities. He used wind tunnel tests in order to study the effect of volume density on the potential of natural ventilation.

Four cases were studied in order to determine if there is an effect on natural ventilation potential when different vertical gaps are created or when a random distribution of heights is made. The first result of this study is that small height differences on the top of buildings do not really increase the air movement at the bottom. Furthermore, the number of gaps does not really influence the ventilation. On the contrary, if the arrangements of gaps create a real 'air path' through the city, then the ventilation performance could be improved by 15 to 20 per cent.

Ng (2009) states that, in Hong Kong, recommendations for air paths through the city have been incorporated within Hong Kong Planning Standards and Guidelines (HKSAR, 2002). The results of these guidelines can be clearly seen on the town plan of Tseung Kwan O, a new town in Hong Kong.

Air and surface temperature in urban canyons

The effect of the urban heat island increases with the size of the urban conurbation (Oke, 1982). However, this temperature refers to the undisturbed wind that flows in the urban boundary layer. The temperature distribution in the urban canopy layer is greatly affected by the radiation balance. Solar radiation incident on urban surfaces is absorbed and then transformed to sensible heat. Most of the solar radiation impinges on roofs and on the vertical walls of buildings; only a relatively small part reaches ground level. In fact, in the street canyons, the air temperature is much lower than in the boundary layer, partially compensating for the heat island effect.

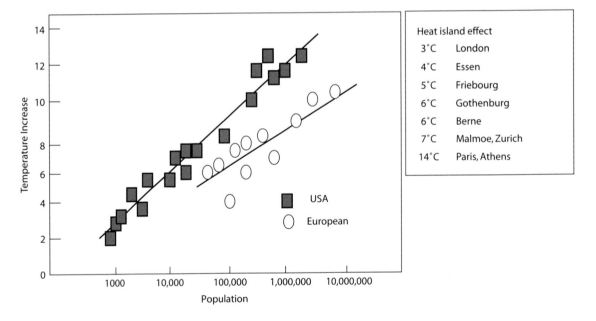

Source: Oke (1982)

Figure 11.9 *Maximum differences in urban and rural temperature for US and European cities*

The optical and thermal characteristics of materials used in urban environments, especially the albedo for solar radiation and emissivity for long-wave radiation, have a very important impact upon the urban energy balance. The use of high albedo materials reduces the amount of solar radiation absorbed in building envelopes and urban structures and keeps their surfaces cooler. Materials with high emissivity are good emitters of long-wave radiation and readily release the energy that has been absorbed as short-wave radiation. Lower surface temperatures decrease the temperature of the ambient air because heat convection intensity from a cooler surface is lower (Santamouris, 2001; Doya and Bozonnet 2007).

Experimental measurements of surface temperature have shown that the maximum simultaneous difference of the two façades was up to 10°C to 20°C at the highest measured levels of the canyon, while the highest difference was close to 7°C at 20m above ground level (Georgakis and Santamouris, 2003). Comparison of the maximum difference of daily temperatures of the building façades and the surface temperature of the street shows that at street level, temperature was 7.5°C higher than the lower parts of the canyon. The surface temperature stratification observed during the day period was between 30°C to 50°C on the south-east wall and 27°C to 41°C on the north-west wall. The temperature differences between opposite surfaces during the day were higher at the highest location of the façade.

The air temperature at street level was 3°C higher than that at the lower parts of the canyon, but no specific temperature distribution pattern with the canyon height has been found. The absence of air temperature stratification inside canyon agrees with the almost identical mean values of surface temperatures for all the measuring spots in the canyon. A possible explanation for this very good air temperature diffusion into the space between buildings is the high advection. The fact that air temperature outside the canyon is higher than inside can be due to street orientation, which permits a lot of hours with shadow in the canyon and the very good airflow inside the canyon due to the large aspect ratio (H/W = 3.3). The air temperatures recorded inside the canyon were about 3.5°C lower than outside.

Noise level and natural ventilation potential in street canyons

High external noise levels are often used to justify the use of air conditioning in commercial and residential buildings. Methods of estimating noise levels in urban canyons are necessary if the potential for naturally ventilating buildings is to be assessed. These estimated levels can then be compared to the level of noise at which building occupants might be motivated to close windows in order to keep out the noise, but also to compromise natural ventilation strategy. Studies concerning the noise attenuation in street canyons were carried out by Nicol and Wilson (2003) under the framework of the URBVENT project. A synthesis of their findings is presented below.

A series of daytime noise measurements were made in canyon streets in Athens with aspect ratios (H/W) varying from 1.1 to 5.3. The main purpose of the measurements was to examine the vertical variation in noise in the canyons in order to give advice on natural ventilation potential. A simple model of the noise level has been developed using a linear regression analysis of the measured data. The model can be used to predict the fall-off (attenuation) of the noise level with height above street level.

The attenuation is found to be a function of street width and height above the street; but the maximum level of attenuation (at the top of the canyon) is almost entirely a function of the aspect ratio, except in narrow streets. Background noise (L_{90}) suffers less attenuation than foreground noise (L_{10}) with height.

The attenuation results are compared to results from acoustic simulation. The simulation gives comparable values for attenuation in the canyons. The simulation is used to estimate the effectiveness of balconies for reducing external noise levels in canyon streets. Measurements in a survey throughout Europe are used to estimate the potential for natural ventilation in canyon streets in Southern Europe.

The survey and simulations are used to assess the effect of noise on the natural ventilation potential of canyon-type streets, and to suggest limitations to the use of natural ventilation as a function of canyon geometry.

Noise in street canyons

Canyon-like streets in cities such as Athens vary considerably in the width and height of the buildings that border them. The ratio of the height of the buildings (H) to the width of the street (W) is known as the 'aspect ratio' (AR) of the street. While the assumption is that the two sides of the street are of the same height, this is frequently not the case. Nicol and Wilson (2003) have taken the average height of the street façades to give $AR = (h_1 + h_2)/2w$ (where h_1 and h_2 are the respective heights of the sides of the canyon – assumed to be comparable). The façades themselves also vary considerably, some being plain and some with balconies. Most residential streets have balconies, but even some office buildings are constructed with balconies. At ground level the situation can be more complex. The ground floor is often set back with colonnades. Paper stalls and other objects often litter the pavement.

A simple model of noise in canyons

The purpose of the investigation of Nicol and Wilson (2003) was to provide a method for estimating the fall-off in noise level with the height in street canyons. The traffic noise, as measured at various locations in the canyons, is a combination of the direct sound and quasi-reverberation in the canyon. The term quasi-reverberation is used to denote a type of reverberation which is not diffuse but consists primarily of flutter echoes between the façades lining the street. Thus, the sound pressure, p, is:

$$p^2 \propto P(dc + rc) \qquad [11.16]$$

where P is the sound power, dc is the direct component of the sound and rc is the reverberating component.

The direct component may be treated in two ways depending upon whether the traffic is considered as a line source (where the traffic stream is considered as the source) or point source (where each vehicle is separately responsible for the noise). For a line source, the direct component, dc, is inversely proportional to the distance from the source; for the point source, the direct component, dc, is inversely proportional to the square of the distance. If the street width is W and the height of the measuring position above the ground is H, assuming the source is in the middle of the road, the distance between source and receiver is:

$$d = \left((W/2)^2 + H^2\right)^{1/2} \qquad [11.17]$$

For the reverberating sound, the noise is related approximately to the absorption area. This strictly applies to diffuse sound sources and is only

approximate in this context. The main area for absorption is the open top of the canyon, which is assumed to be a perfect absorber and whose area per metre of street equals W, the width of the street. If the absorption coefficient is 0.05, the absorption area is:

$$W' = W + 0.05W + 2 \cdot 0.05H \qquad [11.18]$$

where the first term corresponds to the top of the canyon, the second to the floor and the third to the two lateral walls. Using the aspect ratio ($AR = W/H$) of the street, Equation 11.18 becomes:

$$W' = W(1.05 + 0.1 \cdot AR) \qquad [11.19]$$

The sound power is assumed proportional to the number of vehicles per hour, n. For a line source, its expression is:

$$p^2 = a\frac{n}{d} + b\frac{n}{W'} + c \qquad [11.20]$$

For a point source, its expression is:

$$p^2 = a\frac{n}{d^2} + b\frac{n}{W'} + c \qquad [11.21]$$

where a, b and c are constants related to the direct component, the reverberating component and to any background environmental noise entering the canyon, respectively. In general, the contribution of c will be small. Measurements on the rooftop of a building in a pedestrian area behind vehicular streets in the centre of Athens gave $L_{Aeq} = 55$dB. In the vehicular streets, few noise levels below $L_{Aeq} = 70$dB were recorded. L_{90} averaged 66dB. The expressions were developed into the form:

$$L_p = 10\log_{10}\left(n\left(\frac{a}{d_1} + \frac{b}{W'}\right) + c\right) \qquad [11.22]$$

where, by the normal definition of sound level in dB, L_p is the noise level for a sound pressure level p and is equal to $10\log_{10} p$, and d_1 is d or d^2 (see Equations 11.20 and 11.21), depending upon the assumption about the shape of the noise source.

In Equation 11.22, the value of L_p relates to height above the canyon floor, H, through the variable d_1. An estimation of the values of the constants a, b and c will enable the change of L_p with H to be determined. The values of the constants a, b and c have been estimated using multiple regression analysis.

Correlation analysis suggested that the line source of sound was a better model for these data. The correlation between measured p^2 and calculated direct noise levels (ignoring the reverberating component) were 0.86 for the linear source assumption as against 0.68 for the point source. Further tests showed that there was little change in correlation whether W or W' were used. The advantage of using W (the width of the street) is its simplicity while W' (the absorption area) would allow the computation of any increase in the absorption coefficient of the façade. However, there is no measured data to evaluate any change of absorption.

Regression analysis gives optimal values for the constants a, b and c for Equation 11.20: which becomes:

$$p^2 = 17.4 \cdot 10^4 \cdot D_2 + 5.34 \cdot 10^4 \cdot RV - 411 \cdot 10^4 \quad [11.23]$$

Then:

$$L_{eq} = 10 \log_{10} p^2 \quad [11.24]$$

where L_{eq} is the noise level at height H above the street; D_2 is a function of three variables, H, W and n, the number of vehicles (n assumed to be proportional to the noise generated). Two of these variables (n and W) are also included in RV together with the aspect ratio, AR, of the canyon. There is a logical problem with a negative value for c since the value of p^2 cannot be negative. This value may be due to a curvature in the relationship, which the linear regression cannot take into account. The effect of c on the value of p^2 is, in any case, generally small. This shows that the measured value is well predicted by the calculated value ($R^2 = 0.75$).

In order to facilitate the visualization, a simplifying assumption has been made that the traffic level is a function of street width. In these data, the correlation between traffic intensity, expressed in number of vehicles per hour, n, and street width W (m) was $R = 0.88$ and the regression relationship was as follows:

$$n = 137W - 306 \quad [11.25]$$

Using this simplifying assumption, values of expected noise level at different heights for a particular value of street width W can be calculated.

Assuming that the traffic in the canyons follows the relationship shown in Equation 11.25, the expected

daytime noise level becomes purely a function of the geometry of the street. Figure 11.10 shows the expected noise levels in Athens at different street widths and heights above the streets and the implication of this for the natural ventilation potential of office units at a height H above street level.

The results introduced above from the SCATS project (McCartney and Nicol, 2002) suggest that the tolerable noise level in European offices is around 60dB. At the same time, the noise attenuation at an open window is accepted as 10dB to 15dB. Thus, an outdoor noise level of 70dB or less is likely to be acceptable. Using special methods and window designs, a further 3dB to 5dB attenuation is possible. For the traffic conditions of Athens, street widths that will give acceptable conditions at different heights above the street are indicated by 'OK' in Figure 11.10. Street widths that will give unacceptable conditions for buildings with open windows near street level are also indicated by 'Not OK'. Between these two, there are possibilities for acceptable conditions with careful design.

Because the noise measurements reported here were exclusively taken during the day, the implications on natural ventilation potential for evening or night-time can only be guessed, though it should be remembered that in *unoccupied* offices, the outdoor noise level will be irrelevant to the use of night ventilation. The limitation to natural ventilation potential by noise will be important at night in residences. While overall noise levels will almost certainly be lower at night, the reduction will be offset by the greater sensitivity to noise. In addition, the occasional passing vehicle will be almost as loud, although as a point source its attenuation with distance above the street will be according to Equation 11.21 and will be greater than for daytime noise. Notice that the attenuation of the loudest daytime noises (as suggested by the attenuation of the L_{10}) is greater than the attenuation of the L_{eq} for similar reasons.

Outdoor–indoor pollutant transfer

Outdoor air pollution is commonly considered as another barrier for using natural ventilation since filters cannot be used as in mechanical or air-conditioning systems. Nevertheless, two aspects are important in this assessment: the improvement of outdoor air quality with economic development, and the different nature of outdoor and indoor pollutants.

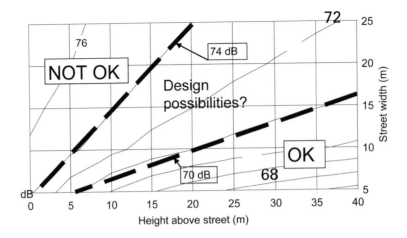

Source: Ghiaus et al (2006)

Figure 11.10 *Contours of noise level at different heights above the street and street widths: configurations in which natural ventilation is possible are indicated (OK), as are those in which it is ruled out (NOT OK) – between these two extremes is a region in which there are possibilities for design solutions*

First, economic growth has the tendency to ameliorate outdoor air quality after its initial negative effect (see Figure 11.11a). While material progress is sought, pollution increases with economic growth. But when the financial and technological resources are enough, the cost of pollution counts in evaluating quality of life, and actions to reduce it are enforced. The decrease of overall outdoor pollution, regardless of income, is also noticeable.

Second, the type and concentration level of pollutants are different indoors and outdoors. The World Health Organization (WHO) issued health-based guidelines for air quality in which recommended values are given for the 'key' pollutants: sulphur dioxide (SO_2), nitrogen dioxide (NO_2), carbon monoxide (CO), methane (O_3) suspended particle matter and lead (Pb). Guideline values for these pollutants are given in WHO (2000). Indoor pollutants include environmental tobacco smoke, particles (biological and non-biological), volatile organic compounds, nitrogen oxides, lead, radon, carbon monoxide, asbestos, various synthetic chemicals and others. Indoor air pollution has been associated with a range of health effects, from discomfort and irritation to chronic pathologies and cancers. In an effort to conserve energy, modern building design has favoured tighter structures with lower rates of ventilation (WHO, 2000). The impact of indoor pollution upon health is much more important than that of outdoor pollution (see Figure 11.11b). Indoor pollution problems differ in developed and developing countries. For the first, the cause is low ventilation rates and the presence of products and materials that emit a large variety of compounds, while for the latter the cause is human activity, especially combustion processes.

Epidemiological studies show associations between health events (such as death and admission in hospitals) and daily average concentrations of particles, ozone, sulphur dioxide, airborne acidity, nitrogen dioxide and carbon monoxide. Although the associations for each of these pollutants were not significant in all studies, taking the body of evidence as a whole, the consistency is striking. For particles and ozone it has been accepted by many that the studies provide no indication of any threshold of effect and an assumption of linearity was made when defining the exposure–response relationships (WHO, 2000).

Indoor air quality is related to the outdoor air pollutant concentration through the rate of air change and reactivity of the pollutant. The façade air tightness, as an intrinsic characteristic of the building, represents a key factor in this relation because it is the main link between indoor and outdoor environments, as well as being an important characteristic of the natural ventilation property of buildings.

Experimental study of outdoor–indoor pollutant transfer

The key outdoor pollutants (SO_2, NO_2, CO, O_3, suspended particle matter and Pb) are usually monitored in large cities. The mean levels of sulphur dioxide and lead are equal indoors and outdoors. Ozone and nitrogen dioxide react with the building material, resulting in a lower concentration indoors than outdoors when the building is airtight. The particle matter transfer depends upon the particle size. The experimental results show that the ratio between indoor and outdoor concentration (I/O) also depends upon the outdoor concentration of the pollutant.

The indoor–outdoor ratio was studied for ozone, nitrogen dioxide and particle matter under the framework of the URBVENT project and of the French programme PRIMEQUAL. A literature review shows that the ozone concentration is less indoors than outdoors and that the ratio increases with airflow rate (see Figure 11.12a). In the case of closed windows (shown as CW in Figure 11.12a), the transfer is more complex. Our experimental results confirm that this complexity comes from the air tightness of the building façade. Other studies showed that the indoor–outdoor ratio also depends upon the outdoor concentration (see Figure 11.12b). These two parameters were considered as explanatory variables in the prediction of the I/O ratio.

Outdoor–indoor transfer mapping

The indoor–outdoor concentration ratio (I/O) is mapped on outdoor concentration, C_o, and the three main levels of air tightness of the façade: 'airtight', $Q_{4Pa} \approx 0m^3/h$; 'permeable', $Q_{4Pa} \approx 150m^3/h$; and 'very permeable', $Q_{4Pa} \approx 300m^3/h$ (see Figure 11.13). The I/O ratio was determined for closed windows (measurements during night). Since the room volume was about $150m^3$, the maximum air change per hour was about 2ach.

Ozone

The I/O ratio diminishes with the outdoor concentration for the airtight façades and increases for the other two types of façades (see Figure 11.14). Two clusters were found: the first is situated in the zone of

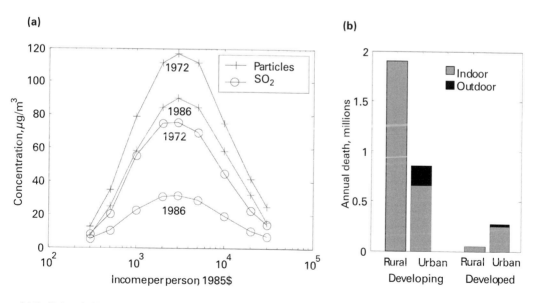

Source: (a) Shafik (1994); (b) WHO (1997); Lomborg (2001)

Figure 11.11 *Relationship between pollution and development: (a) particles and SO_2 pollution in relation to income; (b) estimated global annual deaths from indoor and outdoor pollution*

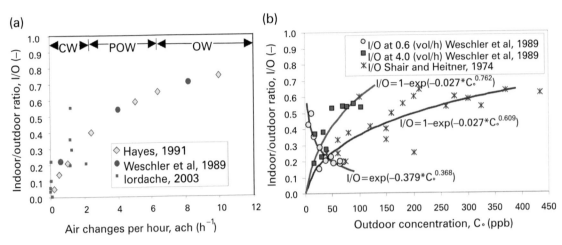

Figure 11.12 *The variation of indoor–outdoor ozone ratio as a function of (a) air changes per hour (CW = closed window; POW = partially opened window; OW = open window); (b) outdoor concentration*

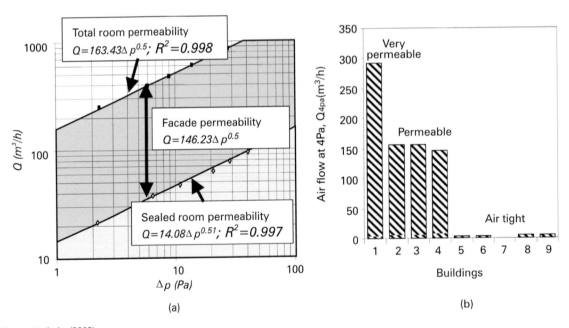

Figure 11.13 *Building classification according to permeability*

the airtight façade ($c_{Q4Pa} \approx 5m^3/h$) and middle-ranged outdoor concentration ($c_{Co} \approx 28ppb$); the second one is placed in the zone of the 'most permeable' façades ($c_{Q4Pa} \approx 292m^3/h$) for middle-ranged outdoor concentration ($c_{Co} \approx 36ppb$). The two peaks of the model are placed in the zone of 'airtight' façade with low outdoor O_3 concentration and the zone of the 'most permeable' façade with high outdoor O_3 concentration (see Figure 11.14a). The second map (see Figure 11.14b) presents the precision of the model expressed by the dispersion of the points in the database. The map shows that the smallest dispersion of the I/O value is 0.18, while the higher dispersion is 0.38 (see Figure 11.14b). The third map presents the credibility of the first two maps (see Figure 11.14c). It is higher in the zones where more measurement points were collected (i.e. in the proximity of the two clusters). The highest credibility zone (CR > 0.5) corresponds to the middle-ranged outdoor O_3 concentrations, between the centres of the two clusters, while the lowest credibility zones (CR < 0.25) are for the 'most permeable' façade with low outdoor concentrations and 'airtight' façade with high outdoor concentrations.

Nitrogen dioxide

The same three parameters were calculated for nitrogen dioxide. The I/O ratio diminishes with the outdoor concentration regardless of the façade air tightness. The values of the I/O ratios corresponding to the airtight façades are slightly higher then those corresponding to 'permeable' or 'very permeable' façades (see Figure 11.15a). The model precision is almost the same for all of the domain (see Figure 11.15b). The credibility is higher in the zones where more measurement are available (i.e. in the proximity of the clusters). Two clusters were found for lower outdoor concentration (Co_{NO2} < 15ppb): one cluster corresponds to the 'airtight' buildings while the second one corresponds to

the 'very permeable'. The credibility parameter diminishes with the rise of the outdoor concentration, having values between 0 and 0.5 for outdoor concentrations higher than 20ppb (see Figure 11.15c).

Particle matter

The same three values are estimated for the penetration indoors of three different size intervals of particulate matter: 0.3–0.4μm, 0.8–1μm and 2–3μm. Similar conclusions can be drawn for all three particle sizes.

The I/O ratios diminish with the outdoor concentration regardless of the building façade air tightness or the size of the particles. For the size interval 0.3–0.4μm (see Figure 11.16a), the model surface is relatively plane, so the I/O ratio diminishes linearly with the outdoor concentration. For the other two sizes, the model maps present a concavity in the model surfaces for the small values of the outdoor concentration and the 'permeable' façades (see Figure 11.16d and g). Contrary to the first two size intervals, the model surface of the class 2–3μm presents I/O ratios of 0.65 corresponding to high outdoor concentration and a 'very permeable' façade. However, the prediction credibility index is very small for that zone.

The dispersion of the I/O ratio presents almost constant values for all outdoor pollution range and façade permeability. The value of the index characterizing this dispersion is about 0.33 for the first

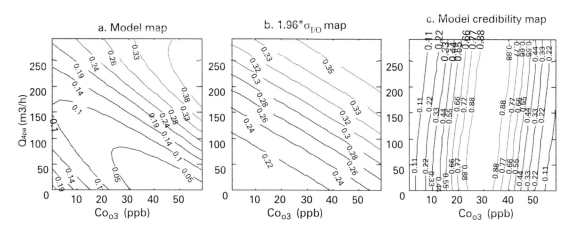

Source: Ghiaus et al (2005)

Figure 11.14 *Ozone outdoor–indoor transfer: (a) I/O ratio; (b) precision; (c) degree of confidence*

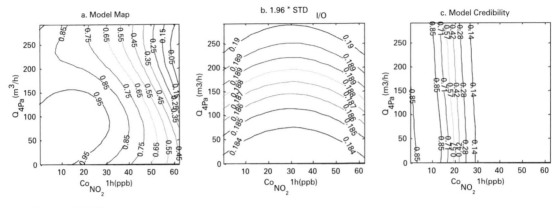

Source: Ghiaus et al (2005)

Figure 11.15 *NO$_2$ outdoor–indoor transfer: (a) I/O ratio; (b) precision; (c) degree of confidence*

size interval (see Figure 11.16b), while it is twice that for the last two size intervals (see Figure 11.16e and h). The prediction credibility presents the same diminishing trend with the outdoor concentration (see Figure 11.16c, f and i).

Summary

Outdoor and indoor pollution have a different nature and usually refer to different types of pollutants. After a threshold in wealth is attained, when the financial and technological means are available, outdoor pollution diminishes with economic development.

In the joint framework of the URBVENT project and the French PRIMEQUAL programme, an experimental study of outdoor–indoor pollution transfer of was conducted in nine schools. The pollutants studied were ozone, nitrogen dioxide and 15 sizes of particle matter. Three maps were calculated for every pollutant: the I/O ratio, the precision of this estimation, and the degree of confidence in the I/O ratio and precision. The ratio of indoor–outdoor concentration was determined as a function of airflow through the façade and of the outdoor concentration. The indoor concentration was less inside than outside. Ozone presented the lowest I/O ratio (0.1–0.4). The I/O ratio for nitrogen dioxide was the highest, between approximately 0 and 0.95. The I/O ratio for particle matter depended upon the particle size. The most important variation (0.25–0.70) was measured for particles of small size (0.3–0.4μm); particles of larger size (0.8–3μm) represented lower, but comparable, variation of the I/O ratio (0.3–0.7).

Natural ventilation strategies in a dense urban environment

The use of natural ventilation in dense urban environments should take into account the lower wind velocity, but also noise and pollution. Ventilation systems cannot rely on low-level inlets since outdoor air at street levels may be contaminated and inlets will be shielded from winds.

Balanced stack ventilation

A number of ancient Middle Eastern strategies using both roof-level inlets and exhausts – including the traditional Iranian wind towers or *bagdir* and the Arabian and Eastern Asian wind catchers or *malkaf* – are being reconsidered for broader application and technical refinement.

In these *balanced* stack ventilation schemes, air is supplied in a cold stack (i.e. with air temperatures maintained close to outdoor conditions through proper insulation of the stack) and exhausted through a warm stack (see Figure 11.17).

Let us consider, for example, the loop through the second level of Figure 11.17. The equation for this

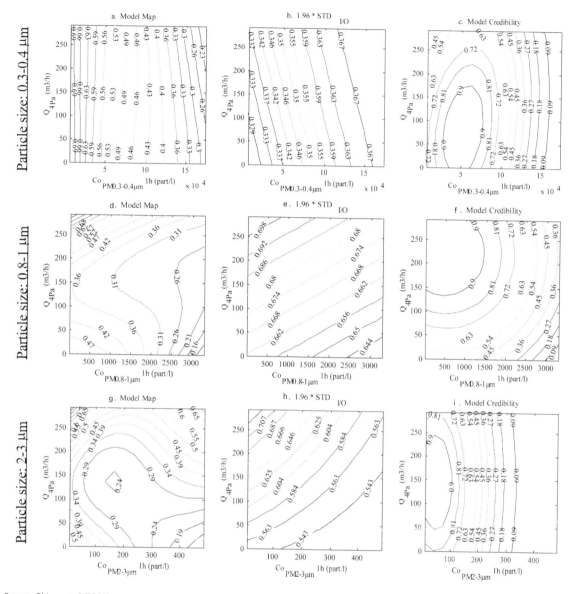

Source: Ghiaus et al (2005)

Figure 11.16 *Particulate matter outdoor–indoor transfer: (a, d, g) I/O ratio; (b, e, h) precision; (c, f, i) degree of confidence*

pressure loop will be similar in form to the case of combined wind- and buoyancy-driven ventilation:

$$\Delta p_s + \Delta p_w = \Delta p_{inlet} + \Delta p_{internal} + \Delta p_{exhaust} \quad [11.26]$$

The stack pressure is determined by the indoor-to-outdoor air density difference and the height difference

from the stack exhaust and the floor-level inlet locations, $\Delta p_s = (\rho_o - \rho_i)g\Delta z$, if air temperatures within the cold stack can be maintained close to outdoor levels. Airflow through each floor level will, therefore, be identical to that expected in the simpler single-stack scheme if the airflow resistance of the supply stack (and its inlet and outlet devices) is similar to that provided by the air inlet

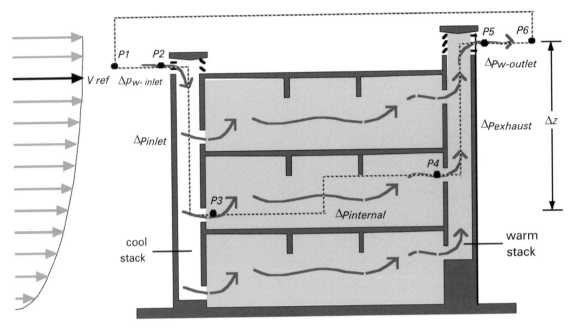

Source: Axley (2001)

Figure 11.17 *Top-down or balanced stack natural ventilation systems use high-level supply inlets to access less contaminated air and to place both inlet and outlets in higher wind velocity exposures*

devices. The driving wind pressure is determined by the difference between inlet and exhaust wind pressure coefficients and the kinetic energy content of the approach wind velocity $\Delta p_w = (C_{p-inlet} - C_{p-exhaust})\rho v_{ref}^2/2$. However, in this case, the high location of the inlet ensures a higher inlet wind pressure and insensitivity to wind direction. This, combined with the potential of a wind-direction insensitive exhaust stack, makes this scheme particularly attractive for urban environments. Balanced stack systems have been commercially available in the UK for, apparently, over a century (Axley, 2001), although these commercially available systems have, until recently, been designed to serve single rooms rather than whole buildings. The Windcatcher natural ventilation systems distributed by Monodraught Limited in the UK (see Figure 11.18) offer air change rates as high as five air changes per hour under relatively low wind conditions (3m/s) measured 10m above the building (www.monodraught.com/WindCather). These systems may also be supplied with co-axial fans to provide mechanical assistance during extreme weather conditions.

In cold conditions, it is possible to achieve ventilation air heat recovery with *top-down* schemes by using coaxial supply.

Passive evaporative cooling

An improvement of the *balanced stack* ventilation system, also based on ancient Middle Eastern and Eastern Asian solutions, consists of adding evaporative cooling to the supply stack. Traditionally, evaporative cooling was achieved through water-filled porous pots within the supply air stream or the use of a pool of water at the base of the supply stack (Santamouris and Asimakopoulos, 1996; Allard and Alvarez, 1998). In more recent developments, water sprayed high into the supply air stream cools the air stream and increases the supply air density, thereby augmenting the buoyancy-induced pressure differences that drive airflow (Bowman et al, 2000).

The loop analysis of this so-called *passive downdraught evaporative cooling* scheme is similar to

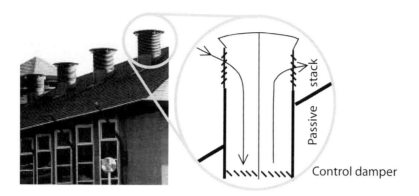

Source: photo reproduced with permission from Monodraught Limited

Figure 11.18 *Windcatcher for natural ventilation systems*

that of the *balanced-stack* scheme; but now the buoyancy effects of the increased moisture content must be accounted for. Consider the representative diagram of such a system shown in Figure 11.19. Two height differences must now be distinguished: z_a – the height above the room inlet location of the moist air column in the supply stack; and z_b – the height of the exhaust above this moist column.

The air density in the moist air supply column, ρ_s, will approach the saturation density corresponding to the outdoor air wet bulb temperature; more specifically, experiments indicate these supply air conditions will be within 2°C of the wet bulb temperature. Hence, the loop equation describing the (time-averaged) ventilation airflow in this system becomes:

$$\left(\Delta p_{inlet} + \Delta p_{internal} + \Delta p_{exhaust}\right) = \Delta p_s + \Delta p_w \quad [11.27]$$

where:

$$\Delta p_s = \left[\rho_o z_b + \rho_s z_a - \rho_i (z_a + z_b)\right]g \quad [11.28]$$

$$\Delta p_w = \left(C_{p-inlet} - C_{p-exhaust}\right)\frac{\rho v_r^2}{2} \quad [11.29]$$

For a quantitative measure of the impact of this strategy, let us consider a case similar to the one discussed above for wind- and buoyancy-induced natural ventilation, but with a cool moist column height that equals the stack height of 10m (i.e. $z_a \approx 0$m and $z_b \approx 10$m). If the outdoor air has a temperature of 25°C and a humidity of 20 per cent RH (i.e. with a density of approximately 1.18kg/m³) and is evaporatively cooled to within 2°C of its wet bulb temperature (12.5°C), its dry bulb temperature will drop to 14.5°C, while its density will increase to approximately 1.21kg/m³ and relative humidity to 77 per cent. If internal conditions are kept just within the thermal comfort zone for these outdoor conditions (i.e. 28°C and 60 per cent RH), using an appropriate ventilation flow rate given internal gains, then internal air density will be approximately 1.15kg/m³. Consequently, the buoyancy pressure difference will be:

$$\Delta p_s = \left(1.18\ \frac{kg}{m^3}(0\ m) + 1.21\ \frac{kg}{m^3}(10\ m) - 1.15\ \frac{kg}{m^3}(0 + 10\ m)\right)9.8\ \frac{m}{s^2} = 6.4\ Pa \quad [11.30]$$

Without the evaporative cooling (i.e. with $\Delta z_a \approx 10$ and $\Delta z_b \approx 0$ m):

$$\Delta p_s = \left(1.18\ \frac{kg}{m^3}(10\ m) + 1.21\ \frac{kg}{m^3}(0\ m) - 1.15\ \frac{kg}{m^3}(10 + 0\ m)\right)9.8\ \frac{m}{s^2} = 2.9\ Pa \quad [11.31]$$

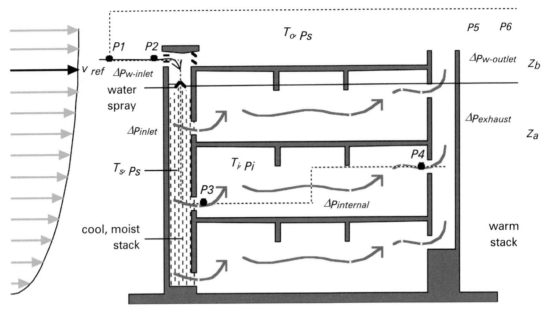

Source: Axley (2001)

Figure 11.19 *Passive downdraught evaporative cooling stack ventilation*

Thus, in this representative example, evaporative cooling more than doubles the buoyancy pressure difference while, at the same time, providing adiabatic cooling.

This principle was applied for the first time during 1994 to 1999 on a large scale at Torrent Research Centre, Ahmedabad, India, designed by Abhikram, Nimish Patel and Parut Zaveri, consultant Brian Ford. During the summer, temperatures are below 32°C, although the outdoor temperature reaches 44°C, which gives a temperature difference of 12°C. The indoor temperature varies by 3°C to 4°C, while the outdoor temperature variations are of 14°C to 17°C. The investment cost was about 13 per cent higher than for a standard solution. The payback period for all the supplementary investment is less than 15 years.

Double-skin façade

The double façade system was first introduced in France during the early 1930s. During this time, Le Corbusier (1887–1965) designed a multiple glass layer wall called 'Mur Neutralisant', which acts as an air duct to neutralize the effect of the cold or sun.

Unfortunately, this idea was never implemented due to the high initial cost. However, this innovative concept

has been employed in many modern buildings. The double façade system was used in the US during the 1980s and is now common in Europe. Examples of buildings using this system include the Occidental Chemical Center (1980), New York, US, by Cannon Design with Hellmuth Obata and Kassabaum; The Lloyd's Building (1986), London, UK, by Richard Rogers Partnership; the Business Promotion Centre (1993), Duisburg, Germany, by Sir Norman Forster and Partners; Headquarters for RWE AG (1996), Essen, Germany, by Ingenhoven, Overdiek, Kahlen and Partners; and Commerzbank Headquarters (1996), Frankfurt, Germany, by Sir Norman Forster and Partners. Even renovated buildings, such as the BCT Telus Communications Operation Building in Vancouver, Canada, also transform the original wall into a double-glazed system.

References

Allard, F. and Alvarez, S. (1998) 'Fundamentals of Natural Ventilation' in F. Allard (ed.) *Natural Ventilation in Buildings*, James and James, London

Allard, F. (ed) (1997) *Natural Ventilation in Buildings: A Design Handbook*, James and James, London

Arnfield, A. J. and Mills, G. (1994) 'An analysis of the circulation characteristics and energy budget of a dry, asymmetric, east, west urban canyon: I. Circulation characteristics', *International Journal of Climatology*, vol 14, pp119–134

ASHRAE (2001) *ASHRAE Handbook Fundamentals*, ASHRAE, Atlanta, FL

Awbi, H. (1998) 'Ventilation', *Renewable and Sustainable Energy Reviews*, vol 2, pp157–188

Axley, J. (2001) *Application of Natural Ventilation for US Commercial Buildings, Climate Suitability and Design Strategies and Methods*, GCR-01-820, National Institute of Standards and Technology Gaithersburg, MD

Baker, N. and Standeven, M. (1996) 'Thermal comfort for free-running buildings', *Energy and Buildings*, vol 23, pp175–182

Berlund, L. B. (2001) *Thermal Comfort*, ASHRAE, Atlanta, GA

Bowman, N. T., Eppel, H., Lomas, K. J., Robinson, D. and Cook, M. J. (2000) 'Passive Downdraught Evaporative Cooling', *Indoor and Built Environment*, vol 9, no 5, pp284–290

Doya, M. and Bozonnet, E. (2007) Theoretical Evaluation of Energy Performance Achieved by 'Cool' Paints for Dense Urban Environment, CLIMAMED, Genova

Dabberdt, W. F., Ludwig, F. L. and Johnson, W. B. (1973) 'Validation and applications of an urban diffusion model for vehicular emissions', *Atmospheric Environment*, vol 7 pp603–618

de Dear, R. and Brager, G. (2002) 'Thermal comfort in naturally ventilated buildings: Revision of ASRHAE Standard 55', *Energy and Buildings*, vol 34, pp549–561

de Dear, R., Brager, G. and Cooper, D. (1997) *Developing an Adaptive Model of Thermal Comfort and Preference, Final Report, ASHRAE RP- 884*, American Society of Heating, Refrigerating and Air-Conditioning Engineers, Inc, and Macquarie Research, Ltd, Sydney

DePaul, F. T. and Sheih, C. M. (1986) 'Measurements of wind velocities in a street canyon', *Atmospheric Environment*, vol 20, pp445–459

Georgakis, G. and Santamouris, M. (2003) *Urban Environment*, Research report, URBVENT Project, European Commission Athens, Greece

Ghiaus, C. (2003) 'Free-running building temperature and HVAC climatic suitability', *Energy and Buildings*, vol 35, no 4, pp405–411

Ghiaus, C. (2006a) 'Experimental estimation of building energy performance by robust regression', *Energy and Buildings*, vol 38, pp582–587

Ghiaus, C. (2006b) 'Equivalence between the load curve and the free-running temperature in energy estimating methods', *Energy and Buildings*, vol 38, pp429–435

Ghiaus, C. and Allard, F. (2006) 'Potential for free-cooling by ventilation', *Energy and Buildings*, vol 80, pp402–413

Ghiaus, C., Iordache, V., Allard, F. and Blondeau, P. (2005) 'Outdoor–indoor pollutant transfer' in C. Ghiaus and F. Allard (eds) *Natural Ventilation in the Urban Environment*, Earthscan, London

Ghiaus, C., Allard, F., Santamouris, M., Georgakis, C. and Nichol, F. (2006) 'Urban Environment Influence on Natural Ventilation Potential, *Building and Environment*, vol 41, no 4, pp395–406

Hayes, S. R. (1991) 'Use of an Indoor Air Quality Model (IAQM) to estimate indoor ozone levels', *Journal of the Air and Waste Management Association*, vol 41, no 2, pp161–170

HKSAR (2002) Monthly Digest, Buildings Department, Hong Kong, January to December

Hoydysh, W. and Dabbert, W. F. (1988) 'Kinematics and dispersion characteristics of flows in asymmetric steet canyons', *Atmospheric Environment*, vol 22, no 12, pp2677–2689

Iordache, V. (2003) *Etude de l'impact de la pollution atmosphérique sur l'exposition des enfants en milieu scolaire – Recherche de moyens de prédiction et de protection*, PhD thesis, University of La Rochelle, France, pp138–139

ISO 7243 (1982) *Hot Environments – Estimation of the Heat Stress on Working Man, based on the WBGT Index (Wet Bulb Globe Temperature)*, International Organization for Standardization, Geneva

Lee, I. Y., Shannon, J. D. and Park, H. M. (1994) 'Evaluation of parameterizations for pollutant transport and dispersion in an urban street canyon using a three-dimensional dynamic flow model', in *Proceedings of the 87th Annual Meeting and Exhibition*, Cincinnati, Ohio, 19–24 June

Liébard, A. and De Herde, A. (2006) *Traité d'architecture et d'urbanisme bioclimatiques: Concevoir, édifier et aménager avec le développement durable*, Editions du Moniteur, France

Lomborg, B. (2001) *The Skeptical Environmentalist*, Cambridge University Press, Cambridge, MA

McCartney, K. and Nicol, F. (2002) 'Developing an adaptive control algorithm for Europe: Results of the SCATS project', *Energy and Building*, vol 34, no 6, pp623–635

Nakamura, Y. and Oke, T. R. (1988) 'Wind, temperature and stability conditions in an E–W oriented urban canyon', *Atmospheric Environment*, vol 22, no 12, pp2691–2700

Ng, E. (2009) 'Policies and Technical Guidelines for Urban Planning of High-density Cities – Air Ventilation Assessment (AVA) of Hong Kong, *Building and Environment*, vol 44, no 7, pp1478–1488

Nicol, F. and Wilson, M. (2003) *Noise in Street Canyons*, Research report, URBVENT Project, European Commission London

Nunez, M. and Oke, T. R. (1977) 'The energy balance of an urban canyon', *Journal of Applied Meteorology*, vol 16, pp11–19

Oke, T. R. (1982) 'Overview of interactions between settlements and their environment', in *Proceedings of the WMO Experts Meeting on Urban and Building Climatology, WCP-37*, World Meteorological Organization (WMO), Geneva

Oke, T. R. (1987) 'Street design and urban canopy layer climate', *Energy and Buildings*, vol 11, pp103–113

prEN 13779 (2004) Ventilation for Buildings: Performance Requirements for Ventilation and Air-Conditioning Systems, CEN, Technical Committee 156, Brussels

Santamouris, M. (2001) *Energy and Climate in the Urban Built Environment*, James and James Science Publishers, London

Santamouris, M. and Asimakopoulos, D.N. (eds) (1996) *Passive Cooling of Buildings*, James and James, London

Santamouris, M., Papanikolaou, N., Koronakis, I., Livada, I. and Asimakopoulos, D. N. (1999) 'Thermal and airflow characteristics in a deep pedestrian canyon under hot weather conditions', *Atmospheric Environment*, vol 33, pp4503–4521

Santamouris, M. and Georgakis, C. (2003) 'Energy and Indoor Climate in Urban Environments: recent trends', Journal of Building Services Engineering Research and Technology, vol 24, no 2, pp69–81

Serageldim, I., Cohen, M. A. and Leitmann, J. (eds) (1995) *Enabling Sustainable Community Development*, Environmentally Sustainable Development Proceedings, Series no 8, World Bank, Washington DC

Shafik, N. (1994) 'Economic development and environmental quality: An econometric analysis', *Oxford Economic Papers*, vol 46, pp757–773

Shair, F. H. and Heitner, K. L. (1974) 'Theoretical model for relating indoor pollutant concentrations to those outside', *Environmental Science and Technology Journal*, vol 8, no 5, p444

United Nations Population Fund (UNFPA) (1998) Annual Report, UNFPA, New York

United Nations Population Fund (UNFPA) (2001) Annual Report, UNFPA, New York

United Nations Population Fund (UNFPA) (2006) *The State of World Population*, UNFPA, New York

Wedding, J. B., Lombardi, D. J. and Cermak, J. E. (1977) 'A wind tunnel study of gaseous pollutants in city street canyons', *Journal of Air Pollution Control Association*, vol 27, pp557–566

Weschler, C. J., Shields, H. C. and Naik, D. V. (1989) 'Indoor ozone exposures', *Journal of Air Pollution Control Association*, vol 39, pp1562–1568

WHO (World Health Organization) (1997) *Health and Environment in Sustainable Development: Five Years after the Earth Summit*, WHO, Geneva

WHO (2000) *Air Quality Guidelines*, WHO, Geneva

Yamartino, R. J. and Wiegand, G. (1986) 'Development and evaluation of simple models for the flow, turbulence and pollution concentration fields within an urban street canyon', *Atmospheric Environment*, vol 20, pp2137–2156

12

Sound Environment: High- versus Low-Density Cities

Jian Kang

In Europe over 30 per cent of the population are exposed to road traffic sound pressure levels (SPLs) above that recommended in World Health Organization (WHO) guidelines (55dBA), and in high-density cities this percentage is often much higher. A recent survey in Hong Kong revealed that about one sixth of the local population are affected by traffic noise over 70dBA (Hong Kong EPD, 2007). There are many potential health effects of environmental noise, which, in turn, can lead to social handicaps, reduced productivity and accidents. In this chapter, the sound environment in high-density cities is examined by comparing it with that in low-density cities through a series of case studies. Three key facets are considered – namely, sound distribution, sound perception and noise reduction.

Sound distribution

In order to examine the sound distribution in urban environments, it is important to consider two scales – namely, the micro-scale, such as a street canyon or a square, and the macro-scale, which includes a large number of street blocks.

Street canyon

A significant feature of high-density cities is that the buildings are normally tall and, thus, deep street canyons are formed. In order to analyse the characteristics of sound propagation in street canyons, a comparison has been made between hypothetical UK and Hong Kong streets (Kang et al, 2001) using three computer simulation models – namely, the image source model, the radiosity model and commercial software Raynoise, for geometrically reflecting (i.e. acoustically smooth) boundaries, for diffusely reflecting boundaries, and for

mixed boundaries, respectively (Kang, 2000, 2001, 2002a, 2002b, 2005).

For the UK situation, two street types are considered based on a number of actual streets in a typical low-density city: Sheffield. One type contains two-storey semi-detached houses on both sides. Each building block is 10m wide, 7m deep and the gap between the buildings is 5m. The building height is 8.5m and the street width is 20m. The other type contains terraced houses on both sides. The buildings are continuous along the street, and are 7m deep and 8.5m high. For comparison, two street widths, 12m and 20m, are considered. For the sake of convenience, the roofs are assumed to be flat. In both types of street, the walls are brick or stone, the roofs are covered with tiles, and the ground is concrete. The street length is considered as 160m for both street types. In Figure 12.1 the configurations used are illustrated.

For the Hong Kong situation, two street types are also considered based on the typical streets in the

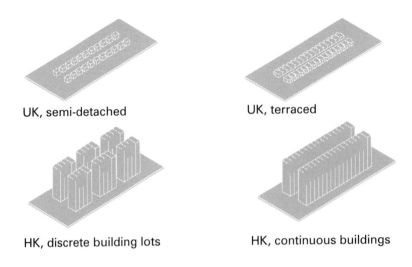

UK, semi-detached   UK, terraced

HK, discrete building lots   HK, continuous buildings

Source: Author

Figure 12.1 *Typical street canyon configurations used in the simulation*

Mongkok area. One is a street with discrete building lots on both sides. The lots are 20m apart, 20m deep, and each lot is 40m long. The buildings are 65m high and the street width is 20m. The other type is a street with continuous buildings on both sides, and the buildings are 20m deep and 65m high. For comparison, two street widths, 20m and 30m, are considered. For both street types, the street length is 160m and the building roofs are flat. Two kinds of façade material, concrete and glass, are considered, and the ground is concrete.

The sound distributions in the UK and Hong Kong street canyons with geometrically reflecting boundaries are compared in Figure 12.2, where a single point source is assumed, located outside the street and 20m from a street end. It is along the street centre, at 0.5m high (also see Figure 12.5). The results are useful for investigating the fundamental characteristics of sound fields, and are representative of certain types of urban noise, such as low-density traffic, especially during night-time. They are also useful for considering noise propagation from a junction into a street. The absorption coefficient of all the boundaries is assumed to be 0.05, except where indicated. It can be seen that in comparison with the UK streets, in the Hong Kong streets the SPL is generally lower, mainly due to the greater street width. The effect of street width can be seen by comparing the UK streets with two widths, 12m and 20m, where the difference is about 1.6dB on

average. The SPL at the top level (1m from the façade) is lower than that at the ground level (i.e. 1.5m above ground), as expected, especially for the Hong Kong streets, although the difference decreases with increasing source–receiver distance. For Hong Kong streets, the SPL difference is about 1dB between concrete and glass façades, with the façades' absorption coefficient assumed as 0.05 and 0.02, respectively.

The calculation also shows that in the UK cases the reverberation time (RT) is systematically shorter than that in the HK cases, typically by 50 to 100 per cent. Again, the difference is caused by the difference in street width. The difference in reverberation between different boundary absorption coefficients is much greater than that in SPL, given that the latter depends mainly upon early reflections, whereas the former is dependent upon multiple reflections. Overall, the reverberation time in these streets could be as high as five to ten seconds, which may cause significant noise annoyance.

If the boundaries are diffusely reflective, which is closer to the actual situation since there are always some irregularities on building or ground surfaces, the results can be rather different. Figures 12.3 and 12.4 compare the SPL and RT30 between the UK and Hong Kong streets, where the two streets have the same width, but the heights are 8.5m and 65m, respectively. Again, the absorption coefficient of all the boundaries is assumed as 0.05. It can be seen that at the ground level, in

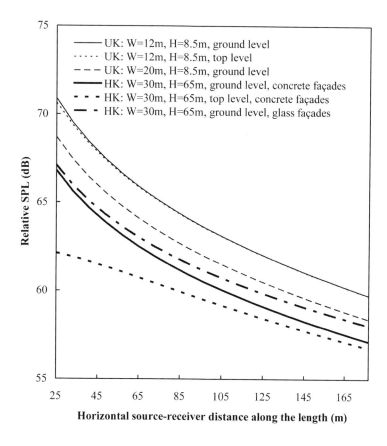

Source: Author

Figure 12.2 *Comparison of the sound pressure levels (SPLs) between UK and Hong Kong streets with geometrically reflecting boundaries*

comparison with the UK street, in the Hong Kong street the SPL is generally 3dB to 5dB higher. At the top level, it is interesting to note that in the Hong Kong street, although the actual source–receiver distance is considerably greater than that in the UK street, the SPL is systematically higher beyond about 40m. In terms of reverberation, Figure 12.4 demonstrates that in the Hong Kong street the RT30 is substantially longer than that in the UK street.

The situation with mixed boundaries is examined using Raynoise, considering the actual boundary absorption within 63Hz to 8kHz. The ground is assumed to be geometrically reflective, and a diffuse coefficient of 0.3 is applied to all the façades. Figure 12.5 compares the SPL distribution between UK and Hong Kong streets at the ground level (i.e. 1.5m above the ground) in the case of a single source, where the street

width is 20m. It can be seen that the SPL is systematically increased by the increased building height, and this SPL increase becomes greater with increasing source–receiver distance. As expected, in comparison with continuous buildings, with discrete lots the SPL is lower, typically by 3dBA to 5dBA.

A line source along the street centre is also considered, at 1.5m high, with its spectrum corresponding to typical traffic noise. Figure 12.6 shows the SPL distribution on a vertical receiver plane at 1m from a façade. Contrary to the situation with a single source, in Figure 12.6 the SPL in the UK streets is almost the same as, or only slightly lower than, that in the Hong Kong streets. Clearly this is due to the effect of direct sound. It is noted, however, that the results in Figure 12.6 are based on the assumption that the sound power level (or, in other words, the traffic flow) is the same in the

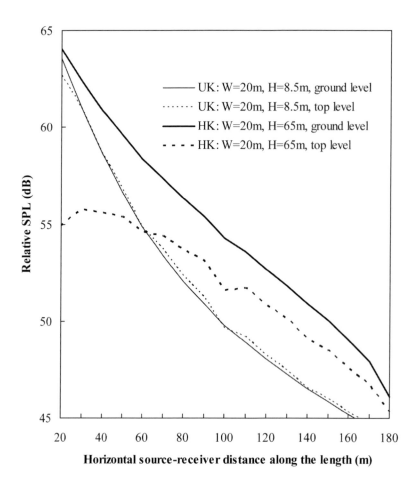

Source: Author

Figure 12.3 *Comparison of the SPLs between UK and Hong Kong streets with diffusely reflecting boundaries*

UK and Hong Kong streets. If the traffic flow is doubled, the SPL will increase by 3dB. Figure 12.6 also illustrates the effect of the gaps between buildings, which is about 2dBA, as well as the SPL attenuation along the street height, which is about 6dBA in the Hong Kong streets. For a side wall, the sound attenuation along the height is greater, at about 10dBA.

Urban morphology

In addition to the greater building height, high-density cities may differ from low-density cities in terms of the urban texture. In order to examine the effects of urban morphological characteristics on the sound distribution, noise maps are compared

between two typical cities – Sheffield in the UK and Wuhan in China – with a number of representative urban areas (Wang et al, 2007), as shown in Figure 12.7. While both cities are among the top ten largest cities in their country, the population in Wuhan is 8.3 million, much greater than that in Sheffield, at 0.6 million. In the sampling process the urban morphological characteristics, the classification of road traffic and the noise source types have all been taken into account. Each sampled area is 500m × 500m. The noise maps are calculated using software package Cadna/A, by considering traffic noise sources only, including roads, trams and light rail. The volume of traffic flow is based on site surveys of some typical roads. A Matlab program has also been

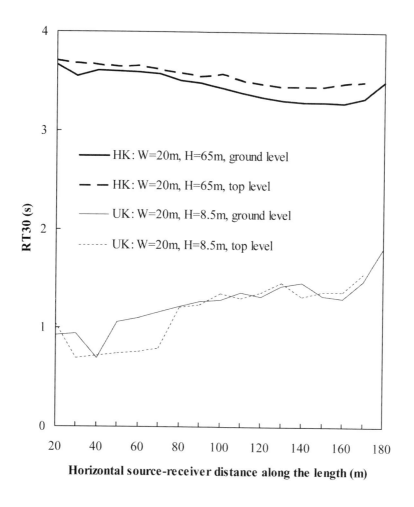

Source: Author

Figure 12.4 *Comparison of the RT30 between UK and Hong Kong streets with diffusely reflecting boundaries*

developed to obtain a series of indices from the maps such as the noise levels at 1m from the façade, road-side noise levels, noise levels in open spaces, spatial (rather than temporal, as conventionally defined) statistical sound levels L_{max}, L_{10}, L_{avg}, L_{50}, L_{min} and L_{90}, as well as some urban morphological indices. An analysis of the urban morphological indices of the sampled areas shows that for the road coverage there is no systematic and considerable difference between the two cities. In terms of the building coverage Wuhan is much higher than that in Sheffield by up to about 70 per cent except in the industrial areas, whereas for the accessible space coverage, Sheffield is much higher than that in Wuhan, by 15 to 65 per cent in various areas.

Figure 12.8 compares the noise distribution between Sheffield and Wuhan, in terms of L_{max}, L_{10}, L_{avg}, L_{50}, L_{min} and L_{90}. For Sheffield, since there are notable variations in traffic volume, especially in the small roads, a reduced traffic volume is also considered for the residential area from 1500 (value used in Figure 12.7) to 800 per hour. For Wuhan, given that the number of vehicles per person is still much lower than that in Sheffield by tenfold (Wuhan Transportation Authority, 2006), the SPL is also shown by assuming doubled traffic volume. In Figure 12.8a, it is very interesting to note that the average noise levels L_{avg} in all of the sampled areas are lower than those in Sheffield by 2dBA to 11dBA. For L_{50}, the result is similar to that of L_{avg}. In terms of L_{min} and L_{90}, as shown in Figure 12.8b,

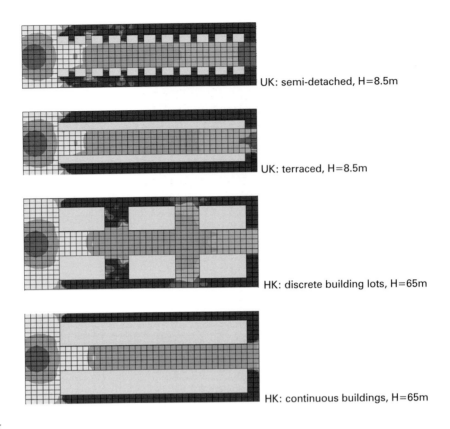

UK: semi-detached, H=8.5m

UK: terraced, H=8.5m

HK: discrete building lots, H=65m

HK: continuous buildings, H=65m

Source: Author

Figure 12.5 *Comparison of the SPLs between the UK and Hong Kong streets with mixed boundaries; each shade represents 5dBA*

the difference is even greater – for example, up to 15dBA in the area with a motorway. Conversely, for L_{max} and L_{10}, the difference between Sheffield and Wuhan is much smaller, as can be seen in Figure 12.8c, and it is important to note that the L_{max} in Sheffield is up to 5dBA to 10dBA lower than that in some Wuhan areas. Similarly, in terms of L_{10}, the SPL in Sheffield is only slightly lower than, or the same as, that in Wuhan.

A main reason for the differences between Sheffield and Wuhan is that in Sheffield the roads are relatively evenly distributed, and the vehicles can access a wide range of roads, whereas in Wuhan the main roads, with a typical spacing of 350m to 500m (Zhao, 2002), take a heavy traffic load, making the sound distribution in the area rather uneven and, at the same time, creating large areas of quiet zones. Indeed, in many typical residential areas in Wuhan the vehicle access is for residents and visitors only, and the traffic volume of typical roads is 10 to 60 times lower than that of the

main roads. Moreover, the high-density and high-rise buildings, especially those along the main roads, often act as effective noise barriers for the residential areas, although the reflections from building façades can also significantly increase the noise level inside the street canyons. Nevertheless, the width of the main roads in Wuhan is generally greater than that in Sheffield, which is helpful for reducing the impact of direct sound to a certain degree. Overall, the comparison between Sheffield and Wuhan clearly demonstrates the effectiveness of urban morphology on the noise distribution.

Sound perception

It has been demonstrated by a number of studies that correlations between noise annoyance and acoustic/physical factors are often not high (Kang, 2006). In addition to the acoustic parameters, other aspects,

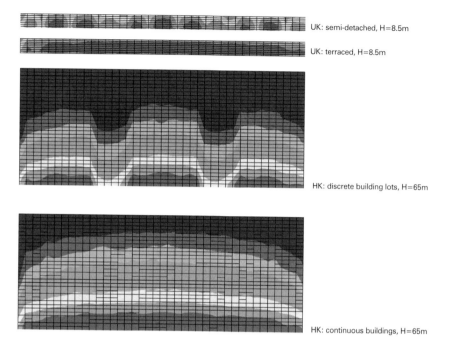

UK: semi-detached, H=8.5m

UK: terraced, H=8.5m

HK: discrete building lots, H=65m

HK: continuous buildings, H=65m

Source: Author

Figure 12.6 *Comparison of the SPLs in front of a façade between the UK and Hong Kong streets with mixed boundaries, in the case of a line source; each shade represents 1dBA*

including social, demographical, psychological, economical and cultural factors, play an important role in the evaluation of the sound environment. In this section, sound perception is compared between typical high-density cities in Asia and low-density cities in the UK, from the viewpoint of noise annoyance as well as soundscape.

Noise annoyance

A series of comparative surveys have been carried out in Sheffield, Beijing and Taipei, aiming at comparing the perception of the sound environment between high- and low-density cities (Xing and Kang, 2006; Yu and Kang, 2006a, 2006b). Three residential areas were sampled in each city, representing typical urban textures as well as residents' social/demographical/cultural backgrounds. The three Sheffield sites were:

1   Springvale Road area, located just outside the city centre, with semi-detached and terraced houses;
2   Walkley area, located along the busy South Road/Highton Street, with high-density terraced

houses and convenient amusement facilities and shops; and
3   West One, a contemporary urban living complex in the city centre area with a large number of flats within the middle/high-rise buildings.

The three sites in Beijing included:

1   XiZhiMen DeWai, a typical Chinese high-density, high-rise middle-class living area, located beside the busy Second Ring road;
2   DongXiLianZi HuTong, an old residential area located in the heart of the city, with terraced houses and traditional Chinese courtyard houses; and
3   BaiWanZhuang, an urban living area built during the 1950s with three-storey low-rise terraced residential blocks, well protected from the busy urban surroundings.

The three Taipei sites included JianGuo S Road, GuoXing Road and ZhangXing E Road, all residential areas near one or more busy roads.

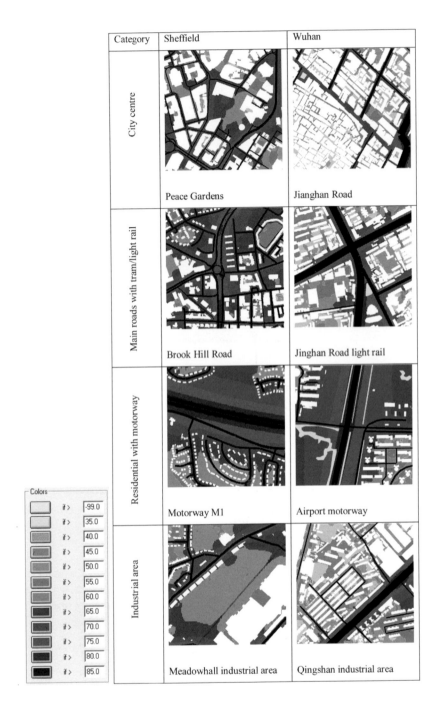

Source: Author

Figure 12.7 *Noise maps of the sampled areas in Sheffield and Wuhan*

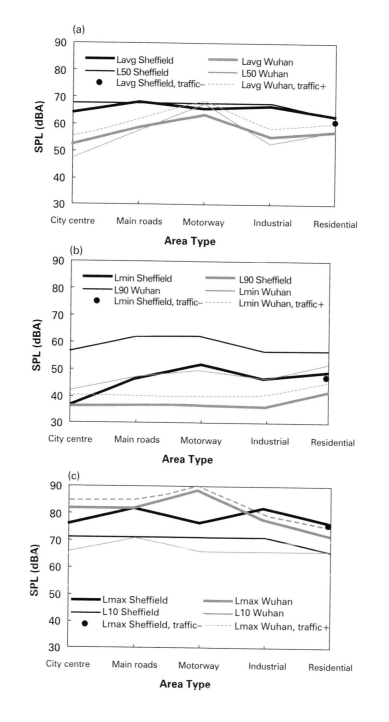

Source: Author

Figure 12.8 *Comparison of the SPLs between Sheffield and Wuhan in the sampled urban areas: (a) L_{avg} and L_{50};*
(b) L_{min} and L_{90}; (c) L_{max} and L_{10}

For each area 30 to 50 interviews were carried out, and SPL measurements were also made considering various typical time periods. In a follow-up study (stage two), general surveys were carried out in Sheffield and Taipei, with 200 samples per city. For both stages, the interviewees were selected at random, and the statistical analysis carried out using the software SPSS shows that the distribution of gender, age, occupation and income was rather representative.

The survey questions asked about the importance of various factors in choosing a living environment, with a 5-level linear scale, from –2 (do not mind) to 2 (very important). The results are shown in Figure 12.9. It has been demonstrated that there are generally significant differences between the three cities for most factors ($p < 0.01$). Quietness was ranked as the sixth important factor in Sheffield, fourth in Taipei and seventh in Beijing, among 11 factors. In Taipei the mean evaluation score was 1.49 and 1.45 (stage 2), significantly higher that in Sheffield, at 0.71 and 0.73 (stage 2), and in Beijing, 0.79 ($p < 0.000$). While the differences among the three cities might be caused by the noise level differences in the case study sites, between Taipei and Beijing another possible reason is that the latter is still at developing stage and, thus, relatively less attention is paid to noise issues.

The interviewees were asked to rank four pollutants – namely, water, air, noise and waste (see Table 12.1 for the mean ranking orders). It can be seen that the rank of noise is second (stage 1) or first (stage 2) in Sheffield; second (stages 1 and 2) in Taipei; and third in Beijing. This generally corresponds to the results in Figure 12.9.

Table 12.2 compares the evaluation of interviewees among the three cities on the general living environment, sound quality of the living area, and sound quality at home, with a 5-level linear scale, from 1 (very comfortable) to 5 (very uncomfortable). It is interesting to note that the scores in Taipei and Beijing are all significantly ($p < 0.01$) higher than those in Sheffield by about 0.5. Moreover, it has been shown that the evaluation of the living environment is significantly correlated ($p < 0.01$) to the evaluation of sound quality as well as the measured SPL. Corresponding to the evaluation of the living environment and sound quality, Taipei and Beijing residents also found their health conditions less satisfactory compared to that in Sheffield.

The main activities at home are shown in Table 12.3. It can be seen that in the three cities there is a high percentage of activities that could potentially be disturbed by noise. It is interesting to note that in Sheffield the percentage of reading and music is considerably higher than that in Taipei and Beijing,

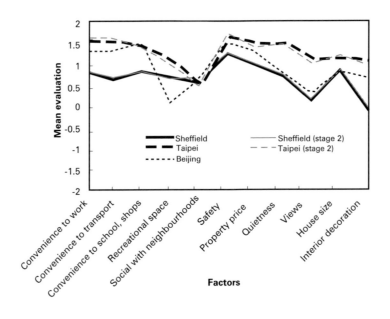

Source: Author

Figure 12.9 *Importance of various factors in choosing a living environment*

Table 12.1 *Mean ranking orders of various environmental pollutants, with the standard deviations shown in brackets*

Pollutants	Sheffield	Taipei	Beijing	Sheffield (stage 2)	Taipei (stage 2)
Water	3.26 (0.96)	2.81 (1.30)	1.97 (0.94)	3.06 (1.13)	2.49 (1.25)
Air	2.09 (0.90)	2.29 (1.01)	1.50 (0.60)	1.96 (0.91)	1.92 (0.97)
Noise	2.12 (1.20)	2.33 (1.12)	2.59 (0.84)	1.81 (1.12)	2.08 (1.08)
Waste	2.53 (1.02)	2.94 (1.34)	3.59 (0.92)	2.20 (1.09)	3.07 (1.18)

Source: Author

Table 12.2 *Mean evaluation of the general living environment, sound quality and health status, with the standard deviations shown in brackets*

	Sheffield	Taipei	Beijing	Sheffield (stage 2)	Taipei (stage 2)
General living environment	1.81 (0.53)	2.43 (0.90)	2.81 (0.65)	1.82 (0.53)	2.36 (0.87)
Sound quality of living area	2.16 (0.65)	2.44 (0.93)	2.57 (0.72)	1.79 (0.86)	2.49 (0.78)
Sound quality of home	1.95 (0.53)	2.59 (0.88)	2.33 (0.81)	2.13 (0.60)	2.65 (0.96)
Health	1.75 (0.83)	2.54 (0.75)	2.25 (0.80)	1.97 (0.53)	2.69 (0.89)

Source: Author

Table 12.3 *Main activities at home (percentage), where multiple choices were allowed*

Activities	Sheffield	Taipei	Beijing	Sheffield (stage 2)	Taipei (stage 2)
Reading	61	35	23	63	38
TV	54	85	75	57	81
Music	55	9	1	57	5
Others	41	29	11	45	29

Source: Author

suggesting that Sheffield people could be more sensitive in terms of noise disturbance.

Since various sources in an urban environment could have rather different impacts upon people, in the questionnaire the noticeability (from –2, none, to 2, very significant), annoyance (from –2, not annoyed, to 2, very annoyed) and sleep disturbance (from –2, not disturbing, to 2, very disturbing) of typical sound sources in residential areas were asked. Figure 12.10 shows the comparison in noticeability among the three cities. It can be seen that people in Sheffield tend to have a relatively high noticeability on various noises, although the average SPL values measured at the Sheffield sites are about 2dBA to 5dBA lower than those in Beijing and over 10dBA

lower than those in Taipei. This might be caused by the nature of people's long-term living environment. Most of the residential spaces in Sheffield feature a relatively low background noise level; hence, people are more likely to be affected by intrusive noise, whereas in Taipei and Beijing people have perhaps adapted their environment to a certain degree. In Taipei two-wheelers are on the top list of the noticed noise sources, as well as talking, music and television, both from neighbours and from their own homes, whereas in Beijing and Sheffield the most noticeable sounds are traffic, possibly caused by the characteristics of the sample sites. There are generally high correlations between noticeability, annoyance and sleep disturbance, with correlation coefficients

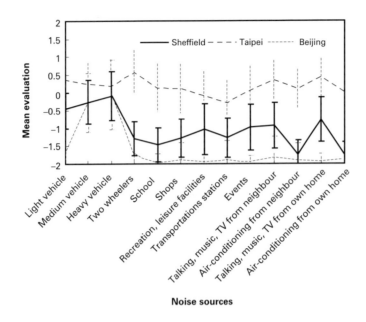

Noise sources

Source: Author

Figure 12.10 *Noticeability of typical sound sources in residential areas; the standard deviations are also shown*

typically over 0.7 to 0.9. It is interesting to note that annoyance evaluation scores are generally systematically lower than those for noticeability, showing people's tolerance, which is similar to the case in urban open public spaces (Yang and Kang, 2005a, 2005b). While most mean evaluation scores are negative, as shown in Figure 12.10, it should be noted that the standard deviations are also high, indicating that there are still a number people in the categories with positive evaluation numbers.

The urban soundscape includes not only negative but also positive sounds. Sound preference was therefore also studied, where the interviewees were asked to select from a list the sounds they would like to hear in their living environment. Table 12.4 shows the results. Significant differences have been found between the three cities in terms of natural sounds, including birdsong and water sounds ($p < 0.001$). For example, 70 per cent of people in Sheffield chose birdsong as a preferred sound in their living environment, whereas only 32 per cent of Taipei citizens and 25 per cent of Beijing citizens ticked the box. Conversely, many people in Taipei (26 per cent) and in Beijing (43 per cent) tended to prefer music in their living environment, while only 4 per cent of the interviewees in Sheffield showed the same interest.

Table 12.4 *Mean preference of various potential positive sounds, with 1 as yes (selected) and 2 as no; standard deviations are shown in brackets*

Type of sounds	Sheffield	Taipei	Beijing	Sheffield (stage 2)	Taipei (stage 2)
Bird songs	1.30 (0.46)	1.68 (0.48)	1.75 (0.44)	1.28 (0.45)	1.70 (0.88)
Insect sounds	1.96 (0.19)	1.79 (0.42)	1.90 (0.30)	1.97 (0.18)	1.93 (0.80)
Water	1.69 (0.47)	1.89 (0.32)	1.90 (0.30)	1.73 (0.45)	1.93 (0.96)
Music from outside	1.96 (0.19)	1.74 (0.45)	1.57 (0.50)	1.96 (0.21)	1.65 (0.89)
Other Sounds	1.71 (0.46)	1.89 (0.57)	1.78 (0.42)	1.71 (0.45)	1.94 (0.65)

Source: Author

Soundscape in urban open public spaces

Urban open public spaces are vital components of modern cities, and the soundscape quality is an important part of overall physical comfort (Zhang and Kang, 2007; Yu and Kang, 2008). Being different from conventional noise reduction, research in soundscape and acoustic comfort concentrates on the way in which people consciously perceive their environment – namely, the interactions between people and sounds. Between the urban open public spaces in high- and low-density cities there are often considerable differences in soundscape. For example, in Beijing, group dancing is a rather common sound type, whereas this sound is rare in typical low-density cities within Europe. Through a comparative study between Sheffield and Beijing, the soundscape evaluation as well as the key factors characterizing the soundscape have been examined (Zhang and Kang, 2006).

A series of semantic differential indices have been compiled (see Table 12.5), where both connotative meanings of urban environmental sounds, such as calming–agitating, interesting–boring and like–dislike, as well as denotative meanings such as quiet–noisy,

sharp–flat and smooth–rough, are included. The indices also cover various aspects of soundscape, such as satisfaction, strength, fluctuation and social aspects. With these indices, soundscape evaluation was carried out in two Sheffield sites (namely, Barkers Pool and Peace Gardens) and two Beijing sites (namely ChangChuenYuan Culture Square and XiDan Cultural Square). These sites represented typical soundscapes in urban open public spaces, including continuous and intermittent sounds, man-made and natural sounds, meaningful and meaningless sounds, and pitched and varied sounds. In each square about 250 to 300 interviews were made, for semantic differential analysis and also for a general evaluation of acoustic comfort and sound preference. The interviewees were the users, not passers-by, of the squares and were selected randomly.

In Figure 12.11 the subjective evaluation of sound level and acoustic comfort is shown, both at a 5-level linear scale – namely, for sound level: 1 (very quiet); 2 (quiet); 3 (neither quiet nor noisy); 4 (noisy); 5 (very noisy); and for acoustic comfort: 1 (very comfortable); 2 (comfortable); 3 (neither comfortable nor uncomfortable); 4 (uncomfortable); 5 (very uncomfortable). It is interesting to note that in Sheffield the average scores for acoustic

Table 12.5 *Factor analysis of the soundscape evaluation in Sheffield (Kaiser-Meyer-Olkin (KMO) measure of sampling adequacy: 0.798)*

Indices	Factors			
	1 (26%)	2 (12%)	3 (8%)	4 (7%)
Comfort–discomfort	.701	.164	.138	
Quiet–noisy	.774			
Pleasant–unpleasant	.784	.258	.157	
Interesting–boring	.435	.272	.274	.103
Natural–artificial	.532	.102	.240	
Like–dislike	.519	.575	.247	.151
Gentle–harsh	.502	.531	.123	
Hard–soft				.812
Fast–slow				.827
Sharp–flat	.220		.345	.488
Directional–everywhere	.234		.441	.267
Varied–simple	.115		.674	.167
Echoed–dead	.204		.531	
Far–close			.550	
Social–unsocial		.672	.462	
Meaningful–meaningless	.126	.585	.469	
Calming–agitating	−.143	.708	.286	
Rough–smooth		.683	.396	

Source: Author

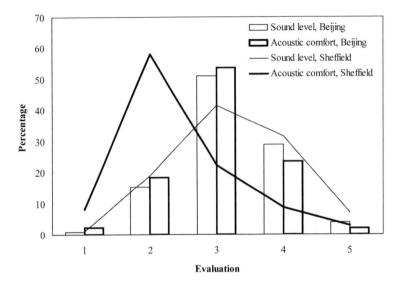

Figure 12.11 *Comparison between the evaluation of sound level and acoustic comfort in Sheffield and Beijing*

comfort are significantly lower than those for sound level ($p < 0.05$), indicating that although people may feel that the sound environment is noisy/loud, they could still find it acoustically comfortable, whereas in Beijing the difference between the two evaluations is insignificant. A possible reason is that in one of the Beijing sites, XiDan Square, the soundscape is dominated by high levels of traffic sounds. Overall, the difference between the evaluation of sound level and acoustic comfort reveals the effects of sound source type and, consequently, the potentials of designing various sounds.

Table 12.5 shows the factor analysis for the two Sheffield sites, where the Varimax-rotated principal components analysis (PCA) is employed to extract the orthogonal factor underlying the 18 adjective indices. With a criterion factor of eigenvalue > 1, four main factors are determined. Factor 1 (26 per cent) is mainly associated with relaxation, including comfort–discomfort, quiet–noisy, pleasant–unpleasant, natural–artificial, like–dislike and gentle–harsh. Factor 2 (12 per cent) is generally associated with communication, including social–unsocial, meaningful–meaningless, calming–agitating and smooth–rough. Factor 3 (8 per cent) is mostly associated with spatiality, including varied–simple, echoed–dead and far–close. Factor 4 (7 per cent) is principally related to dynamics, including hard–soft and fast–slow.

Correspondingly, the factor analysis for the two Beijing sites is shown in Table 12.6. It can be seen that factor 1, including comfort–discomfort, quiet–noisy, natural–artificial, like–dislike and gentle–harsh, is again mainly related to relaxation, although sharp–flat and far–close are also included in this factor. While the other three factors could be related to communication (with factor 2 including pleasant–unpleasant, interesting–boring, social–unsocial and meaningful–meaningless), spatiality and dynamics (with factor 4 including echoed–dead and factor 3 including hard–soft, fast–slow, directional– everywhere, varied–simple and calming–agitating), the factor order and the indices included in each factor are different from the Sheffield situation. In Figure 12.12 the scatter plot of factor 1 and 2 is shown for the Sheffield and Beijing case study sites. It can be seen that although the two graphs have similar patterns, for the Beijing sites the division between factor 1 and 2 is clearer.

Overall, although the soundscape evaluation in urban open public spaces is rather complicated, it is still possible to identify several major factors for both the Sheffield and Beijing situations; interestingly, these factors cover the main facets of designing the acoustics of an urban open public space: function (relaxation and communication), space and time. It is noted that the four factors cover only 53 per cent of the total variance in the Sheffield sites and 56 per cent in the Beijing sites.

Table 12.6 *Factor analysis of the soundscape evaluation in Beijing (KMO measure of sampling adequacy: 0.860)*

Indices	Factors			
	1 (31%)	2 (12%)	3 (7%)	4 (6%)
Comfort–discomfort	.770	.193		−.146
Quiet–noisy	.776	.201		
Pleasant–unpleasant	.358	**.687**		
Interesting–boring	.299	**.732**		
Natural–artificial	**.687**	.136		.288
Like–dislike	**.744**	.235	.100	−.167
Gentle–harsh	**.700**	.306		
Hard–soft		.129	**.513**	.354
Fast–slow	.135		**.503**	.271
Sharp–flat	**.636**	.259		
Directional–everywhere	.380		**.609**	−.284
Varied–simple			**.741**	−.117
Echoed–dead				**.666**
Far–close	.529	.127		.400
Social–unsocial	.242	**.802**		
Meaningful–meaningless	.196	**.762**	.147	
Calming–agitating	−.201	−.439	**.538**	.284
Rough–smooth	−.109	.389	**.457**	.387

Source: Author

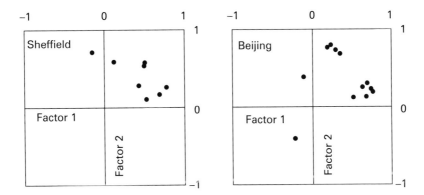

Source: Author

Figure 12.12 *Comparison of the scatter plot with factor 1 and 2 between Sheffield and Beijing*

This is lower than most results in product sound quality studies and general environmental noise evaluation, perhaps due to the significant variations in urban open public spaces in terms of the number and type of sound sources, as well as their characteristics.

Noise reduction

Environmental noise barriers are a commonly used mitigation measure; but in high-density cities its effectiveness is often limited since the barrier height required to form shadow zones is often too great to achieve. One possible solution is to use reactive barriers, such as a series of parallel grooves in the ground (Van der Haijden and Martens, 1982). It has been shown that strategically designed rib-like structures can be very effective in providing insertion loss, typically 10dB to 15dB over a rather wide frequency range (Bougdah et al, 2006), although at frequencies lower than the limiting frequency, the attenuation could be negative at certain receiver locations due to surface wave generation. Alternatively, building forms can be designed to be self-protective from external noise to a certain extent (Kang, 2006). As illustrated in Figure 12.13a, a podium, usually for commercial use, can act as a noise barrier for the main building, which is typically residential. The balconies of high buildings can also effectively stop direct sound from source to windows/doors (Mohsen and Oldham, 1977; Hothersall et al, 1996), as shown in Figure 12.13b.

It is of great importance to develop noise reduction techniques and strategies using sustainable measures. Vegetation, although normally not so effective in reducing noise transmission in open fields unless the depth is significant, could be more effective in urban areas, such as in a street canyon or in a square (Kang, 2006) through three possible mechanisms – namely, sound absorption and sound diffusion, which occur when a sound wave impinges upon the vegetation and is then reflected back; and sound level reduction when a sound wave is transmitted through the vegetation. When vegetation is used on building façades or on the ground, the effectiveness of absorption can be greatly enhanced since there are multiple reflections. Similarly, due to multiple reflections, the diffusion effect of vegetation will be significant even when the diffusion coefficient is relatively low. While the transmission effect in an open field may not be significant unless the density and depth are considerable, the effectiveness could again be significant if multiple reflections are considered.

The influence of urban texture on sound distribution has been demonstrated, as shown in Figures 12.1 to 12.8. In this respect, appropriate prediction tools are of great importance. In Europe, following the European Union directives on the assessment and management of environmental noise, large-scale noise-mapping software packages have been developed and applied extensively in practice, and various prediction methods for sound propagation in micro- and meso-scale urban areas have also been explored. Those prediction models and algorithms, however, have been developed based on the urban texture in Europe, and their applicability is doubtful in high-density cities (Kang and Huang, 2005), where there are often many narrow street canyons formed by high-rise buildings. Moreover, there are numerous canyons of non-uniform height and canyons formed between flyovers (inclined or horizontal). The situation could be further complicated by curved or non-straight street canyons, which are common in hilly cities such as Hong Kong. As a result, there is still a need to systematically examine those special features and their effects on sound propagation, and to develop more generalized numerical noise propagation prediction schemes that can fit worldwide applications.

There have been many other developments in urban noise reduction techniques and strategies, from using low-noise road surfaces, to producing quieter vehicles, to applying acoustic windows (Kang and Brocklesby, 2004; Kang and Li, 2007). Moreover, it is important to consider sound perception. A recent study

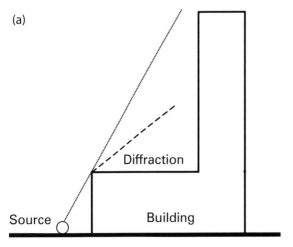

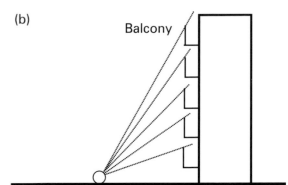

Source: Author

Figure 12.13 *Examples of self-protection buildings: (a) podium as a noise barrier; (b) using balconies to stop direct sound*

has shown that the effectiveness of noise barriers is correlated with the level of public participation (Joynt and Kang, 2002). Furthermore, high-density cities often have many other special features, such as underground spaces, where the noise reduction and sound environment design are especially important.

Acknowledgements

The results presented in this chapter have been financially supported by the European Commission, UK EPSRC, UK Royal Society, British Academy, Chinese Natural Science Foundation, KC Wong Foundation and Hong Kong TDG. The author is also indebted to Dr C. Yu, Dr M. Zhang, B. Wang, Z. Xing, S. Lam, Dr W. Yang and Prof. J. Tsou for their contribution.

References

Bougdah, H., Ekici, I. and Kang, J. (2006) 'An investigation into rib-like noise reducing devices', *Journal of the Acoustical Society of America (JASA),* vol 120, no 6, pp3714–3722

Hong Kong EPD (Environmental Protection Department) (2007) 'An overview on noise pollution and control in Hong Kong', www.epd.gov.hk/, assessed 15 January 2008

Hothersall, D. C., Horoshenkov, K. V. and Mercy, S. E. (1996) 'Numerical modelling of the sound field near a tall building with balconies near a road', *Journal of Sound and Vibration (JSV),* vol 198, pp507–515

Joynt, J. L. R. and Kang, J. (2002) 'The integration of public opinion and perception into the design of noise barriers', in *Proceedings of the 19th International Conference on Passive and Low Energy Architecture (PLEA),* Toulouse, France, pp885–890

Kang, J. (2000) 'Sound propagation in street canyons: Comparison between diffusely and geometrically reflecting boundaries', *Journal of the Acoustical Society of America (JASA),* vol 107, no 3, pp1394–1404

Kang, J. (2001) 'Sound propagation in interconnected urban streets: A parametric study', *Environment and Planning B: Planning and Design,* vol 28, no 2, pp281–294

Kang, J. (2002a) *Acoustics of Long Spaces: Theory and Design Guide,* Thomas Telford Publishing, London

Kang, J. (2002b) 'Numerical modelling of the sound field in urban streets with diffusely reflecting boundaries', *Journal of Sound and Vibration (JSV),* vol 258, no 5, pp793–813

Kang, J. (2005) 'Numerical modelling of the sound fields in urban squares', *Journal of the Acoustical Society of America (JASA),* vol 117, no 6, 3695–3706

Kang, J. (2006) *Urban Sound Environment,* Taylor & Francis Incorporating, Spon, London

Kang, J. and Brocklesby, M. W. (2004) 'Feasibility of applying micro-perforated absorbers in acoustic window systems', *Applied Acoustics,* vol 66, pp669–689

Kang, J. and Huang, J. (2005) 'Noise-mapping: Accuracy and strategic application', in *Proceedings of the 33rd International Congress on Noise Control Engineering (Internoise),* Rio de Janeiro, Brazil

Kang, J. and Li, Z. (2007) 'Numerical simulation of an acoustic window system using finite element method', *Acustica/Acta Acustica,* vol 93, no 1, pp152–163

Kang, J., Tsou, J. Y. and Lam, S. (2001) 'Sound propagation in urban streets: Comparison between the UK and Hong Kong', *Proceedings of the 8th International Congress on Sound and Vibration (ICSV),* Hong Kong, pp1241–1248

Mohsen, E. A. and Oldham, D. J. (1977) 'Traffic noise reduction due to the screening effect of balconies on a building façade', *Applied Acoustics,* vol 10, pp243–257

Van Der Haijden, L. A. M. and Martens, M. J. M. (1982) 'Traffic noise reduction by means of surface wave exclusion above parallel grooves in the roadside', *Applied Acoustics,* vol 15, pp329–339

Wang, B., Kang, J. and Zhou, J. (2007) 'Effects of urban morphologic characteristics on the noise mapping: A generic comparison between UK and China', in *Proceedings of the 19th International Conference on Acoustics (ICA),* Madrid, Spain

Wuhan Transportation Authority (2006) *Annual Report of Wuhan Transportation Development,* China

Xing, Z. and Kang, J. (2006) 'Acoustic comfort in residential areas – a cross-cultural study', in *Proceedings of the Institute of Acoustics (IOA),* UK, vol 28, no 1, pp317–326

Yang, W. and Kang, J. (2005a) 'Acoustic comfort evaluation in urban open public spaces', *Applied Acoustics,* vol 66, no 2, pp211–229

Yang, W. and Kang, J. (2005b) 'Soundscape and sound preferences in urban squares', *Journal of Urban Design,* vol 10, no 1, pp61–80

Yu, C. and Kang, J. (2006a) 'Comparison between the UK and Taiwan on the sound environment in urban residential areas', in *Proceedings of the 23rd International Conference on Passive and Low Energy Architecture (PLEA),* Geneva, Switzerland

Yu, C. and Kang, J. (2006b) 'Effects of cultural factors on the environmental noise evaluation', in *Proceedings of the 34th International Congress on Noise Control Engineering (Internoise),* Honolulu, Hawaii

Yu, L. and Kang, J. (2008) 'Effects of social, demographic and behavioural factors on sound level evaluation in urban open spaces', *Journal of the Acoustical Society of America (JASA)*, vol 123, pp772–783

Zhang, M. and Kang, J. (2006) 'A cross-cultural semantic differential analysis of the soundscape in urban open public spaces', *Technical Acoustics,* vol 25, no 6, pp523–532

Zhang, M. and Kang, J. (2007) 'Towards the evaluation, description and creation of soundscape in urban open spaces', *Environment and Planning B: Planning and Design*, vol 34, no 1, pp68–86

Zhao, Y. J. (2002) 'From plan to market: Transformation in the microscale roads and land use pattern', *City Planning Review*, vol 26, pp24–30 (in Chinese)

13
Designing for Daylighting

Edward Ng

Introduction

More than 20 cities in the world have 10 million inhabitants or more; in the downtown areas of these cities, taller buildings and higher-density living are now the norm. Finding ways of optimizing the city and architectural design for the inhabitants' enjoyment of daylight is now an increasingly demanding design challenge. Design tools are needed. It is sometimes dangerous to extrapolate existing tools beyond their limits when situations change. Hence, there is a constant need to review and update the tools that we require to design appropriately as the urban morphology of the city changes from low to high density.

This chapter traces the development of tools and methods that planners and architects have been using to aid design decision-making. It then reveals that as the city moves towards high-density design, many of these tools and methods are no longer adequate – many of them are even inappropriate. The chapter then highlights some fundamental principles that a new generation of tools for high-density city design could be based on. The case study of the unobstructed vision area (UVA) that is now being used in high-density city design in Hong Kong by the Hong Kong government – based on a new performance-based professional practice note PNAP 278 within the framework of the Hong Kong building regulations, illustrates the concept.

The chapter puts forward the notion that in high-density city design, the horizontal sustained angle of a window of habitable space for daylight may be a more important and effective parameter than the traditional parameter of using vertical sustained angles.

Context

Vitruvius must be credited as one of the first, if not the first, writer giving advice on the design of daylight for buildings:

> We must take care that all buildings are well lighted… Hence we must apply the following test in this matter. On the site from which the light should be obtained let a line be stretched from the top of the wall that seems to obstruct the light to the point at which it ought to be introduced, and if a considerable space of open sky can be seen when one looks up above that line, there will be no obstruction to the light in that situation. (Vitruvius, c. 25BC [1960])

There was no precise definition of what 'considerable space of open sky' means. However, it is evident that given the built circumstances of Roman town houses, the quality and the availability of the admitted daylight is more important than the exact quantity – if that was known. Vitruvius then went on further in his *Ten Books* to describe the type of daylight that should be admitted into buildings. For instance, he suggested that the library should have the morning light and the dining room a gentler and softer evening light.

Echoing Vitruvius was another writer, M. Cetius Faventinus (AD 300), who recommended that kitchens should be provided with 'northward-facing windows, and out houses for the cattle lighted by windows facing the sunrise'. This, he reckoned, could give a 'better and more artistic' effect. The artistic effect, so celebrated by Faventinus, could also be interpreted as giving the room its appropriate amount of daylight at the right time (Plommer, 1973).

It is apparent that in those days of daylight design the qualitative aspects of getting the orientation right – that the window must face into the open sky, and so on – were sufficient for the Roman townscape that Vitruvius had in mind. There was little need to be too precise.

Later, Palladio (1738) in his *Four Books on Architecture*, wrote:

> It is to be observed in making the windows that they should not take in more or less light, or be fewer or more in number, than what necessity requires; therefore, great regard ought to be given to the largeness of the rooms, which are to receive the light from them because it is manifest that a great room requires much more light to make it lucid and clear than a small one; and if the windows are made either less or fewer than which is convenient, they will make the places obscure, and if too large, they will scarce be habitable, because they will let in so much hot and cold air, that the places, according to the season of the year, will either be exceeding hot or very cold, in case the part of the heavens which they face does not in some manner prevent it.

Palladio's (1738) focus on the importance of daylight in buildings is even more evident when he proposed, perhaps, the world's first quantitative method for designing daylight: 'the windows ought not to be wider than the fourth part of the breadth of the rooms, or narrower than the fifth, and to be made two squares and a sixth part of their breadth more in height'.

Another attempt to quantitatively design for daylight was made by William Salmon. In his *Country Builder's Estimator* published in 1727, he put forwarded an equation:

> … and hence it is to be observed that most windows when of a proper size have between 20 and 30 feet in the superficial content of each, viz. from 3 to 4 feet in breadth, and from 6 to 8 feet in height; so … suppose a room is a cube … and admit that to be 12 feet, which being multiplied each by the other, the product will be 1728, whose square root will appear to be 41 feet 6 inches and a half near, and should have 2 windows therein, containing 20 of 9 inches and a quarter superficial in each … this rule is universal for all rooms whatsoever.

Later, Sir William Chambers (1791) in his treatise devoted an entire chapter on the subject of windows and recommended the following for buildings in Britain (taking into account the text by Palladio):

> I have generally added the depth and height … of the rooms on the principal floor together, and taken one eighth part thereof for the width of the windows; a rule to which there are few objections; admitting somewhat more light than Palladio's, it is, I apprehend, fitter for our climate than his rule would be.

Further to Sir William's understanding of the importance of sky in window design, Robert Kerr (1865) proposed a table of 'lighting for a wall window' that contains an embryonic version of the sky component concept. The table divides the sky into 32 portions each with its contribution of light to the window. Depending upon the portion of the sky, a point inside a room could 'see' through the window opening; thus, the corresponding amount of daylight available to that point could be estimated.

Graphical tools for design

In a nutshell, the parameters of designing for daylight so far include:

- the sky component that the room can 'see', taking into account obstructions;
- the orientation of the room;
- the window size as related to the façade, as well as the interior space; and
- the type of sky component of the locality.

The foundation for designing daylight for building interiors has already been laid. Later, illumination pioneers such as Waldram (1923), Moon (1936), Walsh (1961), Hopkinson et al (1966) and Lynes (1968), and so on, added to the basic understanding with better and more precise methodologies, and perhaps easier-to-use tools. To supplement the earlier defined design parameters, the following elements are added to the methodology:

- the shape of the window;
- the position of the window as related to the task;
- the shape of the interior space; and
- the colours of the internal decoration.

It is important to emphasize the need for 'easier-to-use tools'; ultimately, whatever tool is scientifically developed, it still needs to be easily applied by design professionals such as architects and planners, who may not have a deep grounding in sciences but who mostly operate graphically when designing.

Four particular graphical tools are worth noting as they primarily concern the effects of external obstruction to the room's availability of daylight through a window. The first is the Waldram diagram. This tool allows one to calculate the sky factor of a window graphically, taking into account any external obstructions.

The second is the Lynes pepper-pot diagram. This concept is similar to the Waldram diagram except that there is no need to construct the complicated

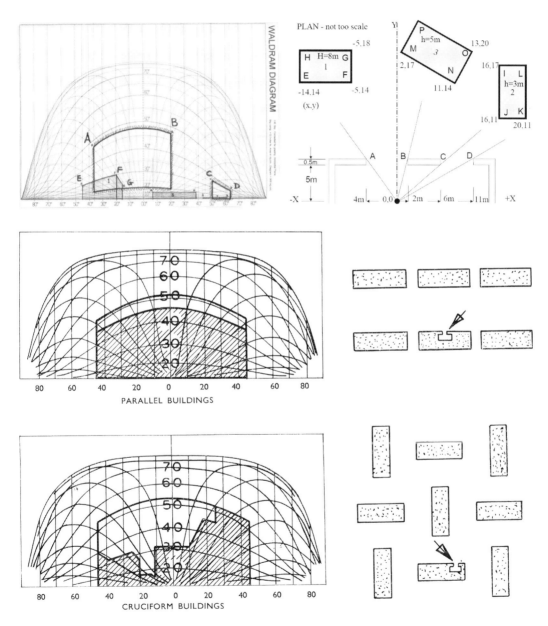

Source: Hopkinson (1963, p34)

Figure 13.1 *Waldram diagram for estimating daylight factor*

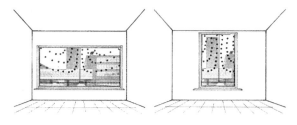

Figure 13.2 *Lynes pepper-pot diagram for estimating daylight factor*

projection of the shape of the windows and the external obstructions. A normal photograph looking towards the window may be used. This greatly simplifies the checking process for a designer and, hence, is much more user friendly.

The third graphical tool is by R. G. Hopkinson. It is known as the Daylight Code promulgated by the Ministry of Housing and Local Government, UK, with advice from the Building Research Station. The code contains a set of permissible height indicators that can be used to test adjacent buildings for daylight obstruction for town planning purposes. The tool allows planners to work mainly on plan-based information. It also allows one to quickly establish the usefulness of gaps between buildings for daylight.

Last, but not least, although not exactly a daylight design tool, the concept of the solar envelope developed by Ralph Knowles is an elegant method. Essentially, the solar envelope concept defines the maximum volume of the building that could be erected on a site without the building casting unacceptable shadows onto its neighbours between a certain time period. Based on cut-off lines extended from the shadow fences of the neighbouring properties, the roof shapes of the volume of the building of a site are trimmed. The resultant pyramid shape is the maximum volume within which designers will have to design their buildings.

The need for daylight

Tools allow one to gauge more accurately or more conveniently the amount or the quality of light to be admitted into building interiors. The next question is: how much? The Foreword of the British Standard BS8206, Part 2 (BSI, 1992) states this adeptly: 'Daylighting design [is] to enhance the well-being and satisfaction of people in buildings.' The standard then outlines a number of design criteria, such as view, enhancement of the appearance of interiors and

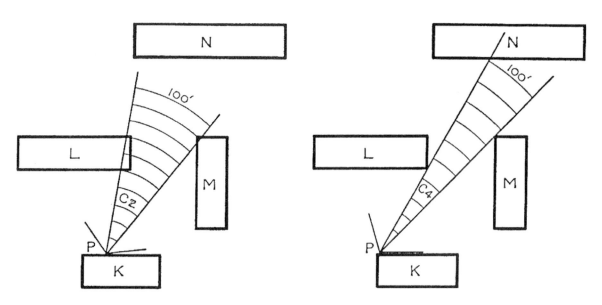

Figure 13.3 *Hopkinson projectors for understanding building obstructions with tall buildings*

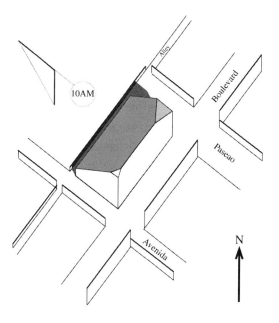

Winter Solstice: 10 am

Winter Solstice: 2 pm

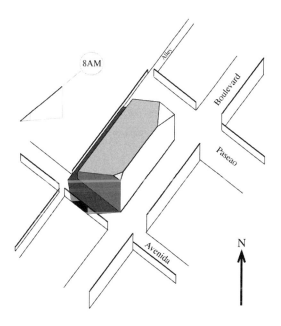

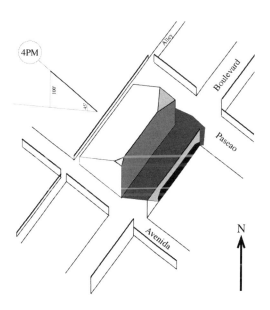

Summer Solstice: 8 am

Summer Solstice: 4 pm

Source: Professor Ralph Knowles. www-rcf.usc.edu/~rknowles/index.html

Figure 13.4 *Solar envelopes during different times of the year: two student projects from the studio of Knowles showing cardboard solar envelopes and the finished design proposals*

illumination of tasks. For the illumination of tasks, the standard further stipulates that daylight is to supplement electric light and offer the occupants a choice during daytime hours to opt for one or the other. It is apparent that the standard is primarily concerned with the psychological well-being of people, and not so much with the level of illumination.

Daylight factor (DF) has been used in the standard as the parameter. For rooms that need a day-lit appearance, the criteria are:

- 5 per cent average DF for rooms without supplementary electric lighting;
- 2 per cent for rooms with supplementary electric lighting.

For rooms in dwellings, the criteria are:

- 1 per cent average DF in bedrooms;
- 1.5 per cent average DF in living rooms; and
- 2 per cent average DF in kitchens.

The standard does not provide the rationale for the recommendation. For task illumination, numerous researchers – for example, Luckiesh (1924), Weston (1962) and Hopkinson and Kay (1969) – have earlier provided some basis. For dwellings, it appears that the standard may have made reference to a set of user survey experiments conducted in 1945. The kitchen was regarded as 'working space' and therefore users preferred a higher level of daylight (HMSO, 1944).

Towards high density

As the world population increases, more mega- and high-density cities will emerge. Today, around 20 cities in the world have 10 million inhabitants or more. This number will continue to increase in years to come. In cities such as these, buildings are fighting each other for natural light and ventilation. Developing ways of optimizing design for light and air becomes an important task for architects, engineers and industry stakeholders. The key questions nowadays are that when cities become denser and buildings become more closely packed, with associated modern lifestyle changes, are the parameters and criteria defined for daylight design still effective in offering designers some reference guidelines? And do these parameters offer regulators a means of control?

Hong Kong is one of the most densely populated cities in the world. It boasts a development density of 2500 individuals per hectare. Typically, residential buildings are built to a plot ratio of 9 and above with site coverage of at least 50 per cent. This leads to very tall buildings built very closely together.

Hong Kong, the ultra high-density city, like many cities in the world, has its own set of building regulations governing the provision of daylight to interior spaces. The regulations, formulated in 1956, are still in use today and were modelled based on the UK system as follows. For habitable rooms, including living and bedrooms:

- 10 per cent window area to floor area ratio;
- maximum room depth of 9m;
- minimum window height of 2m; and
- an unobstructed open space known as the rectangular horizontal plane (RHP) outside of the window.

For high-density city design, the more important requirement to note is the concept of RHP outside the window. Essentially, the RHP regulates the distance permissible between a window of a habitable room and the obstructing building directly in front of it. For example, in Hong Kong, it is required that a habitable space, such as a living room, be provided with a window that has an RHP directly outside that has a plan size not less than 2.3m multiplied by one third of the height of the building above the window. As such, the sustaining vertical unobstructed angle (no sky line) of the window is controlled.

Using the sustaining vertical unobstructed angle to control the separation of buildings can be dated back to Vitruvius. It has been the easiest and most effective way for regulators to state the need, and for designers to visualize the requirement. Various cities in the world have their own requirements.

For higher-density cities such as Singapore and Hong Kong, the permissible vertical sustaining angle can be up to 76 degrees. The vertical sustaining angle concept is basically an extrapolation of the lower angles historically practised in cities such as London. This seems to be a logical move. However, scientifically, one has to be very careful trying to extrapolate and at the same time not err against the very fundamental basis of the original concept. Take the sky component table of a Commission Internationale de l'Eclairage (CIE) overcast sky as the basis. It is apparent that most of the

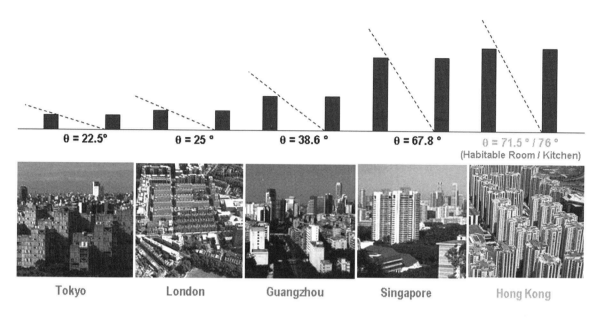

θ = 22.5°   θ = 25 °   θ = 38.6 °   θ = 67.8 °   θ = 71.5 ° / 76 °
                                                                    (Habitable Room / Kitchen)

Tokyo   London   Guangzhou   Singapore   Hong Kong

Source: Author

Figure 13.5 *Vertical obstruction angle restrictions in different cities*

available daylight to a window is from the area of the sky 15° to 35° vertically from the horizon, and 20° either way perpendicular to the window pane.

In order to secure good daylight access for a window, it is prudent to ensure that the sky component is not seriously obstructed. The easiest way to regulate this would be to state an angle, say 20°, beyond which the sky should not be obstructed, as has been done in Tokyo and London. If a vertical sustaining angle of 25° is set, the maximum available sky component (SC) is around 20 per cent. Assuming the horizontal global illuminance of the overcast sky is 5000 lux, the vertical window pane has access to some 1000 lux of daylight.

When this vertical sustaining angle of requirement is progressively extrapolated to, say, 40°, the available SC would be decreased to around 12 per cent. When the angle is further increased to 70°, the available SC would be a scant 1 per cent – that is to say, once the vertical sustaining angle is increased beyond the area of the sky that gives the most daylight to a window, any extrapolation would make little sense at all. This is the key issue of daylight design and regulation for high-density cities. The use of regulatory tools originally developed for low-density cities is, thus, inappropriate. New tools are needed.

Apart from the need for new tools, there is a further need to establish the requirements of inhabitants living in high-density cities. Human adaptation of an environment is a known phenomenon. That is to say, people have the ability to acclimatize in order to cope with different living and environmental conditions. For example, it is known that people are more likely to accept high indoor temperatures in a free-running building in the tropics than in cities of high latitudes. In hotter climates, people also prefer a dimmer indoor environment since, psychologically, it is associated with cooler spaces.

Quoting an extensive user survey conducted in Hong Kong, the acceptable daylight factor of habitable space is observed to be merely around 0.5 per cent. This is a far cry from the 1 to 2 per cent that the British Standard stipulated for the UK. The finding indicates great tolerance regarding the availability of daylight to interiors. One reason for this is environmental acclimatization; the other has to do with the inhabitants' access to convenient and cheap artificial light sources, as well as to their living patterns in coping

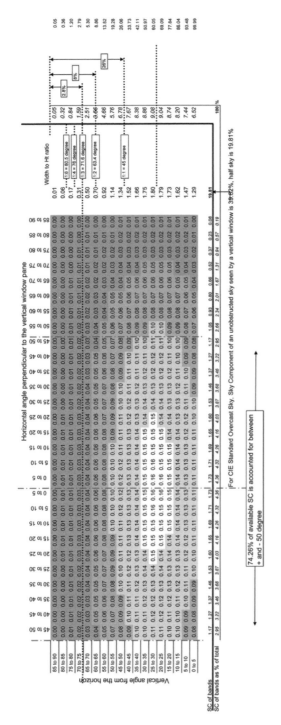

Source: Author

Figure 13.6 *A sky component table in 5° intervals based on CIE overcast sky*

with the lifestyle of a high-density city. For example, where people work late, they only need to access the kitchen occasionally for quick meals (Ng, 2003). This does not mean that daylight can be forgotten in high-density city design. The survey also highlighted that although the acceptable threshold is low, there is still a lower limit, and beyond this limit, people will complain. The survey indicates that this limit for inhabitants of Hong Kong for living rooms and bedrooms is around 8 per cent vertical daylight factor (VDF) available to the window pane. To compare, in the UK, the recommendation made by the Building Research Establishment (BRE) is 23 per cent sky component (Littlefair, 1991).

A tool for high density

Today, sophisticated computational tools are available that very accurately predict the daylight availability of building interiors. Software such as Radiance is one of the *de facto* software programmes of the industry known to be able give reasonable results (Larson and Shakespeare, 1998). Based on an association of related circumstances without experimental proofs, Mardaljevic (1995) proposed that it should therefore also be adequate for high-density city design conditions. However, the issue at hand is not the availability of sophisticated 'evaluative' tools, but the need for simple 'design and regulatory' tools in the early stages of the design process so that regulators can easily and quickly assess a design visually and graphically.

Based on the earlier observation of the available sky component of the CIE overcast sky, and making reference to Hopkinson's Daylight Code, the concept of unobstructed vision area (UVA) has been developed in Hong Kong. Basically, the concept takes into account the typical practice of using only the building plan and building height information as the basis of regulatory control (Ng, 2001).

Tregenza earlier proposed a three-dimensional sky component overlay method (Ng, 2001). For high-density environments where surrounding buildings are tall, the sky component that could be captured above the top of buildings is insignificant. Instead, daylight that may be available through gaps between buildings may be more useful; this could be evaluated using plan information. Tregenza's method essentially overlays the sky component as dots on a semi-circle in front of the window to be tested; based on how much of the sky component can be viewed through

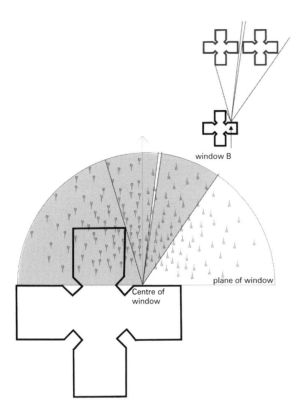

Source: Unpublished drawing by Professor Peter Tregenza given to the author

Figure 13.7 *A study of daylight factor based on Tregenza's dot method*

the gaps, the amount of daylight available to a window is then estimated. The method may be further simplified by replacing the number of dots representing SC with the amount of open 'area' in front of the window. This area is dubbed the unobstructed vision area.

In order to obtain an adequate amount of light on the vertical surface of the window plane, the window must face into an outdoor open area. The larger this open area is, the more daylight it is likely to receive. The UVA method considers an area in the shape of a cone that is 100° wide – beyond 100° the efficacy of light entering the window is reduced. The length of the cone is equal to the height of the building above the window. When such a cone is overlaid onto the site plan, the surrounding buildings will obstruct part of

the area. The resultant area is the unobstructed vision area that the window 'sees'. The formula that relates UVA to the height of building is as follows:

$$UVA = kH^2 \hspace{3cm} [13.1]$$

where:

- UVA = unobstructed vision area (m²);
- k = constant;
- H = building height (m).

The value k is a constant and it depends upon the daylight performance (VDF) required. k is worked out parametrically and statistically based on tests using built and theoretical examples that rely on computational results (Ng et al, 2003). For example, if the vertical daylight factor (VDF) required is 8 per cent, k = 0.24. The higher the VDF required, the higher the value of k. For example, based on test results, it can be stated that if a window located on the surface of a building 100m high could achieve a UVA of 2400 square metres, there is a 75 per cent chance that the window could achieve a VDF of 8 per cent.

The UVA method has been tested for building heights from 90m to 130m. Further tests may be needed to establish the value of k for higher buildings. However, it is not anticipated that the value would change more than 20 per cent of the stated value. In order to apply the UVA tool appropriately, the following conditions must be satisfied. First, the buildings must be high relative to the distance between them. Typically, this is in the order of 2:1 or above. The UVA tool will underestimate daylight availability if buildings are low. For low-rise buildings, other tools should be used. Second, the heights of buildings within the vicinity of the window to be tested must be similar in height.

The UVA method is not an evaluation tool: it is not a tool for evaluating the availability of VDF based on the UVA. For example, it does not say that if one were to design a UVA of 8000m in front of the window, it will give 8 per cent VDF. Actually, in many cases the VDF will be higher – sometimes much higher. The method merely states that if an 8000m UVA can be provided, then there is a 75 per cent chance that the VDF of the window would be 'at least' 8 per cent. The concept of 'at least' is the key spirit of the tool for

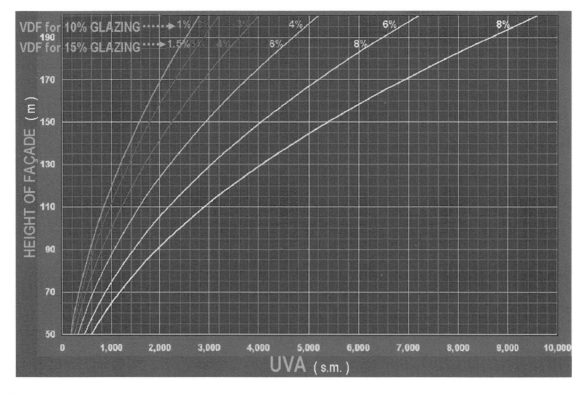

Source: Author

Figure 13.8 *A graph showing the relationship between unobstructed vision area (UVA) and façade heights with various achievable vertical daylight factors*

regulatory purpose, which is the main reason for the development of the tool (Chung and Cheung, 2006).

The UVA method can be a simple regulatory tool. It has been adopted by the regulatory authority in Hong Kong as a means of controlling the high-density built environment (Buildings Department HKSAR, 2003).

In this example, a window in a high-rise tower needs to be assessed. A vertical daylight factor of 8 per cent is needed. Based on the graphs relating the height of façade to UVA, an area of, say, 3000 square metres is needed. A cone 50° left and right to the perpendicular of the window (total 100°) is drawn and extends to a distance H from the window (H being the height of the tower from the window). This is the vision area of the window. Obstructions to the area that the window can 'see' will be deducted. The leftover space is the unobstructed vision

area of the window. If the UVA is more than 3000 square metres, then the window satisfies the regulations. If the UVA is less, than the designer can either reposition the tower to gain further UVA, or enlarge the window area to compensate (as below).

The way forward

If one were to examine further the design logic of UVA, it is not difficult to realize that given the same building bulk, building taller but slimmer and well-spaced towers on a building site may be a better strategy for daylight than building, say, shorter but fatter towers. Designed properly, the strategy of 'tall and thin' has a better chance of gaining more UVA for the windows – mainly through building gaps between towers.

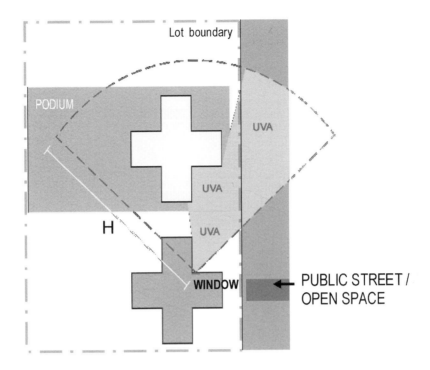

Source: Author

Figure 13.9 *A diagram showing the concept of UVA*

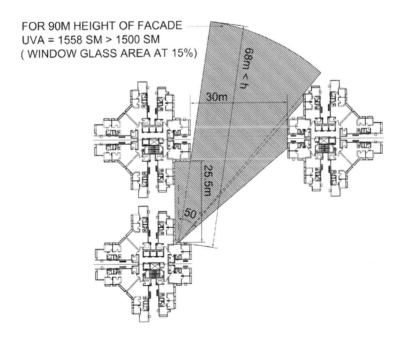

Source: Author

Figure 13.10 *A real-life application of UVA in a housing estate design with 15 per cent glazing area*

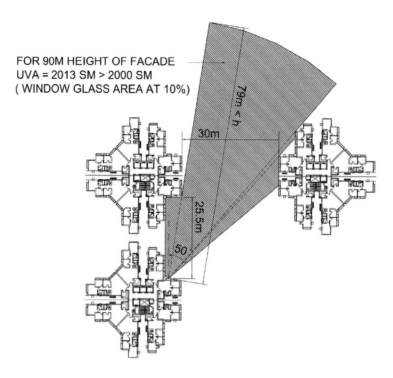

FOR 90M HEIGHT OF FACADE
UVA = 2013 SM > 2000 SM
(WINDOW GLASS AREA AT 10%)

Source: Author

Figure 13.11 *A real-life application of UVA in a housing estate design with 10 per cent glazing area*

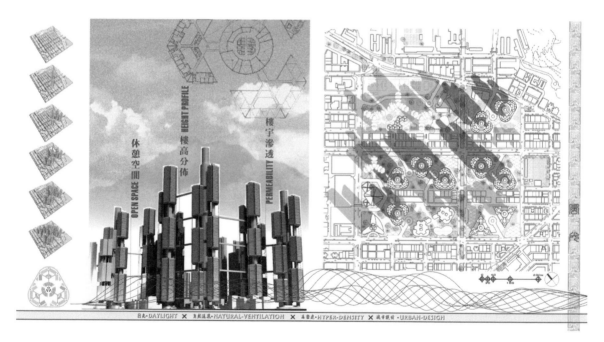

Source: Drawn by Tak-Yan Chan as part of his design thesis for his MArch degree

Figure 13.12 *A design hypothesis based on maximizing UVA*

Furthermore, based on parametric studies of building heights, it has been established that when designing tall buildings in a neighbourhood, designing towers of different building heights is advantageous. Given the same building bulk, on average, daylight availability to windows can improve by some 40 per cent (Ng and Wong, 2005).

Conclusions

The chapter first reviewed historical daylight design tools that have been developed since Vitruvius. It then suggested that for high-density cities, a fundamental change of guiding parameter is needed. The concept of unobstructed vision area (UVA) based on the horizontal sustainable angle has been proposed and explained.

The UVA method is a simplified method. It is relatively easy to use. In practice, it will probably cope with most of the high-density housing developments in Hong Kong. However, like the use of rectangular horizontal plane (RHP) before it, it will not be able to deal with all design cases. Alternative methods must be allowed by the buildings departments for regulatory control. The onus rests on designers to prove that their designs achieve a vertical daylight factor (VDF) of no less than the standard and that the method used is robust and proven. The following methods, if used properly, should be able to deal with more complicated circumstances that the UVA method may not address:

- Any three-dimensional method for estimating sky component (SC) could be used. These methods include the use of the Waldram diagram, the Lynes pepper-pot diagram or other suitable stereographic diagrams. Factor in an external reflected component (ERC) based on r (reflectance) = 0.2 to arrive at VDF.
- The modified split flux formula developed by Peter Tregenza could be used (Tregenza, 1989). This formula is capable of accounting accurately for conditions where the skyline is complicated.
- Computational simulation – to obtain good results, it is important to set the files and configure the variables correctly.
- Measurements using mini-cells, scale models and CIE overcast artificial sky may be used.

For high-density city design, it may be advantageous to design tall, thin and well-spaced buildings. Varying building heights is also a useful design strategy. Today, city design needs to provide more than daylight. Designers should balance various considerations in order to achieve a more liveable city.

References

BSI (1992) *BS8206 Part 2: Lighting for Buildings – Code of Practice for Daylighting*, BSI, UK

Buildings Department HKSAR (2003) *Lighting and Ventilation Requirements – Performance Based Approach*, PNAP278, Government of the Hong Kong Special Administrative Region, China

Chambers, W. (1969) *A Treatise on the Decorative Part of Civil Architecture* (facsimile reprint of the London edition 1791), Farnborough, Hants, Gregg Press Ltd, p116

Chung, T. M. and Cheung, H. D. (2006) 'Assessing daylight performance of buildings using orthographically projected area of obstructions', *Journal of Light and Visual Environment*, Japan, vol 30, no 2, pp74–80

HMSO (1944) *Post-War Building Studies, No 12: The Lighting of Buildings*, HMSO, London

Hopkinson, R. G. (1963) *Architectural Physics: Lighting*, HMSO, London, p34

Hopkinson, R. G., Pethernridge, P. and Longmore, J. (1966) *Daylighting*, Heinemann, London, p423

Hopkinson, R. G. and Kay, J. D. (1969) *The Lighting of Buildings*, Faber and Faber, London

Kerr, R. (1865) *On Ancient Light*, John Murray, London

Larson, G. W. and Shakespeare, R. A. (1998) *Rendering with Radiance – The Art and Science of Lighting Visualization*, Morgan Kaufmann Publishers, San Francisco, USA

Littlefair, P. J. (1991) *Site Layout Planning for Daylight and Sunlight – A Guide to Good Practice*, BRE, UK

Luckiesh, M. (1924) *Light and Work*, D. Van Nostrand Company, New York, NY

Lynes, J. A. (1968) *Principles of Natural Lighting*, Elsevier, London, p147

Mardaljevic, J. (1995) 'Validation of a lighting simulation program under real sky conditions', *Lighting Research and Technology*, vol 27, no 4, pp181–188

Moon, P. (1936) *The Scientific Basis of Illuminating Engineering*, McGraw-Hill Book Co Inc, New York

Ng, E. (2001) 'A simplified daylight design tool for high density urban residential buildings', *Lighting Research and Technology*, CIBSE, vol 33, no 4, pp259–272

Ng, E. (2003) 'Studies on daylight design of high density residential housing in Hong Kong', *Lighting Research and Technology*, CIBSE, vol 35, no 2, pp127–140

Ng, E. and Wong, N. H. (2005) 'Parametric studies of urban design morphologies and their implied environmental performance', in J. H. Bay and B. L. Ong (eds) *Tropical*

Sustainable Architecture: Social and Environmental Dimensions, Architectural Press, London

Ng, E., Chan, T. Y., Leung, R. and Pang, P. (2003), 'A daylight design and regulatory method for high density cities using computational lighting simulations', in M. L. Chiu, J. Y. Tsou, T. Kvan, M. Morozumi and T. S. Jeng, (eds) *Digital Design – Research and Practice*, Kluwer Academic Publishers, London, pp339–349

Palladio, A. (1738) *Four Books on Architecture*, translated by Issac Ware, Dover Publication Inc (1965), London, Book 1, Chapter 25, p30

Plommer, H. (1973) *Vitruvius and Later Roman Building Manuals*, Cambridge University Press, pp41–43, pp61–65

Salmon, W. (1727) *Country Builder's Estimator*, London, p88

Tregenza, P. R. (1989) 'Modification of the split flux formulae for mean daylight factor and internal reflected component with large external obstructions', *Lighting Research and Technology*, vol 21, no 3, pp125–128

Vitruvius (c. 25BC) *De Architectura*, English edition (1960) translated by Morris Hicky Morgan as *The Ten Books on Architecture*, Dover Publications, Book 9, Chapter 3, pp264–265

Walsh, J. W. T. (1961) *The Science of Daylight*, Macdonald and Co Ltd, London

Waldram, P. J. and Waldram, J. M. (1923) 'Window design and the measurement and predetermination of daylight illumination', *The Illuminating Engineer*, vol 16, no 45, pp86–7, 122.

Weston, H. C. (1962) *Sight, Light and Work*, 2nd edition, H. K. Lewis & Co Ltd, London

14

Designing for Waste Minimization in High-Density Cities

Chi-Sun Poon and Lara Jaillon

Introduction: Waste management and waste minimization

Worldwide, the building industry consumes and generates a significant amount of building materials and construction waste. The annual production of building materials and components consumes about 3 billion tonnes of raw materials, which represents about 40 to 50 per cent of the total flow in the global economy (Roodman and Lenssen, 1995; Anink et al, 1996). In the US, 40 per cent of raw materials are used in buildings (USGBC, 2003), and annual construction waste generation accounts for about 136 million tonnes per year, of which 50 per cent is incinerated or disposed of at landfills (Franklin, 1998). The management of construction waste is a key environmental issue as land available for its disposal is scarce in many countries such as Hong Kong. Waste minimization is therefore a priority for the construction industry to tackle the problem at source. A recent study (Innes, 2004) demonstrated that about 30 per cent of construction waste might be directly influenced by design concepts and decisions. Waste reduction at source involves both design concepts and building technology/materials selection (Poon and Jaillon, 2002a). With the introduction of recent legislation in Hong Kong enforcing the polluter pays principle, both architects and contractors are required to pay more attention towards waste minimization practices.

This chapter introduces ways of reducing construction waste arising from both construction and demolition activities, principally through design measures and the use of low-waste building technologies. Significant issues associated with construction waste management and disposal in high-density cities such as Hong Kong are also discussed.

Definitions

Differentiating between waste management and waste minimization

Although the definition of waste management is well established, the distinction between waste management and minimization needs clarification. According to the Organisation for Economic Co-operation and Development report entitled *Considerations for Evaluating Waste Minimization in OECD Member Countries* (OECD, 1996), waste minimization comprises preventive measures and some waste management measures (see Figure 14.1). This definition includes priorities for waste minimization such as preventing and/or reducing the generation of waste at the source; improving the quality of waste generated, such as reducing the hazard; and encouraging reuse, recycling and recovery. Waste minimization is a process that avoids, eliminates or reduces waste at its source or permits reuse/recycling of the waste for benign purposes (Riemer and Kristoffersen, 1999).

The waste management hierarchy is used to show the desirability of adopting various waste management strategies and involves the following, in order of preference: avoidance, minimization, recycling/reuse,

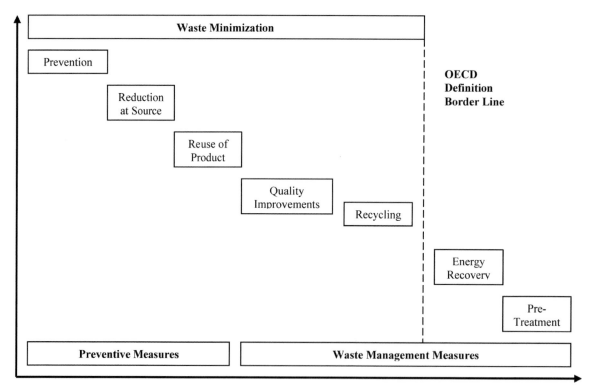

Source: Riemer and Kristoffersen (1999)

Figure 14.1 *OECD working definition on waste minimization*

treatment and disposal. As shown in Figure 14.2, priority is given to the waste minimization concept

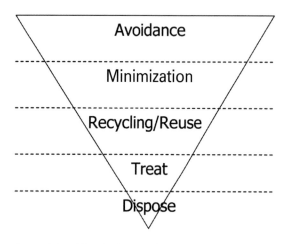

Source: Adapted from Environmental Protection Department, www.epd.gov.hk/epd/misc/cdm/management_intro.htm

Figure 14.2 *Waste minimization hierarchy*

comprising avoidance, minimization and recycling/reuse of waste.

Defining construction waste

Worldwide, the definition of construction waste, also called construction and demolition debris, varies according to countries or states. In Hong Kong, construction waste, or construction and demolition (C&D) materials, is generally defined as a mixture of inert and non-inert materials arising from construction, excavation, renovation, demolition and roadwork (EPD, 2007). The composition of construction waste varies and is highly dependent upon the type and scale of construction activities generating waste. The composition of construction waste is subdivided in two major categories: inert and non-inert materials. Inert materials comprise soft inert materials such as soil, earth and slurry, and hard inert materials such as rocks and broken concrete. Recently in Hong Kong, soft inert materials have accounted for about 70 per cent of all construction waste and are only suitable for reuse as fill materials in reclamation and earth-filling works (Legislative Council, 2006). However, hard inert materials, which account for about 12 to 15 per cent of all construction waste, can be either reused in reclamation works or recycled for construction works as granular materials, drainage bedding layers and concrete application (Legislative Council, 2006). Non-inert waste, such as timber, plastics and packaging waste, account for about 15 to 18 per cent of all construction waste and are recycled or disposed of at landfills. A recent study (Poon et al, 2004) revealed that timber formwork, wet trades of finishing work, and concrete and masonry works were the major contributors to construction waste in building sites. Table 14.1 shows the average percentage of wastage arising from various trades in construction sites.

Waste management in Hong Kong

Hong Kong is a compact city and one of the most densely populated places in the world. The built environment occupies only 20 per cent of the whole territory. Available space is limited, land is expensive and, thus, the construction of high-rise building is a common practice in Hong Kong to maximize profit as well as land use. With such compactness, environmental sustainability is of increasing concern and environmental issues, such as air quality and waste management, have become significant.

In 2005, about 21.5 million tonnes of construction waste were generated, of which 11 per cent was disposed of at landfills (about 6556 tonnes per day) and 89 per cent at public filling areas (about 52,211 tonnes per day). Public filling areas are designated areas that accept surplus inert construction wastes (public fills) for reclamation purposes. Over the last decade, the generation of construction waste has more than doubled (see Figure 14.3). The management of construction waste is a significant issue, as Hong Kong has limited space available for the disposal of waste at both landfills and public filling areas. During recent years, construction waste has accounted for about 38 per cent of the total intake at landfills. With the current waste generation rate, landfills will be completely full within five to nine years (EPD, 2007). In addition, the generation of public fill has recently surpassed demand as currently only a limited number of reclamation projects are in progress. Therefore, since 2002, inert materials have been stored at two temporary fill banks. The fill banks are areas allocated for short-term stockpile of public fills for later use. At the end of February 2006, the remaining capacity of these two temporary fill banks was about 7 million tonnes (Legislative Council,

Table 14.1 *Wastage percentage of various trades for public housing projects and private residential developments*

Trade	Material	Wastage percentage	
		Public housing (%)	Private residential (%)
Concrete	Concrete	3–5	4–5
Formwork	Timber board	– (large panel formwork & precasting)	100
Reinforcement	Steel bars	3–5	1–8
Masonry	Brick & block	3	4–8
Dry wall	Fine aggregate	3	–
Wall screeding	Ready-mix cement	7	4–20
Floor screeding	Ready-mix cement	1	4–20
Wall plastering	Plaster	3	4–20
Ceiling plastering	Plaster	3	4–20
Wall tiling	Tiles	8	4–10
Floor tiling	Tiles	6	4–10
Installation of bathroom fitting	Sanitary fittings	6	1–5
Installation of Kitchen joinery	Kitchen joinery	1	1–5

Source: Poon et al (2001)

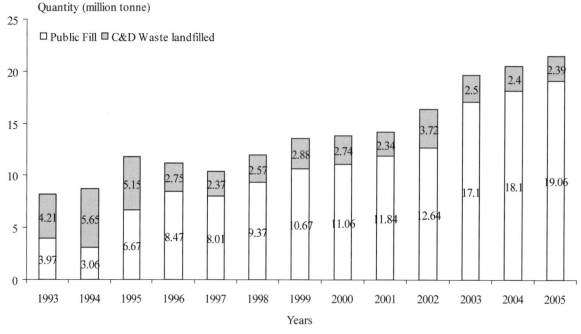

Source: Environmental Protection Department, www.wastereduction.gov.hk/en/materials/info/msw2007.pdf

Figure 14.3 *Construction waste disposed at landfills and public filling areas since 1993*

2006). With the current waste generation rate, the capacities of fill banks will be exhausted by 2008. There is pressing need for further waste reduction measures in the Hong Kong construction industry to tackle the issue of waste management and, thus, to promote sustainable construction.

The Hong Kong government has recently implemented construction waste minimization measures in the construction industry (see Table 14.2). The waste management plan and the trip ticket system adopted in public works contracts encourage on-site sorting and ensure that each type of waste is directed to the appropriate facility for reuse, recycling or disposal. The waste management plan, which is prepared by the contractor before the commencement of work, provides an overall framework for waste reduction and management. It identifies major types of waste and strategies for waste reduction.

Additionally, waste recycling strategies have been promoted by the government. The recycling of hard inert materials was carried out from 2002 to 2005 through the installation of a pilot construction waste recycling plant, producing about 0.53 million tonnes

of recycled aggregates and rock fills for use in government projects. This pilot project demonstrated the viability of using the recycled aggregates in construction.

The introduction of construction waste disposal charges in 2006 provided an economic incentive for developers and contractors to reduce the generation of construction waste. As presented in Table 14.3, the charges are HK$125/tonne for landfills, HK$100/tonne for sorting facilities, and HK$27/tonne for public fill reception facilities. Two off-site sorting facilities have been set up to facilitate the reuse and recycling of construction waste (see Figure 14.4). These two facilities help waste producers, especially when the construction sites are small and limited space is available to carry out on-site sorting. Until 2006, a reduction of about 37 per cent of the amount of construction waste disposed at landfills was noticed (see Figure 14.5) compared to the disposal rate in 2005. Furthermore, the charging scheme for construction waste disposal has already generated about HK$55 million (Chui, 2007). However, the risk in adopting the polluter pays principle is the possible increase in illegal dumping.

Table 14.2 *Drivers towards waste minimization in the Hong Kong construction industry*

Environmental issues and waste generation	Waste minimization measures in Hong Kong construction industry		
	Economic benefits	Construction industry	Regulations and policies
In Hong Kong, the construction industry consumes and generates significant amount of building materials and waste. In 2005, about 21.5 million t of construction waste were generated, of which 11% was disposed of at landfills (6556 t/day) and 89% at public filling areas (52,211 t/day). Limited disposal capacity at landfills and public filling areas (reclamation projects, temporary fill banks). Recently, construction waste accounted for about 38% of total intake at landfills. The landfill capacity will be exhausted within 5–9 years. The generation of public fill has recently surpassed the demand. Two temporary fill banks were created since 2002. The capacity of the fill banks will be exhausted by 2008.	Prior to 2005, the disposal of construction waste was free of charge, requiring the government to pay for its disposal. The total capital cost for the 3 landfills was about HK$5,900M, and the total maintenance cost was estimated to HK$435M/yr. Since December 2005, a disposal charge was introduced, applying 'polluters pay principle'. Charges are HK$125/t for landfills, HK$100/t for sorting facilities and HK$27/t for public fill reception facilities. This scheme has already generated up to HK$55M. Since 2006, a reduction of 37% of the amount of construction waste disposed at landfills was noted. With waste reduction, significant savings can be achieved in material cost, waste disposal cost and transportation cost for materials and waste.	In 2001, the CIRC published the report 'Construct for Excellence'. The report included 109 recommendations for improving the performance of the construction industry. Prefabrication was recommended as a solution to on-site environmental issues (including construction waste generation) associated with conventional construction and the use of timber formworks. A wider use of standardisation in component design & processes was also recommended to eliminate waste and inefficiencies (CIRC, pp104). Some large developers and contractors adopt waste management plans and waste reduction measures on sites. But little consideration to waste minimization at the source, in design principles; little integration of design and construction towards waste minimization, early in the design process.	1998: Waste Reduction Framework Plan (WRFP) 1998–2007. Setting targets for the construction industry: reduction by 25% of construction waste disposed at landfills. Recommendations of implementing construction waste charging scheme, waste management plans to the private sector, and training courses. In December 2005, a waste disposal charge for construction waste was introduced. *Public Sector:* Implementation of: 2000: Waste management plan. 1999: Trip ticket system to minimize illegal dumping. Since 2002, the government promotes the use of recycled aggregates derived from construction waste. A pilot facility produced about 0.53M t of recycled aggregates. *Private Sector:* In 2001 and 2002, the government introduced the Joint Practice Notes 1 and 2. These incentive schemes include green features that may be exempted from GFA calculations under the Building Ordinance. Non-structural prefabricated external wall is one of the green features proposed.

Source: Adapted from Jaillon et al (2009)

Table 14.3 *Government waste disposal facilities and disposal charge*

Government waste disposal facilities	Charge per tonne	Type of C&D waste accepted
Public fill reception facilities	HK$27	Consisting entirely of inert construction waste
Sorting facilities	HK$100	Containing more than 50% by weight of inert construction waste
Landfills	HK$125	Containing not more than 50% by weight of inert construction waste
Outlying islands transfer facilities	HKS125	Containing any percentage of inert construction waste

Source: Environmental Protection Department, www.epd.gov.hk/epd/misc/cdm/scheme.htm

Another waste reduction initiative from the Hong Kong government was the implementation of incentives schemes, with gross floor area (GFA) calculation exemption granted for the use of green and innovative building technologies (Buildings Department, 2001, 2002). The objectives are to:

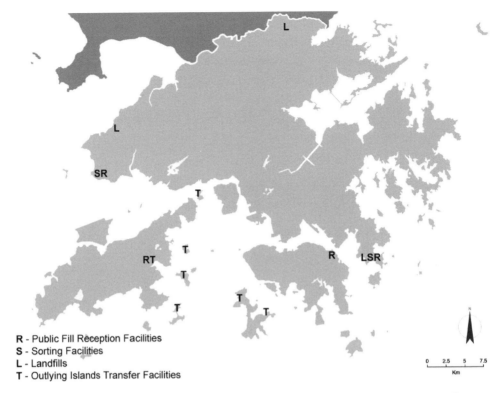

R - Public Fill Reception Facilities
S - Sorting Facilities
L - Landfills
T - Outlying Islands Transfer Facilities

Source: Adapted from the Environmental Protection Department, www.wastereduction.gov.hk/en/materials/info/msw2007.pdf

Figure 14.4 *Existing facilities for construction waste management and disposal*

- encourage a holistic life-cycle approach to planning, design, construction and maintenance;
- maximize the use of natural renewable resources and recycled/green building materials; and
- reduce energy consumption as well as construction and demolition waste generation.

The Joint Practice Note 1 was introduced in February 2001 and included incentives for the use of green features in private developments such as balconies, wider common corridors, and lift lobbies and communal sky gardens. The government issued the second package of incentives, the Joint Practice Note 2, in February 2002. This included further incentives for the construction of various green features such as the use of non-structural prefabricated external walls. Since then, prefabrication techniques are increasingly used in the private sector.

Designing for waste minimization

There is a general observation that not only do designers pay little consideration to waste generation in design concepts, but the selection of building materials and construction methods are hardly geared towards waste minimization in the design stage (Poon et al, 2002a, 2004; Osmani et al, 2006). However, the impact of design decisions on waste minimization is significant. A recent study (Innes, 2004) demonstrated that design decisions might be the indirect cause of about 30 per cent of the construction waste in building projects. Various design concepts may be adopted to minimize waste arising from construction and demolitions activities, and they are discussed below in terms of designing for reducing waste and construction methods/material selection.

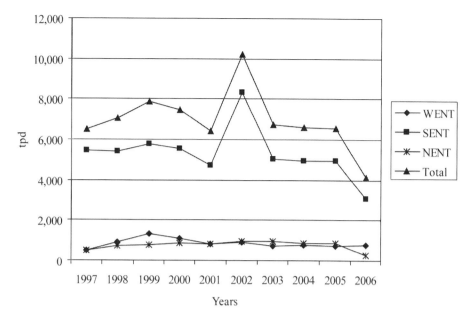

Source: Environmental Protection Department, www.wastereduction.gov.hk/en/materials/info/msw2007.pdf

Figure 14.5 *Construction waste disposed at the three strategic landfills since 1997, in tonnes per day (tpd)*

Designing for reducing waste from demolition works

Optimizing building lifespan

A recent study (Poon and Jaillon, 2002b) showed that, in general, buildings in Hong Kong have an average service life of about 40 years. In this study, it was found that the major causes that reduce the lifespan of a building in Hong Kong were (in order of importance) construction faults, material failures, redevelopment pressure and design faults. The study revealed that the construction faults were mainly due to the shortage of skilled labour and the short construction schedules at the time of construction. Material failures were caused by poor-quality concrete and lower construction standards used in the past. Redevelopment pressures are significant in a compact city such as Hong Kong where available land is scarce and land price is exorbitant. Also, with the implementation of new plot ratio requirements and regulations, redevelopment may be a more profitable option for the developers.

The study also concluded that by extending the building lifespan to 75 years, the amount of waste arising from building demolition can be significantly reduced by half. Although waste is generated during regular maintenance works, the main building structure remains and demolition waste is kept away from the waste stream for a longer duration. There are various design concepts to optimize the lifespan of a building, such as providing flexibilities and adaptabilities in the design, reusing building structures and designing for deconstruction.

Design flexibility and adaptability

Although proper maintenance works promote the optimization of a building's lifespan, providing flexibility and adaptability in the building system is also an important factor. In a recent study, as described above (Poon and Jaillon, 2002b), it was found that design flexibilities that allow future fitting-out modifications can reduce waste generation in both residential buildings and office/commercial buildings.

However, it was argued that in Hong Kong it might be difficult to allow design flexibility in residential buildings due to the restrictive building regulations. In addition, most residential units in Hong Kong are already quite small in size and may not be able to accommodate changes in the structure or layout. The term 'open building system' is well known and defines the principles of ordering and combining subsystems by which interference between subsystems is minimized. This design principle allows flexibility and changes (modifications in fitting out) without demolition of the whole building structure. NEXT21 (Osaka Gas, 2000), an experimental housing project in Japan, adopted a highly flexible architectural system providing flexible layout of internal partitions and external walls. Major renovation works were carried out to respond to individual users' requirements without demolition of the building structure, contributing to significant waste reduction. In this building, the building structure has a long lifespan, and the infill, cladding and piping systems are flexible and can be easily modified.

Reusing buildings

The reuse of existing building structures and adaptive reuse also promote the optimization of a building's lifespan. Previous studies (Poon and Jaillon, 2002b) showed that the reuse of buildings, such as adaptive reuse, is rare in Hong Kong due to the lack of flexibility in the design regulation and plot ratio requirements. The Electrical and Mechanical Services Department (EMSD) headquarters refurbishment project demonstrates a viable and practical way of reusing existing building structures through adaptive reuse (see Figure 14.6). The former air cargo terminal at Kai Tak Airport in Kowloon was converted into an office building and vehicle workshops area. The benefits were significant. By reusing the existing building structure, the project saved about HK\$600 million to HK\$700 million in demolition and development costs (Tam, 2006). In addition, a huge volume of demolition waste (equivalent to the volume of a five-storey football pitch) was avoided, thus conserving landfill space. The adaptive reuse design strategy saves costs for

Source: Pictures provided by the Hong Kong Polytechnic University

Figure 14.6 *Electrical and Mechanical Services Department headquarters in Kowloon; adaptive reuse of the former air cargo terminal of Kai Tak Airport*

redevelopment such as infrastructure and land costs. The California Integrated Waste Management Board (CIWMB) quoted the case study of the Southern California Gas Company, which saved about US$3.2 million in infrastructure, building materials and land costs by reusing an existing building to create the Energy Resource Centre (CIWMB, 1996). However, a building reuse strategy may not be a practical and viable option for every building because such strategies depend upon the building conditions, site location and the programme of the new building, etc.

Design for deconstruction: Reuse and recycle

Deconstruction is the process of disassembling a building structure with the priority of preserving building materials or components that may be reused or recycled. The consideration of a deconstruction strategy in the design phase may reduce waste generation. A recent study (Osmani et al, 2006) confirmed that design for deconstruction was rarely implemented in building projects. Architects also felt that designing for reuse and recycling requires new knowledge, such as new techniques for dismantling of building components (Poon and Jaillon, 2002b).

Designing for reducing waste from construction works

Dimensional coordination and standardization

The adoption of standard dimensions and materials may significantly reduce material wastage, thus resulting in considerable savings. Previous studies (Poon et al, 2001) demonstrated that a significant amount of waste does result from the excessive cuttings of building materials during the construction process. A recent study (Osmani et al, 2006) also stated that off-cuts from cutting materials were a major cause of waste during the construction phase. In this study, it was found that the use of standard dimensions and units, and the use of standard materials to avoid cutting, were rarely implemented in design projects.

Public housing projects in Hong Kong have adopted various standard block designs and standard building components over the years. Recent projects have evolved towards a modular design approach with the use of standard building components such as prefabricated façades, staircases, etc, and standard residential unit configuration/size (e.g. one-bedroom

unit, two-bedroom unit, etc.). The redevelopment of Upper Ngau Tau Kok (see Figure 14.7), comprising six 40-storey towers, adopts a site-specific approach by taking into account site characteristics and environmental issues in the configuration of blocks, while using modular design, symmetries and standard building components, thus resulting in significant waste reduction. On average, public housing projects achieve a waste reduction of about 57 per cent when compared with conventional construction in Hong Kong.

Minimizing temporary works

Temporary works generate a significant amount of waste on site; therefore, alternative forms of design and construction methods should be considered to reduce their need. Poon et al (2004) revealed that timber formwork was the major contributor to construction waste, accounting for about 30 per cent of all wastes. Timber formwork is widely used in Hong Kong for the construction of high-rise buildings. Although timber has various advantages (inexpensive, flexible, etc.), its low durability and reusability compared to system formworks are causing significant wastage on site. Alternatives such as system formworks (metal or aluminium formworks) and prefabricated elements (façades, slabs, staircases, etc.)

Source: Adapted from Hong Kong Housing Authority, building plans of Upper Ngau Tau Tok Redevelopment

Figure 14.7 *Redevelopment of Upper Ngau Tau Kok completed in 2008, using a site-specific design approach and standard building components and unit configurations*

should be considered to reduce waste. A recent residential project in Hong Kong, comprising the construction of three 68-storey towers, achieved a 40 per cent waste reduction when compared to conventional construction by adopting metal formworks. The wastage level was about 0.19 tonnes per square metre. Construction floor area (CFA) system formworks and prefabrication techniques are highly appropriate to the construction of high-rise buildings due to repetitions and symmetries in design.

Avoiding late design modifications

Late modifications in the design, occurring during the construction phase, may generate a large amount of construction waste especially if the building is almost completed. A previous study (Poon et al, 2004) showed that the major causes of design changes were due to last-minute client requirements, complex design, a lack of communication between parties and insufficient design information. Another recent study (Osmani et al, 2006) has confirmed that the major causes of waste during the design phase were the last-minute changes due to clients' requirements. In Hong Kong, clients may include design modifications during the construction phase to best match market conditions.

Construction methods/material selection: Low-waste building technologies

According to the study previously mentioned (Poon and Jaillon, 2002b), waste minimization is the least important factor affecting construction method selection (see Figure 14.8). The use of low-waste building technologies, on site and/or off site, should be considered in the waste minimization process.

On site: System formworks, hoarding and scaffolding

A previous study (Poon and Jaillon, 2002a) revealed that the four main building work components that are considered to be the most waste-producing are, in order of importance, formwork; packaging and protection; finish work; and material handling. This shows that the generation of waste on site is mainly related to the construction methods selection, the availability of on-site sorting facilities and the education and training of workers. The use of system formworks (metal or aluminium), steel hoarding and metal scaffolding helps to reduce waste generation on site.

Another study (Osmani et al, 2006) also maintains that improper storage space and methods is the major cause of waste during site operations. Material control is therefore essential for waste minimization on site. This includes strategies to reduce material loss or damage through good design, specification and procurement, packaging, careful transportation, reception handling, storage and coordination (Ferguson et al, 1995).

Off site: Prefabrication techniques

Prefabrication construction is commonly used in public housing projects in Hong Kong and was introduced during the mid 1980s. The most commonly used prefabricated elements are precast façades, staircases, partition walls, semi-precast slabs and, more recently, volumetric prefabrication such as bathrooms and structural walls. In contrast, in the private sector, prefabrication was promoted only recently, since 2001, through the introduction of incentives schemes (Buildings Department, 2001, 2002).

Poon et al (2004) revealed that timber formwork was the major contributor to waste on site in Hong Kong, accounting for about 30 per cent of all wastes. Wet trades such as plastering and tiling, and concrete/masonry works accounted for about 20 and 13 per cent, respectively. The use of precast construction can significantly reduce waste generation on site. With prefabrication, most of the trades generating waste on site are carried out off site. Furthermore, the waste generated off site is easier to reuse and recycle in a factory environment. Prefabrication also contributes to improved quality control that may reduce the need for maintenance work during the operation of the building, thus reducing waste. The Orchards (see Figure 14.9), a private residential development in Hong Kong comprising two 48-storey towers, is a demonstration project for the private sector exemplifying the use of prefabrication. The project was completed in 2003 and included the use of prefabricated elements (up to 60 per cent), such as precast façades and sun-shading devices, semi-precast balconies, and lost form panels (a permanent formwork). The project achieved a significant waste reduction percentage (of about 30 per cent) when compared with conventional construction (Fong et al, 2004).

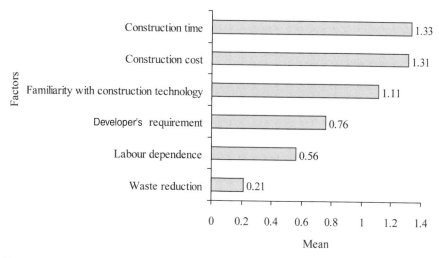

Source: Poon et al (2004)

Figure 14.8 *Factors affecting building technology selection*

Source: Pictures provided by the Hong Kong Polytechnic University

Figure 14.9 *Prefabrication construction adopted at The Orchards in 2003*

However, the use of prefabrication requires changes in the design process, such as early collaboration between designers and builders, as well as early decisions in finalizing the design. In addition, considerations such as transportation limitations (limited site access) and site limitations (small sites and limited storage areas for precast components) are essentials in dense urban areas such as Hong Kong. Chu and Wong (2005) argue that the storage area on site could be kept to a minimum with the implementation of the just-in-time delivery principle.

Conclusions

Worldwide, the construction industry is generating a significant amount of construction waste. Construction waste management and its disposal are pressing issues as available space for its disposal is scarce in many countries. Although the construction industry is aware of the pressing waste management issue, there is little consideration of waste minimization, especially in the design phase. With the implementation of new regulations and the polluter pays principle, both architects and contractors are required to pay more attention to waste minimization practices. The impact of design decisions on waste minimization is significant, as discussed in this chapter, and design decisions may be the cause of about 30 per cent of the construction waste in building projects (Innes, 2004).

Various design concepts may be adopted to minimize waste arising from construction and demolitions activities. Waste from demolition works may be reduced by designing with a focus on optimizing building lifespan, allowing flexibility and adaptability, reusing existing building structures, and designing for deconstruction. Waste arising from construction activities may be minimized by design concepts such as implementing dimensional coordination and standardization, minimizing temporary works and avoiding late design modifications. Careful selection of construction methods and building materials is also essential in the waste minimization process. The use of off-site manufacturing techniques such as prefabrication can significantly reduce waste on site.

Overall, there is a need for further legislation and incentives to promote waste minimization in the construction industry and in the design process. Zero waste strategy is not an idealized utopia but, indeed, a reality already implemented in some countries.

References

Anink, D., Boonstra, C. and Mark, J. (1996) *Handbook of Sustainable Buildings*, James and James Science Publishers, London

Buildings Department (2001) *Joint Practice Note No 1: Green and Innovative Buildings*, Hong Kong

Buildings Department (2002) *Joint Practice Note No 2: Second Package of Incentives to Promote Green and Innovative Building*, Hong Kong

Chu, R. P. K. and Wong, W. H. (2005) 'Precast concrete construction for buildings in Hong Kong', in *Proceedings of the First Shanghai and Hong Kong Symposium and Exhibition for Sustainable Building, Green Building Design*, Shanghai, China, pp216–222

Chui, T. (2007) 'Fly-tipping of building materials on the rise', *The Standard*, 27 March, Hong Kong

CIWMB (California Integrated Waste Management Board) (1996) *Gas Company Recycles Itself and Pilots Energy Efficient, Recycled Products Showcases*, California Integrated Waste Management Board Publication No 422-96-043, California

EPD (Environmental Protection Department, Hong Kong) (2007) www.epd.gov.hk/epd/misc/cdm/introduction.htm, www.epd.gov.hk, accessed 2007

Ferguson, J., Kermode, N., Nash, C. L., Sketch, W. A. J and Huxford, R. P. (1995) *Managing and Minimizing Construction Waste: A Practical Guide*, Institute of Civil Engineers, London

Fong, S., Lam, W. H. and Chan, A. S. K. (2004) 'Building distinction green design and construction in The Orchards', in *Proceedings of the Symposium on Green Building Labelling*, Hong Kong, 19 March, pp69–77

Franklin Associates (1998) *Characterization of Building Related Construction and Demolition Debris in the United States*, US EPA Report, US

Innes, S. (2004) 'Developing tools for designing out waste pre-site and on-site', in *Proceedings of Minimising Construction Waste Conference, Developing Resource Efficiency and Waste Minimization in Design and Construction*, New Civil Engineer, London

Jaillon, L., Poon, C. S. and Chiang, Y. H. (2009) 'Quantifying the waste reduction potential of using prefabrication in building construction in Hong Kong', *Waste Management*, vol 29, no 1, pp309–320

Legislative Council (2006) *Environmental Affairs: Progress Report on the Management of Construction and Demolition Materials*, 24 April, Hong Kong

OECD (Organisation for Economic Co-operation and Development (1996) *Considerations for Evaluating Waste Minimization in OECD Member Countries*, OECD

Osaka Gas (2000) *NEXT21: Osaka Gas Experimental Residential Complex*, www.osakagas.co.jp/rd/next21/htme/reforme.htm, accessed September 2009

Osmani, M., Glass, J. and Price, A. (2006) 'Architect and contractor attitudes to waste minimisation', *Waste and Resource Management*, vol 2, no 1, pp65–72

Poon, C. S. and Jaillon, L. (2002a) *A Guide for Minimizing Construction and Demolition Waste at the Design stage*, Hong Kong Polytechnic University, Hong Kong

Poon, C. S. and Jaillon, L. (2002b) 'Minimizing construction and demolition waste at the design stage', *Journal of the Hong Kong Institute of Architects*, vol 33, no 3, pp50–55

Poon, C. S., Yu, T. W. and Ng, L. H. (2001) *A Guide for Managing and Minimizing Building and Demolition Waste*, Hong Kong Polytechnic University, May, Hong Kong

Poon, C. S., Yu, A. T. W and Jaillon, L. (2004) 'Reducing building waste at construction sites in Hong Kong', *Construction Management and Economics*, vol 22, no 5, pp461–470

Riemer, J. and Kristoffersen, M. (1999) 'Information on waste management practices: A proposed electronic framework', Technical Report 24, July European Environmental Agency, Copenhagen, Denmark, www.eea.europa.eu/publications/TEC24

Roodman, D. M. and Lenssen, N. (1995) *A Building Revolution: How Ecology and Health Concerns Are Transforming Construction*, World Watch Paper, vol 124, Washington, DC

Tam, A. (2006) *Sustainable Building in Hong Kong: The Past, Present and Future*, Insitu Publishing Limited, Hong Kong

USGBC (2003) *Building Momentum: National Trends for High-Performance Green Buildings*, US Green Building Council, Washington, DC

15

Fire Engineering for High-Density Cities

Wan-Ki Chow

Introduction

Many tall buildings, deep underground railway tunnels and large halls are built in high-density cities (Chow, 2003a, 2005a, 2007; Tsujimoto, 2008). Structural elements are either concrete with steel reinforcement or steel framework with fire protection. There are new architectural features of green or sustainable buildings. Although combustible natural materials such as timber are not allowed as building materials in some cities such as Hong Kong, internal partitions used to be made of timber products (Buildings Department, 1995, 1996a, 1996b; Fire Services Department, 1998). Such timber partitions would cause fire problems as demonstrated before by fires in Karaoke venues (Chow et al 2008a). There are also many new materials made from plastic composites with fire-retardant systems (Wang and Chow, 2005). Such materials passing the fire tests specified in codes such as ease of ignition (British Standards, 1979) might not necessarily be safe in real fires under high radiation heat fluxes in post-flashover fires (Chow et al, 2003a). Radiative heat flux up to $440kWm^{-2}$ was measured in high-rack storage spaces (Wu, 2005). Several double-decker bus fires burning up all combustibles within 15 minutes, which occurred in Hong Kong (Chow, 2003b) and Shanghai (*Beijing Times*, 2005), are good examples that envelope materials with good thermal insulation are not safe in a fire. Buildings with thermal insulation might give new fire safety problems on having shorter time to flashover (Chow, in preparation). Large accidental fires have occurred in old high-rise buildings such as the big Garley Building fire (Chow, 1998), cross-harbour tunnels and buses in Hong Kong, and in many old high-rise buildings and new shopping malls in China

(Chow, 2001, 2003b). Non-accidental fires reported over the world included the terrorist attack fires in the World Trade Centre on 11 September 2001 (WTC-911) in the US (Federal Emergency Management Agency, 2006); arson fires in universities in Beijing; and underground railway arson fires in South Korea and Russia. Several arson fires were reported in Hong Kong in a bank (Chow, 1995), a karaoke venue (Chow and Lui, 2001) and an underground train vehicle (Chow, 2004c). Fire safety is therefore a concern for buildings in high-density cities.

It is generally agreed that buildings in compliance with fire codes will have appropriate safety levels. Fire codes in many high-density cities are basically prescriptive. Taking Hong Kong as an example, the codes were developed decades ago (Buildings Department, 1995, 1996a, 1996b; Fire Services Department, 1998), featuring two parts. The first part is for passive building construction, including fire-resisting construction, means of access for fire-fighting and means of escape. The second part is on active fire protection systems or fire service installations. Some parts of these codes are demonstrated to be good for fire safety provisions in buildings that are relatively simple and not for complex usage.

New architectural features for 'green or sustainable buildings' have given new challenges to fire safety design (Hung and Chow, 2002; Chow and Chow, 2003). Those modern architectural design features might have difficulty in complying with fire safety codes. Even if the fire safety provisions satisfied the code requirement, these buildings might not necessarily be safe as the codes are not yet demonstrated to work for such design. As reviewed, architectural features of high-rise buildings, deep-plan framed structures and sealed enclosures are commonly found (CIBSE/ASHRAE, 2003; Rose, 2003). Fire safety of these four features should be considered carefully. Taking window openings for introducing natural ventilation as an example, wind action might generate pressure difference across the building envelope (Chow, 2004a). When a fire occurs, the openable windows for air distribution might provide a pathway for spreading smoke. A negative pressure might be generated on the leeward side of the building. Flame and smoke would then spread out through the windows easily to other levels or even to adjacent buildings. Note that natural ventilation provisions had not yet been put in the new wind engineering code ASCE 7-05 (ASCE/SEI, 2006).

Therefore, fire codes should be updated in order to cope with the new design features for high-density cities. Buildings are closely packed and, therefore, horizontal flame spread due to wind action might result in a mass fire (Pitts, 1991). Buildings with special features would require individual design considerations. An obvious example is super-tall buildings with heights of over 400m (Chow, 2007). But upgrading codes without strong scientific fire research for local safety provision is impossible. For such building features that have difficulty in complying with the prescriptive fire codes, performance-based design (PBD) (British Standards, 2001; SFPE, 2001; National Fire Protection Association, 2003) was implemented.

Possible fire hazards

Building fire hazards that must be considered in relation to high-density cities are as follows:

- *Horizontal fire spreading.* Note that buildings in high-density cities are closely packed together as land is very expensive. When one building experiences a substantial fire like the one at Garley Building (Chow, 1998), flame can spread horizontally to adjacent buildings through strong thermal radiation and wind effects (Pitts, 1991). A fire wind tunnel should be used to forecast the possible hazard scenarios. Mathematical models on fire spread across buildings are useful for fire safety design (Cox, 1995).
- *Crowd movement and control.* Crowd density is high in many areas of high-density cities such as railway stations during rush hour (see Figure 15.1).

Source: Author

Figure 15.1 *Crowd movement in a railway station, Shinjuku, Tokyo, Japan*

Evacuation patterns to safe places (British Standards, 2001; Li and Chow, 2008), modelling of crowd movement, and integration with fire detection systems and global positioning systems should be carefully considered. The dynamics of crowd movement include not only motion analogy to track 'fluid particles'. Human factors will be different for different countries, races and styles of living. 'Full evacuation' or 'refuge evacuation' strategies should be considered. Evacuation to the refuge floors should be further reviewed after the World Trade Centre incident in 2001 (Federal Emergency Management Agency, 2006). The use of personal protection equipment and emergency escape equipment in high-rise buildings should be monitored. Such equipment might not be useful.
- *Impact to structural elements.* Structural members are required to stand the loading under a fire for some time. Structural stability is assessed by the fire resistance period (FRP) (British Standards, 1990). Concerns exist regarding not including thermal radiation heat flux in tests, and on the importance of the heat release rate of burning

different materials. In an enclosure fire, air will not be sufficient after flashover. There is too much fuel and the fire can be classified as a ventilation-controlled fire. Any exposure to ambient air, such as through the breaking of glass, will supply air for combustion. The heat release rate will thus be substantially increased. In this way, the structural members are exposed to a much more severe thermal environment and may not be able to bear the loading and sustain for the FRP as specified. This was clearly demonstrated in the World Trade Centre 2001 incident (Federal Emergency Management Agency, 2006), where the FRP of four hours could not be sustained under such an enormous fire. Some related works on structural fires (Harada et al, 2004; Chow, 2005–2006) have been reported during the past few years.

- *Light structure design.* Light structures are used in super-tall buildings to reduce dead weight. Both wind loading under extreme weather and wind-induced vibration (AWES, 2007) have to be monitored. In addition, the fire behaviour of such light structures (Chow, 2007) is a substantial concern.

- *Fire-safe materials.* Passive building construction (Buildings Department, 1995, 1996a, 1996b) for compartmentalization, fire-resisting constructions, means of escape and means of access are key points. Fire-safe materials (Kashiwagi et al, 2000) and furniture should be used. The use of fire retardants (Wang and Chow, 2005) for delaying ignition times and reducing heat release rates should be developed through more in-depth studies. Smoke aspects for burning plastic materials and use of smoke suppressants are suggested (Chow et al, 2002–2003).

- *Active fire protection systems.* Adequate active fire protection systems should be provided in non-residential buildings (Fire Services Department, 1998). New technology (Chow, 2007) on fire detection and fire suppression for reducing the heat release rate should be developed for tall buildings, deep underground stations and large halls. Equipment for quicker movement of firemen and rescues, new designs to consume oxygen, heat reduction and installing water network systems through urban areas for fire-fighting should be considered.

- *Fire safety management.* A fire safety plan (Malhotra, 1987) with a maintenance plan, a fire action plan, a staff training plan and a fire prevention plan should be worked out based on scientific studies. Care should be taken in dealing with dense populations, crowd movements and mass evacuation under heavy traffic conditions. Fire engineering tools (Cox, 1995) can be applied, as illustrated by working out risk management for gas station explosions in dense urban areas (Chow, 2004b). Fire safety management should be included in the codes and regulations.

Fire safety provisions

Hardware fire safety provisions are required in buildings. Essentially, they are based on two parts (Buildings Department, 1995, 1996a, 1996b; British Standards, 1996; Fire Services Department, 1998): passive building construction and active fire protection systems.

Passive measures can provide effective fire protection to the construction elements of buildings. Items covered in most of the fire codes (Buildings Department, 1995, 1996a, 1996b; British Standards, 1996) include compartmentalization, fire-resisting construction, means of escape for occupants and means of access for fire-fighters. The objective is to reduce the occurrence of accidental fires by making the building materials and components more difficult to ignite. Even if the material is ignited, only a small amount of heat will be given out at the early stage of a fire. It is targeted at confining the fire within the place of origin without affecting the adjacent areas. The spreading rate should be slowed down through compartmentalization and protected corridors, lobbies and staircases. The building structure should be able to withstand the fire for some time so that occupants can evacuate.

Active fire protection systems (British Standards, 1996; Fire Services Department, 1998) are necessary for detecting a fire and giving early warnings; controlling, suppressing or extinguishing the fire; operating smoke management systems to give visibility and more tenable conditions; and operating other emergency systems, such as emergency lighting and standby generators. Therefore, they are divided into detection and alarm systems (as in Figure 15.2a), suppression systems (as in Figure 15.2b), smoke management systems, and auxiliary systems such as essential power supply systems, exit signs (as in Figure 15.2c) and emergency lighting, etc. All of the fire protection systems are checked and inspected before

(a)

(b)

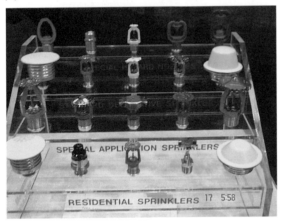

(c)

Source: Author

Figure 15.2 *Active fire protection systems: (a) alarm system; (b) selected sprinkler heads; (c) exit signs*

issuing an occupant permit in Hong Kong and in many other high-density cities. An example of evaluating the performance of smoke exhaust systems through a hot smoke test is shown in Figure 15.3.

Passive building construction and active fire protection systems hardware must be controlled by appropriate fire safety management software (Malhotra, 1987; British Standards, 2001). However, fire safety management is not considered carefully without implementing associated codes in many countries. Good fire safety management should ensure that even if a fire occurs, it can be confined to a small area, occupants can be evacuated within a short time and damage to the building can be minimized. A more detailed description can be found in performance-based design (British Standards, 2001). A fire safety plan (Malhotra, 1987) clearly outlining the procedures for maintaining protection equipment, staff training, fire prevention and evacuation procedures must be worked out scientifically.

Essentially, building fire safety codes deal with accidental fires. As a consequence of the World Trade Centre 2001 incident (Federal Emergency Management Agency, 2006), as well as many arson fires, there are concerns over whether non-accidental fires should be considered. With so many political and social issues, there will be a higher possibility of terrorist attacks and arson fires than before. Therefore, the objectives on protecting against accidental fires, arson fires, terrorist attack fires and disaster fires due to earthquakes should be clarified.

Source: Author

Figure 15.3 *Testing smoke management system*

The total fire safety concept (Chow, 2002, 2004d) in buildings is suggested by implementing software fire safety management to monitor hardware on passive building construction and active fire protection systems.

Performance-based design

Prescriptive fire codes are easier to implement since professionals and fire authorities are familiar with the system. But the specification might not work for the new architectural features discussed above (Chow, 2003a). Performance-based design (PBD) (British Standards, 2001; SFPE, 2001; National Fire Protection Association, 2003) has to be applied as prescriptive codes cannot be updated rapidly to cope with such changes. A new subject discipline on fire safety engineering (FSE) has been established, with first degree programmes proposed (Magnusson et al, 1995; Chow, et al, 1999). This new profession is different from designing traditional fire engineering based on prescriptive codes.

The approaches and methodology of PBD are beginning to be documented in many countries (British Standards, 2001; SFPE, 2001; National Fire Protection Association, 2003). There are many debates on design data, engineering tools (particularly fire models) (Cox, 1995) and acceptance criteria. Since no large accidents have occurred in these PBD projects, statistical data available is still not adequate to work out fire risk parameters.

The following should be clarified in PBD, especially when demonstrating safety equivalent to the prescriptive codes:

- fire safety objectives (goals are life safety design for both occupants and fire-fighters, protection of property, non-disturbance to business and environmental protection) not in compliance with prescriptive codes;
- the issue of protecting against accidental fires and the necessity of protecting against non-accidental fires in some buildings, such as karaoke venues;
- safety level expected for the design, such as with high hazards, ordinary hazards and light hazards;
- engineering approach and tools adopted for hazard assessment;
- actions to adopt hardware passive building construction and fire service installation;
- importance of fire safety management.

Fire safety objectives were earlier discussed by Rasbash in 1977, but published in 1996. In defining fire safety objectives, both the nature of risk and the acceptability of risk should be considered. There are two reasons for working out the objectives:

1   The technical nature of the risk itself varies; therefore, a different balance of fire precautions is required.
2   Different targeted fire safety requires different resource allocation.

Based on the above argument, ten fire safety objectives for building control have been listed. The most important objective is to protect the public as a whole from anxiety following disquieting incidents.

Carrying out full-scale physical experiments for fire hazard assessment (ASTM, 2000) is very expensive and may only be appropriate for measuring empirical parameters, validating theories and for fire investigations. Fire engineering tools (Cox, 1995) including correlation relations and fire models are then applied. Fire models have been developed for studying different stages of a fire:

- Ignition model with thermal conduction dominates the early stage; however, thermal radiation becomes more important at the later stage. Combustion chemistry with intermediate reactions is also required.
- Modelling of fire plume is very useful in studying smoke movement.
- The results from pre-flashover fire may be used to understand the fire environment before severe damage occurs and can be applied in assessing fire service systems such as the response of fire detectors.
- Transition to flashover, including application of non-linear dynamics, is another significant model.
- Post-flashover fire assesses the consequences to buildings and is important in studying the fire resistance of construction elements.

There are difficulties in developing these models practically, although numerous efforts have been made. Knowledge of the pre-flashover stage of a compartmental fire is of great interest to building professionals. Many fire models have been developed for studying pre-flashover fires and have been reported in the literature (Cox, 1995). They can be classified as zone models (CFAST, 2007), field models – application of computational fluid dynamics (CFD) or numerical heat transfer (NHT) models (Chow and Tao, 2003) – and airflow network models (Klote and Milke, 1992). If used carefully, they are suitable for simulating the fire environment for design purposes.

It is obvious that it is difficult to simulate a complicated physical system described by a set of partial differential equations using a set of relatively simple linear equations derived from the finite difference method or the control volume method (in most cases). There is still substantial developmental work required (McGrattan, 2005). Careless application of the technique may lead to incorrect results.

At least three elements should be considered in simulating fire-induced airflow in a simple building of rectangular shape using CFD/NHT:

1 The physical principles behind turbulence should be reviewed. Current turbulence closure models might provide many parameters that can be used in fine-tuning. This becomes even more complicated when combustion processes of the burning object or the evaporation effects of a sprinkler water spray are studied.
2 The schemes for isolating the set of equations have to be considered carefully if the finite difference method is used. The control volume method together with different schemes might not be the only solution.
3 The algorithms in solving the system of pressure-linked equations should to be reviewed.

Debates have centred on different issues when applying such fire models. Verifications and validations of fire models are necessary (AIAA, 1998; Mok and Chow, 2004; Gritzo et al, 2005). Professionals have been criticized for being unfamiliar with fire models (Ho et al, 2002). However, the topic itself is developing actively. Even researchers experience difficulty in catching up with the rapid development of approaches other than their own.

Atrium sprinkler

Atriums have been built in large buildings (Chow, 1996) in the Far East since the development of Tsimshatsui East in Hong Kong during the early 1980s. Since then, tall atriums up to 100m in height are found in shopping malls, banks, public transport terminals and multipurpose complexes in other big cities.

Automatic sprinkler systems have of necessity been installed on the high ceiling during the past 20 years (see Figure 15.4). There are many problems, as discussed in Chow (1996) and shown pictorially in Figure 15.5. There are adverse effects on reducing the buoyancy of smoke due to cooling. Air dragging effects through momentum transfer with water droplets disturb the stability of the smoke layer. Smoke logging is dangerous for people staying on the atrium floor.

The level of combustibles may be very high on the atrium floor (Chow, 2005b) (see Figure 15.6). There might, for example, be catering areas with associated cooking risks. The heat release rate of the fire can escalate to high values at a very rapid rate when the atrium floor is full of such combustibles. Recent full-scale burning tests on a news-stand showed that the heat release rate might be over 8MW. This sort of fire cannot be controlled by traditional sprinkler designs. Appropriate fire suppression systems must be installed to control such fires at a certain size. Installing a traditional sprinkler system is not appropriate in tall spaces. Long-throw sidewall sprinklers (see Figure 15.7) (Chow et al, 2006a) are appropriate and should be installed in many new large and tall shopping malls in Hong Kong.

Structural members under substantial fires

Structural members are required to be stable in a substantial fire for some time. The domino effect (Chow, 2007) of fire spreading to adjacent buildings is a threat if the building under fire does not collapse vertically, as in the 2001 World Trade Centre incident. Structural stability is assessed as specified in building codes (Buildings Department, 1996a) in high-density cities such as Hong Kong. The fire resistance period (FRP) has to be determined by British Standards BS 476 (British Standards, 1990). Values of FRP are 0.5 hours, 1 hour, 2 hours or 4 hours for different applications.

There are at least three points of concern in adopting such standard fire tests:

1 Structural members are commonly tested by a fire furnace only with a standard temperature–time

(a)

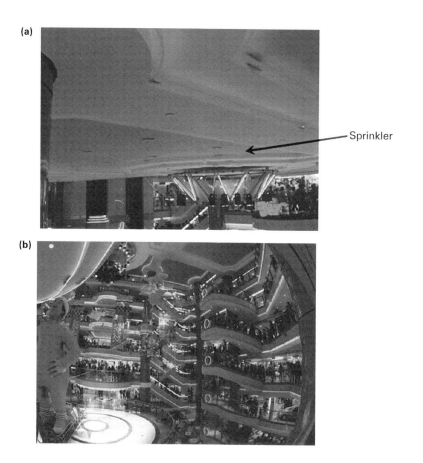

Sprinkler

(b)

Source: Author

Figure 15.4 *Atrium sprinkler: (a) the sprinkler; (b) the atrium*

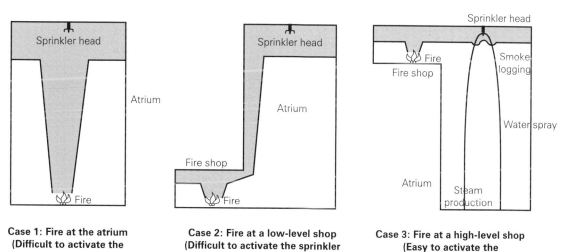

**Case 1: Fire at the atrium
(Difficult to activate the
sprinkler head)**

**Case 2: Fire at a low-level shop
(Difficult to activate the sprinkler
head except high Heat Release Rate,
But useless!)**

**Case 3: Fire at a high-level shop
(Easy to activate the
sprinkler head)**

Source: Chow (1996)

Figure 15.5 *Adverse effects of an atrium sprinkler*

Source: Author

Figure 15.6 *Combustibles in an atrium*

curve. The effects of thermal radiation heat flux have not yet been included (Harada et al, 2004; Chow, 2005–2006).

2   The standard temperature–time curve is determined from experiments in compartment fires with wood. Different values of fire load density and ventilation factors of the room are tested. Heat release rates are not measured. The effects of burning other materials such as plastic composites are commonly not included.

3   Equivalent FRP for fire with higher temperatures as estimated by the empirical rule should be monitored.

In an enclosure fire, air will not be sufficient after flashover: there is too much fuel and the fire should be classified as a ventilation-controlled fire. Any exposure to ambient air through, for example, the breaking of glass, will supply air for combustion. A substantial fire of a long duration might result from storing large

(a)

(b)

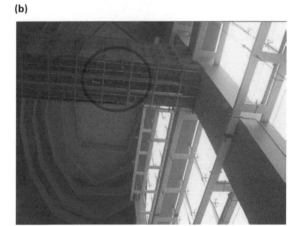

(c)

Source: Author

Figure 15.7 *Longthrow sprinkler: (a) water pattern; (b) installation; (c) testing*

amounts of combustibles, up to $1135MJ/m^{-2}$ (Buildings Department, 1995; Fire Services Department, 1998). The heat release rate will thus significantly increase. In this way, structural members are exposed to a much more severe thermal environment. They may not be able to bear the loading and sustain for the FRP as specified. This was clearly demonstrated in the 2001 World Trade Centre incident (Federal Emergency Management Agency, 2006), where the FRP of four hours could not be sustained under such an enormous fire.

A fire shutter of a two-hour FRP was evaluated under a substantial fire (Chow, 2005–2006), as demonstrated in Figure 15.8. The fire shutter cracked in less than two hours under a 10MW gasoline fire.

Super-tall buildings

Many tall buildings with heights of over 400m have been constructed in the Far East (Chow, 2007). Symbolic high-rise buildings are built up to over 500m in height in Taipei. Among the top 100

(a)

(b)

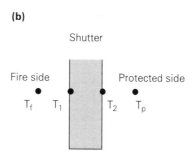

(c)

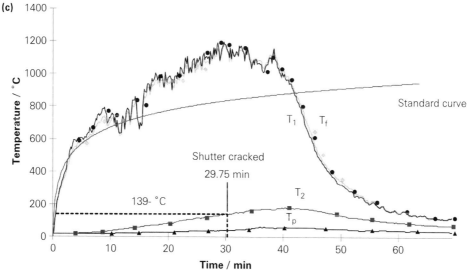

Source: Author

Figure 15.8 *Substantial fire test: (a) the substantial fire; (b) positions of thermocouples; (c) temperature–time curve*

high-rise residential buildings in the world, over half exist in Hong Kong. Numerous problems regarding fire safety have been pointed out by professionals and evacuation is identified to be a major concern. Nobody likes to stay at the refuge floor (Buildings Department, 1996b) waiting for rescue since the terrorist attack on the World Trade Centre in 2001 (Federal Emergency Management Agency, 2006). Fire safety debates regarding safety in super-tall buildings have previously focused on evacuation patterns, designing means of escape and means of access, and sprinkler systems. Concerns regarding fire safety (Chow, 2007) have highlighted that the total evacuation time might be up to 30 minutes, even when using lifts and orderly evacuation (Guo et al, 2004). Even the substantial fire that occurred in the old high-rise Garley building of less than 15 levels during the replacement of lifts led to a serious disaster (Chow, 1998).

It is clear that fire safety for new super-tall building projects should be worked out carefully. In-depth investigation supported by full-scale burning tests under substantial fires is necessary (Chow, 2008b). It is evident that 'full evacuation' time for super-tall buildings might be up to two hours. Evacuation strategies to refuge levels were adopted with total evacuation time reduced (see Figure 15.9).

More emergency exits should be provided for super-tall buildings. However, it is difficult to allocate additional space for putting in more staircases. Some super-tall buildings might even have fewer staircases as specified in building codes while going through PBD! Elevators are not yet designed for fire evacuation in Hong Kong, although there is interest in doing so.

The only way to provide safety for existing super-tall buildings is to upgrade active systems. At least three elements should be considered (Chow, 2007):

1   *Quick detection.* The fire has to be detected rapidly with appropriate zoning design in super-tall buildings.
2   *Quick suppression.* New suppression systems with clean agents are now a design criterion (Chow et al, 2004; Choy et al, 2004). The performance of the system must be evaluated carefully. Upgrading passive fire-resisting construction elements by applying appropriate protection coating is useful.
3   *Quick removal* of contaminants after discharging suppressive agent from the fire zone.

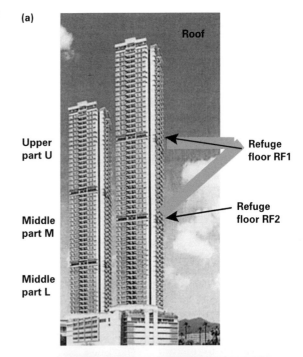

(a)

(b)

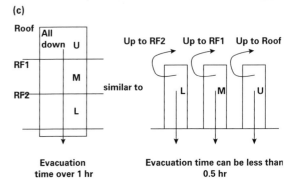

(c)

Source: Author

Figure 15.9 *Evacuation to refuge floor: (a) refuge floors; (b) other examples in Hong Kong; (c) reduction in evacuation time*

Glass façade

Architectural features with glass constructions might result in additional fire safety problems (Hung and Chow, 2003; Chow et al, 2007). Although glass is not combustible in a fire, it will be weakened when heated up to a certain temperature (Glass and Glazing Federation, 1978; Hassani et al, 1995; Loss Prevention Council, 1999; British Standards, 2005). Toughened glass is able to endure higher temperatures, but might be fragile after exceeding its critical limit. Glass itself is a poor conductor: it is difficult to transfer heat from the area exposed to the fire to the other region. The temperature difference between the hot and cool sides will result in thermal expansion. Cracking will occur when heated up to 295°C (Glass and Glazing Federation, 1978) as the induced thermal stress reaches the critical value (Hassani et al, 1995). The framework of aluminium windows will be weakened when heated up to 200°C and will melt at about 550°C. Severe distortion may induce stresses across the glass plate being held up by the frame. The whole glass panel might even fall down (Loss Prevention Council, 1999; Chow et al, 2007).

Cracking and falling of glass panels and failure of the fittings for fixing the glass panels in a fire would supply a higher air intake rate to sustain combustion (Chow et al, 2007). There would be higher heat release rates, causing severe damage. In such cases, substantial fires have resulted, as observed in many buildings with glass façades (Chow and Han, 2006). Wind action might induce fire whirls (Battagliax et al, 2000) or even result in a mass fire (Pitts, 1991) due to horizontal spread of fire to adjacent buildings (Chow et al, 2007)

Flashover occurs with flames coming out at many levels. A substantial fire occurred in a new building with glass features in Dalian, Liaoning, China, on 18 September 2005. As observed by Chow and Han (2006), glass panels fell down (see Figure 15.10). The fire safety of glass façades has already attracted public concern (Chow, 2008a). The fire safety of glass features with double skin façades is a common concern (Chow and Hung, 2006). Smoke, heat and even flames might be trapped inside air gaps. The consequence is very serious when interior glass panels, rather than external ones, are broken.

Source: Author

Figure 15.10 *Fire in a glass building in Dalian, Liaoning, China, 18 September 2005*

Application of performance-based design in Hong Kong

Taking Hong Kong as an example of a high-density city, PBD has been accepted for designing passive construction elements since 1998 (British Standards, 2001; SFPE, 2001; National Fire Protection Association, 2003). This is known as the fire engineering approach (FEA) (Buildings Department 1998; Chow, 2003a, 2005a). Knowledge of fire science and engineering should be applied together with practical experience under local conditions in FEA. Mathematical fire models (Cox, 1995) were used to assess the consequence of different fire scenarios. Full-scale burning tests, scale-model studies and site measurements on evacuation pattern might be required to demonstrate that the design works as expected (Chow et al, 2003a; Chow, 2004e). Essentially, three levels of study for FEA design were observed in hazard assessment (Chow, 2003a):

1   *Basic study.* Basic study projects are those which can get the results easily. Empirical correlation equations from fire engineering are used. Most likely, there are past cases with similar designs. An example is to study the wall at the sides of a link pedestrian bridge higher than the specified value of 1.2m in the fire-resisting construction code (Buildings Department, 1996a).

2   *Intermediate study.* Intermediate study projects are those which can be analysed by using established

fire engineering tools. Similar projects, although not exactly the same, have been carried out before, so that past experience can be shared. An example is to assess the safety aspects for a car park having a 'travel distance' slightly longer than the values specified in the prescriptive evacuation codes (Buildings Department, 1996b).

3   *Advanced study.* Advanced study projects are those involving full-scale burning tests, fire models in assessing the consequences of different fire scenarios and evacuation models for studying the minimum evacuation time required. The problem itself might not necessarily be complicated; but no previous studies or past track record of the design exist. Therefore, it is difficult to identify the problems for reference. An example is whether the vertical spandrel can be substituted by a horizontal apron. CFD/NHT studies would be applied with full-scale burning tests carried out to demonstrate the design works as expected.

All three levels of projects should be analysed carefully as safety provision is an important issue. A detailed report will be submitted to clarify how the safety problems encountered will be solved. Assessment by the authority is very vigorous and the study report must be of a high quality. Design fire is the input parameter for almost all fire models and the importance of this has been pointed out (Yung and Benichou, 2002). Since there is no database for local materials, a very small 0.5MW design fire has even been proposed in a big railway terminal hall.

Examples are reported in the literature with some on joint studies through the Society of Fire Protection Engineers in the US (Chow et al, 2006b, 2008b).

Necessity of full-scale burning tests

Fire engineering tools as described above might not be applicable for some projects. Verification and validation are required for fire models (AIAA, 1998; Mok and Chow, 2004; Gritzo et al, 2005). Hazard assessment under flashover fire is necessary (Chow, 2008b). Full-scale burning tests with bigger fires are suggested (Chow et al, 2003a; Chow, 2004e). Such tests are very cheap in comparison with the consultancy fee for substantial projects requiring PBD, as raised in

an international conference in Hong Kong (Dowling et al, 2007). The cost of measuring heat release rate is much lower than the land price and construction and compensation costs after major fires.

An example is the cabin design (Law, 1990) commonly used in big public transport terminals (Lam, 1995). The design might give better utilization of space without providing sprinkler and smoke exhaust systems in the entire large volume space. However, there are always concerns about not providing smoke exhaust systems to the building as a whole. As demonstrated in the airport terminal in Hong Kong before operation, the whole hall filled up with smoke (*Tin Tin Daily News*, 1998) even under a small fire (see Figure 15.11). It took over two hours for fire-fighters to locate the fire source. Therefore, there are dangers in not providing a smoke exhaust system for the hall space.

A 'full' cabin commonly had a sprinkler to control fire and a smoke exhaust system to remove smoke inside a small space. However, very few systematic experimental studies have focused on this type of design or on measuring how much heat can be removed by operating the sprinkler (Beever, 1998; Law, 1998). It is difficult to conclude that a retail shop fire in a cabin can be controlled at low values such as 2MW even with the operation of a sprinkler (Chow, 1997). Experimental studies in Sweden (Arvidson, 2005) on retail shop fires indicate that burning potato crisps would give a fast t^2-fire up to 6MW.

A long-term research programme on cabin fires was initiated in 1998, in collaboration with several research groups in China (Chow, 2006). The project began with a theoretical analysis on the fire environment inside a 'bare cabin' and the possibility of flashover and shop spill plume. Experiments on bare cabin fires and smoke spilling out to the hall were then carried out. The performance of sprinkler and smoke exhaust systems in the cabin was then studied. Results on this project were summarized, with experimental results reported (Chow, 2006).

Preliminary experimental studies on the performance of these full 'cabins' with the operation of the installed mechanical smoke exhaust and sprinkler system were completed. A cabin of length 3.5m, width 4m and height 3m was considered. It was observed that a sprinkler operating under normal design conditions could not extinguish small fires with low heat release rates of 1.3MW. All combustibles inside were burned out even with the sprinkler operating.

(a)

(b)

Source: (a) *Tin Tin Daily News* (30 April 1998); (b) *South China Morning Post* (1 May 1998)

Figure 15.11 *Airport fire, 1998: (a) full of smoke; (b) not allowed to enter*

An alternative proposal is to put in a water mist fire suppression system (Chow et al, 2003b). Another set of tests with water mists in real scale was used for

evaluating system performance. A news-stand was burned with a heat release rate up to 8MW. A water mist system was installed. Discharging water mist was found to be able to suppress the fire.

The above full-scale tests suggest that sprinklers might not be able to control a cabin fire, especially in retail shops with far too many combustibles. Installing a water mist system might be a solution. In particular, open cabins with only sprinklers inside but no fire suppression system in the outside hall are very dangerous. This is because flashover inside a small cabin can be onsetted easily. The study is in progress, with further results to be reported. Further tests on full cabin fires due to burning retail shops should be carried out, measuring heat release rate (Chow et al, 2003a; Chow, 2004e).

Fire engineering as a new profession

PBD (British Standards, 2001; SFPE, 2001, National Fire Protection Association, 2003) is required for projects with special buildings that have failed to comply with the prescriptive fire codes (British Standards, 1996). However, it takes a long time to train sufficient numbers of qualified fire engineers and officers. The subject of fire engineering (previously, fire safety engineering; Magnusson et al, 1995; Chow et al, 1999) is only fairly well developed in the literature without adequate numbers of engineers. PBD might only be feasible in the transition period when the prescriptive fire codes are not yet updated and should be applied in complement to prescriptive fire codes.

Professional recognition for fire engineering is important. There is a professional society for fire protection engineers in the US with most of the members registered professional engineers (Chow et al, 2008c). Very high-level research and development work is actively being carried out on fire safety. Examples are big hotels with casinos, long and deep underground tunnels, large subway stations, rapid transit systems, marine vehicles and spacecraft. There is also a professional fire engineering institution in the UK, mainly composed of fire officers. Japan is considering proposing a fire engineering profession, as reported at the third international symposium on the 21st Century Centre of Excellence Programme (Centre for Fire Science and Technology, Tokyo University of Science, Japan, 10–11 March 2008).

There are both first and Masters degree programmes at the Hong Kong Polytechnic University under the leadership of the author (Hong Kong Polytechnic University, 1998, 2000). Although the first degree programme was suspended, the Masters degree programme takes in 50 students every year. A fire engineering discipline was established at the Hong Kong Institution of Engineers at the end of 2005, and a fire engineering division in September 2007. There are six topics (HKIE, 2008): fire science; human psychology and physiology; active fire protection systems analysis; passive fire protection systems analysis; law, regulations and standards; and fire risk management. Whether grouping in this way is appropriate or not is currently being monitored. However, the development might be too fast as there are still no first degree programmes offered by local universities for high school students – the fire engineering profession can only be developed with such first degree programmes (Magnusson et al, 1995; Hong Kong Polytechnic University, 1998; Chow et al, 1999).

Conclusions

Rapid development of the construction industry due to the growing number of people living in such high-density cities is a key issue. New architectural features (CIBSE/ASHRAE, 2003; Rose, 2003), such as deep-plan, high-rise framed structures and well-sealed buildings, the use of new materials, and new styles of living, are identified as new fire safety concerns.

Substantial fires reported in the past have provided painful lessons. After the major fire at the Garley Building (Chow, 1998), the Hong Kong government took the following actions:

- Old high-rise buildings (i.e. those erected before 1972 without tight fire regulations) were requested to upgrade their fire safety provisions.
- The Fire Safety Inspection Scheme (Buildings Department, 1997) on structural stability, external finishes and fire safety must be implemented.
- A new Fire Services Ordinance (Services Ordinance, 2004) on sprinkler systems was set up.
- A request was made to install temporary doors with adequate fire resistance in the lift shaft while replacing the lift.

Fire codes, prescriptive (British Standards, 1996) or performance based (British Standards, 2001; SFPE, 2001; National Fire Protection Association, 2003), should be established based on the concept of total fire safety (Chow, 2002, 2004d).

Essentially, many works on fire engineering, including those unpublished consultancy reports on big construction projects, started from the implementation of PBD on fire safety during 1980s. Some activities were supported after several major fires happened during the late 1990s. Another bigger theme is on protecting the environment by using halon substitutes, both for fire engineering systems and fire retardants.

Further investigations on tall buildings, underground subway stations and large halls are urgently required (Chow, 2003a, 2005b, 2007; Tsujimoto, 2008). The following concerns are worth considering for fire engineering in high-density cities:

- The fire safety of buildings with glass façades is a concern (Hung and Chow, 2003; Chow et al, 2007). Note that such buildings in tropical countries would have higher cooling loads and utilize more artificial lighting after shading windows.
- The use of heat release rates (Yung and Benichou, 2002) instead of fire load density to quantify contributions due to combustibles in the fire codes is important (Buildings Department, 1995, 1996a, 1996b; Fire Services Department, 1998).
- Geometrical arrangements of different buildings in complexes in light of natural ventilation provision, evacuation and fire spreading must be considered.
- Is there possible non-compliance with fire codes?
- Have new green and sustainability designs been incorporated (Chow, 2003a)?
- It is important to select appropriate clean agents (Chow et al, 2004; Choy et al, 2004) for gas protection systems and fire retardants. Environmental assessments with and without appropriate agents should be carried out. For example, extinguishing a fire rapidly with halon might be better than discharging gas agents that cannot even control a fire. Much more smoke will be emitted and a mass fire might result!

Acknowledgements

The research for this chapter was funded by the Croucher Foundation for the Active Fire Protection in Super-Tall Buildings project, account number PolyU 5-2H46.

References

AIAA (American Institute of Aeronautics and Astronautics) (1998) *Guide for the Verification and Validation of Computational Fluid Dynamics Simulations*, AIAA G-077-1998, Reston, VA

Arvidson, M. (2005) 'Potato crisps and cheese nibbles burn fiercely', *Brand Posten*, no 32, pp10–11

ASCE/SEI (American Society of Civil Engineers/Structural Engineering Institute) (2006) *Minimum Design Loads for Buildings and Other Structures*, ASCE/SEI, Reston, VA

ASTM (American Society for Testing and Materials) (2000) *ASTM E-1546 Standard Guide for Development of Fire-Hazard-Assessment Standards*, ASTM, US

AWES (Australasian Wind Engineering Society) (2007) *Proceedings of the 12th International Conference on Wind Engineering ICWE12*, 1–6 July 2007, Cairns, Australia

Battagliax, F., McGrattan, K. B., Rehm, R. G. and Baum, H. R. (2000) 'Simulating fire whirls', *Combustion Theory and Modelling*, vol 4, pp123–138

Beever, P. (1998) 'On the "Cabins" fire safety design concept in the new Hong Kong airport terminal building', *Journal of Fire Sciences*, vol 16, no 3, pp151–158

Beijing Times (2005) 'Bus fire at Shanghai', *Beijing Times*, http://auto.china.com/zh_cn/carman/ceshi/11032065/20050718/12492690.html, accessed 18 August 2005

British Standards (1979) *BS 476 Fire Tests on Building Materials and Structures – Part 5: Method of Test for Ignitability*, British Standards Institution, London

British Standards (1990) *BS 476 Fire Tests on Building Materials and Structures – Part 20: Method for Determination of the Fire Resistance of Elements of Construction (General Principles)-AMD 6487*, 30 April 1990, British Standards Institution, UK

British Standards (1996) *BS 5588:1996 Fire Precautions in the Design, Construction and Use of Buildings – Part 0: Guide to Fire Safety Codes of Practice for Particular Premises/Applications*, British Standards Institution, London, UK

British Standards (2001) *7974: 2001 Application of Fire Safety Engineering Principles to the Design of Buildings – Code of Practice*, British Standards Institution, London

British Standards (2005) *BS 6262 Part 4 Code of Practice for Glazing for Buildings – Safety Related to Human Impact*, British Standards Institution, UK

Buildings Department (1995) *Code of Practice for Provisions of Means of Access for Firefighting and Rescue Purposes*, Buildings Department, Hong Kong

Buildings Department (1996a) *Code of Practice for Fire Resisting Construction*, Buildings Department, Hong Kong

Buildings Department (1996b) *Code of Practice for Provisions of Means of Escape in Case of Fire and Allied Requirements*, Buildings Department, Hong Kong

Buildings Department (1997) *Fire Safety Inspection Scheme*, Hong Kong, April

Buildings Department (1998) *Practice Note for Authorized Persons and Registered Structural Engineers: Guide to Fire Engineering Approach*, Guide BD GP/BREG/P/36, Buildings Department, Hong Kong Special Administrative Region, March

CFAST (2007) *Consolidated Model of Fire Growth and Smoke Transport*, www.bfrl.nist.gov/866/fmabbs.html# CFAST, accessed 2007

Chow, C. L. (in preparation) 'Fire safety concern for green or sustainable buildings with better thermal insulation'

Chow, C. L., Han, S. S. and Chow, W. K. (2002–2003) 'Smoke toxicity assessment of burning video compact disc boxes by a cone calorimeter', *Journal of Applied Fire Science*, vol 11, no 4, pp349–366

Chow, W. K. (1995) 'Studies on closed chamber fires', *Journal of Fire Sciences*, vol 13, no 2, pp89–103

Chow, W. K. (1996) 'Performance of sprinkler in atria', *Journal of Fire Sciences*, vol 14, no 6, pp466–488

Chow, W. K. (1997) 'On the "Cabins" fire safety design concept in the new Hong Kong airport terminal building', *Journal of Fire Sciences*, vol 15, no 4, pp404–423

Chow, W. K. (1998) 'Numerical studies on recent large high-rise building fire', *ASCE Journal of Architectural Engineering*, vol 4, no 2, pp65–74

Chow, W. K. (2001) 'General aspects of fire safety management for tunnels in Hong Kong', *Journal of Applied Fire Science*, vol 10, no 2, pp179–190

Chow, W. K. (2002) 'Proposed fire safety ranking system EB-FSRS for existing high-rise non-residential buildings in Hong Kong', *ASCE Journal of Architectural Engineering*, vol 8, no 4, pp116–124

Chow, W. K. (2003a) 'Fire safety in green or sustainable buildings: Application of the fire engineering approach in Hong Kong', *Architectural Science Review*, vol 46, no 3, pp297–303

Chow, W. K. (2003b) 'Observation on the two recent bus fires and preliminary recommendations to provide fire safety', *International Journal on Engineering Performance-Based Fire Codes*, vol 5, no 1, pp1–5

Chow, W. K. (2004a) 'Wind-induced indoor air flow in a highrise building adjacent to a vertical wall', *Applied Energy*, vol 77, no 2, pp225–234

Chow, W. K. (2004b) 'Application of computational fluid dynamics: Fire safety awareness for gas station in dense urban areas with wind effects', Paper presented to ASME Heat Transfer/Fluids Engineering Summer Conference, 11–15 July 2004, Charlotte, NC, Paper HT-FED04-56699

Chow, W. K. (2004c) 'Fire safety in train vehicle: Design based on accidental fire or arson fire?', *The Green Cross*, March/April

Chow, W. K. (ed) (2004d) *Proceedings of the Fire Conference 2004: Total Fire Safety Concept*, 6–7 December 2004, Hong Kong

Chow, W. K. (2004e) *International Journal on Engineering Performance-Based Fire Codes, Special Issue on Full-Scale Burning Tests*, vol 6, no 3

Chow, W. K. (2005a) 'Building fire safety in the Far East', *Architectural Science Review*, vol 48, no 4, pp285–294

Chow, W. K. (2005b) 'Fire hazard assessment of combustibles in big terminals', *International Journal of Risk Assessment and Management*, vol 5, no 1, pp66–75

Chow, W. K. (2005–2006) 'Assessing construction elements with lower fire resistance rating under big fires', *Journal of Applied Fire Science*, vol 14, no 4, pp339–346

Chow, W. K. (2006) 'A long-term research programme on studying cabin fires', Invited Speaker – Fire Asia 2006 – Best Practices in Life Safety, 15–17 February 2006, Hong Kong Convention and Exhibition Centre (HKCEC), Hong Kong

Chow, W. K. (2007) 'Fire safety of supertall buildings and necessity of upgrading active protection systems', Paper presented to International Colloquium on Fire Science and Technology 2007, Seoul, Korea, 25 October

Chow, W. K. (2008a) Correspondences with TVB reporter on possible fire hazards in buildings with glass façades, February

Chow, W. K. (2008b) 'Necessity of testing combustibles under well-developed fires', *Journal of Fire Sciences*, vol 26, no 4, pp311–329

Chow, W. K. and Chow, C. L. (2003) 'Awareness of fire safety for green and sustainable buildings', *Fire Prevention and Fire Engineers Journal*, September, pp34–35

Chow, W. K. and Han, S. S. (2006) 'Report on a recent fire in a new curtain-walled building in downtown Dalian', *International Journal on Engineering Performance-Based Fire Codes*, vol 8, no 3, pp84–87

Chow, W. K. and Hung, W. Y. (2006) 'Effect of cavity depth on fire spreading of double-skin façade', *Building and Environment*, vol 41, no 7, pp970–979

Chow, W. K. and Lui, G. C. H. (2001) 'A fire safety ranking system for karaoke establishments in Hong Kong', *Journal of Fire Sciences*, vol 19, no 2, pp106–120

Chow, W. K. and Tao, W. Q. (2003) *Application of Fire Field Modeling in Fire Safety Engineering: Computational Fluid Dynamics (CFD) or Numerical Heat Transfer (NHT)?*, CPD lecture, 29 March

Chow, W. K., Wong, L. T., Chan, K. T., Fong, N. K. and Ho, P. L. (1999) 'Fire safety engineering: Comparison of a new degree programme with the model curriculum', *Fire Safety Journal*, vol 32, no 1, pp1–15

Chow, W. K., Zou, G. W., Dong, H. and Gao, Y. (2003a) 'Necessity of carrying out full-scale burning tests for post-flashover retail shop fires', *International Journal on Engineering Performance-Based Fire Codes*, vol 5, no 1, pp20–27

Chow, W. K., Gao, Y., Dong, H., Zou, G. W. and Meng, L. (2003b) 'Will water mist extinguish a liquid fire rapidly?', *Architectural Science Review*, vol 46, no 2, pp139–144

Chow, W. K., Lee, E. P. F., Chau, F. T. and Dyke, J. M. (2004) 'The necessity of studying chemical reactions of the clean agent heptafluoropropane in fire extinguishment', *Architectural Science Review*, vol 47, no 3, pp223–228

Chow, W. K., Gao, Y., Zou, G. W. and Dong, H. (2006a) 'Performance evaluation of sidewall long-throw sprinklers at height', Paper presented at the 9th AIAA/ASME Joint Thermophysics and Heat Transfer Conference, 5–8 June 2006, San Francisco, CA, Paper AIAA-2006-3288

Chow, W. K., Fong, N. K., Pang, E. C. L., Lau, F. K. W. and Kong, K. S. M. (2006b) 'Case study for performance-based design in Hong Kong', Paper presented to 6th International Conference on Performance-Based Codes and Fire Safety Design Method, Project Presented, 14–16 June 2006, Tokyo, Japan, pp148–161

Chow, W. K., Han, S. S., Chow, C. L. and So, A. K. W. (2007) 'Experimental measurement on air temperature in a glass façade fire', *International Journal on Engineering Performance-Based Fire Codes*, vol 9, no 2, pp78–86

Chow, W. K., Leung, C. W., Zou, G. W., Dong, H. and Gao, Y. (2008a) 'Flame spread over plastic materials in flashover room fires', *Construction and Building Materials*, vol 22, no 4, pp629–634

Chow, W. K., Tsui, F. S. C. and Ko, S. L. L. (2008b) 'Performance-based design analysis – High-rise apartment building', Paper presented to 7th International Conference on Performance-Based Codes and Fire Safety Design Methods, Auckland, New Zealand, 16–18 April

Chow, W. K., Fleming, R. P., Jelenewicz, C. and Fong, N. K. (2008c) *Fire Protection Engineering, SFPE and Common*

Problems in Performance-Based Design for Building Fire Safety, CPD lecture, Hong Kong Polytechnic University, Hong Kong, China, 12 April

Choy, R. M. W., Chow, W. K. and Fong, N. K. (2004) 'Assessing the clean agent heptafluoropropane by the cup burner test', *Journal of Applied Fire Science*, vol 12, no 1, pp23–40

CIBSE/ASHRAE (2003) *The 2003 CIBSE/ASHRAE Conference Building Sustainability, Value and Profit*, Edinburgh International Conference Centre, Scotland, 24–26 September

Cox, G. (1995) *Combustion Fundamentals of Fires*, Academic Press, London

Dowling, V. P., White, N., Webb, A. K. and Barnett, J. R. (2007) 'When a passenger train burns, how big is the fire?', Paper presented to 7th Asia-Oceania Symposium on Fire Science and Technology, Invited Speech, 20–22 September 2007, Hong Kong

Federal Emergency Management Agency (2006) *World Trade Center Building Performance Study*, US, May

Fire Services Department (1998) *Code of Practice for Minimum Fire Service Installation and Equipment*, Fire Services Department, Hong Kong

Glass and Glazing Federation (1978) *Glazing Manual*, Glass and Glazing Federation, London

Gritzo, L. A., Senseny, P. E., Xin, Y. B. and Thomas J. R. (2005) 'The international FORUM of fire research directors: A position paper on verification and validation of numerical fire models', *Fire Safety Journal*, vol 40, no 5, pp485–490

Guo, D. G., Wong, K., Kang, L., Shi, B. and Luo, M. C. (2004) 'Lift evacuation of ultra-high rise building', in *Proceedings of the Fire Conference 2004 – Total Fire Safety Concept*, 6–7 December 2004, Hong Kong, China, vol 1, pp151–158

Harada, K., Ohmiya, Y., Natori, A. and Nakamichi, A. (2004) 'Technical basis on structural fire resistance design in building standards law of Japan', *Fire and Materials*, vol 28, no 2–4, pp323–341

Hassani, S. K. S., Shields, T. J. and Silcock, G. W. (1995) 'Thermal fracture of window glazing: Performance of glazing in fire', *Journal of Applied Fire Science*, vol 4, no 4, pp249–263

HKIE (2008) 'Fire Division – Introduction to the Division', www.hkie.org.hk/~Eng/html/AboutTheHKIE/Disciplines/fir.htm80Fire, accessed April 2008

Ho, D. C. W., Lo, S. M., Tiu, C. Y., Cheng, W. Y. and To, M. Y. (2002) 'Building officials' perception on the use of performance-based fire engineering approach in building design – A second stage study', *International Journal on Engineering Performance-Based Fire Codes*, vol 4, no 4, pp119–126

Hong Kong Polytechnic University (1998) *BEng(Hons) in Building Services Engineering with Specialism in Fire Engineering*, Hong Kong Polytechnic University, Hong Kong, China

Hong Kong Polytechnic University (2000) *MSc in Fire Safety Engineering*, Hong Kong Polytechnic University, Hong Kong, China

Hung, W. Y. and Chow, W. K. (2002) 'Architectural features for the environmental friendly century', Paper presented to New Symbiotic Building and Environmental Technology – The Future Scope in Subtropical Region, Sustainable Building 2002: 3rd International Conference on Sustainable Building, 23–25 September 2002, Oslo, Norway, Paper 011

Hung, W. Y. and Chow, W. K. (2003) 'Fire safety in new architectural design associated with the extensive use of glass', in *Proceedings of the International Symposium on Fire Science and Fire-Protection Engineering*, 12–15 October 2003, Beijing, China, pp389–396

Kashiwagi, T., Butler, K. M. and Gilman, J. W. (2000) *Fire Safe Materials Project at NIST*, NISTIR 6588, National Institute of Standards and Technology, Gaithersburg, MD

Klote, J. H. and Milke, J. (1992) *Design of Smoke Management Systems*, ASHRAE Publications 90022, Atlanta, GA

Lam, C. M. (1995) 'Fire safety strategies for the new Chek Lap Kok International Airport', in *Conference Proceedings of Asiaflam '95*, 15–16 March 1995, Hong Kong, pp63–68

Law, M. (1990) 'Fire and smoke models – Their use on the design of some large buildings', *ASHRAE Transactions*, vol 96, no 1, pp963–971

Law, M. (1998) 'On the "Cabins" fire safety design concept in the new Hong Kong airport terminal building', *Journal of Fire Sciences*, vol 16, no 3, pp149–150

Li, J. and Chow, W. K. (2008) 'Key equations for studying emergency evacuation in performance-based design', Paper presented to the 3rd International Symposium on the 21st Century Centre of Excellence Programme, Centre for Fire Science and Technology, Tokyo University of Science, Japan, 10–11 March

Loss Prevention Council (1999) *Fire Spreading in Multi-Storey Buildings with Glazed Curtain Wall Façades*, LPC 11, Loss Prevention Council, Borehamwood, UK

Magnusson, S. E., Drysdale, D. D., Fitzgerald, R. W., Motevalli, V., Mowner, F., Quintiere, J., Williamson, R. B. and Zalosh, R. G. (1995) 'A proposal for a model curriculum in fire safety engineering', *Fire Safety Journal*, vol 25, no 1, pp1–88

Malhotra, H. L. (1987) *Fire Safety in Buildings*, Building Research Establishment Report, Department of the Environment, Building Research Establishment, Fire Research Station, Borehamwood, Herts, UK

McGrattan, K. (2005) 'Fire modelling: Where are we now, and where are we going?', Paper presented to 8th International Symposium on Fire Safety Science, Invited Lecture 3, Tsinghua University, Beijing, China, 18–23 September 2005, International Association for Fire Safety Science

Mok, W. K. and Chow, W. K. (2004) 'Verification and validation in modeling fire by computational fluid dynamics', *International Journal on Architectural Science*, vol 5, no 3, pp58–67

National Fire Protection Association (2003) *NFPA 5000 Building Construction and Safety Code*, NFPA, Quincy, MA

Pitts, W. M. (1991) 'Wind effects on fires', *Progress in Energy and Combustion Science*, vol 17, no 2, pp83–134

Rasbash, D. J. (1996) 'Fire safety objectives for buildings', *Fire Technology*, vol 32, no 4, pp348–350

Rose, E. (2003) 'Communication called industry's weakness', *ASHRAE Journal*, vol 45, no 11, pp6, 8, 55–56

Services Ordinance (2004) *Laws of Hong Kong and Its Sub-Leg Regulations*, Hong Kong Special Administrative Region, Hong Kong, Chapter 95

SFPE (Society of Fire Protection Engineers) (2001) *SFPE Engineering Guide to Performance-Based Fire Protection Analysis and Design of Buildings*, Society of Fire Protection Engineers, Bethesda, MD

Tin Tin Daily News (1998) 'No 3 alarm fire at the new Hong Kong International Airport passenger terminal', *Tin Tin Daily News*, Hong Kong, 30 April

Tsujimoto, M. (2008) Paper presented to The Future of the 21st COE Programme of TUS, 3rd International Symposium on the 21st Century Centre of Excellence Programme, Centre for Fire Science and Technology, Tokyo University of Science, Japan, 10–11 March

Wang, J. Q. and Chow, W. K. (2005) 'A brief review on fire retardants for polymeric foams', *Journal of Applied Polymer Science*, vol 97, no 1, pp366–376

Wu, P. K. (2005) 'Heat flux pipe in large-scale fire tests', Paper presented to 8th International Symposium on Fire Safety Science, Tsinghua University, Beijing, China, 18–23 September 2005, International Association for Fire Safety Science, Paper MM-3

Yung, D. T. and Benichou, N. (2002) 'How design fires can be used in fire hazard analysis', *Fire Technology*, vol 38, no 3, pp231–242

16

The Role of Urban Greenery in High-Density Cities

Nyuk-Hien Wong and Yu Chen

Introduction

With rapid urbanization, there has been a tremendous growth in population and buildings in cities. The high concentration of hard surfaces has triggered many environmental issues. The urban heat island (UHI) effect, for example, is a phenomenon where air temperatures in densely built cities are higher than those in suburban rural areas. One of the first reports on UHI was written by meteorologist Luck Howard (1833) in London more than a century ago. After many years of subsequent research, people now well understand the UHI effect in cities. The primary root of UHI is rapid urbanization, which replaces natural landscapes with enormous hard surfaces, such as building façades, roads and pavements in cities. First, these hard surfaces in built environments re-radiate solar energy in the form of long-wave radiation to the surroundings. A lack of extensive vegetation further incurs the loss of a natural cooling means, which cools surrounding air through evapotranspiration. In addition, the UHI is aggravated by a lack of moisture sources due to the large fraction of impervious surfaces in cities. Rainwater is discharged quickly. Finally, heat generated from anthropogenic heat originating from combustion processes and the use of air-conditioning coupled with the greenhouse effect of pollutants also contributes to an increase in temperatures. Such increase in temperatures with the presence of air pollutants can result in the accumulation of smog, damages the natural environment and jeopardizes human health. It also costs consumers more money

because it takes more energy to cool buildings. According to Landsberg (1981), the urban heat island, as the most obvious climatic manifestation of urbanization, can be observed in every town and city worldwide. Temperatures can be higher by as much 10°, as has been observed in many big cities in the world, such as Los Angeles, Shanghai, Tokyo, New Delhi and Kuala Lumpur (Nichol, 1996; Tso, 1996).

Green areas in cities are considered ecological measures to combat concrete jungles since plants can create an 'oasis effect' and mitigate urban warming at both macro- and micro-levels. As soon as a bare hard surface is covered with plants, the heat-absorbing surface transfers from the artificial layer to the living one. Leaves can seize most of the incoming solar radiation – for example, trees were observed to intercept 60 to 90 per cent of incoming radiation (Lesiuk, 2000). Except for a very small portion transformed into chemical energy through photosynthesis, most of the incident solar radiation can be transformed into latent heat, which converts water from liquid to gas, resulting in a lower leaf temperature, lower surrounding air temperature and higher humidity through the process of evapotranspiration. At night, the energy of the outgoing net radiation from a green surface is fed from the thermal heat flux and the latent heat flux. Therefore, the temperature around the green area is lower than that within the built environment. On the other hand, any surface covered with plants has a lower Bowen ratio than a mineral surface. According to Santamouris (2001, p146), the Bowen ratio is typically around 5 in a built environment. However, it ranges from 0.5 to 2 in a planted area. Lower Bowen ratios mean that lower ambient air temperatures can be achieved when the similar incident radiation is absorbed by an area. Furthermore, when greenery is arranged throughout a city in the form of natural reserves, urban parks, neighbourhood parks or rooftop gardens, the energy balance of the whole city can be modified through adding more evaporating surfaces. It actually provides sources of moisture for evapotranspiration. More absorbed radiation can be dissipated to be latent rather than sensible heat, hence, urban temperatures can be reduced.

In a built environment, the UHI effect can be described as a conflict between buildings and the urban climate. By considering the positive impacts of plants upon the 'conflict', a conceptual model was been proposed by Chen and Wong (2005) to further understand the interactions among the three critical components in the built environment (see Figure 16.1). The model consists of not only the three components, but their interactions (PB, PC, BC and CB). PB is the amount of vegetation introduced into a built environment. It could be reinforced when more greenery is introduced into the built environment. PC is the ability of plants to mediate the urban climate. BC and CB are the interactions between climate and buildings. Two hypotheses are subsequently generated from the model (see Figure 16.2). When climate and buildings are largely modified by plants, the overlapped shaded area between them decreases, which means fewer conflicts occur or less active energy is consumed to mitigate the conflicts (see hypothesis 1). On the

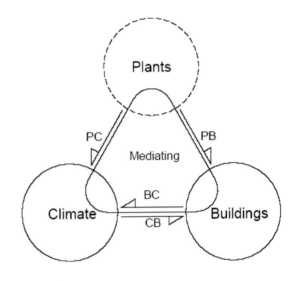

Figure 16.1 *Model of environment (plants are considered to be the major component of environmental control)*

other hand, the shaded area expands when plants have less influence on climate and buildings. This indicates that more negative conflicts occur or more active energy is used for mitigating the negative effects (see hypothesis 2). In order to uncover the benefit of greenery in a built environment on the UHI effect, the two hypotheses should be proved quantitatively.

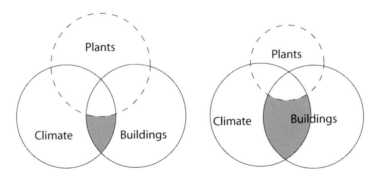

Figure 16.2 *Graphical interpretation of hypothesis 1 (left) and hypothesis 2 (right)*

Reducing ambient air temperature with plants

Urban parks

Although a single tree can already moderate the climate well, its impacts are limited to the microclimate. Large urban parks can extend these positive effects to the surrounding built environment. Two parks, Bukit Batok Natural Park (BBNP), which is a 36ha park located in the centre of Singapore, and Celmenti Woods Park (CWP), which is 12ha park located in the western part of Singapore, have been investigated in order to research thermal benefits in a tropical climate (Chen and Wong, 2006).

In BBNP, five measurement points were selected within the park, while another five points were chosen in surrounding residential blocks. All measurement points were lined up with an interval of around 100m. In order to explore the cooling effect of BBNP, the average temperatures obtained at different locations were compared (see Figure 16.3). Within BBNP, it can be found that most average temperatures were relatively lower than those measured in the residential blocks. From locations 1 to 4, the average temperatures range from 25.2°C to 25.5°C. For location 5, the average temperature is slightly higher since it located at the edge of BBNP where anthropogenic heat generated by vehicles (car parks and highways) may probably influence the readings. On the other hand, there is an orderly elevation of average temperatures for locations within surrounding Housing Development Board (HDB) blocks. It shows that the park has a cooling impact upon its surroundings, but depends very much upon the distance. The highest average temperature was observed at location 9. It is about 1.3°C higher than the average temperature obtained at location 6, which is the nearest location to BBNP. Another interesting difference between the temperatures measured in the park and the surrounding HDB blocks is their standard deviations. The standard deviations obtained in the park range from 1.8 to 2.1 (locations 1 to 4), while they range from 2.0 to 3.2 (locations 5 to 10) in the built environment. This indicates that the extensive plants may have a better ability to stabilize the fluctuation of ambient air temperature throughout the day.

Measurements in BBNP were conducted over a period of 26 days. The lower temperatures were always observed within BBNP, which can, in this case, be

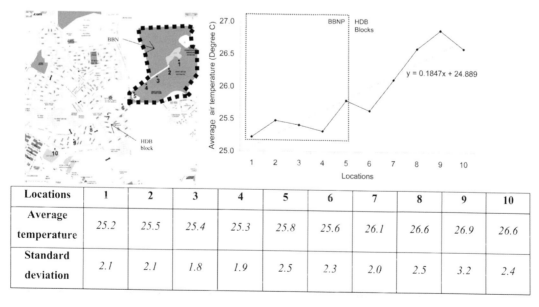

Locations	1	2	3	4	5	6	7	8	9	10
Average temperature	25.2	25.5	25.4	25.3	25.8	25.6	26.1	26.6	26.9	26.6
Standard deviation	2.1	2.1	1.8	1.9	2.5	2.3	2.0	2.5	3.2	2.4

Source: Author

Figure 16.3 *The comparison of average air temperatures measured at different locations in Bukit Batok Natural Park (BBNP) (11 January–5 February 2003)*

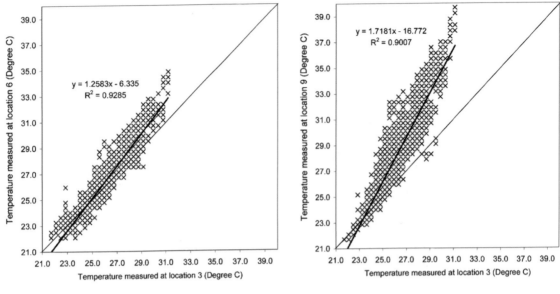

Figure 16.4 *Correlation analysis of locations 6 and 3, as well as locations 9 and 3*

defined as a 'cooling source'. In order to determine the relationship between the cooling source and the locations within buildings, a comparative correlation analysis was conducted. Location 3 has been defined as a reference point since it has lower average temperatures and the lowest standard deviation over a period of 26 days. The elevation of ambient temperatures can be observed at the locations away from the park in terms of the gradients. Figure 16.4 highlights the gradient differences between the location near the park (location 6) and the location further away from the park (location 9). The consistency of the temperature elevation among the locations that were set beyond the vicinity of the park over a long period can be observed.

In order to further explore the pattern of energy consumption of a typical commercial building near BBNK, a simulation programme EDSL TAS: Environmental Design Solutions Limited (EDSL) Thermal Analysis Simulation software (TAS) was used. A typical eight-storey commercial building was built and some general assumptions were made in terms of the internal condition of the building:

- The air conditioning is turned on from 8.00 am to 6.00 pm.

- The temperature ranges from 22.5°C to 25.5°C.
- Relative humidity is less than 70 per cent.
- Lighting gain is 15W/m².
- Occupancy sensible and latent heat gain are 15W/m².
- Equipment sensible heat gain is 20W/m².

The cooling load of the commercial building was consecutively calculated when it was placed inside the park, and 100m, 200m, 300m and 400m away from the park. The calculated cooling loads for different locations within or near the BBNP are presented in Figure 16.5. A clear difference among cooling loads can be observed. The lowest load, 9077kWh, was observed when the building was placed inside the park, while the highest one, 10,123kWh, was experienced when the commercial building was built 400m away from the park (location 9 in the filed measurement). It is unrealistic for a commercial building to be built inside a national park. However, it is possible for the building to be located near a park or greenery. It is encouraging that energy savings can be achieved when a building is located near a park.

In Celmenti Woods Park, the lowest average temperature, 25.7°C, was observed at location 1 where

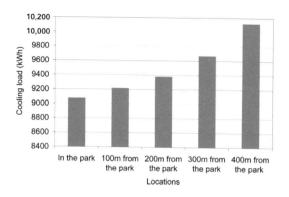

Source: Author

Figure 16.5 *Comparison of cooling loads for different locations*

very extensive trees are planted. Average temperatures ranging from 27.2°C to 27.5°C were observed at the rest of the locations within CWP. The temperature difference between location 1 and the other locations in CWP can be explained by the density of the trees planted in the vicinity of the park. Except for the comparison of ambient air temperatures, the correlation analysis between solar radiation and air

temperatures among different locations has also been made (see Figure 16.6). The solar radiation data was taken from the weather station located near the CWP. Essentially, temperatures will be increased with the elevation of solar radiation at all locations. The trend line of location 1 is at the bottom of the profile. Those trend lines derived within CWP and nearby areas are at the middle of the profile. The trend lines obtained from locations further away from the park, such as locations 9, 11 and 13, are at the top of the profile. These findings accord with the previous analysis; but the interesting phenomenon is that the gradients of these trend lines are more or less the same. In other words, the determining factor seems to be solar radiation, which can easily blur the other impacts.

In order to have an impression of how the existence of CWP influences the surroundings, three scenarios – retaining the park, removing the park and replacing the park with buildings – were created within the simulation programme ENVI-met.

Figure 16.7 shows the comparison of the section views of the three scenarios observed at 12.00 am. It is obvious that the planted area can create a low-temperature zone at its leeward area. The length of the area is almost similar to the length of the green area. Of course, the closer the distance to the green area, the

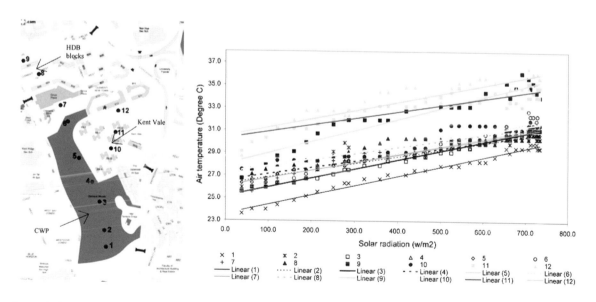

Source: Author

Figure 16.6 *The correlation analysis between solar radiation and air temperatures at all locations*

lower the temperature obtained. The maximum height of the low-temperature zone is around 70m to 80m. In this simulation model, the height of the tallest buildings (HDB point block) is 66m. Therefore, it can be concluded that both upper and lower parts of tall buildings receive cooling benefit from vegetation at

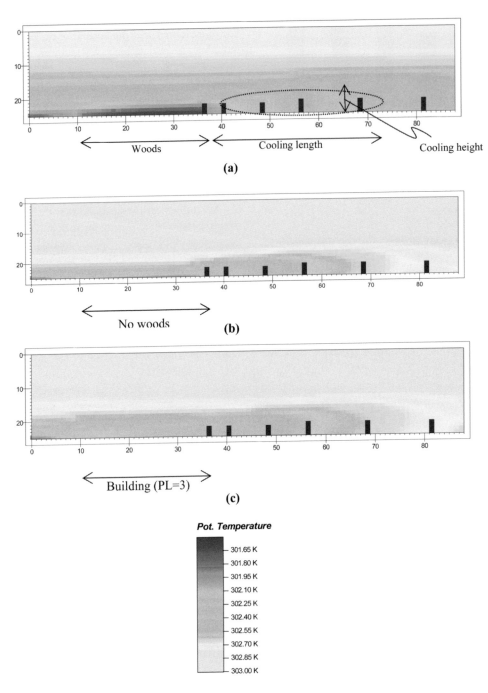

Figure 16.7 *The comparison of section views at 12.00 am of scenarios: (a) with woods; (b) without woods; and (c) with buildings replacing woods*

night if they are located near the green area. When the vegetation is completely removed from the woods, only a very small patch of the low temperature zone is found in the built environment. When plants are completely replaced with buildings, the low-temperature zone is replaced by a high-temperature zone.

Road trees

Trees planted along roadsides are very common in Singapore. The original purpose was to provide shading for pedestrians and visual beauty. However, the thermal effect of road trees on surroundings cannot be ignored, especially in an environment with low-rise buildings and mature trees. In Singapore, measurements were conducted in Tuas, which is an industrial area. Three streets with different densities of road trees were selected (see Figure 16.8). Tuas Avenue 2 and Tuas Avenue 8 are two parallel main streets in the area. Tuas Avenue 2 has very extensive mature trees planted along the roadsides, while Tuas Avenue 8 has fewer trees. Both the two streets have busy traffic during the daytime. Tuas South Street 3 is further away from Tuas Avenue 2 and 8 down to the southern part of Tuas. Compared with Tuas Avenue 2 and 8, Tuas South Street 3 is a relatively narrow street with very minimal young trees and light traffic. Altogether, 21 measuring points were evenly distributed in the three streets with an interval of roughly 100m.

A long-term (over 28-day) comparison is shown in Figure 16.9. It is very interesting that the mean or the median values obtained from Tuas Avenue 2, Tuas Avenue 8 and Tuas South Street 3 are in a sequence according to their density of road trees planted. The lowest mean temperature was observed along Tuas Avenue 2 and it was lower than those of Tuas Avenue 8 and Tuas South Street 3 by 0.5°C and 0.6°C, respectively. The mean or median temperature obtained from Tuas Avenue 8 is slightly lower than that derived from Tuas South Street 3, although it has much denser road trees compared with the almost bare Tuas South Street 3. A possible reason for this is due to the interference from heavy traffic on Tuas Avenue 8 (evidence of this is found in the maximum upper-whisker observed in Tuas Avenue 8). Normally the maximum temperature is experienced during daytime when incident solar radiation is strong. With relatively dense road trees, higher ambient temperatures during the daytime do not make sense if the anthropogenic heat from the traffic is not considered.

In order to explore the extreme conditions, a comparison of the average temperatures derived from the three streets was carried out on a clear day. The ranges of the average temperatures are from 23.2°C to 34.0°C, from 24.4°C to 36.1°C, and from 25.2°C to 34.9°C in Tuas Avenue 2, Tuas Avenue 8 and Tuas South Street 3, respectively. A clear sequence was still observed among the three Tuas streets during night-time. Tuas Avenue 2, as expected, had the lowest average temperature, followed by those in Tuas Avenue 8 and Tuas South Street 3. During the daytime, especially from 10.00 am to 5.30 pm, the interference from heavy traffic can be easily observed in Tuas Avenue 2 and Tuas Avenue 8, where higher temperature profiles were measured.

A simulation was subsequently carried out by TAS according to the data derived from the above measurements. The model built up in TAS is based on

Source: Author

Figure 16.8 *Three streets selected in Tuas area: (left) Tuas Avenue 2; (middle) Tuas Avenue 8; (right) Tuas South Street 3*

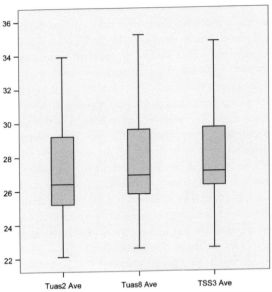

	Tuas 2 Ave	Tuas 8 Ave	TSS 3 Ave
Mean	27.3	27.8	27.9
Median	26.4	26.9	27.1
SD	2.6	2.7	2.4

Source: Author

Figure 16.9 *Box plot of average temperatures (°C) obtained from different locations in the Tuas area over a period from 21 March to 14 April 2005*

a standard stand-alone factory, which is commonly seen in industrials areas. Several assumptions were made:

- The factory building is fully air conditioned.
- The indoor temperature is set to 24°C.
- The working hours are from 7.00 am to 7.00 pm.
- There is no internal heat source (avoiding possible interference from the internal environment).

Simulations were conducted by modifying the climate data through adopting boundary conditions measured from the field measurements. The factory model was put into four cases with reference to the corresponding filed measurements' results. Case 1 is the environment of Tuas South Street 3, where only young trees without effective tree shading could be observed. Case 2 is the environment of Tuas Avenue 8, where medium density of road trees and very heavy traffic during the daytime were experienced. Case 3 and case 4 were derived from

the environment of Tuas Avenue 2. The difference is that case 3 employed the average temperature of the whole street, while case 4 used the lowest temperature profile among all the locations in the street. Figure 16.11 shows the result of the simulation. It is clear that cooling energy saving can be achieved when the stand-alone factory is placed in an environment with extensive road trees. By using case 1 as the benchmark, it can be observed that 5 per cent of energy can be saved in an environment with fairly dense road trees and up to 23 per cent of energy savings can be achieved in an environment with extremely dense road trees on a clear day. Road trees can also contribute to energy savings on a cloudy day (11 and 38 per cent energy savings, respectively, for the above two cases). For case 2, the potential saving is almost zero. The reason is due to the heavy traffic occurred on the street during the daytime.

Landscape within the vicinity of buildings

The landscape within the vicinity of buildings can provide aesthetic benefits as well as a natural scale to residents. A psychological link with the natural environment can also be given to residents who stay in concrete jungles. Two measurements were carried out in two business parks and two residential neighbourhoods in order to explore the role of plants in mediating ambient air temperatures within the vicinity of buildings. Two business parks with relatively extensive landscapes were chosen: Changi Business Park (CBP) and International Business Park (IBP). Since CBP is still under construction, it is possible to set up a reference point (green point) in the vacant area where more extensive greenery can be observed. Except for the measuring points within the boundary of CBP, another two measuring points had been placed in a traditional industrial area, which is quite near CBP. Overall, there were 17 measurements points set up within IBP, CBP and the nearby area (see Figure 16.12).

The average temperatures calculated at different locations over a period of 20 days were compared (see Figure 16.13). It can be seen that the average temperature obtained from the vacant area with relatively extensive greenery is significantly lower (1.5°C–1.8°C) than the other locations. Meanwhile, there is also around a 0.2°C to 0.3°C slight difference

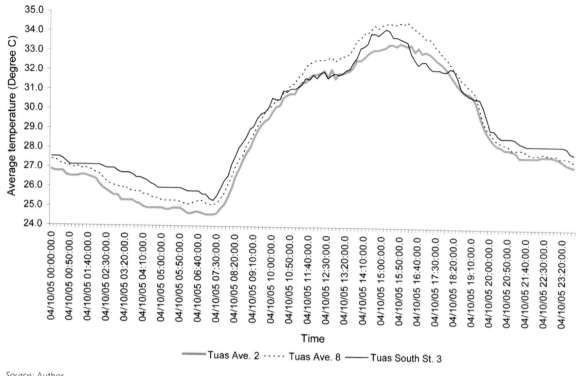

Source: Author

Figure 16.10 *The comparison of average temperatures measured in the Tuas area on 10 April 2005*

between business parks (IBP and CBP) and the traditional industrial area.

The long-term comparison actually shows the two extremes as the result of landscaping built environments. With more extensive greenery, the ambient temperature tends to be lower, whereas it can rise up to around 1.8°C higher with minimal planting. The potential cooling impacts caused by the current plants in the two business parks can be easily blurred by the strong solar radiation during daytime. Plants have to balance not only the direct incident solar radiation, but the indirect radiation reflected from the surrounding buildings. It may explain why only a slight difference can be observed between the two business parks and the traditional industrial area.

Whether plants should be integrated within buildings in concentrated or scattered form is another major concern. At present, the arrangement of planting within the vicinity of buildings is very much governed by aesthetic considerations instead of thermal ones.

In order to reconsider it from the thermal benefit point of view, ENVI-met was employed to simulate the two scenarios, one with a concentrated landscape and the other with a scattered one. The total amount of greenery is the same in the two scenarios. It can be observed that the concentrated landscape, like a huge cooling source, has an obvious low-temperature area. With the help of proper air movement, buildings located near it can benefit from a better thermal condition (see Figure 16.14). On the other hand, the impact of the scattered greenery is much more localized. The small portion of greenery is not sufficient to balance the negative impacts of the harshly built environment, especially during the daytime when the incident solar radiation is strong. The best solution is that some concentrated greenery can be arranged at a reasonable distance within a built environment. Buildings can benefit from the continuous low-temperature buffers that exist between the concentrated greenery.

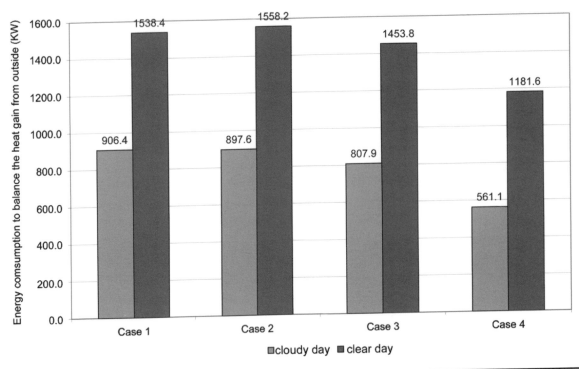

	Case 1	Case 2	Case 3	Case 4
cloudy day	0%	1%	11%	38%
clear day	0%	-1%	5%	23%

Source: Author

Figure 16.11 *The comparison of cooling energy consumptions to balance the heat gain from outside and potential energy saving caused by road trees*

Two residential neighbourhoods had also been chosen to explore the thermal difference caused by greenery within them: Punggol and Seng Kang (see Figure 16.15). Punggol site is a developed residential site with moderate vegetation on the ground level. Seng Kang site is also a developed residential site, but with considerably less vegetation. Calculations have shown that the Punggol site has roughly three times more vegetation coverage than the Seng Kang site.

Measurements were conducted over a two-week period. Figure 16.16 shows the comparison of maximum, minimum and average temperatures between the two sites on a clear day. For a short period in the morning until around 9.06 am, both sites featured quite similar average ambient air temperature readings due to the limited insolation. For the time period of between 9.06 am and 7.12 pm, the temperatures at Seng Kang site had higher temperatures than those at the Punggol site. The temperature in Seng Kang rose more rapidly than in Punggol and reached the maximum average air temperature of 34.63°C at 3.54 pm, with a maximum average temperature of 32.46°C at 3.48 pm. All of these differences are due to the lack of a densely distributed landscape on site. The maximum average temperatures of the two sites were found to occur at around the same time. The maximum average temperature difference of 2.32°C between the two sites was observed at 4.06 pm. In fact, the temperature difference reflected in the two sites indicates the shading effect of the trees planted in the residential area during the daytime. The temperature in Seng Kang began to decrease at 5.12 pm and reached similar readings to Punggol site at around 7.12 pm.

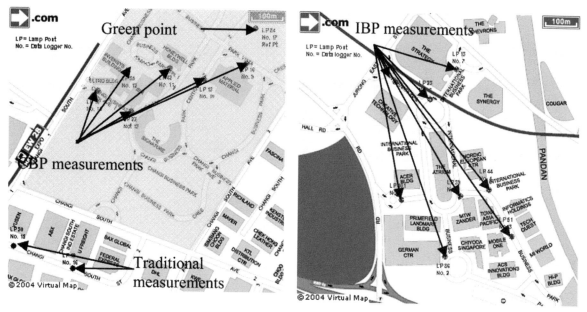

Source: Author

Figure 16.12 *The measurement points in Changi Business Park (CBP) (left) and International Business Park (IBP) (right)*

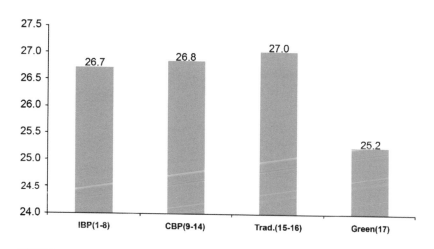

	IBP(1-8)	CBP(9-14)	Trad.(15-16)	Green(17)
Ave T	26.7	26.8	27.0	25.2
SD	2.1	1.9	1.9	2.2

Source: Author

Figure 16.13 *Comparison of average air temperatures (°C) obtained at different locations over a period of 20 days*

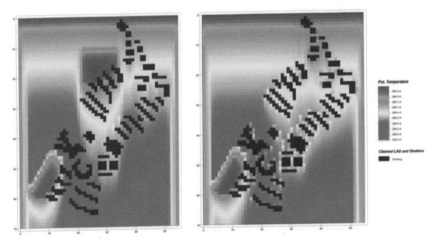

Note: Black areas represent buildings, while other shading indicates temperature ranging from low (dark) to high (light).
Source: Author

Figure 16.14 *Simulation results at midnight: (left) concentrated landscape; (right) scattered landscape*

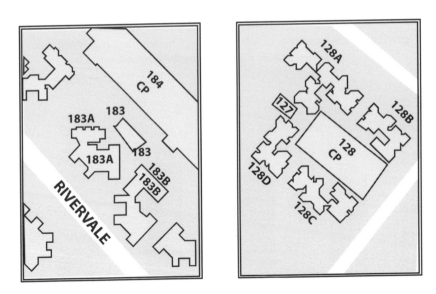

Source: Author

Figure 16.15 *Punggol site (left) and Seng Kang site (right)*

Rooftop gardens

Except for landscaping on the ground, plants strategically introduced into buildings can also benefit the surrounding environment by reducing the ambient air temperature. In order to explore the cooling impacts of rooftop gardens, some field measurements were conducted.

The first measurement was carried out over a period of two weeks on two multi-storey car parks (Wong et al, 2002). One was covered with intensive garden landscaping and was defined as C2 (see Figure 6.17). The other had not been planted by then and was named as C16 (see Figure 6.18). Figure 6.19 shows the respective comparisons of ambient air temperatures and relative humidity (RH) measured at C2 and C16 over

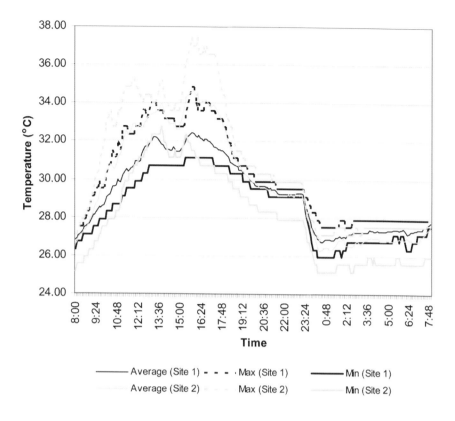

Source: Author

Figure 16.16 *The comparison of temperatures between two sites: (site 1) Punggol site; (site 2) Seng Kang site*

Source: Author

Figure 16.17 *Rooftop garden C2 with vegetation*

Source: Author

Figure 16.18 *Rooftop garden C16 without vegetation*

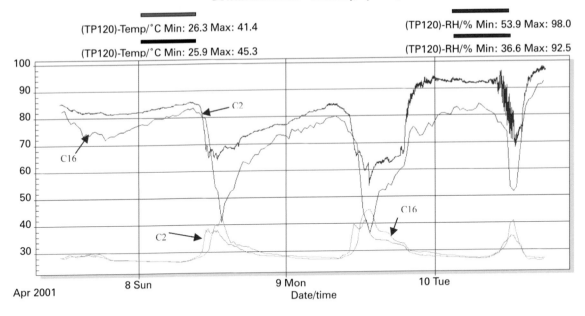

Source: Author

Figure 16.19 *Air ambient temperature and relative humidity plotted over three days*

three days. At night, the ambient temperatures measured at C2 and C16 were quite similar, both at about 28°C. The clear difference could be observed during the daytime, especially at around 1.00 pm, when the solar radiation was at its peak. Throughout the day, the maximum temperature difference between the two sites was about 3°C. Furthermore, the ambient air temperature was consistently lower at C2 due to the presence of plants. On the other hand, a higher relative humidity in the immediate vicinity was observed. It was caused by the process of evapotranspiration on site, which increased the moisture in the air.

A more complicated measurement was carried out on the extensive rooftop garden of a low-rise commercial building that has plenty of plants (see Figure 16.20) (Wong et al, 2003). The measurement points are illustrated in Figure 16.21. The ambient air temperatures were measured at different heights (300mm, 600mm and 1000mm) above the hard surface and the vegetation, respectively. For ambient air temperatures measured above both hard surface and vegetation, higher air temperatures were observed at lower heights during the daytime. It indicates that both

hard surface and vegetation, which were exposed to the strong solar radiation, had elevated surface temperatures, which subsequently influenced the ambient air temperature at a distance. Ambient air temperatures measured at 1m heights above both hard surface and vegetation were obviously lower than that measured at lower levels during the daytime and tended to be uniform. This indicates the limit of the cooling impact caused by the plants in the rooftop garden. Most plants on the rooftop are shrubs and it is understandable that their cooling impact is limited compares to trees on the ground. Figure 16.22 shows the 'cooling effect' of the shrubs that can be found from afternoon to sunrise of the next day. As the cooling effect of vegetation was restricted by distance, the temperature decrease caused by plants measured at a height of 1m was not as obvious as that measured at 300mm. The maximum temperature difference was 4.2°C, measured at a 300mm height, around 6.00 pm.

Based on the ambient air temperatures, global temperatures and air velocity measured at 1m above the rooftop, the mean radiation temperatures (MRTs) were calculated (see Figure 16.23). Maximum differences of

Figure 16.20 *Rooftop garden of the low-rise building*

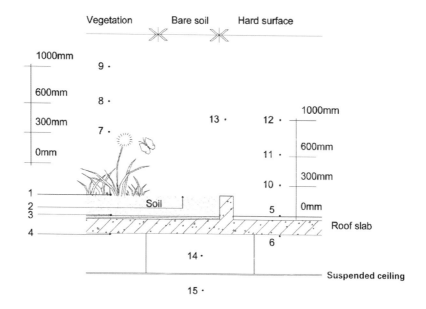

Figure 16.21 *Positions of the field measurements*

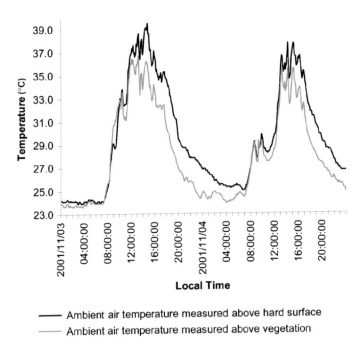

Figure 16.22 *Comparison of ambient air temperatures measured with and without plants at a height of 300mm on 3 and 4 November*

the global temperature and the MRT were 4.05°C and 4.5°C, respectively, just after sunset (between 6.00 pm and 7.00 pm). Without direct sunshine, the radiative load mainly depends upon the amount of long-wave radiation emitted from surrounding surfaces. Since it was heated by solar radiation during the daytime, the hard surface had a higher surface temperature and emitted more long-wave radiation to the surrounding environment at night. Green plants, on the other hand, can absorb part of the incoming solar radiation and protect the surface beneath from high surface temperatures. The long-wave radiation emitted from the vegetation, therefore, is much less than that emitted from the hard surface. Meanwhile the irradiated and reflected radiation from both the hard surface and vegetation were also measured. Radiation measured above vegetation was absolutely lower than that measured above hard surfaces during the daytime. The maximum variation of 109W/m² was found at noon when the incoming solar radiation was the strongest of the day. This is consistent with the fact that green plants irradiated and reflected less solar heat than hard surfaces.

Comparison of calculated mean radiation temperature (MRT) with and without plants

Measurements were also carried out on some extensive rooftop gardens. However, no significant improvement was observed in terms of reducing ambient temperature. It is understandable when the observation is linked back with the formatting of extensive rooftop gardens. Normally, turf is planted on extensive rooftop systems. The cooling impact of turf upon ambient air is very much localized. Meanwhile, the growing media employed is commonly thin and lightweight. If it is exposed to the strong incident radiation, its surface temperature can be increased rapidly during the daytime. All of these factors can easily blur the weak cooling impact caused by turf on rooftops and trigger higher ambient air temperatures.

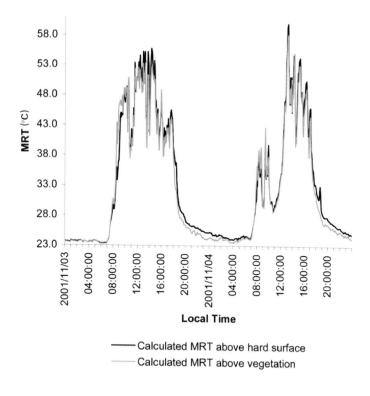

Source: Author

Figure 16.23 *Comparison of mean radiation temperatures (MRTs) calculated with and without plants at a height of 1m on 3 and 4 November*

Summary

From the above measurements and simulations, it can be concluded that plants can reduce high ambient temperature in a built environment. This is an effective way of mitigating the UHI effect in Singapore. At the macro-level, lower temperature can be achieved by parks, road trees and landscapes planted within the vicinity of buildings. At the micro-level, intensive rooftop gardens can also benefit the environment by reducing ambient air temperature; but its cooling impact is much localized. In other words, mitigating the UHI effect by reducing air temperature mainly relies on introducing large-scale greenery. The temperature contrast between the urban area and the rural area can be reduced only when a large amount of greenery can be introduced into the built environment in the form of parks, road trees and different types of landscapes.

Reducing surface temperature with plants

Rooftop gardens

Intensive rooftop garden

The measurements carried out on the intensive rooftop garden mentioned previously also provide evidence of reducing the surface temperatures of the roof. Figure 16.24 compares surface temperatures measured with different plants, only spare soil, and a spare hard surface. Without plants, the maximum temperature of the hard surface can reach around 57°C. The maximum daily deviation of surface temperature was around 30°C. For bare soil, the surface temperature measured during the daytime was not as high as that of the hard surface. The maximum surface temperature of bare soil was around

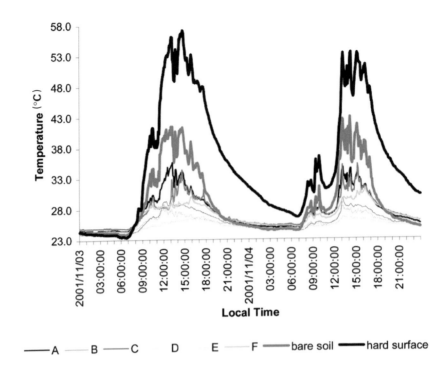

Figure 16.24 *Comparison of surface temperatures measured with different kinds of plants, only soil, and without plants on 3 and 4 November*

42°C and the maximum daily variation of surface temperature was around 20°C. The reason could be due to the evaporation of moisture in the soil that led to the reduction of surface temperatures during the daytime. With the presence of vegetation, surface temperature was greatly reduced.

Figure 16.24 shows that the shading ability of the different plants is highly dependent upon the leaf area index (LAI) since higher temperatures were usually found under sparse foliage, while lower temperatures were detected under dense ones. The maximum temperature measured under all kinds of plants was no more than 36°C. For the densest shrub, the maximum daily variation of surface temperature was less than 3°C and the maximum surface temperature was only 26.5°C, which is much lower than those measured on the hard surface and the bare soil. From a thermal protection point of view, it is desirable to have vegetation planted on a rooftop garden with a larger leaf area index, such as dense trees and shrubs. On the other hand, trees and shrubs can also increase the roof structural load and maintenance. The selection of vegetation on the rooftop therefore requires a balance among these environmental, structural and maintenance considerations. The direct thermal effect of plants was further translated to the heat flux through a typical roof and planted roofs (see Figure 16.25). Compared with the planted roofs, considerably higher heat flux was observed on the typical roof for the whole day. The maximum heat flux, 19.76W/m², was found at around 2.00 pm. Plants played an important role in reducing thermal heat gain through their sun-shading effects during the daytime. At night, however, small and similar values were found on roofs with bare soil and roofs with plants. It is worth mentioning that total heat gain over a day was remarkably reduced to 164.3kJ (around 22 per cent of the heat gain through the bare roof) under the dense shrubs.

Based on the above data, an energy simulation was carried out (see Figure 16.26). It could be concluded that the roofing materials had a great impact upon cooling energy consumption.

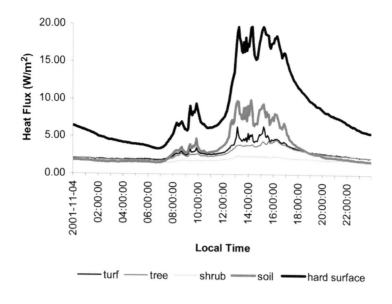

Figure 16.25 *Comparison of heat flux transferred through different roof surfaces on 4 November*

The comparison between the exposed roof and rooftop gardens (the exposed roof as base case) revealed that the installation of a rooftop garden on an exposed roof has significantly reduced the heat gain into the building. The annual energy consumption has reduced by 19MWh (9.5 per cent) (rooftop covered by 100 per cent turfing) to 29MWh (19.5 per cent) (rooftop covered by 100 per cent shrubs) for the five-storey commercial building. The space cooling loads reduced by 92.94MWh (47.1 per cent) (rooftop covered by 100 per cent turfing) to 155.85MWh (79 per cent) (rooftop covered by 100 per cent shrubs), and the peak space cooling load reduced by 43.1kWh (46.9 per cent) (rooftop covered by 100 per cent turfing) to 72.48kWh (78.9 per cent) (rooftop covered by 100 per cent shrubs). The reductions in the annual energy consumption with the installation of the rooftop gardens on an exposed rooftop imply that the overall running cost of the building will decrease.

The comparison between the typical flat roof and rooftop gardens (the typical flat roof as base case) revealed that the installation of the rooftop garden on a typical flat roof also reduced the heat gain into the building, but the reductions were less significant than those caused by the installation of a rooftop garden on

the exposed roof. The annual energy consumption can be reduced by 1MWh (0.6 per cent) (rooftop covered by 100 per cent turfing) to 3MWh (1.8 per cent) (rooftop covered by 100 per cent shrubs) for the five-storey commercial building. The space cooling loads can be reduced by 7.91MWh (17.0 per cent) (rooftop covered by 100 per cent turfing) to 21.86MWh (47.1 per cent) (rooftop covered by 100 per cent shrubs), and the peak space cooling load can be reduced by 3.69kWh (17.0 per cent) (rooftop covered by 100 per cent turfing) to 12.66kWh (58.2 per cent) (rooftop covered by 100 per cent shrubs).

The simulated results revealed that although installation of vegetation on the exposed roof and the typical flat roof would both result in the reduction of heat gain into the five-storey commercial building, the reductions caused by a rooftop garden on the exposed roof (the exposed roof as base case) were more significant than those on the typical flat roof (the typical flat roof as base case). The results also show that for the comparison of the three types of vegetation, shrubs have the most significant reduction of heat gain into the building, while turfing experiences the least reduction. This might be due to the higher value of the leaf area index (LAI) of shrubs and the relatively lower LAI value of turfing.

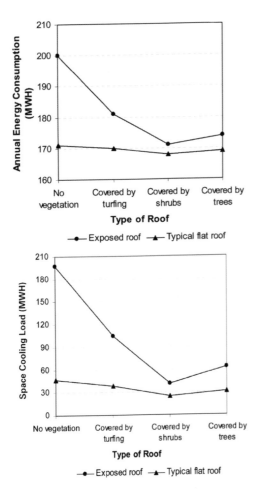

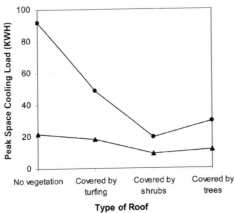

Source: Author

Figure 16.26 *Comparison of annual energy consumption, space cooling load component and peak space cooling load component for different types of roofs for a five-storey commercial building*

Extensive rooftop garden

To explore the thermal impacts of four extensive rooftop greenery systems, a before measurement and an after measurement was carried out in a multi-storey car park in a housing estate (see Figure 16.27). The rooftop of the multi-storey car park was divided into four equivalent areas named as G1, G2, G3 and G4. They were subsequently planted with four different and extensive systems.

The surface temperatures were measured on an exposed rooftop and on the same locations subsequently covered by different extensive systems. Surface temperatures measured on G4 were used to interpret the thermal condition (see Figure 16.28). A maximum of over 18°C of surface temperature decrease was observed at around 2.00 pm.

The surface temperatures of the different substrates (soil) and the exposed surface were compared as well (see Figure 16.29). The maximum difference in surface temperature between exposed surface and substrate surface was around 20°C, which was observed in G3. The obvious benefit of implementing rooftop greening is the thermal protection provided by the holistic system to the building. Heat flux through the roof slab *before* and *after* was calculated with reference to surface temperatures and the thermal characteristics of the structure (see Table 16.1). Heat gain refers to the heat transfer from above the slab to below the slab, while heat loss is the reverse process. It is clear that overall heat gain through the slab is greatly reduced due to the installation of extensive systems. G3 performs very well in terms of preventing heat gain. Over 60 per cent of heat gain can be reduced. In terms of thermal protection provided by vegetation, G3 is not the best case. The combined effect of the whole system, especially the green roof system, results in less heat transferred through the system.

In order to visually compare the performances of four systems, a group of infrared pictures was taken (see Figure 16.30). The difference between G1 and G3 can easily be observed from Figure 16.30. In general, the surface temperatures of G3 were lower than those of G1. However, high surface temperatures could still be observed at some locations where the substrate was exposed. The maximum temperature difference between the well-planted area and the exposed substrate in G3 could be up to 20°C. G1 was covered by clusters of shrubs and the substrate was not well

Source: Author

Figure 16.27 *The multi-storey car park without (left) and with (right) an extensive rooftop system*

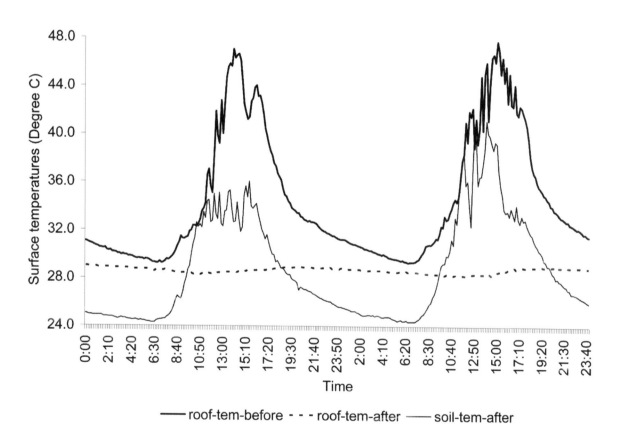

Source: Author

Figure 16.28 *Comparison of surface temperatures measured on G4 during the rainy period*

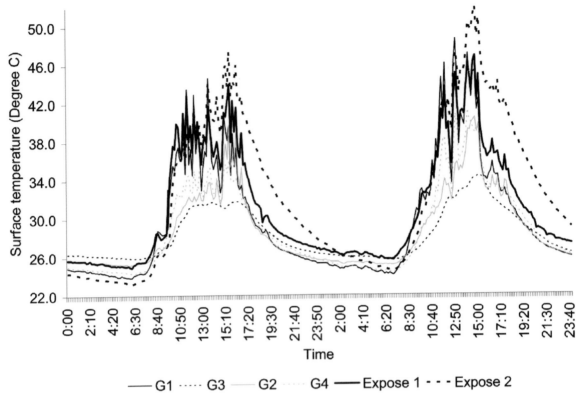

Source: Author

Figure 16.29 *Comparison of substrate surface temperatures with exposed surface temperatures*

covered at some locations where a higher surface temperature was also experienced. The differences between G2 and G4 can be observed in Figure 16.31. G2 was better than G4 in terms of greenery coverage. Therefore, surface temperatures observed in G2 were relatively lower. On the other hand, high surface temperatures were observed in G4 since it was mostly exposed and the substrate colour was dark. The visual comparisons of four roof systems indicate that the coverage of greenery plays an important role in

Table 16.1 *Comparison of total heat gain/loss over a clear day (22 February 2004) on the rooftop, before and after*

Location	Total heat gain/m² over a day (KJ)	Total heat loss/m² over a day (KJ)
G1 before	1681.8	0
G1 after	1072.0	301.8
G3 before	2638.9	0
G3 after	864.6	213.1
G2 before	2079.1	0
G2 after	1335.7	1.2
G4 before	2117.0	0
G4 after	864.5	561.7
The thickness of the concrete slab is 250mm and its R value is calculated to be 0.17m² K/W		

Source: Author

Source: Author

Figure 16.30 *Comparison of G1 and G3 (1 April 2004)*

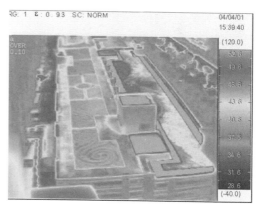

Source: Author

Figure 16.31 *Comparison of G2 and G4 (1 April 2004)*

achieving good thermal performance. Lower surface temperature was observed where extensive greenery was presented. On the other hand, systems with substrates exposed to strong sunshine may incur high surface temperatures and experience worse thermal conditions during the daytime. Occasionally the surface temperature of exposed substrate was even higher than the exposed concrete surface.

Another measurement was carried out on a metal roof with the extensive rooftop system. Surface temperatures were measured on the exposed metal surface as well as under different types of plants (see Figure 16.32).

First, the surface temperatures obtained on the green metal roof measurement were analysed in a long-term run (see Figure 16.33). The effect of LAI values on the surface temperature fluctuation can be clearly

noted from the variations observed from dense plants, sparse plants and weed. The mean surface temperatures ranged from 27.1°C to 30.4°C and the standard deviations ranged from 1.4 to 3.5. The benefits of reducing the surface temperature by greenery can also be observed from mean surface temperature differences between the hard metal surface and those below the plants. They are 4.7°C, 1.9°C and 1.4°C with the presence of the dense plants, the sparse plants and the weeds, respectively. The benefits of greenery are also reflected in preventing the surface temperature from fluctuating. Without plants, the metal surface can be up to 60°C to 70°C during the daytime (observed from the high whisker of the hard surface) and lower than 20°C at night (observed from the low whisker of the

Source: Author

Figure 16.32 *Exposed metal surface and three types of plants measured on the metal roof*

hard surface). Even the 50 per cent observations are distributed between 23°C to 39°C. With plants, the maximum surface temperature observed below the dense plants is around 32°C and the minimum one is around 24°C. To further uncover the pattern during the daytime, a long-term analysis was carried out based on the data derived during the daytime (from 7.00 am to 7.00 pm; see Figure 16.34). A significant increase in terms of the mean surface temperatures can be observed on the hard surface – up to 7.8°C, while only a 0.3°C to 1.6°C increase was observed under the plants. This indicates that the exposed metal roof had experienced high surface temperatures during the daytime. Subsequently, the observation has been zoomed into a clear day when the performance of plants can be easily found (see Figure 16.35). It can be observed that the surface temperatures of the exposed mental roof are very sensitive to solar radiation.

The solar radiation profiles were followed during the daytime. The peak value was around 60°C, which was observed at 12.30 pm when solar radiation also reaches its peak value. The maximum difference between the surface temperatures of the exposed metal roof and below the dense plants is 35.1°C during the daytime. At night, the inverse situation occurred and the surface temperatures of the exposed metal roof dropped dramatically. These temperatures are lower than all temperatures measured below the rooftop greenery. The maximum surface temperature difference between the exposed metal roof and the dense plants is 4.74°C at night. A comparison of surface temperatures measured on the metal roof was also conducted on a cloudy day (see Figure 16.36). Differences can still be observed during the daytime. The surface temperatures of the exposed metal roof can be very low with the decrease of solar radiation during the daytime. But they are still higher than those measured under the dense plants. A maximum temperature difference of nearly 5°C can still be detected between the dense plants and the other plants and the hard surface during the daytime.

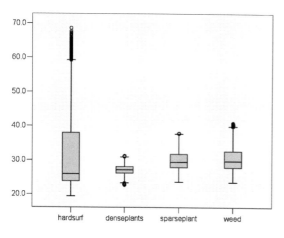

	Hard surface	Dense plants	Sparse plants	Weed
Mean	31.8°C	27.1°C	29.9°C	30.4°C
Standard Deviation	11.6	1.4	2.8	3.5

Source: Author

Figure 16.33 *Long-term analysis of the surface temperatures measured above the green metal roof*

Vertical landscaping

Building façades are also vulnerable to the strong incident radiation in tropical climates. High surface temperatures can be observed and, subsequently, heat can find its way inside buildings, increasing cooling energy consumption. Vertical landscaping is a passive way of solving this problem. Unfortunately, the thermal benefit of vertical landscaping has not been commonly recognized and its implementation is still at the preliminary stage. In order to explore the shading effect of plants on façades, some pilot measurements have been carried out on several low-rise buildings where trees are planted close to the façades. Trees planted along the eastern orientation of a factory (named F2) were measured and compared with a factory (named F1) without any protection from trees (see Figure 16.37). The colour of the measured factories is light grey.

The comparison of the external and the internal surface temperatures measured on the façades of the two factories can be found in Figures 16.38 and 16.39. Generally, the surface temperatures measured on the

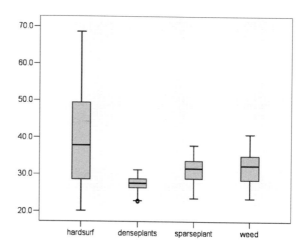

	Hard surface	Dense plants	Sparse plants	Weed
Mean	39.6°C	27.5°C	31.2°C	32.0°C
Standard Deviation	11.9	1.6	3.1	4.0

Source: Author

Figure 16.34 *Long-term analysis of the surface temperatures measured above the green metal roof (excluding night-time) from 7.00 am to 7.00 pm*

external walls of F2 were lower than those on the external walls of F1 (tree-shading effect). The differences were around 1°C to 2°C at night and around 4°C to 8°C during the daytime. It seems that internal temperatures also reflect the variation of external temperatures. The evidence is that F2 had lower internal surface temperatures than those of F1 by around 2°C all day long. It is worth noting that the surface temperature difference was very significant during the morning (due to the tree-shading effect).

Another two factories with and without trees planted at western orientations were also measured (see Figure 16.40). The façade colour for the two factories is dark blue.

A long-term comparison of the temperature variations with and without trees is presented in Figure 16.41. The outstanding shading effect of trees can be reflected by a narrow span of temperature variation. It can be observed that the reduction occurs mainly at the maximum whiskers, which should be detected during the daytime when solar radiation is strong. The trees

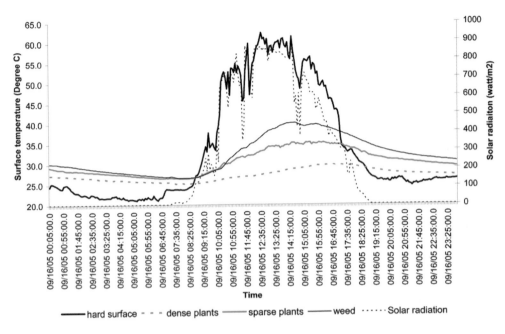

Source: Author

Figure 16.35 *Comparison of surface temperatures measured on the green metal roof on a clear day (16 September 2005)*

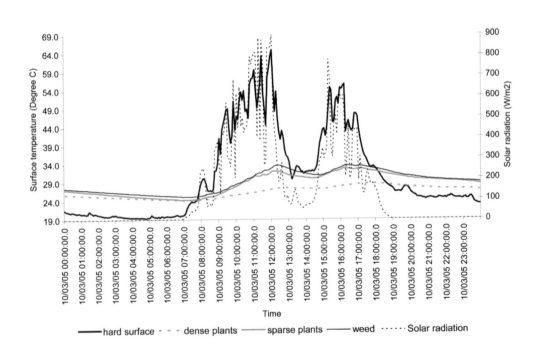

Source: Author

Figure 16.36 *Comparison of surface temperatures measured on the green metal roof on a cloudy day (3 October 2005)*

Source: Author

Figure 16.37 *The two factories involved in the measurements in Changi South Street 1*

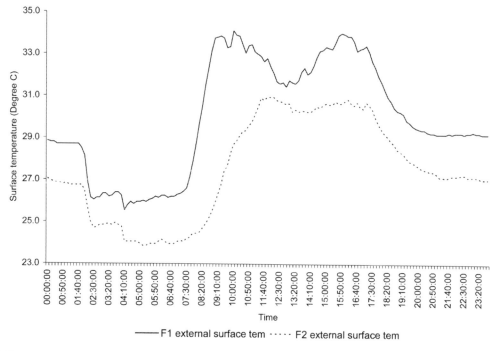

Source: Author

Figure 16.38 *Comparison of surface temperatures measured on the external walls of F1 and F2 on a clear day (20 July 2005)*

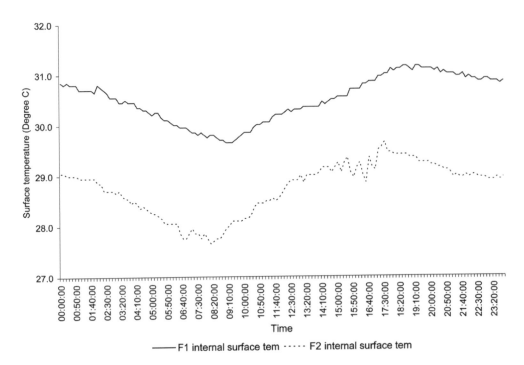

Source: Author

Figure 16.39 *Comparison of surface temperatures measured on the internal walls of F1 and F2 on a clear day (20 July 2005)*

Source: Author

Figure 16.40 *The two factories involved in the measurements in Woodlands Link*

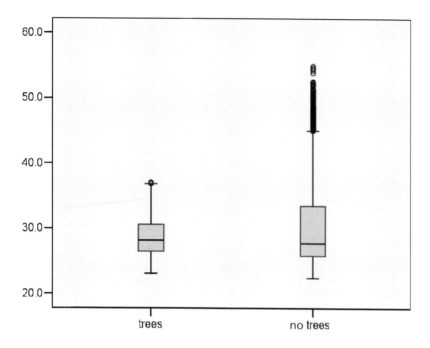

Source: Author

Figure 16.41 *A long-term comparison of the surface temperature variations with and without trees from 21 September to 7 December*

can effectively intercept the incident solar radiation and generate a lower surface temperature behind them on the façade. On the other hand, no significant difference can be observed between the two minimum whiskers. This indicates that the impacts caused by trees at night are not obvious. The mean surface temperature derived behind the trees is 28.7°C, while that obtained from the exposed façade is 30.1°C.

In order to have a close look at the performance of the trees in reducing the surface temperatures along the western orientation, two days were selected. Figure 16.42 shows a comparison made on a relatively clear day. The shading effect caused by trees over the western orientation can easily be observed during the daytime. Due to the effect of orientation, there is a time lag between the peak solar radiation and the peak external surface temperatures measured on the western façades. The maximum temperature difference can be up to 13.6°C at around 3.30 pm. Figure 16.43 shows a comparison made on a relatively overcast day. Without

much direct radiation, the shading effect of trees is mainly reflected in reducing the diffused radiation on the spot. A temperature difference of 7°C can still be observed at around 3.50 pm. This finding highlights that the impact of vertical shading upon building façades is not only reflected during clear days, but also during overcast conditions. On the other hand, the surface temperatures are inversely distributed at night compared with those observed during the daytime. The difference is constantly around 2°C. Without the blockage of foliage, the heat can be easily dissipated by the exposed façade to the surroundings. Compared with the significant reduction of surface temperatures during the daytime, the limitations that occur at night can be ignored.

Decreased surface temperatures on buildings can reduce cooling energy consumption in buildings. In order to explore the energy saving impacts of strategically introduced plants around the factory, simulations were carried out by TAS. Five cases overall

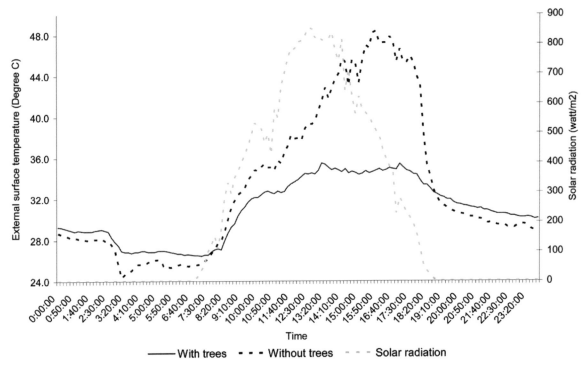

Figure 16.42 *Comparison of solar radiation and surface temperatures measured with and without shading from trees on 1 November 2005*

were simulated. Case 1 is the bare factory without any protection from plants. Case 2 has tree shading at both the eastern and the western façades. Case 3 has an extensive rooftop garden system. Case 4 has both tree shading along the unfavourable orientations and an extensive rooftop garden on the roof. Case 5 is actually case 4 placed in the best scenario in the first round of simulations (with very extensive road trees).

The impacts from plants at the different locations were translated into the equivalent thermal resistance values (R values), which were estimated and calculated with the results derived from the above measurements. The model for the different cases was modified by changing the R values at the different locations.

Figure 16.44 shows the results of cooling energy consumption in the factory. In general, there is an impressive reduction of energy consumption when different strategies are applied to the building. With tree shading along the unfavoured orientations (east and west), 10 per cent cooling energy can be saved. Another 18 per cent energy can be saved with an extensive rooftop greenery system on the metal roof. The combined strategic introduction of plants on unfavoured façades as well as a metal roof can result in an overall 28 per cent energy saving. Finally, with additional help from extensive trees at the macro-level, 48 per cent energy can be saved. It is encouraging that nearly half of the cooling energy can be saved with the help of plants at different levels.

Summary

From the above measurements and simulations, it can be concluded that strategically placed plants can also reduce higher surface temperatures experienced on buildings' roofs and façades. This is an indirect way to

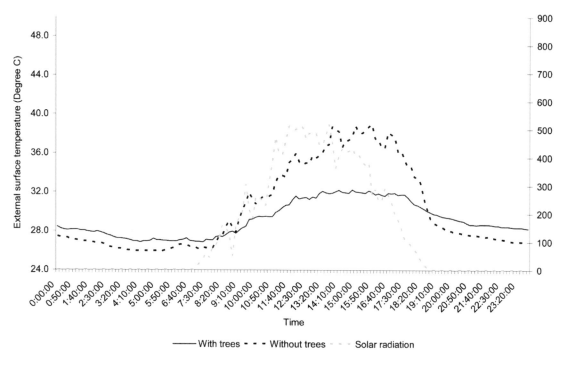

Figure 16.43 *Comparison of solar radiation and surface temperatures measured with and without shading from trees on 15 November 2005*

mitigate the UHI effect. High surface temperature directly associates with high ambient temperature during the daytime and indirectly links with high ambient temperature at night when heat absorbed by buildings release long-wave radiation to their surroundings. Meanwhile, high surface temperature is always the major concern for cooling energy consumption and thermal comfort in every individual building. It is obvious that surface temperature can be reduced by rooftop gardens and vertical landscaping at the micro-level. Therefore, mitigating the UHI by reducing surface temperature mainly relies on the greening of individual buildings.

Challenges in incorporating urban greenery in high-density cities

In high-density cities, land scarcity becomes a reality and there is very little provision of space for the incorporation of urban greenery such as urban parks and landscaping. The integration of urban greenery with buildings also faces many constraints. For example, the provision of rooftop gardens in super-tall skyscrapers would mean that the area that could be covered by greenery is fairly limited. Ways of increasing the greenery coverage include the provision of intermediate sky gardens and vertical green walls.

Compared with green roofs, vertically arranged greenery can probably cover more exposed hard surfaces in a dense urban environment when high-rise buildings are predominant. Ken Yeang (1996) believes that:

This will significantly contribute towards the greening of the environment if a skyscraper has a plant ratio of one to seven, then the façade area is equivalent to almost three times the site area. So if you cover, let's say, even two-thirds of the façade you have already contributed towards doubling the extent of vegetation on the site. So, in fact, a skyscraper can become green. And if you green it, you're actually increasing the organic mass on the site.

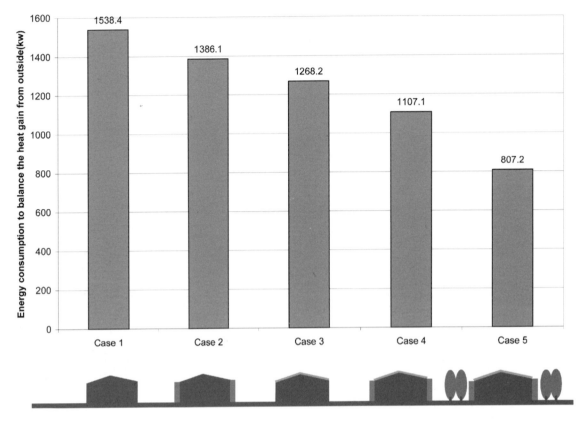

Source: Author

Figure 16.44 *Comparison of cooling energy consumption to balance the heat gain from outside for a factory*

Plants introduced vertically into buildings are not a new concept. However, strategically introducing plants into building façades is still a challenge due to the lack of research and development in the area.

According to species of plants, types of growing media and construction method, vertical green walls can be simply divided into three major categories as wall-climbing type, hanging-down type and module type (see Table 16.2). The wall-climbing type is a very common vertical landscaping method (see Figure 16.45). Climbing plants can cover the walls of buildings naturally (time consuming) or they can grow up with the help of a trellis or other supporting systems. The hanging-down type (see Figure 14.46) is a popular vertical landscaping method – it is a quick way to green whole façades of buildings since plants can be planted at every storey to make a complete green wall. Finally,

the module type (see Figure 16.47) is a fairly new concept compared with the previous three types. More complicated designs and considerations are necessary to set up and maintain such a system. In terms of cost, it is probably the most expensive method among the four types.

The incorporation of vertical green walls poses some major integration issues with the other building systems such as the envelope, interior, mechanical and structural systems, and these walls may have serious impacts upon building performance.

Vertical green walls can be integrated as an unseparated part of the envelope system. The thermal performance is strongly influenced by the arrangement of vertical planting and the characteristics of plants. Eastern and western orientations featuring solar protection through vegetation are necessary since the

Table 16.2 *Comparison of four types of vertical landscaping methods*

Type	Plants	Growing media	Construction type
Tree-against-wall type	Trees	Soil on the ground	No supporting structure
Wall-climbing type	Climbing plants	Soil on the ground or planted box	Supporting structure needed sometimes
Hanging-down type	Plants with long hanging-down stems	planted box	Supporting structure needed sometimes
Module type	Short plants	Light-weight panel of growing media (such as compressed peat moss)	Supporting structure needed

Source: Author

Source: Author

Figure 16.45 *Wall-climbing type on a hotel (left: natural style) and on an office building (right: artificial style), Singapore*

solar radiation is particularly strong during early morning and late afternoon, respectively. Plants used for the interception of solar radiation depend upon their leaf area index (the total area of leaves per unit area). Dense foliage and multiple layers (higher LAI) can obstruct solar radiation, while open and sparse foliage (lower LAI) can filter part of the incoming solar radiation. On the other hand, moisture produced by plants will influence the indoor thermal environment. For a dry climate, an indoor environment with a higher humidity could be obtained through planting vegetation near windows and openings. For a humid climate, on

Source: Author

Figure 16.46 *Hanging-down type on a car park (left) and on a university building (right), Singapore*

Source: Author

Figure 16.47 *Module-type outside hoarding (left) and on a university building (right), Singapore*

the other hand, higher humidity should be avoided through planting vegetation away from windows/openings and encouraging natural ventilation. The position of vertical planting will also significantly influence visual performance. The opaque part of the façade, like the solid wall, is the place where vegetation can be simply planted mainly for solar control and amenity. But the transparent part of the façade, like windows and openings, are the places where plants should be carefully placed to avoid the blockage of daylight and ventilation, and simultaneously promote solar and glare control. The possible solution to such an approach can be overhanging and vertical fin-like planting.

The integration of a vertical landscape and envelope system will also influence spatial performance. Some usable space will be occupied by supporting structures, rooting materials, maintenance systems and plants (see Figure 16.48). Therefore, proper design of a vertical landscape is the key to best support the needs of activities expected by users.

Figure 16.48 *The terrace occupied by vertical landscape*

The vertical green wall is primarily an envelope/structure combination. The structure system bears the load caused by vertical planting (rooting materials and plants). The integration issue here is to ensure structural strength and stability as well as safety. Ensuring that vertical planting is not structurally dangerous for inhabitants is crucial for tall buildings since a successful supporting structure for a vertical landscape should consider both dead loads and wind loads. The structural design should make use of the radiation protection provided by plants and simultaneously prevent the possible damage caused by the roots of plants. The integration of vertical landscape and structure can contribute to the spatial performance through forming green space for users' activities. Such an arrangement of a 'garden in the air' provides users who live in the upper part of tall buildings an opportunity to access nature.

Successful maintenance is crucial for vertical landscape due to the high degree of exposure and the limited soil depth (Yeang, 1996, p106). For tall buildings, irrigation of the vertical landscape will mostly depend upon the mechanical system. Nutrients and water can be transported through an integrated system of pipes and drains. An innovative example is a 'vertical swamp' by fixing rows of swamp grasses in planters down the vertical sides of a building. Irrigation is completed though a system of pipes and drains. Water is released from the top planter and is subsequently filtered through successive layers of grasses.

Thermal performance and indoor air quality may be influenced by the integration of a vertical landscape and mechanical system. The condensers of air conditioners exposed vertically can be shaded by the vertical landscape; therefore, less energy use for cooling and a better indoor thermal environment may be achieved. Indoor air quality will be enhanced when the combination of vertical landscape and the fresh air inlet appears on the vertical façade. A vertical landscape contributes to indoor air quality through generating oxygen and filtering air pollutants around the fresh air inlet. However, care must be taken to ensure that pollen from the plants is not introduced into the indoor spaces via the air-conditioning systems.

The relationship between vertical planting and interior system will influence thermal, visual and acoustical performance and indoor air quality. Performance needs significantly depend upon the placement of vertical planting and the layout of the interior space. The integration of vertical landscape and interior system must solve the direct demands that people make on the building and provide comfort in supporting human activities. Therefore, the design of vertical planting should respect the functional use of interior space. For example, the application of a vertical landscape should pay attention to less blockage of wind flow near windows and openings outside a naturally ventilated room; the placement of plants should avoid blocking daylight but prevent glare near windows, while enhancing the aesthetic environment in an office; extensive solar protection of vertical planting should be applied to a room with a large area of exterior walls, such as theatres and seminar room, for more cooling energy conservation.

The interior system can also be more closely linked with a vertical landscape when plants are introduced into interior spaces. The continuous greening of both exterior and interior spaces will bring many related benefits to occupants who live here that are far beyond the influence of the conventional landscape on the ground.

It is obvious that the application of vertical green walls will have significant impacts upon all four systems. Therefore, a conscious integration approach is crucial at the early stage of tall building design. Since the vertical green wall is not yet a mature technology, more research should be conducted in this area. Cooperation among architects, engineers, botanists and other professionals is also the key for a successful vertical landscape project.

References

Chen, Y. and Wong, N. H. (2005) 'The intervention of plants in the conflict between building and climate in the tropical climate', in *Proceedings of Sustainable Building 2005,* Tokyo, Japan

Chen, Y. and Wong, N. H. (2006) 'Thermal benefits of city parks*', Energy and Buildings*, vol 38, pp105–120

Howard, L. (1833) *The Climate of London*, vols I–III, London

Landsberg, H. E. (1981) *The Urban Climate*, Academic Press, New York, NY

Lesiuk, S. (2000) '*Biotecture II: Plant–building interaction*', http://forests.org/ric/good_wood/biotctll.htm, accessed September 2000

Nichol, J. E. (1996) 'High-resolution surface temperature related to urban morphology in a tropical city: A satellite-based study', *Journal of Applied Meteorology*, vol 35, pp135–146

Santamouris, M. (ed) (2001) *Energy and Climate in the Urban Built Environment*, James and James Science Publishers, London

Tso, C. P. (1996) 'A survey of urban heat island studies in two tropical cities', *Atmospheric Environment*, vol 30, pp507–519

Wong, N. H., Wong, V. L. Chen, Y., Lee, S.E., Cheong, K. W., Lim, G. T., Ong, C. L. and Sia, A. (2002) 'The thermal effects of plants on buildings', *Architectural Science Review*, vol 45, pp1–12

Wong, N. H. Chen, Y., Ong, C. L. and Sia, A. (2003) 'Investigation of thermal benefits of rooftop garden in the tropical environment', *Building and Environment*, vol 38, pp261–270

Yeang, K. (1996) *The Skyscraper: Bioclimatically Considered*, Academy Editions, London

17

Energy in High-Density Cities

Adrian Pitts

Introduction

There can be no doubt that the future energy prospects for the planet offer something very different from that which has developed over the last 200 years and its extreme reliance on fossil fuels. This change will be forced by an increasing scarcity of supplies to meet an increasing demand scenario, and by restrictions on use that are being introduced in an attempt to mitigate the effects of carbon dioxide-induced global climate change. The current fossil-fuel era should thus be viewed as a transient stage of human and, indeed, architectural, history. This chapter deals with both energy supply and with energy use associated with buildings, and what the future may hold.

The world's population is becoming increasingly urbanized and pressure for high-density living is enormous in some parts of the globe. In high-density cities apartment blocks of 40 storeys in height or more are common with perhaps 8 to 12, or even 16, apartments per floor, and a population in a single block equivalent to a rural area village. This kind of urban development concentrates resource use in small land areas and suggests a reliance on certain types of energy that can be delivered to such a concentrated area. The situation for high-density cities presents opportunities and difficulties, and careful planning, regulation and encouragement will be needed to address the issues in an optimum manner. Hui (2001) has previously analysed the positive and negative effects of urban density on energy demand and indicated that a variety of outcomes was possible. Chen et al (2008) have also recently detailed potential energy benefits as well as costs of compact cities. It is therefore essential to encourage and optimize positive benefits over negative impacts.

Clearly, human-induced climate change is a factor affecting many energy-related issues and this has been extensively investigated by the Intergovernmental Panel on Climate Change (IPCC). One of the most recent IPCC reports included a chapter that addressed mitigation measures associated with residential and commercial buildings (Levine et al, 2007). This concluded that carbon dioxide (CO_2) emissions from building energy use could be substantially reduced by using mature existing technologies, and that net benefits, rather than costs, could be clearly demonstrated using life-cycle analysis. Some pessimism was expressed, however, that although buildings offered significant opportunities, enhanced programmes and policies would be needed to encourage buildings towards a lower-carbon future. The need to take action is reinforced by some evidence that energy consumption in some of the newer, major dense urban areas is higher than elsewhere and increasing (Gao et al, 2004).

In the following sections a number of pertinent subjects will be discussed, commencing with energy demands and how these might be reduced or offset. Potential energy supply technologies will then be addressed, including a range of sources and how these can be better matched to demand. Some suggestions and recommendations regarding operation and systems optimization for high-density cities are then itemized.

Energy demand

Buildings are major consumers of energy and are often quoted as using between 40 and 50 per cent of all energy consumption in developed countries, and frequently even higher percentages of electrical energy. The major demands for a high-density city arise from the services (heating, cooling, lighting, air conditioning, electrical equipment, etc.) utilized in its buildings (residential and commercial), and from the transportation required for movement of people between buildings. Although high-density cities are spread around the globe, a majority exist between the tropics or in subtropical climates and thus have requirements more dominated by the provision of cooling than heating. As global warming develops, the demand for cooling will therefore be increasingly the major service requirement.

There are also major energy uses associated with the construction of buildings and for urban area industry and manufacturing; industrial energy use falls outside the remit of this chapter, however, as it is predicated on numerous external factors. Energy costs associated with building products, construction and infrastructure may actually be less in high-density cities because of more efficient use of those materials and systems that are installed (Chen et al, 2008). Transport issues are not dealt with here, although there is general agreement (see, for example, DETR, 1999) that high density leads to better utilization of public transport systems, which, in turn, become more efficient and more frequent, and thus reduce demand for energy-wasteful private transport. In the following sections, influences on demand and how they may be modified are considered and there are many points of linkage with other chapters in this book dealing with specific issues.

Heat island effects and density

The concentration of energy use in dense urban areas has long been known to produce increased temperatures – the so-called 'heat island effect'. Santamouris et al (2001) found that for the city of Athens the heat island effect could exceed a $10°C$ increase in summer ambient temperature. During winter periods the benefits of the higher temperatures are valuable in reducing heating demand (by up to 30 per cent). In summer periods the increased temperature will also have a consequential impact upon the efficiency of air-conditioning systems through reductions in coefficients of performance; however, not all studies have been so negative. Some findings (such as those of Stone and Rogers, 2001) indicated that lower density may increase radiant heat flows that contribute to heat island formation, although the city

with which they were concerned (Atlanta, US) cannot be said to have the extreme high densities of some in this text.

A further consideration is that in dense cities, the area of exposed surface for any single dwelling is likely to be small, resulting in lower envelope surface areas through which heat gains and losses could flow. The protection afforded by adjacent dwellings or office units would therefore tend to reduce energy demands providing that internal heat gains are not excessive in summer.

Passive design

Simple so-called 'passive' techniques for reducing energy requirements for heating, cooling, lighting and ventilation of buildings have been known for centuries, if not millennia. Historical evidence shows that the earliest builders/architects understood how to match their building to the climate; however, in modern times this connection seems to be less strong. The orientation of the building and its positioning within the site both have important impacts for solar radiation absorption and daylighting availability; there is also an impact upon natural ventilation potential. Many techniques exist to help optimize these aspects of design; but the parameters must be set for the location, and high-density cities present problems and restrictions on what may be achieved through site and orientation features alone.

Many texts have addressed the passive design of buildings in suitable formats for application, such as Smith and Pitts (1997), and further detailed studies have been performed by a number of authors such as Chrisomallidou (2001); it is not intended to repeat such detailed information here. For the particular case of high-rise apartments, Cheung et al (2005) computed comparisons of using alternatives for passive envelope design in the climate of Hong Kong and were able to determine a reduction in annual cooling load of up to 36.8 per cent and peak cooling load reduction of up to 31.4 per cent. This was arrived at by using combinations of improved thermal insulation and thermal mass, glazing type and size, shading, and wall colour.

As the use of computer simulation and prediction techniques becomes both more common and more accurate, passive measures are likely to be investigated in more detail in order to find optimum combinations of parameters to produce building envelopes optimized for heat, cooling and lighting energy use. In high-density cities the surface of the external envelope is a key feature and, at the very least, qualitative analyses are required to indicate optimum configurations for designers, with the main emphasis on envelope and glazing features.

Building envelope design

The building envelope is the prime mediator between internal and external environments incorporating impacts of glazing, shading and lighting admission for transparent components, and thermal insulation and thermal mass for opaque components.

The main environmental link between the interior and exterior of a building is provided by the window glazing – this element allows admission of solar heat gain (which can be used to provide or offset heating needs in cool seasons) and of natural daylight (which can reduce the need for energy use in artificial lighting and also reduce consequent internal heat gains). Glazing can, of course, also be the source of overheating itself and Niu (2004) identified this heat gain as the predominant issue for high-rise buildings with a clear need for appropriate shading. Cheung et al (2005) suggested the limiting of window areas and the incorporation of reflective coatings on glazing as a means of controlling heat gain in high-density cities.

Santamouris (2006) has reported on envelope design techniques that can be employed to reduce the impact of solar heat gain and also to reduce urban heat island effects. These include use of novel 'cool' coatings for key surfaces to produce less absorption, with indicative values of a 5°C lowering in temperature.

Cheung et al (2005) also incorporated the impacts of using additional thermal insulation and thermal mass into their computer-based study of energy use in high-rise apartments. An interesting finding was that maximum reduction in annual cooling demand arose with insulation added to the internal surface, whereas maximum reduction in peak demand occurred with insulation added to the outside of the wall. Different recommendations resulted depending upon whether the building was occupied or not during the daytime.

Construction techniques and materials choices can also be made in order to minimize embodied energy and environmental impacts.

Ventilation

Full air-conditioning systems are energy expensive and in recent years there has been encouragement to make more use of natural ventilation. Unfortunately, trends in cities seem to be leading to increased air conditioning rather than less, which may be the result of several factors particularly related to high-density cities. First, the high density may reduce wind speeds, thus diminishing the potential for natural ventilation; second, the height of buildings may mean that natural ventilation is variable and unpredictable – especially at higher levels; third, the density is also likely to increase noise and air pollution levels, which may inhibit occupants from opening windows (Niu, 2004); and, finally, the uniform arrangement of blocks may also hinder turbulence and reduce wind speeds that could aid natural ventilation (Santamouris et al, 2001). In all cases there is clearly a need to be more aware of ventilation potential and performance, and to design not only apartments and blocks with this in mind, but also whole city neighbourhoods. Airflows must be permitted across buildings and not just limited to one side – this will require some layout redesign.

A technique that has gained in popularity is the use of night-time ventilation when the air temperature is lower so as to precondition the fabric of the buildings for the following day. In such systems the role of thermal mass and its location is also important. To reduce temperatures further, ventilation air might be allowed to pass through underground ducts, or evaporative cooling systems might be incorporated within the airflow in certain climates. In high-density buildings such sophisticated airflow routes and systems may not be possible; but appropriate ventilation should certainly be matched to optimize performance.

A further influence related to ventilation concerns the availability of external spaces such as balconies for clothes drying: the sealed monotonous façades of some high-density blocks exclude such spaces, meaning that drying may take place indoors, with consequent increases in humidity levels (Niu, 2004).

Heating, ventilating and air-conditioning (HVAC) systems

Whatever the integration of passive measures within the design of a building, there are always likely to be times and conditions when artificial means of creating comfort are required through heating, ventilating and air-conditioning systems. As a matter of course, such systems should be chosen to be the most efficient available, and these might be sourced through renewable energy or specific types of supply systems discussed in later sections of this chapter. Centralized systems may well be preferred both to provide better control and optimum efficiency.

The tendency in many dense urban buildings is for the installation of individual split-system air-conditioning units that are unsightly, cause nuisance from condensate runoff, and are also less efficient than centralized systems (Niu, 2004). Perhaps a hybrid centrally sourced but individually operated system is required.

Mixed-mode systems that can take advantage of natural ventilation when external air temperature is suitable should also be incorporated within the design, with sealed fully air-conditioned buildings used sparingly if at all.

Controls and metering

A further area in which advantage of developments should be taken is that of smart metering and control systems. These have previously been associated with rather complex commercial buildings; but their use should be extended to the domestic scale where the combined impact over a large apartment block should permit economies and better understanding of performance. Smart controls are also a precursor to the wider use of renewable energy systems, which are naturally more variable in output and with greater needs for energy storage. The use of smart controls should permit better matching of supply and demand by predicting and shifting demand patterns where possible. It may be necessary for the systems to be outside the control of individual system users in order to achieve the best performance, and this may cause some difficulties in implementation.

Energy supply

Conventional fossil-fuel energy sources are likely to become increasingly scarce in the next ten years; even the head of one of the world's major oil companies was reported as being concerned that demand would outstrip supply by as early as 2015 (*Times* online, 2008).

This, along with pressures to reduce carbon dioxide emissions, means that alternatives must be sought, developed and exploited – in particular, renewable energy sources. A frequent problem, however, as will be stated below, is the lack of suitable space and surfaces in dense urban areas where such renewable systems can be installed. This arises from the relatively low energy density of renewables and the enormous demands created by cities. A further complication is posed by the mismatch between availability of the energy (with climate and weather variations) and the demand for use; this means more attention will need to be paid to energy storage systems and the means to adjust supply and use profiles. Boyle (2004) has outlined the details of all major renewable energy sources; an interesting discussion of some more speculative energy devices and options can be found in Smith (2007). Although it is unlikely that all of the possibilities will come to the market at price and availability to meet the needs of large-scale dense urban development, city planners and developers need to be aware of future potential and how the form and design of a city can affect its ability to embrace new energy sources.

Solar thermal energy

A number of options for supplying energy to buildings in dense urban areas exist, and solar thermal heat can be a component of passive heat gain, mentioned earlier. The thermal energy from the sun also offers opportunities for more active utilization for heating using flat-plate or evacuated tube collectors. Evacuated tubes are more expensive but able to produce higher temperatures at greater efficiency than their simpler flat counterparts. The main end-use for the energy derived from thermal collectors is in the provision of domestic hot water. Typically 3 square metres to 5 square metres of collector would be required for each dwelling to provide this service, along with some suitable heat storage system (such as a hot water cylinder). The costs of such systems have been found to be economic in a range of (but not all) locations and climates.

For the collection of sufficient energy to provide space heating for cool/cold climate buildings, much larger areas would be required and potentially much larger heat storage systems. Urban blocks in high-density cities have relatively small overall surface areas (such as the roof) on which to mount the collectors, and are very unlikely to be able to collect and store sufficient energy to meet the needs of the whole building. As a result, while solar thermal systems should be encouraged to be installed in apartment or office blocks, they will need to be supplemented by alternative systems to produce sufficient hot water for the total building needs. It is also difficult to conceive of circumstances where space heating could be provided by the surface areas available, except in very modest demand situations, and it is likely that money available to spend would be better invested in passive measures to reduce heating needs.

Should land outside the high-density city area be available, it is possible that a large-scale collector system could be installed, and warmed water transmitted to the city. There are some systems in existence, mainly in Northern Europe, in which a large collector area is used to provide heat to district heating schemes, but not on the scale suitable for a very high-density and populous major city. This would require substantial capital investment in the system and insulated pipework, as well as pumping systems, and is probably not practical at the present time.

A further type of solar thermal system in which the heat of the sun is concentrated or focused (using mirrored surfaces) to create higher temperatures offers the possibility of an energy source from which a power cycle, producing electricity, might operate. Such systems require not only high levels of solar radiation but also relatively constant levels, as might be found nearer to the equator and in clear sky conditions. Few sites except those on the edges of deserts are able to meet such requirements, and at present although this technology has been proven in pilot and modest-scale plants, it would not seem to offer what is needed for high-density cities.

Photovoltaics

Photovoltaic (PV) systems involve the production of electrical energy by direct conversion of the energy in daylight from the phenomenon known as the photovoltaic effect. PV devices have traditionally been constructed using silicon materials, and typical efficiencies for crystalline devices are in the range of 14 to 17 per cent (but less than half of this for cheaper amorphous cells). Specialist laboratory cells have been created with efficiencies of over 40 per cent; but their cost is many times that of cells viable for use in the built environment.

At present, costs – even for lower-efficiency systems – are still relatively high; however, much technical effort is being put into developing new forms of energy conversion (third and fourth generation devices), and economies of scale in production are being realized in some of the newer large-scale plants in places such as China. Systems are already seen as economically viable in remote off-grid locations where no other form of electrical energy is easily available, although such systems are generally on a small scale. Building-integrated photovoltaics are an area of current expansion, but are generally found in lower-density urban locations. In such circumstances interesting design effects are possible as well as energy production, and some of the costs can be offset by savings on conventional cladding materials.

A further difficulty in the use of PV in urban areas is that already mentioned in relation to other technologies: there is a lack of availability of suitable mounting surfaces of sufficient size and orientation, which also avoid over-shading by other buildings (a typical dwelling and its occupants would require 20 square metres or more of unobstructed and suitably located PV to meet energy needs). Such a requirement simply cannot be achieved in high-density environments; as a result it would be possible to derive only a small fraction of the electrical energy requirements. Nevertheless, it may be possible to introduce PV systems where they form an integral part of a façade design and/or where they may be used for provision of window shading; a full costing appraisal would be needed and decisions taken on a broader basis.

If suitable land was available away from the city, then a PV power station could feasibly be constructed with the intention of transmitting energy by power cables into the city. This would require substantial investment, and although there are some examples of city areas with large-scale PV systems, at present it seems unlikely that photovoltaics will provide a full and immediate answer to the energy needs of a high-density city at an affordable cost.

Wind energy

The number of wind turbines installed has increased rapidly in many countries during recent decades. The size of the largest turbines has been increasing; most wind farms now use individual turbines with outputs of the order of at least 1MW or 2MW, and the largest devices can now produce as much as 5MW or 6MW, with rotor blade diameters of 120m or more. Installation is generally at remote windy locations and rarely close to major urban centres; however, it is possible to transmit the power through electricity grid systems.

At the other end of the scale are much smaller devices with blades of 1m or so in diameter offering output in the range 300W to 1500W. These turbines have been postulated and promoted for use attached to buildings in many locations to provide domestic power when grid connected. A number of observers have expressed concern that many such devices are unsuited to urban locations because of the disruption to wind flow caused by nearby buildings and the consequent poor performance. This would indicate their use to be very limited within dense cities; even if placed on rooftops, they are likely to be able to produce only a small amount of the power needed by the whole multi-storey edifices to which they are attached. Medium-scale turbines on top of a city centre block may be more attractive from an energy point of view, but may raise many objections from residents (e.g. of noise and safety issues).

As a result of the above, the most likely scenario for incorporation of wind power is by generation some way distant from the city; this is both the most efficient and most economic way of accessing a power source that is already seen as cost effective in a number of countries. A valid criticism made of wind turbines is their variable output; however, if viewed as part of a larger integrated renewable energy grid-connected systems approach, their used is more justified. The question for dense cities is, therefore, whether a suitable location can be found close to the city for a wind farm of sufficient scale and wind resource, and if this energy source can be integrated with others to meet demand.

Biofuels and energy from waste

The Earth's biomass consists of the organic material of its flora and fauna; this undergoes a continuous process of regeneration mainly as a result of the solar energy that falls on the Earth's surface, permitting plant growth. This organic material can be used as an energy source and if the process is well managed it can be a totally renewable process. Throughout the planet's history, human beings have used biomass in the form of wood as a primary energy source; however, in many places the use has far exceeded the potential to replace it by new growth, with consequent effects, such as deforestation. In renewable biomass two main sources are available: cultivated fast-growing crops (such as willow, miscanthus and poplar) or the use of wastes from agricultural, industrial or human sources.

Renewable biomass sources have made important impacts in recent years; however, significant areas of land are required both for the cultivation of specific crops or associated with the agricultural industries producing wastes (such as from sugar cane, maize and other crops). Clearly the space for such does not exist within the boundaries of a high-density city and so reliance on such options could only be considered if there were considerable land areas available external but close to the city. Experience of the urbanization process would suggest, however, that such land is likely to be in danger of incorporation within the city and cannot be relied upon without definite planning action and consideration for delivery of energy to its end-use location (perhaps from grid-connected remote biomass power plants).

The further option is to utilize municipal wastes (the products of the city itself, as well as wastes of its human occupants) to produce energy. Wastes of certain types might be incinerated to produce heat and power, although there may be competition as to whether the most environmentally friendly option is to recycle materials (such as paper and some plastics) or to burn them. A full life-cycle analysis may be required in which the transport and other costs of removing/recycling materials is also taken into account. In any case, it is necessary to establish an efficient and effective system for collection of the material and this is something often poorly designed into rapidly urbanizing high-density cities. Some examples of fairly sophisticated systems have been produced, such as at the bo01 exhibition development in Malmö, Sweden (reported in Pitts, 2004).

Other human wastes, such as might be collected by an effective sewage system, and compostable organic wastes can also form the basis of decomposition to produce methane for burning as well as, ultimately, a material suitable as a land fertilizer. Again, however, waste, water and sewage systems may not be sufficiently well developed in high-density cities and so must be paid attention in order both to remove a potential environmental hazard as well as to derive an alternative energy source.

Hydropower, wave and tidal power

Hydropower has been well exploited in a number of locations around the world and through electricity transmission systems the energy can be delivered to major cities. There are still some locations in developing countries where further installations may be built and, thus, serve the needs of new high-density cities. Such development is not without cost, however, since valuable land may need to be flooded and whole communities displaced, as well as causing much damage to the natural environment. In recent years a number of controversial schemes have been enacted and it is important to have a balance to check if the overall impact is matched by benefits. Smaller-scale schemes may also be possible; but the micro-scale developments that are becoming common in rural communities will not transfer to a large urban scale. Important decisions must therefore be taken about whether hydropower schemes to supply major cities should go ahead.

Two other 'water-based' renewable energy technologies involve extracting energy from the movement and flow of water in the tides and ocean currents, and from wave energy. Tidal power schemes can have major environmental impacts, but may also offer significant predictable energy resource if suitable locations exist. Wave power may be seen as suitable for coastal cities. Cities where wave or tidal energy might be used are also likely to have ports for which the movement of shipping might impact upon the viability of projects.

Heat pumps (ground, air and water) and geothermal energy

Heat pumps are devices based on the same thermodynamic devices and processes as are present in refrigeration systems. They operate on the basis of a modest energy input (usually in the form of electricity to a compressor) to move heat between lower and higher temperatures. Thus, in air-conditioning systems they remove heat from a room and exhaust it to the exterior environment. The systems can be used in reverse to extract heat from the ambient environment and emit it inside a building when heating is required. These systems could be said to be air-sourced heat pumps linking, as they do, with the exterior air; similarly, systems which exchange heat with the ground or with water are ground- and water-source heat pumps, respectively, and these can be more effective due to the energy density of earth and water as compared to air.

Water-source pumps have been used for many years where a suitable water course such as a river is available; and ground-source heat pumps are becoming increasingly popular where the temperature stability a few metres below the Earth's surface can be used both as a source of heat in winter and cooling in summer. Clearly, a limitation will be the energy capacity of the material to which the heat pump is attached and many metres of underground pipework and/or deep borehole systems may be required in the ground or large heat exchanger areas in water courses. Both of these have potential in high-density cities, but need to be designed in conjunction with the city development. Additionally, since an energy source is required to power the system, efforts should be made to ensure that this is itself a renewable source; this can be electrical, but it is also possible to use heat absorption refrigeration cycles in suitable circumstances.

Geothermal energy systems are not the same as ground-source heat pumps, though they are often confused. True geothermal energy systems use heat rising to the Earth's surface from geological sources deep underground. Such energy is conveniently available only in certain locations around the world and is so site specific that it is not possible to examine it in detail here; suffice to say, if available in or near to major cities, such energy should be utilized.

District heating/cooling and combined heat and power (CHP) systems

In some countries regulations that influence energy supply are formulated at individual building or development level. When considering high-density developments, the most appropriate scale may be significantly larger with schemes for the provision of heating and cooling, and possibly linked to electrical energy production in combined heat and power systems. Such larger schemes have not only the potential for greater efficiency, but also potential to use fuels and sources (such as biomass) that would be impractical for individual dwellings in high-density cities. Combined heat and power systems are likely to increase in use significantly and may be operated off site by energy service companies (ESCos) as an efficient means of producing electricity for high-density living as well as heat. The possible question in this scenario arises from a need (in, perhaps, warmer climates more associated with high-density cities) to bring together matching heat and electricity demands to be met by such systems.

Nuclear power

An alternative energy source often grouped together with renewable energy is that of nuclear power. Current nuclear power stations use the fission of nuclear materials to generate heat from which electricity can be produced through a suitable fluid cycle. The apparently low carbon emissions from a nuclear power station in operation, together with the need to sustain power supplies in a post fossil-fuel period, are quoted as a justification for new development. Unfortunately, new nuclear plant is likely to be able to produce only a short respite since estimates of fissile material suggest between 40 to 85 years' availability at 2002 rates of consumption.

The goal of nuclear fusion appears some way off at present, and with both fusion and fission cases, although energy can be supplied to high-density cities, the co-location of power plant and city may result in concerns for safety. Nuclear power is certainly a supply option for high-density cities, but it is also the case that nuclear plants operate most efficiently when supplying base energy loads and are not very responsive to changes in demand; thus, there will remain a need for other complementary energy sources.

Energy storage systems

A key element in the development of energy sources of the future will be in the matching of supply to demand. This will be a particularly difficult task in systems with greater reliance on a number of variable renewable energy sources. As a result, sophisticated energy storage options will be needed. These will include devices such as fuel cells that are being developed to use renewable energy to generate hydrogen as a fuel store that can later be recombined to produce electricity; pumped hydroelectric schemes in which excess energy is used to pump water to a higher reservoir for later release and regeneration of power; flywheels and flow batteries for storage and reuse of energy in kinetic and chemical forms; and inter-seasonal, perhaps subterranean, thermal storage, whereby heat from summer can be stored for use in winter and coolth from winter stored for use in summer.

Options and opportunities for high-density cities

Some studies (Durney and Desai, 2004; Sullivan et al, 2006) of potential energy solutions for urban locations have suggested utilizing a range of energy supply and demand options. Some of this work has been driven by changes in UK-based regulations requiring developers to make better use of renewable energy and the aims embodied in the Code for Sustainable Homes (DCLG, 2006).

Taking an overall view of the opportunities and options, a range of measures might be considered for high-density cities that would include the following:

- city-wide planning of both regulations to control energy use, and also of installation of appropriate infrastructures for supply and demand management;
- implementation of all possible suitable passive building design measures to reduce energy requirements for heating, lighting and cooling to a minimum;
- connection to major large-scale off-site wind farms and use of medium-scale wind turbines within city boundaries, if appropriate;
- use of biomass- or gas-powered combined heat and power plants (sufficient to supply hot water and also electrical needs if wind is unavailable);
- installation of solar technologies, where possible, on building façades to provide a modest input to the supply base;
- use of heat pumps linked to inter-seasonal thermal storage;
- anaerobic digestion of waste materials to produce energy from wastes (methane);
- grid connection to other energy supply systems outside the city to allow for balancing of supply and demand;
- longer-term development of other renewables in conjunction with fuel cells.

Whatever options are chosen, it is clear that high-density cities face many challenges in terms of energy supply and demand and that appropriate steps will need to be incorporated with some degree of urgency if comfort and current lifestyles are to be maintained.

References

Boyle, G. (ed) (2004) *Renewable Energy*, Oxford University Press, Oxford, UK

Chen, H., Jia, B. and Lau, S. S. Y. (2008) 'Sustainable urban form for Chinese compact cities: Challenges of a rapid urbanized economy', *Habitat International*, vol 32, pp28–40

Cheung, C. K., Fuller, R. J. and Luther, M. B. (2005) 'Energy-efficient envelope design for high-rise apartments', *Energy and Buildings*, vol 37, pp37–48

Chrisomallidou, N. (2001) 'Guidelines for integrating energy conservation techniques in urban buildings', in M. Santamouris (ed) *Energy and Climate in the Urban Built Environment*, James and James Science Publishers, London, pp247–309

DCLG (Department for Communities and Local Government) (2006) *The Code for Sustainable Homes*, DCLG, UK

DETR (Department of Environment, Transport and the Regions) (1999) 'Towards an Urban Renaissance', in Lord Rogers of Riverside (ed) *Final Report of the Urban Task Force*, UK DETR and E & F N Spon, London

Durney, J. and Desai, P. (2004) *Z Squared: Enabling One Planet Living in the Thames Gateway*, Bioregional Development Group Report, London

Gao, W., Wang, X., Haifeng, L., Zhao, P., Ren, J. and Toshio, O. (2004) 'Living environment and energy consumption in cities of Yangtze Delta area', *Energy and Building*, vol 36, pp1241–1246

Hui, S. C. M. (2001) 'Low energy building design in high density urban cities', *Renewable Energy*, vol 24, pp627–640

Levine, M., Ürge-Vorsatz, D., Blok, K., Geng, L., Harvey, D., Lang, S., Levermore, G., Mongameli Mehlwana, A.,

Mirasgedis, S., Novikova, A., Rilling, J. and Yoshino, H. (2007) 'Residential and commercial building', in B. Metz, O. R. Davidson, P. R. Bosch, R. Dave and L. A. Meyer (eds) *Climate Change 2007: Mitigation, Contribution of Working Group III to the Fourth Assessment Report of the Intergovernmental Panel on Climate Change*, Cambridge University Press, Cambridge, UK, and New York, NY

Niu, J. (2004) 'Some significant environmental issues in high-rise residential building design in urban areas', *Energy and Buildings*, vol 36, pp1259–1263

Pitts, A. C. (2004) *Planning and Design Strategies for Sustainability and Profit*, Architectural Press, Oxford, UK

Santamouris, M. (2006) 'Natural techniques to improve indoor and outdoor comfort during the warm period – A review', in *Proceedings of NCEUB Conference Comfort and Energy Use in Buildings – Getting Them Right*, Windsor, April 2006

Santamouris, M., Papanikolaou, N., Livada, I., Koronakis, I., Georgakis, C., Argiriou, A. and Assimakopoulos, D. N. (2001) 'On the impact of urban climate on the energy consumption of buildings', *Solar Energy*, vol 70, no 3, pp201–216

Smith, P. F. (2007) *Sustainability at the Cutting Edge: Emerging Technologies for Low Energy Buildings*, Architectural Press, Oxford, UK

Smith, P. F. and Pitts, A. C. (1997) *Concepts in Practice: Energy – Building for the Third Millennium*, Batsford, London

Stone, B. Jr. and Rogers, M. O. (2001) 'Urban form and thermal efficiency: How the design of cities influences the urban heat island effect', *Journal of the American Planning Association*, vol 67, no 2, pp186–198

Sullivan, L., Mark, B. and Parnell, T. (2006) 'Lessons for the application of renewable energy technologies in high density urban locations', in *Proceedings of the PLEA2006 23rd Conference on Passive and Low Energy Architecture*, Geneva, Switzerland

Times online (2008) 'Shell chief fears oil shortage in seven years', *Times* online, 25 January 2008, http://business.timesonline.co.uk/tol/business/economics/wef/article3248484.ece, accessed February 2008

18

Environmental Assessment: Shifting Scales

Raymond J. Cole

Introduction

We live in a time of increased scientific understanding of human-induced stresses on natural systems, as well as unprecedented access to information about these impacts. But information is only a means to an end – it has to be interpreted and translated into effective decision-making, whether in the political realm or within the day-to-day activity of building design and construction. Indeed, how we choose to act on the current understanding of resource use and environmental degradation over the next decade or so will prove decisive in any rational transition towards sustainable patterns of living. Moreover, within the current context of rapid and widespread urbanization, it is equally critical to understand the implications of design decisions across a variety of scales – from individual buildings to whole cities. Although profound changes in the design of buildings and human settlement patterns are unlikely until there is a fundamental shift in societal values and expectations, two key mechanisms for improving building performance are regulation and voluntary market-based programmes.

The regulatory approach assumes that increased international attention and public concern surrounding environmental issues will translate into political intent. This will then manifest as more demanding environmental policy and, subsequently, as increasingly stringent environmental regulations. Legislation, if possible to enforce, has historically been viewed as the most appropriate means of combating acute, localized environmental transgressions, particularly if sufficient

information is available to formulate workable regulations, set targets and measure their effectiveness (Aggeri, 1999). Environmental standards and regulations related to buildings can be equally very effective; but they have historically only defined minimally acceptable level of performance and are not, therefore, normally a vehicle for encouraging high levels of performance. Moreover, regulation typically only covers specific environmental performance issues such as energy use or greenhouse gas reduction. That stated, recent developments in the UK with the introduction of the *Code for Sustainable Homes* (DCLG, 2006), point to the changing nature of building environmental regulations and their relationship to voluntary mechanisms. The code was prepared by the government in close working consultation with the Building Research Establishment (BRE) and the Construction Industry Research and Information Association (CIRIA), and became a mandatory requirement for all new homes in 2008. The code has a scoring system of six levels made up by achieving both the appropriate mandatory minimum standards for homes together with a proportion of the 'flexible' standards. A full assessment is a rating requirement across six key issues: energy efficiency/CO_2; water efficiency; surface water management; site waste management; household waste management; and use of materials. However, only the energy/CO_2 emissions criteria are mandatory, operating through phased changes to the building regulations with carbon neutral new houses mandated by 2016 (Banfill and Peacock, 2007). A similarly demanding requirement has been set for all new non-domestic buildings in the UK to be carbon neutral by 2019 and, of broader consequence, the European Parliament amended the 2002 Energy Performance of Buildings Directive to require that all buildings built after 31 December 2018 must be net-zero energy.

By far the most significant improvements in building environmental performance over the past decade have occurred through the introduction of voluntary building environmental assessment and labelling programmes that have significantly increased discussion and application of 'green' building practices. The primary objective of these mechanisms is to stimulate market demand for buildings with improved environmental performance. An underlying premise is that if the market is provided with improved information and mechanisms, discerning clients can and will provide leadership in environmental responsibility and others will follow suit to remain competitive.

A considerable amount of experience now exists regarding the development and use of voluntary assessment methods at the building level. Perhaps the most consistent issue is the reconciliation of providing a comprehensive, objective building assessment and the time, effort and cost involved in doing so. However, there is increasing interest in understanding environmental issues across a range of scales – from the building to the urban scale. This chapter examines the changing and expanding role of building environmental assessment methods within the context of sustainable urban development. The purpose here is not to critique the emerging parallel body of work that has evolved regarding environmental/sustainability assessment and development of indicators at the urban scale (Brandon, et al, 1997; Deakin, et al, 2002; Adinyira, et al, 2007). Rather, it is directed at identifying and exploring the ways in which the larger scale of the city provides a new and necessary context for rethinking scope and structure of building environmental assessment methods. The chapter subsequently considers how the characteristics of high-density urban situations create further consequences for the scope and emphasis of building environmental assessment methods.

Building environmental assessment methods

The term *building environmental assessment method* is used here to describe a technique that has building environmental assessment as one of its core functions, but which may be accompanied by third-party verification before issuing a performance rating or label, include reference to or use of a number of tools and supporting educational programmes for design professionals. The terms 'system' or 'scheme' are often used interchangeably with 'method'.

Building environmental assessment methods evaluate performance across a range of resource use, ecological loadings and indoor environmental quality criteria. They generally have recognizable 'frameworks' that organize or classify environmental performance criteria in a structured manner with assigned points or weightings. More importantly, assessment methods are managed by and operate within known organizational contexts – for example, the Building Research Establishment Environmental Assessment Method (BREEAM) is operated by the UK Building Research Establishment; the Leadership in Energy & Environmental Design (LEED®) rating system by the US Green Building Council. Although parts of an assessment method may be used selectively by design professionals at their discretion, full engagement of a method involves some form of registration or certification. This characteristic represents a critical distinction between assessment *tools* and assessment *methods* since the third-party verification and scrutiny invariably brings additional layers of constraints, bureaucracy and costs to the process (Cole, 2005).

There is little doubt that building environmental assessment methods have contributed enormously to furthering the promotion of higher environmental expectations and are directly and indirectly influencing the performance of buildings. Assessment methods have enjoyed considerable success and their widespread awareness has created the critical mass of interest necessary to cement their role in creating positive change. 'Success' is used here in reference to the adoption of assessment methods into the parlance of the building industry rather than to the number of actual 'assessed' or 'certified' projects, which are currently relatively low compared to the total volume of annual building construction. A number of factors have collectively generated the early success of assessment methods:

- The prior absence of any means to both discuss and evaluate building performance in a comprehensive way left open a distinct niche within an emerging 'culture of performance assessment'.

- The simple, seemingly straightforward declaration of the requirements of a limited number of performance measures presented a complex set of issues in a manageable form. This was attractive to the building industry that is risk averse and prefers simple, unambiguous messages regarding what to do rather than why it should be done. By offering a recognizable structure for environmental issues, assessment methods have provided a focus for the debate on building environmental performance.
- Public-sector building agencies have used them as a means of demonstrating commitment to emerging environmental policies and directives, and declare an industry expectation of what constitutes 'green' building design and construction.
- Manufacturers of 'green' building materials and products have been given the opportunity to make direct and indirect associations with the relevant performance criteria.

The 'success' of building environmental assessment methods has dwarfed all other mechanisms for instilling environmental issues within the building industry. Indeed, they are increasingly positioned not only as the most potent mechanism for affecting change, but, seemingly and unfortunately, as the sole focus of the current building–environmental debate.

The structure and organization of performance issues in current assessment methods is premised on them being used for individual buildings and acting autonomously. It is increasingly understood that single tools cannot be expected to serve all the different conditions and requirements needed to infuse sustainability considerations into the market. Indeed, a meaningful infusion of sustainability thinking into the building process cannot, as Kaatz et al (2004) suggest, be effectively achieved through stand-alone methods and tools, and *ad hoc* assessments. As such, the relationship between an assessment method and other complementary mechanisms assumes considerable importance. While the current generation of assessment methods are being expected to fulfil multiple roles and, to an extent, being quite successful in doing so, it remains uncertain whether they can retain this potency as the field further matures (Cole, 2006). Indeed, as the urgency of addressing climate change becomes a greater political issue, clarifying the complementary nature of regulatory and voluntary mechanisms will become equally important. Moreover,

in the context of this chapter, the ways and extent that building environmental assessment methods dovetail with their counterparts to evaluate sustainability issues at the community and city scale will prove critical in formulating comprehensive approaches to design and planning.

Building environmental assessment methods have provided definitions of 'green building' and associated best practice. But change occurs through the use of such tools, raising a host of questions regarding the demands that they make, the challenging of norms, the acquisition of new knowledge and skills, and, more broadly, how they affect the culture of all those responsible for delivering buildings. Again, by bridging cross-scale, assessment methods offer the potential to enhance dialogue between a broader range of stakeholders associated with building, community and city planning.

Life-cycle assessment methods

The notion of *life-cycle assessment* (LCA) has been generally accepted within the environmental research community as the only legitimate basis on which to compare alternative materials, components and services. Applied to buildings, life-cycle assessment encompasses the analysis and assessment of the environmental impact of building materials, components and assemblies throughout the entire life of the building construction, use and demolition.

The life cycle of buildings is more complex than that of other products in that it involves the aggregate effects of a host of life cycles of their constituent materials, components, assemblies and systems. The full life-cycle environmental impacts of building materials and components can be broken down into distinct phases: first, the detailed assessment of the acquisition and production impacts and resource use; second, the impacts and resource use throughout the useful life of the completed building; and, finally, the demolition and disposal impacts. Whereas the first is specific to the material, component or assembly alone, the second and third are specific to a material, component or assembly *and* their application within the context of a specific design. Detailed life-cycle analyses often only embrace the more general first phase and make relatively scant reference to the latter phases.

Life-cycle assessment tools currently exist alongside building environmental assessment methods. A recurring debate is how and to what extent LCA tools should be more *integral* to the building environmental assessment methods. This occurs in two distinct ways:

1   Using LCA-based environmental assessment tools such as the *Athena Environmental Impact Estimator* (developed by the Canadian Athena Sustainable Materials Institute) and *Envest* (developed by the UK BRE) as the basis of evaluating materials, components or assemblies or other strategic options and generating ranked data sets. Assessment methods give credit for selecting highly ranked products or assemblies from these pre-rated lists based on LCA environmental profiles provided by these tools (e.g. BREEAM using the UK *Green Guide to Specifications* that provides a rating of the environmental profiles of building assemblies based on Envest).

2   Giving credit for decisions based on the use of an LCA tool by the design team – for example, the Canadian *Green Globes*™ offers credit for selecting materials that reflect the results of a 'best-run' life-cycle assessment for foundation and floor assembly and materials; column and beam or post and beam combinations, and wall; roof assemblies; and other envelope assembly materials (cladding, windows, etc.) (Green Globes, 2004).

Many building environmental assessment methods reference the notion of life cycle by offering versions specific to a phase within the life cycle – for example, the proposal for the Hong Kong *Comprehensive Environmental Performance Assessment Scheme* (CEPAS), which emphasizes the key issues and responsibilities at each stage of the design process and permits acknowledgement of the roles of the respective players (design team, contractor, etc.) within that process. Such a structuring demonstrates the way that life-cycle thinking is increasingly entering the parlance of building design and the formulation of environmental assessment methods.

Sustainability assessment

There can be no such thing as a 'sustainable building' or 'sustainable city.' They can, however, be designed to support sustainable patterns of living and the opportunities for doing so increase with the scale of development. Within this context, buildings will probably

be judged by the way in which various systems perform synergistically both internally and through the type and extent of creative connections with adjacent buildings. Similarly, while the three domains of environmental, social and economic are typically used to frame sustainability, it is their points of intersection that are equally critical (i.e. the ways and extent to which they positively or negatively influence each other). Simply adding social criteria to the current mix of environmental performance measures, as is beginning to occur, will not expose/highlight the way in which one influences and is influenced by others. As discussed later, it can only do so if the method or tool is used as part of the deliberations between various stakeholders (i.e. the use of the tool rather than the tool itself).

While most current building environmental assessment methods now reference 'sustainability', only a few were designed specifically at the outset to evaluate the social and economic consequences of buildings, such as the following:

•   The South African *Sustainable Building Assessment Tool* (SBAT) published through the Council for Scientific and Industrial Research (CSIR) organizes 15 main performance areas arranged under the headings of environmental, economic and social (Gibberd, 2001). The use of weightings is extended to these three dimensions in order to obtain an overall 'sustainability' score. SBAT aims at assessing not only the performance of buildings in terms of sustainability, but also the extent of the building's contribution to supporting and developing more sustainable systems around it.

•   The *Sustainable Project Assessment Routine* (SPeAR®), developed by Ove Arup and Partners Ltd in 2000, functions as a project assessment methodology to enable a rapid review of the sustainability of projects. *SPeAR®* does not attempt to provide a basis for comparing a project's sustainability performance with other buildings, but relative to the strengths and weaknesses within a particular context. It uses an appraisal matrix: the site is evaluated in accordance with the declared set of indicators and is concerned with making before and after comparisons associated with a new project (i.e. the exercise will rate the project sustainability value against the *status quo*). Many of the performance issues are qualitative and results of the assessment exercise will therefore reflect the knowledge and views of the assessor. While this degree of subjectivity is probably acceptable for a system that focuses on assessing changes/improvements in a specific case study, it is problematic when making comparisons between buildings.

Furthermore, whereas the majority of current building environmental assessment methods use scoring systems that evaluate performance *relative* to typical practice, the extent to which they can reference absolute metrics to climate stabilization and other critical environmental issues may prove decisive in the tool's relevance within a context of increasing societal concern around climate change.

Shifting scales

While the framing of assessment methods is clearly broadening, most assessment tools still focus on *individual* buildings. Many of the major building environmental assessment methods offer a suite of products each targeted at a specific building type, phase or situation. The sequence in the development of assessment methods is important in revealing the increasing acknowledgement of a broader context. The majority began with a version for new office buildings and then subsequently expanded the range of products to include existing office buildings, multi-unit residential and then other broader applications – schools, homes, etc. Several existing systems have recently introduced versions that address a broader context – for example, the US Green Building Council's (USGBC's) *LEED for Neighbourhood Development* (LEED-ND®) is currently being piloted and *CASBEE for Urban Development* (CASBEE-UD) was released in 2006. The fact that these were developed *after* gaining experience with assessing individual buildings is remarkably telling – development has been from the scale of individual buildings upwards to a larger scale rather than setting building performance within the overarching context of a neighbourhood, community or city. This, one can argue, would have significantly influenced the design of each.

LEED for Neighbourhood Development (LEED-ND®)

The US Green Building Council (USGBC), the Congress for the New Urbanism (CNU), and the Natural Resources Defense Council (NRDC) partnered to develop a national set of standards for neighbourhood location and design based on the combined principles of smart growth, new urbanism and green building. The goal of this partnership was to establish these standards for assessing and rewarding environmentally superior development practices within the rating framework of the Leadership in Energy and Environmental Design (LEED®) Green Building Rating System.

LEED for Neighbourhood Development (LEED-ND®) was designed to 'certify exemplary development projects that perform well in terms of smart growth, new urbanism, and green building' (USGBC, 2007) and was conceived to be able to assess situations as small as two buildings up to the scale of an entire new town, with the primary objective of encouraging mixed-use development. The three major performance areas of LEED-ND® – smart location and linkage, neighbourhood pattern and design, and green infrastructure and buildings – emphasize where to build, what to build and how to build to enhance neighbourhood development. Unlike other LEED products that focus primarily on the environmental performance of individual buildings, with relatively few credits-related site selection and design, LEED-ND® 'places emphasis on the design and construction elements that bring buildings together into a neighbourhood, and relate the neighbourhood to its larger region and landscape' (USGBC, 2007). LEED-ND® is directed at developers, development teams and, secondarily, planners and local government, and 'provides a label and guidelines for design and decision-making, to serve as an incentive for better location, design and construction of new residential, commercial and mixed use developments' (USGBC, 2007). LEED-ND® was initially released for pilot testing in 2007 with the expectation that the final post-pilot version of the rating system be launched in late summer, 2009.

CASBEE for Urban Design (CASBEE-UD)

The Japanese *Comprehensive Assessment System for Building Environmental Efficiency* (CASBEE), while employing an additive/weighting approach, breaks away from the simple addition of points achieved in *all* performance areas to derive an *overall* building score, which has been the dominant feature of all previous methods. It distinguishes between the *environmental loading* (resource use and ecological impacts) and *environmental quality and performance* (indoor environmental quality and amenities), scoring them separately to determine the building environmental efficiency (i.e. the ratio of environmental quality and performance to environmental loading). Conceptually, therefore, building assessment is presented not as a representation of the environmental characteristics of the building as a 'product', but, rather, more explicitly as a measure of the environmental implications associated with providing a set of 'services.'

CASBEE for Urban Design (CASBEE-UD) is an environmental performance assessment focusing on the issues related to larger urban developments and the associated outdoor spaces. In doing so, it can contribute to enhancing sustainability in urban plans by regional authorities. CASBEE-UD can be applied to situations involving a small group of buildings on two or three adjoining plots up to those covering hundreds or thousands of building sites, roads and parks in developments such as 'new towns.' The key distinction made on the standard floor–area ratio for the project is as follows:

- city centre = high usage development (floor–area ratio 500 per cent or more);
- general = general developments (floor–area ratio below 500 per cent).

If the project spans two areas of differing ratios, an area-weighted average is used.

CASBEE-UD retains the eco-efficiency concept where both environmental quality and performance in urban development and the outdoor environmental loads in urban development are scored separately. Each comprise three main categories, and the assessment results for the designated area are presented in various forms, such as bar charts and radar charts, for the scores in these six categories. An indicator for building environmental efficiency in urban development is given by:

$$BEE_{UD} = Q_{UD}/L_{UD} \qquad [18.1]$$

where BEE_{UD} is building environmental efficiency in urban development; Q_{UD} is environment quality and performance in urban development; and L_{UD} is environmental load in urban development. CASBEE-UD is a stand-alone system, independent of whether a building-scale CASBEE assessment has earlier been made, although future work will be required to develop

assessment methods that integrate the two assessment levels. As with CASBEE-UD, the expectation is that the experience gained with LEED-ND® will inform other LEED products.

Environmental programming of urban development

New systems are emerging that place the environmental performance of buildings within a broader context. The Norwegian *Environmental Programming of Urban Development* (Støa and Kittang, 2006), for example, is a web-based tool developed in 2005. Performance issues are organized hierarchically where four main topics (area and infrastructure; green areas; buildings; and construction) collectively include 18 environmental aspects. For each environmental aspect, the tool suggests several operational objectives, and it is at this level that the environmental performance requirements are defined. Energy demand is, for instance, an environmental aspect within the topic of buildings with the objective of reducing energy demand and the use of electricity for heating. The tool currently offers more than 80 operational objectives.

A key emphasis of the Environmental Programming of Urban Development appears to be one of positively influencing the development process:

- Help to determine environmental performance requirements for urban areas, facilitate the follow-up of an environmental programme and document if the requirements have been achieved.
- Enable access to relevant information and to support effective dialogue in the programming process.
- Assist relevant actors to make priorities, define operational objectives for urban developments, set relevant performance requirements, and, finally, make a plan for following up the visions.

An important distinction between the above approaches lies in the consistency and robustness of the conceptual frameworks of the methods to embrace assessment at a range of scales. Rees (2002, p253) suggests that, viewed as systems, both the built environment and the ecosphere 'exist in loose, nested hierarchies, each component system contained by the next level up and itself comprising a chain of linked subsystems at lower levels'. Such hierarchical attributes presumably should be equally evidenced in the design of cross-scale assessment tools. Within the majority of the LEED products, environmental issues are structured within five major categories: sustainable sites; water efficiency; energy and atmosphere; materials and resources; and indoor environmental quality. LEED-ND®, however, introduces a different organizational frame to address environmental issues at the larger scale. By contrast, CASBEE-UD applies the same conceptual underpinning as the other CASBEE products in a clear, hierarchical manner.

Blurring boundaries

The environmental design of buildings is almost always constrained by the legal boundaries of their sites. This has made 'self-reliance' in on-site energy use, water, sanitary waste treatment, etc. the current goal of environmental design as far as is technically possible within the constraints and opportunities of the site.

There are considerable advantages in recognizing, challenging and extending boundaries in all areas of enquiry. Picon (2005, p10), for example, identifies three traits evident in the papers presented at the Association of Architectural Historians' 2005 Conference: Rethinking the Boundaries: Architecture across Space, Time and Disciplines: first, an 'affirmation of the decisive importance of the notion of boundary, in all of its forms, in thinking both architectural and urban objects'; second, the 'need to interrogate and even throw into crisis the borders, limits and lines of demarcation that we have inherited, sometimes unconsciously'; and, third, that as soon as boundaries are 'closely examined, they rapidly blur; they fall apart, giving birth to a multitude of traces for which one is tempted to invoke all sorts of images and metaphors borrowed from mathematics, from physics, and from philosophy'.

The notion of boundaries can be interpreted in a variety of ways in the context of environmental issues, whether in terms of where conflicting conceptual ideas meet, the definition of system limits in LCA analyses, or at the interface between different ecosystems. In an ecological context, for example, Van der Ryn, (2005, p151) identifies that 'ecotones' – those places where two kinds of natural systems come together, such as where forest meets grassland or where tidal waters meet land, 'are typically places of maximum biological diversity and productivity'. This suggests that the realm that separates or links entities is as important as the entities themselves. In all cases, the boundaries of limits

of a system are entirely dependent upon the 'observer's viewpoint in defining the purpose and activities of the system' (Williamson et al, 2002, p82).

The urban context permits a number of opportunities to 'blur boundaries' that are not permissible or possible at the scale of individual buildings, including exploiting synergies between buildings and other systems and accounting for the social and economic consequences of buildings. These have consequence for the future development of building environmental assessment methods.

Exploiting synergies

Solutions to complex environmental problems that involve a wide range of scales of influence and timeframes require systems thinking – the ability to appreciate and address linkages and interrelationships between a broad range of often conflicting requirements. It is increasingly recognized that while the improvement of individual buildings is important, a potentially greater set of performance gains lie in synergies between buildings and between systems, together with the consequences for urban infrastructure systems. Indeed, it is the expectation that many of these will be captured in LEED-ND® and CASBEE-UD.

Capturing synergies between performance issues in building assessment methods has proved to be a difficult task given the need to offer clearly defined performance credits that can be attained independently of others, eliminate 'double-counting' and permit consistent evaluation by third-party assessors. Gladwin et al (1997) suggest that wholes need to be emphasized over constituent parts, relationships over specific entities, processes and transformations over physical structure, quality over quantity, and inclusiveness over exclusiveness. These are not the underpinnings of most current building environmental assessment methods and are not easily superimposed on them.

Accounting for social and economic issues

The need to address the rate and scale of environmental degradation has become increasingly recognized and institutionalized in building design in the form of environmental assessment methods. While many of the environmental performance issues – energy use, water use, greenhouse gas emissions – can be relatively simply aggregated across scale, the social and economic consequences cannot.

As mentioned earlier, given the current legal constraints that define ownership and site boundaries, environmental performance has led to autonomy or self-reliance becoming an overall goal, whether explicitly or implicitly. Bringing broader social and economic considerations into the mix creates a wider range of consideration into any negotiation. Negotiation literature typically focuses on trade-offs of interests among parties who are already in agreement on the basic nature of the dispute and seldom explicitly challenge the underlying values. Robinson (2004, p380) suggests that the 'need to develop methods of deliberation and decision-making that actively engage the relevant interests' of stakeholders will become increasingly important to infuse sustainability considerations into day-to-day conduct and practice. Given the current multiplicity of conflicting views, he further suggests that the 'power' of sustainability lies 'precisely in the degree to which it brings to the surface these contradictions and provides a kind of discursive playing field in which they can be debated' and subsequently encourage the 'development of new modes of public consultation and involvement intending multiple views to be expressed and debated' (Robinson, 2004, p382).

High-density urban contexts

High-density urban environments present a qualitatively different context for building environmental assessment. While methods have been developed by organizations that have experience in high-density contexts (e.g. HK-BEAM in Hong Kong), they are primarily concerned with large high-rise buildings rather than their consequence within a high-density urban context. Several key issues emerge for building environmental assessment in high-density contexts.

Valuing density

Newman and Kenworthy (1989, 1999) demonstrated that cities with high urban density, such as Tokyo and Hong Kong, have significantly lower gasoline consumption per capita than those with relatively low urban density, such as Houston and Phoenix in the US. This strong negative correlation established the axiom that increasing density will thereby lead to reduced transportation energy use. Clearly, a host of other

supporting factors are of importance, such as an efficient and multi-mode public transport system and culture of using public transit (e.g. Hong Kong has a comprehensive system of railways, trams, buses, public light buses, taxis and ferries that support more than 11 million daily passenger trips).

Compact and appropriately mixed-use urban developments with well-designed buildings served by efficiently engineered systems and infrastructure can offer considerable environmental, social and economic benefits. Density is now considered a critical component in sustainable urban development in North America and is central to many of the credits within LEED-NC® and LEED-ND®. However, given that high-rise and high-density compact cities can create air and noise pollution, limited access to daylight and natural ventilation, and limited space for vegetation, how these are acknowledged and accommodated within cross-scale assessment is critical.

Accounting for public space

Building environmental assessment methods cover those performance issues over which owners and the design team exercise some level of control. The consequence of buildings on, and the benefits derived from, public amenities such as public space, maintaining solar and wind access for adjacent properties, noise control and air quality are exacerbated in high-density contexts and are not typically accounted for in current methods. Again, it is the expectation that these will be addressed in LEED-ND® and CASBEE-UD.

Under the *2001 Government Policy Objectives*, the Buildings Department of the Hong Kong Special Administrative Region Government commissioned, in 2002, a consultancy to develop a new Comprehensive Environmental Performance Assessment Scheme (CEPAS). Requirements of the consultancy study were that the system be 'user friendly' and 'tailor made for Hong Kong taking into consideration the local characteristics such as high urban density, and hot and humid climate' (Hui, 2004, p54). Ove Arup and Partners Hong Kong Ltd developed the programme, which, after discussion forums, wider consultation and trial cases, was completed in 2005.

CEPAS is structurally different from the existing Hong Kong Building Environmental Assessment Method (HK-BEAM) in that it introduces and organizes performance criteria that make a clear distinction between 'human' and 'physical' performance issues, as well as between 'buildings' and their 'surroundings'. This manifests as eight performance categories: resource use; loadings; site impacts; neighbourhood impacts; indoor environmental quality; building amenities; site amenities; and neighbourhood amenities. The provision of site and neighbourhood amenities (e.g. open areas, greenery, landscapes and communal facilities, and neighbourhood amenities) is lacking in many old districts. The inclusion of neighbourhood impacts and amenities acknowledges the value placed on these amenities within the high-density building context of Hong Kong.

Conclusions

This chapter has explored the notion of building environmental assessment in the context of sustainable urban development. While both the breadth and the timeframe have increased, future tools are likely to link across varying scales – building, neighbourhood, city, region, etc. – to permit the comprehensive framing of sustainability assessment and to enable trade-offs to be explored between building design and infrastructure requirements. There are clear indications that this development is under way but, with the exception of CASBEE, does not appear yet to have strong conceptual underpinnings.

Boundaries, whether implicit or explicit, are both useful and constraining in the ways that environmental issues are considered in research and practice. Clear demarcation of a problem or scope of work permits clarity in definition and responsibilities. However, the increasing acknowledgement of sustainability as an overriding requirement and the associated shift towards systems thinking has placed greater emphasis on understanding links and synergies between constituent elements of systems as much as the elements themselves. This is relevant in terms of the design of building environmental assessment methods.

Prior to the introduction of building environmental assessment methods, discussion centred on individual performance issues such as energy use. Having accepted the challenge of comprehensive environmental assessment, it seems necessary to follow this through to its logical conclusion and create frameworks that explicitly accommodate temporal and spatial dimensions within which performance issues

and stakeholder interests can be appropriately positioned. The more comprehensive bounding will identify issues deserving greatest attention and permit more informed judgements to be made regarding the accuracy needed to evaluate them. More importantly, perhaps, it will help to identify the range, type and combinations of tools and mechanisms needed to create and maintain positive change.

References

Adinyira, E., Oteng-Seifah, S. and Adjei-Kumi, T. (2007) 'A review of urban sustainability assessment methodologies', in M. Horner, C. Hardcastle, A. Price and J. Bebbington (eds) *Web-Proceedings International Conference on Whole Life Urban Sustainability and its Assessment*, Glasgow, Scotland

Aggeri, F. (1999) 'Environmental policies and innovation – a knowledge-based perspective on cooperative approaches', *Research Policy*, vol 28, pp699–717

Banfill, P. F. G. and Peacock, A. D. (2007) 'Energy efficient new housing – the UK reaches for sustainability', *Building Research and Information*, vol 35, no 4, pp426–436

Brandon, P., Lombardi, P. and Bentivegna, V. (1997) *Evaluation of the Built Environment for Sustainability*, E & F N Spon, London

Cole, R. J. (2005) 'Building environmental methods: Redefining intentions', *Building Research and Information*, vol 35, no 5, pp455–467

Cole, R. J. (2006) 'Editorial: Building environmental assessment – changing the culture of practice', *Building Research and Information*, vol 34, no 4, pp303–307

DCLG (Department for Communities and Local Government) (2006) *Code for Sustainable Homes: A Step-Change in Sustainable Home Building Practice*, DCLG, December, London

Deakin, M., Lombardi, P. and Mitchell, G., (2002) 'Urban sustainability assessment: A preliminary appraisal of current techniques', *Urbanistica*, vol 118, pp50–54

Gibberd, J. (2001) 'The Sustainable Building Assessment Tool–assessing how buildings can support sustainability in Developing Countries', Continental Shift 2001, IFI International Conference, 11–14 September, Johannesburg, South Africa

Gladwin, T. N., Newberry, W. E. and Reiskin, E. D. (1997) 'Why is the Northern elite mind biased against community, the environment and a sustainable future', in H. Bazerman, D. M. Messick, A. E. Tenbrunsel and K. A. Wade-Benzoni (eds) *Environment, Ethics and Behaviour*, The New Lexington Press, San Francisco, CA, pp227–234

Green Globes (2004) *Design for New Buildings and Retrofits Rating System and Program Summary*, ECD Energy and

Environment Canada Ltd, www.greenglobes.com, accessed December 2004

Hui, M. F. (2004) 'Comprehensive environmental performance assessment scheme', in *Proceedings of the Symposium on Green Building Labelling*, Hong Kong, China, 19 March 2004, pp54–60

Kaatz, E., Root, D. and Bowen, P. (2004) 'Implementing a participatory approach in a sustainability building assessment tool', in *Proceedings of the Sustainable Building Africa 2004 Conference*, 13–18 September 2004, Stellenbosch, South Africa (CD Rom, Paper No 001)

Newman, P. W. G. and Kenworthy, J. R. (1989) *Cities and Auto Dependency: A Source Book*, Gower Publishing Co, Aldershot, UK

Newman, P. W. G. and Kenworthy, J. R. (1999) *Sustainability and Cities: Overcoming Automobile Dependence*, Island Press, Washington, DC

Picon, A. (2005) 'Rethinking the boundaries: Architecture across space, time and disciplines', *Newsletter of the Society of Architectural Historians*, vol 49, no 6, December 2005, pp10–11

Rees, W. E. (2002) 'Globalisation and sustainability: Conflict or convergence?', *Bulletin of Science, Technology and Society*, vol 22, no 4, August, pp249–268

Robinson, J. (2004) 'Squaring the circle? Some thoughts on the idea of sustainable development', *Ecological Economics*, vol 48, pp369–384

Støa, E. and Kittang, D. (2006) 'Presentation of a tool for environmental programming', ENHR Conference on Housing in an Expanding Europe: Theory, Policy, Participation and Implementation, Ljubljana, Slovenia, http://enhr2006ljubljana.uirs.si/publish/W13_Stoa.pdf, accessed July 2006

USGBC (US Green Building Council) (2007) *LEED for Neighborhood Development Rating System – Pilot*, USGBC, Washington, DC

Van der Ryn, S. (2005) *Design for Life: The Architecture of Sim Van der Ryn*, 1st Edition, G. Smith, Salt Lake City

Williamson, T. J., Radford, A. and Bennetts, H. (2002) *Understanding Sustainable Architecture*, E & F N Spon Press, London

Part IV

High-Density Spaces and Living

19

The Social and Psychological Issues of High-Density City Space

Bryan Lawson

Introduction

Many have tended to assume that high density inevitably brings with it a variety of social ills that result purely from cramming people together in what might be regarded as unnaturally restricted spaces. The implication here is that there is some minimum space required to sustain human life. This is not an argument about the very basic needs to grow food, manufacture goods and generate energy. It can be assumed in our modern technologically advanced world that these needs can be met by developments outside the high-density city. Whether organizing ourselves like this is sustainable at a planetary scale is dealt with by other authors in this book. The question here is about the social and psychological sustainability of high-density cities. This rather populist argument would have it that it is not possible to design healthy spaces and places at higher densities. But does such an idea really stand up in terms of what we know today?

The notion that high density was somehow fundamentally undesirable probably started to gain credence when Calhoun famously coined the term 'behavioural sink'. His work (Calhoun, 1962) coincided with the house-building boom in Europe that followed on from the decade of deprivation caused by World War II. Suddenly cities were being rebuilt at what some saw as alarmingly high densities. Calhoun's work was, of course, based on rats not people; but it offered some remarkable parallels with the breakdown of behavioural standards observed in newly constructed high-density cities.

Calhoun protected a pair of Norwegian rats from predators and provided them with an unlimited food supply. He did, however, restrict the area available to them and his findings showed a remarkable response to this limitation of space. Given their reproductive capability, Calhoun could have ended his study with 50,000 rats. In fact, the population stabilized at around only 150 organized in a dozen social groups of around 12 located in identifiable places within the enclosure. This appeared to facilitate the protection of pregnant females and newly delivered mothers, as well as the rearing and weaning of the young. It was as if somehow this society of rats was able collectively to control its population at some ideal level. This notion was reinforced by the next stage in Calhoun's study when he intervened to double the population. Social order quickly broke down. The result was violence, harassing of females, failure to complete nest building, abortions and many other socially pathological features of what Calhoun called the 'behavioural sink'. Since Calhoun had still maintained adequate food supply and protection from predators the conclusion seemed inevitable. The rats simply needed a certain amount of room in order to conduct their territorial social structures in space.

As economic prosperity fuelled a human building boom, many voices suggested that we, too, might see this sort of breakdown in our society. By the 1970s the island city-state of Singapore had embarked upon what remains one of the most remarkable social housing programmes ever attempted. It was simply to create public housing for the vast majority of the population.

Although the Housing Development Board (HDB) of Singapore has been hugely successful in statistical terms, some began to question the social well-being of the residents. By 1978 Walter was commenting on the lack of a sense of community in the Singaporean HDB high-rise blocks. He compared the lives of the people living here to the traditional Kampong villages still in use across the causeway in Malaysia, and asked what was causing this deterioration in quality of life (Walter, 1978).

In fact, Walter suggested a number of reasons. What is interesting here is that the main cause of this lack of community seems to be only indirectly to do with density. Walter compared the actual design of space in HDB developments with Kampongs. He found that the Kampong naturally focused people onto communal outdoor space not available in the HDB high-rise blocks. In the hot tropical climate of South-East Asia there is no real need to divide indoors from outdoors in the manner so automatically adopted in the temperate climates of North America and Europe from which so much 20th-century architectural influence derives. This leads to a special form of architecture.

As Ken Yeang has so well documented (Yeang, 1978), the traditional Malay house uses a more permeable structure with deep overhangs, shuttered windows and open verandas that facilitate cross-ventilation. In the Kampong there are few, if any, fences and the verandas of dwellings typically look onto communal space. Although not achieving the densities of high rise, these arrangements are often sufficiently compact for residents to converse with each other from their verandas. The whole works rather like a flock system ensuring social protection from intruders. Thus, life revolves around communal space that serves really practical purposes, as well as building a sense of belonging and togetherness.

There is another interesting problem that arises from such an architectural study of space. The traditional architecture of so many countries in which high-density cities have recently become established simply does not provide a precedent for them. London is not now regarded as one of the highest-density cities; but it has a history of relatively high density. Several hundred years ago London was one of the highest-density cities in the world. It was not high rise, but it was high density. It evolved a form of architecture that allowed buildings to be jammed close together. We

would find something similar elsewhere – in Cairo, for example, though with a very different architectural language. But in cities such as Kuala Lumpur, Jakarta and Bangkok, we would not have found this. Essentially, the traditional architecture of this part of the world was of pavilions standing in the landscape. This has posed huge problems for the new 20th-century high-density versions of these great capital cities. In raising their density they also had to import a foreign architectural language. It is not just that HDB blocks in Singapore are higher density than their neighbouring Kampungs, they are also essentially Western in their cultural language.

Around the same time as HDB were building so rapidly in Singapore, Oscar Newman was developing his theory of defensible space in American high-density cities (Newman, 1973). Newman showed that crime was correlated with building height in residential blocks in New York. Just as Walter was suggesting that the problem was not density *per se* in Singapore, Newman was concluding that it was not the height itself that was the problem in New York. Newman showed that the increased levels of crime in the higher-rise blocks tended to occur not inside dwellings nor in outdoor spaces, but in the unsupervised indoor circulation spaces. It was the very design of these blocks that increased the proportion of space that was public and yet not overlooked, he argued, that caused the problems. The notion of 'defensible space' was thus developed, and we began to realize that this may be intrinsically more difficult to achieve in some housing layouts than others. It may well be that some of the architectural responses to high density have encouraged layouts that also have less defensible space; but this is not directly the result of high density.

Jane Darke studied a series of award-winning public-sector housing developments in the UK and found no correlation between resident satisfaction and density (Darke and Darke, 1979). It was beginning to look as if the actual arrangement of space was more critical than simple indicators such as ratios of people per hectare or acre. A series of famous and highly influential housing blocks was constructed in Sheffield in the UK (Lynn, 1962). The most well known of these, Park Hill, was described by one of its high-profile architects, Jack Lynn, as having 'streets in the air'. He argued that Le Corbusier's ideas in the famous *Unite d'Habitation* were not suitable for England, where:

Centuries of peace and 100 years of housing reform in this country had given us the open street directly approachable from either end off which every house was entered directly through its own front door.

Lynn (1962) went on to ask: 'Does gregariousness depend on the open air? Why is there so little conversation in tube trains and lifts? Are there social and anti-social forms of housing?'

Attempting answers to Lynn's more rhetorical questions is hardly likely to be of help here; but his final question is actually worth taking seriously. At first sight the design of the Park Hill, Hyde Park and Kelvin blocks in Sheffield appeared to offer a solution; but on further inspection we can see that it fundamentally missed the point. These famous buildings were deck access, but sadly far from being the 'streets in the air' that were claimed. The front doors did, indeed, open off them; but they were not overlooked by any windows. You would be very lucky ever to see your neighbours coming and going, never mind be able to converse with them. The 'streets', which were in reality more like open-sided single-banked corridors, were classic examples of indefensible space.

The communal refuse chutes and lifts, which were romantically described by Lynn as the 'modern equivalent of the village pump', were, of course, no better at providing a social focus. Sadly, these buildings have proved to generate significant social problems and the worst of these, Kelvin, has been demolished, but not before residents were injured by disused televisions and refrigerators discarded from the upper-level 'streets'.

Sheffield was later to build some other deck access housing schemes. but with significantly different plans. At Stannington the living rooms, which were glazed more or less wall to wall and floor to ceiling, overlooked the decks. Decks were also kept to lengths of less than a dozen or so dwellings. Recent interviews with residents have revealed minimal levels of crime and high levels of socialization and a sense of community among neighbours (Lawson, 2001).

Privacy

What distinguishes the Stannington plans from the Park Hill plans is the extent to which privacy or community has been allowed to form the generative ideas. It has been accepted that privacy is a generally rather important human need and that a lack of privacy often leads to behaviour that can be seen as anti-social (Pederson, 1997). However, such an argument has often led inaccurately to the assumption that privacy means individual isolation. In fact, studies suggest very strongly that privacy is really about the ability to control the amount and type of contact we have with others. What, in turn, this implies for the design of high-density cities is the even more acute need to provide boundaries that people control in order to create and operate hierarchical social contact. This is, of course, as true inside the home as it is outside. However, the creation of graded spaces from private through semi-private and semi-public to the public domain becomes increasingly difficult as density rises.

At the other end of the scale there is a common assumption that increased density leads to an increased sense of loneliness and a reduced sense of belonging to a socially rewarding neighbourhood (Skjaeveland and Garling, 1997). Certainly, there is evidence that overall dwelling density is inversely correlated with supportive behaviour towards neighbours. However, the mechanism for this seems interesting from a design perspective. The likelihood of meeting large numbers of strangers in the home territory public domain would seem to increase an unwillingness to trust people and, thus, to support them. Increased density could thus be a depressing factor on social trust and on neighbourly behaviour unless the public domain is designed in a hierarchical and localized way. Thus again, while increased density makes this more difficult and critical, it may not in itself be the chief causal factor.

If we see privacy and loneliness on some sort of scale of the social interaction of places, then it is also important here to recognize that there is not some special point along this scale which is universally good. What feels right will depend upon at least three major factors. First, there is no doubt that there is a cultural variation here. Many have observed that personal space seems to reduce as one moves generally eastwards from the UK, through Europe and on into Asia. But there are also cultural differences about the extent to which we allow individuals to be 'private in public'. Certainly, ignoring others very close to you in space is culturally much more acceptable in England than in the US, and far more than in many Asian and Arabic cultures (Hall, 1966). We would be foolish indeed not to recognize the very obvious effect of personality here. Some people are simply more gregarious than others. There is obviously, too, an effect of context. We feel more or less in need of privacy depending upon the context of activity – although, curiously, modern hospitals seem to remove privacy at the very time it might be assumed to be most needed. They have been influenced by a generation of thought coming straight from Florence Nightingale, after whom the design of open wards is named (Nightingale, 1860). She emphasized not privacy or dignity, but surveillance; the ability of the nurse to see all her patients was the generating factor. This offers a nice architectural metaphor for the problem of the design of both private space and defensible space in high-density cities. Conversely, much modern high-density housing, such as Park Hill, has been designed from the privacy angle.

Public policy

The studies of Malaysian Kampong housing, Walter's investigation of Singaporean HDB residences, Newman's study of American housing and the Park Hill scheme in Sheffield show a common thread. Problems are not so much to do with density or absolute numbers, but with spatial geometry. In particular, the notion of private, public and semi-public space plays a central role here.

Territoriality offers a rather appealing concept for explaining and understanding much of the behaviour that seems to underpin commonly observed high-density social ills. Territoriality is essentially a spatial theory of social structure (Ardrey, 1967). One of the difficulties, and there are several, of applying such a theory to human behaviour is that territoriality has its origins in ethology. Ethology is based on studying animals in their natural habitats and, of course, we no longer know what the natural habitat of the human species is. The assumption in applying such ideas is that we have developed technically and economically far faster than any evolutionary process could keep up with and therefore our social patterns still show earlier and more basic patterns of behaviour not yet adapted to our contemporary condition. Others feel that such analysis leans too far towards the nature side of the nature–nurture debate that has characterized the development of psychology and prefer explanations that stress the choices we learn to make rather than instinctive behaviour. However, the vast majority of species sharing this planet with us show territorial behaviour of one kind or another. In fact, humans seem to exhibit all of the many varieties of territorial behaviour. We certainly exhibit the pair-bond and family territory, seem to love to hate our neighbours (the *noyau*) and build cities that share the conventions of arena behaviour.

Our attachment to particular places and our willingness and even enthusiasm for defending them is well documented. The almost irrational desire felt by football fans to beat their local neighbours rather than win any other game is entirely characteristic of territorial behaviour. The propensity that children show for building dens and secret hideaways is known to us all. The sad proliferation of wars between neighbouring nations about land that seems less than essential economically or culturally is blazoned across the front of our daily newspapers. We may sympathize with Einstein when he rails against nationalism describing it as 'an infantile disease', and as being 'the measles of mankind'. However, the nation is, deep down, one of the many faces of territoriality that we seem locked into. It is when the wish to identify ourselves as part of a nation oversteps the mark and becomes 'nationalism' that we show the weakness in our make-up. It is a line the human race has still not yet learned to avoid crossing from time to time no matter how civilized other aspects of our culture may have become.

Numerous anthropological studies of those primitive societies that still exist around the world show that these tribes can almost invariably accurately describe what they consider to be their territory and where the borders with the neighbouring territories can be found. In many cases, the cultures of such tribes cannot be understood without reference to their concept of territory and their sense of belonging in a special place that they regard as exclusively theirs. Other evidence of the strength of our territorial drive comes from reports of those who have tried to live without individual territories. A study of the Israeli kibbutz described the limits many members would go to contrive a way of cultivating their own plot of land. An analysis of the performance of the agricultural industry in Soviet Russia offers another form of evidence. In 1975 it was claimed that private land, which amounted to less than 1 per cent of cultivated areas, was actually responsible for generating over half of the food supply of the Soviet Union! It seems that a willingness to work hard and territoriality are bound together in a kind of virtuous circle.

Work by Alan Lipman on the behaviour of residents in a nursing home also reinforces the strong underlying need for permanently defended territory. Here we might imagine that the residents might have lost what territories they originally had before moving into the home. Lipman recorded that although the home had a definite policy of not allowing chairs in the communal sitting rooms to be exclusively reserved, this could not be enforced. So strong was the defence of territorial chairs by these elderly residents that the staff eventually had to bow to this wish and allow the practice even though this contradicted policy (Lipman, 1970).

Sadly, in the modern city, territorial problems are often triggered by an ambiguity resulting directly from spatial design, or lack of it. Unclear boundaries and tracts of land that cannot easily be defended can cause enormous distress to some people and make the lives of many others quite unpleasant. When this happens it is all too easy to put the problem down to density rather than design. Lawyers are reputed to make more money from neighbourly disputes than any other form of legal quarrel, save for divorce. The history of architecture throughout the 20th century surely shows an inexorable move away from defining the family home and its garden towards larger aggregated buildings and communal open space.

It is often assumed that such arrangements achieve higher densities; but, in fact, they often do not. During the 1970s Aston University demolished many streets of lovely terraced houses on its Birmingham, UK, city centre campus and replaced them with tower blocks for student residences. The houses were known as back-to-back since each terrace backed onto a set of yards and then the next terrace. Although they had become unsanitary and needed renovation, they were solidly built and could easily have been adapted to student life. Such a proposal would have achieved comparable densities to the high-rise blocks and allowed for a more graduated social structure.

Perhaps one of the features of territoriality as a theory that makes it more controversial in the modern world is the way in which it often depends upon conventionalized gender roles. In many forms of territorial behaviour males compete for territories and females find them attractive in relation to the quality of the acquired real estate. What is undeniable is that the territory is a remarkably effective device. In evolutionary terms it simultaneously ensures that a species distributes itself evenly in the environment, thus maximizing use of the food supply, and promotes the survival of the fittest and strongest. However, in social terms it also creates social structures that provide protection against predators.

Ardrey (1967) has also argued that it exquisitely provides the three big environmental needs of stimulation, identity and security. We can certainly see all three in the following of a local football team: the stimulation that comes from beating your opponents; the identity served through the wearing of emblems and replica clothing; and the security from belonging to a 'tribe' that has shared values, interests and behavioural norms.

The city territory

In environmental terms, territories are usually defined by two important features: their borders with other territories and their heartland. Human nations are thus recognizable through their frontiers and their capital city. The reunification of Germany and the need to re-establish Berlin as the national capital is an example of the symbolic importance of such things. In Malaysia, the capital Kuala Lumpur was originally built on the Klang River that indirectly gives it its name (Kuala Lumpur means muddy river). It has become extremely congested with the transportation infrastructure lagging behind, though now catching up. The capital must be the most important city and acts as an icon for a nation. If the nation is defined by it borders and capital, so the capital is defined by both its own boundary and its core. In many capital cities there is a building or perhaps a few buildings that act as the icon of the city. The Eiffel Tower in Paris, St Paul's Cathedral in London and Hagia Sofia in Istanbul are all very obvious examples. So important are these icons that again we lavish attention on them in quite extravagant ways. Several hundred years ago it seems that the architect of St Paul's, Christopher Wren, knew that he was building a national symbol and not just a church. According to his grandson, Stephen Wren, he wrote: 'Architecture has its political use, public buildings being the ornament of the country; it establishes a nation, draws people and commerce, and makes people love their native country' (Wren, 1750).

The construction of the world's tallest building (at the time) in the Petronas Towers by Cesar Pelli was surely an attempt to 'draw people and commerce' to

Kuala Lumpur rather than a response to a need for floor space. There was no particular need for such a huge building, and certainly no imperative to build so high. The result has put enormous added strain on the ground-level infrastructure.

In Australia the competition to design a new opera house on a very prominent site in the harbour was famously won by Jorn Utzon, whose wonderful creation has become the icon of Sydney. However, it is said that he submitted drawings late, in the wrong format, and broke many other rules of the competition. Initially the design was unbuildable, took far longer and cost many times the budget to construct, and it remains hugely problematic in terms of its circulation and acoustics. But Utzon realized what others did not. Sydney wanted a city heartland symbol and, in turn, one for the whole nation.

These great cities seem also themselves to be the product of a rather dramatic form of territorial behaviour known as the 'arena'. The arena is a specific area of land making the breeding ground for some species. It is through the mechanism of this special place that Darwinian principles of selection for breeding are enabled. The arena is, thus, a territory or, more strictly, a whole set of territories over which the males of some species compete. The winners of the battles take ownership of the most central and prized territories and thus become attractive to the females. Thus, the strongest and most dominant males are selected for reproductive purposes.

The prestige and consequent associated high land values of a city centre can be seen as parallels with the most desirable central places in the arena. An important company will require its offices to be centrally located, not for convenience or necessity, but for symbolic reasons. A quick tour around the central business districts of any of the world's great capital cities today tends to reveal many familiar names. These huge multinational banks, manufacturers, service providers and so on need to maintain the image of their potency and power through their location and address. But there is far more to it than just economics. We expect our cities to have an increasing intensity towards their core. This is where 'it all happens'. Great cities depend upon this centralism for their very character and attraction. Thus, density, or, more accurately, intensity, must increase towards a recognizable core.

So we may expect to see a continuation of high-density cities. A few, of course, are the product of restricted space, with Singapore and Hong Kong being obvious examples. However, many cities achieve high density normally accelerating towards the core, most often the central business district, in an arena-like fashion. London is a notable exception, with a ring of higher-density districts surrounding a lower-density centre. But then London was originally, and essentially remains, a collection of villages, each with their own arena-like qualities. Perhaps nowhere in the world does your address matter so much as in the UK. An ex-student of mine who, for a while, became a colleague, left to return to London saying that he missed the feeling of being at the centre of things just too much to stay in Sheffield.

Evidence-based design

We now have a number of tools for measuring the extent to which space is interconnected, allows for natural surveillance, enables defence and protects against escape of criminals and such matters. Such ideas have been pioneered by Hillier under the generic heading of space syntax (Hillier and Hanson, 1984). What is interesting about such tools is that they show the common characteristics of space from the individual building, through the street to the housing development and right up to the city. While such tools are, in reality, no more than statistical descriptions of space, they can be used to correlate spatial characteristics of design with the less desirable features of some modern high-density city life. Such ideas now inform the design of individual buildings, such as hospitals and the regeneration of urban areas in problematic cities.

There is now a considerable body of evidence that views of nature and access to outdoor places with substantial natural landscape are both significant factors in contributing to psychological well-being (Ulrich, 1986). Since high density is potentially an inhibiting force in the provision of such places, this needs careful consideration.

Simply having views of nature has been shown to be important in specialized settings such as healthcare facilities, schools, offices and housing. However, there is now so much evidence that many of these findings can be taken to have generic value. In particular, heath outcomes are now clearly linked to the relationship of patients to landscape (Ulrich, 1999). Terminal cancer patients show significant preferences for rooms with views of nature and showed better affective states when they had them (Baird and Bell, 1995). College students whose dormitory rooms looked out onto natural landscape settings were shown to perform better on attention-demanding tasks (Tenessen et al, 1995). Inmates have been found to make fewer demands on healthcare facilities in prisons if they have cells with views of vegetation (Moore, 1981).

But such work is not restricted to specialized building types. Views of natural landscape have been shown to correlate significantly with residents expressing satisfaction with their neighbourhood and sense of well-being (Kaplan, 2001). Much of the evidence demonstrates not just nice feelings, but real psycho-physiological changes in people who have views of nature (Ulrich, 1981). Hospital patients even appear to experience less pain (Diette et al, 2003) and take less medication (Lawson and Phiri, 2003) when exposed to the sights and sounds of nature.

All of this research reinforces the notion that open spaces having a high degree of natural landscape are extraordinarily valuable features of the urban environment. In high-density places where pressure on space increases, it perhaps becomes vitally important to maintain such places. This is, in turn, reinforced by more recent research on London (Burdett et al, 2004). Open landscaped areas in the form of parks or other green spaces seem to be one of the most significant factors in perceived quality of life in big cities. The London study suggested that having access to 'large coherent pieces of well-landscaped and well-maintained open space within a 10 to 15 minute walk' seems to sum up the expressed need.

Perception of density and satisfaction

Density needs to be thought of not as a statistic but as an experience. People living in high-density urban places do not necessarily experience a sense of density proportional to the arithmetic ratios of people to area. The message here must surely be that it is about perception and experience. A large part of the life of such residents is necessarily spent inside their dwellings, and research shows that their overall expressed feelings are strongly related to the way in which space is structured within the dwelling itself. For example, the evidence strongly suggests that people who are provided with clearly defined private space are more

likely to be social and less withdrawn. By contrast, depriving residents of the ability to retreat into entirely private space when desired is likely to increase aggressive boundary-control behaviour in public (Zimring, 1981). A study of London suggested that residents perceive their locality as having higher density when their own home is congested. By contrast, localities having overall high densities but larger homes are rated more highly (Burdett et al, 2004).

This study of London found that the accessibility and quality of public transport was a major concern of residents, as were the issues of safety and level of anti-social behaviour. London is particularly interesting as it has quite variable levels of density, unlike some other similarly sized capitals. The study found that actual density did not correlate with the levels of expressed satisfaction of residents. In fact, the highest levels of dissatisfaction were found in both the densest and least dense wards of the city. What this study showed was that high density is perceived to offer both advantages and disadvantages. Perceived advantages include diversity, availability of housing, transport and other facilities. Perceived disadvantages include parking problems, crime and vandalism, noise and restricted living spaces. In fact, residents often seem to be quite poor judges of the relative densities of parts of their cities. High-rise is often assumed incorrectly to mean high density. In many UK cities, public housing in the later half of the 20th century was often high rise, but at lower overall densities than the terraced housing it replaced.

A commonly held notion is that high density causes a lack of visual privacy and intrusion. Studies suggest, however, that noise may be perceived as more of a problem than overlooking. While many countries and authorities have adopted clear design guidelines on distance and overlooking, perhaps attention to the attenuation of urban noise has been less thorough.

What have we learned?

All of this evidence appears to suggest a number of important lessons for planners, architects and the makers of policy in high-density cities.

First, the pure statistical ratio of people per unit area does not seem to be the most important factor in determining how people feel about living in high-density cities. It is what is in these places and how space is designed that matters. It is much more a matter of design than of statistics. Arranging space to create a feeling of retreat and privacy both within homes and in the public domain is likely to have very positive outcomes. The availability and quality of facilities and, especially, transport are clearly significant. The provision of open space and contact with nature remains a fundamentally important and positive factor, in general. While there may also be some individuals who rate such things as relatively unimportant, the research suggests that, overall, they are pretty fundamental. The creation of space in such a way as to minimize the opportunities for vandalism and anti-social behaviour also seem important factors.

While density itself, then, is perhaps not the key issue here, it remains true that the higher the density, the harder we have to work to design our cities in such a way that they remain pleasant and fulfilling places in which to live. It is certainly true that the closer their proximity, the greater potential people have to annoy one another.

Above all, increases in density make it even more essential to move towards an evidence-based approach to design. Developing a new generation of architects and urban designers who can understand the evidence, work with it and interpret it creatively is probably one of the greatest challenges facing us. This has implications for the way in which such professionals are educated and go on to practise; but that is another story.

References

Ardrey, R. (1967) *The Territorial Imperative: A Personal Inquiry into the Animal Origins of Property and Nations*, Collins, London

Baird, C. L. and Bell, P. A. (1995) 'Place, attachment, isolation and the power of a window in a hospital environment: A case study', *Psychological Reports*, vol 76, pp847–850

Burdett, R., Travers, T., Czischke, D., Rode, P. and Moser, B. (2004) *Density and Urban Neighbourhoods in London*, Enterprise LSE Cities, London

Calhoun, J. B. (1962) 'Population density and social pathology', *Scientific American*, vol 206, pp139–146

Darke, J. and Darke, R. (1979) *Who Needs Housing?*, Macmillan, London

Diette, G. B., Lechtzin, N., Haponik, E., Devrotes, A. and Rubin, H. R., (2003) 'Distraction therapy with nature sights and sounds reduce pain during flexible bronchoscopy', *Chest*, vol 123, pp941–948

Hall, E. T. (1966) *The Hidden Dimension*, The Bodley Head, London

Hillier, B. and Hanson, J. (1984) *The Social Logic of Space*, Cambridge University Press, Cambridge

Kaplan, R. (2001) 'The nature of view from home: Psychological benefits', *Environment and Behaviour*, vol 33, no 4, pp507–542

Lawson, B. R. (2001) *The Language of Space*, Architectural Press, Oxford

Lawson, B. R. and Phiri, M. (2003) *The Architectural Healthcare Environment and Its Effects on Patient Health Outcomes*, The Stationery Office, London

Lipman, A. (1970) 'Territoriality: A useful architectural concept?', *RIBA Journal*, vol 77, no 2, pp68–70

Lynn, J. (1962) 'Park Hill redevelopment', *RIBA Journal*, vol 69, no 12

Moore, E. O. A. (1981) 'Prison environment's effect on healthcare service demands', *Journal of Environmental Systems*, vol 11, no 1, pp17–34

Newman, O. (1973) *Defensible Space: People and Design in the Violent City*, Architectural Press, London

Nightingale, F. (1860) *Notes on Nursing*, Harrison and Sons, London

Pederson, D. M. (1997) 'Psychological functions of privacy', *Journal of Environmental Psychology*, vol 17, pp147–156

Skjaeveland, O. and Garling, T. (1997) 'Effects of interactional space on neighbouring', *Journal of Environmental Psychology*, vol 17, pp181–198

Tenessen, C., Cimprich, C. M. and Cimprich, B., (1995) 'Views to nature: Effects on attention', *Journal of Environmental Psychology*, vol 15, pp77–85

Ulrich, R. S. (1981) 'Nature versus urban scenes: Some psychophysiological effects', *Environment and Behaviour*, vol 13, no 5, pp523–556

Ulrich, R. S. (1986) 'Human responses to vegetation and landscapes', *Landscape and Urban Planning*, vol 13, pp29–44

Ulrich, R. S. (1999) 'Effects of gardens on health outcomes: Theory and research', in C. Cooper Marcus and M. Barnes (eds) *Healing Gardens*, John Wiley & Sons, New York, NY, pp27–86

Walter, M. A. H. B. (1978) 'The territorial and the social: Perspectives on the lack of community in high-rise/high density living in Singapore', *Ekistics*, vol 270, pp236–242

Wren, S. (1750) *Parentalia or Memoirs of the Family of the Wrens*, Gregg Press, London

Yeang, K. (1978) *Tropical Urban Regionalism: Building in a South-East Asian City*, Mimar, Singapore

Zimring, C. M. (1981) 'Stress and the designed environment', *Journal of Social Issues*, vol 37, no 1, pp145–171

20

Sustainable Compact Cities and High-Rise Buildings

Sung Woo Shin

History and background

The growth of cities and environmental problems after the Industrial Revolution

Industrialization has been spreading across Europe after its first Industrial Revolution in England during the 18th century. Thus, agrarian society has been transformed into industrial cities, which were part of the market and expanded social infrastructures. Many people gathered to the city for its convenience of roads, water supply, drainage, electricity and increased employment due to industrialization. Economic scale also expanded compared to pre-existing cities. This industrialization has expanded all around the world. The development of cities provided convenience and abundance to citizens; but numerous problems arose when people gathered to the city for its benefit. Cities were expanding, but there was only limited space, which led to housing, water and air pollution problems due to manufacturing activities, and created the greenhouse effect by development on greenfield sites. In addition, an increase in the transportation system, which was to connect cities, resulted in serious traffic problems. As shown in Figure 20.1a, these environmental problems are deviating from city deterioration, and turning into city centre cavitation ('the doughnut phenomenon').

The eco-city: Avoiding environmental problems (Shin, 2008a)

The most serious problem in cities is environmental pollution. Environmental pollution not only affects one nation, but the livelihood of the whole planet – the Earth. Thus, in order to adopt a more natural environment, the concept of the eco-city was introduced during the 20th century. Environmentally friendly energy was used and the city was developed to exhaust less carbon dioxide (CO_2), which is the main cause of global warming. However, in order to maintain the eco-city, roads were constructed, and water, electricity and drainage system ware installed; thus, construction costs escalated. Moreover, a burden was imposed on transporting and linking logistics, schools and hospitals between the big cities and the eco-city. This resulted in excessive energy, which caused heavy burdens on the environmental load. And this kind of urban sprawl damaged nature irreversibly.

Creation of the sustainable compact city

During the 21st century, therefore, the direction of cities was redirected as compact cities and this developed specifically under the concept of the sustainable compact city (see Figure 20.1b). The idea is to construct the urban elements in an efficient way but within compact limits. This has been categorized into reducing urban energy consumption to combat global warming; and revitalizing the traditional city centre, which has gone into decline as a result of suburbanization (AIJ and IBEC, 2002). In order to achieve the sustainable compact city, high-rise or tall buildings are seen as one of the best solutions because of the benefit of centralizing numerous functions of the city in one place, as shown in Figure 20.1b. The first high-rise building was the 15-storey reliance building constructed in Chicago, which was built to take care of housing problems in the city. As more apartments were built to solve the housing problem, more functions were required in the city to satisfy the people living there. However, since the space of the city is limited to absorb all these problems, high-rise buildings accommodated all of these complex city functions. During the 1920s in New York, along with the development of cities and in order to display the national prestige of America, the 102-storey Empire State Building was constructed. This showed that high-rise buildings can control city expansion and create many other value-added functions. At the end of the 20th century, the high-rise building boom centre has shifted from the US to Asia and now is expanding to all global cities (CTBUH, 2008) or to other international cities defined by super-tall buildings or high-rise buildings that are more than 50-storeys tall or over 200m. During the 21st century (as shown in Figure 20.1b), these high-rise buildings will effectively utilize the land of the metropolis, which was a densely populated city, to solve city population problems. In addition, their function is expected to result in energy savings by using environmentally friendly energy, by increasing the area of greenery in a city, and by decreasing transportation costs and air pollution due to the easing of traffic congestion.

Current status, direction and effect of high-rise buildings

Current status of high-rise buildings

World-class metropolitan cities such as Tokyo, New York, Shanghai, London, Paris, Hong Kong and Seoul are using high-rise buildings according to the compact city plan to solve problems originating in the city and in order to become the key growth engines for the city and nation. Until 2000, super-tall buildings were mostly 100 storeys tall and were recognized more as local landmarks. However, for the past seven to eight years since 2000, the height of the buildings increased significantly, as shown in Table 20.1, and there are five ultra-high-rise buildings (i.e. building over 1000m) in progress. Thus, our society should be socially and environmentally prepared for this change to adopt high-rise buildings as part of the vertical city.

Direction of high-rise buildings

Until now, a city's highest building was a significant representative symbol and a milestone. However, after the 20th century, from the start of European Union unification, the world has been categorized into blocks and has changed to city competition, like medieval cities of Europe, from international competition. Cities

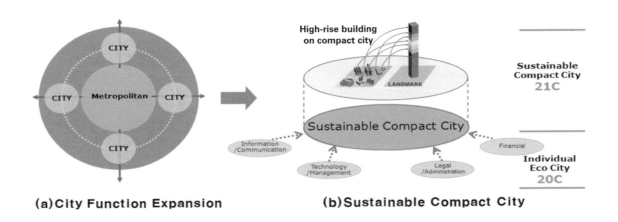

(a) City Function Expansion   **(b) Sustainable Compact City**

Source: Shin (2008b)

Figure 20.1 *City development process: (a) city function expansion; (b) sustainable compact city*

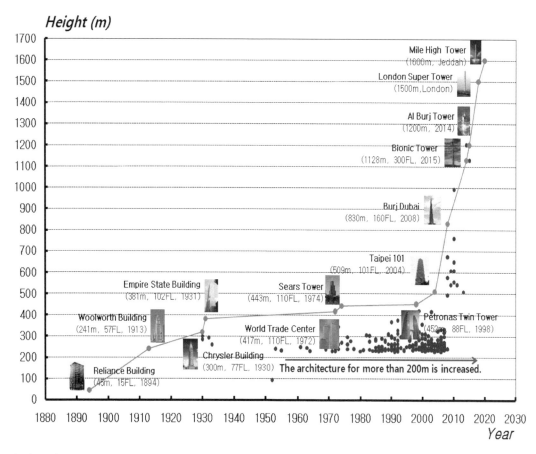

Height (m)

Source: Shin (2008a)

Figure 20.2 *Global trend and plans of high-rise buildings*

are now being developed to represent the nation. This kind of competition between cities is most effective by integrating the function of the city, and the most significant method of doing so is through the high-rise building. The high-rise building is not only significant in its height, but provides a variety of ripple effects – environmental, social, technical, cultural and economic (see Table 20.2).

High-rise building ripple effect

The environmental, social, technical, cultural and economic ripple effects of high-rise building are as shown in Table 20.2. This demonstrates the shift from the highest symbol since the early 20th century to complex functions as a vertical city in the 21st century (Shin, 2008a).

Urban development cases utilizing high-rise buildings

While the high-rise building exhibits ripple effects, these effects can be synergized when they are combined with the surrounding city's competitiveness. High-rise buildings are most effective when the city changes from an expanding metropolis to a compact city, and when they are aligned with the competitiveness of the city. The following case studies represent some of the world's best-known examples of effective city competitiveness management.

Case 1: Tokyo – Roppongi Hills

Roppongi Hills introduced the 'culture city' concept. The construction of the Roppongi Hills project dates

Table 20.1 *World high-rise buildings – status and plan*

No	Name	City	Floors	Height(m)	Completed
1	Mile High Tower	Jeddah	300	1600	Unsettled
2	London Super Tower	London	Unsettled	1500	Unsettled
3	Al Burj Tower	Dubai	Unsettled	1200	2014
4	Bionic Tower	Shanghai	300	1128	Unsettled
5	Silky City Mubarak Tower	Kuwait	250	1101	Unsettled
6	Nakheel Tower	Dubai	200+	1000+	2020
7	Burj Dubai	Dubai	160+	800+	2009
8	Seoul Lite	Seoul	133	640	2014
9	Pentominium	Dubai	122	618	2012
10	Russia Tower	Moscow	118	612	2012
11	151 Inchon Tower	Inchon	151	610	2012
12	Chicago Spire	Chicago	150	609	2012
13	China 117 Tower	Tianjin	117	600	2014
14	Mekkah Royal Clock Tower Hotel	Mekkah	76	577	2010
15	Lotte Super Tower	Seoul	112	555	Unsettled
16	Doha Convention Center Tower	Doha	112	551	2012
17	World Trade Center One	New York	82	541	2013
18	Busan Lotte World 2 Tower	Busan	118	510	2013
19	Burj Al Alam	Taipei	108	510	2011
20	Taipei 101	Taipei	101	509	2004
21	Federation Towers – Vostok Tower	Moscow	95	509	2010
22	Shanghai World Financial Center	Shanghai	101	492	2008
23	International Commerce Centre	Hong Kong	106	484	2010
24	Petronas Tower 1, 2	Kuala Lumpur	88	452	1998
25	Nanjing Greenland Financial Center	Nanjing	69	450	2009

Source: Shin (2008a); CTBUH (2009)

back to 1986, when the area was designated as a 'redevelopment priority zone'. Construction was initiated in 2000 and was completed in April 2003. This is Japan's representative urban redevelopment project, which utilized two high-rise buildings: the 54-floor Mori Tower and the 43-floor Roppongi Hills Residences. This project used the land in Tokyo effectively, although the Japanese were critical of high-rise building due to the threat of earthquakes (Je, 2006).

Case 2: London – Canary Wharf

Canary Wharf, located on the Isle of Dogs, is a large business development in London's city centre on the old West India Docks in the London Docklands. Rivalling London's traditional financial centre, Canary Wharf contains the UK's three tallest buildings and is known as London's best skyline: One Canada Square (235.1m, usually known as Canary Wharf Tower); HSBC Tower and Citigroup Centre (199.5m); and Swiss Re Building (41 floors, 180m), completed in 2004. The Swiss Re Building was built under the eco-concept rather than

during the development of the city and the first floor was converted into a community area. In this respect, Canary Wharf is known as the single strongest symbol of the changed economic geography of the UK and provides a representative function that integrated the city's competitiveness (Je, 2006).

Case 3: Paris – La Défense

La Défense is a new town within Paris, 6km to the north-west of the old town centring on the Arc de Triomphe. During the 1960s, Paris experienced the limits of city expansion and attempted vertical expansion. However, in light of Paris's artistic and historical significance, there was a need to solve the traffic problem and to maintain historical buildings. The initial development started as a satellite city in order to provide labour in Paris. The year 2000 saw the start of the Paris redevelopment plan, which centred on the La Défense district, which expanded upon the old town's historical axes. Over 115,000 people live in the La Défense area (744ha). The district holds a 30-storey building that is 180m high, and limitations

Table 20.2 *Ripple effect of high-rise buildings*

Category	Details
Environmental ripple effect	*Positive effect* – Minimal change of pre-existing environment, restoration and preservation of ecosystem *Negative effect* – Increase in use of raw material and energy consumption
Social ripple effect	*Positive effect* – Surrounding environment development by 50,000 people moving daily (100-storey building) – Milestone function / national pride *Negative effect* – Possibility of traffic congestion in the surrounding area
Technical ripple effect	*Positive effect* – Uplift of technology in storm-resistance, earthquake-resistance and sound-proofing for high-rise building construction – Develop material for high-rise building / facility technology / construction technology / curtain wall technology
Cultural ripple effect	*Positive effect* – Increased prospect and corporate representation – Construction site as tourist spot *Negative effect* – Cultural refusal on gigantism
Economical ripple effect	*Positive effect* – Additional increase of added value: brand recognition, etc – Other industry production generation effect US$4320 trillion (taller than 100-storey building construction expense US$1800 trillion) – Employment (42,000 people) / revitalization of the surrounding subsidiary facilities *Negative effect* – Extreme investment cost – Construction cost : two 30-floor buildings → one 60-floor building: 1.3–1.4 times increase 　　　　　　　　　　two 50-floor buildings → one 100-floor building: 1.7–2 times increase

Source: Shin (2008a), Leigh (2008)

Source: Je, 2006

Figure 20.3 *Roppongi Hills model, Tokyo*

regarding the building's construction shape have been removed save for the criterion that the axes of the city should not be destroyed. Thus, it was possible to maintain the historical aspect of the old town. After removing the construction shape limitation, private investors began to invest and a variety of designs were applied, which eventually led to the construction of a symmetrical building mass and La Grande Arche. Phare Tower, which has been designed by Morphosis, to be completed by 2012, will contribute an organic configuration to the city. The Tour Signal, which is designed by Jean Nouvel, is also scheduled to be completed by 2014 and with the Phare Tower will form La Défense's high-rise building group. Along with London (Canary Wharf), Paris–La Défense is one of the EU's most compact cities utilizing high-rise buildings (see http://en.wikipedia.org/wiki/La_D%C3%A9fense, accessed December 2008).

Source: Shin, 2008d

Figure 20.4 *Canary Wharf and London metropolitan skyline, London*

Source: Shin, 2008d

Figure 20.5 *La Défense, Paris*

Case 4: New York – 3D city management system

New York's building height limit has been flexible according to the development of the city and the change of local conditions. New York developed a skyline centred around the city to symbolize the image of the city. Midtown, which is known by the Empire State Building, and Lower Manhattan, which featured the World Trade Centre before the 11 September 2001 attacks, shows the symbolic New York skyline and are representative of a modern city model (Shin, 2008d).

In order to continuously enhance New York's city image, building height limit considers scenery, construction and intercultural aspects along with its three-dimensional (3D) city management system. Under this concept, the reconstruction of the World Trade Centre was reviewed as four 55-floor buildings instead of two 110-floor buildings, and has been finalized as the Freedom Tower, which has 173 floors and is 541m in height.

Case 5: Shanghai – Pudong

Pudong is a new development area that has been established through the Shanghai government's significant support. Based on the 1990 Pudong development plan, the Oriental Pearl Tower (the tallest building in Pudong) and many other buildings, including Shanghai International Centre, the World Financial Centre and the World Trade Square, were erected. Recently, Jin Mao Building, which is now the tallest building, was completed. In 2008, the design plan for Shanghai's centre (the Shanghai Tower, with 160 floors) was announced. Along with Dubai, Shanghai is being promoted as the world's best high-rise building compact city. Even at this moment, high-rise buildings are under construction (see http://en.wikipedia.org/wiki/Pudong, accessed December 2008).

High-rise buildings – their trend and efficiency in terms of the sustainable compact city

Sustainable compact city utilizing high-rise buildings

Nowadays the world topic for city development is 'sustainability'. Sustainability is a concept that requires

Source: Shin, 2008d

Figure 20.6 *Freedom Tower, New York*

the integration of environmental, economical and societal dimensions for intergenerational equity. In Europe, it is being promoted as environmentally sound and sustainable development (ESSD) and in the US it is known as 'growth management' or 'smart growth'. Thus, it is of the utmost importance to establish city development plans to reuse ground resources; promote environmentally friendly land-use efficiency; decrease transportation and infrastructure costs; suppress fossil-fuel use; and minimize environment and landscape damage. And as part of city development strategy execution plans, interest in development density or height should be newly defined as a method to accomplish high-rise–high-density concentration, shifting from high-rise–high-density or low-rise–low-density

Source: Shin, 2008a

Figure 20.7 *Shanghai Pudong skyline*

dichotomy. Sustainable high-rise building can contribute to society by reducing pollution and environmental loads and facilitating economic growth. Under this 'sustainability concept', expansion of the city has turned towards the compact city, and one of the most effective methods to accomplish this is through the construction of sustainable high-rise buildings, as mentioned earlier. World global cities are being developed at the city-nation competitiveness level. Next is the efficiency of high-rise buildings with respect to environment, social and economic considerations. High-rise building construction should establish social and economic sustainability, as well as build artistic and culturally sustainable high-rise buildings through design multiplicity.

Efficiency of sustainable high-rise buildings

Environmental efficiency

Environmental efficiency can be described as:

* the reuse of land resources and protection of the environment;
* energy savings and reduction of environmental cost (air pollution) (Choi, 2007).

Land resource is a finite natural resource and thus it should be reused by increasing the input of resources (buildings). Before developing greenfield sites, brownfield resources should be reused. This means promoting the 'compact city'. In other words, by balancing development and preservation, nature can be protected and development can reach its full effect. In addition, through the three-dimensional complex use of high-rise buildings located in the city, if a one-stop service (i.e. provides business, commerce, entertainment, culture and other services in the most efficient areas) becomes available, public transportation can be actively used, decreasing reliance on personal vehicles. Through revitalization of public transportation, parking spaces can be reduced and the usage of roads can also lessen. This will lead to a reduction in traffic expenses, save energy and reduce air pollution by decreasing the energy input. Lastly, if we use the building integrated photovoltaic system (BIPVS), the double-skin system and the wind turbine system that are being applied in certain high-rise buildings, we can save much more energy.

Economic efficiency

Economic efficiency is represented by:

- land usage based on land price;
- 24-hour usage of land through complex use;
- the creation of economic added value through three-dimensional complex usage.

Effective use of land does not mean high-density use or constructing tall buildings unconditionally. According to economic theory, in an area where there is more demand for land and, accordingly, high land prices, there is a necessity for more high-density use or the construction of tall buildings. On the other hand, where there is less demand and, accordingly, low land prices, the use of the land should be the opposite. Land price represents comparative scarcity in the market. High land price infers that there is less land and, therefore, it should be economically used. Thus, input of resources (building) should be increased to use the land intensively. On the contrary, low land price means using the land with more room. Land should be used more extensively by increasing the input of land compared to resources (building). In addition, places with high land price should not limit their use of land during the daytime or night-time, but make full use of it, which is known as 'round the clock' occupancy. To use the land for 24 hours, mixed-use development (MXD) should be a priority. Given this fact, high-rise buildings are effective at integrating diverse uses (such as businesses, residences, accommodation, entertainment and culture) three dimensionally and vertically. Accordingly, land resource can be used day (business and commerce) and night (residence, accommodation, entertainment, etc.). As a result, high-rise construction increases the intensity of the usage of land and can be a method of promoting efficient use of the land. In addition, three-dimensional and vertical use of land has the potential for new economy. Three-dimensional use of high-rise buildings has a landmark effect and increases the city's brand value, which can promote tourism. Complex use of land can also prevent inner-city decline and can encourage night activities to revitalize the local economy.

Societal efficiency

Societal efficiency involves:

- reduction of traffic expenses;
- reduction of infrastructure expenses;

- security of open and walking spaces;
- security of a city's sense of freedom.

Complex use of land through high-rise buildings enables one-stop service (i.e. providing business, commerce, entertainment, culture and other services) that encourages multipurpose trips, which can effectively reduce traffic expenses. In addition, by constructing high-rise buildings in the middle of the city, where there is already developed infrastructure such as subways and water systems, this can save a city's infrastructure cost. In other words, it is better to fix and expand the already existing facilities than incurring additional new infrastructure by expanding the function of the city horizontally. This is more cost effective and can promote sustainable city development. To improve the city's environment where there are many buildings, it is important to secure as much open space as possible. Generally, towards the outer limits of the city there is relatively more green space; but it lacks usable open space where people can easily approach. Nevertheless, there is still a high building-to-land ratio, which uses low-storey buildings and high-density use of the land, in the centre of the city. In this respect, high-rise buildings secure idle space and increase the quality of public space. Lastly, considering the eye level of pedestrians, the additional increase in the height of the building rarely creates a feeling of being hemmed in by pedestrians. Instead, it is more important to control the width of the building, which extends beyond the human scale. By promoting a tower-shape type of building rather than a box-shape type of building, one can secure a view corridor or vertical public space, as shown in Figure 20.8. Moreover, sustainable high-rise buildings secure open spaces between buildings and can contribute to the quality of a city's outer limits (Yeo, 2008). This occurs more frequently in the building's middle-upper level. And high-rise buildings provide a vertical void within the same floor space index, which creates a wind road and view corridor.

Sustainable high-rise buildings: Plan and cases

High-rise buildings require increased construction costs and use more energy. This is due to the different weather conditions (e.g. strong winds) at the upper level of the buildings and their natural closed skin structure. In order to keep the inside of such buildings

Source: Yeo, 2008

Figure 20.8 *Singapore city high-rise building for vertical public space*

similar to the floors downstairs, a mechanical system is required and this results in increased use of energy and in high maintenance costs, as well as decreasing living conditions. Recently, there have been innovative technology developments to minimize these kinds of high-rise buildings' decreased living conditions or to optimize energy. The following sub-sections outline the

relationship between the height of the building and an increase of mass and energy consumption. Energy saving systems are also highlighted.

Energy consumption in buildings

Office
Figure 20.9 shows the yearly energy costs of 92 office buildings. It can be noted that although they have similar exterior conditions, based on environmentally friendly designs, construction and operation, there is a 15-fold difference in costs (Leigh, 2008; Musau and Steemers, 2008).

Area
Figure 20.10 shows US commercial building energy consumption in 2003, categorized by the scale of the building. Note that even though it has fewer storeys, an increase in building floor space contributes to a significant increase in energy consumption. In addition, as the height of the building increases, energy consumption per unit space increases as well (Energy Information Administration, 2006).

Mass
Figure 20.11 is based on research conducted on Chinese buildings by the Building Energy Research Centre in TsinghuaHua University. It shows the correlation between energy consumption and the scale of the building. Note that as the building becomes larger, each element of energy consumption increases as well (Building Energy Research Centre, 2007).

Energy savings in sustainable high-rise buildings – various systems

Building Integrated Photovoltaic System (BIPVS)
Recently, much progress has occurred in utilizing solar energy, as is evidenced in a variety of sustainable high-rise building technologies. BIPVS uses solar energy in high-rise buildings. Since high-rise buildings feature larger areas that can absorb sunlight, they are much more advantageous than ordinary buildings. In addition, by increasing the exterior space of buildings, as shown in Figure 20.12, a variety of designs can be applied. A BIPV panel can advance a diversity of designs because it is fairly easy to apply different colours (Pank et al, 2002):

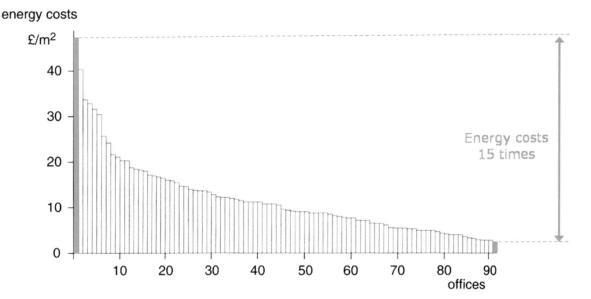

Source: Musau and Steemers, 2008

Figure 20.9 *Energy costs of 92 office buildings*

- BIPV systems contribute to the electronic energy supply of buildings themselves.
- BIPV provides an opportunity for a clear path of direct sunlight.

- There is sufficient area to install a photovoltaic (PV) panel.
- BIPVS is easy to incorporate in high-rise buildings as a result of:

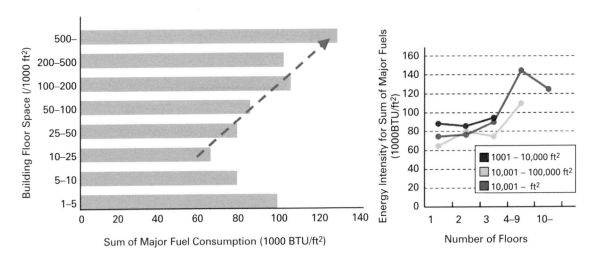

Source: Leigh, 2008

Figure 20.10 *Consumption pattern based on the nature of construction*

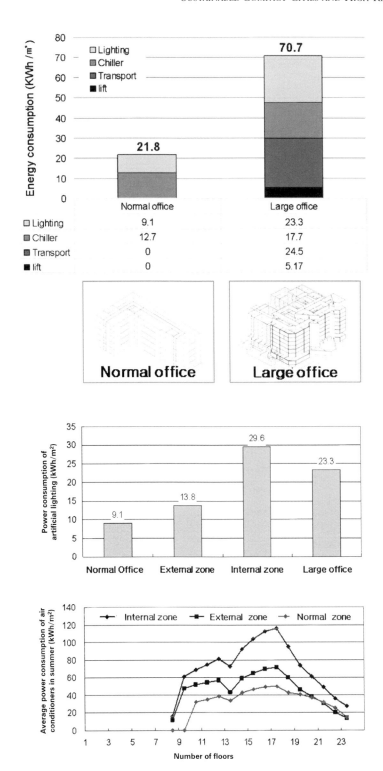

Source: Leigh, 2008

Figure 20.11 *Energy consumption ratios within large buildings*

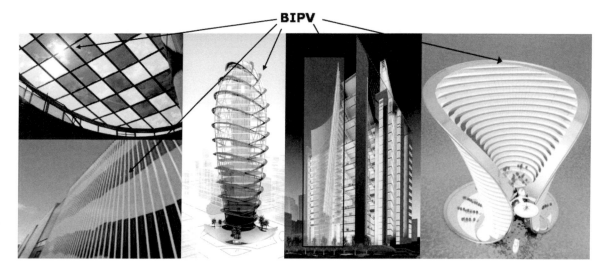

Figure 20.12 *Building integrated photovoltaic system with design variation on a high-rise building*

- natural ventilation (improves energy efficiency and is good for health);
- economical efficiency: initial investment increases by 8.5 per cent, but energy consumption decreases by 40 per cent, while a low life-cycle cost (LCC) is required.

Double-skin system

The double-skin system uses natural ventilation as a basic facility to increase energy efficiency and is also known to be good for health. In addition, it is very economical – initial construction costs increase by 8.5 per cent; but in the end energy consumption is reduced by 40 per cent (low life-cycle cost). Examples that have applied this system are shown in Figures 20.13, 20.15, 20.18 and 20.19 (Pank et al, 2002).

Wind turbine system

High-rise buildings have been criticized by people due to their overuse of energy. However, wind turbines can now be installed on top or in the middle of buildings to adapt to the wind current, as is shown in Figures 20.14 and 20.17, and are being used as a form of alternative energy. Recently, as shown in Figure 20.19, there is a new system that utilizes the rising current of air from the middle part and lower parts of buildings (Pank et al, 2002):

- Aerodynamic modelling is used to determine the optimum tower height, control systems, number of blades and blade shape.

Sustainable high-rise buildings: Cases

Phare Tower

Phare Tower is an example of the sustainable design of a high-rise building that applied a variety of sustainable design methods. The tower satisfies the condition of a high-rise building by meeting its purpose as a place for sales, exhibitions and halls. The total floor area of abundant tree planting and balconies is almost the same as the total floor area of the building. Trees have been planted along the slope from the first floor to the top of the building (see http://en.wikipedia.org/ wiki/Phare_Tower, accessed December 2008). Important features include the following:

- eco-friendly landmark in the redevelopment of La Défense, Paris, France, by Morphosis – to be completed by 2012;
- extends to a height of 300m and 68 floors;
- double-skin system with a wind turbine on the roof.

Source: Shin, 2009

Figure 20.13 *Double-skin system design concept and cases*

Source: Shin, 2009

Figure 20.14 *Wind turbine system cases*

Bishopsgate Tower

Bishopsgate Tower, in London, England, although not yet completed, is noticeable for its application of an environmentally friendly sustainable design by Ken Yeang. In order to promote environmental sustainability, the building fully took into consideration its surrounding environment and systems. The building also aimed to minimize the building system and applied the following concepts (see http://en. wikipedia.org/wiki/Bishopsgate_Tower, accessed December 2008):

- KPF(Kohn Pedersen Fox)–BIPV panels and natural ventilation;
- continuous landscape;
- a circulation and water recycling system;
- extends to a height of 288m and 63 floors.

Bahrain World Trade Center

Three wind turbines are expected to provide 10 to 15 per cent of the Bahrain World Trade Center's towers' total power consumption, and the construction cost for

Source: Shin, 2009

Figure 20.15 *Phare Tower*

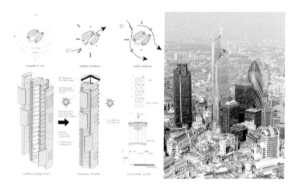

Source: Leigh, 2008

Figure 20.16 *Bishopsgate Tower*

Source: Shin, 2009

Figure 20.18 *Guanzhou Pearl River Tower*

Source: Shin, 2009

Figure 20.17 *Bahrain World Trade Centre*

Source: Shin, 2009

Figure 20.19 *Seoul LITE building*

turbines was approximately 3 per cent of the total construction cost. In order to increase the function of the turbines, the sail-shaped buildings on either side increase the speed of wind passing through the turbines. Other features include:

- features wind turbines;
- project managed by WS Atkins plc;
- extends to 239 m and 53 floors.

See http://en.wikipedia.org/wiki/Bahrain_world_trade_center for further information.

Guanzhou Pearl River Tower

Two wind turbines are located within the Guanzhou Pearl River Tower in China, and the BIPV system features solar energy outside of the building (Ali and Armstrong, 2008). Features include the following:

- extends to a height of 239m and 71 floors;
- will be completed by 2012;
- architects are SOM (Skidmore, Owings & Merrill LLP);
- wind turbines;
- double-skin system;
- geothermal heat sinks;
- ventilated façades;
- waterless urinals;
- integrated photovoltaics;
- condensate recovery;
- daylight-responsive controls.

Seoul LITE

More than 90 wind turbines are applied in the Seoul LITE building, Korea, for the rising current of air inside the building's inner core. The outer side is constructed by using a double-skin system and photovoltaic power generation (Chul and Choi, 2008; Shin, 2008b). Features include the following:

- extends to a height of 640m and 133 floors;
- a wind turbine system;
- BIPV panel;
- to be completed by 2014;
- double-skin system;
- architects are SOM, Y-Group, SAMOO, MOO YOUNG.

Conclusions

Over time, the construction of high-rise buildings has become more meaningful than just the symbol of height. The concept of a city that evolves alongside industrial and economic growth has brought diverse environmental problems requiring prompt solutions. Society has responded by constructing tall buildings and turning them into a vertical city. Modern cities need to promote effective communication of information and logistics. In addition, due to reckless development on the ground, there is a lack of land area, and residences are deteriorating. City development plans were initiated to promote the eco-city

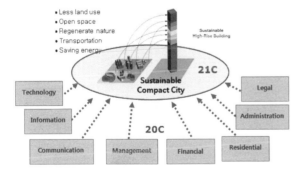

Source: Shin (2008b)

Figure 20.20 *Sustainable compact city concept utilizing high-rise buildings*

(developing new cities near metropolitan areas or spreading functions across cities to solve the overcrowding of a specific city). However, with mass energy consumption and a shift in the city paradigm, the concept of the compact city has been re-established (see Figure 20.20) as the sustainable vertical city. Efforts are also being made to consider environmental, social and economic concerns.

Nevertheless, there is a lack of synthesized analysis of sustainable compact cities that use sustainable high-rise buildings based on thorough and sufficient research and studies. This chapter has focused on positive environmental, social and economic approaches to the sustainable compact city that utilizes sustainable high-rise buildings; however, enough feedback from these exemplary cities is not yet available. If sufficient research and studies are to be conducted in the near future, environmental, social and economic efficiency can be improved and the function of cities within nations will be strengthened.

We now need to focus on practical execution plans or design according to research and studies on sustainable compact cities that are based on sustainable high-rise buildings in order to establish sustainable cities and, more importantly, a sustainable Earth.

Acknowledgements

The research for this chapter was initiated by the Sustainable Building Research Centre of Hanyang University (supported by the SRC/ERC programme, MEST Grant R11-2005-056-010003-0) and the Korea Super Tall Building Forum.

References

AIJ and IBEC (2002) *Architecture for a Sustainable Future*, Architectural Institute of Japan, Tokyo, pp78–80

Ali, M. M. and Armstrong, P. J. (2008) 'Overview of sustainable design factors in high-rise buildings', Paper presented to the CTBUH 8th World Congress 2008, Dubai, pp9–10

Building Energy Research Centre (2007) 'Living style: The key factor for building energy efficient', Presentation, Building Energy Research Centre, Tsinghua University, China

Choi, M. J. (2007) 'The meaning of super tall building within city space structure', in *Proceedings of the Super Tall Building and City Development Plan Policy Debate*, Korea Planners Association (KPA), Korea, May 2007, pp5–19

Chul, W. and Choi, S. O. M. (2008) 'Plan of Sang-am DMC Landmark Tower on Seoul', in *Proceedings of the 10th International Symposium of Korea Super Tall Building Forum*, Federation of Korean Industries (FKI), Korea, pp130–139

CTBUH (Council on Tall Buildings and Urban Habitat) (2008) *CTBUH Tall Building Database*, www.ctbuh.org/HighRiseInfo/TallestDatabase/tabid/123/Default.aspx, accessed December 2008

CTBUH (2009) *100 Tallest Buildings in the World*, www.ctbuh.org/Portals/0/Tallest/CTBUH_Tallest100.pdf, accessed January 2009

Energy Information Administration (2006) *2003 Commercial Buildings Energy Consumption Survey*, Energy Information Administration, US

Je, H.-S. (2006) 'Super tall buildings and urban competitive power', in *Proceedings of the 7th International Symposium of the Korea Super Tall Building Forum*, Federation of Korean Industries (FKI), Korea, pp35–67

Leigh, S.-B. (2008) 'The method to increase sustainability in tall buildings', in *Proceedings of the 10th International Symposium of the Korea Super Tall Building Forum*, Federation of Korean Industries (FKI), Korea, pp67–84

Musau, F. and Steemers, K. (2008) 'Space planning and energy efficiency in office buildings: The role of spatial and temporal diversity', *Building Research Energy Conservation Support Unit*, UK

Pank, W., Girardet, H. and Cox, G. (2002) *Tall Buildings and Sustainability Report*, Corporation of London, London, pp38–47

Shin, S. W. (2008a) 'Industry of super tall buildings as new growth power', in *Proceedings of the 10th International Symposium of the Korea Super Tall Building Forum*, Federation of Korean Industries (FKI), Korea, pp2–11

Shin, S. W. (2008b) 'Economic, environmental impact and urban competitiveness of sustainable tall buildings', Paper presented to Sustainability in Tall Buildings Special Session, XXII UIA Congress, Torino, Italy, 2 July 2008

Shin, S. W. (2008c) 'Current work and future trend for sustainable buildings in South Korea', Paper presented to the *SB08 Melbourne World Sustainable Building Conference*, IISBE, Australia, 22 September 2008

Shin, S. W. (2008d) 'Super tall building with Hangang and urban competitiveness', in *Proceedings of the 9th International Symposium of Korea Super Tall Building Forum*, Federation of Korean Industries (FKI), Korea, pp2–19

Shin, S. W. (2009) 'A Way to Sustainable Super Tall Building Industry', proceedings of 11th international symposium of Korea Super Tall Building Forum, Architectural Institute of Korea, Korea, pp3–19

Yeo, Y.-H. (2008) 'Industry of super tall buildings as new growth power', in *Proceedings of the 10th International Symposium of Korea Super Tall Building Forum*, Federation of Korean Industries (FKI), Korea, pp52–65

21

Microclimate in Public Housing: An Environmental Approach to Community Development

John C. Y. Ng

Introduction

Well-planned communities contribute to social cohesion, improved health and better use of resources. Housing plays a key role in urban renewal and local regeneration. Adequate and affordable housing is an indicator of social and economic stability. The Hong Kong Housing Authority (HKHA) aims to make public housing estates a better place in which to live, and to ensure that tenants enjoy a quality living environment with a focus on safety and hygiene. Housing planning and design can help to promote more sustainable use of resources and better meet people's changing needs so that we can keep buildings longer before pulling them down. During a building's construction and over its whole life cycle, we should be able to contribute to a more sustainable future by being more energy efficient, using fewer resources and generating less waste in the process.

As the agent that provides and manages rental dwellings for nearly one third of Hong Kong's population, the HKHA is in a unique position to help drive the industry towards sustainable development. The HKHA started early and has been a forerunner in green construction and housing management practices:

- use of large panel formwork for reduced timber use;
- use of prefabricated façades, staircases, dry panel walls for better quality control and reduction of construction wastes;
- segregation of waste material in demolition sites for the recycling of materials and land reclamation use;
- use of a refuse compaction system in handling the large volume of domestic wastes;
- implementation of the Green Delight in Housing Estate Programme in collaboration with green groups to increase residents' awareness of environmental protection and waste recovery.

Since the late 1990s, the HKHA has ventured into the concept of sustainable development in the planning and design of public housing. In 1999, The housing authority formally established its environmental policy, which requires the HKHA to 'promote healthy living, green environment and sustainable development' in the provision of public housing and its related services. The HKHA has since broken away from the norm of using standard housing blocks and has embarked on site-specific block designs to optimize development potential.

Microclimate is the local modification of the general climate that is imposed by the special configuration of a small area. It is influenced by topography, ground surface, plant cover and man-made forms. In 2001, the HKHA initiated the application of microclimate studies in the planning and design of public housing. These studies enabled optimization of the development potential and enhancement of the built environment of the neighbourhood.

This chapter discusses the experience of the HKHA in blending microclimate studies with planning and design and how it contributes to the development of a sustainable community.

Sustainable community: A holistic approach

One of the HKHA's key missions is to deliver affordable quality housing and a healthy living environment to its tenants. This, we believe, in turn allows our tenants to contribute more effectively to the community and the local economy. In a broader perspective, we are contributing to the sustainability of Hong Kong as a whole. In order to achieve this vision, we have been striving for better design that integrates environmentally friendly, functional and cost-effective considerations into a holistic solution.

Sustainable housing balances the economical, environmental and social needs of our communities. All three dimensions of sustainability are addressed in our planning and design process in a holistic manner. We address these elements in the entire process from master layout to specification stage, and at different levels of details. We tackle these issues in the earliest instance and capture the valuable opportunities for community enhancement available at early stages of development.

We cannot achieve this alone. We engage our stakeholders and collaborate with them; sustainable community needs the widest base upon which to stand and grow.

Community development: In pursuit of economic sustainability

The economic performance of an organization provides the key to its success and sustainability. Cost effectiveness is a critical consideration on many aspects of the housing programme, from planning and design, through to construction, operation and maintenance. We optimize site potential, respond to site characteristics and microclimate conditions, and improve building and structural efficiency. By designing in harmony with the site, we aim to economize on resources, reduce energy consumption and waste, and remove processes with potentially adverse environmental impacts.

Domestic blocks are designed to maximize natural ventilation and light, facilitate mechanized construction for speed and accuracy, and to provide good-quality, flexible living space for tenants. Comfortable homes provide the base for our physical as well as mental health. They enhance the sense of belonging to the estate and facilitate community development.

During 2002 to 2005, the HKHA commissioned consultants to carry out a study on life-cycle assessment

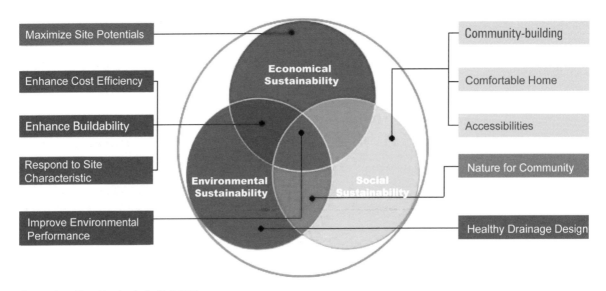

Source: Hong Kong Housing Authority (HKHA)

Figure 21.1 *The three dimensions of sustainability*

(LCA) and life-cycle costing (LCC) of building materials and components. Designers are now using the LCA and LCC software to help them make decisions on the choice of materials in new designs. With the life-cycle cost optimized, economic sustainability is enhanced and the living environment is improved. This also facilitates the development of sustainable community in public housing.

Community development: In pursuit of social sustainability

Over the past five decades, the HKHA's public housing programme has promoted social stability, economic prosperity and has fostered harmony in the community. Serving one third of the population in some 240 housing estates is a challenging task. It requires planning, design and management practices that place the welfare of our tenants in the forefront. The HKHA aims to make public housing estates a better place in which to live and to ensure that our tenants enjoy a quality living environment with a focus on safety and hygiene. Community development and social cohesion are enhanced through community engagement and participation. Sustainable housing can only be achieved through working with people.

Engaging the community is an important step in enhancing community development during the planning and design stages. We have piloted several models to explore people-oriented design on estates at Yau Tong Estate, Ma Hang Headland, Upper Ngau Tak Kok Estate and Lam Tin Estate. A variety of identified groups of stakeholders have been engaged: academics, residents, concern groups, district councillors, schools and non-governmental organizations (NGOs) were briefed on the constraints and opportunities of the project in a series of facilitated workshops. The workshops help them to understand the concerns and aspirations of their built environment. Microclimate studies serve as an objective tool in predicting environmental performance. It is particularly useful in public engagement and demonstrates how environmental concerns are being taken care of.

In one of our pilot projects, we worked with professional facilitators to develop a model for this purpose, and conducted a series of community workshops and briefing sessions with the aim of incorporating community wisdom within the project. The workshop was an open forum for people to voice their concerns and to develop design proposals in an organized and rational manner. Participants were divided into smaller groups for discussions. Various options were then explored and evaluated. The workshop allowed future users and stakeholders to understand from a perspective of competing interests and priorities. Participants contributed to decisions made about their community so that there was a sense of collective ownership. They also found opportunities to express creativity to shape their own living environment. The workshop established a sense of trust and was very well received by residents. It also demonstrates care and sensitivity to their well-being and responds to their genuine concerns. We also ran exhibitions to strengthen public awareness and appreciation of local heritage, and instilled a greater sense of belonging in the community.

Community development: In pursuit of environmental sustainability

The HKHA is the largest developer in Hong Kong with a stock of over 680,000 flats. We have a construction programme of approximately 15,000 new flats every year and our day-to-day operations could have a great impact upon the local environment. Given our high-density, high-rise environment with enormous political, technical, time and cost constraints, we design, construct and manage for better environmental performance for the benefit of our tenants and the community at large.

Since 2004, all our designs for new estates have adopted microclimate studies to assess the performance of the estates by applying various simulation programmes and computational fluid dynamics techniques. Designers are able to refine the master layout plan and scheme design to maximize the advantages of the built form, orientation and disposition of buildings and thereby optimize performance of local wind patterns, natural ventilation to buildings, dispersion of pollutants, daylighting standards, thermal comfort, and provide a basis for improved energy efficiency. The studies help us to provide a natural, healthier and more user-friendly living environment for our tenants and the community.

We have already applied these microclimate modelling techniques on 30 projects. The first project, Upper Ngau Tau Kok Estate phases 2 and 3, which was due for completion in early 2009, has been assessed under the

Hong Kong Building Environmental Assessment Method (HK-BEAM) and has achieved the provisional top-level platinum rating. This was followed by Lam Tin Estate phase 7 and 8, which is due for completion in 2009.

Wind environment

A healthy lifestyle has become a great concern of Hong Kong society after the severe acute respiratory syndrome (SARS) crisis in 2003. The wind environment of a housing development not only affects the health condition of the living environment, but also determines the thermal comfort of the domestic dwellings, common areas within the blocks, pedestrian circulation, external open spaces and nearby neighbourhoods. It is one of the key considerations in designing communal spaces to encourage people to gather, meet, encounter, chat and interact socially. We use the microclimate studies as an urban design tool to optimize estate planning, disposition/ orientation of blocks, built form and building permeability to enhance the overall wind environment within the housing development and its surroundings.

Site wind availability data

It is necessary to account for the characteristics of the natural wind availability of each individual housing development site. We make use of wind data from weather stations of the local observatory to estimate qualitatively the prevailing wind directions and magnitudes. For sites with weather stations nearby, a wind rose of prevailing directions covering most of the time in a typical reference year is vital for microclimate studies, whereas for those with specific site topography and remote from weather stations, it will be more appropriate to make use of wind tunnel simulation tests to determine the local wind pattern.

Air ventilation assessment (AVA)

Air ventilation assessment is an indicator that relates the wind availability of a city and urban geometry, and assesses the built form's capability of optimizing available wind. This indicator addresses what minimum wind environment, and in what form, is needed to guide design and planning in order to achieve a better wind penetration into and, hence, air ventilation of the city, especially at the pedestrian level.

Wind environmental initiatives

In order to assess the wind environment of a new development, we apply computational fluid dynamics (CFD) analysis to study the wind flow pattern and magnitude at low, mid and high zones of the high-rise

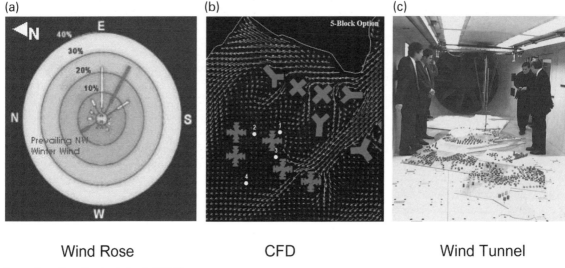

| (a) | (b) | (c) |
| Wind Rose | CFD | Wind Tunnel |

Source: Hong Kong Housing Authority (HKHA)

Figure 21.2 *Simulation tools: (a) wind rose; (b) computational fluid dynamics; (c) wind tunnel*

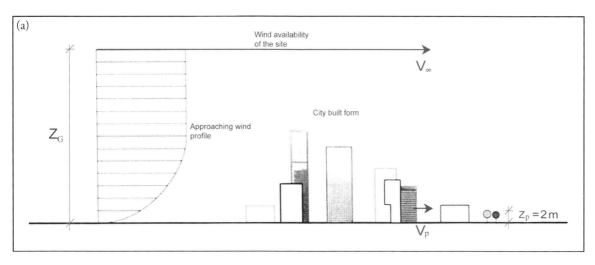

(b)

$$VRw = \frac{Vp}{V\infty}$$

Velocity Ratio at pedestrian level

Source: Department of Architecture, Chinese University of Hong Kong (2005)

Figure 21.3 *Air ventilation assessment to ensure ventilation performance at the pedestrian level*

Note: The effectiveness of the wind corridor design, in quantitative terms, for enhancing site permeability for prevailing wind is identified by comparing simulation results of 'before' and 'after' implementation of the development. The increase in air velocity with wind corridor under the prevailing wind condition creates a pleasant environment for social gathering and interaction in plaza and pedestrian circulation areas within the estate, as well as various activities in open spaces.
Source: Author

Figure 21.4 *Wind corridor to enhance the wind environment of the plaza*

domestic towers for different enhancement measures in site planning and building design options, external circulation and open spaces, and impact upon surroundings. By comparing the microclimate study results of various green initiatives, the most optimal planning and design option is worked out objectively on both a qualitative and quantitative basis.

Natural ventilation and pollutant dispersion

Energy-efficient homes and well-planned communities reduce energy consumption and contribute to social cohesion. We use the microclimate studies as a building design tool to optimize the configuration of blocks, as well as detailed architectural layout and window openings to enhance natural cross-ventilation in domestic units and public areas.

Natural ventilation initiatives

By simulating the wind flow pattern and magnitude of typical domestic units, lobbies and public areas at low, mid and high zones, an optimized design option is developed to enhance natural ventilation with effective pollutant dispersion from toilets and refuse rooms.

Daylight and sun shading

Daylight is essential for psychological well-being and increases the comfort level of spaces. We use microclimate

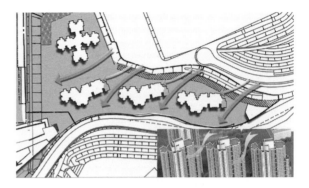

Note: For constrained sites of narrow linear configuration, design options for disposition and orientation (deviation up to 10°) of high-rise domestic blocks are compared in microclimate studies to streamline the wind flow across the development. The wind speed in the open spaces between domestic towers increases substantially by 100 to 133 per cent by adopting the master layout. This enhances the wind environment at the promenade in the front and attracts more social interaction and pedestrian circulation.

Source: Hong Kong Housing Authority (HKHA)

Figure 21.6 *Enhancement of wind environment at a pedestrian promenade through built form refinement and disposition of domestic blocks*

studies as a design tool to optimize daylight penetration in domestic units and public areas for energy efficiency, comfort and health, and to optimize the planning of passive and active open spaces within the development.

Natural lighting initiatives

The amount of daylight on the surface of a building façade is related to the extent of its exposure. In high-density and high-rise developments, much of the daylight penetrating through window openings at the lower floors of domestic blocks come from reflected light from the surrounding surfaces. We adopt the performance-based approach using the vertical daylight factor (VDF) (a ratio in percentage of the total amount of illuminance falling onto a vertical surface of a building to the instantaneous horizontal illuminance from an overcast sky) as a design indicator for optimizing natural lighting performance.

Sun-shading initiatives

Sun-shading is one of the key considerations in designing external open spaces to encourage people to

Note: The environmental design in estate planning and disposition/orientation of blocks enhance the wind environment of the housing development, as well as that of nearby neighbourhoods.
Source: Hong Kong Housing Authority (HKHA)

Figure 21.5 *Wind corridor to enhance the wind environment of the housing development and nearby neighbourhoods*

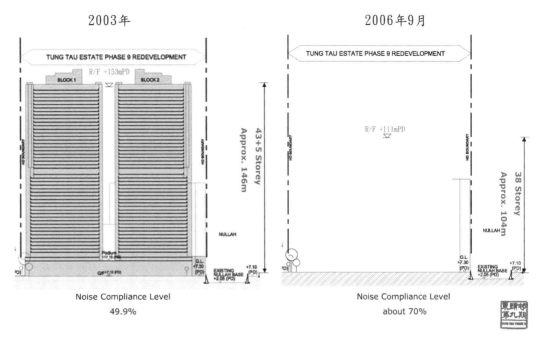

Note: Site-specific design options 'with' and 'without' a podium are compared for identification of the significant variance in building permeability for air ventilation at the pedestrian level. The average wind speed and velocity ratio at street level (leeward side) increases by 13 and 14 per cent, respectively without a podium.

Source: Hong Kong Housing Authority (HKHA)

Figure 21.7 *Podium option discarded for better wind environment at the pedestrian level*

Note: A double-height green deck garden is sandwiched at the first-floor level of a high-rise domestic tower to enhance building permeability and to extend the ground floor garden into the habitable spaces. This deck garden integrates the social spaces inside and outside the block, provides additional amenity spaces for social, cultural and heritage use, creates a special identity for the estate, and increases the tenants' sense of belonging to the community. With the deck garden open for the enjoyment of the residents from nearby estates, it serves as a platform for social interaction and enhancement of the social cohesion of the community. Nearby urban greening filters airflow and provides additional shade and cooling.

Source: Hong Kong Housing Authority (HKHA)

Figure 21.8 *The deck garden enhances the microclimate of the domestic tower and integrates the social activities at the ground level*

**Proposed Redevelopment
(WITH cross-ventilated
re-entrants)**

**Before Redevelopment
(WITHOUT cross-ventilated
re-entrants)**

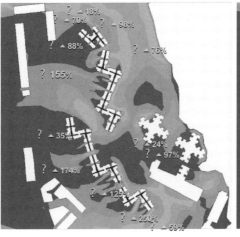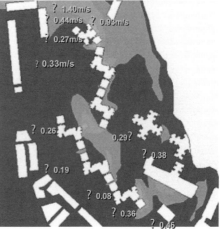

Note: The effectiveness of a cross-ventilated re-entrant design for enhancing building permeability is reflected by quantitative results obtained from the 'with' and 'without' models. The increase in air velocity with cross-ventilated re-entrants at selected points around the development, under the prevailing east wind condition, ranges from 18 to 250 per cent.
Source: Hong Kong Housing Authority (HKHA)

Figure 21.9 *Cross-ventilated re-entrants improve building permeability and facilitate social interaction among tenants at common areas within the domestic blocks*

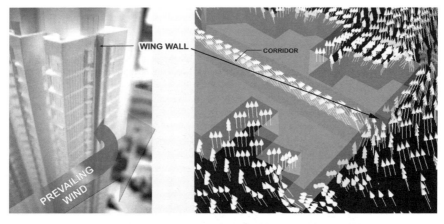

Note: The effectiveness of the wing wall as wind deflector for enhancing natural ventilation of domestic blocks at sites with a low ventilation rate is reflected in the quantitative results of 'with' and 'without' scenarios. Wing wall increases the air velocity inside corridors by 2.5 per cent.
Source: Hong Kong Housing Authority (HKHA)

Figure 21.10 *Wing wall enhances natural ventilation in common corridors, improves comfort level and facilitates social interaction among tenants in common areas*

gather, meet casually, encounter, chat and interact. Simulation of an annual three-dimensional sun path diagram dedicated to the local context identifies the sunlight and shade pattern at external areas at different times of the day and in different seasons of the year. It is an integrated design approach for optimizing the sunlight exposure to green areas, morning exercise and outdoor laundry space, sun-shading for leisure sitting,

Note: Microclimate studies verify the effectiveness of modular design flats in quantitative terms for enhancing natural ventilation. Better natural ventilation implies the reduction of energy consumption in mechanical ventilation and air conditioning. It improves comfort and provides a healthy wind environment.
Source: Hong Kong Housing Authority (HKHA)

Figure 21.11 *Modular design of domestic flats*

and children's play and ball courts, particularly for west-facing open spaces.

Comprehensive performance-based open space planning is adopted. Activities that benefit from shading (e.g. children's play area and foot massage trail) are planned along adequately shaded areas. Areas exposed to the sun during most of the day would be shaded by adding trees or shelters. This is to create a pleasant environment for various outdoor activities.

In some projects, greening of open spaces is extended and brought into the development both physically and visually through careful planning based on sun-shading simulation results and sensitive landscape design. This gives the estate an individual ambience and a specific identity.

Solar heat gain

A comfortable home provides the base for our physical as well as mental health. We use microclimate studies as a design tool to minimize solar heat gain in domestic units in order to achieve higher energy efficiency and better human comfort.

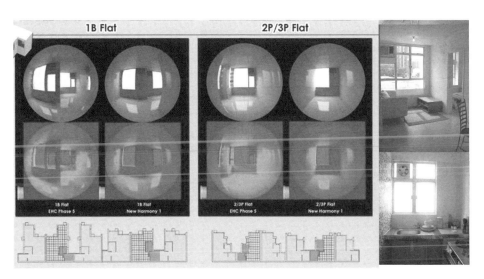

Note: The effectiveness of the modular design for enhancing daylight penetration into domestic flats is reflected by performance assessment. Better daylight for the dwelling units implies a reduction of energy consumption for artificial lighting. It also provides a good ambience and comfortable environment for indoor activities.
Source: Hong Kong Housing Authority (HKHA)

Figure 21.12 *Daylight simulation for modular flats*

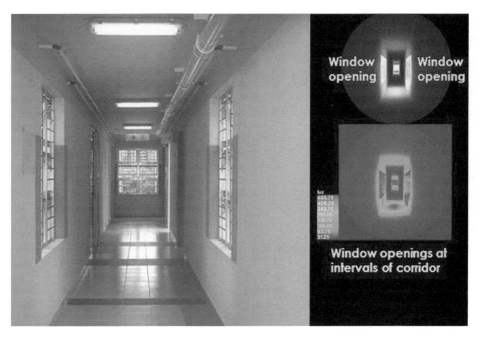

Note: The effectiveness of window openings for enhancing daylight penetration into public areas is reflected by performance-based assessment. The windows in cross-ventilated corridors yield energy cost savings of approximately 13 per cent, while facilitating social interaction among tenants in common areas.
Source: Hong Kong Housing Authority (HKHA)

Figure 21.13 *Cross-ventilated window openings improve daylight penetration*

Source: Hong Kong Housing Authority (HKHA)

Figure 21.14 *Sun-shading simulation results for external open space*

Overall thermal transfer value (OTTV) as an indicator

The façade of a building is a complex system, comprising a range of components that act together to create a healthy internal environment. The amount of energy saved by adopting a cost-effective and high-performance façade design to maintain a thermally acceptable environment could be quantified through the overall thermal transfer value (OTTV), which

Source: Hong Kong Housing Authority (HKHA)

Figure 21.15 *Environmental façade with design approach to reduce energy consumption*

relates to fabric thermal mass, glazing, passive solar design, window design and shading devices. The OTTV, other than as an effective indicator, can be used as a good reference for external wall colour scheme design.

Environmental façade design initiatives

We apply simulation technology and a computer program that consists of modules for ventilation, thermal comfort and building energy analysis for computing the temperature profiles of the internal environment of habitable rooms. The façade features, which affect cooling load, achievable ventilation rates and daylight illuminance, comprise and relate closely to wall/roof construction, window/wall area ratio, glazing type, building orientation, configuration and separation, floor level, external wall finishes and colour, shading device, etc. We apply the study to design solar shading devices for reducing solar heat gain both on the building façade and in individual dwellings in order to reduce the energy consumption related to air conditioning and other mechanical ventilation means. In order to optimize the life-cycle cost, the shading fins are integrated within the precast façade panels, as well as taking into consideration the transportation economy and loading for on-site installation.

The unique environmental façade design brings visual meaning to the domestic towers in relation to their microclimatic conditions. It also gives identity to individual flats, which enhance the sense of belonging and ownership, promoting tenants' pride in being part of the community.

Conclusions

Public housing in Hong Kong has made a substantial contribution towards the quality of the built environment and the well-being of the community. With the availability of advanced simulation technology, microclimate studies have proven to be a useful design tool and are instrumental in improving the environmental performance of housing development. Such studies bring long-term benefits to the built environment and the quality of living of the community as a whole.

Environmental performance of new housing developments is causing increasing public concern regarding high-density urban development. A political debate occurs when people start to become concerned about how a neighbouring development will affect their existing environment. Microclimate studies could serve as a practical approach and an objective tool in predicting resultant environmental performances at an early stage.

These studies are useful in public engagement and consultation, demonstrating how environmental concerns are being taking care of. The government has pledged a vision of 'blue sky and social harmony' through direct enhancement of the environment. As a platform for the community engagement process, microclimate studies could be part of effective policy implementation.

A healthy built environment directly enhances the well-being of the community. It saves energy and associated health-related costs. Through community participation and engagement of the public in the development process, it involves people in developing an environment and a community that is sustainable and carries ownership.

Reference

Department of Architecture, Chinese University of Hong Kong (2005) *Final Report: Feasibility Study for Establishment of Air Ventilation Assessment System*, Department of Architecture, Chinese University of Hong Kong, November, Hong Kong

Designing for High-Density Living: High Rise, High Amenity and High Design

Kam-Sing Wong

High-density living: Best or worst?

It is the best of times and it is the worst of times. High-density living has been the wholehearted pride of many Hong Kong people for decades. Whether luxury, middle class, or public, Hong Kong housing is high rise and high density. However, it has ironically become the worst connotation of the dense local built environment during the past few years in the eyes of many citizens. Here is a tale of Hong Kong and these two apparently opposite views.

In recent years, Hong Kong has faced an unprecededly high level of public criticism against newly planned and newly built high-density developments, especially those residential projects near the harbour front or on top of mass transit railway stations. Such strong protests have been reported as frequent headline news over a prolonged period of time. Kowloon Station Development (see Figure 22.1) is one of the classic controversial examples.

This extraordinary public pressure is forcing the government to respond to the grave concerns of high density. The years 2007 to 2008 signify a historic turning point in Hong Kong in which, for the first time, the Policy Address of the Chief Executive of the Hong Kong Special Administrative Region (HKSAR) included an unprecedented section on 'lowering development density'. Under the heading 'Quality city and quality life', the top official of the HKSAR government introduced the term 'progressive development', which means overall progress rather than economic development alone, and specifically pointed out the following local concerns and counter-measures in Hong Kong:

> Over the past few years, the public has raised concerns about the 'wall effect' caused by high-density buildings, which affects ventilation and leads to a rise in temperature. Despite the absence of a scientific definition of the 'wall effect', we believe that a slight reduction of development density can increase the distance between buildings and upgrade building design. This will enhance the vista of the buildings and improve ventilation.

> The government will review the outline zoning plans of various districts in a step-by-step manner and, where justified, revise the relevant planning parameters to lower the development density. We will also review the approved schemes of above-station property development projects at the Nam Cheong Station and the Yuen Long Station along the West Rail, with a view to lowering their development densities. Such measures will inevitably lead to a reduction in public revenue; but I am convinced that it is well worth it for the better living environment that will be created for our people.

While the latest policy on 'quality city and quality life' is taking shape step by step, its actual effect is yet to be seen at this juncture since the concerned large-scale developments will take years to complete. Nonetheless, it is timely to review Hong Kong's lesson of designing for high-density living.

Note: A strong contrast is evident between the recent high-density property development above Kowloon Station and its surrounding high-density developments in the older district.

Source: Author

Figure 22.1 *Kowloon Station Development*

1993 – Hong Kong architecture: The aesthetics of density

In 1993, Vittorio Magnago Lampugnani et al edited a classic publication entitled *Hong Kong Architecture: The Aesthetics of Density*. The book, coined as the first comprehensive overview of recent trends and developments in this teeming city, covers an in-depth historical review of Hong Kong's urban development, which has been moving towards increasing building density for over a century and results in shaping an exceptionally compact urban form. Hong Kong has been praised as a model city that can achieve high efficiency in the use of land, energy, infrastructure, transit and various other resources while conserving three-quarters of the territory undeveloped. About 40 per cent of the total land mass is reserved as scenic country parks and nature reserves. In contrast, the intensely urbanized areas are vibrant day and night.

In the foreword, Edward George Pryor, the principal government town planner at that time (when Hong Kong's airport was still at the heart of the city), described Hong Kong as follows:

> Flying in to Hong Kong's International Airport at Kai Tak provides a unique opportunity to take in, at a glance, a densely packed high-rise city fringed by steep mountains overlooking a magnificent deep-water harbour. Around

the harbour, the urban conglomeration of the Metro area comprising the northern shoreline of Hong Kong Island, Kowloon, New Kowloon and Tsuen Wan–Kwai Tsing covers a total of about 7250ha and is the home of some 4 million people. The overall density of population in the built-up areas of the Metro area is in the order of 550 persons per hectare; but in certain districts, such as Mong Kok, the gross density reaches as high as 1170 [persons per hectare]. These crude indices of congestion raise questions of how people cope with the resulting pressures. The answer is found partly in the psychological adaptation of the Chinese people to living in tightly knit communities over many centuries, and partly in the innovative skills of planners, engineers and architects in being able to produce high-density urban forms that are well designed, well built and well managed.

Pryor has further highlighted that, in many ways, Hong Kong can be regarded as an 'urban laboratory', where there has been a willingness to try out new ideas. From an urban design point of view, however, there has been a price to pay. Within the space of four decades or so, the city form has been turned from a horizontal to a vertical plane. Older buildings of five to six storeys have been replaced by high-rise megaliths of concrete and steel, frequently designed in frugal ways to achieve minimum costs and maximum returns. The profit motive has unashamedly been a primary driving force; but that motive is an integral part of Hong Kong's cultural heritage. At any rate, from the experience gained in Hong Kong, there could be valuable lessons to be learned by other cities that face increasing pressures of hyper-urbanization within shrinking limits of space suitable for urban expansion. Generally speaking, the typical height of high-rise residential buildings in Hong Kong can be described as 20 storeys, 30 storeys, 40 storeys, and 50 storeys and above during the 1970s, 1980s, 1990s and 2000s, respectively. Given the technological advancement in both structure and building services, the momentum for building taller high-rise homes seems to be ceaseless. Apparently, the sky is the limit.

Projecting into the future, Lampugnani et al (1993) cited a number of planned high-density developments, including Verbena Heights and Kowloon Station Development. The overall comments have been optimistically positive about Hong Kong's high-density trend in development that adopts a high-rise built form and high-quality design for creating urban living with a high amenity.

Verbena Heights (see Figure 22.2), completed between 1996 and 1997 in two phases, is a high-density public housing estate based on a plot ratio of 8 on a site of 2ha. It houses about 3000 families or a total population of 8000 people (i.e. a population density of approximately 4000 persons per hectare).

The project is intended to be a showcase of sustainable design for high-rise living in the humid subtropical climate. Supported by microclimate studies, the stepping building height coupled with permeable massing is designed to optimize the harnessing of the prevalent summer breeze for the health and comfort of most occupants, as well as those in the surroundings.

On the other hand, Kowloon Station Development (see Figure 22.1) has been completed to a large extent by the time of writing. The project, planned directly over a mass transit railway station, comprises a mixture of apartments, offices, hotels and shopping malls on site of 14ha. The plot ratio for this large site is also approximately 8, with over half assigned for domestic development. The tallest residential blocks, up to 270m high or about 70 storeys, are aligned along the harbour front in order to optimize the sea view for the apartment units. The outcome is highly controversial, particularly with respect to the impact of the overly dense built form of the surroundings.

Note: Verbena Heights is a high-density public housing estate based on a plot ratio of about 8. The design model in 1993 indicates a pioneering approach towards sustainable high-rise development.

Source: Anthony Ng Architects Ltd (1993)

Figure 22.2 *Verbena Heights public housing estate*

2003 – Hong Kong's dark age: The outbreak of severe acute respiratory syndrome (SARS)

In the inner cover of Lampugnani's *Hong Kong Architecture: The Aesthetics of Density* (1993), the experience of flying into Hong Kong is described as an unforgettable one given the gleaming city of skyscrapers. The sheer density of buildings – hemmed in by rocky hills and open water – is truly breathtaking.

Not far away from the former Hong Kong International Airport at Kai Tak, the outbreak of severe acute respiratory syndrome (SARS) at Amoy Gardens in March 2003 is not less breathtaking in the history of urban development in Hong Kong.

Amoy Gardens (see Figure 22.3) is located in the Ngau Tau Kok area of Kowloon, in the north-east of Kowloon Peninsula of Hong Kong. It is a classic high-density middle-class housing estate in Hong Kong completed between 1980 and 1987. It comprises 19 apartment blocks – namely Blocks A to S – above a three-storey podium as a shopping mall. The apartment blocks typically have 33 storeys, with eight flats per floor. The flat size roughly ranges between 34 square metres to 56 square metres, with an average of about 45 square metres. It was the most seriously affected location during the 2003 SARS outbreak, with over 300 infected people.

Towards the end of March 2003, an outbreak of SARS occurred among residents of Amoy Gardens. As of mid April 2003, there were a total of 321 cases of SARS in the estate. A concentration of cases was recorded in Block E, accounting for 41 per cent of the cumulative total. Block C (15 per cent), block B (13 per cent) and block D (13 per cent) recorded the second, third and fourth highest incidence of SARS infections. The other cases (18 per cent) were scattered in 11 other blocks. Most of the initial 107 patients from Block E lived in flats that were vertically arranged. All residents were subsequently moved out for isolation.

The estate was eventually decontaminated before the residents could return. During mid 2003, the authority concerned found that there were serious problems of leaky drainage pipes located at the narrow re-entrant space that may have contributed to the spread of SARS.

Amoy Gardens represents the most common form of high-rise apartment buildings in the private-sector development throughout Hong Kong from the 1980s to 1990s. The classic features include the cruciform plan shape at the residential level, which typically comprises eight flats per floor, and the disposition of domestic blocks on top of a non-domestic podium.

In Hong Kong, besides the high overall building density that can be permitted up to a domestic plot ratio of 8 to 10 under the Buildings Ordinance, the habitation spaces are mostly densely packed around a central core of lifts, staircases and services and result in forming very narrow semi-enclosed external spaces in between flats. Such narrow, vertical chimney-like spaces are commonly called 're-entrants' in Hong Kong, which is design trick for allowing natural lighting and ventilation into the kitchen and bathroom of each apartment unit with a view to meeting the minimum prescriptive requirements under the building regulations. The width of the re-entrant in this kind of cruciform block design can be as narrow as 1.5m (or sometimes can be even narrower, as found in the case of Amoy Gardens), while its depth is several metres or more since there is no statutory control on the depth and height of this kind of re-entrant. Given a combination of extreme narrowness, depth and height, re-entrant spaces can be very dark and stuffy.

Although the cause of the SARS outbreak remains unclear in the eyes of many researchers and professionals, the planning and design for high-density living clearly becomes a highly debatable and crucial issue for review with a view to providing a healthy and liveable urban environment in Hong Kong.

The outbreak of SARS in 2003 represented a 'dark age' in Hong Kong, affecting not only the residents of Amoy Garden, but all people throughout the entire territory. It was the worst of times, but has triggered some positive changes.

At the building level, the Buildings Department has subsequently issued a series of practice notes to guide better design in terms of natural lighting and ventilation for habitable spaces and kitchens, mechanical ventilation and drainage design for bathrooms, and disposition of drain pipes in the common area for ease of inspection and maintenance; all of these are intended to tailor for healthy living in the specific high-density context of Hong Kong.

At the planning level, the Planning Department has conducted a feasibility study for establishing an air ventilation assessment (AVA) system in Hong Kong.

Notes: Amoy Gardens represents the most common form of high-rise apartment buildings in the private-sector development throughout Hong Kong during the 1980s to 1990s – densely packed cruciform tower blocks on top of a podium. A notable feature is the narrow re-entrant space that runs vertically like a semi-enclosed chimney in between each pair of apartment wings.

Source: Author

Figure 22.3 *Amoy Gardens*

As an initiative to identify measures to improve the living environment, Team Clean, commissioned by the chief executive and led by the chief secretary, promulgated a *Final Report on Measures to Improve Environmental Hygiene in Hong Kong* in August 2003. Amongst the recommendations, Team Clean proposed examining the practicality of stipulating AVA as one of the considerations for all major (re)development proposals and in future planning, including, in particular, the standards, scope and mechanism for application of the assessment system.

2004 – Hong Kong's turning point: The rise of 'green sense'

After the outbreak of SARS in 2003, the government took new initiatives at both building and planning levels in an attempt to improve environmental hygiene – which is of significance from the viewpoint of the general public as well as experts in the new age. However, coupled with the effect of global climate change, local meteorological conditions have, in fact, been deteriorating.

According to C. Y. Lam, director of the Hong Kong Observatory, Hong Kong SAR government, in his report to the Professional Green Building Council's Symposium 2006 on Urban Climate and Urban Greenery:

In tandem with urbanization in Hong Kong, urban temperature has risen faster than [in] the countryside, winds have [slowed], visibility has deteriorated, less solar radiation is

[is] reaching the ground, evaporation rate[s] [have] gone down, and so on. But does it matter?... For people with lesser means, especially the old and the weak, it could, however, become a life-threatening issue... They also have to fear the attack of more germs than used to be since their natural enemies, viz fresh air and sunshine,

have been reduced in strength. Unfortunately, the underprivileged have to look forward to even more tall buildings along the shore or even right at the heart of the urban areas to block the little wind and sunshine left. Buildings are meant to benefit people. But we have seen in the meteorological records presented above that buildings have collectively modified the urban climate in a way unfavourable to healthy living. It is high time for us to rethink the fundamentals about [what] urban living should look like.

In view of the deteriorating urban climate conditions and the rising building bulk and height in new development/redevelopment sites, there has been a growing societal reaction to such adverse trends. This is evidenced by the increasing popularity of a local green group called Green Sense, which was only founded in 2004. Despite its infancy and small set-up, a key advocacy of this non-governmental organization (NGO) is to fight against the so-called 'wall effect' developments.

Notes: All of these high-rise residential developments, mostly built in 2000, are typically 50 to 60 storeys tall on top of a large podium. Except through the limited wind corridor spaces, reserved in the zoning plan, the developments collectively block the sea breeze to the inner part of the new town, which provides a home for over 300,000 people.

Source: Author

Figure 22.4 *Wall effect developments along the waterfront of Tseung Kwan O New Town*

By 2007, Hong Kong was evidently suffering more significant and widespread impacts from the wall-like developments that sprang up in various urban areas, especially near the harbour front, largely due to the revenue-driven land policy and the deficiencies in both town planning and building regulation mechanisms. Although there is not yet consensus on a precise definition of the 'wall effect', the fact is that various large-scale residential estates are developed in the form of huge multi-storey podiums covering the entire site and a long row of continuous towers above for maximizing possible sea views.

Such kinds of 'wall effect' developments are commonly found not only in the new urban areas and new towns such as West Kowloon (see Figure 22.1) and Tseung Kwan O New Town, (see Figure 22.4), but also in older districts subject to urban renewal or redevelopment (see Figure 22.5). The tower height is typically up to about 60 storeys (i.e, twice that in Amoy Gardens). In most cases, there is also no (or minimal) gap in between individual residential blocks. For a linear row of 15 towers in one of the estates in Tseung Kwan O, the resultant mass is in the range of 600m long and 200m high – indeed, a 'great wall' of mountain height.

This 'wall effect' development trend has become controversial in Hong Kong. The NGO Green Sense has also become a key player in voicing public concern through various channels, from protest to court appeal. However, for those developments that have been cast in concrete, their environmental impacts upon the neighbourhood are irreversible during their lifespan (decades).

Given the rise of public feeling for a greener and more liveable urban environment, the government has eventually begun to admit the problem and has considered stepping up policy, as mentioned in the Policy Address of the Chief Executive in 2007. 'Quality city and quality life' is the policy statement. Initial measures include lowering the development intensity of sensitive sites, especially those facing the harbour front or on top of railway stations, controlling building height and introducing strategic breezeways to cut through individual development sites.

Note: Various districts in Kowloon have been subject to the pressure of redevelopment after the lifting of stringent height control upon the relocation of the airport away from the urban area since the late 1990s. Many of these developments are huge in scale and height, as well as wall like, dwarfing the existing urban fabric and significantly modifying the microclimate, including both air and light.

Source: Author

Figure 22.5 *Districts in Kowloon*

2008 and beyond – Hong Kong's sustainable future: High rise, high amenity and high design

Looking forward, the design for living in future Hong Kong should embrace key aspects – namely, high rise coupled with 'eco-density'; high amenity; and high design.

First, the design for living will focus on high rise, but strive for a more sustainable development pattern with 'eco-density'. The approach can be echoed by the Eco-Density Charter adopted by Vancouver City Council in June 2008. The charter commits the City to make environmental sustainability a primary goal in all city planning decisions – in ways that also support housing affordability and liveability. The underlying concept of eco-density is an acknowledgement that high-quality and strategically located density can make the city more sustainable, liveable and affordable. The right kind of quality density in the right places can help to address climate change, as well as lower our ecological footprint. The development of an urban climatic map for the urban area of Hong Kong will help to define the disposition of quality density in the right places.

Second, the quality of high amenity as captured in the current high-density developments on top and around mass transit stations should be maintained and even further improved. Such quality is conducive to high convenience and affordability in terms of public transit, 'walkability', shopping, open spaces, community facilities and other amenity services. Dense mixed-use neighbourhoods with a high-quality public realm and accompanying amenities are great places in which to live.

Last, but not least, the challenge of higher design quality for high-density, high-rise development demands innovative and appropriate solutions that will not only provide a healthy indoor living environment, but also take care of the liveability of urban living spaces in the surroundings. Design quality can be upheld through upgrading the planning and building control systems to set new requirements, such as site coverage of greenery, building permeability, building setback from narrow streets, and even green building rating. Innovative and high-quality design approaches can also be learned from award-winning projects, such as new constructions, research and planning schemes honoured by the Professional Green Building Council's Green Building Award.

High-density living: Our dream city?

Figure 22.6 shows the state of Lohas Park in late July 2008, where the 50-storey superstructure in the first phase has been topped out. Formerly named Dream City, it was renamed Lohas Park. Integrated with the mass transit station, Lohas Park is a planned mass residential development of the MTR Corporation, situated in Tseung Kwan O New Town. The 330,000 square metre estate will comprise 50 residential towers and a comprehensive range of amenity and supporting facilities, offering over 20,000 apartments to accommodate 58,000 residents in the site area. The project is divided into many phases, which are to be completed between 2009 and 2015. Upon its completion, it will be the largest residential development in the territory.

Lohas is an acronym for 'lifestyle of health and sustainability'. The MTR Corporation designated it as an 'environmentally friendly city' when planning for it began in 2002. After the SARS epidemic in 2003, the element of 'health' was incorporated. Following controversy over 'wall effect' buildings in 2007, the corporation further promised to review the air ventilation performance of the master layout plan.

Since this large-scale project takes more than a decade from initial planning to overall completion, its changes, from naming to design, somehow reflect the shifting aspirations of Hong Kong people with respect to high-density living. It may represent a notable 'urban laboratory' to test whether our dream city is a matter of *dream* or reality.

On the opposite side of the Earth, in July 2008, the Skyscraper Museum in New York launched an exhibition on Vertical Cities: Hong Kong and New York. The exhibition highlighted a number of comparisons between Hong Kong and New York under the theme 'Future City: 20/21':

Hong Kong and New York are the world's iconic vertical metropolises. Both island cities with perfect harbours, they evolved from colonial ports into dominant centres of international finance and commerce. As they grew, each embraced the skyscraper as the principal instrument of modern urbanism.

Many of the visionary ideas that New York architects proposed in the 1920s came to fruition decades later in Hong Kong. Raymond Hood's or Hugh Ferriss's ideas of tower clusters linked by high-speed public transportation can be seen now in Hong Kong projects like the International Commerce Centre, and the elevated

Note: In late July 2008, 'Lohas Park' has its first five 50-storey apartment towers already topped out, while the remaining 45 towers of similar height will be further built on top of a mass transit station, depot and adjoining land. It represents another large-scale 'urban laboratory' of high-density living for 58,000 residents.

Source: Author

Figure 22.6 *'Lohas Park'*

walkways, multilevel transit, and mid-level escalators echo Harvey Wiley Corbett's dream of multi-level transit. Hong Kong, in many ways, can be seen as a 'hyper New York', where the ideas and dreams of New York's early 20th-century architects were enacted and surpassed. Despite their similarities, the Asian and American cities differ significantly in their geography, history and culture in ways that affect their vertical expression. Today, Hong Kong has surpassed New York in terms of the number of high rises, population density, efficiency of mass transit... Hong Kong's vertical density piles people on a small percentage of the land: throughout the mountainous territory, more than three-quarters of the area is preserved as natural landscape. As a result, the cumulative built area of Hong Kong is only 100 square miles. Thus, the 7 million citizens live at an average density of 70,000 per square mile. The average density of Manhattan is likewise 70,000, meaning that all of the population of Hong Kong – on the island or in distant transit-based New Towns – [live] at the density of Manhattan.

While Hong Kong conserves three-quarters of the territory as country parks or natural landscapes and has superb urban amenities and facilities, such as elevated walkways, mass transit and so on, the form of high rise and the disposition of population density should be subject to urgent, critical review with respect to the design and desire for a sustainable future. Our dream should be more than being a 'hyper-New York'. If 'Quality city and quality life' is our common dream, a more solid policy and action plan to implement an integrated consideration of 'high rise, high amenity and high design' is imminently needed. Hong Kong's best of times is yet to come.

References

Chief Executive of the Hong Kong Special Administrative Region (2007) 'Years 2007–08 policy address', www.policyaddress.gov.hk/07-08/eng/policy.html, accessed August 2008

Green Sense (2008) 'Hong Kong', www.greensense.org.hk/, accessed August 2008

Lam, C. Y. (2006) 'On Climate Changes Brought About by Urban Living', in Wong, K. S. and Cheng, J. (eds) PGBC Symposium 2006 on Urban Climate and Urban Greenery, Professional Green Building Council, Hong Kong

Lampugnani, V. M. et al (eds) (1993) *Hong Kong Architecture: The Aesthetic of Density*, Prestel, München, New York

Skyscraper Museum (2008) *Vertical Cities: Hong Kong/ New York*, www.skyscraper.org/EXHIBITIONS/VERTICAL_CITIES/walkthrough_intro.php, accessed August 2008

Vancouver City Council (2008) *Eco-Density Charter*, www.vancouver-ecodensity.ca, accessed August 2008

Index

acoustic conditions   109–110
  see also noise
additive transformation   48–49
advection   138, 149
aesthetic factor   234–235, 291, 322–323
Africa   27, 71, 137
agriculture   20–24, 42
  fertilizers for   23–24
  organic   24
  urban   20, 24
air-conditioning systems   28–29, 36, 63, 119, 227,
    264–265
  see also HVAC systems
air flow   214
  see also ventilation
air paths/breezeways   79–81, 104–105, 122, 125,
    130–131, 133, 148
air pollution   28, 36–37, 43, 59, 71–72, 137, 172–173,
    227
  compact cities and   293–294
  nitrogen dioxide (NO_2)   152, 155–156
  noise *see* noise
  outdoor-indoor transfer   151–156
  outdoor-indoor transfer mapping   153
  outdoor-indoor transfer study   153
  ozone   152–156
  particle matter   152, 155–157
  and ventilation   119, 143, 151–156, 314
air quality   139–141, 151–156, 261, 280
air-source heat pumps   269
air speed, indoor   96–104, 139
air temperature   71, 73, 75
  and greenery   229–243
  and thermal comfort   87–105
air tightness of buildings   138, 141, 155
air traffic   29
albedo   71, 80, 149
Amoy Gardens (Hong Kong)   323–324
ancient cities   27, 156, 158, 264
apartment blocks   31–32, 263–266
  in property market   31–32
  see also public housing
architecture
  iconic role of   289–290
  and perceived density   12–13
  social/psychological aspects of   286–288

Ardrey, R.   289
arenas   288, 290
ASHRAE (American Society of Heating, Refrigerating and
    Air-Conditioning Engineers)   97, 139
Asia   27, 47, 71, 137, 287
Astana (Kazakhstan)   31
ASV (actual sensation vote)   110–111, 116
Athens (Greece)   109, 145, 148–151, 264
atriums   214
Australia   24, 290
AVA (air ventilation assessment, Hong Kong)   125–130,
    135, 312, 324
  implementation   130
  methodology   126, 128–129
  wind velocity ratio (VRw) in   126–128

Bahrain World Trade Centre   305–307
Baker, N.   108
balanced stack ventilation   156–158
Bangkok (Thailand)   90, 103–104, 286
Banham, R.   20
Barcelona   45
Basiago, A.D.   43
BBNP (Bukit Batok Natural Park, Singapore)   229–230
behavioural sink   285
Beijing (China)   169–177
Bender, R.   46
Beveridge Report (1941)   30
biofuel/biomass   19, 22, 268–270
BIPV (building-integrated photovoltaic) systems   301–304,
    307
Bishopsgate Tower (London, UK)   305–306
Bonnes, M.   13
Bowen ratio   227–228
Boyle, G.   266
Brazil   43
BRE (Building Research Establishment)   273–274, 276
BREEAM (BRE Environmental Assessment Method)   274,
    276
breezeways *see* air paths
Britain   50, 221
  building height in   32, 34–36
  Daylight Code/standard   184, 186–188
  food production in   20–21, 24–25
  human/thermal comfort in   109–111, 115–116
  inequality in   30

measurement of density in   4, 14
minimum density in   6
natural ventilation in   158
noise in   163–166
property market in   30–31
refurbishment in   28
rural density in   8
social/psychological issues in   287–288
sustainability in   43, 270, 273–274
  see also Cambridge; London; Sheffield
Brundtland Commission   41
building consumption patterns   301–303
building density
  measurment   5–6, 9
  and people density   14–15
  and urban morphology   9–12
building disposition   131–133, 145, 264
building durability   27–28
building envelope design   264
building façades   160, 219, 222, 251–257, 267, 270
  environmental   319
building form   50
  and noise reduction   177–178
building height   9–11, 13, 32–37
  and daylight   189–193
  differentials   122, 124
  and fire regulations   32–33
  and ventilation   131
building insurance   29
building lifespan   201
  see also LCA
building regulations   28, 32, 130
  and sustainability   270, 273–274
Bukit Batok Natural Park *see* BBNP
Burj Dubai Tower   34, 36, 295–296
business parks   234–235, 237

Cairo (Egypt)   137, 286
Calhoun, J.B.   285
Cambridge (UK)   109–110, 112–113
Canada   21, 160, 276, 327
Canary Wharf (London, UK)   296–298
capitalism   24–25, 45, 50
carbon neutral buildings   273–274
car parks   31, 220, 229, 238–240, 299
cars   24
  dependency on   42
CASBEE for Urban Design (CASBEE-UD, Japan)   28, 277–280
CBP (Changi Business Park, Singapore)   234–235, 237
Celmenti Woods Park *see* CWP
centralization   7–8
CEPAS (Comprehensive Environmental Performance Assessment Scheme)   276, 280

CFD (computational fluid dynamics)   112, 214, 220, 311–314
Chambers, William   182
Cheng, V.   90–96
Chen, H.   263
Chen, Y.   228
Cheung, C.K.   264–265
China   24, 28–29, 33, 66–67, 209, 267, 301, 303
  see also Beijing; Guanzhou; Shanghai; Wuhan
Chow, W.K.   215
CHP (combined heat and power) systems   269–270
Chrisomallidou, N.   264
city centres   7, 46, 290, 293
city competitiveness   294–296, 299
city development plans   298–300, 307–308
city function expansion   294
Clark, T.W.   29
Cleveland (Ohio, US)   31
climate change   28, 35–38, 55–61, 72, 275
  and energy demand   263–264, 293
  evaporation   59–60
  hot nights   60, 63–64
  modelling   71–72
  rate   55–57
  sky turbidity/visibility   57–59, 63
  wind factors   57, 60
  see also UHI
CO_2 emissions   19, 35–37, 263, 293
comfort zones   81, 88, 108, 110, 139–140
  for daylight   187
Commoner, B.   19, 24
communal facilities   4, 9
community development   310–319
  and economic sustainability   3, 310–311
  and environmental sustainability   311–319
  and social sustainability   311
compact cities   42, 197
  sustainable/high-rise   293–308
Compagnon, R.   110
complexity   46
computational fluid dynamics *see* CFD
construction materials   33–34, 63, 195, 203, 264, 275
  and fire engineering   209–211
  storage/management of   204, 206
construction and waste reduction   195, 203–206
  composition of waste   196–197
  and design modifications   204
  low-waste technologies   204–206
  need for   195, 197–198
  off-site/prefabrication   200, 204–206
  on-site   204
  private sector   197, 199–200, 204
  standard dimensions/materials for   203, 206
  temporary works and   203–204

continuity 49
convection 87–88
cooling loads 5, 230–231, 244–245, 264
cooling systems 36, 141–143, 158–160, 227, 264
Cooper-Marcus, C. 13
Le Corbusier 20, 160, 286–287
crime 29–30, 43, 286
crowding 12, 14
crowd management 210
Crown Las Vegas (US) 34
Curitiba (Brazil) 43
CWP (Celmenti Woods Park, Singapore) 229–233
cycling 15, 20, 24, 43

dams 35
Darke, Jane 286
data collection 74–78, 80–82, 89–92
daylight, designing for 13, 181–193, 264–265, 314, 324
    daylight factor (DF) in 186
    graphical tools for 182–185, 193
    in high-density cities 181, 186–193
    history of 181–182
    psychological/lifestyle factor in 187–188
    RHP (rectangular horizontal plane) concept 186
    sky component (SC) 187–188, 193
    and standards/regulations 184–186
    strategy for 190–193
    UVA concept 181, 188–193
    vertical daylight factor (VDF) 188–189, 193
    vertical sustaining angle and 186–187
dead building syndrome 30–31
decentralization 7–8
deck access housing schemes 286–287
deep street canyons see street canyons
La Défense project (Paris, France) 296–297, 304
defensible/indefensible space 286–287
densification 48–49
density gradient 6–8
density, measurement of 3–12
    quantitative/qualitative 45
density perception see perceived density
density profile 7–8
desalination plants 36
design briefing 5
developing countries 43, 152
    alternative energy in 137–138
    energy demands in 137
    sanitation in 27
development budgeting 5
DF (daylight factor) 186
Dinh Cong (Hanoi, Vietnam) 47
disease 28, 59–60
    see also SARS

dissonance/unevenness 45
dog-sledge strategy 46
double skin façade system 160, 299, 304, 307
doughnut phenomenon 293
drainage 15, 293
Dubai 31, 34, 36

eco-cities 293
'eco-density' 327
ecology, Commoner's laws of 19
economic development 24, 152
economic sustainability 41, 43, 50, 310–311
education 19, 274
electricity
    demand 137, 263–266
    generation/consumption 36
    prices 35
    renewable see renewable energy
    subsidies 36
elevators 35–36, 218
Empire State Building (New York, US) 294–295, 298
employment 38, 48, 50
energy in high-density cities 37, 263–271, 280
    and building envelope design 264
    CHP/district systems 269–270
    control/metering of 266
    demand 137, 263–266
    nuclear 270
    options/opportunities for 270–271
    and passive design 264–265, 270
    renewable see renewable energy
    subsidies 36
    and UHI 264
    and ventilation 265
energy performance of buildings 141, 273–274
Energy Performance of Buildings Directive (EU, 2002) 274
Envest 276
ENVi-met model 112, 231, 235
environmental assessment 273–281
    boundaries and 279–281
    broad applications of 274–275, 277–279, 281
    CASBEE-UD approach 277–281
    Environmental Programming of Human Development 278–279
    in high-density context 280–281
    LEED-ND approach 274, 277–280
    life-cycle (LCA) 263, 268, 275–276, 279
    methods 274–275
    six key issues in 273
    social/economic issues in 276–277, 279–280
    sustainability 276–277
    synergies in 279, 281
    voluntary/labelling schemes 274

environmental degradation   137, 273
environmental diversity maps   112–114
environmental efficiency   299–300
environmental sustainability   41, 43, 274–275, 310–319
ESSD (environmentally sound and sustainable
        development)   299
ethanol   22
European cities   19–20, 29, 49, 160
    climate change in   71
    noise in   149–151, 163, 178
    urban diversity/human comfort in   107–117
European Commission/Union   42, 274, 297
evaporation   6, 59–60, 71, 119
    and natural ventilation   158–160
    sweat   88, 91–92, 139
evapotranspiration   227–228, 240

factor analysis   175–177
factories   251–256
Faventinus, M. Cetius   181
FEA (fire engineering approach)   219–220
fertilizers   23–24
fire alarms   211–212
fire engineering   209–222
    active protection systems   211–213, 222
    airflow factor   214
    approach (FEA)   219–220
    and building materials   209
    detection systems   210–211, 213, 218
    evacuation plans   210–212, 218
    fire resistance period see FRP
    and glass façades   219, 222
    hazards addressed by   210–211, 222
    and models/experiments   213–214, 219–221
    and PBD   210, 213, 218–220, 222
    professional qualifications in   221–222
    safety management (FSM)   211–213
    sprinkler systems   212, 214–215
    and structural elements   210–211, 214–218
fire regulations   32–33, 209
Flachsbart, P.G.   13
flats see apartment blocks
flooding   20
floor area ratio   5, 42, 278
Fong, K.E.   96–99
food footprint   21
food production   20–24, 37
    energy for   21–22
    fertilizer for   23–24
fossil fuels   19, 22–23
    depletion of   19–20, 38, 263, 266
    see also oil
France   25

Frankfurt (Germany)   72, 75
free-running temperatures   141–143
FRP (fire resistance period)   210–211, 216–217
FSM (fire safety management)   211–213
fuel cells   270
fuel poverty   28, 31, 137

Gardaiha (Algeria)   74, 76
garden city   24, 42
Garley Building fire (Hong Kong)   209–210, 218,
        222
Georgakis, G.   145
geothermal energy   269, 307
Germany   50, 73, 111, 160, 289
Gideon, S.   29
GIS (geographical information system) data   78–79
Givoni, B.   119, 125
Gladwin, T.N.   279
glass façades   219, 222
globe temperature   91, 99–100, 109–112, 139
Goyette, J.   110
'green building'   209–210, 275, 277
greenfield development   42, 293, 299
green roofs/walls   81, 200
    see also rooftop gardens; vertical landscaping
Green Sense   325–326
green spaces   15, 20, 43, 89
    see also parks; trees
Greenwich Village (New York)   45
ground coverage ratio   124
ground-source heat pumps   269
growth management   209
Guanzhou Pearl River Tower (China)   306–307

Hall, P.   42, 45
Hanoi (Vietnam)   47–48
Hansen, James   36–37
Haussmann, George-Eugene   29
Hawaii   28–29
health considerations   5, 28, 38, 43, 80, 119
    in public housing   309–310
    see also pollution; SARS
health facilities   19
heat emissions   63
heating/cooling curve   141, 143
heat pumps   269–270
height-to-space ratio   13
height to width ratios see H/W
high density   13–16
    and infrastructure   15
    personal/social elements of   15–16
    and transport systems   15
    and urban use   14–15

high-rise buildings   9–11, 15, 204, 264–265, 293–308, 322–323, 327
  case studies   295–298
  commercial viability of   34–36
  and compact cities   295, 298–307
  and dead building syndrome   31
  energy demand of   33–34, 263
  energy efficiency of   299–307
  and fire hazard   211, 217–218
  refurbishment of   28
  ripple effect of   295, 297
  social/psychological aspects of   286, 291
  'wall effect'   325–327
  see also super-tall buildings
HK-BEAM (Hong Kong Building Environmental Assessment Method)   280–281, 312
HKHA (Hong Kong Housing Authority)   309–312
HKO (Hong Kong Observatory)   55–60, 64, 125
HKPSG (Hong Kong Planning Standards and Guidelines)   130–135, 148
home environment   99–103
  factors in choice of   172
  noise and   169–174
Hong Kong   14, 29, 290, 294, 321–328
  air ventilation assessment in *see* AVA
  building/people density in   14, 124
  climate change measurement in   55–60, 64
  compactness of   197, 322
  daylight levels in   181, 186–193
  environmental assessment in   276, 280–281
  fire engineering in   32–33, 209–210, 214, 218–220, 222
  food production for   21–23
  ground coverage ratio in   124
  health/disease in   28, 125
  high-rise trend in   322–323, 325–327
  H/W ratio in   123
  measurement of density in   3–4, 6–7
  noise in   163–166, 178
  PET distribution in   74, 76
  property market in   31–32
  public housing in   310–319
  thermal comfort in   89–99
  UHI in   64–68, 72, 75
  urban climatic map of   80–81
  urban fabric of   124–125
  ventilation assessment of *see* AVA
  ventilation guidelines for *see* HKPSG
  waste management in   196–200
  wind environment of   123–135
Hong Kong, Chinese University of   90–96
Hong Kong, City University of (CityU)   93, 96–99
Hopkinson projectors   184

Hopkinson, R.J.   182, 186
Hopkinson's Daylight Code   188
hot climate cities   104–105, 107, 119
Howard, E.   24
Howard, Luck   227
Hui, M.F.   280
Hui, S.C.M.   263
human comfort   107–117
  and choice/control   108
  and city density   116
  and climatic models   107–108
  comfort chamber research   107–108
  field monitoring kit   109
  and metabolic rate   108, 110, 138–139
  modelling/mapping   107–108, 111–116
  monitoring   107–116
  socio-cultural elements in   107–110, 169
  survey methodologies   107–108, 116
  survey results   110–116
  and urban diversity   107–108, 117–118
  see also quality of life; thermal comfort
humidity   59, 72, 138, 265, 323
  and thermal comfort   91–92, 96, 99, 101, 103, 110
  and urban greenery   238, 240, 259–261
HVAC (heating, ventilation and air-conditioning) systems   29, 141–142, 265–266
H/W (height to width) ratios   107, 112, 122–123, 145
  and noise levels   149–152, 163–165
hydrogen fuel cells   270
hydropower   21, 35, 269–270

IBP (International Business Park, Singapore)   234–235, 237
India   28–29, 33, 43, 160
Indonesia   89
indoor environment
  air speed   96–104, 139
  and density perception   12–13, 43
  thermal comfort in   89, 96–104, 125, 138–139
  ventilation in *see* natural ventilation
  see also home environment; offices
industrialization   293
industry   31, 63, 264
inequality   29–31, 36
  and climate change   60–61
informality   50–51
infrastructure   15, 19, 27, 38, 300
  and suburban sprawl   42
  see also roads; transport systems
insulation   265
IPCC (Intergovernmental Panel on Climate Change)   37, 263
Israel   14, 105, 288
Italy   50, 111

Jacobs, Jane   45
Jaillon, L.   201–202
Japan   50, 119, 202, 221
    see also CASBEE; Tokyo

Kampong (Malaysia)   286, 288
Kang, J.   163, 169, 175
Kassel (Germany)   77, 79, 81–82
    human comfort survey in   109–110
Katz, E.   275
Kay, J.D.   186
Kazakhstan   31
Kenworthy, J.R.   280
Kerala (India)   43
Kerr, Robert   182
Khedari, J.   103–104
Kim Lien (Hanoi, Vietnam)   47–48
King's Park (Hong Kong)   57
Knowles, Ralph   184
Korea   49–50
Kowloon (Hong Kong)   323–324, 326
Kowloon Station Development (Hong Kong)
    321–323
Krieger, S.   35
Kuala Lumpur (Malaysia)   227, 286, 289–290
Kuwait   36
Kwok, H.   31–32

LAI (leaf area index)   244–245, 259
Lam, C.Y.   325
Lampugnani, Vittorio   322–323
landfills   197–200
Landsberg, H.E.   71, 227
landscape   125, 234–237
    vertical   251–256
land use   19, 49, 78, 299–300
    for food production   21
    mixed   43, 45–47
    planning   9
land-use zoning   5, 42
Las Vegas (US)   34–35
latent heat   139, 228
Latin America   27–29, 71–72, 137
Lau Fau Shan (Hong Kong)   55–56
LCA (life-cycle analysis)   263, 268, 275–276, 279
leaf area index *see* LAI
LEED for Neighbourhood Development (LEED-ND, US)
    274, 277–280
leisure facilities   19, 317–318
Leung, Y.K.   59–60, 64
Levine, M.   263
libraries   9
life-cycle analysis *see* LCA

lifts   35–36, 218, 222
lighting   211, 264–265
light levels   13, 59
Lipman, Alan   289
Li, Y.   28
local authorities   28, 277
local facilities   43
Lohas Park (Hong Kong)   327–328
London (UK)   20, 23, 160, 186–187, 286,
    289–291, 294
    Bishopsgate Tower   305–306
    Canary Wharf   296–298
    UHI in   64, 71, 73, 148
loose-fit environment   46–48
low-rise cities   19–20, 47–50
Luckiesh, M.   186
Lykoudis, S.   107
Lynes pepper-pot diagram   183–184, 193
Lynn, Jack   286–287

McGrath, S.   29
Malaysia   286, 288–290
maps
    SVFs   80, 111–113
    UC-AnMap/UC-ReMap   74, 77–78
    urban climate   74–82
    urban diversity   111–116
Mardaljevic, J.   188
master plan   5, 78
Maya (modelling tool)   112
Mayer, H.   79, 124
Mayhew, H.   23
mean radiant temperature *see* MRT
Medieval cities   19–20, 25, 27, 294
medium-rise development   9, 44
megacities   71, 137, 181
mega-projects   46
Melbourne (Australia)   33
metabolic rate   108, 110, 138–139
Mexico   43, 50
microclimates   79, 91–92, 107–117
    modelling   311
    in public housing   309–320
micro-scale planning   78–79
Middle East   36, 156, 158, 287
mixed-use areas   43, 45–47, 50, 277, 300, 304
modernist approach   20, 42
Mongkok (Hong Kong)   57, 133, 164–166
mould   29, 138
MRT (mean radiant temperature)   88, 99, 110–111, 139,
    240–242
multi-storey development *see* high-rise buildings
Murakami, Shuzo   125

natural ventilation 119, 138–143, 264–265, 304, 314
  airflow rates 139–141
  and air quality 139–141, 151–156
  comfort indices for 139
  cooling potential of 141–144
  double skin façade system 160
  and heating/cooling curves 141, 143
  and indoor pollutants 152
  and noise 149–152
  and outdoor air/pollution 141, 151–156
  passive evaporative cooling 158–160
  stack 138, 156–158
  strategies 138, 156–160
  and street canyons 144–151
  and thermal comfort 138–139, 142
  and weak wind 147–148
Nayarit (Mexico) 43
neighbourhood relations 16
neighbourhoods 107, 281, 286–287
  micro-climates in 79, 265
  planning for 78, 277
Nevada (US) 35
Newman, Oscar 286, 288
Newman, P.W.G. 280
new towns 42, 277
New York 16, 29, 32, 45, 160, 286, 288, 294, 327–328
  3D city management system 298
New Zealand 22
Ngau Tau Kok (Hong Kong) 203, 311–312
Nicol, F. 149–151
Nightingale, Florence 288
Nikolopoulou, M. 107, 109
Nipkow, J. 35
nitrogen dioxide (NO$_2$) 152, 155–156
Niu, J. 265
noise 43, 137, 143, 163–179, 280
  and acoustic comfort 175–177
  annoyance caused by 164, 169–177
  distribution 163–168
  domestic 173–174
  factor analysis of 175–177
  health effects of 163, 172
  maps 166–167, 170, 178
  micro-/macro-scale 163
  modelling 163, 166–167, 178
  and natural ventilation 149–152
  in open public spaces 174–177
  perception of 169–179
  positive 174
  reduction 177–179
  reverberation time (RV) 164
  sound pressure levels see SPL
  and sound quality 172–173

  and street canyons 149–152, 163–166
  in underground spaces 179
  and urban morphology 166–168
  and urban texture 166, 169, 178
Norway 278
nuclear power 270

occupancy rate 5
occupational density 4–5
OECD countries 137, 195–196
offices 267, 301–302
  and noise levels 149–152
  property market for 30–31, 33
  thermal comfort in 96–99, 108, 138
oil 35–36
  peak 19
  price 33, 35–36
open spaces 79–80
  high-/low-density differences in 175
  linking 130, 133
  soundscape in 175–177
optimal density 37–38, 43
Osmani, M. 203–204
OTTV (overall thermal transfer value) 318–319
overcrowding 14
over-determination 46–47
ozone 152–156

Palladio, A. 182
Paris (France) 29, 42, 45, 148, 289, 294
  La Défense project 296–297, 304
  Phare Tower 297, 304, 306
Park Hill (Sheffield, UK) 286–288
parks 89, 105–106, 291
  cooling effect of 229–233
passive evaporative cooling 158–160
pavements, and thermal comfort 80, 88
PBD (performance-based design) 210, 213, 218–219, 222
peak oil 19
Pearlmutter, D. 107
pedestrians 15, 20, 24, 42–43, 300, 327
  wind environment 120–121, 125, 127–128, 133–135
people density 4–5, 42
  and building density 14–15
  occupancy 4–5
  regional 4, 6
  residential 4, 6
  and stress/social conflict 16
perceived density 3, 12–13, 43, 291
  and environmental cues 13
  and spatial/social density 12
Pérez de Arce, Rodrigo 48–49

permeability   82, 121, 124–125
   and building classification   154
personal space   285–288
PET (physiological equivalent temperature)   72–74, 78
Phare Tower (Paris, France)   297, 304, 306
photovoltaic (PV) energy   267, 299, 301–304
physical density   3–8
   building see building density
   gradient/profile   6–8
   people see people density
Picon, A.   279
Pitts, A.C.   264
planning
   law   78
   measures of density in   6
   and sustainability   41–42, 275
plot ratio   5, 9–11, 14, 323
podiums   131, 133, 315
polluter pays principle   195, 198
pollution see air pollution
Poon, C.S.   201–204
population growth   19, 27–33, 37, 137
Potcher, O.   105
poverty   29–31, 36, 137
   and climate change   60–61
PRIMEQUAL programme   153, 156
private space   48
property market   30–32
Pryor, Edward George   322
psychological factors   187–188, 287–288
public housing   28, 35–36, 285–286, 291
   construction projects   197, 203–204, 285–287
   deck access   286–287
   economic sustainability in   310–311
   environmental sustainability in   311–319
   microclimate in   309–320
   social sustainability in   311
   wind environment of   312–314
public spaces   42–43, 48, 50, 107
   diversity in see urban diversity
   environmental assessment of   280–281
   and fire engineering   214
public transport   20, 24, 38, 264, 280, 291, 299
   and dispersal strategies   42
   and fire engineering   209–211, 220–222
Pudong (Shanghai, China)   298–299
Punggol (Singapore)   236, 239

quality of life   33, 38, 42, 137–138, 152

radiation   88, 138
rail transport   36
   and fire hazard   209–211, 221–222

rainfall   68
Rapoport, A.   13
Rees, W.E.   278–279
refurbishment   28
regional density   4, 6
renewable energy   20–22
   biofuels/waste products   19, 22, 268–270
   geothermal/heat pumps   269–270
   hydro-/wave/tidal power   21, 35, 269–270
   solar   20, 35, 266–267, 270
   storage systems   270
   wind   21–22, 267–268, 270
renovation of buildings   202–203
residential density   4, 6
resource depletion   33–36, 137
   and building materials   33–34
   oil   35–36
   water   34–35
resource flows   25
reverberation time (RV)   164
roads   15, 168, 178, 293, 299
Robinson, J.   280
Rogers, M.O.   264
roofs
   cool   80
   solar power systems on   266–267
rooftop gardens   238–250, 256–257
   extensive   246–250
   intensive   243–245
   load/maintainance of   244
   plant selection for   244–245
   substrate temperatures   246–248
Roppongi Hills project (Tokyo, Japan)   295–297
Roth, M.   66–67
rural density   8
RUROS (Rediscovering the Open Realm and Open Spaces)
   project   109
RV (reverberation time)   164

Salmon, William   182
sanitation   5, 27, 37, 137
Santamouris, Mat   125, 137, 145, 227–228, 264–265
Sarkissian, W.   13
SARS (severe acute respiratory syndrome) virus   28, 125,
   312, 323–324, 327
Saudi Arabia   36
SBAT (Sustainable Building Assessment Tool, South Africa)
   276
scaffolding   204
Schalcher, M.   35
Schiller, S.   79
Scotland   28, 31, 35–36
sea breezes   80–81

seasonal factors   66–68, 71–72, 106, 110, 115–116, 264

security   28–29, 38, 43

self-adjustment   46, 50

Selman, P.   41

Seng Kang (Singapore)   236, 239

Sennett, R.   45–46

sensible heat   138–139, 228

Seoul (Korea)   49–50, 66, 294
    LITE building   296, 307

sewage
    as energy   268–270
    as fertilizer   23–24
    management   5, 27, 37, 137

Shanghai (China)   46, 209, 227, 294
    Pudong development   298–299

Sheffield (UK)   163–177, 286–288, 290

shopping malls   214

shops, local   43, 48

sick building syndrome   138

signage   13, 133–135

Singapore   32, 64, 186–187, 229–243, 290, 301
    business parks in   234–237
    public housing in   285–286, 288
    residential districts in   236
    roadside trees in   233–234
    thermal comfort in   89–90, 93, 99–103, 119
    urban parks in   229–233

site coverage   6, 9, 11

skylines   193, 296, 298

Skyscraper Museum (New York, US)   327–328

sky turbidity   57–59

sky view factors see SVFs

smart growth   299

smart meters/controls   266

Smith, P.F.   264

smoke management systems   211–212

social housing see public housing

social life in cities   15–16, 42–43, 45, 50, 107, 109–110,
    285–292
    architecture/design and   286–288, 290–291
    boundaries and   287, 289
    and compact/high-rise cities   300
    crime   29–30, 43, 286
    and environmental assessment   276–277, 279–280
    and perception of density   12–13, 43, 291
    personal space   285–288
    privacy   16, 287–288
    public policy and   288–289
    sense of community   286–287
    territoriality and   288–290

social segregation/cohesion   46, 50

social sustainability   41, 43, 285, 310–311

sol-air temperature   142, 144

solar envelopes   184–185

solar heat gain   265, 317, 319

solar obstruction   9–11, 63–64, 67–68
    see also sun shading

solar power   20, 35, 266–267, 270

solar radiation   59, 64, 88–89, 91, 110–111, 148–149
    shading from see sun shading
    and urban greenery   231, 242

solar thermal energy   266–267

sound see noise

sound pressure levels see SPL

South Africa   276

space cooling load   5, 244–245

space openness/complexity   13

Spain   64

SPeAR (Sustainable Project Assessment Routine)   276–277

SPL (sound pressure levels)   164–166, 168–169, 171

sprinkler systems   212, 214–215

stack ventilation   138, 156–158

Stamps, A.   13

Standeven, M.   108

Stone, B. Jr   264

storms   20

street canyons   120, 122–123, 143–151
    airflow in   144–145
    air/surface temperature in   148–149
    noise in   149–152, 163–166, 177
    wind direction in   145–147
    wind speed in   146

Street Farmers group (London, UK)   20

streets   20, 29, 107
    in the air   286–287
    grain   46
    hierarchy of   45–46
    orientation of   105, 107, 122–124, 130, 132, 149
    width   13, 125

street signs   13, 133–135

substitution, scale of   49

suburban sprawl see urban/suburban sprawl

sunlight see solar radiation

sun shading   64, 79–80, 89, 92–94, 109, 112, 124–125,
    314–317, 319
    and urban greenery   236, 244–245, 251–255
    see also solar obstruction

super-tall buildings   34, 36, 210–211, 257, 294–296
    fire engineering and   217–218
    iconic role of   289–290, 294

sustainability   19–22, 27–50, 323
    of compact/high-rise cities   293–308
    in construction industry   198, 270
    defined   41
    density and   42–50
    and diversity/flexibility   45–46

and 'eco-density'   327
in environmental assessment   274–275
history of   42
holistic approach to   310
and over-determination   46–47
and planning   41–42
and pollution   36–37
and population growth   27–33
in public housing   309–310
and quantitative/qualitative density measures   45
and resource depletion   27, 33–36
and size/complexity   46
three dimensions of   41, 43, 310
Sustainable Homes Code (UK)   270, 273–274
SVFs (sky view factors)   80, 111–113
sweat evaporation   88, 91–92, 139
Switzerland   111
synergies   279, 281
system formworks   204

Taipei (Taiwan)   169–174, 217
Ta Kwu Ling (TKL, Hong Kong)   55–56, 64, 67
Tanamas, J.   99–103
taxation   30
temperature effects see climate change; thermal comfort;
     UHI
terraced housing   20, 289
territoriality   288–290
terrorism   28, 30, 209, 212
Thailand   89, 103–104
thermal comfort   60, 63–64, 71, 80, 87–117
     and air speed/evaporative cooling   88
     and building design   104–106
     clothing factor   87, 90–91, 96, 108–110, 125, 139–140
     in cold climates   105–106, 110
     computer modelling   112
     and convection   87–88, 138
     defined   87
     and heat exchange of body   87, 138–139
     in hot climates   104–105
     index for (PET)   72–74, 78
     indices   139
     indoor   89, 96–104, 125, 138–141
     monitoring   107–116
     and natural ventilation   138–139
     and radiation   88, 138
     research methodology for   89–90, 109–110
     research on   90–104
     subjective sensation formulae   94–97, 100–103, 119
     sun shading and see sun shading
     and urban diversity   107–117
     and urban planning   104–105
     ventilation for   125

wind speed and see under wind speed
     see also human comfort
thermal mass   264–265, 319
thermal stress   72, 79, 81, 119
three dimensional (3D) management system   298, 300
Titmuss, Richard   30
TKL see Ta Kwu Ling
TKL (Ta Kwu Ling, Hong Kong)   55–56, 64, 67
Tokyo (Japan)   71, 73, 119, 187, 227, 280, 294
     Roppongi Hills project   295–297
traditional cities   42, 45, 47, 49
traffic   13, 15, 29, 43, 168, 293
     hierarchical system of   45–46
     noise see noise
transport systems   15, 37–38, 43, 63, 264, 293
     energy for   19–20
     for food   20
     and urban sprawl   42
     see also public transport; rail transport; roads
travel   43
trees   20, 74, 80, 105, 227, 251–255, 304
     roadside   233–234, 236
     see also parks
Tregenza, P.R.   188–189, 193
Treloar, G.J.   33
Tse, C.-Y.   31–32
Tseung Kwan O (Hong Kong)   148, 326–327

UC-AnMap/UC-ReMap   74, 77–78
UCI (urban cool island)   64
UCL (urban canopy layer)   79, 119–120, 144–145
UHI (urban heat island)   59–60, 63–68, 71–74, 137, 148
     conditions favourable to   67, 119, 227
     and density   71
     diurnal variation of   64–68
     and energy demands   264
     factors in   63–64
     health problems and   72
     mitigation of   72, 74, 80, 265
     profile   72
     seasonal variation of   66–68, 71–72
     and thermal/human comfort   89, 104, 107
     and urban greenery   227–228, 243, 256
underground spaces   179
     and fire engineering   209, 211, 221–222
United Nations (UN)   42
United States (US)   28–29, 31, 50, 287, 294, 301–302
     building height in   33–34
     construction industry in   195, 203
     environmental assessment in   274, 277, 280
     fire engineering in   220–221
     measurement of density in   4, 14
     resource depletion in   34–35

suburban sprawl in 20, 24, 45
ventilation in 138, 160
World Trade Centre attack (2001) 29, 209–211, 217
see also New York
urban boundary layer 119, 144–145, 148
urban climate 71–82
and GIS data 78
health problems and 72
maps 74–82
and open spaces 79–80
PET distribution 72–74, 78
and planning 78–82
positive/negative effects on 79
and vegetation 74, 79–80, 105, 227–228
see also thermal comfort; UHI
urban density 42
urban diversity 45–51, 107–117
and choice 108, 116
and city density 116
mapping/modelling 111–116
optimum 116
profiles 114–115
seasonal factors 110, 115–116
urban fabric 124–125
urban form 41–42, 44, 49–51, 107–108
diversity in *see* urban diversity
urban greenery 15, 20, 43, 80, 89, 227–262, 291
and ambient air temperature 229–243
in business parks 234–235, 237
challenges in 257–262
conceptual model for 228
and cooling loads 230–231
evapotranspiration by 227–228, 240
LAI of 244–245, 259
landscapes near buildings 234–237
and MRT 240–242
plant selection/arrangement 235, 238, 244–245, 258–262
in residential areas 236, 239, 315, 317
roadside trees 233–234
shading effect of 236, 244–245, 251–255
shrubs 105, 240
simulated scenarios for 230–231, 234–235, 244–245, 255–256
and surface temperature 242–257
and UHI 227–228, 243, 256
vertical landscaping *see* vertical landscaping
see also parks; trees
urbanization 13, 27–28, 137, 227, 263, 268, 273, 293, 322
and climate change 55–61, 71
and urban heat island effect *see* UHI
urban morphology 9–12

and noise 166–168
and ventilation 120–124
urban regeneration 42, 49
urban/suburban sprawl 20, 24, 42, 293
urban texture 166, 169, 178
urban use 14–15
URBVENT project 146, 149, 153, 156
USGBC (US Green Building Council) 274, 277
Utah (US) 35
UVA (unobstructed vision area) 181, 188–193

vacant spaces 13
Van der Ryn, S. 279
VDF (vertical daylight factor) 188–189, 193, 314
vegetation *see* urban greenery
ventilation 15, 72, 78, 119–160, 312
air paths 79–81, 104–105, 122, 125, 130
building/city morphology for 121–124
and building disposition 125, 131–133
and building height 122, 124–125, 131
deep street canyons 120, 122–123
and disease 28–29
and energy demand 265
and ground coverage ratio 122, 124
in high-density cities 119–120, 137–160
Hong Kong case study 124–135
and H/W ratios 122–123
natural *see* natural ventilation
night-time 265
non-building areas 130
open spaces 130
podiums for 131, 133
and pollution 119
and projecting obstructions 133–135
role of 119, 138
street orientation 105, 107, 122–124, 130, 132
for thermal comfort 125
waterfront sites 129–131
and wind velocity ratio (VRw) 120–121, 123–124, 126–128
see also HVAC systems
Verbena Heights (Hong Kong) 322–323
vertical daylight factor *see* VDF
vertical landscaping 251–262
and air quality 261
challenges of 257–262
in dry/humid climates 259–261
plant selection/methods for 258–262
and structural design 261
Vietnam 47–48
view 32–33, 291, 300
sky *see* solar obstruction
visual comfort 110

Vitruvius   181–182, 186
VRw *see* wind velocity ratio

Waglan Island (Hong Kong)   57
Waldram diagram   183, 193
'wall effect' development   325–327
walls
    cool   80
    greenery on *see* vertical landscaping
Walter, M.A.H.B.   286, 288
waste   19–20
    construction   196–197
    for fuel   268–270
    recycling   195–196, 198, 203
    see also sewage
waste management   37, 137, 195–200
    compaction system   309
    incentives for   198–200
waste minimization   195–206
    and building reuse   202–203
    in construction works   203–206
    defined   195–196
    in demolition works   201–203
    designing for   200–206
    and design modifications   204
    hierarchy   196
    importance of   195, 206
    legislation and   195, 206
    objectives of   198–200
    and waste management   195–196
water   19, 34–35, 37, 293
    access to   27
    and high-rise buildings   36
    recycling/conserving   20
waterfront sites   46, 60, 129–131
water-source heat pumps   269
Weston, H.C.   186
Wharton, William C.   32–33

WHO (World Health Organization)   152, 163
Wilkinson, Richard G   29–30
Williamson, T.J.   279
Wilson, M.   149–151
windbreaks   79, 90, 93, 105
Windcatcher ventilation system   158–159
windows   12–13, 29, 34, 88, 259–261, 265
    and daylight design   181–182, 186–188, 193
    and fire hazard   210
    and thermal comfort   104, 108
    and ventilation/noise   149, 151, 153–154, 178
wind power   21–22, 267–268, 270, 299
    for high-rise buildings   304–305, 307
    small-scale   268
wind profile   120, 312–314
wind speed   57, 60, 63, 68, 72, 265
    modelling   112
    and thermal comfort   88–89, 91–93, 103–104,
        110–111, 125
wind tunnels   99, 124, 129, 146–148, 312
wind velocity ratio (VRw)   120–121, 123–124, 126–128
    spatial average/local spatial average   129
wind ventilation *see* ventilation
Wong, N.H.   99–103, 125, 228
World Health Organization *see* WHO
World Trade Centre attack (2001)   29, 209–211, 217
World War II   20, 24, 30
Wuhan (China)   166–168, 170

Xing, Z.   169

Yeang, Ken   257, 286, 305
Yong, Xue   24
Yu, C.   169, 175
Yu, S.-M.   32

Zacharias, J.   13
Zhang, M.   175